# NEW MEXICO

ZORA O'NEILL

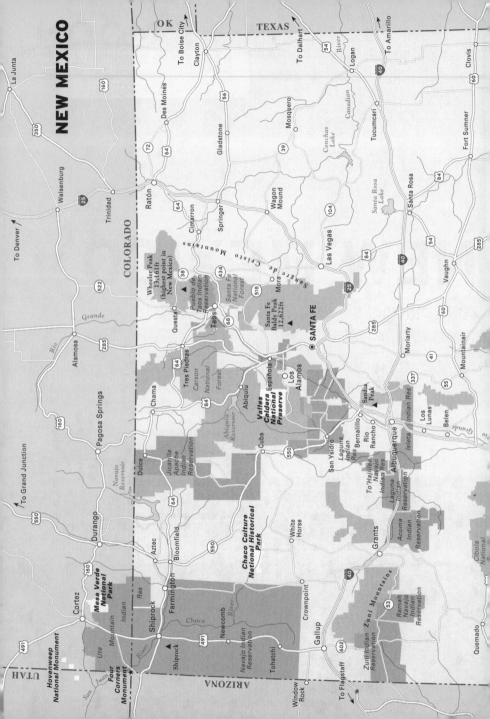

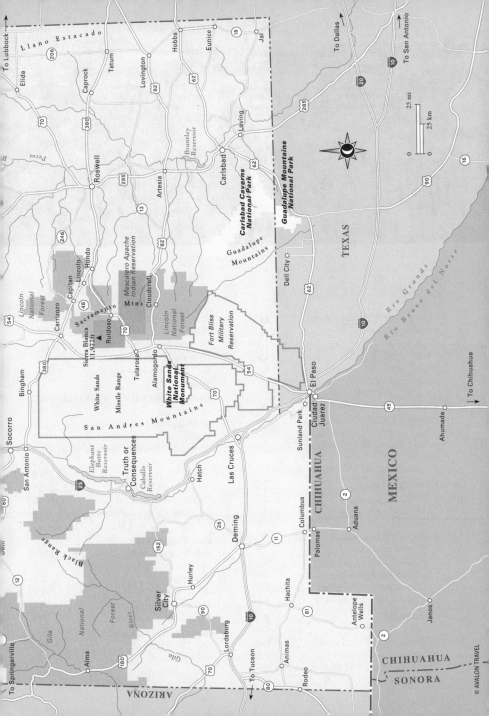

# Contents

DISCOVER
# New Mexico

There's a reason it's called the Land of Enchantment. The smells alone would be entrancing enough: lilacs in spring, ozone after summer thunderstorms, green chiles roasting in supermarket parking lots in fall, and fragrant piñon crackling in woodstoves and corner fireplaces. Listen, too, and you'll hear what makes the state special: Western tanagers warble in the trees, coyotes yelp in the night, and the deep boom of drums and jingle of bells resound at pueblo ceremonies. And that green chile adds a distinct taste to everything—it finds its way onto hamburgers and pizzas and even into ice cream and beer.

But none of that matches the majesty of the view: across austere mesas, down narrow sandstone canyons, or up to snowcapped mountain peaks. Straight above is a cloudless dome the precise hue of the turquoise in the locally crafted jewelry. At night, stars clot the velvety sky, so close you can almost touch them. Many visitors to New Mexico feel disoriented by all this new sensory input—and perhaps by the dizzying altitude, which soars over 13,000 feet at its highest point. And on top of everything, they feel like Alice in Wonderland, ever shrinking, when compared with the vast landscape.

New Mexico is a sort of alternate world, one that lives by different rules. Santa Fe is an adobe-looking utopia where the economy seems to thrive magically on nothing but art and politics. Los Alamos is a hidden city on a hill with a secret that changed the world, and half of Roswell, it seems, is still obsessed with an alleged UFO crash there in 1947. There are settlements named Truth or Consequences and Pie Town.

Visitors might need time to adjust—to the altitude, certainly, and maybe also to the laid-back attitude. But there's a point of entry for everyone. Outdoor adventurers can hike for an hour or a week, along mountainsides thick with yellow-leafed aspens, and camp on the surreal dunes of White Sands National Monument. Culture mavens thrive in Santa Fe, with its world-class art scene and an eclectic calendar of international film and music. History buffs can explore the ruined civilization at Chaco Canyon, spy ruts dug by thousands of passing wagon wheels on the Santa Fe Trail, or bunk down under a buzzing neon motel sign along Route 66.

At the end of the day, you can always pull yourself back into the present with a cold margarita and cuisine with a hot-chile kick—but that's no guarantee you'll shake off New Mexico's spell.

# Planning Your Trip

## Where to Go

### Albuquerque

A modern Western city, Albuquerque sprawls over more than 100 square miles at the base of the Sandia Mountains. It's proud of its Route 66 style, and it's also preserving farmland along the Rio Grande and redesigning itself as a green city. Head north to Santa Fe via the ghost towns of the Turquoise Trail, the hot springs in the Jemez Mountains, or the solitary wilderness of the Valles Caldera.

### Santa Fe

New Mexico's picturesque capital has a human scale and a golden glow (partly from the loads of money spent here). Museums are a major draw—for state history, folk art, and more—as are the scores of galleries. Outside of town are the cliff dwellings at Bandelier National Monument; the scenery of Abiquiu, which inspired painter Georgia O'Keeffe; and Los Alamos, birthplace of the A-bomb.

spring in Santa Fe

### If You Have . . .

- **FIVE DAYS:** Visit Santa Fe, with an overnight trip to Taos.

- **ONE WEEK:** Cruise the Navajo Nation in the northwest, or concentrate on Albuquerque and Santa Fe.

- **TWO WEEKS:** Follow the New Mexico Road Trip itinerary, or cover most of the southwest and southeast.

- **THREE WEEKS:** Go crazy: You have time for backpacking, rafting trips, or other wilderness excursions.

### Taos and
### North Central New Mexico

Taos melds artists, spiritual seekers, and ski bums—plus centuries-old Spanish and American Indian families. Make time to enjoy the atmosphere, cultivated in coffee shops and creative restaurants. A good day drive is the Enchanted Circle, a loop of two-lane roads with Wheeler Peak, the highest in New Mexico, at the center. Or head over the mountains to Chama, home to a historic steam train that forges the pass to Colorado.

### Las Vegas and the Northeast

Past the Pecos Mountains, Las Vegas, a.k.a. Meadow City, is a well-preserved historic town, often used as a Western film set. From there, the terrain, where the Santa Fe Trail

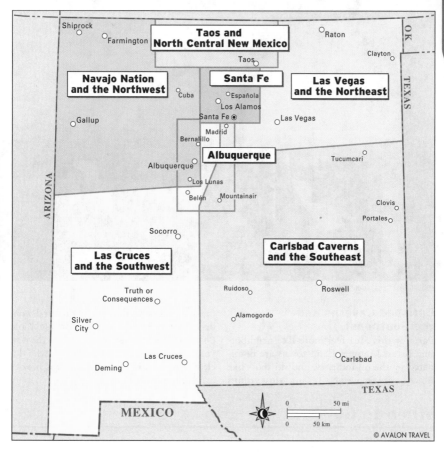

Taos and
North Central New Mexico

Navajo Nation
and the Northwest

Santa Fe

Las Vegas
and the Northeast

Albuquerque

Las Cruces
and the Southwest

Carlsbad Caverns
and the Southeast

Shiprock
Farmington
Raton
Clayton
Taos
Cuba
Española
Los Alamos
Santa Fe
Las Vegas
Gallup
Madrid
Bernalillo
Tucumcari
Albuquerque
Los Lunas
Belén
Mountainair
Clovis
Portales
Socorro
Truth or
Consequences
Ruidoso
Roswell
Alamogordo
Silver
City
Las Cruces
Carlsbad
Deming

ARIZONA

TEXAS

OK

TEXAS

MEXICO

0      50 mi
0      50 km

© AVALON TRAVEL

once ran, is all short-grass prairie, once the western edge of the Dust Bowl. To get a view, drive the spiral road up Capulin Volcano, then soar across gorgeous Johnson Mesa to the mountain burgs of Raton and Cimarron.

## Navajo Nation and the Northwest

Stark volcanic landscape, lonesome roads, and tall mesas—this is some of the most dramatic desert terrain in the state, along with its oldest cultures. This quadrant (often called Four Corners, as it abuts three other states) is where the Ancestral Puebloans lived in Chaco Canyon, and where Gallup is the

self-proclaimed American Indian capital. The city is surrounded by hiking and mountain biking trails.

## Las Cruces and the Southwest

This corner of the state has both the rugged Gila Wilderness and the mesmerizing Chihuahuan Desert. It's a long drive between the river-fed farmland around Las Cruces and colorful, artsy Silver City, tucked in the mountains, but worth it—especially for the food-focused, who will find a number of excellent restaurants. Truth or Consequences reels in the curious, delivering hot springs and quirkiness.

sunset near Taos Mountain

### Carlsbad Caverns and the Southeast

Parts of this area feel more like neighboring Texas: Many flatland towns are dominated by the oil industry, and ski spots like Ruidoso are beloved by Texans. Most visitors make a beeline to the amazing natural wonders of White Sands National Monument and Carlsbad Caverns National Park. On the way, you can track outlaw Billy the Kid, who dueled in the mountain town of Lincoln, now an excellent outdoor museum.

## When to Go

Summer (June through September) is high season in northern New Mexico, though it's prettiest late in the season, when the so-called monsoon rains, which usually start in late June, have revived the landscape. Summer is the only time to hike at higher elevations, as snow finally melts, but lower elevations are baking and sleepy. Be prepared for a temperature drop from the 90s to as low as the 60s after sunset, especially outside of cities, and bring an umbrella.

Fall is the most beautiful time across the state, with crisp temperatures, clear skies, and brilliant leaves in the mountains. For New Mexico's most temperate season, pack a sweater and a windbreaker to keep out the nighttime chill.

Winter is busy (and pricier) in ski towns like Taos, but traditional celebrations preceding Christmas are wonderful. Many sights are closed or have limited hours, however. Towns at lower elevations, such as Truth or Consequences and Carlsbad, remain balmy, and prices in these places hold steady year-round. Be prepared for temps below freezing, even in southern desert areas. If you think you'll attend winter pueblo dances, pack mittens, long underwear, double-thick wool socks, and a hat with earflaps—there's a lot of standing around outside.

The cheaper shoulder seasons are March, April, and May, and, to a lesser extent, November, before ski season starts. Spring

# Plan Ahead

Ready for the grand entry at the annual Taos Pueblo Powwow.

New Mexico is a just-show-up kind of place, but a few elements require some forethought.

- **Ceremonial dances:** Attending a ceremonial dance is worth planning a trip around. Dances are held at New Mexico pueblos year-round; check the schedules for Albuquerque (page 44), Santa Fe (page 87), Taos (page 142) and Zuni (page 212), Laguna and Acoma Pueblos (page 204) in advance.

- **Georgia O'Keeffe House:** The house in Abiquiu is open to guided tours mid-March through November; book at least a month in advance (page 111).

- **Santa Fe Opera:** Online ticket sales start in October for the July and August summer season; book in the winter for the best seat selection (page 85).

- **Santa Fe Indian Market** (August), **Spanish Market** (July), and **Christmas:** Book Santa Fe hotels six to eight months ahead.

- ***The Lightning Field:*** Visiting this extraordinary land art requires advance overnight reservations (May-Oct., $150-250 pp). Guests leave their vehicles in Quemado; casual visitors are not allowed and the road to the site is unmarked. Reservations open in March; book immediately and if your dates are full, ask to be put on a waiting list (page 253).

is perhaps the harshest time in the state—weather can be extreme, switching from snowfall and mud to dry, hot winds (pack boots for rural or muddy areas, and a clean pair of shoes for around town). But it is a good season for river rafting. Book a hotel at least six months in advance for the week between Christmas and New Year's, Santa Fe's summer art markets, or the Albuquerque balloon fest in October.

Be prepared for a wide range of temperatures whenever you go, and always pack sunglasses, sunscreen, and a brimmed hat. Local "formal" wear is only clean jeans and boots; when visiting churches and pueblos, women should cover their shoulders.

# New Mexico Road Trip

You could conceivably explore New Mexico for a month or so, seeking out ever more obscure towns, but two weeks gives just enough time to appreciate the distinct character of the cities and enjoy a few bumpy back roads. This itinerary involves a lot of driving to cover the state's most scenic routes, but you'll still have opportunities for leisurely lunches and other out-of-car activities. If you want to cut down on the driving, you could fly out of El Paso, Texas, about one hour south of Las Cruces and substantially closer to White Sands—in this case, stay in Albuquerque for the first few days, then head out to explore.

## Day 1

Arrive at Albuquerque's Sunport airport; transfer to a hotel in the city or one of the rural-feeling bed-and-breakfasts in the North Valley. Have drinks and dinner in Nob Hill.

## Day 2

Visit the Indian Pueblo Cultural Center, then head west to Acoma Pueblo. Lunch in Grants and stay the night in Gallup.

## Day 3

Get an early start for the long, bumpy ride along the back road to Chaco Culture National Historical Park. When you're done exploring, grab a late lunch at El Bruno's in Cuba, then take Highway 96 over the mountains to Abiquiu, where you'll spend the night.

## Day 4

If you like hiking, explore Abiquiu's red rocks at Ghost Ranch or drive down the road to Bandelier National Monument. If you prefer the city, head in to Santa Fe and the excellent museums around the plaza. In either case, stay

The curves and shadows of San Francisco de Asis Church have fascinated artists for a century.

# Best Drives

vintage car buffs cruise the Mother Road

There's hardly a bad road in New Mexico, but these drives are outstanding.

- **Turquoise Trail:** (55 miles, 1.5 hours) From Albuquerque to Santa Fe, Highway 14 offers great vistas around every curve and ghost towns to break up the drive (page 58).

- **Highway 4:** (32 miles, 1 hour) The road through Jemez Springs to Valles Caldera is especially good in fall, with yellow aspens highlighted against red rock (page 61).

- **U.S. 84:** (93 miles, 1 hour 45 minutes) North of Santa Fe, ascend through the red rocks of Abiquiu (page 111), then past the Brazos Cliffs near Tierra Amarilla (page 153).

- **La Frontera del Llano Scenic Byway:** (26 miles, 30 minutes) Highway 39 zigzags across the northeastern plains, from Roy to Abbott, with pronghorns and ruined homesteads along the way (page 183).

- **Highway 72:** (37 miles, 1 hour) This tiny road between Raton and Folsom soars over bucolic Johnson Mesa (page 186).

- **U.S. 180:** (98 miles, 2 hours) From Silver City to Reserve, this highway passes largely through national forest (page 295).

- **Sunspot Highway:** (17 miles, 30 minutes) Highway 6563 winds south from Cloudcroft to Sunspot National Solar Observatory, with White Sands visible below (page 330).

the night there, at classic La Fonda or more modern Hacienda Nicholas.

## Day 5

Take in Santa Fe's contemporary culture, with shopping, gallery-hopping, or a visit to the Museum of International Folk Art. Round out a colorful day with dinner at Café Pasqual's.

## Day 6

Head to Taos via the high road, with stops at the chapel in Chimayó, where you can also pick up some delicious tamales, and in the villages of Truchas and Las Trampas. Settle into your hotel in Taos after a de rigueur margarita at the Adobe Bar.

## Day 7

Start with an early visit to San Francisco

Aliens rule the streets of Roswell.

de Asis Church, followed by breakfast at Ranchos Plaza Grill. Then head to the Taos Art Museum for background on the town's art scene. Spend the afternoon at Taos Pueblo, then get a local-produce dinner at The Love Apple.

## Day 8
Drive the first leg of the Enchanted Circle, turning east at Eagle Nest to reach Cimarron. Lunch at The Porch, then head down to Las Vegas via I-25. Check in at the Plaza Hotel, and walk down Bridge Street and over to El Fidel Restaurant for dinner.

## Day 9
Today is a long day of driving, but you'll pass through pretty old villages like Villanueva and the plains around Vaughn. Have a late lunch in Roswell, and visit the International UFO Museum & Research Center or the Anderson Museum of Contemporary Art. You're bunking down at Carlsbad's Trinity Hotel & Suites.

## Day 10
Head out early to Carlsbad Caverns National Park. Back in town, have dinner at Danny's

Place BBQ and take in a movie at the Fiesta Drive-In, then head back to the Trinity for bed.

## Day 11
Head west to Alamogordo and White Sands National Monument, winding up in Las Cruces that evening. Have dinner in historic Mesilla.

## Day 12
Drive up I-25 to return to Albuquerque, stopping in Truth or Consequences for coffee and a snack and a dip in the hot springs. Plan on lunch at the Owl Bar & Café in San Antonio. You should be in Albuquerque by nightfall—check out the scene downtown.

## Day 13
Take it easy today, and take one last look at the Southwestern scenery, either with a dawn hot-air balloon ride, or a sunset tram ride to Sandia Peak.

## Day 14
Fuel up for your flight with breakfast at The Frontier, where you can also grab some house-made tortillas to take home.

# Not Just Hot Tamales

Hazel's green chile at El Bruno's

## BEST TRADITIONAL NEW MEXICAN

"Red or green?" is the official state question, referring to the dilemma diners face when they order enchiladas, huevos rancheros, or anything else that can be drowned in an earthy red-chile sauce or a chunky, vegetal green one.

- **Mary & Tito's Café:** An Albuquerque institution, this family restaurant was named a James Beard American Classic in 2009. Red chile is the star here (page 55).

- **San Felipe Restaurant:** In the category of restaurants in a gas station, this one's a winner: big enchilada platters, as well as pueblo favorites like blue-corn mush (page 65).

- **Tia Sophia's:** The alleged inventors of the breakfast burrito, in Santa Fe (page 96).

- **Zuly's:** A dreamy rich, deep red sauce bathes enchiladas and burritos at this café in the bucolic village of Dixon (page 115).

- **El Bruno's:** The restaurant in Cuba processes all its green chile by hand (page 241).

## BEST GREEN-CHILE CHEESEBURGER

- **Santa Fe Bite:** Ten-ounce burgers, from meat that's hand-ground every-day. Legendary (page 97).

- **The Frontier:** With the all-you-can-ladle pot of green-chile stew, you can add as much heat as you want to your burger at this colossal Albuquerque diner (page 54).

- **Owl Bar & Café:** A twofer in the village of San Antonio: not only the old-school Owl, but rival Buckhorn Burgers is right across the street (page 254).

- **Big D's Downtown Dive:** An outpost of gourmet fast food in Roswell, this place does a succulent burger, with garlic fries on the side (page 320).

## BEST LOCAL AND ORGANIC

- **La Merienda:** The restaurant at historic farm inn Los Poblanos serves a few perfect dishes each evening; overnight for the full farm-life experience in Albuquerque (page 52).

- **Vinaigrette:** This "salad bistro" in Santa Fe and Albuquerque grows its own greens on a nearby farm and can vouch for every ingredient on its menu (page 52).

- **The Love Apple:** At this candlelit New Mexican bistro, a chalkboard displays the sourced ingredients: Tucumcari cheese, Pecos beef, and more (page 150).

- **Gallup flea market:** As local as it gets: grilled lamb from sheep raised here, with a roasted green chile, on fry bread made with flour from Colorado (page 218).

- **The Curious Kumquat:** Chef Rob Connoley applies global spices to local goodies, and the occasional line-caught salmon flown in by friends from Alaska (page 290).

# A Week in the Wild West

Gunslingers, cattle rustlers, and Apache warriors made New Mexico a colorful, if violent, place in the 19th century, and relics of that frontier lifestyle are still visible everywhere. History buffs can visit old forts, count bullet holes in saloon ceilings, and trace the fortunes of prospectors in ghost-town graveyards. Though the major cities have their share of history, this route takes you away from the modern centers and into emptier quarters on the east side of the state. It can be expanded with a stop in Santa Fe or a more leisurely pace up to Las Vegas (Highway 3, which connects I-40 to I-25, for instance, is exceptionally pretty, if a bit out of the way).

## Day 1

Arrive in Albuquerque. Take in the western sunset at the base of the Sandia Peak Tramway, in the foothills, then come back to the center of the city for dinner at the appropriately named and Western-themed The Frontier restaurant. Bed down at the Los Poblanos Inn, amid horse farms in the North Valley.

## Day 2

Head southeast to Mountainair and the rustic-bizarre Shaffer Hotel; you'll also pass the Salinas Pueblo Missions. By mid-afternoon, you should be in Lincoln, where Billy the Kid earned his greatest notoriety. Tour the buildings here, then settle in for the evening at the Wortley Hotel.

## Day 3

After breakfast, you're headed north to Fort Sumner to see Billy the Kid's grave and a memorial to Navajo internment in the 1860s. Take an afternoon dip in the Blue Hole in Santa Rosa to fortify yourself for the last leg of the drive, to Las Vegas, where you'll stay and dine at the wonderfully restored Plaza Hotel.

## Day 4

Tour the Meadow City's historic buildings in the morning, with lunch at Abraham's Tiendita, then head for sprawling Fort Union National Monument in the afternoon—the slanting sun should highlight the ruts of the

In the film *Young Guns*, Cerrillos stood in for Lincoln, where Billy the Kid escaped from jail.

# Very Retro

one of New Mexico's tastiest roadside attractions

"Get your kicks," advises Nat King Cole's classic anthem of the Mother Road. Though officially decommissioned, Route 66 (now traced by I-40) is still alive in New Mexico in the form of neon signs and cruising culture. And even off that iconic highway, many parts of the state foster nostalgia for the mid-20th century.

Hit the road, preferably in a convertible, to enjoy good old-fashioned fun like **drive-in movie theaters** (page 176) in Las Vegas (summers only) and Carlsbad. The car is still king in Clovis, where you'll find original drive-ins, such as **Foxy** (page 310), complete with carhops—this is the way burgers and fries were meant to be eaten.

Clovis is also where 1950s crooner Buddy Holly recorded his early hits—check out the **Norman & Vi Petty Rock & Roll Museum** (page 308), or plan a trip for the September **Clovis Music Festival** (page 309). Hot-rod fans can see one of Elvis's Caddies at **B-Square Ranch** (page 225) in Farmington (the taxidermy museum here also seems like a relic of another age). And capture the real spirit of a road trip by heading out U.S. 60 to

remote **Pie Town** (page 252), so named because it served intrepid motorists sweets in the 1930s. Two cafés keep this slice (pun intended) of Americana alive with mixed berry, chocolate cream, and more at the ready. For more sweets, head to **Carrizozo** (page 346), where Roy's mixes up chocolate ice cream sodas at an old fountain. Don't miss the very groovy early-1960s signage on the short main street.

The best legacy of the Route 66 era is the motels. Tuck yourself into 1939 at the **Blue Swallow Motel** (page 307) or the slightly newer **Motel Safari** (page 307) in Tucumcari, or at **El Rancho Hotel & Motel** (page 219) in Gallup, which hosted Ronald Reagan and other Western movie stars. Farther afield, in Raton, the **Maverick Motel** (page 192) is meticulously preserved, and the **Budget Host Melody Lane Motel** (page 192) has vintage saunas in the rooms. In Truth or Consequences (a town named for a 1950s radio show), the owners of **Blackstone Hotsprings** (page 260) have decorated rooms as homages to *The Twilight Zone* and Lucille Ball. Sleep tight, and dream of the charm of yesteryear.

# Weird and Wonderful

Sometimes New Mexico feels like an entirely different planet. Here's where to see the state at its most eccentric.

## TRUTH OR CONSEQUENCES

From its attention-grabbing name (a 1950 publicity stunt) to its downtown of hot baths, odd shops, and the labyrinthine **Geronimo Springs Museum** (page 256), this is a small town with more than its share of character.

## MADRID

It's pronounced MAD-rid, which gives you an idea about this **ghost-town-turned-galleryville**'s wacky residents, who have brought the place back from the dead since the 1970s. South of here is **Tinkertown Museum** (page 58), a miniature wonderland whittled from wood, cobbled together from bottle caps and bits of string.

## SANTA FE AND TAOS

Poll your fellow hot-tubbers at **Ten Thousand Waves** (page 93) about their past lives, or ask your neighbor at the **World Cup** (page 149) coffee shop if he can hear the "Taos hum." Check out the **Greater World Earthship Development** (page 138), an off-the-grid suburb of Taos where the buildings crafted from beer cans and tires look straight off a *Star Wars* set.

## LOS ALAMOS

This mesa-top town is where the **atomic bomb** was devised and scientists now toil in secrecy and one **museum** (page 103) here touts the joys of nuclear science. Round out your visit to "the Hill" with a jaunt south to **Trinity Site** (page 346), where the bomb was first tested in July 1945; it's open to visitors only two days a year.

## ROSWELL

Ever have cryptic dreams about green creatures with big heads and long, skinny arms? You'll feel right at home at the **International UFO Museum & Research Center** (page 316), where alien visitations are treated as a matter of course. The work at the outstanding **Anderson Museum of Contemporary Art** (page 317) depicts all manner of alternate realities.

## PLAINS OF SAN AGUSTIN

If Roswell gets you in the mood to peer into the solar system, cruise out to this installation of radio telescopes that make up **The Very Large Array** (page 251). They don't actually receive messages from across the galaxy, but the images they take of deep space are nearly as illuminating.

Tinkertown Museum

Santa Fe Trail off to one side. Return to Las Vegas for the evening.

## Day 5

I-25 north takes you to Raton, where you turn east to Capulin Volcano National Monument, which affords a grand view over the plains. Loop back via Folsom (site of numerous train robberies) and the awesome, empty expanse of Johnson Mesa. Have a late lunch in Raton at Boomers BBQ, or farther down the road at the ultimate Western roadhouse, Colfax Tavern. Then cruise down the road to Cimarron, where you'll spend the night in the spooky St. James Hotel.

## Day 6

Depending on your interests, hang out in Cimarron in the morning until the Old Mill Museum opens, or make a beeline through dramatic Cimarron Canyon to Eagle Nest and on to Taos. The long way around the Enchanted Circle yields the best views and takes you past abandoned Elizabethtown, site of the state's first gold rush. In Taos, the Wild West is alive and well at the Sagebrush Inn—a must for drinks, after you've had a decadent dinner at Antonio's or Lambert's. The Historic Taos Inn or Hotel La Fonda de Taos both wear their years well.

## Day 7

Drive south back to Albuquerque via the low road and, if you have the time, the Turquoise Trail—you can have lunch at San Marcos Café, then stop in Cerrillos, which has been used as a Western film set. If you don't have to meet a flight out, plan on stopping in Madrid too, for burger or a beer at the Mine Shaft Tavern.

# Black Stone, White Sands

Temperate climates, plain old "pretty" landscapes—who needs 'em? New Mexico's extreme terrain, from stark lava beds to gleaming fields of gypsum, is much more exciting. Snowcapped peaks are just a short drive from arid deserts, and you can spot hardy animals,

odd birds, and stunning rock formations everywhere in between. Whether remote wilderness areas or lesser-known routes in popular parks, these otherworldly spots are almost always empty.

Every corner of the state holds some

sunset at White Sands National Monument

enticing natural adventure, but due to long driving distances, you're better off limiting your exploration to one quadrant at a time. This way, you'll spend less time in the car and more time on the land. Which ones you visit depends on what time of year it is and, equally important, what altitude you can handle. When you arrive, it's tempting to put on your boots and head straight out, but unless you're coming from a comparable elevation, stick to clambering in foothills and scenic drives for the first couple of days. Drink plenty of liquids, and head to bed early.

## Wheeler Peak

From Red River, a hike up the state's highest mountain typically requires a few days. Or you can take the short, steep route from Taos Ski Valley, doable in a long afternoon. Either way, don't go any time other than June, July, or August.

## Bisti/De-Na-Zin Wilderness

Top-heavy hoodoos—precarious, windswept sandstone towers—are the hallmark of this barren landscape south of Farmington. There are no trails and no services, and virtually no other hikers, so come prepared with plenty of water, a compass, and an appreciation for solitude. Don't want to hike? Head to nearby Angel Peak Scenic Area instead, for fine views.

## Valles Caldera National Preserve

The lush alpine meadows that line this ancient volcanic basin are some of the state's most pristine. Every season here is beautiful, whether the trout streams are high with spring runoff or the knee-deep snow is prime for snowshoeing. But if you plan just to hike on your own, without a larger group tour, plan to come between June and September, before the cold snap.

## Kiowa and Rita Blanca National Grasslands

Once the edge of the brutal Dust Bowl, this protected prairie now looks a bit more hospitable, brushy and green. The real surprise comes when you drive down to Mills Canyon, a red-striped chasm with a lush bottom. Camping in this hidden spot, with hawks wheeling overhead, is like being hidden away from the world.

lava frozen mid-flow at Valley of Fires National Recreation Area

### Sky Islands

The mountains that spike out of the flat, hot Chihuahuan Desert are little-visited crags, each fostering its own flora and fauna. The most accessible are the Organ Mountains in Las Cruces; the Florida Mountains near Deming harbor bighorn sheep and vivid wildflowers; and Cave Creek Canyon (technically in Arizona) near Rodeo teems with birds.

### Valley of Fires
### National Recreation Area

The volcano that produced these badlands exploded just yesterday, relatively speaking—the blackened landscape hardened about 1,500 years ago, setting in wedges, whorls, and fantastically odd lumps. Come at the end of the summer rain season to see them at their surprising greenest.

### White Sands National Monument

After you've slid down the gypsum dunes, really get to know this amazing place on a ranger-led car tour to the sands' source, Lake Lucero, or a hike on Alkali Flats Trail. Better still, camp here overnight after taking a hike or mountain biking tour under the full moon. Try to avoid the boiling peak of summer and midwinter, when periods of heavy rain can close off parts of the park.

### Carlsbad Caverns National Park

Go deeper—literally—than the average day-tripper by signing up for the hardcore Spider Cave tour, on which you'll wiggle through tiny tunnels into lofty halls. The park supplies helmets and headlamps, but it's BYOB: bring your own batteries. Handily, the temperature underground holds steady year-round; just book ahead during peak summer months.

# Native New Mexico,
# Ancient and Modern

The culture that developed before the arrival of the Spanish in the 16th century is visible in both ruined and inhabited pueblos and in excellent museums that hold some of the state's finest treasures. Even if you're visiting only a small area on your trip, there's a lot of American Indian history to see in and around each place—but definitely try to schedule a visit around a dance ceremony at a pueblo, as this will give you the most memorable impression of the living culture. If you're serious about purchasing art and jewelry, you may want to time your visit with the Santa Fe Indian Market, which takes place every August and showcases more than 1,200 artisans. But you'll also have a chance to buy directly from craftspeople in Zuni, Acoma, Crownpoint, and Santa Fe. If you have plenty of time to explore, you could also head south of Albuquerque to the Salinas Pueblo Missions, the Gila Cliff Dwellings, and the Bosque Redondo Memorial at Fort Sumner.

### Albuquerque

The Indian Pueblo Cultural Center should be your first stop, for its good museum and information on all the American Indian settlements. Also pay a quick visit to Petroglyph National Monument on the west side, to see ancient rock carvings and get a great view across the city. The Hyatt Regency Tamaya resort, on the north side of town, is owned by Santa Ana Pueblo.

### Acoma Pueblo

West of Albuquerque, this weathered fortress village atop a mesa is accessible only by guided tour. At the base is an excellent cultural museum, which displays the pueblo's specialty, delicate white pottery painted with

examining the goods at the Crownpoint Rug Auction

fine black lines. You can grab lunch here, or down the road in Grants.

## Zuni Pueblo

This is the only pueblo where you can stay overnight, at the Inn at Halona. It's also the source of beautiful jewelry. Take a walking tour of the mission church, with its resplendent kachina murals, and check out the A:shíwi A:wan Museum. The dance ritual Shalako, in late November or early December, is amazing, but you must book at the inn many months ahead.

## Gallup

Hosting a huge annual powwow, Gallup has the largest native population in the state, as well as the small WWII Navajo Code Talkers Museum. Visit on a Saturday, for the funky and diverse flea market. About an hour's drive away is Crownpoint, which hosts a monthly rug auction—a must-visit even if you don't buy anything.

## Shiprock and Farmington

Head into the Navajo Nation via U.S. 491, passing the Toadlena Trading Post, which displays beautiful rugs. Shiprock offers another

chance at a Saturday flea market, or traditional mutton stew at the fast-food joints—or hold out till Farmington and Ash-Kii's Navajo Grill. Farmington is usually the base for visiting Chaco Culture National Historical Park, a little over two hours south—though you can also camp at the site, under starry skies.

## Taos

Taos Pueblo is as much a relic as Acoma but still regularly used. If your visit doesn't coincide with a ceremonial dance there, stop by the Best Western Kachina Lodge in the early evening to see a demonstration performance (summer only)—but you should stay across the road at El Pueblo Lodge, a well-tended motel.

## Santa Fe

Check out the modern arts scene at the Museum of Indian Arts & Culture and the Museum of Contemporary Native Arts, as well as several galleries representing pueblo artists. And don't miss the jewelry vendors under the portal at the Palace of the Governors. A short drive away are the ruins at Bandelier National Monument and the Puyé Cliff Dwellings, where Santa Clara residents lead the tours.

# ALBUQUERQUE

As a tourist destination, Albuquerque has long labored in the shadow of the jet-set arts colonies to the north, but that has slowly started to change, as visitors discover a city that's fun, down-to-earth, and affordable. If Santa Fe is the "City Different" (a moniker Albuquerqueans razz for its pretentiousness), then New Mexico's largest city, with a population of 850,000

© ZORA O'NEILL

# HIGHLIGHTS

LOOK FOR 【 TO FIND RECOMMENDED SIGHTS, ACTIVITIES, DINING, AND LODGING.

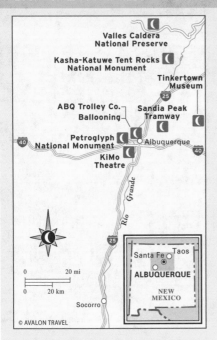

© AVALON TRAVEL

【 **ABQ Trolley Co.:** The best tour in the state, aboard an open-sided, faux-adobe tram-on-wheels, with the lively, knowledgeable owners sharing Albuquerque lore (page 30).

【 **KiMo Theatre:** A fantasia of Southwestern decorative styles, this former cinema is one of the few examples of Pueblo Deco style. Restored and run with city money, it's the showpiece of downtown (page 34).

【 **Sandia Peak Tramway:** Zip up the world's longest single-cable tram to the crest of the mountain that looms over the east side of Albuquerque. At the top, you'll get a vertigo-inducing view across the whole metro area and out to the hazy western horizon (page 38).

【 **Petroglyph National Monument:** The city's west mesa is covered with fine rock carvings made centuries ago by the ancestors of the local Pueblo people. Don't miss the views across the city from the dormant volcanoes that stud the top of the ridge (page 40).

【 **Ballooning:** In the American capital for hot-air balloons, enjoy the silent city on a dawn flight. You'll get a true bird's-eye view, and dip down to skim the Rio Grande (page 45).

【 **Tinkertown Museum:** An enthralling collection of one man's lifetime of whittling projects, this folk-art exhibit is inspiring for adults and a delight for kids (page 58).

【 **Valles Caldera National Preserve:** In the crater formed by a collapsed volcano, some 89,000 acres of grassy valleys are set aside for very controlled public access. You must make reservations to hike here, but it's worth planning ahead (page 64).

【 **Kasha-Katuwe Tent Rocks National Monument:** A great attraction off the otherwise unremarkable freeway to Santa Fe—drive a few miles west to hike in this eerie canyon landscape (page 64).

in the greater metro area, is proudly the "City Indifferent," unconcerned with fads and flawless facades.

Which is not to say the city doesn't have its pockets of historic charm—well away from the traffic-clogged arteries of I-40 and I-25, which intersect in the center in a graceful tangle of turquoise-trimmed bridges. The Duke City was founded three centuries ago, its cumbersome name that of a Spanish nobleman but its character the product of later eras: the post-1880 downtown district; the University of New Mexico campus, built in the early 20th century by John Gaw Meem, the architect who

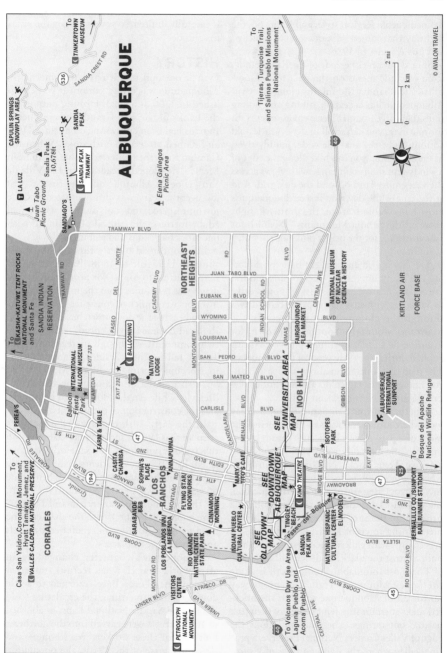

# ALBUQUERQUE

© AVALON TRAVEL

defined Pueblo Revival style; and Route 66, the highway that joined Albuquerque to Chicago and Los Angeles in 1926.

Spread out on either side of the Rio Grande, from volcanic mesas on the west to the foothills of the Sandia Mountains along the east, Albuquerque has accessible hiking and biking trails that run through diverse environments. In the morning, you can stroll under centuries-old cottonwood trees near the wide, muddy river; in the afternoon, you can hike along the edge of a windswept mountain range with views across the vast empty land beyond the city grid. And at the end of the day, you'll see Albuquerque's most remarkable feature, the dramatic light show on the Sandia Mountains—Spanish for "watermelon," for the bright pink hue they turn at sundown.

The city is also an excellent base for exploring the many interesting pueblos and natural attractions nearby, and it's just an hour's drive to Santa Fe, with easy day trips or scenic drives through the mountains in between. In the Manzano Mountains southeast of town, for instance, lie a series of ruined pueblos, last inhabited during the early years of the Conquest. The road that links them also winds past a canyon known for its fall colors and a historic hotel in a distinctly New Mexican style.

Whether en route to Santa Fe or as a day loop, there are several ways to head north. The most direct is I-25, which cuts through dramatic rolling hills; take a short detour to Kasha-Katuwe Tent Rocks National Monument, where pointed white rocks tower above a narrow canyon. Beginning east of Albuquerque, the historic Turquoise Trail winds along the back side of the Sandias, then through the former mining town of Madrid, resettled as an arts colony, with galleries occupying the cabins built against the black, coal-rich hills.

The most roundabout route north is along the Jemez Mountain Trail, a scenic byway northwest of Albuquerque through the brick-red rocks surrounding Jemez Pueblo, then past natural hot springs. The road runs along the edge of Valles Caldera National Preserve, a pristine valley where the daily number of visitors is carefully limited, so you can enjoy the vistas in solitude.

## HISTORY

Even before tourists beat a path to points north, Albuquerque was a way station. It was established in 1706 as a small farming outpost on the banks of the Rio Grande, where Pueblo Indians had been cultivating crops since 1100, and named after a Spanish duke. When the Camino Real, the main trade route north from Mexico, developed decades later, the Villa de San Felipe de Alburquerque (the first "r" was lost over the years) was ideally situated, and the town prospered and soon outgrew its original adobe fortress, the central plaza ringed with one-story haciendas and a church.

Life continued quietly through the transition to U.S. rule in 1848. But in 1880 the railroad came to town—or near enough. The depot was two miles from the main plaza, and investors were quick to construct "New Town," which became the downtown business district. Railroad Avenue (now Central) connected the two communities, though increasingly "Old Town" fell by the wayside, its adobe buildings occupied primarily by the Mexican and Spanish population maintaining their rural lifestyle, while Anglos dominated commerce and the construction of the new city.

In the early 20th century, Albuquerque's crisp air was lauded for its beneficial effect on tuberculosis symptoms, and sanatoriums flourished. By 1912, these patients made up nearly a quarter of the state's population. Then Route 66 was laid down Central Avenue in the 1930s. By the next decade, car traffic and business were booming; by the 1950s, the characteristic neon signs on the numerous motor-court hotels and diners were in place.

Albuquerque's character changed again after World War II, when recruits trained at Kirtland Air Force Base returned to settle down. At the same time, the escalating Cold War fueled Sandia National Labs, established in 1949. Streets were carved into the northeast foothills for these workers' tract homes, and over the course of the 1940s, the population exploded from 35,000 to 100,000; by 1959, 207,000 people lived in Albuquerque.

Growth has been steady ever since, and recent development has been spurred by an Intel manufacturing plant, a growing film industry, and other technical innovations. Subdivisions have spread across the West Mesa, and small outlying communities have become suburbs—though portions along the river retain a village feel that's not too far from the city's roots as a farming community three centuries back.

## PLANNING YOUR TIME

Because it's not so full of must-see historic attractions, Albuquerque fares best as the primary focus of a trip, when you have time to enjoy the natural setting, the food, and the people. Ideally, you would spend a leisurely four or five days here, soaking up a little Route 66 neon, enjoying the downtown entertainment, hiking in the Sandias, taking scenic drives, and bicycling along the Rio Grande.

If you're also planning to visit other parts of the state, it is difficult to recommend more than a couple of days in Albuquerque—preferably on the way out, as the city's modern, get-real attitude is best appreciated after you've been in the adobe dreamland of Santa Fe for a bit. Spend a day visiting the Salinas pueblos, then the next relaxing and knocking around Old Town and the shops in Nob Hill. Or if you prefer a last dose of open sky, take the tramway up to Sandia Peak and hike along the crest trail—at the end of your trip, you'll be able to handle the elevation with no problem.

Any time of year is enjoyable in the city proper—winters are mild in the low basin around the river, though the Sandias often get heavy snow. As elsewhere, summer heat is broken by heavy afternoon rainstorms. And because Albuquerque is seldom at the top of tourists' lists, there's never a time when it's unpleasantly mobbed. Hotel prices are higher in summer, but not a dramatic hike from low-season rates.

## ORIENTATION

Albuquerque's greater metro area covers more than 100 square miles, but visitors will likely see only a handful of neighborhoods, all linked by Central Avenue (historic Route 66), the main east-west thoroughfare across town. Visitors typically start in Old Town: The best museums are clustered here, a few blocks from the Rio Grande, which runs north-south through the city. East from Old Town lies downtown, with most of the city's bars and clubs, along with the bus and train depots. Central continues under I-25 and past the University of New Mexico campus, followed by the Nob Hill shopping district, which occupies about 10 blocks of Central. After this, the rest of Albuquerque blurs into the broad area known as the Northeast Heights; the main attractions up this way are hiking trails in the foothills and the Sandia Peak Tramway. The other notable parts of town—technically, separate villages—are Los Ranchos de Albuquerque and Corrales. These are two districts in the North Valley—the stretch of the river north of Central—that contain a few of the city's better lodging options; from Old Town, head north on Rio Grande Boulevard to reach Los Ranchos, then jog west over the river and north again to Corrales.

To get your bearings, do as the locals do and keep your eyes on the mountain, along the east side of the city. Street addresses are followed by the city quadrant (NE, NW, SE, SW); Central Avenue divides north and south, while the east-west border is roughly along 1st Street and the train tracks. When locals talk about "the Big I," they mean the relatively central point where I-40 and I-25 intersect. You won't need to use the freeways for much until you head east to the foothills or west to Petroglyph National Monument.

# Sights

## OLD TOWN AND THE RIO GRANDE

Until the railroad arrived in 1880, Old Town wasn't old—it was the *only* town. The labyrinthine old adobes have been repurposed as souvenir emporiums and galleries; the city's major museums are nearby on Mountain Road. Despite the chile-pepper magnets and cheap cowboy hats, the residential areas surrounding the shady plaza retain a strong Hispano flavor, and the historic Old Town buildings have a certain endearing scruffiness—they're lived-in, not polished. Because there are few formal sights but plenty of lore in the neighborhood, the free walking tour with the Albuquerque Museum of Art and History is recommended. A few blocks west of Old Town runs the Rio Grande,

a ribbon of green through the city and a quiet reminder of the city's agricultural history.

## ◖ ABQ Trolley Co.

To cruise the major attractions in town and get oriented, put yourself in the hands of the excellent locally owned and operated **ABQ Trolley Co.** (303 Romero St. NW, 505/240-8000, www.abqtrolley.com, Apr.-Oct., $25). Even if you're not normally the bus tour type, you'll find this one special. Not only is it in a goofy faux-adobe open-sided trolley-bus, but the enthusiastic owners give the tours themselves, and their love of the city is clear as they wave at pedestrians and tell stories about onetime Albuquerque resident Bill Gates.

All tours depart from Old Town. The

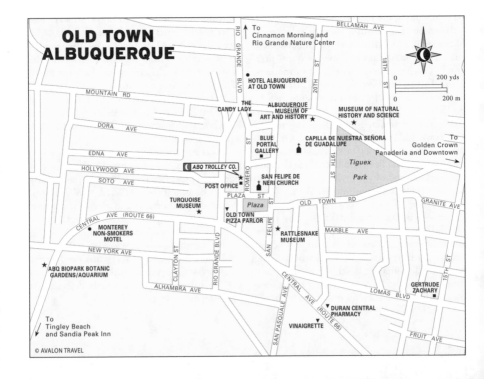

OLD TOWN ALBUQUERQUE

© AVALON TRAVEL

© ZORA O'NEILL

The ABQ Trolley tour takes a quirky look at the city's neighborhoods.

75-minute standard tour (11am and 1pm Tues.-Sat., 1pm Sun., $25) runs through downtown and some off-the-beaten-track old neighborhoods, passing many TV and movie locations. There's also a weekly *Breaking Bad* tour (3.5 hours, $65) that's hugely popular—book well in advance for this. Or join one of the monthly nighttime theme tours—such as "Albucreepy," a tour of supposedly haunted locations, or a pizza crawl—which draws locals as well. Buy tickets online to guarantee a spot; they also give you discounts around town.

### ABQ BioPark

The kid-friendly **ABQ BioPark** (505/768-2000, www.cabq.gov/biopark, 9am-5pm daily, till 6pm Sat.-Sun. June-Aug.) has three components. On the riverbank just west of Old Town (2601 Central Ave. NW) is a single complex that contains, on one side, an **aquarium,** with a giant shark tank, a creepy tunnel full of eels, and displays on underwater life from the Gulf of Mexico and up the Rio Grande. The other

half is **botanic gardens,** including a desert hot-house and a butterfly habitat. The most New Mexico-specific installation, and the most interesting, is the 10-acre Rio Grande Heritage Farm, a re-creation of a 1930s operation with heirloom apple orchards and rare types of livestock, such as Percheron horses and Churro sheep, in an idyllic setting near the river.

A few blocks away is the **zoo** (903 10th St. SW), which you can reach from the aquarium via a miniature train. The zoo is not particularly groundbreaking, but there's plenty of space for kids to run around among trumpeting elephants and screeching peacocks. The window into the gorilla nursery is probably the most fascinating exhibit. Tickets for each section (zoo or aquarium/gardens) are $12.50, and a combo ticket for entry at all three, which includes the mini-train ride, is $20.

Between the zoo and aquarium, on the east bank of the river, south of Central, so-called **Tingley Beach** (1800 Tingley Dr. SW, sunrise-sunset, free) is 18 acres of paths and ponds for fishing; you can also rent pedal boats and bicycles here.

### Albuquerque Museum of Art and History

The **Albuquerque Museum of Art and History** (2000 Mountain Rd. NW, 505/243-7255, www.cabq.gov/museum, 9am-5pm Tues.-Sun., $4, free 9am-1pm Sun.) has a permanent collection ranging from a few choice Taos Society of Artists members to contemporary work by the likes of Nick Abdalla, whose sensual imagery makes Georgia O'Keeffe's flower paintings look positively literal. The history wing covers four centuries, with emphasis on Spanish military trappings, Mexican cowboys, and Albuquerque's early railroad years. Free guided tours run daily around the sculpture garden, or you can join the informative **Old Town walking tour** (11am Tues.-Sun. mid-Mar.-mid-Dec.).

### American International Rattlesnake Museum

You'd never guess that a small storefront just off the plaza houses the **American International**

## Breaking Bad

Walter White and Jesse Pinkman may be gone from television, but their legacy lives on in Albuquerque. The AMC show about a high school chemistry teacher turned meth cook, *Breaking Bad* was originally written for a California setting, but production moved to Albuquerque following tax incentives. It was a happy accident, and unlike other productions shot here anonymously, *Breaking Bad* was explicitly down with the 505.

Dedicated fans should book the monthly "BaD Tour" with the **ABQ Trolley Co.** (303 Romero St. NW, 505/240-8000, www.abqtrolley.com, Apr.-Oct., 3.5 hours, $65)–though its standard route passes a few filming locations as well. The bike rental company **Routes** (1102 Mountain Rd. NW, 505/933-5667, $50) offers several "Biking Bad" tours every other Saturday; each route follows a different character.

Other sights around town include:

- The **Dog House** hot-dog stand, with its exceptionally fine neon sign, is at 1216 Central Avenue Southwest, near Old Town.

- **Los Pollos Hermanos** is actually Twisters, at 4257 Isleta Boulevard Southwest, but the PH logo is painted on the wall outside.

- Walt and Skyler's **car wash** is at Menaul and Eubank.

- **The Grove,** where Lydia loved her Stevia too well, is a popular café downtown.

As souvenirs of your Albuquerque visit, **Great Face & Body** (123 Broadway SE, 505/404-6670) sells Bathing Bad blue bath salts. **The Candy Lady** (524 Romero Ave. NW, 505/243-6239), which cooked the prop "meth" for a few episodes, sells its blue hard candy in zip-top baggies.

**Rattlesnake Museum** (202 San Felipe St. NW, 505/242-6569, www.rattlesnakes.com, 10am-6pm Mon.-Sat., 1pm-5pm Sun. June-Aug., $5), the largest collection of live snakes in the world. To see the real critters, you have to wade through an enormous gift shop full of plush snakes, wood snakes, little magnet snakes, and snakes on T-shirts. You'll also see some fuzzy tarantulas and big desert lizards, and the reptile-mad staff are usually showing off some animals outside to help educate the phobic. In the off-season, September-May, weekday hours are 11:30am-5:30pm (weekends are the same).

### Capilla de Nuestra Señora de Guadalupe

One of the nifty secrets of Old Town, the tiny adobe **Capilla de Nuestra Señora de Guadalupe** (404 San Felipe St. NW) is tucked off a small side alley. It's dedicated to the first saint of Mexico; her image dominates the wall facing the entrance. The dimly lit room, furnished only with heavy carved seats against the walls, is still in regular use, and the air is sweet with the smell of votive candles. Despite the building's small scale, it follows the scheme of many traditional New Mexican churches, with a clerestory that allows sunlight to shine down on the altar.

### Indian Pueblo Cultural Center

Just north of I-40 from Old Town, the **Indian Pueblo Cultural Center** (2401 12th St. NW, 505/843-7270, www.indianpueblo.org, 9am-5pm daily, $6) is a must-visit before heading to any of the nearby Indian communities. The horseshoe-shaped building (modeled after the Pueblo Bonito ruins in Chaco Canyon in northwestern New Mexico) houses a large museum that traces the history of the first settlers along the Rio Grande. It depicts the Spanish Conquest as a faintly absurd enterprise, and is illustrated with some beautiful artifacts and showcases the best craftwork from each pueblo.

The central plaza hosts **dance performances** (11am and 2pm Apr.-Oct., noon Nov.-Mar.), one of the only places to see them outside of the pueblos themselves. The extensively stocked

© ZORA O'NEILL

Seek out the hidden Capilla de Nuestra Señora de Guadalupe chapel in Old Town.

gift shop is a very good place to buy pottery and jewelry; you can also have a lunch of *posole* and fry bread at the Pueblo Harvest Café. Don't miss the south wing, which contains a gallery for contemporary art. At the information desk, check on ceremony schedules and get directions to the various pueblos.

## Museum of Natural History and Science

The **Museum of Natural History and Science** (1801 Mountain Rd. NW, 505/841-2800, www. nmnaturalhistory.org, 9am-5pm daily) is a large exhibit space containing three core attractions: a **planetarium** and **observatory**; a wide-format **theater** screening the latest vertigo-inducing nature documentaries; and a presentation of Earth's geological history. This latter section devotes plenty of space to the crowd-pleasers: dinosaurs. New Mexico has been particularly rich soil for paleontologists, and several of the most interesting finds are on display, such as *Coelophysis* and *Pentaceratops*. In addition, the *Startup* exhibit details the early history of the personal computer in Albuquerque and elsewhere. The show was funded by Paul Allen, who founded Microsoft here with Bill Gates, *then* moved to Seattle. Admission is $7 to the main exhibit space or the planetarium and $10 for the theater, though there are discounts if you buy tickets to more than one.

## Rio Grande Nature Center State Park

Familiarize yourself with river ecology at the **Rio Grande Nature Center State Park** (2901 Candelaria St. NW, 505/344-7240, www.rgnc. org, 8am-5pm daily, $3/car), in the center of town. You enter the sleek, concrete **visitors center** (10am-5pm daily) through a drainage culvert. Beyond an exhibit on water conservation and river ecology is a comfortable glassed-in "living room," where you can watch birds on the pond from the comfort of a lounge chair, with the outdoor sounds piped in through speakers. Outside, several **paved trails** run across irrigation channels and along the river, shaded by towering cottonwoods. In the spring and fall, the area draws all manner of migrating birdlife. Borrow binoculars from the staff if you want to scout on your own, or join one of the frequent **nature walks** (including full-moon tours) that take place year-round.

### San Felipe de Neri Church

Established in 1706 along with the city itself, **San Felipe de Neri Church** (2005 N. Plaza St. NW) was originally built on what would become the west side of the plaza—but it dissolved in a puddle of mud after a strong rainy season in 1792. The replacement structure, on the north side, has fared much better, perhaps because its walls, made of adobe-like *terrones* (sun-dried bricks cut out of sod) are more than five feet thick. As they have for two centuries, local parishioners attend Mass here, conducted three times a day, once in Spanish.

Like many religious structures in the area, San Felipe de Neri received a makeover from Eurocentric Bishop Jean Baptiste Lamy of Santa Fe in the second half of the 19th century. Under his direction, the place got its wooden folk Gothic spires, as well as new Jesuit priests from Naples, who added such non-Spanish details as the gabled entrance and the widow's walk. The small yet grand interior has brick floors, a baroque gilt altar, and an elaborate pressed-tin ceiling with Moorish geometric patterns. A tiny **museum** (9:30am-5pm Mon.-Sat., free), accessible through the gift shop, contains some historic church furnishings.

### Turquoise Museum

The **Turquoise Museum** (2107 Central Ave. NW, 505/247-8650, tours 11am and 1pm Mon.-Sat., $10), a modest-looking place in a strip mall, is much more substantial than it looks. Exhibits present the geology and history of turquoise, along with legendary trader J. C. Zachary's beautiful specimens from all over the world. But most folks can't help but think how this relates to all the jewelry they plan to buy. So come here to learn the distinction between "natural" and "real" turquoise and otherwise arm yourself for the shopping ahead. Admission is by **guided tour** only (1.5 hours).

## DOWNTOWN

Albuquerque's downtown district, along Central Avenue between the train tracks and Marquette Avenue, was once known as bustling New Town, crowded with mule-drawn streetcars, bargain hunters, and wheeler-dealers from the East Coast. Then, in the 1950s and 1960s, shopping plazas in Nob Hill and the Northeast Heights drew business away. By the 1970s, downtown was a wasteland of government office buildings and utterly desolate after 5pm. But thanks to an aggressive urban-renewal scheme initiated in 2000, the neighborhood has regained some of its old vigor, and Central is now a thoroughfare best known for its bars and lounges. By day, you won't see too many specific attractions, but a stroll around reveals an interesting hodgepodge of architectural styles from Albuquerque's most optimistic era.

### ( KiMo Theatre

Albuquerque's most distinctive building is the **KiMo Theatre** (423 Central Ave. NW,

© ZORA O'NEILL

The splendid KiMo Theatre is preserved and managed by the city.

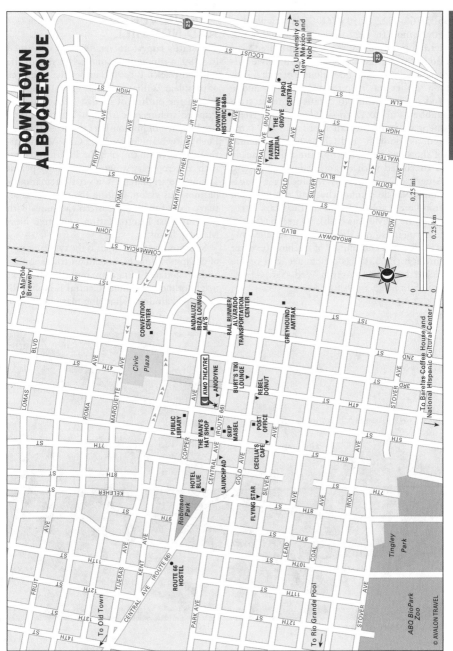

# DOWNTOWN ALBUQUERQUE

To Marble Brewery

To Old Town

CONVENTION CENTER

Civic Plaza

Robinson Park

PUBLIC LIBRARY

THE MAN'S HAT SHOP

HOTEL BLUE

LAUNCHPAD

ROUTE 66 HOSTEL

ANDALUZ/ IBIZA LOUNGE/ MA'S

KIMO THEATRE

ANODYNE

BURT'S TIKI LOUNGE

SKIP MAISEL

CECILIA'S CAFÉ

POST OFFICE

FLYING STAR

REBEL DONUT

RAIL RUNNER/ ALVARADO TRANSPORTATION CENTER

GREYHOUND/ AMTRAK

DOWNTOWN HISTORIC B&Bs

FARINA PIZZERIA

THE GROVE

PARQ CENTRAL

To University of New Mexico and Nob Hill

To Barelas Coffee House and National Hispanic Cultural Center

ABQ BioPark Zoo

Tingley Park

To Rio Grande Pool

© AVALON TRAVEL

0.25 mi

0.25 km

505/768-3522 or 505/768-3544, www.cabq.
gov/kimo). In 1927, local businessman and
Italian immigrant Carlo Bachechi hired Carl
Boller, an architect specializing in movie pal-
aces, to design this marvelously ornate building. Boller was inspired by the local adobe
and native culture to create a unique style
dubbed Pueblo Deco—a flamboyant treatment of Southwestern motifs, in the same
vein as Moorish- and Chinese-look cinemas
of the same era. The tripartite stucco facade
is encrusted with ceramic tiles and Native
American iconography (including a traditional Navajo symbol that had not yet been
completely appropriated by the Nazi Party
when the KiMo was built). To get the full effect, you must tour the interior to see the cow-
skull sconces and murals of pueblo life; enter
through the business office just west of the
**ticket booth** (11am-8pm Wed.-Sat., 11am-
3pm Sun.).

## THE UNIVERSITY AND NOB HILL

The state's largest university was established
in 1889, a tiny outpost on the far side of the
railroad tracks. By 1909, under the guidance
of president William George Tight, it had acquired the outline of its distinctive pueblo-
inspired architecture (though Tight was then
fired in part for his non-Ivy League aesthetics).
Pueblo Revival pioneer John Gaw Meem carried on the vision through the 1940s, and even
with contemporary structures now interspersed
among the original halls, it's still a remarkably
harmonious vision, uniting the pastoral sanctuary feel of the great Eastern campuses with
a minimalist interpretation of native New
Mexican forms.

Surrounding the campus is the typical scrum
of cheap pizza places, bohemian coffeehouses,
and dilapidated bungalow rentals. The next
neighborhood east along Central is Nob Hill,
developed around a shopping plaza in the late

the University of New Mexico

© ZORA O'NEILL

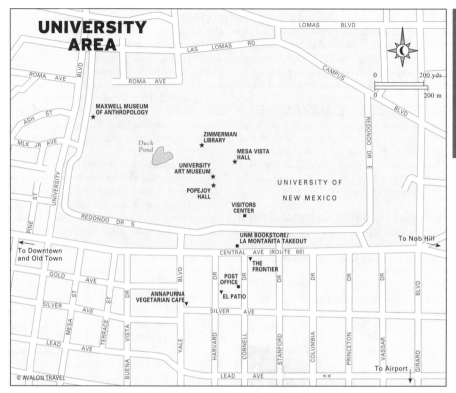

UNIVERSITY AREA

© AVALON TRAVEL

1940s and still showing that decade's distinctive style in marquees and shop facades.

## The University of New Mexico

Nearly 25,000 students use the **University of New Mexico** campus, which sprawls for blocks beyond the old core bounded by Central Avenue and University Boulevard. Visitors can park in a complex just inside the UNM campus across from Cornell Street. The info center, where you can pick up a detailed map, is in the southwest corner of the structure. Just across the way, the **University Art Museum** (505/277-4001, 10am-4pm Tues.-Sat., $5 donation) displays treasures from the permanent fine art collection of more than 30,000 pieces from all over the globe.

Wandering around the grounds, you'll see such classic Meem buildings as **Mesa Vista**

**Hall** (now the Student Services Building) and **Zimmerman Library.** Rest up at the bucolic duck pond, then head for the **Maxwell Museum of Anthropology** (off University Blvd., north of M. L. K. Jr. Blvd., 505/277-4405, 10am-4pm Tues.-Sat., free), a Meem building designed as the student union. The museum has a particularly good overview of Southwestern Indian culture.

## Nob Hill

Gates trimmed in neon mark the **Nob Hill** district on Central Avenue at Girard Street and at Washington Boulevard. The area began to grow after 1937, when Route 66 was rejiggered to run along Central. The Nob Hill Shopping Plaza, at Central and Carlisle, signaled the neighborhood's success when it opened as the glitziest shopping district in town a decade later. The area went through a slump from the 1960s through the mid-1980s, but it's again lined with brightly painted facades and neon signs, a lively district where the quirk factor is high—whether you want designer underwear or an antique Mexican mask, you'll find it here.

## ALBUQUERQUE METRO AREA

Beyond these neighborhoods, Albuquerque is a haze of houses and shopping centers built during the 1960s and later—decades dubbed Albuquerque's "Asphalt Period" by one local journalist. A few sights are well worth seeking out, however.

### National Hispanic Cultural Center

Just south of downtown (but not within walking distance) on 4th Street, the modern **National Hispanic Cultural Center** (1701 4th St. SW, 505/246-2261, www.nhccnm.org, 10am-5pm Tues.-Sun., $3, free on Sun.) lauds the cultural contributions of Spanish speakers the world over. It has had a positive influence in the down-at-the-heels district of Barelas (even

one of the performance halls at the National Hispanic Cultural Center

the McDonald's across the street mimics its architecture), but numerous houses—occupied by Hispanics, no less—were demolished for its construction. One woman refused the buyout, and her two small houses still sit in the parking lot, almost like an exhibit of their own.

The central attraction is the **museum**, which shows work ranging from the traditional santos and *retablos* by New Mexican craftspeople to contemporary painting, photography, and even furniture by artists from Chile, Cuba, Argentina, and more. If you can, visit on Sunday, when the *torreón* (tower) is open (noon-4pm) to show Frederico Vigil's amazing fresco *Mundos de mestizaje*, a decade-long project depicting the many strands—Arab, Celtic, African—that have contributed to Hispanic culture today.

Adjacent to the museum is the largest Hispanic genealogy library in existence, as well as the giant Roy E. Disney Center for Performing Arts.

### National Museum of Nuclear Science & History

The spiffy **National Museum of Nuclear Science & History** (601 Eubank Blvd. SE, 505/245-2137, www.nuclearmuseum.org, 9am-5pm daily, $8) covers everything you wanted to know about the nuclear era, from the development of the weapon on through current energy issues. Exhibits cover the ghastly elements of the atomic bomb, but also wonky tech details (check out the display of decoders, set in suitcases for emergency deployment) and pop-culture artifacts, such as "duck and cover" films from the Cold War. Don't miss the beautiful posters by Swiss American artist Erik Nitsche.

### ◖ Sandia Peak Tramway

The longest tramway of its type in the world, the **Sandia Peak Tramway** (505/856-7325, www.sandiapeak.com, $1 parking, $20 round-trip, $12 one-way) whisks passengers 2.7 miles along a continuous line of Swiss-made cables, from Albuquerque's northeast foothills 4,000 feet up to the crest in about 15 minutes. If the wind is blowing, the ride can be a bit

© ZORA O'NEILL

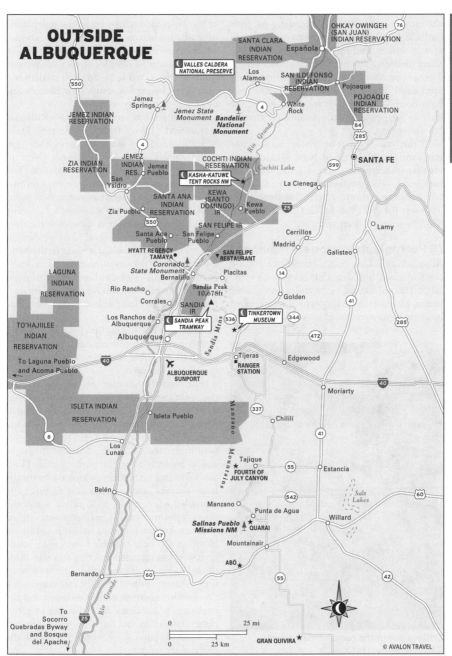

# OUTSIDE ALBUQUERQUE

OHKAY OWINGEH (SAN JUAN) INDIAN RESERVATION

Española

SANTA CLARA INDIAN RESERVATION

VALLES CALDERA NATIONAL PRESERVE

Los Alamos

SAN ILDEFONSO INDIAN RESERVATION

Pojoaque

POJOAQUE INDIAN RESERVATION

JEMEZ INDIAN RESERVATION

Jemez Springs

Jemez State Monument

**Bandelier National Monument**

White Rock

Rio Grande

ZIA INDIAN RESERVATION

JEMEZ INDIAN RES.

Jemez Pueblo

COCHITI INDIAN RESERVATION

Cochiti Lake

La Cienega

**SANTA FE**

San Ysidro

KASHA-KATUWE TENT ROCKS NM

KEWA (SANTO DOMINGO) IR

Kewa Pueblo

SANTA ANA INDIAN RESERVATION

Zia Pueblo

Cerrillos

Lamy

SAN FELIPE IR

Madrid

Galisteo

Santa Ana Pueblo

San Felipe Pueblo

**HYATT REGENCY TAMAYA**

SAN FELIPE RESTAURANT

LAGUNA INDIAN RESERVATION

**Coronado State Monument**

Bernalillo

Placitas

Rio Rancho

Sandia Peak 10,678ft

Golden

Corrales

SANDIA IR

Los Ranchos de Albuquerque

**SANDIA PEAK TRAMWAY**

TINKERTOWN MUSEUM

TO'HAJIILEE INDIAN RESERVATION

Albuquerque

Sandia Mtns

To Laguna Pueblo and Acoma Pueblo

ALBUQUERQUE SUNPORT

Tijeras

RANGER STATION

Edgewood

Moriarty

ISLETA INDIAN RESERVATION

Isleta Pueblo

Manzano Mountains

Chilili

Los Lunas

Estancia

Tajique

**FOURTH OF JULY CANYON**

Salt Lakes

Belén

Manzano

Punta de Agua

Willard

**Salinas Pueblo Missions NM**

QUARAI

Mountainair

Bernardo

Rio Grande

ABÓ

GRAN QUIVIRA

To Socorro Quebradas Byway and Bosque del Apache

0        25 mi

0        25 km

© AVALON TRAVEL

alarming—or thrilling, depending on your outlook. It's a convenient way to get to the ski area in winter, and in summer, you can hike along the crest a few miles to the visitors center. The service runs frequently year-round (9am-9pm daily June-Aug., 9am-8pm Wed.-Mon., 5pm-8pm Tues. Sept.-May)—but check the website for periodic maintenance closures in fall and spring.

At the base of the tram, there's a small free museum about skiing in New Mexico, and even from this point, the view across the city is very good—you may want to come to the casual Mexican restaurant here, **Sandiago's** (38 Tramway Rd., 505/856-6692, 11am-8pm daily, $13), for a sunset margarita.

## ◖ Petroglyph National Monument

Albuquerque's west side is bordered by 7,500 acres of black boulders that crawl with some 20,000 carved lizards, birds, and assorted other beasts. Most of the images, which were created by chipping away the blackish surface "varnish"

Critters adorn the rocks at Petroglyph National Monument.

of the volcanic rock to reach the paler stone beneath, are between 400 and 700 years old, while others may date back three millennia. A few more recent examples of rock art include Maltese crosses made by Spanish settlers and initials left by explorers (not to mention a few by idle 20th-century teenagers).

Stop in first at the **Petroglyph National Monument** (Unser Blvd. at Western Trail, 505/899-0205, www.nps.gov/petr, 8am-5pm daily) visitors center for park maps, flyers on flora and fauna, and general orientation. You can see some of the largest groupings on two major trails: **Boca Negra Canyon,** a short paved loop, and in **Rinconada Canyon,** a 1.25-mile one-way hike. Boca Negra Canyon is the only fee area ($1/car on weekdays, $2 on weekends), and there are restrooms and water in the parking area. The Rinconada trailhead is less developed; the walk can be tedious going in some spots because the ground is sandy, but it's relatively flat. The clearest, most impressive images are in the canyon at the end of the trail. Keep an eye out for millipedes, which thrive in this stark environment; dead, their curled-up shells resemble the spirals carved on the rocks—coincidence?

The back (west) side of the parkland is the **Volcanoes Day Use Area** (9am-5pm daily), where three cinder cones distinguish Albuquerque's western horizon. Access is via Atrisco Vista Boulevard (exit 149) off I-40; turn right (east) 4.3 miles north of the highway at a dirt road to the parking area. From this vantage point, you can look down on the lava "fingers" that stretch east to form the crumbled edges of the escarpment where the petroglyphs are found. The fingers were formed when molten rock flowed between sandstone bluffs, which later crumbled away. The volcanoes were last reported emitting steam in 1881, though a group of practical jokers set smoky fires in them in the 1950s, briefly convincing city-dwellers of an impending eruption. But the peaks are not entirely dead: Patches of green plants flourish around the steam vents that stud the hillocks, particularly visible on the middle of the three volcanoes.

© ZORA O'NEILL

## Anderson-Abruzzo Albuquerque International Balloon Museum

Boosters of Albuquerque's hot air balloon scene—which has been flourishing since the first rally in 1972—include locals Ben Abruzzo, Larry Newman, and Maxie Anderson, who in 1978 made the first Atlantic crossing by balloon in the *Double Eagle II* helium craft. Abruzzo and Anderson also crossed the Pacific and set a long-distance record (5,678 miles) in the *Double Eagle V*. These pioneers are honored at the so-called **BaMu** (9201 Balloon Museum Dr. NE, 505/880-0500, www.balloonmuseum. com, 9am-5pm Tues.-Sun., $4), in Balloon Fiesta Park just off Alameda Boulevard. The displays are a great mix of historical background, interactive physics lessons, and inspiring footage of record-setting balloon ventures. As long as you don't dwell too long on the zeppelin exhibit, complete with salt-and-pepper cellars from the *Hindenburg,* you'll likely come away inspired by the grace of balloons and wanting to take a ride in one yourself.

## Los Ranchos and Corrales Scenic Byway

For a pretty drive (or bike ride) through these villages that have been all but consumed by greater Albuquerque, head north from Old Town on Rio Grande Boulevard; you first reach **Los Ranchos**, then cross the river at Alameda to Corrales Road and continue up the west bank. These districts remain pockets of pastoral calm where horses gambol and 18th-century acequias water organic herb gardens—a practical melding of old agricultural heritage with modern suburban bliss. The only real sights are in central Corrales, two blocks west of the main road. The folk Gothic **Old San Ysidro Church** (505/897-1513, 1pm-4pm Sat.-Sun. June-Oct.) stands where the center of the village was in 1868, when its bulging adobe piers were first constructed. Every spring, the church gets a fresh coat of mud from the community.

Across the road, **Casa San Ysidro** (505/898-3915, www.cabq.gov/museum, $4) was owned by obsessive collectors Alan and Shirley Minge, who lived in the place from 1952 to 1997, heating with firewood and squirreling away New Mexican antiques and craftwork. The Albuquerque Museum gives tours of the interior, with its beautiful brickwork and wood carving, June-August (9:30am and 1:30pm Wed.-Fri., 9:30am, 10:30am, and 1:30pm Sat., 2pm Sun.) and a little less frequently September-November and February-May (9:30am and 1:30pm Wed.-Sat., 2pm Sun.). You can just turn up, but it's a good idea to call to confirm the times.

## Coronado State Monument

Though named for Spanish explorer Francisco Vásquez de Coronado, who camped on this lush spot by the river during his 1540 search for gold, the **Coronado State Monument** (485 Kuaua Rd., Bernalillo, 505/867-5351, 8:30am-5pm Wed.-Mon., $3) is actually a Native American relic, the partially restored pueblo of Kuaua (Tiwa for "evergreen"), inhabited between 1300 and the early 1600s. The centerpiece is the partially sunken square kiva, its interior walls covered with murals of life-size human figures and animals in ritual poses. What you see are reproductions—the originals have been removed for preservation, and a few are on display in the visitors center. While not exactly worth its own special trip, the site is a good place to stop on your way up to Jemez, and the setting is pleasant for a picnic. Facing the river and the mountains, with the city hidden from view behind a dense screen of cottonwoods, you get a sense of the lush, calm life along the Rio Grande in the centuries before the Spanish arrived. To reach the monument, exit I-25 in Bernalillo and head west on Highway 550; Kuaua Road is on your right, before the Santa Ana Star casino.

# Entertainment and Events

## NIGHTLIFE

When the city government promoted downtown as the nightlife district, it may have created too much of a good thing. Now it's the city's main bar and club scene, packed in a few square blocks, which makes for handy hopping (or staggering) from place to place. Many bars cater to students, with plentiful beer and other happy-hour specials but a somewhat generic, slightly dressed-up atmosphere. It ends in a rowdy scene after closing time on Fridays and Saturdays and crowds spill out onto several blocks of Central that are closed to car traffic.

The more distinctive places are pure Albuquerque: unpretentious, with a remarkably varied clientele. Because there aren't enough members of any one particular subculture to pack a whole bar, even the most chic-appearing places will see an absentminded professor and a veteran Earth Firster propping up the bar next to well-groomed professionals.

### Downtown

The **Hotel Andaluz lobby** (125 2nd St. NW, 505/242-9090) touts itself as "Albuquerque's living room"—Conrad Hilton's original vision for the place—and it's a comfy spot to sip delectable cocktails (the watermelon-lime cooler is dangerously drinkable) and nibble Spain-inspired snacks, especially if you reserve one of the private "casbahs" on the weekend, when there's also live tango or salsa and a big crowd of dancers. On the second floor, the indoor-outdoor **Ibiza Lounge** (4pm-10pm Mon.-Thurs., 4pm-1am Fri.-Sat.) is a chic scene on weekends, a cooler alternative to the mayhem just over on Central; occasional special events carry cover charges, but usually it's free to enter.

The best all-purpose casual bar downtown is the second-floor **Anodyne** (409 Central Ave. NW, 505/244-1820, 4pm-1:30am Mon.-Fri., 7pm-1:30am Sat., 7pm-11:30pm Sun.), a long, wood-floor room filled with pool tables and a younger crowd sprawled on the thrift-store sofas. Choose from more than a hundred beers, and get some quarters to plug in to the good collection of pinball machines. Happy hour is 4pm-8pm Monday to Thursday, and till 9pm on Friday.

To catch touring indie rockers or the local crew about to hit it big, head to the very professional **Launchpad** (618 Central Ave. SW,

## Traditional New Mexican Music

Blaring mariachi ensembles, scratchy fiddles accompanying the Matachines dancers, booming tribal drums: The musical traditions of New Mexico are diverse. The best place to hear the mix is on **KANW (89.1 FM)** in Albuquerque, a public radio station that devotes most of its day and evening programming to homegrown music, with a heavy emphasis on mariachi, and such stars as Los Reyes de Albuquerque. There's also a vintage country show on Saturday nights, as a nod to Anglo listeners.

On Sunday afternoons, **KUNM (89.9 FM)** turns the airwaves over to *Singing Wire*, where you'll hear traditional Native American music as well as pop anthems like Keith Secola's oft-requested "NDN Kars" and the Black Lodge Singers chanting the Mighty Mouse theme song.

If you're out of range of these stations, look for the excellent Smithsonian Folkways CDs *Music of New Mexico: Hispanic Traditions* (which has the Matachines and Comanches dance songs alongside more widespread Mexican songs like "Las Mañanitas") and *New Mexico: Native American Traditions*, which is all traditional drumming.

505/764-8887, www.launchpadrocks.com). With free live music and a pool table, **Burt's Tiki Lounge** (313 Gold Ave. SW, 505/247-2878, www.burtstikilounge.com, 8:30pm-2am Wed.-Sat.) has a funky feel and an eclectic bill, from British psychedelia to reggae.

Farther out of the downtown fray, the **Marble Brewery** (111 Marble Ave. NW, 505/243-2739, 1pm-midnight Mon.-Sat., 1pm-10:30pm Sun.) is a cool space with a big patio out back, where you might catch a band: salsa, country, whatever—the crowd will dance to it, as their dogs hang out by the picnic tables. Its beers are much better than other brewpubs' in town.

### The University and Nob Hill

In the Nob Hill shopping plaza, **Gecko's** (3500 Central Ave. SE, 505/262-1848, 11:30am-late Mon.-Fri., noon-late Sat.-Sun.) is a good place for a snack (anything from Thai curry shrimp to chipotle hot wings) and a drink in the sidewalk seats. For more street life, **Kellys Brew Pub** (3222 Central Ave. SE, 505/262-2739, 8am-10:30pm Sun.-Thurs., 8am-midnight Fri.-Sat., $9) has ample outdoor seating along the

© ZORA O'NEILL

Kellys Brew Pub is set in a 1940s car dealership.

sidewalk. The food is only so-so—you're really here for the scene, the sun, and the suds.

## FESTIVALS AND EVENTS

The city's biggest annual event is the **Albuquerque International Balloon Fiesta** (505/821-1000, www.balloonfiesta.com), nine days in October dedicated to New Mexico's official state aircraft, with more than 700 hot air balloons of all colors, shapes, and sizes gathering at a dedicated park on the north side of town, west of I-25. During the fiesta, the city is packed with "airheads," who claim this is the best gathering of its kind in the world. If you go, don't miss an early-morning mass ascension, when the balloons glow against the dark sky, then lift silently into the air in a great wave. Parking can be a nightmare—take the park-and-ride bus, or ride a bike (valet parking available!).

In April is the equally colorful **Gathering of Nations Powwow** (505/836-2810, www. gatheringofnations.com), the largest tribal get-together in the United States, with more than 3,000 dancers and singers in full regalia from over 500 tribes crowding the floor of the University Arena. Miss Indian World earns her crown by showing off traditional talents such as spearfishing or storytelling.

Labor Day weekend is dedicated to the **New Mexico Wine Festival** (505/867-3311, www. newmexicowinefestival.com), in Bernalillo. It's well attended by a wide swath of Burqueños; the Rail Runner train runs on a special schedule, sparing stress on designated drivers.

Just after Labor Day, the state's agricultural roots get their due at the **New Mexico State Fair** (www.exponm.com), two weeks of fried foods and prizewinning livestock. It's the usual mix of midway craziness and exhibition barns, along with really excellent rodeos, which often end with shows by country music legends.

Around November 2, don't miss the **Marigold Parade** (505/363-1326, www.muertosymarigolds.org), celebrating the Mexican Day of the Dead. The parade through the South Valley is a procession of skeletons and cars bedecked in flowers.

## Ceremonial Dances

This is only an approximate schedule for dances at Albuquerque-area pueblos—dates can vary from year to year. Annual feast days typically involve carnivals and markets in addition to dances. Confirm details and start times—usually afternoon, but sometimes following an evening or midnight Mass—with the **Indian Pueblo Cultural Center** (505/843-7270, www.indianpueblo.org) before setting out.

- **January 1** - Jemez, Matachines
- **January 6** - Most pueblos: various dances
- **February 2** - San Felipe: various dances for Candlemas (Día de la Candelaria)
- **Easter** - Most pueblos: various dances
- **May 1** - San Felipe: Feast of San Felipe

- **June 13** - Sandia: Feast of San Antonio
- **June 29** - Santa Ana: Feast of San Pedro
- **July 14** - Cochiti: Feast of San Bonaventura
- **July 26** - Santa Ana: Feast of Santa Ana
- **August 2** - Jemez: Feast of Santa Persingula
- **August 15** - Zia: Feast of the Assumption of Our Blessed Mother
- **September 4** - Isleta: Feast of Saint Augustine
- **September 8** - Isleta (Encinal): Feast of the Nativity of the Blessed Virgin
- **November 12** - Jemez: Feast of San Diego
- **December 12** - Jemez: Los Matachines

# Shopping

Albuquerque doesn't have Santa Fe's exotic treasure troves and tony galleries, but it doesn't have the high prices either. Old Town and the environs are where you can pick up traditional American Indian jewelry and pottery for very reasonable prices, while Nob Hill is the commercial center of Albuquerque's counterculture, with body-piercing studios adjacent to comic book shops next to herbal apothecaries. On the first Friday of each month, **Artscrawl** (www.artscrawlabq.org) keeps galleries and shops open late in both neighborhoods and downtown; on the third Friday of the month, the festivities are focused in one neighborhood.

## OLD TOWN AND THE RIO GRANDE

The galleries and gift shops around the plaza can blur together after just a little bit of browsing, but the **Blue Portal Gallery** (2107 Church St. NW, 505/243-6005, 10am-4:30pm Mon.-Sat., 1pm-4pm Sun.) is a nice change, with well-priced and often very refined arts and crafts, from quilts to woodwork, by Albuquerque's senior citizens. And the **street vendors** set up on the east side of the plaza are all artisans selling their own work, at fair prices.

Just outside of Old Town's historic zone, the **Gertrude Zachary** showroom (1501 Lomas Blvd. NW, 505/247-4442, www.gertrudezachary.com, 10am-6pm Mon.-Sat., noon-6pm Sun.) is the place to go for contemporary turquoise-and-silver jewelry. For more traditional work, head to the shop at the **Indian Pueblo Cultural Center** (2401 12th St. NW, 505/843-7270, www.indianpueblo.org, 9am-5:30pm daily); not only are prices reasonable, but the staff is happy to explain the work that goes into various pieces.

## DOWNTOWN

An emporium of American Indian goods, **Skip Maisel's Indian Jewelry & Crafts** (510 Central Ave. SW, 505/242-6526, 9am-5:30pm

Mon.-Sat.) feels like a relic from downtown's heyday. Whether you want a war bonnet, a turquoise-studded watch, or deerskin moccasins, it's all here in a vast, overstocked shop with kindly salespeople. Don't miss the beautiful murals above the display windows and in the foyer; they were painted in the 1930s by local Indian artists such as Awa Tsireh, whose work hangs in the New Mexico Museum of Art in Santa Fe. Another throwback is **The Man's Hat Shop** (511 Central Ave. NW, 505/247-9605, 9:30am-5:30pm Mon.-Fri., 9:30am-5pm Sat.), which stocks just what it promises, from homburgs to ten-gallons.

## THE UNIVERSITY AND NOB HILL

**Mariposa Gallery** (3500 Central Ave. SE, 505/268-6828, 11am-6pm Mon.-Sat., noon-5pm Sun.) is one of the city's longest-established art vendors, dealing since 1974 in jewelry, fiber art, and other crafts. **The A Store** (3500 Central Ave. SE, 505/266-2222, 10am-6pm Mon.-Sat., noon-5pm Sun.) specializes in home furnishings for the Southwestern hipster, such as flower-print Mexican tablecloth fabric

© ZORA O'NEILL

a vintage shop window in Nob Hill

and handmade candles. The jewelry here, much of it by local designers, is very good too.

# Sports and Recreation

Albuquerque is a perfect city for outdoorsy types, with trails running through its several distinct ecosystems. Late summer (after rains have started and fire danger is passed) and fall are the best times to head to the higher elevations on the Sandia Mountains. Once the cooler weather sets in, the scrub-covered foothills and the bare, rocky West Mesa are more hospitable. The valley along the Rio Grande, running through the center of the city, is remarkably pleasant year-round: mild in winter and cool and shady in summer. As everywhere in the desert, always pack extra layers of clothing and plenty of water before you set out, and don't go charging up Sandia Peak (10,678 feet above sea level) your first day off the plane.

## ◀ BALLOONING

You don't have to be in town for the Balloon Fiesta to go up, up, and away. Take advantage of Albuquerque's near-flawless weather to take a hot-air balloon ride almost any morning of the year. A trip is admittedly an investment (and you have to wake up before dawn!), but the sensation of being so far up in the air, without any barriers, is unlike any other sort of ride, as it's free of any speed and adrenaline, and it's almost completely silent. One of the best established operations is **Rainbow Ryders** (505/823-1111, www.rainbowryders.com, $195 pp). Typically, you're up in the balloon for an hour or so, depending on wind conditions, and you get a champagne toast when you're back on solid ground.

A hot-air balloon ride provides a unique perspective on the city.

## BIKING

Albuquerque maintains a great network of paved trails in the city, and the mountains and foothills have challenging dirt tracks. Probably the most visitor-oriented bike store in town is **Routes** (1102 Mountain Rd. NW, 505/933-5667, 9am-6pm Mon.-Thurs., 8am-6pm Fri.-Sun., $15/hour, $35/day), which rents city cruisers, mountain bikes, and more at its handy location between Old Town and downtown; pickup and drop-off from hotels is free. It also runs fun daylong **bike tours,** and rents snowshoes in the winter (when the shop closes 30 minutes earlier).

### City Cycling

Recreational cyclists need head no farther than the river, where the **Paseo del Bosque,** a 16-mile-long, completely flat biking and jogging path, runs through the Rio Grande Valley State Park. The northern starting point is at **Alameda/Rio Grande Open Space** (7am-9pm daily Apr.-Oct., 7am-7pm daily Nov.-Mar.) on Alameda Boulevard. You can also reach the trail through the **Rio Grande Nature Center** (8am-5pm daily, $3/car), at the end of Candelaria, and at several other major intersections along the way. For details on this and other bike trails in Albuquerque, download a map from the city's bike info page (www.cabq.gov/bike), or pick up a free copy at bike shops around town. In the summer, you can rent bikes at **Tingley Beach** (part of ABQ BioPark, 10am-5pm Mon.-Fri., 10am-6pm Sat.-Sun., $8/hour, $20/4 hours) and start biking along the river from there.

Corrales is also good for an afternoon bike ride: The speed limit on the main street is low, and you can dip into smaller side streets and bike along the acequias. The excellent **Stevie's Happy Bikes** (4583 Corrales Rd., 505/897-7900, 10am-6pm Tues.-Sat.) rents comfy cruisers ($25/day) and even tandems ($35/day) and can advise on the best routes on and around the river. You could bike along the road one direction, perhaps stopping at the church and Casa San Ysidro, and then loop back on the riverfront path, an extension of the Paseo del Bosque. In about four hours, you can make a leisurely loop down to Los Poblanos farms and open space and get back up to Corrales.

### Mountain Biking

Mountain bikers can take the Sandia Peak Tramway to the ski area, then rent wheels to explore the 30 miles of wooded trails. Bikes aren't allowed on the tram, though, so if you have your own ride, you can drive around the east side of the mountain. Or stay in the city on the **foothills trails,** a web of dirt tracks all along the edge of the Northeast Heights. **Trail no. 365,** which runs for about 15 miles north-south from near the tramway down to near I-40, is the best run. You can start at either end, or go to the midpoint, at Elena Gallegos Picnic Area, off the north end of Tramway Boulevard at the end of Simms Park Road. Aside from the occasional sandy or rocky patch, none of the route is technical or steep. More complex

© ZORA O'NEILL

Tingley Beach has fishing ponds, as well as walking and biking trails.

trails run off to the east; pick up a map at the entrance booth at Elena Gallegos.

### Road Biking

A popular tour is up to **Sandia Peak** via the Crest Road on the east side—you can park and ride from any point, but cyclists typically start somewhere along Highway 14 north of I-40, then ride up Highway 536, which winds 13.5 miles along increasingly steep switchbacks to the crest. The **New Mexico Touring Society** (www.nmts.org) lists descriptions of other routes and organizes group rides.

## HIKING

Between the West Mesa and the east mountains, Albuquerque offers a range of day hikes. The least strenuous is the *bosque* (the wooded area along the Rio Grande), where level paths lead through groves of cottonwoods, willows, and olive trees. The **Rio Grande Nature Center State Park** (2901 Candelaria St. NW, 505/344-7240, www.rgnc.org, 8am-5pm daily,

$3/car) is the best starting point for any walk around the area.

For a little elevation gain, head to the Sandia foothills, ideal in the winter but a little hot in the summertime. The best access is at **Elena Gallegos Picnic Area** (7am-9pm Apr.-Oct., 7am-7pm Nov.-Mar., $1 weekdays, $2 weekends), east of Tramway Boulevard and north of Academy, at the end of Simms Park Road.

The foothills are also the starting point for the popular **La Luz Trail,** a 7.5-mile ascent to the Sandia Crest Visitor Center. The trail has a 12 percent grade at certain points, and passes through four climate zones (pack lots of layers) as you climb 3,200 vertical feet. Near the top, you can take a spur that leads north to the Sandia Crest observation point or continue on the main trail south to the ski area and the Sandia Peak Tramway, which you can take back down the mountain. Ideally you'd have someone pick you up at the bottom end of the tram, because the 2.5-mile trail along the foothills from the tram back to the trailhead is

## Birding on the Peak

**Sandia Peak** in the dead of winter does not seem hospitable to life in any form, much less flocks of delicate-looking birds the size of your fist, fluffing around cheerfully in the frigid air. But that's precisely what you'll see if you visit in the iciest months, particularly right after a big snowfall. The feathered critters in question are rosy finches, a contrary, cold-loving variety (sometimes called "refrigerator birds") that migrate from as far north as the Arctic tundra between November and March to the higher elevations of New Mexico, which must seem relatively tropical by comparison.

What's special about Sandia is that it draws all three species of rosy finch, which in turn draws dedicated birders looking to add the finches to their life lists. *Birder's World*

magazine praised Sandia Peak as "the world's most accessible location to see all three species of rosy finches." This is a boon for people who are more accustomed to kayaking through swamps and slogging through tropical forests to spot rare species.

So if you see the finches—they're midsize brown or black birds with pink bellies, rumps, and wings—you'll probably also spy some human finch fans. But they might not have time to talk, as it's not unheard-of for the most obsessive birders—those on their "big year," out to spot as many species as possible in precisely 365 days—to fly in to Albuquerque, drive to the crest, eyeball the finches, and drive right back down and fly out in search of even more obscure varieties.

dusty and lacks shade. (You might be tempted to take the tram up and hike down, but the steep descent can be deadly to toes and knees.) La Luz trailhead ($3/car) is at the far north end of Tramway Boulevard just before the road turns west.

To enjoy the views without quite so much effort, drive up the east face of the mountain (I-40 to Highway 14) via scenic byway Highway 536, a.k.a. the Crest Road, and park at the Sandia Crest Visitor Center at the top ($3/car). From there, an easy loop of a little more than two miles runs south along the **Crest Spur Trail,** which dips below the ridgeline to connect to **La Luz,** which in turn goes on to the tram terminal. Then you can hike back to your car via the **Crest Trail.**

## SKIING

**Sandia Peak Ski Area** (505/242-9052, www. sandiapeak.com, $50 full-day lift ticket) is open from mid-December through mid-March, though it often takes till about February for a good base to build up. The 10 main trails,

serviced by four lifts, are not dramatic, but they are good and long. The area is open daily in the holiday season, then Wednesday through Sunday for the rest of the winter.

Sandia Peak also has plenty of opportunities for cross-country skiing. Groomed trails start from **Capulin Springs Snow Play Area** (9:30am-3:30pm Fri.-Sun. in winter, $3/car), where there are also big hills for tubing and sledding. Look for the parking nine miles up Highway 536 to the crest. Farther up on the mountain, **10K Trail** is usually groomed for skiers, as is a service road heading south to the upper tramway terminal; the latter is wide and relatively level, good for beginners. Check the status of the trails at the Sandia **ranger station** (505/281-3304) on Highway 337 in Tijeras.

## SWIMMING

Beat the heat at the **Rio Grande Pool** (1410 Iron Ave. SW, 505/848-1397, noon-5pm daily, $2.25), one of Albuquerque's nicest places to take a dip; the outdoor 25-meter pool is shaded by giant cottonwoods.

# Accommodations

Because Albuquerque isn't quite a tourist mecca, its hotel offerings have languished a bit, but the scene has improved in recent years. There are still plenty of grungy places, but the good ones are exceptional values. Whether on the low or high end, you'll pay substantially less here than you would in Santa Fe for similar amenities.

## UNDER $100

Funky and affordable, the **Route 66 Hostel** (1012 Central Ave. SW, 505/247-1813, www.rt66hostel.com) is in a century-old house midway between downtown and Old Town and has been offering bargain accommodations since 1978; it's clean despite years of budget travelers traipsing through. Upstairs, along creaky wood hallways, are private rooms ($25-35) with various configurations. Downstairs and in the cool basement area are single-sex dorms ($20 pp). Guests have run of the kitchen, and there's a laundry and room to lounge. The most useful city bus lines run right out front. There have been complaints of staff not being on hand for early or late check-ins—be sure to call and confirm before you arrive.

If you're on a budget but have your own car, you can also stay on the east side of the Sandias, about a half-hour drive from the city. The **Cedar Crest Inn** (12231 Hwy. 14, 505/281-4117) is peaceful, with an orchard out back, and very inexpensive lodging, including a dorm option ($20 pp). The dorm area is well kept, though it's screened from the big, shared kitchen only by a curtain. Upstairs are three private rooms ($50-80). Just up the road on the west side, the **Turquoise Trail Campground** (22 Calvary Rd., 505/281-2005, www.turquoisetrailcampground.com, May-Oct.) has tree-shaded spots for tents ($17.50) as well as two small cabins ($36; no water) and one large one with a bathroom and kitchenette ($58), along with showers and laundry facilities.

The only criticism to muster against the

**Sandia Peak Inn** (4614 Central Ave. SW, 505/831-5036, www.sandiapeakinnmotel.com, $60 s, $70 d) is that it's nowhere near the mountain; in fact, it's on the west side of the city, just over the river from Old Town. In all other respects, it's more than you could want in a bargain hotel: large, spotless rooms, all with bathtubs, fridges, microwaves, and huge TVs. Breakfast is included in the rate. There's a small indoor pool and free wireless Internet available throughout.

Central Avenue is strewn with motels, many built in Route 66's heyday. Almost all of them are unsavory, except for **◖ Monterey Non-Smokers Motel** (2402 Central Ave. SW, 505/243-3554, www.nonsmokersmotel.com, $58 s, $68 d), which is as practical as its name implies. Except for a jazzy neon sign, the place doesn't really capitalize on 1950s kitsch—it just offers meticulously clean, good-value rooms with no extra frills or flair. One large family suite has two beds and a foldout sofa. The pool is a treat, the laundry facilities are a bonus, and the location near Old Town is very convenient.

**The Hotel Blue** (717 Central Ave. NW, 877/878-4868, www.thehotelblue.com, $69 d) offers great value downtown. The rooms in this '60s block are a slightly odd mix of cheesy motel decor (gold quilted bedspreads) and bachelor-pad flair (a gas "fireplace"), and the windows don't open. But the Tempur-Pedic beds are undeniably comfortable, and the low rates include breakfast, parking, and a shuttle to the airport. There's also a decent-size outdoor pool, open in summers, and the downtown farmers market is in the park right out front. Request a room on the northeast side for a mountain view.

On the north side of town, **Nativo Lodge** (6000 Pan American Fwy. NE, 505/798-4300, www.nativolodge.com, $74 d) is really convenient only for the Balloon Fiesta, or a cheap off-airport rental car pickup: a Hertz office is in walking distance. But the price is great for this level of comfort and style, with plush pillow-top beds and some rooms designed by local American Indian artists. Definitely request a room in the back, so you're not overlooking I-25.

## $100-150

The exceptionally tasteful ◖ **Downtown Historic Bed & Breakfasts of Albuquerque** (207 High St. NE, 505/842-0223, www.albuquerquebedandbreakfasts.com, $139 d) occupies two neighboring old houses on the east side of downtown, walking distance to good restaurants on Central in the EDo (East of Downtown) stretch. Heritage House has more of a Victorian feel, while Spy House has a sparer, 1940s look—but both are nicely clutter-free. Two outbuildings are more private suites.

The heart of **Cinnamon Morning** (2700 Rio Grande Blvd. NW, 505/345-3541, www.cinnamonmorning.com, $129 s), about a mile north of Old Town, is its lavish outdoor kitchen, with a huge round dining table and a fireplace to encourage lounging on nippier nights. Rooms are simply furnished, with minimalist Southwestern detail—choose from three smaller rooms in the main house, each with a private bath, or, across the garden, a two-bedroom guest house and a casita with a private patio and a kitchenette.

On a narrow road in the rural-feeling Los Ranchos district, **Casita Chamisa** (850 Chamisal Rd. NW, 505/897-4644, www.casitachamisa.com, $105 d) is very informal, and even a little bit worn, but really feels like staying at a friend's house (a friend who happens to have a swimming pool and an orchard). The rambling 150-year-old adobe compound is the sort of place that could exist only in New Mexico: It sits on an old acequia, amid the remnants of a Pueblo community established seven centuries ago. The site was partially excavated by the owner's late wife, an archaeologist.

Another strong option in Los Ranchos, **Sarabande B&B** (5637 Rio Grande Blvd. NW, 505/345-4923, www.sarabandebnb.com, $109 s), has six rooms in three configurations. They can be a bit jammed with

Southwestern tchotchkes, but the owners here are very thoughtful. A small lap pool takes up the backyard.

**Hotel Albuquerque at Old Town** (800 Rio Grande Blvd. NW, 505/843-6300, www.hotelabq.com, $139 d) is a good backup in this category. Sporting a chic Spanish colonial style, the brick-red-and-beige rooms are relatively spacious. Opt for the north side (generally, even-numbered rooms) for a view of the mountains.

## $150-250

A beautiful relic of early 20th-century travel, ◖**Hotel Andaluz** (125 2nd St. NW, 505/242-9090, www.hotelandaluz.com, $159 d) first opened in 1939 by New Mexico-raised hotelier Conrad Hilton. It received a massive renovation in 2009, keeping all the old wood and murals but updating the core to be fully environmentally friendly, from solar hot-water heaters to a composting program. The neutral-palette rooms are soothing and well designed, with a little Moorish flair in the curvy door outlines. The place is worth a visit for the lobby alone; check out the exhibits from local museums on the second-floor mezzanine.

Set in the original AT&SF railroad hospital and sporting a storied past, the stylishly renovated **Parq Central** (806 Central Ave. SE, 505/242-0040, www.hotelparqcentral.com, $139 s, $159 d), opened in late 2010 and is a nice alternative to the Andaluz if you prefer your history in paler shades. The rooms are a bit smaller but feel light and airy thanks to big windows and gray and white furnishings, with retro chrome fixtures and honeycomb tiles in the bath. The hospital vibe is largely eradicated, though whimsical vitrines in the halls conjure old-time medical treatments, and the rooftop bar sports a gurney. Perks include free parking, decent continental breakfast, and airport shuttle.

At Albuquerque's nicest place to stay, you don't actually feel like you're anywhere near the city. ◖**Los Poblanos Historic Inn** (4803 Rio Grande Blvd. NW, 505/344-9297, www.lospoblanos.com, $175 d) sits on 25 acres, the

© ZORA O'NEILL

The farm-fresh food at Los Poblanos Historic Inn is one of its main attractions.

largest remaining plot of land in the city, and the rooms are tucked in various corners of a sprawling *rancho* built in the 1930s by John Gaw Meem and beautifully maintained and preserved—even the huge old kitchen ranges are still in place, as are murals by Taos artist Gustave Baumann and frescoes by Peter Hurd. Main-house guest rooms, accented with Spanish colonial antiques and arrayed around a central patio, retain their old wood floors and heavy viga ceilings. Newer, larger rooms have been added and fit in flawlessly—Meem rooms have a very light Southwest touch, while the Farm rooms have a whitewashed rustic aesthetic, accented by prints and fabrics by modernist designer Alexander Girard, of the folk-art museum in Santa Fe. There's also a saltwater pool and a gym, but the most special feature is access to the extensive gardens

and organic lavender farm that take up much of the acreage. Included breakfast is exceptional (you get eggs from the farm), as are optional light dinners—make sure you plan on at least one.

The smell of piñon smoke and the sound of flute music set the tone at the **Hyatt Regency Tamaya** (1300 Tuyuna Tr., Santa Ana Pueblo, 505/867-1234, www.hyattregencytamaya.com, $179 d), a nicely designed resort that's a joint project with Santa Ana Pueblo. Rooms aren't always maintained as well as they could be, but even the standard ones are quite large, with either terraces or balconies, though the mountain view is worth the premium. Three swimming pools and a full spa offer relaxation; the more active can play golf or tennis, take an archery class, or attend an evening storytelling program with a pueblo member.

# Food

Albuquerque has a few dress-up establishments, but the real spirit of the city's cuisine is in its lower-rent spots where dedicated owners follow their individual visions. A lot of the most traditional New Mexican places are open only for breakfast and lunch, so plan accordingly. Prices given are those of the average entrée.

## OLD TOWN AND THE RIO GRANDE

Aside from the couple recommended here, the restaurants in the blocks immediately adjacent to the Old Town plaza are expensive and only so-so; better to walk another block or two for real New Mexican flavor, which can be found in a number of local hangouts around Old Town and up Rio Grande Boulevard in the North Valley.

### Cafés

Inside the Albuquerque Museum, **Slate Street Café** (2000 Mountain Rd. NW, 505/243-2220, 10am-2:30pm Tues.-Fri. and Sun., 10am-4pm Sat., $8) is great for coffee and cupcakes, as well as more substantial breakfast and lunch, like a chipotle-spiked meatloaf sandwich.

A 10-minute walk from Old Town, **Golden Crown Panaderia** (1103 Mountain Rd. NW, 505/243-2424, 7am-8pm Tues.-Sat., 10am-8pm Sun., $4-9) is a real neighborhood hangout that's so much more than a bakery. Famous for its green-chile bread and bizcochitos (the anise-laced state cookie), it also does pizza with blue-corn or green-chile crust, to take away or to eat at the picnic tables out back. And you'll want a side salad just to watch them assemble it straight from the hydroponic garden that consumes a lot of the space behind the counter. Wash it down with a coffee milkshake.

### Fresh and Local

Founded in Santa Fe, **Vinaigrette** (1828 Central Ave. SW, 505/842-5507, 11am-9pm daily, $13) is a posh-sounding "salad bistro"

that is more substantial than it sounds—and it's a welcome spot of healthy eating around Old Town.

On a barren stretch of North 4th Street, where neighboring businesses are feed stores and car washes, **Sophia's Place** (6313 4th St. NW, 505/345-3935, 7am-9pm Mon.-Fri., 9am-9pm Sat., 9am-2pm Sun., $9) is the sort of bohemian café that serves farm-fresh eggs but doesn't brag about it. Get those eggs on a breakfast sandwich, which you're really ordering for the side of highly addictive red-chile-dusted home fries. Lunch and dinner bring goodies like duck enchiladas with tomatillo sauce.

The restaurant at Los Poblanos resort, **La Merienda** (4803 Rio Grande Blvd. NW, 505/344-9297, 6pm-9pm Wed.-Sat., $26), serves flawless food, a bit Mediterranean in style, but undeniably New Mexican in ingredients like heirloom beans. The short menu changes each night, based on produce. Book well ahead—hotel guests get priority, so tables fill up fast.

If you can't get a table at La Merienda, the next best option is **Farm & Table** (8917 4th St. NW, 505/503-7124, 5pm-9pm Wed.-Thurs., 5pm-10pm Fri., 9am-2pm and 5pm-10pm Sat., 9am-2pm Sun., $30), which has a similar sensibility. Some diners have reported uneven meals and staff, but the setting is bucolic. Plus, the place is kid-friendly, with a big sandbox and plenty of toys within sight of some outdoor tables.

### New Mexican

Don't waste a meal on restaurants around the plaza. Instead, walk a couple of blocks to **Duran Central Pharmacy** (1815 Central Ave. NW, 505/247-4141, 9am-6:30pm Mon.-Fri., $9), an old-fashioned lunch counter hidden behind the magazine rack in this big fluorescent-lit drugstore. Regulars pack this place at lunch for all the New Mexican staples:

huevos rancheros, green-chile stew, and big enchilada plates. Cash only.

For New Mexican food with a heavier American Indian influence, hit the **Pueblo Harvest Café** (2401 12th St. NW, 505/724-3510, 8am-8:30pm Mon.-Thurs., 8am-9pm Fri.-Sat., 8am-4pm Sun., $10), at the Indian Pueblo Cultural Center. The menu has standard burgers and fries, but specialties such as mutton stew with a side of *horno* bread and a green-chile-and-lamb sandwich are rich and earthy and rarely found elsewhere. Breakfast is also good, with blue-corn mush topped with carne adovada, and apple-raisin "Indian toast." The "Rez Breakfast," with Spam on the side, may be a treat for some. There's live music Friday and Saturday evenings, as well as Sunday around noon.

### Italian

Not a destination from elsewhere in the city, but **Old Town Pizza Parlor** (108 Rio Grande Blvd. SW, 505/999-1949, 11am-9pm Mon.-Fri., noon-9pm Sat., noon-8pm Sun., $9) is an unpretentious place to eat in the wasteland of Old Town, with generously topped pizzas, ultra-creamy pastas, and creative "white nachos." The back patio is a bonus.

## DOWNTOWN

With so many bars in this area, there's little room left for food, beyond a couple of solid cafés.

### Cafés

A branch of **Flying Star** (723 Silver Ave. SE, 505/244-8099, 6am-10pm Sun.-Thurs., 6am-11pm Fri.-Sat., $10) occupies a hiply restored 1950 John Gaw Meem bank building.

For a sugar fix, **Rebel Donut** (400 Gold Ave. SW, 7am-4pm Mon.-Fri., 7am-noon Sat., $2) fulfills, with creations like red-chile chocolate-bacon.

Past the railroad tracks in EDo (East Downtown), **The Grove** (600 Central Ave. SE, 505/248-9800, 7am-4pm Tues.-Sat., 8am-3pm Sun., $10) complements its local-organic menu with an indoor-outdoor feel, with big

front windows facing Central and a screened-in patio. The chalkboard menu features big, creative salads (spinach, orange slices, and dates is one combo) as well as sandwiches and cupcakes; breakfast, with farm-fresh local eggs and homemade English muffins, is served all day. It's a notch above Flying Star in price, but you're paying for the especially high-quality ingredients.

### New Mexican

Even though it's in the middle of Albuquerque's main business district, **Cecilia's Café** (230 6th St. SW, 505/243-7070, 7am-2pm daily, $8) feels more like a living room than a restaurant. Maybe it's the woodstove in the corner—as well as the personal attention from Cecilia and her daughters and the food that's clearly made with care. The rich, dark red chile really shines here.

### Italian

A popular hangout for urban pioneers in the EDo neighborhood, **Farina Pizzeria** (510

© ZORA O'NEILL

Cecilia's Café serves homestyle food in the downtown business district.

Central Ave. SE, 505/243-0130, 11am-9pm Mon., 11am-10pm Tues.-Fri., 4pm-10pm Sat., 5pm-9pm Sun., $14) has exposed brick walls and a casual vibe. The pies come out of the wood-fired oven suitably crisp-chewy and topped with seasonal veggies. Make sure you get a cup of the gorgonzola-crème fraîche-chive dip for your crusts—it's the upscale version of the ranch dressing that's more commonly offered. There's usually a pasta special as well.

### Spanish

At press time, **Más** (125 2nd St. NW, 505/242-9090) had just opened in the Hotel Andaluz, under the direction of Chef James Campbell Caruso, best known for his chummy, creative-tapas joint Boca in Santa Fe. If all goes smoothly, this place should do some quality southern Spanish food.

## THE UNIVERSITY AND NOB HILL

Thanks to the large student population, this area has some great and varied spots to grab a cheap bite, but Nob Hill has some upscale options too.

### Cafés

When you walk into **Flying Star Café** (3416 Central Ave. SE, 505/255-6633, 6am-11pm Mon.-Thurs., 6am-midnight Fri.-Sat., $10), you'll be mesmerized by the pastry case, packed with triple-ginger cookies, lemon-blueberry cheesecake, and fat éclairs. But try to look up to appreciate the range on the menu boards: Asian noodles, hot and cold sandwiches, mac-and-cheese, and enchiladas. The food isn't always quite as great as it looks, but with speedy service and locations all over town, it's a handy place to zip in or to lounge around (wireless Internet access is free). You'll find one in nearly every neighborhood, including the North Valley (4026 Rio Grande Blvd. NW, 505/344-6714) and downtown.

Just a few blocks from the university, **Annapurna's World Vegetarian Café** (2201 Silver Ave. SE, 505/262-2424, 7am-9pm Mon.-Fri., 8am-9pm Sat., 10am-8pm Sun., $9) is a vegetarian's delight, serving a menu that's compatible with Ayurvedic dietary recommendations, with giant masala dosas (rice-flour crepes) as well as less strictly Indian dishes such as cardamom pancakes with maple syrup. It has a second branch in the North Valley (5939 4th St. NW, 505/254-2424, 8am-9pm Mon.-Sat., 10am-8pm Sun.).

Pick up goods for a picnic at **La Montañita Co-op** (3500 Central Ave. SE, 505/265-4631, 7am-10pm Mon.-Sat., 8am-10pm Sun.), where quinoa salads and stuffed grape leaves are all the rage; look in the dairy section for "sampler" pieces of locally made cheese. There's a snacks-only operation in the **UNM Bookstore,** across from the Frontier (2301 Central Ave. NE, 505/277-9586, 8am-6pm Mon.-Fri., 10am-4pm Sat.), and a bigger branch in the North Valley (2400 Rio Grande Blvd. NW, 505/242-8800, 7am-10pm daily).

### New Mexican

You haven't been to Albuquerque unless you've been to ◖ **The Frontier** (2400 Central Ave. SE, 505/266-0550, 5am-1am daily, $6), across from UNM. Everyone in the city passes through its doors at some point in their lives, so all you have to do is pick a seat in one of the five Western-themed rooms (Hmm, under the big portrait of John Wayne? Or maybe one of the smaller ones?) and watch the characters file in. You'll want some food, of course: a green-chile-smothered breakfast burrito filled with crispy hash browns, or a grilled hamburger, or one of the signature cinnamon rolls, a deadly amalgam of flour, sugar, and some addictive drug that compels you to eat them despite the hydrogenated goo they're swimming in. If you feel a little unhealthy, you can always get some fresh orange juice and restore your balance by vegging out in front of the mesmerizing tortilla machine.

Near the university, **El Patio** (142 Harvard Dr. SE, 505/268-4245, 11am-9pm Sun.-Thurs., 11am-9:30pm Fri.-Sat., $9) is the kind of old-reliable place that ex-locals get misty-eyed about after they've moved away. The green-chile-and-chicken enchiladas are high on many citywide favorite lists. It doesn't hurt that the setting, in an old bungalow with a shady outdoor space, feels like an extension of someone's home kitchen. The menu is more vegetarian-friendly than most New Mexican joints.

## ALBUQUERQUE METRO AREA

Great places to eat are scattered all over the city, often in unlikely looking strip malls. These places are worth making a trip for, or will provide a pick-me-up when you're far afield.

### New Mexican

Experts agree: **Mary & Tito's Café** (2711 4th St. NW, 505/344-6266, 9am-6pm Mon.-Thurs., 9am-8pm Fri.-Sat., $7) is the place to go for *carne adovada,* the dish of tender pork braised in red chile, particularly good in what they call a Mexican turnover (a stuffed sopaipilla). The meat is flavorful enough to stand alone, but the fruity, bright red-chile sauce, flecked with seeds, is so good you'll want to put it on everything. This place is such a local icon, seemingly untouched since the 1980s (ah, lovely dusty rose vinyl!), it won a James Beard America's Classics award.

Cruise down by the rail yards south of downtown to find **El Modelo** (1715 2nd St. SW, 505/242-1843, 7am-7pm daily, $7), a local go-to for a hangover-curing *chicharrón* burrito, chile-smothered spare ribs, or tamales for the whole family. Because it's really a front for a tortilla factory, the flour tortillas are particularly tender, and you can order either a taco or a whole platter of food. If the weather's nice, grab a seat at a picnic table outside and watch the freight trains go by.

Just two blocks from the National Hispanic Cultural Center, popular **Barelas Coffee House** (1502 4th St. SW, 505/843-7577, 7:30am-3pm Mon.-Fri., 7:30am-2:30pm Sat., $7) is confusing to the first-timer: The attraction is chile, not coffee—especially the red, which infuses hearty, timeless New Mexican standards like *posole, chicharrones,* and *menudo.* The restaurant occupies several storefronts, and even then there's often a line out the door at lunch. But it's worth the wait—this is timeless food.

Out in Corrales, **Perea's Restaurant & Tijuana Bar** (4590 Corrales Rd., 505/898-2442, 11am-2pm Mon.-Sat., $7) is open only for lunch, but it's worth scheduling around if you know you'll be out this way. Everything's home-cooked, from Frito pie to *carne adovada.*

# Outside Albuquerque

Within 45 minutes of the city are some great natural attractions. A winding road through the mountains southeast of town brings you past the ruined Salinas Pueblo Missions, an intriguing bit of early Conquest history, and little visited. To the east is the start of one of routes to Santa Fe, the Turquoise Trail, which leads through some vestiges of New Mexico's mining past. An equally scenic route north is the more circuitous Jemez Mountain Trail, past red rocks and hot springs. Or you can zip directly up the interstate, where you'll pass the windswept region known as Tent Rocks.

## SALINAS PUEBLO MISSIONS NATIONAL MONUMENT

Set on the plains behind the Manzano Mountains, the scenically decaying mud-brick buildings at **Quarai, Gran Quivira,** and **Abó** represent one of the Franciscans' bigger challenges during the early years of the Conquest. The **Salinas Pueblo Missions National Monument** designation applies to three separate sites. The route (starting on Highway 337, beginning in Tijeras, just east of the city) also passes by the little town of Mountainair, as well as one of the area's most beautiful fall hiking spots.

Allow a full day for a leisurely drive—the whole loop route from Albuquerque is about 200 miles, and straight driving time is about four hours. From Albuquerque, take I-40 east to exit 179, to the village of Tijeras (Scissors, for the way the canyons meet here), established in the 1850s. Turn south on Highway 337.

## Fourth of July Canyon

After you pass through the Spanish land grant of Chililí, the terms of which have been contested ever since the Treaty of Guadalupe Hidalgo, Highway 337 runs into Highway 55—make a right and head to Tajique, then turn onto Forest Road 55 to reach **Fourth of July Canyon.** The area in the foothills of the Manzanos, seven miles down the dirt road, is a destination in late September and early October, when the red maples and oak trees turn every shade of pink, crimson, and orange imaginable. (Actually, the place got its name not for this fireworks-like show of colors, but for the date an Anglo explorer happened across it in 1906.) It's also pretty in late summer, when the rains bring wildflowers. You can explore on the short **Spring Loop Trail** or **Crimson Maple Trail,** or really get into the woods on **Fourth of July Trail** (no. 173), which wanders into the canyon 1.8 miles and connects with **Albuquerque Trail** (no. 78) to form a loop.

Forest Road 55 loops back to meet Highway 55, but the second half, after the campground, can be very rough going. It's usually maintained in the fall, but at other times of the year, it's wiser to backtrack rather than carry on, especially if you're in a rental car.

## Quarai

The first ruins you reach are those at **Quarai** (505/847-2290, www.nps.gov/sapu, 9am-6pm daily June-Aug., 9am-5pm Sept.-May, free), a pueblo inhabited from the 14th to the 17th century. Like the other two Salinas pueblos, Quarai was a hardscrabble place with no natural source of water and very little food, though it did act as a trading outpost for salt, brought from small lakes farther east (hence the name). When the Franciscans arrived, they put more

than the usual strain on this community. The 400 or so Tiwa speakers nonetheless managed to build a grand sandstone-and-adobe mission, the most impressive of the ones at these pueblos. The priests also found themselves at odds with the Spanish governors, who helped protect them but undermined their conversion work by encouraging ceremonial dances. At the same time, raids by Apaches increased because any crop surplus no longer went to them in trade, but to the Spanish. *And* there were terrible famines between 1663 and 1670. No wonder, then, the place was abandoned even before the Pueblo Revolt of 1680. Only the mission has been excavated; the surrounding hillocks are all pueblo structures.

## Mountainair

Highway 55 meets U.S. 60 in the village of **Mountainair**, which hosts the **Salinas Pueblo Missions Visitors Center** (505/847-2585, www.nps.gov/sapu, 9am-5pm daily), on U.S. 60 west of the intersection—though it offers not much more information than what's available at the small but detailed museums at each site. The **Mountainair ranger station** (505/847-2990, 8am-noon and 12:30pm-4:30pm Mon.-Fri.) is here as well; coming from the north, follow signs west off Highway 55, before you reach the U.S. 60 intersection.

Mountainair is also home to the weird architectural treasure that is the **Shaffer Hotel** (103 Main St., 888/595-2888, www.shafferhotel.com), a 1923 Pueblo Deco confection with a folk-art twist, built by one Clem "Pop" Shaffer, who had a way with cast concrete—look for his name in the wall enclosing the little garden. In terms of decoration, the real draw is the hotel **restaurant** (10am-8pm Mon., 8am-8pm Tues.-Sat., 8am-4pm Sun., $8). While you're eating your enchiladas (or just peeking in the door), take a long look at the ceiling, Shaffer's masterpiece of carved and painted turtles, snakes, and other critters. As for the hotel itself, it has changed hands several times since its redo in 2005, and early reports on the new team seemed promising. The rooms don't have any particular Pop Shaffer quirks, but the

© ZORA O'NEILL

**"Pop" Shaffer, of Mountainair, was creative with rocks.**

shared-bath ones are a bargain at $30; private-bath rooms start at $65.

Another lodging option: In the hills southwest of Mountainair, the casita at **Two Ponyz Ranch** (505/847-0245, www.twoponyzranch. com, $135), with a full kitchen, is ideal for a weekend getaway in this area.

And another food option: bustling **Alpine Alley** (210 N. Summit Ave., 505/847-2478, 6am-2pm Mon.-Fri., 8am-2pm Sat.), just north of the main intersection on Highway 55. This café is the town living room, serving good baked treats, soups, and creative sandwiches and drinks to a crew of regulars, many of whom have inspired the menu's concoctions.

## Gran Quivira

South from Mountainair 26 miles lies Gran Quivira—a bit of a drive, and you'll have to backtrack, but on the way you'll pass another Pop Shaffer creation, **Rancho Bonito,** his actual home. As it's private property, you can't go poking around, but from the road you can

see a bit of the little log cabin painted in black, red, white, and blue. (If you happen to be in Mountainair in May for its art tour, the house is open then.)

Where Highway 55 makes a sharp turn east, **Gran Quivira** (505/847-2770, www.nps. gov/sapu, 9am-6pm daily June-Aug., 9am-5pm Sept.-May, free) looks different from the other two Salinas pueblos because it is built of gray San Andres limestone slab and finished with plaster that was painted with symbols. It's the largest of three, with an estimated population between 1,500 and 2,000. The array of feathers and pottery styles found here indicate the community was devoted to trade. Like the people of Abó, the residents spoke Tompiro, and the Spanish dubbed them Los Rayados, for the striped decorations they wore on their faces. They appear to have outwardly accepted the Franciscan mission after the first sermon was preached here in 1627. But they took their own religion literally underground, building hidden kivas underneath the residential structures even as they toiled on two successive missions ordered by the Catholics. Nonetheless, the place was deserted by 1671, after more than a third of the population had starved to death.

## Abó

From Gran Quivira, drive back the way you came and turn west on U.S. 60 in Mountainair to reach **Abó** (505/847-2400, www.nps.gov/ sapu, free), nine miles on. The **visitors center** (9am-6pm daily June-Aug., 9am-5pm Sept.-May, free) here has the same hours as the other sites, but the ruins themselves are open all the time—it's nice to drop by here just as the setting sun is lending a red glow to the rocks. Abó was the first pueblo the Franciscans visited, in 1622; the mission here, constructed over more than 60 years, shows details such as old wood stairs leading to the choir loft. (The Franciscans were so dedicated to re-creating the Catholic church experience here in the desert that they brought in portable pipe organs and trained their converts to sing.)

Unlike Gran Quivira, though, Abó seems to have had some agreement regarding kivas, as

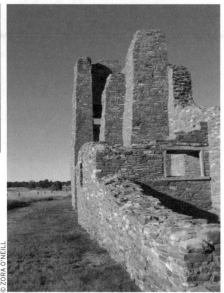

© ZORA O'NEILL

a ruined mission church at Abó

Take I-40 east from Albuquerque to exit 175. For hiking maps of the area, bear right to go into the village of Tijeras and the **Sandia ranger station** (11776 Hwy. 337, 505/281-3304), and to gas up if you need it—it's one of the last stops until close to Santa Fe. Go left to continue directly to the junction with Highway 14, the beginning of the Turquoise Trail.

The four-lane road heads north through alternating communities of old Spanish land grants and modern subdivisions collectively referred to as the East Mountains. Six miles up, you come to a large triangle intersection—to the left is Highway 536, the so-called **Crest Road** up to Sandia Peak, a beautiful winding drive through steadily thinning forests until you reach the exposed top of the mountain, more than 10,000 feet above sea level and more than 5,500 feet above the center of Albuquerque.

### Tinkertown Museum
Even if you don't drive to Sandia Peak, do head 1.5 miles up the Crest Road to **Tinkertown Museum** (121 Sandia Crest Rd., 505/281-5233, www.tinkertown.com, 9am-6pm daily Apr.-Oct., $3), a temple to efficient use of downtime. Ross Ward, an artist, a certified circus-model builder, and a sign painter who learned his trade doing banners for carnivals, was also a master whittler and creative engineer who built, over 40 years, thousands of miniature figures and dioramas out of wood, clay, and found objects. Some of the scenes are even animated with tiny pulleys and levers: A man with a cleaver chases chickens in a circle; circus performers soar; the blacksmith's bellows huff and puff. Much of the building is Ward's creation as well—undulating walls made of bottles and studded with odd collectibles, for instance. The museum, like an amoeba, even seems to have taken over a neighbor's 35-foot wooden boat. Ward died in 2002; his family keeps up the museum, and even though it's no longer growing as it used to, it remains a remarkable piece of pure American folk art.

there is one built right in the center of the *convento* (the compound adjoining the mission), dating from the same period—something that no archaeologist or historian has otherwise explained. The excellent condition of all of these ruins is due in part to the efforts of the family that owned the land from the mid-19th century. One member, Federico Sisneros, is buried near the mission, at his request.

From Abó, continue west through the mountain pass, then down into the long, flat Rio Grande valley on U.S. 60. It runs straight into I-25 at Bernardo, but if you're heading back to Albuquerque, you can take Highway 47 northwest to Belén, about 25 miles closer to the city.

## THE TURQUOISE TRAIL
This scenic back route to Santa Fe, along the east side of the Sandias and up across high plateaus, revisits New Mexico's mining history as it passes through a series of ghost towns. From Albuquerque, it's about 70 miles, and can be driven straight through in just an hour and a half.

© ZORA O'NEILL

Folk artist Ross Ward whittled every colorful character in his Tinkertown Museum by hand.

## Golden

Back on Highway 14, continue north through rolling hills and ever-broader sky. After 15 miles, you reach the all-but-gone town of **Golden**, so named because it was the site of the first gold strike west of the Mississippi, in 1825. But all that's left now is a handful of homes, an attractive adobe church, and **Henderson Store** (10am-3:30pm Tues.-Sat.), a general store open since 1918. It's largely given over to Indian jewelry and pottery, and antique trinkets line the upper shelves, remnants of Golden's moment of glory. One other small attraction: the house across the road, bedecked with thousands of antique bottles.

## Madrid

Thirteen miles beyond Golden, and about midway along the drive, **Madrid** (pronounced MAD-rid) is a ghost town back from the dead. Built by the Albuquerque & Cerrillos Coal Co. in 1906, it once housed 4,000 people, but it was deserted by the end of World War II,

when natural gas became the norm. By the late 1970s, a few of the swaybacked wood houses were squatted by hippies willing to live where indoor plumbing was barely available. Over the decades, Madrid slowly revived. Portable toilets are still more common than flush models, but the arts scene has flourished, and a real sense of community pervades the main street, which is lined with galleries and pretty painted bungalows. In 2006, the village was the setting for the John Travolta film *Wild Hogs,* and the set-piece café built for the production (now a souvenir shop) has become a minor pilgrimage site for bikers.

You can learn more about Madrid's history at the **Old Coal Town Museum** (Hwy. 14, 505/474-0344, www.themineshafttavern.com, 10:30am-4:30pm Fri.-Mon., $5), where you can wander among sinister-looking machine parts and even walk partway down an abandoned mineshaft—a great disciplinary tool for kids who've been acting up in the car. You'll feel the "ghost" in "ghost town" here. There's an Old West costume photo studio in the lobby, and the melodrama-ready **Engine House Theatre,** occasionally used for special events.

A more vibrant remnant of Madrid's company-town days is the **Mine Shaft Tavern** (2846 Hwy. 14, 505/473-0743, 11:30am-10pm daily), where you can belly up to a 40-foot-long pine-pole bar. Above it are murals by local artist Ross Ward, who built the Tinkertown Museum in Sandia Park. "It is better to drink than to work," reads the Latin inscription interwoven among the mural panels, and certainly everyone in the bar, from long-distance bikers to gallery-hoppers, is living by those encouraging words.

For coffee and local gossip, hit **Java Junction** (2855 Hwy. 14, 505/438-2772, www.java-junction.com, 7:30am-close daily), which also rents a guest room ($109 d). For more substance, head straight to ◖**Mama Lisa's Ghost Town Kitchen** (Hwy. 14, 505/471-5769, $10). When it's open (seemingly not on a regular basis, but chances are better in the summer), it's a true treat, a cozy place with an all-over-the-map menu: bison enchiladas, Austrian-style

Madroids get festive at their Fourth of July parade.

pork chops, lemon butter cake, and hibiscus mint tea, which you can enjoy out on the tree-shaded front patio. When it's closed, all you can do is press your face against the window and dream—or go down the street to **The Hollar** (Hwy. 14, 575/471-4821, 11am-7pm Mon.-Wed., 11am-9pm Thurs.-Sun., $9), which dishes out fancied-up Southern standards like po'boys, fried okra, and gooey cheese grits—it's casual by day and more refined in the evening (entrées are about $15). The last option—though not a bad one at all—is the food at the **Mine Shaft Tavern:** "roadhouse cuisine," including green-chile cheeseburgers. The kitchen closes at 7:30pm weeknights and 9pm on Friday and Saturday.

## Cerrillos

**Cerrillos,** said to be the source of turquoise that has been traced to Chaco Canyon, Spain, and Chichén Itzá in Mexico's Yucatán Peninsula, hasn't been gallerified like Madrid, its neighbor down the road. There are a couple of antiques stores (one ghostly, one better dusted), plus a combo **petting zoo-trading post** with some llamas and goats, plus turquoise nuggets and taxidermied jackalopes. And there's barely one bar, **Mary's,** filled with cats and serving as more of a sitting room for the proprietress and namesake, who's in her 10th decade. All this means it's a pretty quiet place to wake up, at the artfully decorated **Cerrillos Hills B&B** (12 3rd St., 505/424-3125, www.cerrilloshills-bedandbreakfast.com, $149), which has three private-feeling guest suites on a tree-shaded back street.

If you want to do something besides wave to the Amtrak train in the afternoon, you can go **horseback riding** (Broken Saddle Riding Co., 505/424-7774, www.brokensaddle.com, $85 for two hours) or hiking in **Cerrillos Hills State Park** (head north across the railroad tracks, www.nmparks.com, $5/car), more than 1,000 acres of rolling hills and narrow canyons that are also good for mountain biking. A visitors center is in the village, but open only 2pm-4pm.

a peacock at the San Marcos Café

## The Home Stretch

After ascending from the canyons around Cerrillos onto a high plateau (look out for antelope), you're on the home stretch to Santa Fe—but you'll pass one more dining option, the **San Marcos Café** (3877 Hwy. 14, 505/471-9298, 8:30am-6pm Mon.-Fri., 8:30am-5pm Sat., 8:30am-2pm Sun., $9), which shares space with a working feed store where chickens and the occasional peacock scratch in the yard. Hearty meals are served in a country-style dining room (complete with potbellied stove); breakfast is especially delicious, with great cinnamon buns, home-made chicken sausage, and a variety of egg dishes.

From here, Highway 14 becomes Cerrillos Road, which runs 10 slow, unscenic miles to the center of Santa Fe. The more direct route is via I-25 to Old Santa Fe Trail. Keep an eye out for the highway on-ramp—signs point to Las Vegas.

# THE JEMEZ MOUNTAIN TRAIL

Beginning just northwest of Albuquerque, the **Jemez** (HAY-mez) **Mountain Trail** is a beautiful drive through Jemez Indian Reservation, the Santa Fe National Forest, and the Valles Caldera National Preserve. It's the least direct way of getting to Santa Fe—from Albuquerque, it covers about 140 miles, and you actually wind up near Los Alamos and must backtrack a bit south to reach town. But anyone in search of natural beauty will want to set aside a full day for the trip, especially in the fall, when the aspen leaves turn gold against the rich red rocks.

The drive begins on U.S. 550, northwest out of the satellite town of Bernalillo, just west of I-25. (Stop here for gas, if necessary—stations are few on this route.) At the village of San Ysidro, bear right onto Highway 4, which forms the major part of the route north.

## Jemez Pueblo

This community of some 1,800 tribal members was settled in the late 13th century, and Highway 4 runs through the middle of the 89,000 acres it still maintains. Before the Spanish arrived, the Hemish people (which the Spanish spelled *Jemez*) had established more than 10 large villages in the area. **Jemez Pueblo** is quite conservative and closed to outsiders except for ceremonial dances. Because Jemez absorbed members of Pecos Pueblo in 1838, it celebrates two feast days, San Diego (November 12) and San Persingula (August 2). It's also the only remaining pueblo where residents speak the Towa language, the rarest of the related New Mexico languages (Tewa and Tiwa are the other two).

The pueblo operates the **Walatowa Visitor Center** (575/834-7235, www.jemezpueblo.com, 8am-5pm daily Apr.-Dec., 10am-4pm Jan.-Mar.), about five miles north of San Ysidro. You might miss it if you're gawking off the east side of the road at the vivid red sandstone cliffs at the mouth of the **San Diego Canyon.** From April till October, another, tastier distraction is the Indian fry bread and enchiladas sold by

© ZORA O'NEILL

© ZORA O'NEILL

fresh frybread in the works on the highway in Jemez

roadside vendors. The center has exhibits about the local geology and the people of Jemez and doubles as a ranger station, dispensing maps and advice on outdoor recreation farther up the road—including the status of trails, campgrounds, and fishing access points following the Las Conchas Fire in 2011. You can take a one-mile guided hike ($5) up into the red rocks; it's a good idea to call ahead and arrange a time.

## Jemez Springs

A charming small resort town, **Jemez Springs** is really just a handful of little clapboard buildings tucked in the narrow valley along the road—and it's also the most convenient place to indulge in the area's springs. Their stew of minerals and trace elements like lithium have inspired tales of miraculous healing since people began visiting in the 1870s. **Giggling Springs** (Hwy. 4, 575/829-9175, www.gigglingsprings.com, 11am-sunset Tues.-Sun., $18/hour or $60/day) has a spring-fed pool enclosed in an attractively landscaped flagstone area right near the Jemez River. In winter, it's open only

Wednesday-Sunday. The **Jemez Springs Bath House** (Hwy. 4, 575/829-3303, www.jemezsprings.org, 10am-7pm daily, $18/hour) is operated by the village. Here, the springs have been diverted into eight soaking tubs. They're private, but they have a somewhat austere feel. Call ahead to reserve; massages and other spa treatments are available as well.

For a bargain place to stay, **Laughing Lizard Inn** (Hwy. 4, 575/829-3108, www.thelaughinglizard.com, $70 d) offers four basic but pretty rooms opening onto a long porch. Hot springs are a short walk away across the road.

For food, head to **Highway 4 Coffee** (17478 Hwy. 4, 575/829-4655, 7am-3pm Mon.-Tues. and Thurs., 7am-5pm Fri. and Sun., 7am-7pm Sat., $5), which has rich homemade pastries and pizza, in addition to caffeine. The only place for dinner in town proper is **Los Ojos Restaurant & Saloon** (17596 Hwy. 4, 575/829-3547, 11am-midnight Mon.-Fri., 8am-midnight Sat.-Sun., $10), where horseshoes double as window grills, tree trunks act as barstools, and the atmosphere hasn't changed in decades.

Burgers are the way to go. The kitchen shuts around 9pm, and bar closing time can come earlier if business is slow, so call ahead in the evenings. You'll find more variety about fifteen minutes up the road at the **Ridgeback Café** (38710 Hwy. 126, 575/829-3322, 8am-8pm daily, $9), which serves elk burgers, enchiladas, and more.

If you're planning to explore the wilderness and missed the Walatowa Visitor Center at Jemez Pueblo, you can stop at the **Jemez Ranger District office** (Hwy. 4, 575/829-3535, 8am-4:30pm Mon.-Fri.) for info. There's a **Valles Caldera National Preserve visitors center** (39201 Hwy. 4, 575/661-3333, 8am-6pm daily) here too—stop in to arrange reservations for the park or to see if there are last-minute openings. Both are on the north edge of town.

## Jemez State Monument

Just north of Jemez Springs, you pass the **Jemez State Monument** (Hwy. 4, 575/829-3530, 8:30am-5pm Wed.-Sun., $3), a set of ruins where ancestors of the present Jemez people settled more than 700 years ago and lived until the Pueblo Revolt of 1680. More striking than the old pueblo, which was named Giusewa, is the crumbling Franciscan mission that rises up in the middle. The convent and church of San José de los Jémez were built around 1620, using forced labor from the pueblo. The result was remarkably grand, but the friars abandoned their work by 1640, probably because they'd thoroughly antagonized their would-be parishioners. Today the remnants of the two cultures have nearly dissolved back into the earth from which they were both built, but the church's unique octagonal bell tower has been reconstructed to good effect. If you pay $5 admission, you can also visit Coronado State Monument, on the north edge of Albuquerque, on the same day.

A couple of curves in the highway past the monument, you reach the rocks of **Soda Dam** off the right side of the road. The pale, bulbous mineral accretions that have developed around this spring resemble nothing so much as the top of a root beer float, with a waterfall crashing through the middle. You can't really get in the water here, but it's a good photo op.

## Hot Springs

Outside Jemez Springs, you pass several other opportunities to take a hot bath. Five miles north, where the red rocks of the canyon have given way to steely-gray stone and Battleship Rock looms above the road, is the start of the East Fork Trail. Two miles along this trail, in a not-too-strenuous climb, are **McCauley Hot Springs.** (Look for the trailhead parking just north of Battleship Rock Picnic Area.) Follow the trail until it meets a small stream flowing down from your left (north), then walk up the creek about a quarter mile to the spring, which has been diverted so it flows into a series of pools of ever-cooler temperatures (only 85°F at most points). Because the trail runs along the streambed, though, it's usually impassable in the high-flow winter and spring.

The most accessible pools are **Spence Hot Springs,** about half a mile north of Battleship Rock. A sign marks a parking area on the east side of the road, and the trail to the springs starts immediately south of the dirt pullout. A short hike (0.4 mile) leads down to the river then up the steep hillside to two sets of 100°F pools. The place is well known, and although there are signs insisting on clothing, don't be surprised if you encounter some people bathing nude.

## Hiking

Several trails run through the Jemez, but damage from the 2011 Las Conchas Fire has made some less scenic. Portions of **East Fork Trail** (no. 137), are still quite nice, however. The route runs between Battleship Rock (on the west end) and Las Conchas (on the east), crossing Highway 4 at a convenient midpoint. If you head west from the highway parking area (about 3 miles after a hairpin turn southeast), you reach Jemez Falls after 1 mile, and then gradually descend to Battleship Rock, in about 6 miles, passing McCauley Springs on the way. Heading east from the highway is fine too, following a stream through a pine forest, though near the end of 4.5 miles, you approach the burned area.

## ◖ Valles Caldera National Preserve

Spreading out for 89,000 acres to the north of Highway 4, the protected **Valles Caldera National Preserve** (866/382-5537, www.vallescaldera.gov) is a series of vast green valleys, rimmed by the edges of a volcano that collapsed into a huge bowl millennia ago. At the center is rounded Redondo Peak (11,254 feet). The park was a private ranch, which the U.S. government purchased in 2000. It's managed with the goal of making the area financially self-sustaining, independent of government funds. To this end, fees are high (starting at $10 pp), and for all but two trails, you must make reservations at least 24 hours ahead online, as there are restrictions on how many people may enter the park each day. The reward is a hike through untouched land, where you will see herds of elk grazing and eagles winging across the huge dome of the sky.

In 2011, the Las Conchas Fire burned about 30 percent of the caldera. Fortunately, most of that was in the easily replenished grasslands. Unfortunately, the burned area also encompasses the two trails (Valle Grande and Coyote Call) that you can hike for free and without a reservation. So until growth returns, hiking Valles Caldera requires planning ahead. The season is best June-September, and in winter months, the park is open for cross-country skiing. There are also limited elk-hunting and fishing seasons. A full roster of guided activities is available too: group day hikes, full-moon snowshoeing and sleigh rides, overnight winter yurt camping, tracking classes, horseback riding, and more.

Past Valles Caldera, Highway 4 leads to Bandelier National Monument in about 20 miles. If you're carrying on to Santa Fe, it's another hour's drive (about 40 miles). Continue on Highway 4 through the town of White Rock and join Highway 502. This leads to U.S. 285, which then goes south to the capital.

## THE INTERSTATE TO SANTA FE

The most direct route north to Santa Fe is along I-25, a drive of about 60 miles and just one hour without stops. The road, which passes through the broad valley between the Sandia and Jemez mountain ranges, is not as scenic as the more meandering routes, but it does cross wide swaths of undeveloped pueblo lands (Sandia, San Felipe, and Kewa, formerly Santo Domingo).

## ◖ Kasha-Katuwe Tent Rocks National Monument

A slight detour takes you to one of the region's most striking natural phenomena where wind-whittled clusters of volcanic pumice and tuff do indeed resemble enormous tepees, some up to 90 feet tall. To reach the **Kasha-Katuwe Tent Rocks National Monument** (Forest Rd.

Kasha-Ketuwe Tent Rocks National Monument

266, 7am-7pm daily mid-Mar.-Oct., 8am-5pm daily Nov.-mid-Mar., $5/car), leave I-25 at exit 259 and head northwest toward Cochiti Pueblo on Highway 22. After about 15 miles, turn south in front of Cochiti Dam. In less than two miles, before you reach the pueblo, turn right on Indian Route 92.

From the monument parking area, you have the choice of two short trails: An easy, relatively flat loop runs up to the base of the rocks, passing a small cave, while a longer option runs 1.5 miles into a narrow canyon where the rock towers loom up dramatically on either side. The latter trail is level at first, but the last stretch is steep and requires a little clambering. Even if you just want to take a quick peek and don't intend to hike, don't come too late in the day: The gates are shut one hour before official closing time.

On your way out from the hike, you can drive through **Cochiti Pueblo,** the northernmost Keresan-speaking pueblo, which claims its ancestors inhabited some of the ruins at Bandelier National Monument. The core of the community is still two ancient adobe kivas; the people who live in the surrounding houses sell craftwork. Nearby **Cochiti Lake** (reached by continuing along Highway 22 past the dam) is a popular summer destination for boaters, though it's not particularly scenic.

## Food

At exit 252, hop off for a meal at the 🄲 **San Felipe Restaurant** (26 Hagen Rd., 505/867-4706, 6am-9pm daily, $8), alongside a gas station and past a short hall of dinging slot machines. Its broad diner-ish menu of spaghetti and meatballs as well as New Mexican favorites is superlative, especially pueblo dishes like *posole* with extra-thick tortillas. The crowd is just as diverse: pueblo residents, daytrippers, long-haul truckers.

# Information and Services

## TOURIST INFORMATION

The **Albuquerque Convention and Visitors Bureau** (800/284-2282, www.itsatrip.org) offers the most detailed information on the city, maintaining a kiosk on the Old Town plaza in the summer and a desk at the airport near the baggage claim (9:30am-8pm daily). You can also get excellent information on events at the **Hotel Andaluz,** at the computer terminals on the second-floor mezzanine. The **City of Albuquerque** website (www.cabq.gov) is very well organized, with all the essentials about city-run attractions and services.

### Books and Maps

The **University of New Mexico Bookstore** (2301 Central Ave. NE, 505/277-5451, 8am-6pm Mon.-Fri., 11am-4pm Sat.) maintains a good stock of travel titles and maps, along with state history tomes and the like. In summer, it closes an hour earlier on weekdays. On the west side, **Bookworks** (4022 Rio Grande Blvd. NW, 505/344-8139, 9am-9pm Mon.-Sat., 9am-7pm Sun.) is a great resource, with a large stock of New Mexico-related work as well as plenty of other titles, all recommended with the personal care of the staff.

### Local Media

The *Albuquerque Journal* (www.abqjournal.com) publishes cultural-events listings in the Friday entertainment supplement. On Wednesdays, pick up the new issue of the free weekly *Alibi* (www.alibi.com), which will give you a hipper, more critical outlook on city goings-on, from art openings to city council debates. The glossy monthly *ABQ The Magazine* (www.abqthemag.com) explores cultural topics, while the free *Local Flavor* (www.localflavormagazine.com) covers food topics.

## Radio

**KUNM** (89.9 FM) is the university's radio station, delivering eclectic music, news from NPR and PRI, and local-interest shows. **KANW** (89.1 FM) is a project of Albuquerque Public Schools, with an emphasis on New Mexican music, plus the most popular NPR programs.

## SERVICES

### Banks

Banks are plentiful, and grocery stores and pharmacies increasingly have ATMs inside. Downtown, look for **New Mexico Bank & Trust** (320 Gold Ave. SW, 505/830-8100, 9am-4pm Mon.-Thurs., 9am-5pm Fri.). In Nob Hill, **Wells Fargo** is on Central at Dartmouth (3022 Central Ave. SE, 505/255-4372, 9am-5pm Mon.-Thurs., 9am-6pm Fri., 9am-1pm Sat.). Both have 24-hour ATMs.

### Post Offices

Most convenient for visitors are the **Old Town Plaza Station** (303 Romero St. NW, 505/242-5927, 11am-4pm Mon.-Fri., noon-3pm Sat.), **Downtown Station** (201 5th St. SW, 505/346-1256, 9am-4:30pm Mon.-Fri.), and an office near **UNM** (115 Cornell Dr. SE, 505/346-0923, 8am-5pm Mon.-Fri.).

### Internet

City-maintained **wireless hotspots** are listed at www.cabq.gov/wifi; many businesses around town also provide service.

# Getting There and Around

## BY AIR

**Albuquerque International Sunport** (ABQ, 505/244-7700, www.cabq.gov/airport) is a pleasant single-terminal airport served by all major U.S. airlines. It's on the south side of the city, just east of I-25, about four miles from downtown. It has free wireless Internet access throughout. Near bag claim is an info desk maintained by the convention and visitors bureau.

Transit from the airport includes the free **Airport Connection shuttle** (a.k.a. city bus Route 250), which only runs weekdays and is timed to meet the Rail Runner train to Santa Fe at the downtown Alvarado Transportation Center, at Central and 2nd Street; weekday departures are at 9:10am, 4:01pm, 5:09pm, and 6:10pm. Another free weekday bus (Route 222) runs to the Bernalillo Rail Runner stop, timed for southbound trains; departures are four times a day (7:10am, 2:21pm, 4:16pm, 5:33pm). Verify online at www.nmrailrunner.com, as the train schedule can change.

If it's Saturday, or you just want to get downtown and don't care about the train, take Route 50 ($1), also to the Alvarado Transportation Center. It runs every half hour 7am-8pm, and on Saturdays every hour and 10 minutes 9:45am-6:50pm; there is no Sunday service. The ride takes about 25 minutes.

## BY TRAIN

**Amtrak** (800/872-7245, www.amtrak.com) runs the Southwest Chief through Albuquerque, arriving daily in the afternoon from Chicago and Los Angeles. The depot shares space with the Greyhound terminal, downtown on 1st Street, south of Central Avenue and the Alvarado Transportation Center.

The **Rail Runner** (866/795-7245, www.nmrailrunner.com) runs from downtown Santa Fe through Albuquerque and as far south as Belén. The main stop in Albuquerque is downtown, at the Alvarado Transportation Center, at Central and 1st

© ZORA O'NEILL

The Rail Runner stops at the Alvarado Transportation Center downtown.

Street. It's fantastic service to or from Santa Fe, if the not-so-frequent schedule fits yours, but within Albuquerque, the system doesn't go anywhere visitors typically go. If you ride, keep your ticket—you get a free transfer from the train to any city bus.

## BY BUS

**Greyhound** (800/231-2222, www.greyhound.com) runs buses from all major points east, west, north, and south, though departures are not frequent. The bus station (320 1st St. SW, 505/243-4435) is downtown, just south of Central Avenue. Cheaper *and* nicer are the bus services that cater to Mexicans traveling across the Southwest and into Mexico, though they offer service only to Las Cruces and Denver; **El Paso-Los Angeles Limousine Express** (2901 Pan American Fwy. NE, 505/247-8036, www.eplalimo.com) is the biggest operator, running since 1966.

With the city bus system, **ABQ Ride** (505/243-7433, www.cabq.gov/transit), it's possible to reach all of the major sights along Central Avenue, but you can't get to the Sandia Peak Tramway or anywhere in the east mountains. The most tourist-friendly bus is (of course) Route 66, the one that runs along Central Avenue, linking Old Town, downtown, and Nob Hill; service runs until a bit past 1am on summer weekends. The double-length red **Rapid Ride** buses (Route 766) follow the same route but stop at only the most popular stops. The fare for all buses, regardless of trip length, is $1; passes are available for one ($2), two ($4), and three ($6) days and can be purchased on the bus. The D-Ride bus is a free loop-route bus around downtown.

## BY CAR

Albuquerque is 60 miles (one hour) south on I-25 from Santa Fe; it is 225 miles (a little more than three hours) north on I-25 from Las Cruces. From Denver, the drive takes about six and a half hours (445 miles); Phoenix is about the same distance west on I-40.

All the major car-rental companies are in a single convenient complex adjacent to the airport, connected by shuttle buses. **Hertz** and **Enterprise** offer service at the Amtrak depot (really just a refund for the cab ride to the airport offices). Hertz's two other city locations are usually less expensive because you bypass the airport service fee; if you're renting for more than a week, the savings can be worth the cab fare.

## BY BIKE

Albuquerque's **bike-route system** (www.cabq. gov) is reasonably well developed, the terrain is flat, and the sun is usually shining. Rent bikes from **Routes** (1102 Mountain Rd. NW, 505/933-5667, www.routesrentals.com, $15/ hour, $35/day).

# SANTA FE

One of Santa Fe's several monikers is "Fanta Se," a play on the name that suggests the city's disconnection from reality. This small cluster of mud-colored buildings in the mountains of northern New Mexico does indeed seem to subsist on dreams alone, as of the 68,000 people who live here, there's a larger proportion of writers, artists, and performers than in any other

# HIGHLIGHTS

LOOK FOR ◖ TO FIND RECOMMENDED SIGHTS, ACTIVITIES, DINING, AND LODGING.

◖ **New Mexico Museum of Art:** See how the state sees itself in this nearly-century-old museum, which displays works old and new, traditional and creative (page 74).

◖ **La Fonda:** The Santa Fe Trail came to an end on the doorstep of this hotel, which has witnessed the city's fluctuating fortunes—and harbored its assorted colorful characters—for centuries (page 79).

◖ **Canyon Road:** More than 200 galleries line this winding street that's the heart of Santa Fe's art scene. It's also the main artery of its social life when it's packed with potential collectors and party-hoppers on summer Friday nights (page 80).

◖ **Museum of International Folk Art:** In the main exhibition hall, all the world's crafts, from Appalachian quilts to Zulu masks, are jumbled together in an inspiring, if slightly overwhelming, display of human creativity (page 82).

◖ **Bandelier National Monument:** The hidden valley of Frijoles Canyon was once home to the ancestors of today's Puebloans, in an elaborate urban complex and cliff-side cave apartments (page 107).

◖ **Ghost Ranch:** The spread where Georgia O'Keeffe kept a studio occupies a patch of dramatic red-rock cliffs and windblown pinnacles. Learn about the dinosaurs unearthed there, and hike up to Chimney Rock for the best view across Abiquiu (page 113).

◖ **Chimayó:** The faith is palpable in this village, where an adobe chapel has become known as "the Lourdes of America," thanks to the healing powers attributed to the holy dirt found in a small "well" in a side room (page 115).

city in the United States. In the local Yellow Pages, "Art galleries" take up five pages, and "Artists" have their own heading. In all, nearly half the city is employed in the larger arts industry. (Cynics would lump the state legislature, which convenes in the capitol here, into this category as well.)

The city fabric itself is a by-product of this creativity—many of the "adobe" buildings in the distinctive downtown area are in fact plaster and stucco, built in the early 20th century to satisfy an official vision of what Santa Fe ought to look like to appeal to tourists. And the mix of old-guard Spanish, Pueblo Indians, groovy Anglos, and international jet-setters of all stripes has even developed a soft but distinct accent—a vaguely Continental intonation, with a vocabulary drawn from the 1960s counterculture and alternative healing.

What keeps Santa Fe grounded, to use the

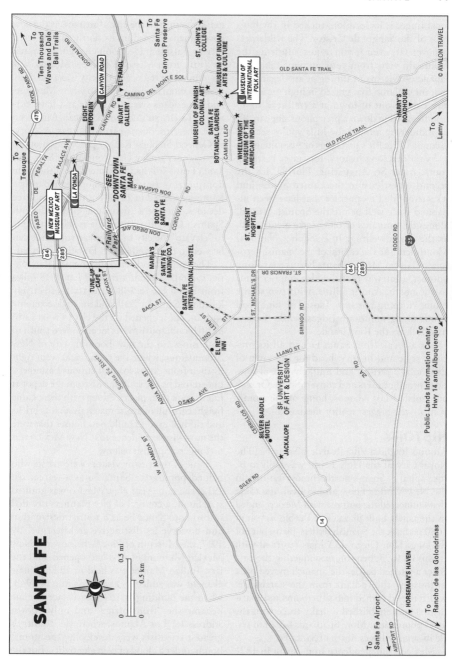

SANTA FE

© AVALON TRAVEL

local lingo, is its location, tucked in the foothills of the Sangre de Cristos. The wilderness is never far, even if you're just admiring the mountain view from your massage table at a Japanese-style spa or dining at an elegant restaurant on lamb that grazed in high meadows. You can be out of town at a trailhead in 15 minutes, skiing down a precipitous slope in 30, or wandering among the hills you've seen in Georgia O'Keeffe's paintings of Abiquiu in 60.

Santa Fe's long history, too, gives it strong roots. After St. Augustine, Florida, it's the second-oldest city in the United States, and it's surrounded by pueblos that have been inhabited since well before the Spanish arrived, alongside remnants of older settlements, such as the cliff dwellings in Bandelier National Monument. As the capital of the Spanish territory of Nuevo México, Santa Fe was a far-flung outpost, a gateway to the wilder, emptier lands to the north. And it still is, with two scenic routes running north to Taos: The high road winds along mountain ridges, while the low road follows the Rio Grande.

For a break from Santa Fe and all its precious style and history, head for the town of Española, a scruffy and unlikely mix of low-rider-proud cruisers and convert Sikhs. Or seek out isolated Los Alamos, home of the atomic bomb—the biggest reality check of all.

## HISTORY

Around 1609, La Villa Real de la Santa Fé (The Royal City of the Holy Faith) was built to be the capital of Spain's northernmost territory in the New World. The Camino Real, the route that connected the outpost with Mexico, ended in the newly built plaza. The Pueblo Revolt of 1680 set back the Spanish settlers' plans, but not for long: Don Diego de Vargas returned with troops in 1693, bent on reconquering the city. After a pitched battle, the Spanish moved back in (ousting the Indians from the statehouse, which they'd turned into storerooms and apartments) and established a shaky truce with the local population. More Spaniards began to settle in small villages north of Santa Fe.

Mexico's independence from Spain in 1821 marked a shift in the city's fortunes, as the new government opened up its northernmost territory to outside trade. Soon enough, the Santa Fe Trail, from Missouri to New Mexico, was booming with trade, and the city was a relatively cosmopolitan commercial hub where Mexicans and Americans swapped goods and hard currency. In the subsequent Mexican-American War, the Americans earned an easy victory, as General Stephen Kearny peaceably brought the territory under U.S. control in 1846. But Santa Feans still had to contend with the more domineering figure of Bishop Jean-Baptiste Lamy, appointed in 1850. For more than three decades, the Frenchman struggled with both Spanish Catholics and Indians. His attempts to "elevate" the city to European standards can be seen in the grandiose St. Francis Cathedral.

The railroad had better luck taming the frontier capital. When it arrived at Lamy, 18 miles from Santa Fe, in 1880, the train effectively killed the Santa Fe Trail (and the trade economy with it), but it opened up the city to what's still its lifeblood: tourism. As locals moved south to do business in the now-booming city of New Albuquerque, where the train tracks went right by their front doors, loads of curious Easterners, undeterred by the spur line up from the depot at Lamy, took their places. Along with them came freight cars full of exotic materials such as bricks and timber, used to build new houses that were the most visible evidence that New Mexico was no longer a Spanish colony.

Some of these early visitors were artists who helped popularize Santa Fe as a retreat. In 1912, the same year New Mexico was granted statehood, a council of city planners decided to promote Santa Fe as a tourist destination and preserve its distinctive architecture. By 1917, the Museum of Fine Arts (now the New Mexico Museum of Art) had opened, and the first Indian Market was held in 1922. A new element was added to Santa Fe's mix in 1943, when the building at 109 East Palace Avenue became the "front office" and only known address for Los Alamos, where the country's greatest scientists were developing the atomic bomb under a cloud of confidentiality. But the

## It's Not *All* Adobe

Santa Fe's distinctive look is the product of the stringent Historic Styles Ordinance, which dictates even the shade of brown stucco finish required for buildings around the plaza. But look closely, and you'll see some variations. **Colonial** is the term applied to adobe (or adobe-look) buildings, usually one story, with their typical rounded edges and flat roofs supported by vigas, the long crossbeams made of single tree trunks. The style was developed by the Spanish colonists in the 16th, 17th, and 18th centuries, based on their previous experience with adobe architecture and forms they saw in the pueblos.

In the 19th century, when New Mexico became a U.S. territory, timber-frame houses came into fashion. These so-called **territorial** buildings were often two stories tall, with balconies, and trimmed with brick cornices and Greek revival details, such as fluted wood columns and pediments above windows. The Catron Building,

on the northeast corner of the plaza, is a fine example.

But the tide turned again in the early part of the 20th century, when the **Pueblo Revival** style brought the Spanish colonial look back in vogue. Architects like John Gaw Meem and Isaac Rapp admired the mission churches and pueblos for their clean-lined minimalism. Because they used frame construction, Pueblo Revival buildings could be taller: Rapp's New Mexico Museum of Art towers on the northwest corner of the plaza, and Meem's additions to La Fonda make it five stories. The trend coincided with an aggressive tourism campaign and the development of a comprehensive look for the city, and in the process many territorial houses were simply covered over in a thick layer of faux-adobe plaster. The result is not precisely historic, but the city planners achieved their goal: Santa Fe looks like no other city in the United States.

rational scientists left little mark on Santa Fe. Right-brain thinking has continued to flourish, and the city is a modern, creative version of its old self, a meeting place where international art dealers swap goods and ideas.

## PLANNING YOUR TIME

Santa Fe is an ideal destination for a three-day weekend getaway. Add a few days more to take a hike outside of town or make the drive to Taos, Los Alamos, or Abiquiu. Crowds descend in July and August, especially for Spanish Market and Indian Market (the latter coincides with closing night at the Santa Fe Opera), but the gallery scene is in full swing—plan to be in the city on a Friday night, when Canyon Road galleries have their convivial openings.

You'll find the city a bit calmer—and the heat less overpowering—in the shoulder seasons. Choose spring if you'll be primarily in the city—lilacs bloom in May, but the surrounding mountains are dry and windswept. Opt for the fall if you plan to do a lot of hiking. The hills

are greener, and in October, dense groves of aspen trees on the Sangre de Cristo Mountains turn bright yellow. Winter is cold and occasionally snowy, but clear; most tourists are here to ski. Late December in Santa Fe is a special time, as houses are decked with paper-bag lanterns (luminarias), and bonfires light Canyon Road on Christmas Eve.

## ORIENTATION

For all the things to see and do in Santa Fe, it's easy to forget you're in a small town. Most of the major sights are within walking distance from the central plaza. Generally, you'll find yourself within the oval formed by Paseo de Peralta, a main road that almost completely circles the central district. On its southwest side it connects with Cerrillos Road, a main avenue lined with motel courts, shopping plazas, and chain restaurants. Compared with the central historic district, it's unsightly, but there are some great local places to eat along this way, as well as the few inexpensive hotels in town.

# Sights

## DOWNTOWN

The city's most visited sights are within a few blocks of the central plaza.

### Santa Fe Plaza

When Santa Fe was established in 1610, its layout was based on Spanish laws governing town planning in the colonies—hence the central plaza fronted by the Casas Reales (Palace of the Governors) on its north side. The **Santa Fe Plaza** is still the city's social hub, and the blocks surrounding it are rich with history. In the center of the plaza is the **Soldiers' Monument,** dedicated in 1867 to those who died in "battles with...Indians in the territory of New Mexico." The word "savage" has been neatly excised, following a policy applied to historic markers throughout the state.

### New Mexico History Museum and Palace of the Governors

Opened in 2009, the **New Mexico History Museum** (113 Lincoln Ave., 505/476-5200, www.nmhistorymuseum.org, 10am-5pm daily June-Sept., 10am-5pm Tues.-Sun. Oct.-May, $9) was intended to give a little breathing room for a collection that had been in storage for decades. Oddly, though, it feels like very few actual objects are on display. The exhibits give a good basic overview, though if you're already familiar with the state's storied past, you might not find much new here.

The museum incorporates the **Palace of the Governors,** the former seat of Santa Fe's government. Built 1610-1612, it's one of the oldest government buildings in the United States, giving it plenty of time to accumulate stories. De Vargas fought the Indian rebels here room by room when he retook the city in 1693, ill-fated Mexican governor Albino Pérez was beheaded in his office in 1837, and Governor Lew Wallace penned *Ben Hur* here in the late 1870s. The exhibits here showcase some of the most beautiful items in the state's collection:

trinkets and photos from the 19th century, as well as the beautiful 18th-century Segesser hide paintings, two wall-size panels of buffalo skin. These works, along with the room they're in (trimmed with 1909 murals of the Puyé cliffs) are worth the price of admission. In a couple of the restored furnished rooms, you can compare the living conditions of the Mexican leadership circa 1845 to the relative comfort the U.S. governor enjoyed in 1893.

**Walking tours** depart from the blue gate on the Lincoln Avenue side of the New Mexico History Museum at 10:15am (Mon.-Sat. mid-Apr.-mid-Oct., $10), covering all the plaza-area highlights in about two hours.

### ◖ New Mexico Museum of Art

Famed as much for its building as for the art it contains, the **New Mexico Museum of Art** (107

© ZORA O'NEILL

**Look for deals under the portal at the Palace of the Governors.**

W. Palace Ave., 505/476-5041, www.nmartmuseum.org, 10am-5pm daily June-Sept., 10am-5pm Tues.-Sun. Oct.-May, $9) is dedicated to work by New Mexican artists. Built in 1917, it is a beautiful example of Pueblo Revival architecture, originally designed as the New Mexico pavilion for a world expo in San Diego two years prior. The curvaceous stucco-clad building is an amalgam of iconic pueblo mission churches—the bell towers, for instance, mimic those found at San Felipe. Inside, the collection starts with Gerald Cassidy's oil painting *Cui Bono?*, on display since the museum's opening in 1917 and still relevant, as it questions the benefits of pueblo tourism. Look out for an excellent collection of Awa Tsireh's meticulous watercolors of ceremonial dances at San Ildefonso Pueblo, alongside works by other local American Indian artists.

On your way out, don't miss the adjacent St. Francis Auditorium, where three artists adorned the walls with art nouveau murals depicting the life of Santa Fe's patron saint. It's rare to see a secular style usually reserved for languorous ladies in flowing togas used to render such scenes as the apotheosis of Saint Francis and Santa Clara's renunciation, and the effect is beautiful.

## Cathedral Basilica of St. Francis of Assisi

Santa Fe's showpiece **Cathedral Basilica of St. Francis of Assisi** (131 Cathedral Pl., 505/982-5619, 7am-6pm daily, free), visible from the plaza at the end of East San Francisco Street, was built over some 15 years in the late 19th century. It was Jean-Baptiste Lamy's folly. The French priest had been assigned by the church to a newly created post that would formally separate New Mexico's Catholics from those in Mexico, but when he arrived in 1851 full of fire and zeal to uplift the barbarous population, he promptly alienated much of his would-be flock.

Lamy was shocked by the locals' religious practices, as the cult of the Virgin of Guadalupe was already well established, and the Penitente brotherhood was performing public self-flagellation. He also disliked their aesthetics. How could a person possibly reach heaven while praying on a dirt floor inside a building made of mud? Lamy took one look at the tiny adobe church dedicated to St. Francis of Assisi, which had stood for 170 years, and decided he could do better. Construction on his Romanesque revival St. Francis Cathedral eventually began in 1869, under the direction of architects and craftsmen from Europe—they used the old church as a frame for the new stone structure, then demolished all of the adobe, save for a small side chapel. Lamy ran short of cash, however—hence the stumpy aspect of the cathedral's facade, which should be topped with spires.

Inside is all Gothic-inspired light and space and glowing stained-glass windows, but the salvaged adobe chapel remains off to the left of the altar. It is dedicated to the figure of La Conquistadora, a statue brought to Santa Fe from Mexico in 1625, carried away by the re-treating Spanish during the Pueblo Revolt, then proudly reinstated in 1693 and honored ever since. She glows in her purple robes, under a heavy viga ceiling—all of which probably

## New Mexico State Museum Pass

One of Santa Fe's better deals is the four-day, $20 pass that grants access to the museums run by the state. These are the **New Mexico Museum of Art** and the **New Mexico History Museum,** both on the plaza, as well as the **Museum of Indian Arts & Culture** and the **Museum of International Folk Art,** on Museum Hill. You can purchase the pass at any of the four participating museums. A one-day pass ($15) admits you to two.

Additionally, all four of these museums have free admission on Friday nights, 5pm-9pm, in summer (Memorial Day through the Balloon Fiesta in early October). The rest of the year, they're free all day on the first Friday of the month. New Mexico residents get discounts, and free admission Sundays as well.

# DOWNTOWN SANTA FE

To Santa Fe Opera, Española, and Taos

To Hwy 599

CLAFOUTIS ▼

285
84

N GUADALUPE ST

PASEO DE PERALTA

SAN FRANCISCO ST

JEFFERSON ST

BUMBLE BEE'S BAJA GRILL ▼

W ALAMEDA ST

LAS PALOMAS

Santa Fe River
Santa Fe River State Park

CASA CHIMAYÓ
W WATER ST

DE FOURI ST

IRVINE ST

CLOSSON ST

SANTUARIO DE GUADALUPE

S ST FRANCIS DR

AGUA FRIA ST

▼ JOSEPH'S

▼ THE COWGIRL

OP. CIT. ■

AZTEC ST

DOUBLE TAKE

JEAN COCTEAU CINEMA ■

MONTEZUMA AVE

RAIL RUNNER/ SANTA FE CVB

ROMERO ST

S GUADALUPE ST

GARFIELD ST

SANDOVAL ST

W MANHATTAN AVE

READ ST

JUANITA ST

MARKET ST

FLYING STAR ▼

ALCALDESA ST

W MANHATTAN AVE

CAMINO DE LA FAMILIA

SANTA FE MOTEL & INN

EL PARADERO B&B ●

FARMERS MARKET ■  ● LEWALLEN

HOTEL SANTA FE ●

▼ OHORI'S

▼ SAGE BAKEHOUSE

ALARID ST

★ SITE SANTA FE

PASEO DE PERALTA

NINITA ST

285
84

Rail Runner

Railyard Park

CERRILLOS RD

DON DIEGO AVE

▼ VINAIGRETTE

CAMINO SIERRA VISTA

SANTA FE SAGE INN ●

LA CHOZA ▼

© AVALON TRAVEL

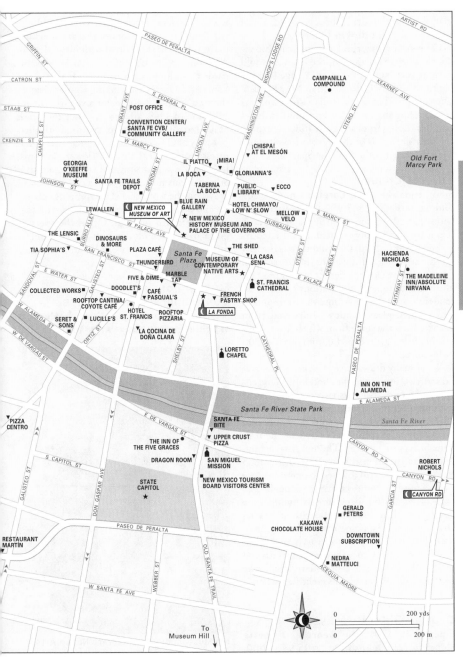

SANTA FE

ARTIST RD
GRIFFIN ST
PASEO DE PERALTA
CATRON ST
KEARNEY AVE
STAAB ST
CHAPELLE ST
S. FEDERAL PL
POST OFFICE
CKENZIE ST
GRANT AVE
CONVENTION CENTER/
SANTA FE CVB/
COMMUNITY GALLERY
W MARCY ST
¡CHISPA!
AT EL MESÓN
Old Fort
Marcy Park
GEORGIA
O'KEEFFE
MUSEUM
IL PIATTO
¡MIRA!
SHERIDAN ST
LINCOLN AVE
WASHINGTON AVE
GLORIANNA'S
LA BOCA
JOHNSON ST
SANTA FE TRAILS
DEPOT
TABERNA
LA BOCA
PUBLIC
LIBRARY
ECCO
LEWALLEN
NEW MEXICO
MUSEUM OF ART
BLUE RAIN
GALLERY
HOTEL CHIMAYO/
LOW N' SLOW
MELLOW
VELO
E MARCY ST
W PALACE AVE
NEW MEXICO
HISTORY MUSEUM AND
PALACE OF THE GOVERNORS
NUSBAUM ST
THE LENSIC
BURRO ALLEY
DINOSAURS
& MORE
PLAZA CAFÉ
Santa Fe
Plaza
THE SHED
OTERO ST
CIENEGA ST
HACIENDA
NICHOLAS
TIA SOPHIA'S
SAN FRANCISCO ST
THUNDERBIRD
MUSEUM OF
CONTEMPORARY
NATIVE ARTS
LA CASA
SENA
THE MADELEINE
INN/ABSOLUTE
NIRVANA
SANDOVAL ST
E WATER ST
GALISTEO ST
FIVE & DIME
MARBLE
TAP
E PALACE AVE
FAITHWAY ST
COLLECTED WORKS
DOODLET'S
CAFÉ
PASQUAL'S
ST. FRANCIS
CATHEDRAL
ROOFTOP CANTINA/
COYOTE CAFÉ
FRENCH
PASTRY SHOP
W ALAMEDA ST
SERET &
SONS
ORTIZ ST
LUCILLE'S
HOTEL
ST. FRANCIS
ROOFTOP
PIZZARIA
LA FONDA
LA COCINA DE
DOÑA CLARA
SHELBY ST
CATHEDRAL PL
LORETTO
CHAPEL
PASEO DE PERALTA
INN ON THE
ALAMEDA
PIZZA
CENTRO
E DE VARGAS ST
E ALAMEDA ST
Santa Fe River State Park
SANTA FE
BITE
Santa Fe River
W DE VARGAS ST
S CAPITOL ST
THE INN OF
THE FIVE GRACES
UPPER CRUST
PIZZA
CANYON RD
ROBERT
NICHOLS
DRAGON ROOM
SAN MIGUEL
MISSION
CANYON RD
GALISTEO ST
DON GASPAR AVE
STATE
CAPITOL
NEW MEXICO TOURISM
BOARD VISITORS CENTER
GARCIA ST
CANYON RD
PASEO DE PERALTA
GERALD
PETERS
KAKAWA
CHOCOLATE HOUSE
DOWNTOWN
SUBSCRIPTION
RESTAURANT
MARTÍN
WEBBER ST
OLD SANTA FE TRAIL
NEDRA
MATTEUCI
ACEQUIA MADRE
W SANTA FE AVE
To
Museum Hill
0       200 yds
0       200 m

makes Lamy shudder in his crypt in front of the main altar (he died in 1888).

On your way out, check the great cast-bronze doors—they're usually propped open, so you'll have to peer behind to see the images depicting the history of Catholicism in New Mexico. One plaque shows the Italian stoneworkers constructing the cathedral, and another shows families fleeing from attack in 1680—perhaps the only depiction of the Pueblo Revolt statewide that's sympathetic to the Spanish.

## Loretto Chapel

Step inside the small **Loretto Chapel** (207 Old Santa Fe Tr., 505/982-0092, 9am-4pm Mon.-Sat., 10:30am-5pm Sun., $2.50) and you leave the Southwest behind. Initiated by Bishop Lamy in 1873, the building was the first Gothic structure built west of the Mississippi. The decorative elements reflect his fondness for all things European: the stations of the cross rendered by Italian masons, the harmonium and stained-glass windows imported from France. Even the stone from which it was built was hauled at great expense from quarries 200 miles south.

What really draws the eye is the elegant spiral staircase leading to the choir loft. Made entirely of wood, it makes two complete turns without a central support pole. It was built in 1878 by a mysterious carpenter who appeared seemingly at the spiritual behest of the resident Sisters of Loretto. These nuns—whom Lamy had summoned from Missouri in 1853 to run a school—had resorted to prayer because Lamy's funding hadn't been quite enough. The carpenter toiled in silence for six months, the story goes, then disappeared, without taking any payment. He was never heard from again—though some historians claim to have tracked him down to Las Cruces, where he met his end in a bar fight. The Sisters of Loretto went broke in 1968; the chapel was de-sanctified when it sold in 1971.

## Georgia O'Keeffe Museum

Opened in 1997, the **Georgia O'Keeffe Museum** (217 Johnson St., 505/946-1000,

www.okeeffemuseum.org, 10am-5pm daily, till 7pm Fri., $12) honors the artist whose name is inextricably bound with New Mexico. The contrary member of the New York avant-garde ("Nothing is less real than realism," she famously said) started making regular visits to the state in the 1920s, then moved to Abiquiu full-time in 1949, a few years after the death of her husband, photographer Alfred Stieglitz.

Many of O'Keeffe's finest works—her signature sensuous, near-abstract flower blossoms, for instance—have already been ensconced in other famous museums, so the collection here draws on the work that she kept, plus ephemera and other work her foundation has amassed since her death in 1986. Often the space is given over to exhibitions on her contemporaries, or those whose work she influenced or admired.

## Museum of Contemporary Native Arts

Set in the city's former post office, the **Museum of Contemporary Native Arts** (108 Cathedral

the Museum of Contemporary Native Arts

© ZORA O'NEILL

Pl., 505/983-8900, www.iaia.edu, 10am-5pm Mon. and Wed.-Sat., noon-5pm Sun., $10) is the showcase for students, professors, and alumni of the prestigious Institute of American Indian Arts. The space is relatively small, and the shows can be hit or miss, which makes it a bit pricey. If your time is limited, the Museum of Indian Arts & Culture is a better bet. But the gift shop stocks items with a good blend of modern and traditional styles that are quite well priced.

### ◖ La Fonda

**La Fonda** (100 E. San Francisco St., 505/982-5511), on the corner of San Francisco Street and Old Santa Fe Trail, has been offering respite to travelers in some form or another since 1607. "The Inn at the End of the Trail" boomed in the early years of the trade route across the West, and also in the later gold-digging era, with a casino and saloon. It hosted the victory ball following General Kearny's takeover of New Mexico in the Mexican-American War. During the Civil War it housed Confederate general H. H. Sibley. Lynchings and shootings took place in the lobby. In the 1920s, it got a bit safer for the average tourist, as it joined the chain of Harvey Houses along the country's railways, and the architect Mary Jane Colter (best known for designing the hotels at the Grand Canyon) redesigned the interior. Since the 1960s, it has been a family-owned hotel.

The stacked Pueblo Revival place you see today dates from 1920, and it hums with history—something about the waxed tile floors, painted glass, and heavy furniture conveys the pleasant clamor of conversation and hotel busyness the way more modern lobbies do not. Guests pick up their keys at an old wood reception desk, drop their letters in an Indian-drum-turned-mailbox, and chat with the concierge below a poster for Harvey's Indian Detour car trips. Also look around—including up on the mezzanine level—at the great art collection. La Plazuela restaurant, in the sunny center courtyard, is a beautiful place to rest (with good *posole*), and the bar is timeless, with live country music many nights.

La Fonda, "The Inn at the End of the Trail"

© VISIONS OF AMERICA LLC/123RF.COM

the New Mexico State Capitol

## NEW MEXICO STATE CAPITOL

A round building with an entrance at each of the cardinal points, the 1966 **New Mexico State Capitol** (491 Old Santa Fe Tr., 505/986-4589) mimics the zia sun symbol used on the state flag. Inside, the Roundhouse, as it's commonly known, houses an excellent collection of art by the state's best-known creative types, all accessible for free. You'll find paintings and photographs in the halls on the senate side, in the upstairs balcony area, and in the fourth-floor Governor's Gallery. In the floor of the rotunda is a mosaic rendition of the state seal: the Mexican brown eagle, grasping a snake and shielded by the American bald eagle. And don't forget to look up at the stained-glass skylight, with its intricate Indian basket-weave pattern.

When the legislature is in session—late January through February in even-numbered years, late January through March in odd—visitors are welcome to sit in the galleries and watch the proceedings.

## ⟨ CANYON ROAD

The intersection of Paseo de Peralta and **Canyon Road** is ground zero for the city's **art market.** This is the beginning of a half-mile strip that contains more than 80 galleries, and in the summer, Canyon Road is a solid mass of strolling art lovers, aficionados and amateurs alike. It's especially thronged on summer Fridays, when most galleries have an open house or an exhibition opening, from around 5pm until 7 or 8pm.

Hard to believe, but the street wasn't always chockablock with thousand-dollar canvases. Starting in the 1920s, transplant artists settled on this muddy dirt road, the area gradually came to be associated with creative exploits, and eventually the art market really boomed in the 1980s. Before that, it was farmland, irrigated by the "Mother Ditch," Acequia Madre, which still runs parallel one block to the south—take a walk up here to get a sense of what the neighborhood used to be like.

There's a city parking lot at the east (upper) end of the road. Public restrooms

(9:30am-5:30pm daily) are near the west end, in the complex at 225 Canyon Road, behind Expressions gallery.

## OLD SANTA FE TRAIL

From the plaza, the historic **Old Santa Fe Trail** trade route, now paved and looking like any other city street, runs off to the east. Just past Paseo de Peralta and the small Santa Fe River, it passes through Barrio de Analco, one of Santa Fe's oldest residential neighborhoods, established by the Tlaxcala Indians who came from Mexico as servants of the first Spanish settlers. The road then runs past the state capitol and to a junction with Old Pecos Trail, the main route to I-25.

### San Miguel Mission

The **San Miguel Mission** (401 Old Santa Fe Tr., 505/983-3974, 9am-5pm Mon.-Sat., 10am-4pm Sun., $1), a sturdy adobe building where Mass is still said in Latin at noon on Sunday, is the oldest church structure in the United States. It was built starting in 1610, then partially reconstructed a century later, after it was set aflame in the Pueblo Revolt.

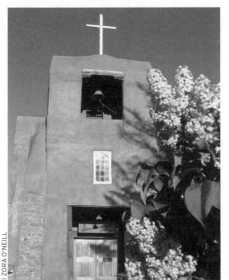
the chapel at San Miguel Mission

© ZORA O'NEILL

Its stone buttresses are the product of a desperate attempt to shore up the sagging walls in the late 19th century. The interior is snug and whitewashed, with painted buffalo hides on the walls and an altar screen that was restored in 1955 after having been covered over in house paint for decades. The late-18th-century work is attributed to the anonymous Laguna Santero, a Mexican artist who earned his name from the intricately carved and painted screen at the Laguna Pueblo church, near Albuquerque.

## GUADALUPE AND THE RAILYARD

This neighborhood southwest of the plaza developed around the depot for the rail spur from the main line at Lamy. Now it's the terminus for the Rail Runner from Albuquerque. The clutch of cafés and shops here are more casual and local, and generally feel different from the plaza, as **Guadalupe** is just outside beyond the reach of the most stringent adobe-look building codes.

South of the train depot is **The Railyard** (www.railyardsantafe.com), a mixed-use district where former warehouses and workshops have been adapted to new business, including a permanent indoor home for the city farmers market. The south side of this area is the green space of **Railyard Park,** nicely landscaped with local grasses and fruit trees.

### Santuario de Guadalupe

Built 1776-1796, the **Santuario de Guadalupe** (100 S. Guadalupe St., 505/988-2027, 9am-4pm Mon.-Sat., free) is the oldest shrine to the Virgin of Guadalupe in the United States. The interior is spare, just folding chairs set up on the wood floor, in front of a Mexican baroque oil-on-canvas altar painting from 1783. Mass is still said regularly and musical groups, particularly the Santa Fe Desert Chorale, make use of the space's excellent acoustics. A museum in the small anteroom displays relics from earlier incarnations of the building, such as Greek-style columns carved in wood. The chapel is closed on Saturdays during the winter.

SANTA FE

## SITE Santa Fe

This boxy, modern exhibition space is dedicated to all things new in the art world, mounting high-concept one-off shows that often transform the interior (and sometimes exterior). **SITE Santa Fe** (1606 Paseo de Peralta, 505/989-1199, www.sitesantafe.org, 10am-5pm Thurs. and Sat., 10am-7pm Fri., noon-5pm Sun., $10) hosts the Santa Fe Biennial in even-numbered years. It's also open Wednesdays in July and August, and entrance is free on Fridays and on Saturday till noon, when the farmers market is on, kitty-corner across the train tracks.

## MUSEUM HILL

These museums, on the southeast side, are worth leaving the plaza area. The new Santa Fe Botanical Garden is also up here, opposite the folk art museum. At press time, it was still in its earliest phases—check to see how it's growing.

### Museum of Spanish Colonial Art

The museum of the **Spanish Colonial Arts Society** (750 Camino Lejo, 505/982-2226, www.spanishcolonial.org, 10am-5pm daily June-Aug., 10am-5pm Tues.-Sun. Sept.-May, $5) exhibits a strong collection of folk art and historical objects dating from the earliest Spanish contact. One-of-a-kind treasures—such as the only signed *retablo* by the 19th-century *santero* Rafael Aragón—are shown alongside more utilitarian items from the colonial past, such as silk mantas, wool rugs, and decorative tin. New work by contemporary artisans is also on display—don't miss Luis Tapia's meta-*bulto, The Folk-Art Collectors.*

### Museum of Indian Arts & Culture

The excellent **Museum of Indian Arts & Culture** (710 Camino Lejo, 505/476-1250, www.miaclab.org, 10am-5pm daily June-Sept., 10am-5pm Tues.-Sun. Oct.-May, $9) is devoted to Native American culture from across the country, with the cornerstone exhibit *Here, Now and Always,* which traces the New Mexican Indians from their ancestors on the mesas and plains up to their present-day efforts at preserving their culture. It displays inventive spaces (looking into

a HUD-house kitchen on the rez, or sitting at desks in a public schoolroom), sound clips, and stories. Another wing is devoted to contemporary art, while the halls of craftwork display gorgeous beaded moccasins, elaborate headdresses, and more. The gift shop has beautiful jewelry and other tidbits from local artisans.

### Museum of International Folk Art

A marvelous hodgepodge, the **Museum of International Folk Art** (708 Camino Lejo, 505/476-1200, www.moifa.org, 10am-5pm daily June-Sept., 10am-5pm Tues.-Sun. Oct.-May, $9) is one of Santa Fe's biggest treats—if you can handle visual overload. In the main exhibition space, some 10,000 folk-art pieces from more than 100 countries are on permanent display in one hall, hung on walls, set in cases, even dangling from the ceiling, juxtaposed to show off similar themes, colors, and materials. The approach initially seems jumbled but in fact underscores the universality of certain concepts and preoccupations.

A separate wing is dedicated to northern New Mexican Hispano crafts (a good complement to the Museum of Spanish Colonial Art) and a lab area where you can see how pieces are preserved. Temporary exhibits take up the rest of the space, usually with colorful interactive shows. Don't skip the gift shop, which stocks some smaller versions of the items in the galleries.

### Wheelwright Museum of the American Indian

In the early 1920s, Mary Cabot Wheelwright, an adventurous East Coast heiress, made her way to New Mexico, where she met a Navajo medicine man named Hastiin Klah. Together they devised the **Wheelwright Museum of the American Indian** (704 Camino Lejo, 505/982-4636, www.wheelwright.org, 10am-5pm Mon.-Sat., 1pm-5pm Sun., free), which opened in 1937 as the House of Navajo Religion. The mission has since incorporated all Native American cultures, with exhibits of new work by individual artists rotating every few months.

The building is modeled after the Navajo hogan, with huge viga timbers supporting the eight-sided structure. The basement gift shop is a re-creation of a 19th-century trading post, which would feel like a tourist trap if it weren't for the authentically creaky wood floors and the beautiful antique jewelry on display.

## SANTA FE METRO AREA
### El Rancho de las Golondrinas

About a 15-minutes' drive southeast, **El Rancho de las Golondrinas** (334 Los Pinos Rd., 505/471-2261, www.golondrinas.org, 10am-4pm Wed.-Sun. June-Sept., $6), the "Ranch of the Swallows," is a 200-acre museum built around a restored Spanish colonial *paraje,* a way station on the Camino Real. Museum staff members in period costumes demonstrate crafts and other aspects of early New Mexican history in the blacksmith shop, the schoolhouse, the mills, and even a rebuilt Penitente *morada* (the docent who works here is a Penitente himself and may sing some of the group's hymns). The ranch hosts big to-dos—a sheep-shearing fair

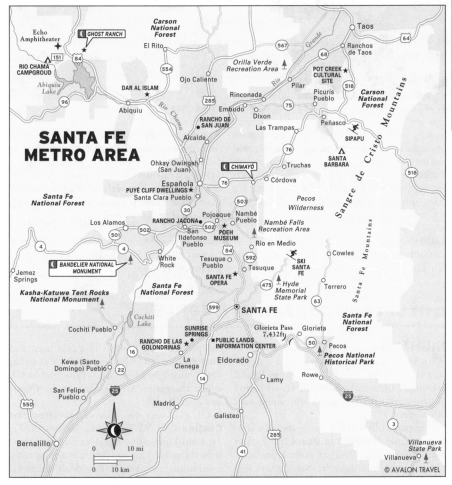

© AVALON TRAVEL

adobe ovens in a courtyard at El Rancho de las Golondrinas

in early June and a frontier-themed horse show in August, among other things—and outside the regular season opens just for special theme weekends. It's a good idea to pack your own picnic; there's a basic café at the ranch, but it's open only on weekends. It takes a few hours to really see the whole place.

### Lamy
Probably only worth the drive if you're a rail fan, this village is little more than a depot,

though it is a mighty fine place to step off a train. Across the road, **Legal Tender** (505/466-1650, 3pm-9pm Thurs.-Sat., noon-late Sun., $15) is a sprawling Old West saloon that's a bit of a destination for weekend road-trippers. It has a small museum inside, and you can look in an old diner car as well.

Take Old Las Vegas Highway (or I-25) southeast out of Santa Fe; six miles out of town, turn south on U.S. 285. After six miles, turn left for the last bumpy mile to Lamy.

# Entertainment and Events

## NIGHTLIFE
With balmy summer evenings and a populace that always seems to be able to knock off work a little early, Santa Fe favors happy hour—bars typically don't stay open past midnight.

The plaza offers two good spots for a sundown drink: **Marble Tap Room** (60 E. San Francisco St., 505/989-3565, noon-11pm Sun.-Thurs., noon-midnight Fri.-Sat.), where you

can perch on the porch with a cold beer, and **Thunderbird** (50 Lincoln Ave., 505/490-6550, 11am-midnight Mon.-Sat., 11am-9pm Sun.), where margaritas are $5 between 4pm-6pm and after 9pm.

On the next block down, the **Rooftop Cantina** (132 W. Water St., 505/983-1615, 11:30am-11pm daily, Apr.-Oct.), at the otherwise skippable Coyote Café, has a long table overlooking the street. But don't drink so much you get hungry—the food here is barely serviceable.

Over at La Fonda hotel, the outdoor **Bell Tower Bar** (100 E. San Francisco St., 505/982-5511, Apr.-Oct.) provides a fine view from its fifth-floor rooftop haunt, but it shuts just after sunset. In wintertime, the regulars decamp to the lobby watering hole, **La Fiesta Lounge,** decorated with portraits of rodeo queens; live local country acts grace the small corner stage.

Near the plaza, and only in New Mexico, **Low n' Slow** (125 Washington Ave., 505/988-4900, 2pm-midnight Mon.-Thurs., noon-1am Fri.-Sun.) is a tribute to cool car culture. Decked out with cool upholstery and hubcap chandeliers, it follows the lowrider theme with cocktails ($10) named after car details. Happy hour is 5pm-7pm. Don't miss the deadly deep-fried, corn-tortilla-wrapped hot dogs, an alleged Chimayó family recipe.

Get an early start on happy hour, 3pm-6pm, on the patio at **The Cowgirl** (319 S. Guadalupe St., 505/982-2565, 11am-midnight daily). But the scene is good later, too, as it segues into live music many nights.

**El Farol** (808 Canyon Rd., 505/983-9912, 11am-midnight Sun.-Thurs., 11am-1am Fri.-Sat.) is a perennial favorite. A bar since 1835, it's the gallery owners' clubhouse, and exuberant dancing occasionally breaks out on the tiny dance floor. There's a nice back patio too.

For margaritas, **Maria's** (555 W. Cordova Rd., 505/983-7929, 11am-10pm Mon.-Fri., noon-10pm Sat.) has been serving a dazzling selection of them since 1952. It's more a restaurant than a bar, but the standard New Mexican food is good enough and gets better with each drink.

Adjacent to the venerable Pink Adobe restaurant, the **Dragon Room** (406 Old Santa Fe Tr., 505/983-7712, 4pm-midnight Tues.-Sun.) is so dim you might not notice at first the huge tree growing up from the left side of the bar. Guys in cowboy hats chat with mountain bikers and dressed-up cocktail drinkers. There's live music Tuesday, Thursday, and Saturday.

Tucked in the middle of a block near the plaza, **Taberna La Boca** (72 W. Marcy St., 505/982-3433, 5pm-11pm daily) is very popular for a glass of wine or sherry and a savory snack. The party often spills out into the courtyard. **¡Chispa! at El Mesón** (213 Washington St., 505/983-6756, 5pm-11pm Tues.-Sat.) has music five nights a week, and a particularly devoted crew of regulars on Tuesday, for tango night. You can order traditional tapas, or bigger dishes from El Mesón's excellent dinner menu at the bar, or just join in the dancing on the small wood floor.

## PERFORMING ARTS

The 2,128-seat **Santa Fe Opera** (U.S. 84/285, 505/986-5900, www.santafeopera.org) is the city's premier arts venue. The elegant open-air amphitheater seven miles north of Santa Fe acts as "summer camp" for the country's best singers to perform a mix of repertory and modern works during July and August. If you think opera is all about tuxes, plush seats, and too-long arias, give the SFO a chance. Half the fun is arriving early to "tailgate" in the parking lot, which involves gourmet goodies, lots of champagne, and time to mill around and check out other attendees' bolo ties. In addition to your picnic dinner, pack blankets to ward off the chill after the sun sets. If you have kids to entertain, time your visit for bargain-priced "family nights" or a special dress rehearsal with extra info to introduce young ones to the art form.

Set in a 1931 Moorish curlicue palace, the **Lensic Performing Arts Center** (211 W. San Francisco St., 505/988-1234, www.lensic.com) is Santa Fe's best stage after the opera house, with 820 seats and an eclectic schedule. The six-week-long **Santa Fe Chamber Music Festival** (www.sfcmf.org) schedules events here, as well as at the St. Francis Cathedral, with performances nearly every day in July and August.

## FESTIVALS AND EVENTS

Santa Fe's summer is packed. In mid-July, the **International Folk Art Market** (505/997-7600, www.folkartmarket.org) showcases traditional crafts from all over the globe, often from the artisans in person. It's set up on Museum Hill,

© ZORA O'NEILL

wearable art at the International Folk Art Market

so the center of the city is not disrupted. On Sunday, tickets are cheap and vendors are ready to make deals.

In late July, **Spanish Market** (505/982-2226, www.spanishcolonialblog.org) takes over the plaza with traditional New Mexican woodwork (especially *santos*), weaving, and furniture. (It happens again right after Thanksgiving.)

Finally, the city's biggest annual event is in late August, when 100,000 visitors come for **Santa Fe Indian Market** (505/983-5220, www.swaia.org). Like Spanish Market, it's centered on the plaza, with some 1,200 Native American artisans selling jewelry, pottery, weaving, and more, in traditional and wildly modern styles. It's a bit of a frenzy, but also festive, due to free music and dance performances.

After all the frenzy of summer tourism, locals celebrate the arrival of fall with the **Burning of Zozobra** (www.burnzozobra.com), a neo-pagan bonfire on the Friday after Labor Day. The ritual kicks off the weeklong **Fiesta de Santa Fe** (505/204/1598, www.santafefiesta.org), which has been celebrated in some form since 1712. It begins with a reenactment of De Vargas's *entrada* into the city, then a whole slew of balls and parades, including the Historical/Hysterical Parade and a children's pet parade—eccentric Santa Fe at its finest. Some downtown businesses close for some of the time, particularly on Zozobra day.

## CINEMA

The delightful little **Jean Cocteau Cinema** (418 Montezuma Ave., 505/466-5528, $10) was shuttered for several years before resident author George R. R. Martin (now known to the TV-watching world as the man behind *Game of Thrones*) bought the place in 2013 and revamped it. Now the 120-seat theater is back to showing the eclectic art-house offerings, to an enthusiastic local audience.

## The Burning of Zozobra

© ZORA O'NEILL

**Old Man Gloom waits for the torch.**

Every fall a raucous chant fills the air in Santa Fe's Fort Marcy Park: "Burn him! Burn him! Burn him!" It's not a witch hunt, but the ritual torching of Zozobra, a 50-foot-tall marionette with long, grasping arms, glowering eyes, and a moaning voice. Old Man Gloom, as he's also known, represents the accumulated sorrows of the populace—aided by the divorce papers, pictures of ex-girlfriends, hospital gowns, and other anxiety-inducing scraps with which he's stuffed. Setting this aflame purges these troubles and allows for a fresh start.

This Santa Fe tradition sounds like a medieval rite, but it dates only from the 1920s, when artist Will Shuster—a bit of a local legend who's also credited with inventing the piñon-juniper incense and starting the tradition of citywide bonfires on Christmas Eve—wanted to lighten up the heavily Catholic Fiesta de Santa Fe. Shuster, who had moved to Santa Fe in 1920 to treat his tuberculosis, was inspired by the Mummers Parade from his native Philadelphia, as well as the Yaqui Indians in Tucson, Arizona, who burn Judas in effigy in the week before Easter.

A 1926 *Santa Fe New Mexican* article describes the spectacle Shuster developed, with the help of the Kiwanis Club:

> Zozobra...stood in ghastly silence illuminated by weird green fires. While the band played a funeral march, a group of Kiwanians in black robes and hoods stole around the figure.... [Then] red fires blazed at the foot ...and leaped into a column of many colored flames.... And throwing off their black robes the spectators emerged in gala costume, joining an invading army of bright-hued harlequins with torches in a dance around the fires as the band struck up "La Cucaracha."

Shuster oversaw Zozobra nearly every year until 1964. In the late 1930s, Errol Flynn, in town with Olivia de Havilland and Ronald Reagan to film *The Santa Fe Trail,* set Zozobra aflame. A few years later, during World War II, the puppet was dubbed Hirohitlomus. In 1950, Zozobra appeared on the New Mexico state float in the Rose Bowl parade and won the national trophy.

Although Zozobra (a.k.a. O.M.G.) has a Twitter account these days and accepts worries-to-burn online, the spectacle is roughly unchanged, with dozens of white-clad children playing "glooms," followed by a "fire dancer" who taunts Zozo until he bursts into flame; fireworks cap it off. It's a fine sight, and a great cross-section of Santa Feans attend. But anyone leery of crowds may want to watch from outside the perimeter of the ball field.

# Shopping

Even people who clutch tight to their purse strings may be a little undone by the treasures for sale in Santa Fe. The most expensive shops are more like free museums; the cheapest are eternally on the brink of "going out of business" and should be avoided. Downtown around the plaza are souvenir shops and a few influential galleries; on Canyon Road, art dealers of all stripes; and on South Guadalupe Street, more funky and fun boutiques. If you buy too much to carry, **Pak Mail** (369 Montezuma Ave., 505/989-7380) can ship it home safely; it even offers free pickup from hotels.

## ART GALLERIES

With seemingly every other storefront downtown occupied by a gallery, Santa Fe's art scene can be overwhelming. The densest concentration of work is on Canyon Road, though it can seem a bit crowded with Southwestern kitsch. Summer hours are given here; in the winter, most galleries are closed at least Monday and Tuesday.

### Local Artists

At the top end of Canyon Road, **Red Dot Gallery** (826 Canyon Rd., 505/820-7338, 11am-6pm Fri., 11am-5pm Sat.-Sun.) is the exhibition space for Santa Fe Community College students and alumni, a nice antidote to the high-toned vibe on the rest of the street. In the convention center, the **Community Gallery** (201 W. Marcy St., 505/955-6705, 10am-5pm Tues.-Fri., 9:30am-4pm Sat.) is run by the Santa Fe Arts Commission and always has a wide mix of work on display.

### Contemporary

Santa Fe's contemporary scene seems to have cooled a bit in recent years, at least in terms of large galleries. But granddaddy **LewAllen** maintains its downtown space (125 W. Palace Ave., 505/988-8997, 10am-6pm Mon.-Sat.), as well as a larger space for more abstract work in

the **Railyard** (1613 Paseo de Peralta, 505/988-3250, 10am-6pm Mon.-Fri., 10am-5pm Sat.).

Off Canyon Road, **Eight Modern** (231 Delgado St., 505/995-0231, 9:30am-5:30pm Mon.-Sat., 11am-4pm Sun.) focuses on colorful, abstract, and pop art. Nearby, **Nüart Gallery** (670 Canyon Rd., 505/988-3888, 10am-5pm Mon.-Sat., daily) showcases Latin American magical realism.

### Native American and Southwestern

Near Canyon Road, **Gerald Peters Gallery** (1011 Paseo de Peralta, 505/954-5700, 10am-5pm Mon.-Sat.) and **Nedra Matteucci Galleries** (1075 Paseo de Peralta, 505/982-4631, 9am-5pm Mon.-Sat.) are the biggies when it comes to Taos Society of Artists and other Western art, though both have contemporary artists too. Even if nothing inside hits the spot, the one-acre sculpture garden in back of Nedra Matteucci is a treat. Smaller **Robert Nichols Gallery** (419 Canyon Rd., 505/982-2145, 10am-5pm Mon.-Sat., 11am-5pm Sun.) specializes in Native American pottery, including some with often funny, boundary-pushing sensibilities.

Near the plaza, **Blue Rain Gallery** (130 Lincoln Ave., 505/954-9902, 10am-6pm Mon.-Sat.) showcases work from many pueblo residents, such as Tammy Garcia's modern takes on traditional Santa Clara pottery forms—she sometimes renders bowls in blown glass or applies the geometric decoration to jewelry.

## CLOTHING AND JEWELRY

Get the Santa Fe look at **Lucille's** (223 Galisteo St., 505/983-6331, 10am-6pm Mon.-Sat., 11am-4pm Sun.), which is stuffed with flowing cotton skirts, bohemian tunics, and chunky jewelry. There's always good stuff on the sale rack.

**¡Mira!** (101-A W. Marcy St., 505/988-3585,

© ZORA O'NEILL

a turquoise necklace in a Santa Fe shop window

9am-9pm Mon.-Sat., noon-6pm Sun.) has a hip mix of clothes and housewares, with T-shirts by local designers ("Fanta Se" in the old Santa Fe Railroad logo, say) as well as cool imports from places like Ghana. In winter, it closes at 6pm, and 5pm on Sunday. Just down the block, **Glorianna's** (55 W. Marcy St., 505/982-0353, 10am-4:30pm Mon.-Tues. and Thurs.-Sat., often closed for lunch 1pm-2pm) is a treasure trove of beads, packed to bursting with veritable eggs of raw turquoise, trays of glittering Czech glass, and ropes of African trade beads.

The city's best consignment shop is **Double Take** (321 S. Guadalupe St., 505/989-8886, 10am-6pm Mon.-Sat., 10am-4pm Sun.), a sprawling two-story space with an excellent selection of boots, as well as cool clothing, rodeo-themed 1950s sofas, Fiestaware, and plenty more.

## GIFT AND HOME
The owner of **Seret & Sons** (224 Galisteo St., 505/988-9151, 9am-5:30pm Mon.-Fri., 9am-6pm Sat., 9:30am-5pm Sun.) is a Santa Fe icon who deals in finely woven rugs, antique doors, and life-size wooden elephants from his cavernous warehouse just south of the plaza.

For funky folk art that won't break the bank, head for the equally gigantic **Jackalope** (2820 Cerrillos Rd., 505/471-8539, 10am-6pm daily), where seemingly acres are given over to mosaic-topped tables, wooden chickens, Mexican pottery vases, and inexpensive souvenirs. Sharing the space is a community of prairie dogs—good distraction for children while adults cruise the breakables.

## OPEN-AIR MARKETS
One of the most familiar sights of Santa Fe is the portal of the **Palace of the Governors,** where American Indian vendors from all over New Mexico spread out their wares as they've been doing for more than 80 years. Some 1,000 vendors are licensed to sell here after going through a strict application process that evaluates their technical skills. Every morning the

© ZORA O'NEILL

Go organic with goodies from the Santa Fe Farmers Market.

63 spots, each 12 bricks wide, are doled out by lottery. Expect anything from silver bracelets to pottery to *heishi* (shell bead) necklaces to freshly harvested piñon nuts. It's a great opportunity to buy direct from a skilled artisan and learn about the work that went into a piece.

The popular **Santa Fe Farmers Market** (1607 Paseo de Peralta, 505/983-4098, www.santafefarmersmarket.com, 7am-noon Tues. and Sat. in summer, 8am-1pm Sat. in winter) is a great place to pick up fresh treats as well as souvenir chile *ristras*. It's in a market hall in the Railyard complex, off Paseo de Peralta near Guadalupe Street. On Sundays, the **Railyard Artisan Market** (www.artmarketsantafe.com, 10am-4pm) takes over the space.

## SWEET TREATS

**Todos Santos** (125 E. Palace Ave., 505/982-3855, 10am-5pm Mon.-Sat.) adds the sweet smell of chocolate to the air in Sena Plaza. The closet-size shop has the perfect (if short-lived) Santa Fe souvenir: *milagros,* the traditional Mexican Catholic prayer charms shaped like body parts, rendered in Valrhona chocolate and covered in a delicate layer of gold or silver leaf. If you prefer nuts and chews, head to long-time candy vendor **Señor Murphy** (100 E. San Francisco St., 505/982-0461, 10am-5:30pm daily) for some "caramales" (chewy balls of caramel and piñon nuts wrapped up in little corn husks) and other New Mexico-inspired sweet treats.

# Sports and Recreation

It's no accident *Outside* magazine has its offices here. On weekends, Santa Feans leave the town to the tourists and scatter into the surrounding mountains on foot or bike. You'll find something to do all four seasons, though hikes above the foothills shouldn't be attempted till mid-May at least (and not until you're acclimated to the altitude). If you're in town in the fall, don't miss the leaves turning on the aspens, usually in mid-October (for a great, low-effort view, ride the lift at the ski basin). The main access route for most activities is Highway 475—it starts out from the north side of Santa Fe as Artists Road, then the name changes to Hyde Park Road, and farther north it's Ski Basin Road.

## Information and Guides
Just off Highway 14, immediately south of I-25, the **Public Lands Information Center** (301 Dinosaur Tr., 505/954-2002, www.publiclands.org, 8am-4:30pm Mon.-Sat.) is the best starting point for any outdoor activity. The staff will also know the latest status on areas affected by wildfires or floods. **Outspire!** (505/660-0394, www.outspire.com) runs guided full- and half-day outings—hiking in summer, snowshoeing in winter. For gear, check **REI** (500 Market St., 505/982-3557) in the Railyard district.

## BIKING
Mountain bikers have fantastic outlets very close to Santa Fe, while those who prefer the open road will love the challenges in the winding highways through the mountains north of the city. **Rob & Charlie's** (1632 St. Michael's Dr., 505/471-9119, 9:30am-6pm Mon.-Sat.,

SANTA FE

## Santa Fe for Kids

Give the little ones a break from museums and galleries. All of the following fun options are open 10am-5pm Monday-Saturday, except where noted.

- **Bee Hive** (328 Montezuma Ave., 505/780-8051, also open noon-4pm Sun.) A lovingly curated kids' bookstore, often with story time on Saturdays.

- **Dinosaurs & More** (137 W. San Francisco St., 505/988-3299, also open Sun.) The owner can tell a story about nearly every meteorite, fossil, and geode in the place.

- **Doodlet's** (120 Don Gaspar St., 505/983-3771) Open since 1955, this corner shop is filled with doodads for kids and adults, from toy accordions to kitchen tchotchkes.

- **Moon Rabbit Toys** (112 W. San Francisco St., 505/982-5373) Worth seeking out inside the Plaza Mercado, for its house-designed strategy games.

- **Play!** (500 Montezuma Ave., 505/820-3338) Stocks wooden and other European-style toys and clothes, with lots of play space and events.

- **Santa Fe Children's Museum** (1050 Old Pecos Tr., 505/989-8359, closed Mon., also open noon-5pm Sun., $9, $5 on Sun.) Hands-on fun, such as pint-size looms, a giant soap-bubble pool, and a dazzling collection of bugs.

- **Toyopolis** (150 Washington Ave., 505/988-5422) The closest toy store to the plaza, for emergency distraction.

- **Warehouse 21** (1614 Paseo de Peralta, 505/989-4423, www.warehouse21.org) This teen arts center hosts a range of workshops, performances, and more.

noon-5pm Sun. in summer) is a reliable shop for road bikers. Closer to the plaza, **Mellow Velo** (132 E. Marcy St., 505/995-8356, 9am-5:30pm Mon.-Sat.) rents mountain and road models, as well as city cruisers (from $20/day).

## Mountain Biking

The **Dale Ball Trails** are a 30-mile network of single-track routes used by both hikers and mountain bikers, winding through stands of piñon and juniper in the foothills. Two trailheads give access to the North, Central, and South Sections of the trail. From the northern trailhead, on Sierra del Norte (immediately off Highway 475 after mile marker 3), the North Section trails vary a bit in elevation, but the Central Section (south from the parking area) is more fun because it's a longer chunk of trails. The southern trailhead, on Cerro Gordo just north of its intersection with Canyon Road, gives access to the Central Section and the South Section, which is for advanced riders only. Note that the trail that starts at the southern trailhead lot, part of the Santa Fe Canyon Preserve, is for foot traffic only—ride your bike one-tenth of a mile down Cerro Gordo to the start of the Dale Ball system.

A local classic, the **Santa Fe Rail Trail** is a paved path starting in Railyard Park, then turns to dirt outside the city limits. Revamped in 2012, the trail is now a lot smoother than it was, and it's a pleasant, relatively easy route along the railroad tracks to Lamy. The trail is about 12.5 miles one-way; except for a grade near I-25, it's fairly level.

## Road Biking

Make sure you're acclimated to the altitude before you set out on any lengthy trip—the best tour, along the high road to Taos, will take you through some of the area's highest elevations. Starting in Chimayó shaves some not-so-scenic miles off the ride and gives you a reasonable 45-mile jaunt to Taos. The annual **Santa Fe Century** (www.santafecentury.com) takes place every May, running a 104-mile loop south down the Turquoise Trail and back north via the old farm towns in the Galisteo Basin, southeast of Santa Fe.

## HIKING

Some hikes start very near the center of town, while others call for a half-hour drive at the most.

## Santa Fe Canyon Preserve

For an easy saunter in town, head for this 190-acre patch of the foothills managed by the **Nature Conservancy** (505/988-3867). The area is open only to people on foot—no mountain bikes and no pets. The preserve covers the canyon formed by the now-diverted Santa Fe River. An easy interpretive loop trail leads around the area for 1.5 miles, passing the remnants of the dam and winding through dense stands of cottonwoods and willows. The trailhead is on Cerro Gordo Road just north of its intersection with Upper Canyon Road.

## Atalaya Mountain

One of the easiest-to-reach trails in the Santa Fe area (you can take the M city bus to the trailhead on the campus of St. John's College) is also one of the more challenging. The hike heads up to a **9,121-foot peak,** starting out as a gentle stroll along the city's edge, then becoming increasingly steep, for a round-trip of approximately seven miles. Allow about four miles for the full up-and-back.

## Aspen Vista

Aspen Vista is the **most popular trail in the Sangre de Cristos.** But don't be put off by the prospect of crowds, as the promised views of golden aspen groves are indeed spectacular—in the densest spots, when the sun is shining through the leaves, the air itself feels yellow. Even though it's at a high elevation, it's an easy hike, on a rough service road with a gradual slope. The full length is 11.5 miles, but it's the first 2.5 miles that are the most aspen-intense. A little under 4 miles in, you get a great view of Santa Fe below; this makes a good turnaround point for a two-hour hike. Look for the parking area on the right of Ski Basin Road (Hwy. 475), just under 13 miles up the road from town.

## SPAS

**Ten Thousand Waves** (3451 Hyde Park Rd., 505/982-9304, www.tenthousandwaves.com, 9am-10:30pm Wed.-Mon., noon-10:30pm Tues. July-Oct.) is such a Santa Fe institution that it could just as well be listed under the city's major attractions. This traditional Japanese-style bathhouse just outside of town has two big communal pools and seven smaller private ones tucked among the trees so as to optimize the views of the mountains all around; many have adjoining cold plunges and saunas. The place also offers full day-spa services, with

©ZORA O'NEILL

Ten Thousand Waves is a Japanese bathhouse with New Mexican touches.

intense massages and luxe facials and body scrubs. Prices are relatively reasonable, starting at $24 for unlimited time in the public baths and $109 for one-hour massages. In the winter (Nov.-June), the baths open at 10:30am (2pm on Tues.) and close earlier on weeknights.

In town, **Absolute Nirvana Spa** (106 Faithway St., 505/983-7942, www.absolutenirvana.com, 10am-6pm Sun.-Thurs., 10am-8pm Fri.-Sat.) offers Balinese treatments and massages. Afterward, you can relax in the gardens with a cup of tea and some organic sweets from the adjacent tearoom.

A bit farther from the center, but very highly rated by locals, **Body of Santa Fe** (333 W. Cordova Rd., 505/986-0362, www.bodyofsantafe.com, 9am-9pm daily) is praised for its affordable treatments (massages from $80/hour) and relaxed atmosphere. There's a nice café on-site too.

## WINTER SPORTS

Sixteen miles northeast of town in the Santa Fe National Forest, **Ski Santa Fe** (Hwy. 475, 505/982-4429, www.skisantafe.com, $69 full-day lift ticket) is a well-used day area with 77 fairly challenging trails. A major selling point: virtually no lift lines.

For cross-country skiers, the groomed **Norski Trails** are about a quarter of a mile before the Ski Santa Fe parking lot, off the west side of the road. The standard route is about 2.5 miles, winding through the trees and along a ridgeline, and you can shorten or lengthen the tour by taking various loops and shortcuts, as long as you follow the directional arrows counterclockwise.

Just seven miles out of town along the road to the ski area, **Hyde Memorial State Park** (www.nmparks.com) has a couple of nicely maintained sledding runs, as well as some shorter cross-country ski routes. **Cottam's Ski Shop** (740 Hwy. 475, 505/982-0495) is the biggest rental operation in the area, handily located on the way to Aspen Vista.

SANTA FE

# Accommodations

Santa Fe offers some great places to stay, but none are cheap. Prices quoted for the bigger hotels are standard rack rates; chances are, you'll be able to find substantially lower ones just by calling or by booking online, at least at the higher-end properties. Prices spike in July and August, often up to holiday rates. If you're coming for Indian Market or Christmas, try to book at least eight months in advance. On the other hand, despite ski season, rates are often quite low in January and February.

## UNDER $100

As hostels go, **Santa Fe International Hostel** (1412 Cerrillos Rd., 505/988-1153, www.hostelsantafe.com) is not the worst, but neither is it one of the more inspiring—unless you clamp on your rose-colored glasses and view it as an old-school hippie project (it *is* run as a nonprofit). The dorms ($18 pp) and private rooms ($25 s, $35 d) are dim, and cleanliness can be spotty, as you're relying on the previous guests' efforts, as part of the required daily chores. The kitchen has free food, but you have to pay for Internet access ($2/day).

For camping, the closest tent sites to the center are at **Hyde Memorial State Park** (Hwy. 475, 505/983-7175, www.nmparks.com), about four miles northwest of the city, with both primitive ($8) and developed sites with electricity ($14).

Wedged in among the chain hotels on Cerrillos, the quirky ◖ **Silver Saddle Motel** (2810 Cerrillos Rd., 505/471-7663, www.santafesilversaddlemotel.com, $62 s, $67 d) plays up the retro charm. Cozy rooms may be pretty basic and have cinder-block walls, but they're decked out with Western accoutrements and kept clean—and the price, which includes breakfast, can't be beat. A handful of later-built rooms have some extra square footage.

## $100-150

The bones of ◖ **Santa Fe Sage Inn** (725 Cerrillos Rd., 505/982-5952, www.santafesageinn.com, $115 d) are a standard highway motel, but the super clean rooms are done in sharp, modern red and black, with Southwestern rugs hung on the walls. Little touches such as free Wi-Fi, plush beds, and an above-average breakfast (fresh bagels, fruit, yogurt, and more) make this an excellent deal—the place even has a swimming pool. It may be on Cerrillos Road, but it's still walking distance to the center, and it's right across the street from the Railyard Park and the farmers market.

Despite its location on uncharming Cerrillos Road, about two miles from the plaza, **El Rey Inn** (1862 Cerrillos Rd., 505/982-1931, www.elreyinnsantafe.com, $105 s, $140 d) counts as one of the more charming hotels in Santa Fe. Built in 1935, it has been meticulously kept up and adjusted for modern standards of comfort, with beautiful gardens, a hot tub, a big swimming pool, and a fireside open-air Jacuzzi. The 86 rooms, spread over 4.5 acres, vary considerably in style (and in price), from the oldest section with snug adobe walls and heavy viga ceilings to airier rooms with balconies. Rooms at the back of the property are preferable, due to noise from the road.

**Santa Fe Motel & Inn** (510 Cerrillos Rd., 505/982-1039, www.santafemotel.com, $149 d) is your best budget bet close to the center, with rooms done up in simple, bright decor that avoids motel sameness despite the generic motor-court layout. A few kitchenettes are available, along with some more private casitas with fireplaces. Lots of nice touches—such as bread from the Sage Bakehouse across the street along with the full breakfast—give the place a homey feel without the tight quarters of a typical bed-and-breakfast.

## $150-250

In a handy location west of the plaza, **Las Palomas** (460 W. San Francisco St., 505/982-5560, www.laspalomas.com, $153 d) is a cluster of four separate complexes—there's usually still room here when smaller B&Bs are full, and on-line booking discounts can be generous. Room layouts vary significantly—the condos at Zona Rosa are good for longer stays, though many have at least a kitchenette. Some casitas have bedrooms facing parking lots, which feels no better than a motel—call to book, to make sure you're not in one of these.

With 12 rooms in an old adobe, plus an adjacent Victorian with two suites, **El Paradero B&B** (220 W. Manhattan St., 505/988-1177, www.elparadero.com, $155 d) is a flexible place: It has a variety of room configurations that can suit families, solo travelers, and friends traveling together. Upstairs rooms have balconies, and a few others have fireplaces. The look throughout is subdued Southwestern, with soothing whitewashed walls.

East of the plaza, twin bed-and-breakfasts under the same ownership offer two kinds of style: The rooms at **Hacienda Nicholas** (320 E. Marcy St., 505/986-1431, www.haciendanich-olas.com, $165 d) have a tasteful Southwest flavor, decorated with a few cowboy trappings and Gustave Baumann prints; most rooms have fireplaces. Across the street, **The Madeleine** (106 Faithway St., 505/982-3465, www.madeleineinn.com, $165 d) is set in a wood Victorian, but the lace curtains are offset with rich Balinese fabrics. In both places, breakfast is a continental spread, but that doesn't mean you'll go away hungry—the banana bread is fantastic.

**Hotel Chimayó** (125 Washington Ave., 505/988-4900, www.hotelchimayo.com, $169 d), offers good value very close to the plaza, though not everyone will like its folky style, done up with wooden crosses and striped rugs from its namesake village. Upstairs rooms have private balconies, and some suites have fireplaces.

**Inn on the Alameda** (303 E. Alameda St., 505/984-2121, www.innonthealameda.com, $215 d) is a good option for people who want adobe style *and* space, and its location near Canyon Road is handy for gallery-hoppers. The big rooms have triple-sheeted beds, wireless Internet access, and overstuffed armchairs that are only lightly dusted with Southwestern flair; most also have a patio or balcony. The continental breakfast spread is generous, and there's a wine-and-cheese hour every afternoon.

Majority-owned by Picurís Pueblo, **Hotel Santa Fe** (1501 Paseo de Peralta, 800/825-9876, www.hotelsantafe.com, $169 d) is both a successful business experiment and a very nice hotel, with one of the few large outdoor pools in town, set against the neo-pueblo hotel walls. The standard rooms are a bit small—the real value is in the ultraluxe Hacienda wing, where the huge rooms with fireplaces and butler service can be as low as $219 online—a steal compared with other high-end places in town.

A rental condo is a great option if you have a family or group, and those at **Campanilla Compound** (334 Otero St., 800/828-9700,

Hotel Santa Fe is a project of Picurís Pueblo.

SANTA FE

© ZORA O'NEILL

www.campanillacompound.com, $225) are especially nice, with whitewashed walls, fireplaces, Mexican-tiled kitchens, and plenty of space inside and out—each one has a private patio or porch. The units are arranged up a hill, and some have excellent views of the city and the sunset. There's a two-night minimum.

The iconic, family-owned **◖ La Fonda** (100 E. San Francisco St., 505/982-5511, www.lafondasantafe.com, $239 d) underwent a major renovation in 2013, which lightened up its guest rooms considerably. They feel slightly more generic and modern as a result, though many do have original folk art, and a few have *latilla* ceilings and kiva fireplaces—along with all the necessary luxuries, such as pillow-top beds. You can soak up most of the place's atmosphere in the public areas, of course, but the location couldn't be better. It helps to have flexible dates—in periods of high demand, the rates can spike to exorbitant levels.

A wonderfully restful spot is **Houses of the Moon** (3451 Hyde Park Rd., 505/992-5003, www.tenthousandwaves.com, $239 d), the guest cottages at Ten Thousand Waves spa. Some have more of a local feel, with viga ceilings and kiva fireplaces, while others are straight from Japan, both samurai era and contemporary anime. Some larger suites have kitchens. Rates include a suitably organic granola breakfast as well as free access to the communal and women's tubs.

## OVER $250

Special occasion? **The Inn of the Five Graces** (150 E. De Vargas St., 505/992-0957, www.fivegraces.com, $650 per suite) can transport you to exotic climes—for at least slightly less than a plane ticket. Outside, it looks like a typical historic Southwestern lodge, a collection of interconnected adobe casitas. But inside, there's a certain air of opium dream—the 24 sumptuous suites are done in antique Turkish kilims, heavy wood doors, and mosaics—all courtesy of the boho dealers Seret & Sons. Rates include a stocked fridge and full breakfast, delivered to your room if you like.

# Food

Dining is one of Santa Fe's great pleasures—considering the tiny population, it offers a dazzling range of flavors, and very high quality. Sure, you can get a cheese-smothered, crazy-hot plate of green-chile-and-chicken enchiladas, but most locals eat more globally than that. "Santa Fe cuisine" cheerfully incorporates Asian, Southwestern, and Mediterranean flavors, with an emphasis on organic and holistic.

## DOWNTOWN

Food is a bit ho-hum on Santa Fe Plaza itself (except for the fajita cart, when it's set up), but the blocks surrounding it, within the ring formed by Alameda Street and Paseo de Peralta, contain some classic Santa Fe spots to which everyone makes a trek at some point, along with a few hidden treats.

## Cafés

**Ecco** (105 E. Marcy St., 505/986-9778, 7am-9pm Mon.-Thurs., 7am-10pm Fri., 8am-10pm Sat., 8am-7pm Sun.) is packed with coffee junkies and Wi-Fi fanatics in the mornings; later, people come in for panini (at the counter next door) and gelato.

The **French Pastry Shop** (100 E. San Francisco St., 505/983-6697, 6:30am-5pm daily, $7) doles out sweet crepes, buttery pastries, *croques monsieurs,* and chewy baguette sandwiches. Early mornings attract a fascinating crew of Santa Fe regulars.

**◖ Tia Sophia's** (210 W. San Francisco St., 505/983-9880, 7am-2pm Mon.-Sat., 8am-1pm Sun., $8) is one of the last places in the plaza area that feels untouched by time and tourists, serving old-time New Mexican plates to a slew of regulars without a touch of fusion—so

## Santa Fe's Finest Dining

In Santa Fe, there is a certain category of restaurant that one reader of this guide dubbed "Vegas-style"–that is, a place where the blingier your bolo tie or cowboy boots, the better. They're not totally superficial–in fact, **Coyote Café** (132 W. Water St., 505/983-1615, 5:30pm-9pm Sun.-Thurs., 5:30pm-10pm Fri.-Sat., $40) deserves a spot in the history books for having pioneered haute Southwestern cuisine in the late 1980s, under Chef Mark Miller.

Today that restaurant is owned by the same team as **Geronimo** (724 Canyon Rd., 505/982-1500, 5:45pm-9pm daily, $39), and both have opted for more generic fine dining with the occasional local nod–chile-rubbed pork chops, haute green-chile mac-and-cheese, etc. **La Casa Sena** (125 E. Palace Ave., 505/988-9232, 11am-9pm Mon.-Wed., 11am-10pm Thurs.-Sat., $24) runs in the same vein, as does **The Compound** (653 Canyon Rd., 505/982-4353, noon-2pm Mon.-Sat. and 6pm-9pm daily, $32), which has perhaps the most substance in this category.

They're all perfectly acceptable, but not a great value, and you'll be dining alongside other visitors, not locals. The best way to see the scene without emptying your wallet is at their bars. The Coyote Café has its lively **Rooftop Cantina** (505/983-1615, 11:30am-11pm daily, Apr.-Oct.), and the snug bar at Geronimo is a good place to put your feet up after a Canyon Road cruise. La Casa Sena is set in a truly dreamy garden courtyard. Order a cocktail and an appetizer, and enjoy the eye candy.

authentic, in fact, the kitchen claims to have invented the breakfast burrito decades back.

**Plaza Café** (54 Lincoln Ave., 505/982-1664, 7am-9pm daily, $11) may look shiny and new, but it's a city institution where residents roll in to read the paper and load up on coffee and great renditions of New Mexican and American diner favorites. This is no greasy spoon, though—the granola is house-made, and the piñon blue-corn pancakes are fluffy and fresh.

For a very casual lunch, stop in at the **Five & Dime General Store** (58 E. San Francisco St., 505/992-1800, 8:30am-10pm Mon.-Sat., 9am-9pm Sun., $5), on the south side of the plaza. In this former Woolworth's where, allegedly, the Frito pie was invented (Frito-Lay historians beg to differ), the knickknack shop has maintained its lunch counter and still serves the deadly combo of corn chips, red chile, onions, and cheese, all composed directly in the Fritos bag. Eat in, or, better, lounge on the plaza grass—and don't forget the napkins.

## American

Burger lovers despaired when legendary Bobcat Bite closed in early 2013, but the resolution is better than could be hoped: **Santa Fe Bite** (311 Old Santa Fe Trail, 505/982-0544, 7am-9pm Tues.-Fri., 8am-9pm Sat., 8am-5pm Sun., $10) is the new incarnation, close to the plaza, in much more comfortable digs. The same 10-ounce burgers, from beef ground fresh every day, on a home-baked bun, are the stars. But there's plenty more, including tacos, big salads, and fish and chips. Wash it down with a cold Mexican Coke; alas, no beer. Hearty breakfasts are served until 2pm.

## Fresh and Local

Open since the late 1970s, **Café Pasqual's** (121 Don Gaspar St., 505/983-9340, 7am-3pm and 5:30pm-9:30pm Mon.-Sat., 8am-3pm and 5:30pm-9:30pm Sun., $28) has defined its own culinary category, relying almost entirely on organic ingredients. Its breakfasts are legendary, but the food is delicious any time of day. Just brace yourself for the inevitable line, as the brightly painted dining room seats only 50 people, and loyal fans number in the thousands. Expect nearly anything on the menu:

smoked-trout hash or Yucatán-style *huevos motuleños* for breakfast; for dinner, mole enchiladas or Vietnamese squid salad.

## Italian

**Rooftop Pizzeria** (60 E. San Francisco St., 505/984-0008, 11am-10pm Sun.-Thurs., 11am-11pm Fri.-Sat., $15) is a good place to enjoy a view along with your meal, on a long balcony overlooking Water Street (enter on the plaza side of the shopping complex and head upstairs). You have the option of a crust with a hint of blue-corn meal, and toppings range from plain old onions to duck and crab, and they come in combinations like the BLT (the lettuce is added after the pie comes out of the oven, luckily). It also has a good selection of wines by the glass. Winter closing time is an hour earlier.

Off the plaza, with a pleasantly rustic atmosphere (nice creaky front porch, often with a live country crooner), **Upper Crust Pizza** (329 Old Santa Fe Tr., 505/982-0000, 11am-10pm daily, $10), next to Mission San Miguel, does regular, whole-wheat, or gluten-free crust. Hot deli sandwiches and big superfresh salads round out the menu.

Locals head to amber-lit **Il Piatto** (95 W. Marcy St., 505/984-1091, 11:30am-10:30pm Mon.-Sat., 4:30pm-10:30pm Sun., $20) for casual Italian and a neighborly welcome from the staff, who seem to be on a first-name basis with everyone in the place. Hearty pastas like *pappardelle* with duck are served in generous portions—a half order will more than satisfy lighter eaters. This is a great place to take a breather from enchiladas and burritos without breaking the bank.

## New Mexican and Mexican

**The Shed** (113½ E. Palace Ave., 505/982-9030, 11am-2:30pm and 5:30pm-9pm Mon.-Sat., $16) has been serving up platters of enchiladas since 1953—bizarrely, with a side of garlic bread. But that's just part of the tradition at this colorful, comfortable, marginally fancy place that's as popular with tourists as it is with die-hard residents. There are perfectly decent distractions like lemon-garlic shrimp and fish tacos on the menu, but it's the red chile you really should focus on.

It can be a bit inconsistent, but **Casa Chimayó** (409 W. Water St., 505/428-0391, 11am-2pm and 5pm-9pm daily, $14) has a bit more of a family-run feel, with recipes from the owner's grandmother. A nice touch: Mexican *chiles en nogada,* and far better dessert options than most New Mexican places. But it's beer and wine only (margaritas are made with agave wine).

The specialty at **Bumble Bee's Baja Grill** (301 Jefferson St., 505/820-2862, 11am-9pm daily, $5) is Baja shrimp tacos, garnished with shredded cabbage and a creamy sauce, plus a spritz of lime and your choice of house-made salsas. Lamb tacos are also delicious, as are the fried-fresh tortilla chips and that Tijuana classic, Caesar salad.

Tucked away in the Santa Fe Village minimall, **◖ La Cocina de Doña Clara** (227 Don Gaspar Ave., 505/983-6455, 9:30am-3pm Mon.-Thurs., 8am-4pm Fri.-Sun., $10) has Mexican goodies like *chilaquiles*—tortilla chips in savory sauce, a great way to start the day—and menudo on weekends.

## Spanish

Cozy creative-tapas joint **La Boca** (72 W. Marcy St., 505/982-3433, 11:30am-10pm daily) starts from Spain, then pulls in other Mediterranean influences: a salad spiked with apricots and figs, Moroccan *merguez*, and more. Ranging from $6 to $14, the little plates can add up fast, unless you're there 3pm-5pm weekdays, when there's a selection for half price. Reserve, ideally, and go early if you're sensitive to noise.

# GUADALUPE AND THE RAILYARD

An easy walk from the plaza, these few square blocks hold some of the better, quirkier dining options in town.

## Cafés

Make room in your morning for an almond

croissant from ◖ **Sage Bakehouse** (535 Cerrillos Rd., 505/820-7243, 7:30am-2:30pm Mon.-Sat., $4). Washed down with a mug of coffee, these butter-soaked pastries will have you set for hours. Before you leave, pick up some sandwiches for later—classic combos like smoked turkey and cheddar on the bakery's excellent crust. And maybe a pecan-raisin wreath. And a cookie too.

A few steps away is **Ohori's Coffee, Tea & Chocolate** (505 Cerrillos Rd., 505/988-9692, 7:30am-6pm Mon.-Fri., 8am-6pm Sat., 9am-2pm Sun.), Santa Fe's small-batch coffee epicures. Their dark-as-night brew makes Starbucks seem weak.

## American

All things Texan are the specialty at **The Cowgirl** (319 S. Guadalupe St., 505/982-2565, 11:30am-10:30pm Sun.-Wed., 11:30am-4pm Thurs., 11:30am-11pm Fri., 11am-11pm Sat., 11:30am-10:30pm Sun., $15)—but it's been a Santa Fe fixture for so long that it doesn't seem like "foreign" food. It's a kitsch-filled spot that's as friendly to kids as it is to margarita-guzzling, barbecue-rib-gnawing adults. Non-meat-eaters won't feel left out: An ooey-gooey butternut squash casserole comes with a salad on the side. Both carnivores and veggies can agree on the pineapple upside-down cake and the ice-cream "baked potato."

## Fresh and Local

Not far out of the Paseo de Peralta loop, the **Tune-Up Café** (1115 Hickox St., 505/983-7060, 7am-10pm Mon.-Fri., 8am-10pm Sat.-Sun., $9) is a homey one-room joint that locals love, whether for fish tacos or a suitably Santa Fe-ish brown-rice-and-nut burger. The Salvadoran *pupusas* are tasty.

## Italian

Sometimes you just want a nice pizza pie, and **Pizza Centro** (418 Cerrillos Rd., 505/988-8825, 11:30am-8:30pm daily, $12) fits the bill, with probably the most East Coast-style crispy crust in town. "Primo" toppings (truffle oil,

house-made meatballs) make it extra special, as do good salads.

## New Mexican

The under-the-radar cousin of The Shed, **La Choza** (905 Alarid St., 505/982-0909, 11am-2:30pm and 5pm-9pm Mon.-Sat., $16) has a similar creative New Mexican menu but is more of a local hangout—though it has become better known now that the rail yard has been developed around it. This also makes it a handy destination if you're coming to Santa Fe on the train—just walk back down the tracks a few minutes.

## Fine Dining

**Restaurant Martín** (526 Galisteo St., 505/820-0919, 11:30am-2pm and 5:30pm-10pm Tues.-Fri. and Sun., 5:30pm-10pm Sat., $34) is run by longtime local hero Chef Martín Rios. His "progressive American" food can be more style than substance, especially for full-price dinners, but it's a good place for a grown-up lunch—smooth service and a mix of full plates as well as a big burger on a cornmeal bun ($14).

A late, but long-awaited entrant: As this book was going to press, **Joseph's Restaurant** (505/982-1272, 428 Agua Fria St., www.josephsofsantafe.com, 5:30pm-10pm Sun.-Thurs., 5:30pm-11pm Fri.-Sat., $24) had just opened to great reviews. Celebrated chef Joseph Wrede (formerly of the great Joseph's Table in Taos) is a fresh-food fanatic (no freezers in his kitchen), known for creative combinations.

## CANYON ROAD

Gallery-hopping can make you hungry—but there are only a handful of places to eat on Canyon Road, and most are more dedicated to getting caffeine into your system.

## Cafés

For morning brew, jog off the strip to **Downtown Subscription** (376 Garcia St., 505/983-3085, 7am-6pm daily), an airy coffee shop that stocks perhaps a million magazines. Chocolate freaks should go a little farther to ◖ **Kakawa Chocolate House** (1050 E. Paseo

Get your chocolate fix at Kakawa.

de Peralta, 505/982-0388, 10am-6pm Mon.-Sat., noon-6pm Sun.), opposite the Gerald Peters Gallery. It specializes in historically accurate hot chocolate, based on ancient and medieval recipes, though you can also get regular coffee drinks, truffles, and pastries here. It's in a tiny adobe house—after one drink, you'll be bouncing off the walls.

For a mellower high, head to the top end of Canyon Road and **The Teahouse** (821 Canyon Rd., 505/992-0972, 9am-9pm daily, $12), where some 13 pages of the menu are devoted to teas, plus organic vittles such as kale salad with sunflower-seed dressing, and a deliciously hearty bowl of oats, rice, and wheat berries for breakfast. The service could be euphemistically described as "very Santa Fe" (i.e., spacey), but the food is good, and it's a great place to put your feet up after a long art crawl. On summer Fridays, it's usually open till 10pm to serve dessert during and after the gallery openings.

### Spanish
The lively evening spot is stalwart **El Farol**

(808 Canyon Rd., 505/983-9912, www.elfarolsf.com, 11am-12:30am Mon.-Thurs., 11am-1:30am Fri.-Sat., 11am-midnight Sun., $8). It's very popular as a bar, but its outside seating, under a creaky wooden portal and on a back patio, is an appealing place for a big stuffed sandwich (tuna and egg with arugula, say) or garlicky Spanish snacks.

## CERRILLOS ROAD
This commercial strip isn't Santa Fe's most scenic zone, but you'll find some great culinary gems out this way.

### Cafés
Don't feel guilty if you're on green-chile-and-cheese overload—just head to ( **Vinaigrette** (709 Don Cubero Alley, 505/820-9205, 11am-9pm Mon.-Sat., $14) and dig into a big green salad, along with half of Santa Fe. The so-called salad bistro uses largely organic ingredients from its farm in Nambé, in imaginative combos, like a highbrow taco salad with chorizo and honey-lime dressing. The setting is pure homey Santa Fe, with tea towels for napkins, iced tea served in canning jars, and local art on the whitewashed walls. There's a pretty patio too. Heading north on Cerrillos Road, turn off just after La Unica Cleaners.

Community activists need caffeine too—and they head to the **Santa Fe Baking Co.** (504 W. Cordova Rd., 505/988-4292, 6am-8pm Mon.-Sat., 6am-6pm Sun., $9) to get it. The scene is talkative (local radio station KSFR broadcasts a live show from here weekday mornings), and vegetarians will find a lot to eat—but so will fans of gut-busters such as chile dogs; breakfast is served all day.

### New Mexican
Green chile has been getting milder over the years—but not at ( **Horseman's Haven** (4354 Cerrillos Rd., 505/471-5420, 8am-8pm Mon.-Sat., 8:30am-2pm Sun., $8), which claims to serve the hottest green chile in Santa Fe. Locals grumbled when it moved out of its gas-station digs into a marginally nicer building just next

door, but the chile continues to knock the socks off.

## SANTA FE METRO AREA

Out on Old Las Vegas Highway, the frontage road for I-25, **Harry's Roadhouse** (96-B Old Las Vegas Hwy., 505/989-4629, 7am-10pm daily, $11) is a good destination, or an easy place to pop off the freeway (at the Old Santa Fe Trail exit). The patio has a great view across the flatlands, there's a full bar, and the menu includes cold meatloaf sandwiches, catfish po'boys, lamb stew, and an awe-inspiring breakfast burrito. Oh, and pie: Chocolate mousse, lemon meringue, and coconut cream pies could be crowding the pastry case at any given time.

# Outside Santa Fe

Less than an hour's drive from Santa Fe are six-century-old ruins of ancestral Puebloan culture at Bandelier and the 20th-century atomic developments in Los Alamos, home of the Manhattan Project. Abiquiu, best known as Georgia O'Keeffe country, is a landscape of rich red rocks along the tree-lined Rio Chama. The most popular outing from Santa Fe is to Taos, but even that presents several possibilities. The main options are the low road along the Rio Grande or the high road that passes through tiny mountain villages. You can also take a more roundabout route through Ojo Caliente, a village built around hot springs.

## THE PUEBLOS

Between Santa Fe and Taos lie seven pueblos, each set on a separate patch of reservation land. Unlike scenic Taos Pueblo, which opens its centuries-old buildings to visitors, most of these are not worth visiting for their ancient architecture—they're typically unremarkable modern housing, and some are closed to outsiders all or part of the year. With the exception of the cliff dwellings at Santa Clara, none of these pueblos merit a visit on an average day—but do make the trip on feast days or for other ceremonial dances if you can.

### Tesuque and Pojoaque

Just north of Santa Fe, the highway overpasses are decorated with the original Tewa names of the pueblos. Tesuque (Te Tesugeh Owingeh, "village of the cottonwood trees") is marked by **Camel Rock,** a piece of sandstone on the west side of the highway that has eroded to resemble a creature that looks right at home in this rocky desert.

Farther north, Pojoaque manages the **Poeh Museum** (U.S. 84/285, 505/455-3334, 8am-5pm Mon.-Fri., 9am-4pm Sun., free), in a striking old-style adobe building. It shows (and sells) local artwork, as well as a permanent installation relating the Pojoaque people's path *(poeh)* through history.

### San Ildefonso

Best known for the black-on-black pottery of María Martinez and her husband, Julian, and now produced by a number of skilled potters, the pueblo of San Ildefonso is off Highway 502, on the way to Los Alamos. Of all the pueblos just north of Santa Fe, it's probably the most scenic, with even its newer houses done in faux-adobe-style, and the main plaza shaded by giant old cottonwoods. You must first register at the **visitors center** (off Hwy. 502, 505/455-3549, 8am-5pm Mon.-Fri., $10/car), then proceed on foot. There is a very small **museum** (8am-4:30pm daily), which is really just an excuse to walk across the village. The only other attractions are pottery shops—which are interesting even if you're not in the market, as it's a chance to peek inside people's homes, and chat a bit.

### Santa Clara

On the land of Santa Clara (Kha P'o, or Shining Water), on Highway 30 south of Española, are

SANTA FE

© ZORA O'NEILL

Camel Rock is a landmark north of Santa Fe.

the beautiful **Puyé Cliff Dwellings** (888/320-5008, www.puyecliffs.com), which were occupied until the early 1600s. They're accessible only by guided tour, and a somewhat expensive one at that: $20 for a one-hour walk either along the cliff side or the mesa top, or $35 for both. But tour leaders come from the pueblo and connect the ancient ruins with current culture in an intimate and fascinating way. At the base of the cliffs is a stone building from the Fred Harvey Indian Detour days of the early 1900s, when carloads of intrepid visitors would trundle off the train and out to these exotic sights; it now houses a small museum. You must buy your tickets at the Puyé Cliffs Welcome Center—better recognized as a gas station on Highway 30, at the turn to the cliffs. **Tours** run on the hour 9am-5pm daily April through September; the rest of the year, tours run 10am-2pm.

### Getting There

From downtown Santa Fe, northbound Guadalupe Street turns into U.S. 84/285, which runs north through Tesuque in five miles and Pojoaque in 15 miles. Though this stretch of casinos and tax-free cigarette shops isn't particularly scenic, don't be tempted to race through it—the area is a major speed trap.

To reach San Ildefonso, turn off U.S. 84/285 in Pojoaque at the exit for Highway 502 to Los Alamos; the turn for the pueblo is about six miles ahead on the right. From San Ildefonso, you can continue to Santa Clara by turning north on Highway 30; the cliff dwellings are seven miles ahead on the left. Or head somewhat more directly to Santa Clara from Santa Fe via Española, then follow signs for Highway 30; the total drive from the edge of Santa Fe is about 23 miles.

## LOS ALAMOS

Unlike so many other sights in New Mexico, which are rooted in centuries of history, Los Alamos, home of the atomic bomb, is a product of the modern age. You may only spend a few hours here, visiting the museum and admiring the view from this high plateau, but you'll still sense a different atmosphere from anywhere else in New Mexico.

During World War II, what had been only an elite, rugged boys' school was requisitioned by the army to become the top-secret base for development of the nuclear bomb, home for a time to J. Robert Oppenheimer, Richard Feynman, Niels Bohr, and other science luminaries. The Manhattan Project and its aftermath, the Cold War arms race, led to the establishment of Los Alamos National Labs (LANL) and the growth of the makeshift military base into a town of about 18,000 people (if you count the "suburb" of White Rock, just down the hill on Highway 4).

The highway up the mountainside is wider than it used to be, but the winding ascent to mesa of "Lost Almost"—as the first scientists dubbed their officially nonexistent camp—still carries an air of the clandestine. The town has a jarring newness about it, with street names like Bikini Atoll Road, and it's only emphasized by the dramatic landscape spreading out in all directions.

## Orientation and Information

Los Alamos is spread over three long mesas that extend like fingers from the mountain behind. Highway 502 arrives in the middle mesa, depositing you on Central Avenue and the main downtown area. The north mesa is mostly residential, while the south mesa is occupied by the labs and two routes running back down the mountain and connecting with Highway 4. (Stray too far off the beaten track, and you start passing ominous Explosive Area signs.) Stop at the **tourist info center** (109 Central Park Square, 505/662-8105, www.visit.losalamos.com, 9am-5pm Mon.-Sat., 10am-3pm Sun.) for maps and advice on hikes that skirt the wildfire damage. There's another helpful office in **White Rock** (35 Rover Blvd., 505/672-3183, 9am-4pm daily), just off Highway 4.

## Los Alamos Historical Museum

Even a manufactured town like Los Alamos has a history. See what the area was like pre-Manhattan Project at the fascinating **Los Alamos Historical Museum** (1050 Bathtub Row, 505/662-6272, www.losalamoshistory.org, 9:30am-4:30pm Mon.-Fri., 11am-4pm Sat.-Sun., free) set in an old building of the Los Alamos Ranch School, the boys' camp that got the boot when the army moved in. The exhibits cover everything from relics of the early Tewa-speaking people up to juicy details on the social intrigue during the development of "the gadget," as the A-bomb was known.

In front of the museum is **Fuller Lodge Art Center** (2132 Central Ave., 505/662-1635, 10am-4pm Mon.-Sat.), originally the Ranch School's dining room and kitchen. It usually has a community art exhibit, but the structure itself, built by John Gaw Meem, is notable too. Meem handpicked the vertical logs that form the walls and designed the cowboy-silhouette light fixtures in the main hall.

The museum is just west of the main street, Central Avenue—you'll see Fuller Lodge on Central, with the museum set back behind it. You can pick up a walking-tour brochure that guides you past other landmarks downtown.

## Bradbury Science Museum

This exhibit by **Los Alamos National Lab** (1350 Central Ave., 505/667-4444, www.lanl.gov/museum, 10am-5pm Tues.-Sat., 1pm-5pm Sun.-Mon., free) on the miracles of atomic energy has the feel of a very high-grade science fair, with plenty of buttons to push and gadgets to play with. There's also an air of a convention sales booth—the museum's mission is definitely to sell the public on LANL's work and nuclear technology in general, though a public forum corner gives space to opposing views. More interesting are the relics of the early nuclear age: Fat Man and Little Boy casings, gadgetry from the Nevada Test Site, and the like.

**Atomic City Van Tours** (505/662-3695, www.buffalotoursla.com, 1:30pm daily, Mar.-Oct., $15) leave from the parking lot in front of the museum. The 1.5-hour tour is a good way to see more of the town, which is otherwise a bit difficult to navigate, and learn some of the history. Call ahead to reserve—or download a short self-guided tour from the website. This

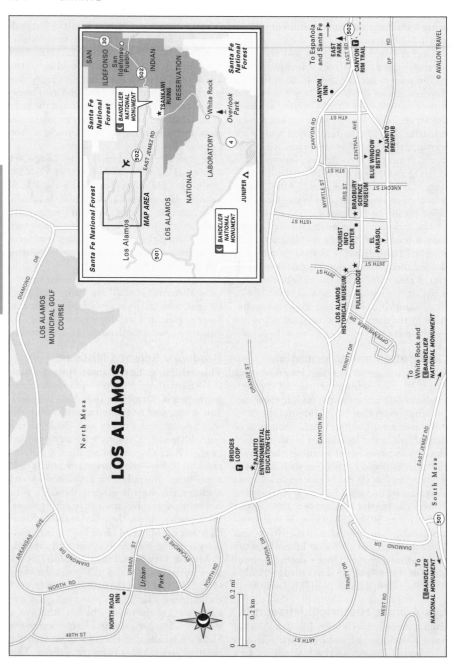

## Ceremonial Dances

This is only an approximate schedule for ceremonial dances at pueblos in the Santa Fe area–dates can vary from year to year, as can the particular dances. Annual feast days typically involve carnivals and markets in addition to dances. Confirm details and start times–usually afternoon, but sometimes following an evening or midnight Mass–with the **Indian Pueblo Cultural Center** (505/843-7270, www.indianpueblo.org) before setting out.

- **January 1** - Ohkay Owingeh (San Juan): cloud or basket dance
- **January 6** - Picurís: various dances; Nambé: buffalo, deer, and antelope dances
- **January 22** - San Ildefonso: vespers and firelight procession at 6pm
- **January 23** - San Ildefonso: Feast of San Ildefonso, with buffalo, Comanche, and deer dances
- **January 25** - Picurís: Feast of San Pablo
- **February 2** - Picurís: various dances for Candlemas (Día de la Candelaria)
- **March/April** (Easter) - Nambé: bow dance; San Ildefonso: various dances
- **June 13** - Ohkay Owingeh (San Juan), Santa Clara, and Picurís: Feast of San Antonio
- **June 24** - Ohkay Owingeh (San Juan): Feast of San Juan Bautista
- **July 4** - Nambé: celebration at the waterfall
- **August 9-10** - Picurís: Feast of San Lorenzo
- **August 12** - Santa Clara: Feast of Santa Clara
- **September 8** - San Ildefonso: corn dance
- **October 4** - Nambé: Feast of San Francisco de Asís
- **November 12** - Tesuque: Feast of San Diego
- **December 12** - Pojoaque: Feast of Nuestra Señora de Guadalupe
- **December 24** - Picurís and Ohkay Owingeh (San Juan): torchlight procession at sundown, followed by Los Matachines; San Felipe, Tesuque, and Nambé: various dances, beginning after midnight Mass
- **December 25** - San Ildefonso, Ohkay Owingeh (San Juan), Picurís, and Tesuque: various dances
- **December 26** - Ohkay Owingeh (San Juan): turtle dance
- **December 28** - Picurís and Santa Clara: children's dances to celebrate Holy Innocents Day

SANTA FE

route takes the free city bus to the main part of LANL, pointing out town landmarks along the way.

## Recreation

The 2011 Las Conchas Fire left a dramatic burn scar on Pajarito Mountain behind the town, but the canyons below Los Alamos were untouched, and offer good hiking. They are crisscrossed with a network of county-maintained hiking trails, easily accessible from the town's main roads. Pick up a map from the visitors center, or look for East Park Trailhead on the right as you drive in on Highway 502—the **Canyon Rim Trail** that starts here is an easy level walk along the North and South Canyons, with a great view down the mountain. The **Bridges Loop,** at the Pajarito Environmental Education Center on Orange Street, is another nice, slightly wilder-feeling walk, of about 45 minutes.

In White Rock, the **White Rock Rim Trail** runs three miles along the cliff edge—you'll have suburban tract homes to your back and a dizzying canyon out in front of you. Even if you don't much feel like a hike, stop by where the walk starts in Overlook Park, just for the view; follow signs from Highway 4 at the first stoplight in town. You can also take a strenuous hike into the gorge along the **Red Dot Trail,** which passes a few petroglyphs on its way down to the Rio Grande; ask at the White

© ZORA O'NEILL

Pine-pole Fuller Lodge is Los Alamos's art center.

Rock visitors center for directions to the trailhead, which is at the back end of a subdivision.

Thanks to the canyon walls, White Rock is also popular with **rock climbers,** who most frequently head to **The Overlook,** a 65-foot basalt wall below Overlook Park. The **Los Alamos Mountaineers** (www.lamountaineers.org) maintains a good website with detailed route guides and information on smaller area walls.

## Accommodations

The few hotels in Los Alamos cater primarily to visiting engineers, which is a shame considering the city's proximity to Valles Caldera National Preserve—it's a handy place to bunk if you want to get an early start on a hike. The chain hotels are functional, and a couple of smaller B&Bs are a nice alternative. A converted apartment complex in a quiet residential area, **North Road Inn** (2127 North Rd., 505/662-3678, www.northroadinn.com, $79 s, $92 d) has large rooms (some are suites with kitchenettes); upper-level rooms are a bit more private. **Canyon Inn** (80 Canyon Rd., 505/662-9595,

www.canyoninnbnb.com, $87 s, $97 d) has four carpeted rooms with wireless Internet and private bathrooms; it's in a convenient location close to downtown. Guests have the run of a shared kitchen and can fix themselves breakfast when they like.

## Food

Los Alamos has a dearth of restaurants; **Starbucks** on Central Avenue is notable just for the deeply scientific conversations on which you can eavesdrop. For lunch, the branch of the Española taco specialists **El Parasol** (1903 Central Ave., 505/661-0303, 7am-6pm Mon.-Fri., 8am-3pm Sat., 9am-2pm Sun., $5) is reliable and well priced.

**Blue Window Bistro** (813 Central Ave., 505/662-6305, 11am-2:30pm and 5pm-8:30pm Mon.-Fri., 5pm-9pm Sat., $18) is the fanciest restaurant in town, which in Los Alamos still doesn't mean too fancy—it's a colorful, bustling place with a bit of outdoor seating. Food is typical fresh American: huge salads and hot sandwiches for lunch, creative pasta and steaks in the evening. If you're headed back down the hill for the night, it's not worth staying for dinner, but if you're here overnight, it's your best option.

Kitty-corner across the parking lot, **Pajarito Brewpub** (614 Trinity Dr., 505/662-8877, 11am-11pm Sun.-Wed., 11am-1am Thurs.-Sat.) is the liveliest (er, maybe only) bar in town, but the food is pricey.

## Getting There

Los Alamos is 36 miles (45 minutes by car) from downtown Santa Fe, via U.S. 84/285 north to Highway 502 west. From Española, it's 20 miles (30 minutes) west on Highway 30 to Highway 502.

**New Mexico Airlines** (888/564-6119, www.flynma.com) flies in to Los Alamos airport (LAM, www.lam.aero) from Albuquerque, on three flights daily. The airport is on Highway 502 at the east edge of town.

## 🄲 BANDELIER NATIONAL MONUMENT

One of New Mexico's most atmospheric ancient sites, **Bandelier National Monument** (www.nps.gov/band, $12/car) comprises 23,000 acres of wilderness, including the remarkable Frijoles Canyon, lined on either side with cave "apartments," while the remnants of a massive settlement from the 16th century occupy the valley floor. Despite recent natural disasters (wildfire in 2011, flooding in 2013), the core of the park is still open and enjoyable; the backcountry will take some time to recover, however.

Nonetheless, the place gets so busy in summer that from Memorial Day through October, the park is accessible only by shuttle van from White Rock. The best way to avoid crowds is to arrive early on a weekday, if possible. Another approach is to join a torch-lit, silent **night walk** ($6) into Frijoles Canyon; they're typically on Friday nights, but call the visitors center or check online for the schedule.

In the park, a **visitors center** (505/672-3861, 8:30am-4:30pm daily June-Oct., 9am-4:30pm daily Nov.-May) has a museum and the usual array of maps and guides; pick up a

Falls Trail guide, as it has good illustrations of the various plants and wildflowers that grow in the area. And you can also get permits and topo maps here. From here, rangers run free **guided walks** around the main loop a few times a day, or you can pick up the trail guide for $1.

## Main Loop Trail and Alcove House Trail

A paved walkway leads out the back of the visitors center into Frijoles Canyon, passing the ruins of the major settlements—or at least the ones that have been thoroughly excavated. You first reach **Tyuonyi** (chew-ON-yee), a circle of buildings that was settled for about 200 years, beginning in the 1300s. Built of bricks cut from tuff (the volcanic rock that makes up most of the area) and adobe plaster, some of the 250 rooms at one time stood several stories tall.

The trail then goes up next to the cliffs, dotted with small caves dug out of the soft stone, and to **Long House,** the remnants of a strip of condo-style buildings tucked into the rock wall. Paintings and carvings decorate the cliff face above. If you're here near sunset, keep an eye on the **bat cave** near the end of the strip, home to thousands of the animals.

Continue another half mile to the **Alcove House,** accessible by 140 feet of ladders. It's well worth the climb up, if you can handle heights. But the kiva at the center of the cliff house was closed for restoration at the time of research.

### Frey Trail

The 1.5-mile **Frey Trail** used to be the main access route to Frijoles Canyon, before the access road was built by the Civilian Conservation Corps in the 1930s. Descending from **Juniper Campground** (just off Highway 4 northwest of the park access road), it's a nice approach to the area, with great views over Tyuonyi, and a general sense of what it must have been like to "discover" the canyon. The trail has no shade, however, so it's best hiked early in the day. The shuttle van can drop you at the trailhead, so you can hike down, then ride back to the depot.

## Tsankawi

Well before you reach the main entrance to Bandelier, you pass **Tsankawi** on the east side of Highway 4. (This area is accessible by car year-round.) Unique pottery excavated in this separate section, disconnected from the main park, suggests that it was inhabited by a different people from those who settled in Frijoles Canyon, and some sort of natural border seems to have formed here, despite a shared cliff-dwelling culture: Today the pueblos immediately north of the Bandelier area speak Tewa, while those to the south speak Keresan. A 1.5-mile loop, with ladders to climb along the way, leads past unexcavated ruins, cave houses, and even a few petroglyphs.

## Camping

**Juniper Campground** ($12), just inside the park's northern border, is usually open year-round, with 94 sites. There are no hookups or showers—you're directed to the Los Alamos YMCA up the hill instead. No reservations are taken, but it's usually not full. The scenery up on the plateau is bleak, due to the fires and floods, but you will get an early start on the day if you overnight here.

## Getting There

Bandelier is 45 miles (one hour) from downtown Santa Fe, via U.S. 84/285 north to Highway 502 and Highway 4 west. From Jemez Springs, it's 41 miles (one hour) via Highway 4 east.

From June through October, 9am to 3pm, access to the park is via **shuttle van** only. The service departs from a **visitors center** (Hwy. 4, 505/672-3183, 8am-6pm daily in summer) in White Rock every 20-40 minutes, with the first shuttle at 8:20am. White Rock is a 40-minute drive from Santa Fe via U.S. 84/285 north to Highway 502 and Highway 4 west. From Jemez Springs, it's about an hour drive via Highway 4 east (but you'll have to drive past the Bandelier entrance, and double back in the shuttle van).

The shuttle van stops at the Frey Trail trailhead en route to the main park. Because the

park is open dawn till dusk, you can enter by car early or late in the day, and of course the rest of the year, November through May.

## ESPAÑOLA

The relatively modern town of Española is a bit haphazard, split across the Rio Grande, and not too attractive along its main roads. Partially due to this seeming lack of history, the town of 10,000 is often the butt of jokes in the rest of northern New Mexico; at least on the surface, it lacks the polish and cosmopolitanism of Taos or Santa Fe. A fine city symbol is on the south end of town: the Saints and Sinners package liquor store, the neon sign of which should get landmark status (yes, they sell souvenir T-shirts).

The town was founded as a stop on the Chili Line railway from Denver, and it's still a crossroads, with highways to Taos, Abiquiu, and Los Alamos. Most people just stop long enough for a good meal: The authentic northern New Mexican cuisine served here is never watered down for interlopers' tastes. But two very nice hotels may entice you to stay overnight—in which case you should keep an eye out for great custom cars. They're rarer than

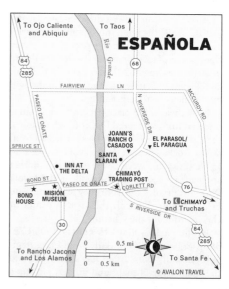

© ZORA O'NEILL

the Chimayó Trading Post in Española

they were, but this is still the state's unofficial lowrider capital.

## Sights

No, you haven't made a wrong turn—you're still in Española. The **Chimayó Trading Post** (110 Sandia Dr., 505/753-9414, 10am-4pm Wed.-Sat.), on the west side of the main highway, relocated here in the 1930s, after several decades at its original location in Chimayó. Now it's a listed landmark, as one of the last remaining historic trading posts, and it has everything you'd expect: creaky wood floors, dim lighting, and a jumbled stock of treasures that includes of course Chimayó rugs, as well as Nepalese silver jewelry; cut-tin candleholders, made locally; skeins of handmade wool yarn; postcards; and even free coffee. The remaining elderly owner (one of a pair of airline employees, back in the real jet-set age) is no longer seriously replenishing his stock, but there are still some nifty finds. Hours can be a bit erratic.

Española's tiny museum, **Bond House** (706 Bond St., 505/747-8535, 1pm-3:30pm Mon.-Wed., noon-4pm Thurs.-Fri., free), devotes half its space to artwork and the other small room to various historic artifacts. Down the hill, past the replica Alhambra fountain, is the **Misión Museum,** another replica, of the town's original mission church, furnished with traditional craftwork from around the valley. It is open sporadically—ask at the Bond House if no one is around.

## Accommodations

Española is not a common overnight stop, but it has some hotels that are so nice, you might rethink your itinerary. The ◖ **Inn at the Delta** (234 Paseo de Oñate, 505/753-9466, www.inatthedelta.biz, $120 s, $160 d) is a beautiful rambling adobe complex built by a long-established local family. The positively palatial rooms are decorated with locally made furniture, and each has a fireplace, a porch, and a jet tub. Rates include a generous breakfast, with homemade bread.

A project of the local pueblo, the **Santa Claran** (460 N. Riverside Dr., 877/505-4949, www.santaclaran.com, $89 d) also has spacious rooms, tastefully done in subdued grays and browns. Perks include fridges and laundry machines, but Internet is wired only in rooms; there's wireless access in the lobby.

South of town, on the road to Los Alamos, C **Rancho Jacona** (277 County Rd. 84, 505/455-7948, www.ranchojacona.com, $165 d) is a working farm dotted with 11 casitas, each with a kitchen and space for three to eight people. You'll likely get some fresh chicken eggs for breakfast, and kids can frolic in the pool. There's a three-day minimum.

## Food

Stop off for a quick bite at **El Parasol** (603 Santa Cruz Rd., 505/753-8852, 7am-9pm Mon.-Sat., $3), a takeout stand with picnic tables under cottonwood trees and a Spanglish menu ("pollo with guacamole taco"). The statelier indoor version is **El Paragua** (505/753-3211, 11am-9pm Mon.-Thurs., 11am-9:30pm Fri.-Sat., 10am-8pm Sun., $15) next door. It's oddly expensive, but the tacos are good. Turn for both of these places at the sign for Highway 76, which is called Santa Cruz Road in town—the restaurants are immediately on the left.

Better value for a sit-down meal is diner-style **JoAnn's Ranch O Casados** (938 N. Riverside Dr., 505/753-1334, 7am-9pm Mon.-Sat., 7am-4pm Sun., $10) which serves breakfast all day, along with very good and inexpensive enchiladas, fajitas, and more. The red chile is rich and mellow, and you can get half orders of many dishes.

## Getting There

Española is about a 45-minute drive from central Santa Fe via U.S. 84/285 north.

Leaving Española, take Highway 68 (also called Riverside Drive) north from here to Taos (45 miles), or cross over the Rio Grande and continue on U.S. 84 to Abiquiu (22 miles) or U.S. 285 to Ojo Caliente (25 miles). From an intersection in the middle of Española, Highway 76 leads east to Chimayó (8 miles), then to Truchas and the other high-road towns on the way to Taos. From the old main plaza

on the west side of the Rio Grande, Highway 30 is the back road to Los Alamos (20 miles).

# OJO CALIENTE

Twenty-six miles north of Española on U.S. 285, Ojo Caliente (Hot Spring) is, like Jemez Springs, an old resort village based around natural mineral water. It's worth a stop if you're driving through, but not necessarily deserving of a day trip from Santa Fe (unless you're tired of Ten Thousand Waves there). The springs are managed by **Ojo Caliente Mineral Springs** (505/583-2233, www.ojospa.com, 8am-10pm daily), a rather lavish resort built around a 1916 hotel building. The various paved pools ($18 Mon.-Thurs., $28 Fri.-Sun., $14/$24 after 6pm), set in front of red cliffs, have different mineral contents; there are also private options, as well as a full spa. Just behind the springs, **Posi Trail** leads into the public land behind the springs; the area is especially popular with mountain bikers. The resort office has trail maps.

If you happen to have forgotten your swimsuit, **Cornelia's** thrift and gift shop, on U.S. 285 north of the turn to the springs, usually has a stock of cheap ones that could work in a pinch.

## Accommodations

You can stay the night at **Ojo Caliente Mineral Springs,** though rates (which include access to the springs the day of arrival, and on departure) are a bit steep for what you get. It's worth noting that the cheapest rooms, in the historic hotel building ($169 d), don't have showers. The next step up are cottages ($209 d), then rather grand suites (from $289 d); but maintenance is not always great. Camping ($20) is an option. It can be better value to stay at the nice bed-and-breakfast just down the road, **The Inn at Ojo** (505/583-9131, www.ojocaliente.com, $95 s, $125 d), and pay for day use of the pools.

## Food

Ojo Caliente Mineral Springs has its own rather grand restaurant, **The Artesian** (505/583-2233, 7:30am-9pm daily, $26), which has lovely ambience, but sometimes its reach exceeds its grasp. Out on the highway, **Red Mountain Café** (35310 U.S. 285, 575/583-2184, 11am-8pm Wed.-Mon., $8) does pizza and other house-baked goods, and **Mesa Vista Café** (U.S. 285, 575/583-2245, 8am-9pm daily, $7) is the old-school New Mexican place, with decent chile.

## Getting There

Ojo Caliente is 50 miles from downtown Santa Fe, about an hour's drive north on U.S. 84/285, then U.S. 285 east where it splits north of Española. From Española, allow 30 minutes' driving time. From Abiquiu, avoid backtracking by going through El Rito; take Highway 554 north to Highway 111 north, coming out on U.S. 285 a few miles north of Ojo Caliente. This route takes about 45 minutes.

From Ojo Caliente, you can continue 41 miles to Taos (about a one-hour drive). Follow U.S. 285 north for 10 miles, then turn right (east) on Highway 567. In nine miles, Highway 567 ends at a T junction; turn left (north) on Taos County Road and continue about eight miles. You will meet U.S. 64 about one mile west of the Rio Grande Gorge; Taos is to the right (east).

## ABIQUIU

Northwest of Española, along U.S. 84, the valley formed by the muddy Rio Chama is one of the most striking landscapes in northern New Mexico. Lush greenery on the riverbanks clashes with bright red mud; roaming sheep and cattle graze by the roadside. The striated hills represent dramatic geological shifts, from 200-million-year-old purple stone formed in the dinosaur era to red clay formed by forests, then gypsum sand dunes, then a layer of lava from only 8 million years back. More recently, Abiquiu became inextricably linked with the artist Georgia O'Keeffe, who made the valley her home for more than 40 years, entranced all the while by the glowing light and dramatic skyline.

Although Abiquiu often refers to the whole river valley, the unofficial town center is **Bode's**

(21196 U.S. 84, 505/685-4422, 6:30am-7pm Mon.-Thurs., 6:30am-8pm Fri., 7am-8pm Sat., 7am-7pm Sun.), pronounced BO-deez. This long-established general store also has gas, pastries and green-chile cheeseburgers, fishing licenses and tackle, and local crafts. In winter, it closes earlier on weekends.

The actual village of Abiquiu, established in 1754 by *genízaros* (Hispanicized Indians) through a land grant from the Spanish Crown, is up the hill on the opposite side of the road. O'Keeffe's house forms one side of the old plaza; on the other is the Santo Tomas de Abiquiu Church, built in the 1930s after the community opted for the legal status of village rather than pueblo. Past O'Keeffe's house is the village *morada*, dramatically set on a hilltop. You're not really welcome to poke around, however—the village maintains a privacy policy similar to those of the pueblos. So it's best to visit on a guided tour of the house.

## Georgia O'Keeffe House

The artist's main residence, where she lived 1949-1984, fronts the small plaza in the village center of Abiquiu. The **Georgia O'Keeffe House** (505/685-4539, www.okeeffemuseum. org) is open to hour-long guided tours mid-March-November. The price, even for the basic tour, can seem a bit steep, but for fans of modernism of any kind, it's a beautiful place to see. The rambling adobe, parts of which were built in the 18th century, is a great reflection of O'Keeffe's aesthetic, which fused the starkness of modernism with an organic sensuality. If you're on a budget, console yourself with the fact that in many ways the surrounding landscape reflects O'Keeffe's work as much as her home does—and be sure to stop at Ghost Ranch, for more (and cheaper) info on the painter.

The schedule depends on the month, but there are five **tours** each day Tuesday, Thursday, and Friday ($35). From June through October, tours are also scheduled on Wednesdays, as well as Saturdays, when the price jumps to $45. Special tours ($55) with Judy Lopez, who worked with O'Keeffe

SANTA FE

© ZORA O'NEILL

cliffs at Plaza Blanca

for more than a decade, run on Thursdays in summer, and a Wednesday-night "behind-the-scenes" tour includes a visit to O'Keeffe's fallout shelter, among other things. Tours depart from the Abiquiu Inn on U.S. 84; you must make reservations at least a month in advance.

## Dar al Islam and Plaza Blanca

In another chapter of New Mexico's long utopian history, a few American converts established **Dar al Islam** (505/685-4515 ext. 21, www.daralislam.org, 10am-4pm Mon.-Fri., free), an intentional religious community, in 1979. A village for about 150 families on 8,300 acres just south of the village of Abiquiu proper, it was meant to be a place in which Muslims could practice their religion in every aspect of life, from education to food. The village concept never quite took off, though, and Dar al Islam has been reinvented as a retreat center that's open to visitors (call ahead to make sure the gate is open). Egyptian architect Hassan Fathy's adobe mosque, all organic sinuous lines,

is beautiful and harmonizes flawlessly with the land surrounding it.

The community's land also includes the towering gypsum formations of **Plaza Blanca** (White Place). The eerie space, bleached as bones, was recorded in a series of Georgia O'Keeffe paintings, and it has also been used for numerous movie shoots. Two main trails lead out from the parking area.

The most direct route to the community is via Highway 554, which runs east from U.S. 84, just south of Abiquiu (follow signs for El Rito). Immediately after crossing the Chama River, turn left on County Road 155. Continue 3.2 miles, and turn right through an arched wooden gate. After less than a mile, the road forks: To the left is the entrance to Dar al Islam; to the right, Plaza Blanca. Leaving, you can continue northwest on County Road 155; in 2.3 miles you reach U.S. 84, half a mile north of Bode's. This stretch of the road is rutted and unpaved, however, so it's slower going.

## Abiquiu Lake

An Army Corps of Engineers dam project created the 4,000-acre **Abiquiu Lake** with fingers running into the canyons all around. The view coming in is marred by the power station, but past that the water glimmers at the base of the flat-topped flint mountain Pedernal Peak, the distinctive silhouette that found its way into so many of O'Keeffe's paintings. ("It's my private mountain," she often said. "God told me if I painted it often enough, I could have it.") The overly paved **campground** (505/685-4433, www.nmparks.com) at the lake is open year-round, but water and electric hookups ($14) are available only in the summer.

## ◖ Ghost Ranch

**Ghost Ranch** (U.S. 84, 505/685-4333, www.ghostranch.org), a 21,000-acre retreat owned by the Presbyterian Church, is famous for several things: First, Georgia O'Keeffe owned a small parcel of the land and maintained a studio here. Then, in 1947, paleontologists combing the red hills discovered about a thousand skeletons of the dinosaur *Coelophysis* ("hollow form," for its hollow, birdlike bones), the largest group discovered in the world.

The grounds are open to visitors, to see the **Florence Hawley Ellis Museum of Anthropology** and the **Ruth Hall Museum of Paleontology** (both 9am-5pm Mon.-Sat., $2), which display the local finds, including remnants of the prehistoric Gallina culture from the ridge above the valley and an eight-ton chunk of *Coelophysis*-filled siltstone in the process of being excavated. Both museums are also open 1pm-5pm on Sundays in the summer.

Guided **tours** (various times, $25-35) of the ranch grounds run mid-March through November, on various topics, from local archaeology to movie settings. One walking tour visits O'Keeffe's painting spot in the red Chinle hills behind the ranch. **Horseback riding** ($75/hour) is available, including lessons for kids.

You can also **hike** on your own after registering at the reception desk. The best trek, which takes about 1.5 hours round-trip, is to **Chimney Rock,** a towering landmark with panoramic views of the entire area. Don't be daunted—the steepest part of the trail is at the start—but do slather on the sunscreen, as there's no shade on this route. **Box Canyon** is an easier, shadier, all-level walk that's about four miles round-trip. **Kitchen Mesa Trail,** which starts at the same point, is much more difficult, requiring some climbing to get up the cliffs at the end (though you could hike the easy first two-thirds, then turn around).

## Echo Amphitheater

**Echo Amphitheater,** a bandshell-shape rock formation, is a natural wonder of acoustics and is a great place to let kids run around and yell to their hearts' content. It's four miles north of Ghost Ranch. There are pleasant picnic areas ($2/car) tucked in the brush.

## Accommodations and Food

The **Abiquiu Inn** (505/685-4378, www.abiquiuinn.com) functions as the area's visitors center. Lodging ($150 d) consists of some pretty casitas at the back of the property, with great views of the river, and a cluster of motel rooms closer to the front (opt for rooms 2-6, which face away from the road). Solo travelers should reserve well ahead for "El Vado Económico," a cozy one-bed room ($110). The inn's restaurant, **Café Abiquiu** (7am-9pm daily, $13) serves steak sandwiches, as well as bigger entrées like fried trout.

You can also stay at **Ghost Ranch** (U.S. 84, 505/685-4333, www.ghostranch.org) when it's not full for retreats, in various room options; the cheapest are cabins with shared bath ($50 s, $90 d, with breakfast), or you can camp for $19.

Thirteen miles down a rocky dirt track, **Christ in the Desert Monastery** (Forest Rd. 151, 801/545-8567, www.christdesert.org, $70 s, $90 d) delivers on solitude. Day visitors are welcome, or you can stay overnight (two-night minimum) for a suggested donation, which includes all meals. Out the same road (at the 11.5-mile mark), **Rio Chama Campground** is remote but beautiful—preferable to Abiquiu Lake if you really want to get away from it all.

SANTA FE

## Getting There

Abiquiu is about 50 miles (one hour) from downtown Santa Fe. From Santa Fe, take U.S. 285/24 north for 26 miles to Española. From Española, continue on U.S. 84 north for 23 miles to Abiquiu. From Abiquiu to Taos, it's about 70 miles, or an hour and a half, via El Rito and Ojo Caliente. Continuing north on U.S. 84, you'll reach the Rio Chama in another 60 miles (one hour).

## LOW ROAD TO TAOS

The lush farmland around the Rio Grande is the highlight of this drive north—the valley filled with apple orchards is as green as New Mexico gets. The road is at first a bit unpromising, as it passes through the modern town of Española, but it soon winds into an ever-narrower canyon and finally emerges at the point where the high plains meet the mountains. This dramatic arrival makes it the better route for heading north to Taos; you can then loop back south via the high road.

## Embudo and Dixon

The village of Embudo is really just a bend in the river, where the Chili Line railroad from Denver used to stop (the old station is across the river). But it offers a random roadside attraction in the **Classical Gas Museum,** a front yard filled with old service station accoutrements. There's also a good eating option: **Sugar's** (Hwy. 68, 505/852-0604, 11am-6pm Thurs.-Sun., $6), a small roadside trailer that doles out seriously big food, such as barbecue brisket burritos. It's takeout only, but there are a few plastic picnic tables where you can sit down.

If you're into wine, keep an eye out for the various wineries just north of here: **Vivác** (2075 Hwy. 68, 505/579-4441, 10am-6pm Mon.-Sat., 11am-6pm Sun.) is on the main highway and **La Chiripada** (505/579-4437, 10am-6pm Mon.-Sat., noon-6pm Sun.) is down Highway 75 a few miles in the pleasant little town of Dixon, known for its dense concentration of artists, organic farmers, and vintners. On summer and fall Wednesdays (4:30pm-7pm)

roadside attractions in Embudo

© ZORA O'NEILL

is the convivial farmers market, and in early November, look for the long-running **Dixon Studio Tour** (www.dixonarts.org). A good year-round reason to make the turn is **(( Zuly's** (234 Hwy. 275, 505/579-4001, 8am-3pm Tues.-Thurs., 8am-8pm Fri., 9am-8pm Sat., $8), serving classic New Mexican food with a bit of hippie flair, and strong coffee; hours cut back slightly in winter.

## Pilar

Beginning just south of the village of Pilar and stretching several miles north, **Orilla Verde Recreation Area** ($3/car) is public land along either side of the Rio Grande, used primarily as a put-in or haul-out for rafting, but you can camp on the riverbanks as well. Petaca and Taos Junction have the best sites ($7 per night).

Running about 1.2 miles one-way along the west edge of the river, the **Vista Verde Trail** is an easy walk with great views and a few petroglyphs to spot in a small arroyo about a third of the way out. The trailhead is located on the other side of the river, half a mile up the hill from the Taos Junction Bridge off the dirt road Highway 567 (turn left off the highway in Pilar, then follow signs into Orilla Verde). Stop first on the main highway at the **Rio Grande Gorge Visitors Center** (Hwy. 68, 575/751-4899, 8:30am-4:30pm daily June-Aug., 10am-2pm daily Sept.-May) for maps and other information.

Across the road, **Pilar Yacht Club** (Hwy. 68, 575/758-9072, 8am-6pm daily mid-May-Aug., 9am-2pm daily Apr.-mid-May and Sept.-Oct.) is the center of the action, selling tubes for lazy floats, serving food to hungry river rats, and functioning as an office for a couple of outfitters.

## Getting There

This low-road route is more direct than the high road to Taos, and has fewer potential diversions. Driving the 70 miles direct from downtown Santa Fe to Taos (on U.S. 84/285 and Hwy. 68), with no stops, takes about an hour and a half. There are no gas stations between Española and Taos.

# HIGH ROAD TO TAOS

Córdova, Truchas, Las Trampas, Peñasco—these are the tiny villages strung, like beads on a necklace, along the winding highway through the mountains to Taos. This is probably the area of New Mexico where Spanish heritage has been least diluted—or at any rate relatively untouched by Anglo influence, for there has been a long history of exchange between the Spanish towns and the adjacent pueblos. The local dialect is distinctive, and residents can claim ancestors who settled the towns in the 18th century. The first families learned to survive in the harsh climate with a 90-day growing season, and much of the technology that worked then continues to work now; electricity was still scarce even in the 1970s, and adobe construction is common. These communities, closed off by geography, can seem a little insular to visitors, but pop in at the galleries that have sprung up in a couple of the towns, and you'll get a warm welcome. And during the **High Road Art Tour** (www.highroadnewmexico.com), over two weekends in September, modern artists and more traditional craftspeople famed particularly for their wood-carving skills open their home studios.

## Nambé Pueblo

A few miles off Highway 503, **Nambé Falls Recreation Area** (505/455-2306, www.nambefalls.com, $10/car) is open to the public for swimming and fishing; it also has beautiful **camping** spots ($25, including day pass). The highlight is the falls themselves, a double cascade through a narrow crevice, marking the break between the Sangre de Cristo Mountains and the Española Basin.

Incidentally, the Nambé line of high-end housewares has nothing to do with this pueblo of 1,700 people—weaving and micaceous pottery are some of the traditional crafts here. The biggest annual event is Fourth of July, celebrated with dances and a crafts market.

## (( Chimayó

From Nambé Pueblo, Highway 503 continues to a T junction; make a hard left to follow the main road and begin the descent into the valley of Chimayó, site of the largest mass pilgrimage in the United States. During Holy Week, some 50,000 people arrive on foot, often bearing large crosses.

The group treks began in 1945, as a commemoration of the Bataan Death March, but the destination, the **Santuario de Chimayó** (www.holychimayo.us, 9am-6pm daily May-Sept., 9am-5pm daily Oct.-Apr.), had a reputation as a healing spot from the start. The small chapel was built in 1814 at the place where a local farmer, Bernardo Abeyta, is said to have dug up a miraculously glowing crucifix.

Unlike many of the older churches in this area, which are now open very seldom, Chimayó is an active place of prayer, always busy with tourists as well as visitors seeking solace, with many side chapels and a busy gift shop. (Mass is said weekdays at 11am and on Sunday at 10:30am and noon year-round.) The approach from the parking area passes chain-link fencing into which visitors have woven twigs to form crosses, each set of sticks representing a prayer. Outdoor pews made of split tree trunks accommodate overflow crowds, and a wheelchair ramp gives easy access to the church.

But the original adobe *santuario* seems untouched by modernity. The front wall of the dim main chapel is filled with an elaborately painted altar screen from the first half of the 19th century, the work of Molleno (nicknamed "the Chile Painter" because forms, especially robes, in his paintings often resemble red and green chiles). The vibrant colors seem to shimmer in the gloom, forming a sort of stage set for Abeyta's crucifix, Nuestro Señor de las Esquípulas, as the centerpiece. Painted on the screen above the crucifix is the symbol of the Franciscans: a cross over which the arms of Christ and Saint Francis meet.

Most pilgrims make their way directly to the small, low-ceiling antechamber that holds *el pocito,* the little hole where the glowing crucifix was allegedly first dug up. From this pit they scoop up a small portion of the exposed red earth, to apply to withered limbs and arthritic

Santuario de Chimayó

© ZORA O'NEILL

joints, or to eat in hopes of curing internal ailments. (The parish refreshes the well each year with new dirt, after it has been blessed by the priests.) The adjacent sacristy displays handwritten testimonials, prayers, and abandoned crutches; the figurine of Santo Niño de Atocha is also said to have been dug out of the holy ground here. (Santo Niño de Atocha has a dedicated chapel just down the road—the artwork here is modern, bordering on cutesy, but the back room, filled with baby shoes, is poignant.)

### ACCOMMODATIONS AND FOOD

If you want to spend the night in the area, or use it as a base for exploring, you have two good options. Not far from the church, off County Road 98, **Rancho Manzana** (26 Camino de Mision, 505/351-2227, www.ranchomanzana. com, $75 s, $105 d) has a rustic feel, with excellent breakfasts (the owner also runs cooking classes). En route to Española, **Casa Escondida** (Hwy. 76, 505/351-4805, www.casaescondida. com, $105 s, $145 d) is a lovely place, with a big backyard, a hot tub, and a sunny garden.

For lunch, head across the parking lot from the Santuario de Chimayó to **Leona's** (505/351-4569, 10am-5pm Fri.-Mon., $3), where you can pick up bulk chile and pistachios as well as delicious tamales and crumbly *bizcochitos*. For a more leisurely sit-down lunch, **⬛ Rancho de Chimayó** (County Rd. 98, 505/351-4444, www.ranchodechimayo. com, 11:30am-9pm daily May-Oct., 11:30am-9pm Tues.-Sun. Nov.-Apr., $12) offers great red chile on a beautiful terrace—or inside the old adobe home by the fireplace in wintertime. The place is also open for breakfast on weekends, 8:30am-10:30am.

## Córdova

From Chimayó, turn right (east) on Highway 76 (west takes you back toward Española), to begin the climb back up the Sangre de Cristo Mountains. Near the crest of the hill, about three miles up, a small sign points to Córdova, a village best known for its austere unpainted santos and *bultos* done by masters such as George López and José Dolores López.

Another family member, **Sabinita López Ortiz** (9 County Rd. 1317, 505/351-4572, variable hours), sells her work and that of five other generations of wood-carvers. **Castillo Gallery** (County Rd. 1317, 505/351-4067, variable hours) mixes traditional woodwork with more contemporary sculpture.

## Truchas

Highway 76 winds along to the little village of Truchas (Trout), founded in 1754 and still not much more than a long row of buildings set into the ridgeline. On the corner where the highway makes a hard left to Taos, the village *morada,* the meeting place of the local Penitente brotherhood, looks onto the expansive valley below.

Head straight down the smaller road to reach **Nuestra Señora del Rosario de las Truchas Church,** tucked into a small plaza off to the right of the main street. It's open to visitors only June-August—if you do have a chance to look inside the dim, thick-walled mission, you'll see precious examples of local wood carving. Though many of the more delicate ones have been moved to a museum for preservation, those remaining display an essential New Mexican style—the sort of "primitive" thing that Bishop Lamy of Santa Fe hated. They're preserved today because Truchas residents hid them at home during the late 19th century. Santa Lucia, with her eyeballs in her hand, graces the altar, and a finely wrought crucifix hangs to the right, clad in a skirt because the legs have broken off.

Just up the road is **The Cordovas Handweaving Workshop** (32 County Rd. 75, 505/689-1124, 8am-5pm Mon.-Sat.), an unassuming wooden house that echoes with the soft click-clack of a broadloom, as this Hispano family turns out subtly striped rugs in flawless traditional style, for quite reasonable prices.

## Las Trampas

Back on Highway 76, the village of Las Trampas was settled in 1751, and its showpiece, **San José de Gracia Church** (10am-4pm Sat.-Sun. June-Aug.), was built nine years later.

the San José de Gracia Church church at Las Trampas

It remains one of the finest examples of New Mexican village church architecture. Its thick adobe walls are balanced by vertical bell towers; inside, the clerestory at the front of the church—a very typical design—lets light in to shine down on the altar, which was carved and painted in the late 1700s. Other paradigmatic elements include the *atrio,* or small plaza between the low adobe boundary wall and the church itself, utilized as a cemetery, and the dark narthex where you enter, confined by the choir loft above, but serving only to emphasize the sense of light and space created in the rest of the church by the clerestory and the small windows near the viga ceiling.

## Picurís Pueblo

The smallest pueblo in New Mexico, Picurís is one of the few Rio Grande pueblos that has not built a casino. Instead, it capitalizes on its beautiful natural setting, a lush valley where bison roam and aspen leaves rustle. You can picnic here and fish in small but well-stocked Tu-Tah Lake. The **San Lorenzo de Picurís Church** looks old, but it was in fact rebuilt by hand in 1989, following exactly the form of the original 1776 design—the process took eight years. As at Nambé, local traditions have melded with those of the surrounding villages; the Hispano-Indian Matachines dances are well attended on Christmas Eve. Start at the **visitors center** (575/587-1099 or 575/587-1071, 9am-5pm Mon.-Sat.) to pick up maps. The pueblo is a short detour from the high road proper: At the junction with Highway 75, turn left, then follow signs off the main road.

## Peñasco

Peñasco is best known to tourists as the home of ( **Sugar Nymphs Bistro** (15046 Hwy. 75, 575/587-0311, 11:30am-2:30pm Wed., 11:30am-2:30pm and 5:30pm-7:35pm Thurs.-Sat., 11am-2:30pm Sun., $12), a place with "country atmosphere and city cuisine," where you can get treats like grilled lamb, fresh-pressed cider, piñon couscous, and staggering wedges of layer cake. An adjoining **Peñasco Theatre** (www.penascotheatre.org) hosts quirky music and theatrical performances June to September. Restaurant hours can be more limited in the winter, so it's best to call ahead.

After making a hard left onto Highway 518, the road climbs again, and you arrive in Taos at its very southern end, on Highway 68. Turn left to see the St. Francis of Asisi church, or turn right for the plaza and Taos Pueblo.

## Getting There

From downtown Santa Fe, the high road route to Taos is about 90 miles. Follow U.S. 84/285 north for 17 miles to Pojoaque. Turn right (east) on Highway 503, following signs for Nambé Pueblo. In about 60 miles you'll arrive in Ranchos de Taos, just north of the church and about three miles south of the main Taos plaza. The drive straight through takes a little more than two hours; leave time to dawdle at churches and galleries, take a hike, or have lunch along the way.

© ZORA O'NEILL

SANTA FE

Stop in Peñasco for a sweet pick-me-up at Sugar Nymphs Bistro.

# Information and Services

## TOURIST INFORMATION

The **Santa Fe Convention and Visitors Bureau** (800/777-2489, www.santafe.org) hands out its visitors guide and other brochures from its offices at the **convention center** (201 W. Marcy St., 8am-5pm Mon.-Fri.) and at the Rail Runner depot in the rail yard (401 S. Guadalupe St., 8:30am-5:30pm Mon.-Fri., 10:30am-6:30pm Sat.-Sun.). The New Mexico Tourism Department runs a **visitors center** (491 Old Santa Fe Tr., 505/827-7336, 8am-5pm Mon.-Fri.) near San Miguel Chapel.

For info on the outdoors, head to the Bureau of Land Management's comprehensive **Public Information Access Center** (301 Dinosaur Tr., 505/954-2000, www.publiclands.org, 8am-4:30pm Mon.-Fri.), just off Highway 14 (follow Cerrillos Road until it passes under I-25). You can pick up detailed route descriptions for area

day hikes, as well as guidebooks, topo maps, and hunting and fishing licenses.

### Books and Maps

Santa Fe has two particularly good bookshops right in the center of town. **Travel Bug** (839 Paseo de Peralta, 505/992-0418, 7:30am-5:30pm Mon.-Sat., 11am-4pm Sun.) specializes in maps, travel guides, gear, and free advice. For more general stock, **Collected Works** (202 Galisteo St., 505/988-4226, 8am-8pm Mon.-Sat., 8am-6pm Sun.) is the place to go for a trove of local-interest titles, and the eclectic new and secondhand stock at **op.cit.** (500 Montezuma Ave., 505/428-0321, 8am-7pm Mon.-Sat., 8am-6pm Sun.), in Sanbusco Center, is endlessly browsable.

### Local Media

The *Santa Fe New Mexican* is Santa Fe's

daily paper, which publishes events listings and gallery news in its *Pasatiempo* insert on Fridays. For left-of-center news and commentary, the *Santa Fe Reporter* is the free weekly rag, available in most coffee shops and cafés.

### Radio
**KBAC** (98.1 FM) is better known as Radio Free Santa Fe, a dynamic community station with eclectic music and talk. Tune in Friday afternoons for news on the gallery scene.

## SERVICES
### Banks
**First National Bank of Santa Fe** (62 Lincoln Ave., 505/992-2000, 9am-5pm Mon.-Fri.) is on the west side of the plaza.

### Post Office
Santa Fe's **main post office** (120 S. Federal Pl., 505/988-2239, 8am-5:30pm Mon.-Fri., 9am-4pm Sat.) is conveniently just north of the plaza, near the district courthouse.

### Laundry
Most self-service laundries are on or near Cerrillos Road. One of the largest and nicest is **St. Michael's Laundry** (1605 St. Michael's Dr., 505/989-9375, 6am-9pm daily), a couple of blocks east of Cerrillos Road. It also has drop-off service.

# Getting There and Around

## BY AIR
**Santa Fe Municipal Airport** (SAF, 505/955-2900), west of the city, receives direct flights from Dallas and Los Angeles with American Eagle, and from Denver with United and Great Lakes. But typically, fares are better to the Albuquerque airport (ABQ), less than an hour's drive away.

**Sandia Shuttle Express** (888/775-5696, www.sandiashuttle.com) does hourly pickups from the Albuquerque airport 8:45am-11:45pm and will deliver to any hotel or B&B ($28 one-way).

## BY TRAIN
The **Rail Runner** (866/795-7245, www.nmrailrunner.com) goes from Albuquerque to downtown Santa Fe—the final stop is at the rail yard in the Guadalupe district (410 S. Guadalupe St.). The 90-minute ride costs $8, or $9 for a day pass (only $8 if you buy it online), and the last train back to Albuquerque leaves at 9pm weekdays, 10pm Saturdays, and 8pm Sundays.

**Amtrak** (800/872-7245, www.amtrak.com) runs the Southwest Chief through Lamy, 18 miles south of Santa Fe and a dramatic place to step off the train—you'll feel very Wild West, as there's no visible civilization for miles around. Trains arrive once daily from Chicago and Los Angeles in the afternoon. Amtrak provides a shuttle van for passengers coming and going to Santa Fe.

## BY BUS AND SHUTTLE
**Santa Fe Pick-Up** (505/231-2573, www.santafenm.gov) is a free shuttle designed primarily for passengers arriving on the Rail Runner, departing from Montezuma Avenue just north of the depot and stopping at the capitol, the St. Francis Cathedral, four points on Canyon Road, Museum Hill, and a few other tourist-friendly spots around town. It makes a 20-minute loop, 6:30am-6pm Monday to Friday and 7:30am-4:30pm Saturday.

The reasonably useful city bus system, **Santa Fe Trails** (505/955-2001, www.santafenm.gov), can take you to all of the major sights from the handy central depot on Sheridan Street northwest of the plaza. The M route goes to Museum Hill; Route 2 runs along Cerrillos Road. Buses on all routes run only every 30 to 60 minutes. The Museum Hill and Cerrillos Road buses run on Sundays. Fare is $1, or you can buy a day pass for $2, payable on board with exact change.

## BY CAR

Ideally, you would not have a car while in Santa Fe itself. The area around the plaza is a maze of one-way streets, and parking is difficult and expensive. **Hertz, Budget, Avis,** and **Thrifty** all have branches on Cerrillos Road.

From Albuquerque to Santa Fe, it's a straight shot north on I-25 for about 65 miles; you'll reach Santa Fe in about an hour.

From Las Vegas to Santa Fe, the 65-mile drive via I-25 takes a little over an hour. Coming from Taos, allow 1.5-2.5 hours, depending on whether you come on the low road (on Hwy. 68 and U.S. 84/285, via Española), via Ojo Caliente (mostly on U.S. 285), or on the high road (mostly on Hwy. 76, via Truchas).

# TAOS AND NORTH CENTRAL NEW MEXICO

Adobe buildings cluster around a plaza. Art galleries, organic bakeries, and yoga studios proliferate. But the town of Taos is much more than a miniature Santa Fe. It's more isolated, reached by two-lane roads along either the winding mountain-ridge route or the fertile Rio Grande valley, and it has a rougher, muddier feel. The glory of the landscape, from looming Taos

© ZORA O'NEILL

# HIGHLIGHTS

LOOK FOR 【 TO FIND RECOMMENDED SIGHTS, ACTIVITIES, DINING, AND LODGING.

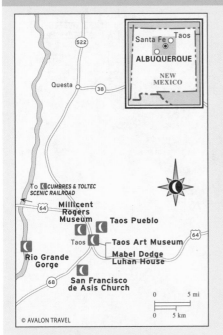

© AVALON TRAVEL

in a fantastical fusion of Tartar, Spanish, and American Indian styles. Today, his paintings hang next to the wood lintels and furniture he carved (page 132).

【 **Millicent Rogers Museum:** A 1950s' socialite amassed an astounding trove of American Indian and Spanish artwork in just a few short years in Taos. Her collection is on view in her former house, and it provides a thorough introduction to the region's oldest cultures (page 132).

【 **San Francisco de Asis Church:** With its massive adobe buttresses and rich earthy glow, this 350-year-old Franciscan mission is one of the most recognizable in the world, thanks to its frequent depiction in paintings and photographs (page 135).

【 **Taos Pueblo:** The stepped adobe buildings at New Mexico's most remarkable pueblo seem to rise organically from the earth. Don't miss the ceremonial dances here, about eight times a year (page 136).

【 **Rio Grande Gorge:** Think how dismayed the first homesteaders must have been when they reached "New Mexico's Grand Canyon," an 800-foot-deep channel cut through the rock to the west of Taos. Think how overjoyed today's white-water rafters are in the spring, when mountain runoff surges through the rift (page 137).

【 **Cumbres & Toltec Scenic Railroad:** Ascending the pass through the Rockies into Colorado on this rumbling old steam train, soot and wind in your hair, you'll feel like you've climbed to the very top of the world (page 155).

【 **Mabel Dodge Luhan House:** See where America's counterculture thrived in the mid-20th century, as encouraged by the arts doyenne who made Taos her home. Countless writers, painters, and actors visited Mabel here in her idiosyncratic home (page 129).

【 **Taos Art Museum:** In the early 1930s, Russian artist Nicolai Fechin designed his home

TAOS

Mountain to the blue mesas dissolving into the flat western horizon, can be breathtaking. The mysticism surrounding Taos Pueblo is intense, as is the often wild creativity of the artists who have lived here. No wonder people flock here on pilgrimages: to the ranch where D. H. Lawrence lived, to the hip-deep powder on the slopes at Taos Ski Valley, to the San Francisco de Asis Church that Georgia O'Keeffe painted. Then they simply wind up staying. The person pouring your coffee at the café probably has a variation on this very story.

Celebrity residents like Julia Roberts have lent the town a certain reputation of wealth

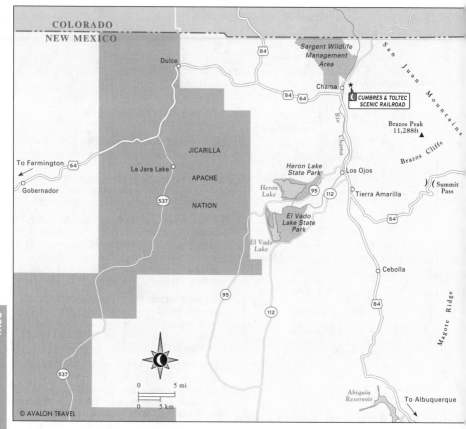

© AVALON TRAVEL

and exclusivity, but this is not typical. Hispano farmers in Valle Valdez scrape by on acequia-fed farm plots as they have for centuries. The same goes for residents of old Taos Pueblo, the living World Heritage Site that still uses no electricity or running water. Add to that a strong subculture of ski bums, artists, off-the-grid eco-homesteaders, and spiritual seekers, and you have a community that, while not typically prosperous, is more loyal and dedicated to preserving its unique way of life than perhaps any other small town in the western United States.

Jump the Taos Gorge on U.S. 64 west out of town for a beautiful drive over the mountains

to Tierra Amarilla, where sheepherding continues as it has for centuries. North from here, you're nearly at the Colorado border in Chama, best known as the depot for a scenic steam train up a narrow mountain pass.

North and east from Taos, the so-called Enchanted Circle byway loops around Wheeler Peak, the highest mountain in New Mexico at 13,161 feet. Unlike the rest of northern New Mexico, the area was settled primarily by miners and ranchers in the late 19th century. Along the way, you can stop at a mining ghost town, a moving Vietnam veterans' memorial, or a couple of less extreme ski resorts.

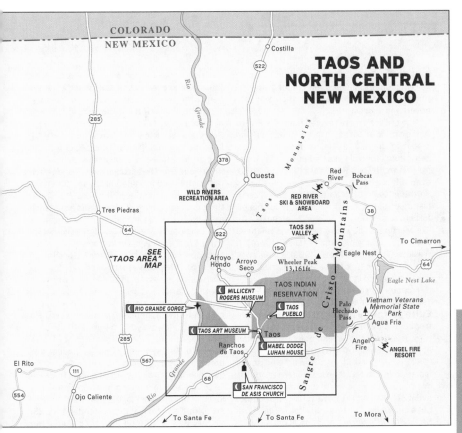

## HISTORY

The first human inhabitants of the area at the base of Taos Mountain were Tiwa-speaking descendants of the Ancestral Puebloans (also called Anasazi) who migrated from the Four Corners area around AD 1000. Taos (how Spaniards heard the Tiwa word for "village") was a thriving village when Spanish explorers, part of Francisco de Coronado's crew, arrived in 1540. By 1615, settlers had arrived.

The Spanish initially had difficulty establishing a toehold. The Pueblo Revolt of 1680 started from a base in Taos and drove settlers out of New Mexico for 12 years. In 1692, under the heavy hand of Governor Diego de Vargas, most of the area was reclaimed, but the Taos

Pueblo Indians held out for four more violent years before they formally surrendered. The only thing that kept the truce was the Puebloans' and Spaniards' mutual need to defend against Comanche and Jicarilla Apache raiders.

By the mid-18th century, Taos was moderately more secure and part of a large trade network, thanks to French fur trappers who had discovered wealth in beaver pelts from the lakes in the surrounding mountains. The little village became a place to gather and swap goods from Mexico and the surrounding wilderness.

Early in the town's history, the population was so small and life so hard that it took only one energetic person to have a significant

## Taos: Fact and Fiction

Just as San Francisco de Asis Church has inspired countless painters and photographers, the people of Taos have found their way into novels and short stories.

One of Taos's more revered figures is **Padre Antonio Martinez,** a popular priest and leader in the mid-1800s. So some Taos residents aren't fond of Willa Cather's *Death Comes for the Archbishop* (New York: Vintage, 1990), even if it is a classic. The 1927 novel is based on the mission of Jean Baptiste Lamy, archbishop of Santa Fe, with sympathy for his efforts to straighten out "rogue" Mexican priests like Martinez. The *padre* gets more balanced coverage in *Lamy of Santa Fe* (Middletown, CT: Wesleyan University Press, 2003), a biography by Paul Horgan that won a Pulitzer Prize after it was published in 1975.

Famous Western novelist Frank Waters, a Taos resident for almost 50 years, fictionalized **Edith Warner,** a woman who ran a small café frequented by the Los Alamos scientists while they developed the nuclear bomb. *The Woman at Otowi Crossing* (Athens, OH: Swallow Press, 1987) is his portrait of a woman who seeks isolation in the New Mexico wilderness but is drawn back into the world through the largest event of her time. The novel is fairly true to life, but a biography, *The House at Otowi Bridge: The Story of Edith Warner and Los Alamos* (Albuquerque: University of New Mexico Press, 1973),

is stricter with the facts. It's by Peggy Pond Church, who lived at Los Alamos for 20 years before the area was taken over by the military.

Another Taos writer, **John Nichols,** earned acclaim for his 1974 comic novel *The Milagro Beanfield War* (New York: Owl Books, 2000), later made into a film by Robert Redford. The war of the title is an escalating squabble in a tiny village over the acequia, the irrigation ditch that's still used in Valle Valdez and other agricultural communities in the area. But if you think it takes comic melodrama and a star such as Redford to make irrigation interesting, look into the beautiful and fascinating *Mayordomo: Chronicle of an Acequia in Northern New Mexico* (Albuquerque: University of New Mexico Press, 1993), **Stanley Crawford**'s memoir about his term as "ditch boss" in the valley where he runs his garlic farm.

If that's all too highbrow, you can find pure pulp in Ruth Laughlin's *The Wind Leaves No Shadow* (Caldwell, ID: Caxton, 1978), a bodice ripper based on the steamy life of **Doña Barcelo Tules,** who was born a pauper but grew up to be a powerful madam and gambling queen in 1830s Taos, then decamped to Santa Fe to run a high-end card house. She was the lover of Manuel Armijo, the last Mexican governor of New Mexico, then attended the U.S. Victory Ball in 1846 on the arm of American General Stephen Kearny. Allegedly.

---

impact. Padre Antonio José Martinez, son of an established trader, was one of the area's most dynamic leaders in the 19th century. In 1835, he acquired the first printing press in the American West and began producing books and a newspaper. He also established a coed school, a seminary, and a law school. Jean-Baptiste Lamy, the Frenchman appointed bishop of Santa Fe in 1853, earned the enmity of Taoseños by curtailing the popular Padre Martinez's work, even filing an order to excommunicate him. Although the papers don't appear to have been processed, Martinez claimed to have been cast out of the church, and he set

up a private chapel at his house, from which he ministered until his death in 1867.

When Mexico declared independence from Spain in 1821, little changed. But in 1846, the transition to U.S. rule, following the Mexican-American War, caused much more upheaval. Wealthy Spanish landowners and Catholic priests (including Padre Martinez) foresaw their loss of influence under the Americans and plotted a rebellion. On January 19, 1847, the leaders incited a mob, many of them American Indian, to kill New Mexico's first American governor, the veteran merchant Charles Bent. Elsewhere in town and the larger region, scores of other Anglo landowners were massacred before U.S. cavalry came from Santa Fe to squelch the uprising.

The latter half of the 1800s saw the start of mining in Twining (now Taos Ski Valley) and a gold rush in nearby Elizabethtown. But in 1879 the railroad arrived in Raton, which bumped Taos from its position as a trading hub, and it slipped into backwater status.

But fortunes turned again in 1898: Bert Geer Phillips and Ernest Blumenschein, two painters on a jaunt from Denver, "discovered" Taos when their wagon wheel snapped near town. Happily waylaid, Phillips stayed and married the town doctor's sister, Rose Martin. Blumenschein eventually returned with others and established the Taos Society of Artists (TSA) in 1915. In the 12 years of the TSA's existence, not only did these and other artists make names for themselves as painters of the American West, but they also put Taos on the map.

The TSA piqued the curiosity of influential East Coasters. One was Mabel Dodge, a well-off, freethinking woman who had fostered art salons in New York City and Florence, then decamped to Taos in 1916. Her name—with "Luhan" appended, after she married Taos Pueblo member Tony Luhan—is now inextricably linked with Taos's 20th-century history because she had an eye for budding artists and writers and encouraged them to come live with and meet one another in Taos. D. H. Lawrence dubbed the place "Mabeltown," and figures as grand and varied as Greta Garbo, Willa Cather, Ansel Adams, Georgia O'Keeffe, Robinson Jeffers, and Carl Jung made the long trek to this dusty mountain town at her behest.

A later generation, in the 1960s, was even more dedicated to living together and sharing ideas. The New Buffalo commune in Arroyo Hondo inspired Dennis Hopper when he filmed *Easy Rider,* which in turn led to another wave of countercultural immigrants. Locals, living by very traditional mores, were horrified at the naked, hallucinogen-ingesting, free-loving, long-haired aliens who had appeared in their midst; more than a decade of antagonism followed. Eventually, however, the most extreme communes disbanded and everyone mellowed a bit with age. Even members of old Spanish families have been known to talk about maximizing the solar gain of their adobe houses.

## PLANNING YOUR TIME

Taos's busiest tourist season is summer, when a day's entertainment can consist simply of gallery-hopping, then settling in to watch the afternoon thunderheads gather and churn, followed by the sun setting under lurid red streaks across the broad western mesas. Wintertime also gets busy with skiers between November and April, but as they're all up on the mountain during the day, museums scale back their hours, and residents reclaim the town center, curling up with books at the many coffee shops. Taos Pueblo also closes to visitors for up to 10 weeks in February and March. By May, the peaks are relatively clear of snow, and you can hike to high meadows filled with wildflowers. Fall is dominated by the smell of wood smoke and the beat of drums, as the pueblo and the rest of the town turn out for the Feast of San Geronimo at the end of September.

From Santa Fe, it's possible to visit Taos as a day trip—as plenty of people do in the summertime—but you'll of course get a better sense of the place if you stay overnight. With a good selection of lodging, it's a great spot for a weekend getaway. A three- or four-night visit gives you time for an afternoon at Taos Pueblo, a couple of mornings at galleries and museums, a hike or skiing, and a day tour of the Enchanted Circle.

For Chama, you can easily make the drive from Taos and back in a day, though if you plan to ride the train, you'll have to get an early start or book a hotel there. As for the Enchanted Circle, the 84-mile loop is typically done as a day trip, but you may want to stay overnight in Eagle Nest or Red River, the better to take in the skiing, hiking, and rock climbing in the area. By no means attempt to visit Taos and do the Enchanted Circle loop in a

TAOS

TAOS

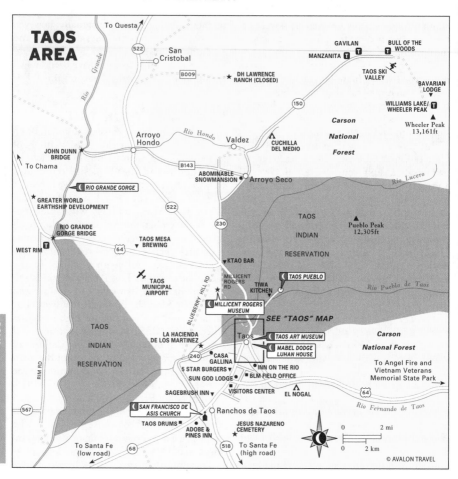

single day—you'd be terribly rushed, and this is hardly the spirit of the place.

## ORIENTATION

The area usually referred to as Taos encompasses not only the historic old town, around the main plaza, but a few surrounding communities as well. If you come via the low road, on Highway 68, you pass first through Ranchos de Taos. Once a separate settlement, it's now connected to Taos Plaza by the least scenic part of town, a stretch of chain stores and cheap motels. Paseo del Pueblo Sur, as Highway 68

is called from Ranchos on, continues north to the central crossroads, the intersection with Kit Carson Road (U.S. 64). The main plaza is west of this intersection; there's a pay parking lot on the east side, or a free lot a few blocks farther east on Kit Carson.

After the light, the street name changes to Paseo del Pueblo Norte. Where it curves west, at the northern end of the central business district, a smaller road continues north about two miles to Taos Pueblo. Paseo del Pueblo Norte carries on through the village of El Prado (now also considered part of greater Taos) to a four-way intersection that will forever be called "the old blinking light," referring to the flashing yellow signal that was replaced with a newfangled three-color job in the 1990s. Here U.S. 64 regains its name, shooting west to the Rio Grande, and Highway 522 leads northwest to the outlying village of Arroyo Hondo, then to Questa and the Enchanted Circle. Highway 150, commonly called Taos Ski Valley Road, goes north to Arroyo Seco, another peripheral town that usually gets lumped in with Taos, and eventually to the base of the ski area.

# Sights

## TAOS PLAZA

The central **Taos Plaza,** enclosed by adobe buildings with deep portals, is easy to miss if you just cruise through on the main road—it's just west of the intersection with Kit Carson Road. Once an informal area at the center of a cluster of settlers' homes, the plaza was established around 1615 but destroyed in the Pueblo Revolt of 1680. New homes were built starting in 1710, but fires repeatedly gutted the block-style homes, so the buildings that edge the plaza all date from around 1930.

In the center is a **monument** to New Mexicans killed in the Bataan Death March of World War II. The U.S. flag flies day and night, a tradition carried on after an incident during the Civil War when Kit Carson and a crew of his men nailed the flag to a pole and guarded it to keep Confederate sympathizers from taking it down. In front of the historic La Fonda hotel, a large bronze statue of local hero Padre Martinez gestures like a visionary—his enormous hands suggest his vast talent and influence. On the plaza's north side, the **old Taos County courthouse** contains a series of WPA-sponsored murals painted in 1934 and 1935 by Emil Bisttram and a team of other Taos artists. The door isn't always open, but definitely try to get in: Enter on the ground floor through the North Plaza Art Center and go upstairs, toward the back of the building.

## Taos Inn

Distinguished by its large glowing thunderbird sign, the oldest neon in town, the inn was as central to previous generations of Taoseños' lives as it is now. Granted, today it's the hotel bar that everyone goes to, but starting in the 1890s, it was the **home of Dr. T. P. Martin**, the first and, for a long time, only doctor in Taos County, who had a good reputation for accepting chickens or venison from his poorer patients in lieu of cash. His home looked out on a small plaza and a well—which has since been covered over and made into the hotel lobby.

## ◖ Mabel Dodge Luhan House

Now used as a conference center and B&B, arts patroness **Mabel Dodge Luhan's home** (240 Morada Ln., 575/751-9686, www.mabeldodge-luhan.com, 9am-7pm daily, free) is open to curious visitors as well as overnight guests. Knock at the main building first; the caretaker will give you information for a self-guided tour of the home's public areas.

Bordering the Taos reservation, the house was built to Luhan's specifications starting in 1918, a year after she moved to New Mexico to be with her third husband (she was Mabel Dodge Sterne at that point), then divorced him. Alongside a small original structure—a low row of adobe rooms that were already a century old at that point—she added a three-story main building, topped with a huge sunroom open on three sides. This, and the similarly glass-enclosed bathroom on the second floor, scandalized her neighbors, the pueblo residents.

One of them, however, didn't seem to mind: Tony Luhan, the foreman of the construction project, became her next husband. But Mabel's custom love nest brought out some latent prurience even in D. H. Lawrence, who objected to the curtainless bathroom windows; to soothe his sensibilities, if not Mabel's, he painted

TAOS

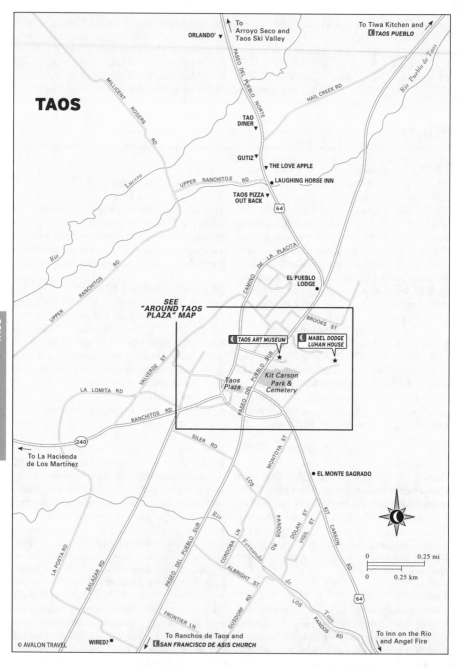

TAOS

To Arroyo Seco and Taos Ski Valley

ORLANDO'

To Tiwa Kitchen and
**TAOS PUEBLO**

MILLICENT ROGERS RD

HAIL CREEK RD

Rio Pueblo de Taos

TAOS

TAO DINER

PASEO DEL PUEBLO NORTE

Lucero

UPPER RANCHITOS RD

GUTIZ

THE LOVE APPLE

LAUGHING HORSE INN

TAOS PIZZA OUT BACK

64

Rio

UPPER RANCHITOS RD

CAMINO DE LA PLACITA

EL PUEBLO LODGE

SEE "AROUND TAOS PLAZA" MAP

BROOKS ST

TAOS ART MUSEUM

MABEL DODGE LUHAN HOUSE

Taos Plaza

PASEO DEL PUEBLO SUR

Kit Carson Park & Cemetery

VALVERDE ST

LA LOMITA RD

RANCHITOS RD

240

SILER RD

To La Hacienda de Los Martínez

EL MONTE SAGRADO

MONTOYA ST

LOS

PANDOS RD

Rio

DOLAN ST

VIGIL ST

KIT CARSON RD

CORDOBA LN

Fernando

LA POSTA RD

SALAZAR RD

PASEO DEL PUEBLO SUR

ALBRIGHT ST

GUSDORF RD

de

Los

Taos

PANDOS RD

64

0        0.25 mi

0        0.25 km

FRONTIER LN

© AVALON TRAVEL

WIRED?

To Ranchos de Taos and
**SAN FRANCISCO DE ASIS CHURCH**

To Inn on the Rio and Angel Fire

© ZORA O'NEILL

early morning on the Taos Plaza

colorful swirls directly on the glass; you can still see them today.

### Kit Carson Park and Cemetery

After seeing where Mabel Dodge Luhan lived, you can also visit her grave, in Taos's oldest cemetery. A shady sprawl of gravestones in a corner of **Kit Carson Park** (on Paseo del Pueblo Norte north of the Taos Inn), the cemetery was established in 1847 to bury the dead from the Taos Rebellion (the melee in which Governor Charles Bent was murdered). It earned its current name when the bodies of Carson and his wife were moved here in 1869, according to his will.

Many of Taos's oldest families, particularly the merchants of the late 1800s, are buried here. Mabel had been a very close friend of the trader Ralph Meyers, and they often joked about being buried together. When Mabel died in 1962, a few years after Ralph, writer Frank Waters recalled their wishes and suggested that Meyers's grave be scooted over to make room for Mabel. She was the last person to be buried in the cemetery, in 1962, and her grave is squeezed into the far southwest corner. Other local luminaries at rest here include Padre Antonio Martinez, who stood up to Catholic bishop Lamy, and Englishman Arthur Manby, whose grave actually stands outside of the cemetery proper, due to his lifetime of shady business deals, land grabs, and outright swindles perpetrated in town. Manby was found beheaded in his mansion in 1929, and the unsympathetic populace was happy to attribute the death to natural causes.

### MUSEUMS

The **Museum Association of Taos** (www. taosmuseums.org) manages five museums in town—all of those listed here except for the Governor Bent House and the Kit Carson Home and Museum. At any of these museums, you can purchase a $25 pass (valid for one year) that grants you a single admission to all five. With individual admissions costing $8 to $10, it will likely pay off if you visit three places.

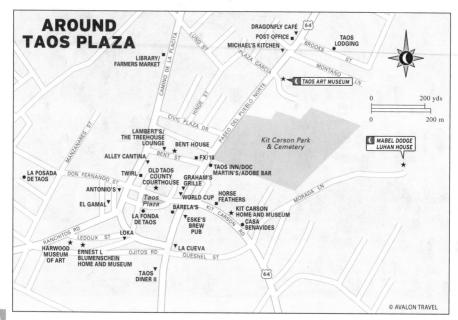

**AROUND TAOS PLAZA**

DRAGONFLY CAFÉ
POST OFFICE
MICHAEL'S KITCHEN
64
BROOKS
TAOS LODGING
ST
LUND ST
CAMINO DE LA PLACITA
LIBRARY/ FARMERS MARKET
PLAZA GARCIA
MONTAÑO
TAOS ART MUSEUM   LN
HINDE ST
PASEO DEL PUEBLO NORTE
CIVIC PLAZA DR
Kit Carson Park & Cemetery
MABEL DODGE LUHAN HOUSE
MANZANARES ST
LAMBERT'S/ THE TREEHOUSE LOUNGE
BENT HOUSE
BENT ST
FX/18
ALLEY CANTINA
TWIRL
OLD TAOS COUNTY COURTHOUSE
GRAHAM'S GRILLE
TAOS INN/DOC MARTIN'S/ADOBE BAR
LA POSADA DE TAOS
DON FERNANDO ST
ANTONIO'S
Taos Plaza
WORLD CUP
HORSE FEATHERS
MORADA LN
EL GAMAL
BARELA'S
KIT CARSON
KIT CARSON HOME AND MUSEUM
LA FONDA DE TAOS
ESKE'S BREW PUB
CASA BENAVIDES
RANCHITOS RD
LOKA
LEDOUX ST
HARWOOD MUSEUM OF ART
ERNEST L BLUMENSCHEIN HOME AND MUSEUM
OJITOS RD
LA CUEVA
QUESNEL ST
64
TAOS DINER II

0      200 yds
0      200 m

© AVALON TRAVEL

All have somewhat more limited winter hours, which can vary.

## Taos Art Museum

This sunny space, the former home of artist and wood-carver Nicolai Fechin, is a showcase not only for a great collection of paintings, but also for Fechin's lovely woodwork. When the Russia native moved to Taos in 1927, hoping to cure his tuberculosis, he purchased seven acres of land, including the small, two-story **Taos Art Museum** (227 Paseo del Pueblo Norte, 575/758-2690, 10am-5pm Tues.-Sun., $8). He proceeded to hand-carve the lintels, staircases, bedsteads, and more, in a combination of Russian Tartar and local styles. His blending of traditions is flawless and natural—a small altar, also in the dining room, is set with Orthodox icons but could just as easily hold local santos.

The collection of paintings shown here is eclectic: Victor Higgins's 1936 *Indian Nude* recalls Gauguin, while Dorothy Brett's *Rainbow and Indians* from 1942 is more enamored of the powerful landscape. One room is dedicated to Fechin's own portrait work, characterized by broad, dynamic brushstrokes and a canny eye for distinctive facial features. One work is an etching of the same set of haggard, mustachioed twins who are rendered in oil by Ernest Hennings on a canvas hanging at the Harwood Museum. After all the work Fechin did on the house, he stayed in Taos only six years, when his wife divorced him. He moved on to Los Angeles with his daughter, Eya (her sunny study, on the ground floor, contains the child-scale furniture that her father made for her). After her father died in 1955, Eya, by then practicing psychodrama and dance therapy, returned to live in the studio (the back building that also houses the gift shop) and helped establish the main house as a museum.

## Millicent Rogers Museum

While today's style makers jet to Dakar and Bhutan for inspiration, Millicent Rogers, a dashing, thrice-married New York City socialite and designer, moved to Taos in 1947 on a tip from a friend, Hollywood actress Janet

## Dennis Hopper in Taos

In 1968, a Taos Pueblo elder told Dennis Hopper, "The mountain is smiling on you!" No wonder the *Easy Rider* actor and real-life renegade made the town into what he called his "heart home." His early years here were wild: He's notorious for having ridden his motorcycle across the roof of the Mabel Dodge Luhan House, which he bought in 1969. Over the decades, he mellowed just a bit, and Taos locals came to think of him as one of their own. In 2009, as part of a 40th-anniversary celebration of the Summer of Love, the Harwood Museum mounted an exhibit of his photography and paintings, along with works by some of his compatriots from that era.

Hopper died not long after, in 2010. His funeral was held at the San Francisco de Asis Church, and attended by fellow 1960s veterans Peter Fonda and Jack Nicholson. Following Pueblo tradition, Hopper was buried in a pine box under a dirt mound, in the nearby **Jesus Nazareno Cemetery.** Fans can pay their respects there; it's off Espinoza Road—look for the turn east from Highway 518, about a quarter mile south of the intersection with Highway 68. From the main gate of the cemetery, Hopper's grave is near the back, on the right-hand side.

© ZORA O'NEILL

mementos on Dennis Hopper's grave

Gaynor. Rogers brought her eye for style with her, adopting Navajo-style velvet broomstick skirts and *concho* belts and donning pounds of turquoise-and-silver jewelry for photo spreads in *Vogue* and *Harper's Bazaar.* Though she died just six years after she moved to Taos, in 1953, at the age of 51, she managed to accumulate a fantastic amount of stuff. The **Millicent Rogers Museum** (1504 Millicent Rogers Rd., 575/758-2462, 10am-5pm daily, closed Mon. Nov.-Mar., $10) was established by her son, Paul Peralta-Ramos, and is set in the warren of adobe rooms that make up her former home.

The collection reflects her discerning taste, with flawless pieces of pottery, rugs, and jewelry—both local works and her own designs. Peralta-Ramos also contributed his own collection, including beautiful pieces of Hispano devotional art. Aside from the works' individual beauty, they make an excellent broad introduction to the crafts of the area, from ancient times to modern. But it's not all rooted in local culture: Rogers's goofy illustrations of a fairy tale for her children fill the last room. The gift shop here is particularly thorough and includes beautiful vintage jewelry and very old rugs.

### Harwood Museum of Art

The **Harwood Museum of Art** (238 Ledoux St., 575/758-9826, 10am-5pm Mon.-Sat., noon-5pm Sun., closed Mon. Nov.-Mar., $10), set in the sprawling Pueblo Revival-style home of the Harwood patrons, tells the story of Taos's rise as an art colony, beginning with Ernest Blumenschein's fateful wagon accident, which left him and his colleague Bert Phillips stranded in the tiny town in 1898.

Modern Taos painters are represented as well in the temporary exhibit spaces upstairs, and it's interesting to see the same material—the mountain, the pueblo, the river, local residents—depicted in different styles over the decades. Also upstairs is a small but very good assortment of Hispano crafts, including a couple of santos by Patrocinio Barela, the Taos wood-carver who modernized the art in the 1930s, and some beautiful 19th-century tinwork. A separate back wing is dedicated to seven ethereal abstractions by painter Agnes Martin.

## Blumenschein Home and Museum

Ernest Blumenschein, one of the founding fathers of the Taos Society of Artists, moved into what is now the **Blumenschein Home and Museum** (222 Ledoux St., 575/758-0505, 10am-5pm Mon.-Sat., noon-5pm Sun., $8) in 1919 with his wife, Mary Shepard Greene Blumenschein, also an accomplished artist. The house's decoration largely reflects her taste, from the sturdy wood furnishings in the dining room to the light-filled studio and the cozy wood-paneled library.

Throughout, the walls are hung with sketches and paintings by their contemporaries. Some of the finest are in the back "Green Room," including a beautiful monotype of Taos Mountain by Oscar E. Berninghaus. The main bedroom, entered through a steep arch, is decorated with Mary's lush illustrations for *The Arabian Nights.* Throughout, you can admire the variety of ceiling styles, from rough-hewn split cedar *(rajas)* to tidy golden aspen boughs *(latillas).* In winter (Nov.-Mar.), the museum closes at 4pm, and all day on Wednesday.

## La Hacienda de los Martinez

The word *hacienda* conjures a sprawling complex and fields, but the reality in 19th-century Taos was quite different, as the carefully restored **La Hacienda de los Martinez** (708

Hacienda Rd., off Lower Ranchitos Rd., 575/758-1000, 10am-5pm Mon.-Sat., noon-5pm Sun., $8) from 1804 shows. Its builder and owner, Severino Martinez, was a prominent merchant who hosted the Taos trade fairs at the hacienda and eventually became the mayor of Taos in the 1820s. His oldest son was Padre Antonio Martinez, the valley leader who clashed with the French bishop Jean-Baptiste Lamy.

Despite the family's high social standing, life was fairly rugged, cramped, and cold: 21 simple rooms arranged around two courtyards allowed room for sleeping, cooking, and, in the single room with a wood floor, dancing. Some of the spaces have been furnished to reflect their original use; others are dedicated to exhibits, such as a very interesting display on slavery in the area, and an especially creepy wood carving of Doña Sebastiana, Lady Death, with her glittering mica eyes, in the collection of Penitente paraphernalia. During the summer, local craftspeople are on hand to demonstrate weaving, blacksmithing, and the like in the house's workshops; in the fall, the trade fair is reenacted. In winter (Nov.-Mar.), the museum closes at 4pm, and all day on Wednesday.

## Kit Carson Home and Museum

Old photographs, memorabilia, and assorted trinkets from the frontier era conjure the spirit of the legendary scout at the **Kit Carson Home and Museum** (113 Kit Carson Rd., 575/758-4945, www.kitcarsonhomeandmuseum.com, 10am-5:30pm daily in summer, 11am-4pm daily in winter, $5), where he lived with his third wife, Josefa Jaramillo, from 1843 until they both died in 1868.

The definitive mountain man, Carson was one of many solitary scouts, trackers, and trappers who explored the American West. He was an intrepid adventurer who, after a childhood on the barely settled edge of Missouri, joined a wagon train headed down the Santa Fe Trail; he arrived in Taos in 1826. His talent for tracking, hunting, and translating from Spanish and various Indian languages soon put him in high demand. Whether he was scouting for John C.

TAOS

© ZORA O'NEILL

the courtyard of the Kit Carson Home and Museum

Frémont as the explorer mapped the trails west to Los Angeles, serving as an officer in the Civil War, or, less heroically, forcing the Navajos on the Long Walk to Fort Sumner, he called Taos home. He bought this house in 1843 with his third wife, Josefa Jaramillo, and they died there in 1868.

## Governor Bent House and Museum

This dusty little backroom exhibit space is odd, but well worth a visit if it happens to be open (the posted hours aren't always maintained). The **Governor Bent House and Museum** (117 Bent St., 10am-5pm daily, $3) is the former residence of Charles Bent who, following the Mexican-American War, was appointed the first governor of the territory of New Mexico in 1846, based on his extensive experience as a Western trader (he and his brother had built Bent's Fort, an important trading center in southern Colorado). But Bent died in 1847, at the hands of an angry mob dissatisfied by the new American government.

Amid the slightly creepy clutter, which includes a malevolent-looking ceremonial buffalo head, Inuit knives, and photos of Penitente rituals from an old *Harper's* magazine, is the very hole in the very wall that Bent's family quickly dug to escape while Bent tried to reason with the murderous crowd. The back room only gets stranger, with surreal taxidermy, sinister doctor's instruments, and lots of old guns. The place may feel like an antiques store where nothing's for sale, but it still gives a surprisingly good overview of the period.

## ◖ SAN FRANCISCO DE ASIS CHURCH

Just as photographs of the Great Pyramid of Cheops seldom show the sprawl of modern Cairo crowding up to its base, **San Francisco de Asis Church** (east side of U.S. 68 in Ranchos de Taos, 575/758-2754, 9am-4pm daily, Mass 7am, 9:30am, and 11:30am Sun., donation) as depicted in, say, Georgia O'Keeffe's paintings or Ansel Adams's photographs, is always a shadow-draped fortress isolated on a hilltop.

© ZORA O'NEILL

The San Francisco de Asis Church gets a fresh coat of mud every year.

So visitors are often surprised to see the cluster of buildings that rings the small plaza in front of the church, which was built in the first half of the 18th century as a Franciscan mission for the farming community of Ranchos de Taos.

It's easy see what has fascinated so many artists: the clean lines, the shadows created by the hulking buttresses, the rich glow of the adobe in the sun. The church is living architecture, as much a part of the earth as something raised above it. As with every traditional adobe structure, it must be refinished every year with a mix of clay, sand, and straw; it is then coated with a fine layer of water and sand, and buffed with sheepskin. This happens over two weeks in June, during which the church is open only at lunchtime and on Sunday.

Inside, the whitewash walls are covered with santos and *retablos*. In the **parish hall** (9am-3:30pm daily, $3) is the 1896 painting *The Shadow of the Cross*, an eight-foot-high canvas in which the figure of Christ can be seen to luminesce—allegedly miraculously.

## TAOS PUEBLO

Even if you've been in New Mexico for a while and think you're inured to adobe, **Taos Pueblo** (575/758-1028, www.taospueblo.com, 8am-4:30pm Mon.-Sat., 8:30am-4:30pm Sun., till 4pm in winter, closed for 10 weeks around Feb.-Mar., $10) is an amazing sight. Two clusters of multistory mud-brick buildings make up the core of this village, which claims, along with Acoma Pueblo, to be the oldest continually inhabited community in the United States. The current buildings, annually repaired and recoated with mud, are from the 1200s, though it's possible that all their constituent parts have been fully replaced several times since then.

About 150 people (out of the 1,200 or so total Taos reservation residents) live here year-round. These people, along with the town's designation as a UNESCO World Heritage Site, has kept the place remarkably as it was in the pre-Columbian era, save for the use of adobe bricks (as opposed to clay and stone), which were introduced by the Spanish, as the main structural material. The apartment-like homes, stacked up at various levels and reached by wood ladders, have no electricity or running water, though some use propane gas for heat and light.

As you explore, be careful not to intrude on private space: Enter only buildings that are clearly marked as shops, and stay clear of the ceremonial kiva areas on the east side of each complex. These round structures form the ritual heart of the pueblo, a secret space within an already private culture.

You're welcome to wander around and enter any of the craft shops and galleries that are open—a good opportunity to see inside the earthen structures and to buy some of the distinctive Taos pottery, which is only very lightly decorated but glimmers with mica from the clay of this area. These pots are also renowned for cooking beans.

### San Geronimo Church

The path from the Taos Pueblo admission gate leads directly to the central plaza, a broad expanse between Red Willow Creek

The earth gapes open at the Rio Grande Gorge due west of Taos.

(source of the community's drinking water, flowing from sacred Blue Lake higher in the mountains) and **San Geronimo Church.** The latter, built in 1850, is perhaps the newest structure in the village, a replacement for the first mission the Spanish built, in 1619, using forced Indian labor. The Virgin Mary presides over the room roofed with heavy wood beams; her clothes change with every season, a nod to her dual role as the Earth Mother. (Taking photos is strictly forbidden inside the church at all times and, as at all pueblos, at dances as well.)

The older church, to the north behind the houses, is now a cemetery—fitting, given its tragic destruction. It was first torn down during the Pueblo Revolt of 1680; the Spanish rebuilt it about 20 years later. In 1847 it was again attacked, this time by American troops sent in to quell the rebellion against the new government, in retaliation for the murder of Governor Charles Bent. The counterattack brutally outweighed what had sparked it. More than 100 pueblo residents, including women and children, had taken refuge inside the church when the Americans bombarded and set fire to it, killing everyone inside and gutting the building. Since then, the bell tower has been restored, but the graves have simply intermingled with the ruined walls and piles of dissolved adobe mud. All of the crosses—from old carved wood to new finished stone—face sacred Taos Mountain.

## RIO GRANDE GORGE

Heading west on U.S. 64 from the "old blinking light," you pass the Taos airstrip on the left; then, after a few more miles, the ground simply drops away. This is the **Rio Grande Gorge** (also called the Taos Gorge), plunging at its most alarming point 800 feet down into malevolent-looking basalt. The river courses below, but it's not just millions of years of rushing water that have carved out the canyon—seismic activity also caused a rift in the earth's surface. The crack extends north to just beyond the Colorado state line and south almost to Española.

The elegant, unnervingly delicate-looking bridge that spans it was built in 1965 to supplement entrepreneur John Dunn's rickety old toll crossing eight miles north. Critics mocked the newer structure as "the bridge to nowhere" because the highway on the western bank had yet to be built, but the American Institute of Steel Construction granted it the Most Beautiful Span award in 1966. At 650 feet above the river, the cantilever truss was a stunning engineering feat; it is still the fifth-highest bridge in the United States. On either side of the bridge is the stretch of white water called the Taos Box, two words that inspire wild tales in any seasoned river-runner. The Class III and IV rapids are considered the best place for rafting in New Mexico.

On the west side of the gorge is a rest area, and the start of the **West Rim Trail,** running south from the parking lot and yielding great views of the bridge to the north.

View the inner workings of an eco-friendly home at the Greater World Earthship Development.

## Greater World Earthship Development

If you brave the slender bridge and continue west on U.S. 64, you soon see some odd apparitions along the right side of the road. These whimsically curved and creatively stuccoed houses are Earthships: modular, low-priced homes that function entirely on collected rainwater and wind and solar power. Whether it's due to the latent hippie culture or the awe-inspiring landscape, the homes have proved very popular, and you'll see them dotted around the area, as well as clustered together here at Greater World, the largest of three local all-Earthship subdivisions. Although they look like fanciful Hobbit homes or Mars colony pods on the outside, Earthships are made of rather common stuff: The walls, usually built into hillsides, are stacks of used tires packed solid with rammed earth, while bottles stacked with cement and crushed aluminum cans form front walls and colorful peepholes.

The Greater World subdivision and Earthship Biotecture office maintains a **visitors center** (575/613-4409, www.earthship.com, 9am-6pm daily in summer,

10am-4pm daily in winter, $5). Look for the green building on the right 1.8 miles past the bridge. This is the most unconventional model home and sales office you'll ever visit. You can take the self-guided tour of a basic Earthship and watch a video about the building process and the rationale behind the design. If you're hooked, you can of course get details on buying a lot in the development or purchasing the plans to build your own place elsewhere. Or try before you buy: You can stay the night in an Earthship here, starting at $130.

## TAOS SKI VALLEY

From the "old blinking light," Highway 150 heads to Arroyo Seco, a small cluster of galleries and stores at a bend in the road. The road then winds relentlessly up through Hondo Canyon, the steep mountain slopes crowded with tall, dense pines that in winter disappear into a wreath of clouds. The road dead-ends at **Taos Ski Valley,** technically an incorporated village.

One sliver of the near-vertical slopes of Taos Ski Valley

finally get out of the car at the base of the ski runs and take in the vertiginous view toward Kachina Peak (elevation 12,481 feet and often white-capped even in July), you'll see why it inspires legions of reverential skiers every winter, when an average of 305 inches of snow falls on the mountain—almost 10 times the amount they get down in town.

And in fact, for decades, it was *only* skiers here. Snowboarders were banned, allegedly because of the seriously precipitous slopes—more than half the trails are rated expert level, and many of them are left ungroomed. But the slopes were finally opened to all in 2008. It was a major adjustment for TSV's loyal customers, and it leaves just three resorts in the country that don't allow snowboarding (Utah's Deer Valley and Alta, and Mad River Glen in Vermont).

In the summertime, Hondo Canyon's many trails make for very good hiking or picnicking. The road is dotted on either side with picnic areas and campgrounds—Cuchilla del Medio is a particularly nice area for a picnic. The **visitors center** (575/776-1413, www.taosskivalley.com) in the ski area parking lot stocks trail descriptions and maps.

But only the mountain, along with the snow on top of it, matters to most people. When you

# Entertainment and Events

Taos is a small town: no glitzy dance clubs, no bars where you're expected to dress up. Nighttime fun is concentrated in a handful of places where, even after a couple of visits, you'll get to know the regulars quickly. The various town-wide celebrations—including music and dancing on the plaza on summer Thursdays—draw a good cross-section of the population.

## NIGHTLIFE
Starting around 5pm, the **Adobe Bar** (125 Paseo del Pueblo Norte, 575/758-2233), in the lobby of the Taos Inn (look for the glowing thunderbird sign), is where you'll run into everyone you've seen over the course of the day, sipping a Cowboy Buddha ($10) or some other specialty margarita—the best in town. Mellow jazz or acoustic guitar sets the mood from 7pm. To give hotel residents a break, the bar closes at 10pm, which forces all the regulars to move on down the road to the next phase of the evening: the dance floor at the **Sagebrush Inn** (1508 Paseo del Pueblo Sur, 575/758-2254). It gets packed with cowboy-booted couples stepping lively to country cover bands whose members always seem to resemble Kenny Rogers. The scene encompasses all of Taos, from artists to pueblo residents to mountain men with grizzled beards. Booze is a bargain, and the fireplace is big.

After the band wraps up around midnight, the most dedicated move on to **The Alley**

© ZORA O'NEILL

## New Mexico's Communes

Something about New Mexico's vast empty spaces inspires utopian thinking, as if the landscape were a blank slate, a way to start from scratch and do things right. Spanish settlers felt it in the 16th century. Gold miners banked on it in the 1800s. And in the 1960s, freethinkers, free-lovers, and back-to-the-landers fled crowded cities and boring suburbs to start communities such as the Hog Farm and the New Buffalo Commune, both near Taos. For a while, New Mexico was the place to be: Dennis Hopper immortalized New Buffalo in his film *Easy Rider*, Janis Joplin chilled out in Truchas, and Ken Kesey drove his bus, *Further*, through the state. At the end of the decade, some 25 communes had been established.

In most of the rest of the United States, these experimental communities and their ideals were just a brief moment of zaniness—their legacy appears to be Hog Farm leader Wavy Gravy's consecration on a Ben & Jerry's label. But in New Mexico, many of the ideals set down by naked organic gardeners and tripping visionaries took root and sprouted in unexpected ways. Yogi Bhajan, a Sikh who taught mass kundalini yoga sessions in New Mexico in 1969, later became a major contributor to the state economy through all the businesses he established. Buddhist stupas dot the Rio Grande Valley, the product of Anglo spiritual seekers working with Tibetan refugees brought to New Mexico by Project Tibet, cofounded by John Allen, who also ran the commune Synergia Ranch near Santa Fe. Allen was also instrumental in building Biosphere 2, the experimental glass dome in the Arizona desert—probably the most utopian vision yet to have sprouted in New Mexico.

**Cantina** (121 Teresina Ln., 575/758-2121) for another hour or so. This warren of interconnected rooms (one of which is supposedly the oldest in Taos...but don't they all say that?) can be potentially baffling after a few drinks. There's shuffleboard for entertainment if you're not into the ensemble onstage—its name usually ends in "Blues Band"; a cover of $5 to $7 applies on weekends. The kitchen is open until 11pm, and it's not a bad place for a lunchtime burger ($6.50) either.

Is your drinking unsustainable? Not if you go to the **KTAOS Bar** (9 Hwy. 150, 575/758-5826 ext. 206, 4pm-9pm Sun.-Thurs., 4pm-11pm Fri.-Sat.), the social wing of the local radio station, which happens to be entirely solar-powered. You can peek into the radio studios, and out to Taos Mountain. Needless to say, live music is a big thing here, with occasional major shows. Kids are welcome, with plenty of room to play.

If your style is cramped by old adobes, head out to **Taos Mesa Brewing** (20 ABC Mesa Rd., 575/758-1900, noon-late daily), on U.S.

64 opposite the airport, where there's plenty of room to groove. The metal Quonset hut looms like a far-flung Burning Man camp, and the entertainment roster is eclectic, from theremin masters to major global artists performing outside (cover from $5 some nights). The crowd is all of Taos's younger hippies, plus hops aficionados of all stripes. The food ($10) is veg- and beer-friendly.

A more upscale newcomer to Taos's bar scene is **The Treehouse Lounge** (123 Bent St., 575/758-1009, 5pm-10pm daily), the upper floor of an adobe house downtown. With a full bar and the creative minds running it, the range of cocktails ($10) is highly stimulating. Highbrow snacks will keep you grounded.

A few other watering holes draw a crowd, usually for live music of some kind. On the plaza, **The Gorge** (103 E. Taos Plaza, 575/758-8866, 11am-midnight daily) has balcony seats overlooking the action—a good place for a sunset margarita. The fancified pub grub ($10 and up) isn't that special, though, so save your appetite for elsewhere. Wood-paneled **Eske's Brew**

**Pub** (106 Des Georges Ln., 575/758-1517) is across from the plaza, tucked back from the southeast corner of the intersection of Paseo del Pueblo Sur and Kit Carson Road. With live music on Fridays and Saturdays, it serves its house-made beer to a chummy après-ski crowd. You're in New Mexico—you should at least *try* the green-chile ale.

## FESTIVALS AND EVENTS

Taos's biggest annual festivity (for which many local businesses close) is the **Feast of San Geronimo,** the patron saint assigned to Taos Pueblo by the Spanish when they built their first mission there in 1619. The holiday starts the evening of September 29 with vespers in the pueblo church and continues the next day with footraces and a pole-climbing contest. La Hacienda de los Martinez usually reenacts a 19th-century Taos trade fair, with mountain men, music, and artisans' demonstrations.

In summer, the town also turns out for the **Fiestas de Taos** (www.fiestasdetaos.com), a mid-July celebration of Santiago de Compostela and Santa Ana that lasts three days, with a parade, food and crafts booths on the plaza, and the crowning of the Fiestas Queen. Also in July is the **Taos Pueblo Powwow** (www. taospueblo.com), a major get-together of Pueblo Indians and tribal members from around the country. Try to be there for the Grand Entry, the massive opening procession. The event takes place at the powwow grounds in El Prado near the Overland Sheepskin store.

Taos galleries put out their finest at the **Taos Fall Arts Festival** (www.taosfallarts.com), a two-week-long exhibition in late September and early October that shows the works of more than 150 Taos County artists. On the first weekend in October, the **Taos Wool Festival** (www.taoswoolfestival.org) has drawn textile artists as well as breeders since 1983. Admire the traditional Churro sheep or an Angora goat and then pick up a scarf made from its wool.

The glow of luminarias and torchlight on snow produces a magical effect—perhaps that's why Taos has so many winter events. On the first weekend in December, the **tree-lighting ceremony** on the plaza draws the whole town, and the rest of the season sees

TAOS

## What to Expect at Pueblo Dances

Visiting a pueblo for a ceremonial dance or feast-day celebration is one of the most memorable parts of a trip to New Mexico. But it's important to remember that a pueblo dance is not at all for the benefit of tourists. It is a ceremony and a religious ritual, not a performance—you are a guest, not an audience.

Keep this in mind as a guide to your own behavior. Applause is not appropriate, nor is conversation during the dance. Queries about the meaning of the dances are generally not appreciated. Never walk in the dance area, and try not to block the view of pueblo residents. The kivas, as holy spaces, are always off-limits to outsiders. During feast days, some pueblo residents may open their doors to visitors, perhaps for a snack or drink—but be considerate of others who may also want to visit, and don't

stay too long. Photography is strictly forbidden at dances (sometimes with the exception of Los Matachines, which is not a religious ritual). Don't even think about trying to sneak a shot with your camera phone, as tribal police will be more than happy to confiscate it.

On a practical level, be prepared for a lot of waiting around. Start times are always approximate, and everything depends on when the dancers are done with their kiva rituals. There will usually be a main, seasonal dance—such as the corn dance at the summer solstice—followed by several others. If you go in the winter, dress very warmly, but in layers—ceremonies usually start with Christmas Eve Mass inside the close-packed, overheated church, and then dances often proceed outside in the cold.

## Ceremonial Dances at Taos Pueblo

In addition to the Feast of San Geronimo, visitors are welcome to attend ceremonial dances. This is only an approximate schedule—dates can vary from year to year, as can the particular dances. Contact the **pueblo** (505/758-1028, www.taospueblo.com) for times, or check the listings in the *Tempo* section of the paper for that week.

Every night May through October, there are demonstration dances at the Best Western Kachina Lodge (413 Paseo del Pueblo Norte)—a little touristy, but nice if your trip doesn't coincide with a ceremonial dance at the pueblo itself.

- **January 1** - Turtle dance
- **January 6** - Deer or buffalo dance
- **May 3** - Feast of Santa Cruz: corn dance
- **June 13** - Feast of San Antonio: corn dance
- **June 24** - Feast of San Juan: corn dance
- **July 25-26** - Feast of Santiago and Santa Ana: corn dances and footraces
- **September 29-30** - Feast of San Geronimo
- **December 24** - Sundown procession and children's dance
- **December 25** - Various dances

numerous celebrations, such as the reenactments of the Virgin's search for shelter, called Las Posadas, which take place at Our Lady of Guadalupe Church west of the plaza on the third weekend in December. At the pueblo, vespers is said at San Geronimo church on Christmas Eve, typically followed by a children's dance. On Christmas Day, the pueblo hosts either a deer dance or the Spanish Los Matachines dance.



# Shopping

Taos Plaza is ringed with less-than-inspiring souvenir stores. Two further clusters of boutiques and art dealers lie just north of the plaza—very pleasant places to browse, though you certainly won't find any bargains. If you're hoping to discover Taos's next big art star, poke around smaller operations on back streets and in Arroyo Seco, or just keep your eyes open when you get your morning coffee—nearly every business doubles as a gallery in this town.

## ARTS AND CRAFTS

Daniel Barela, great-grandson of legendary wood-carver Patrocinio Barela (whose work is on view in the Harwood Museum), can often be found working in **Barela's Traditional Fine Art** (124-A Paseo del Pueblo Sur, 575/779-5720, noon-3pm daily). The raw, casual gallery space houses his and his relatives' hand-carved saint figures, as well as work by several Salazars, another noted woodworking family.

Down in Ranchos de Taos, **Orr's Trading** (2 St. Francis Plaza, 575/779-7283, 10am-5pm daily) is less a store than a repository of traditional skill. Elderly proprietor Dell Orr spends much of his time making ceremonial headdresses from porcupine hair, sewing buckskin with deer tendon, and other nearly forgotten indigenous crafts. He can also sell you beads and other materials, as well as some finished products.

**Taos Drums** (3956 Hwy. 68, 800/424-3786, 10am-5pm Mon.-Fri., 11:30am-5pm Sun.) is a giant shop and factory dedicated to making Taos Pueblo-style percussion instruments, from thin hand drums to great booming ones made of hollow logs. Trying out the wares is encouraged. The shop is located on the west side of the highway five miles south of the plaza.

## CLOTHING AND JEWELRY

Gussy yourself up in Western trappings from **Horse Feathers** (109-B Kit Carson Rd., 575/758-7457, 10:30am-5:30pm daily), where you can pick up a full cowpoke getup, from ten-gallon hat to jingling spurs. The big money is in the vintage cowboy boots, but you can find less expensive, eclectic gift items, such as giant belt buckles or campfire cookbooks from 1900.

## GIFT AND HOME

**FX/18** (103-C Bent St., 575/758-8590, 11am-6pm Mon.-Sat., noon-5pm Sun.) has a great selection of goodies: groovy housewares, lively kids' stuff, nifty stationery. And the selection of contemporary Southwest-style jewelry is particularly good.

Up Highway 150, **Arroyo Seco Mercantile** (488 Hwy. 150, 575/776-8806, 10am-5pm Mon.-Sat., 11am-5pm Sun.) is the town's former general store, now a highly evolved junk shop that has maintained the beautiful old wood-and-glass display cases. Its stock ranges from the practical (books on passive-solar engineering and raising llamas) to the frivolous, with lots of the beautiful, like antique wool blankets.

## KID'S STUFF

Taos is also home to an exceptionally magical toy store, **Twirl** (225 Camino de la Placita, 575/751-1402, www.twirlhouse.com, 10am-6pm daily). Tucked in a series of low-ceiling adobe rooms, it's crammed with everything from science experiments to wooden trains to fairy costumes. Even the kiva fireplace gets a fantastical 1,001 Nights treatment, and there's a big roster of activities in the huge play space out back.

# Sports and Recreation

The wild setting presses in all around Taos, and the mountains loom up behind every town view. Downhill skiing is the main draw in the winter, but you can also try more solitary snowshoeing and Nordic skiing. In summer, peak-baggers will want to strike out for Wheeler, the state's highest, while rafters, rock climbers, and mountain bikers can head the other direction, to the dramatic basalt cliffs of the Rio Grande Gorge. In the water, river-runners challenge the churning rapids of the legendary Taos Box (late May and early June is the best season for this).

## Information

Stop in at the **Carson National Forest Supervisor's Office** (208 Cruz Alta Rd., 575/758-6200, 8:30am-4:30pm Mon.-Fri.) for booklets on recommended trails and maps. Just down the street, the **Bureau of Land Management Taos Field Office** (226 Cruz Alta Rd., 575/758-8851, 8am-4:30pm

Mon.-Fri.) can help you prepare for a rafting or longer camping trip, with plenty of maps and brochures.

Sudden thunderstorms are common in the summer months, as are flash floods and even freak blizzards. Well into May, snow can blanket some of the higher passes, so wherever you go, always carry more warm clothing than you think you'll need, and don't skimp on the sunscreen, even when it's below freezing.

## BIKING

Taos has several great trails for mountain biking. A popular ride close to town is **West Rim Trail** along the Rio Grande Gorge, either from the gorge bridge up to John Dunn Bridge, about 15 miles round-trip, or from the gorge bridge south to the Taos Junction bridge near Pilar, about 18 miles out and back. Either way, you'll have great views and fairly level but rugged terrain.

For road touring, you can make a pleasant 25-mile loop from Taos through Arroyo Hondo and Arroyo Seco. With no steep grades, it's a good way to get adjusted to the altitude. Head north up Paseo del Pueblo Norte, straight through the intersection with Highway 150, then turn right in Arroyo Hondo onto County Road B-143. Cross Highway 230, and you arrive in Arroyo Seco behind the Abominable Snowmansion. Turn right on Highway 150 to loop back to Taos. The standard challenge is the 84-mile Enchanted Circle; every September sees the **Enchanted Circle Century Tour,** sponsored by the Red River Chamber of Commerce (800/348-6444 for info) and drawing more than a thousand riders. A mountain-biking race takes place the day after.

**Gearing Up** (129 Paseo del Pueblo Sur, 575/751-0365) rents mountain and hybrid bicycles for $50 per day. If you're bringing your bicycle with you, consider having it shipped here, and they'll reassemble it and have it waiting when you arrive.

## HIKING

With Taos Mountain in the backyard, you can ramble along winding rivers or haul up 2,000 feet in less than four miles. Be prepared for a cold snap or storm at any time, and don't plan on anything before May—it takes that long for the snow to thaw, though even in high summer, you can still hit some of the white stuff in the alpine meadows.

A variety of trails course through **Taos Canyon** east of town, with numerous campgrounds and trailheads off U.S. 64, including the **South Boundary Trail,** 22 miles up and over the pass, with views onto Moreno Valley.

More varied trails are along the road to Taos Ski Valley (Hwy. 150). Just before you reach the parking lot for the ski area, **Gavilan Trail** (no. 60) leads off the north side of the road. It's plenty steep but leads to a high mountain meadow. The route is five miles round-trip, or you can connect with other trails once you're up on the rim.

Purists will want to head for **Wheeler Peak Summit Trail** (no. 67), which scales New

on the Williams Lake Trail

© ZORA O'NEILL

Mexico's highest in about four miles (one-way). The first two miles of the route is the relatively easy and popular **Williams Lake Trail** (no. 62), which starts near the end of Twining Road, a narrow dirt road that leads out of the top of the Taos Ski Valley parking lot. (Before starting up Twining Road, stop first at the visitors center in the parking lot, for trail descriptions.) Williams Lake is a nice destination and pleasant hiking, once you get past the early stretch, strewn with mid-size rocks. From near the lake, the Wheeler Peak route continues on another two miles or so.

If all that sounds too strenuous, you can take the **chairlift** (10am-4:30pm Thurs.-Mon. June-Aug., $15) up to the top of the mountain then wander down any of several wide, well-marked trails, all with stunning views.

## RAFTING AND TUBING

The **Taos Box,** the 16-mile stretch of the Rio Grande south of John Dunn Bridge down to near Pilar, provides perhaps the best rafting in New Mexico, with Class III rapids with ominous names like Boat Reamer and Screaming Left-Hand Turn. The river mellows out a bit south of the Taos Box, then leads into a shorter Class III section called the Racecourse—the most popular run, usually done as a half-day trip. Beyond this, in the Orilla Verde Recreation Area around Pilar, the water is wide and flat, a place for a relaxing float with kids or other water newbies; you can flop in an inner tube if you really want to chill out. North of the John Dunn Bridge, there's another intermediate run called La Junta that's a half-day trip.

**Los Rios River Runners** (575/776-8854, www.losriosriverrunners.com) leads trips to all these spots as half-day outings ($54), day trips (from $105), and overnight trips. (Kokopelli also runs a daylong float trip in a lesser-traveled section of the river north of the Taos Box.) **Far-Flung Adventures** (575/758-2628, www.farflung.com) is another outfitter and can add on rock climbing and horseback riding. With both organizations, you can choose whether you want a paddle boat—where you're actively (and sometimes strenuously) paddling—or an oar boat, where guides row, and you can sit back. The best season is late May and early June, when the water is high from mountain runoff.

## WINTER SPORTS

**Taos Ski Valley** (866/968-7386, www.ski-taos.org, $77 full-day lift ticket) is a mecca for downhill skiing. The resort is open from late November through the first weekend in April, with 113 trails served by 14 lifts and snowmaking capacity on all beginner and intermediate areas in dry spells. The dedicated can hike to Kachina Peak, an additional 632 feet past where the lift service ends. The highly regarded Ernie Blake Snowsports School is one of the best places to learn the basics or polish your skills. Novice "yellowbirds" can take one ($110) or two ($175) days of intensive instruction specially geared to new skiers.

For cross-country skiing and snowshoeing, **Enchanted Forest** (575/754-6112, www.enchantedforestxc.com, $18 full-day pass), between Elizabethtown and Red River on the Enchanted Circle loop, offers miles of groomed trails. There are also easy ski access points in the Carson National Forest—at Capulin Campground on U.S. 64, for instance, five miles east of Taos and along **Manzanita Trail** in the Hondo Canyon on the road to the ski valley.

Don't have your own gear? **Cottam's Ski & Outdoor** (207-A Paseo del Pueblo Sur, 575/758-2822, 7am-7pm Mon.-Fri., 7am-8pm Sat.-Sun.) has the biggest stock of rental skis, snowboards, and snowshoes. The shop also sells everything else you'll need to get out and enjoy the snow; there's another location at the ski valley (575/776-8719) and one at Angel Fire (575/377-3700).

# Accommodations

Taos hotels can be a bit overpriced, especially at the lower end, where there are few reliable bargains. But because Taos is awash in centuries-old houses, bed-and-breakfasts have thrived. For those skeptical of B&Bs, don't despair: The majority of them have private bathrooms, separate entrances, and not too much country-cute decor. Certainly, just as in Santa Fe, the Southwestern gewgaws can be applied with a heavy hand, but wood-burning fireplaces, well-stocked libraries, hot tubs, and big gardens can make up for that.

For better deals, consider staying outside of Taos proper. Arroyo Seco is about a half-hour drive from the plaza, as is the Earthship subdivision, and rates here and in Ranchos de Taos can be a little lower. In the summer, the lodges near the ski valley cut their prices by almost half—a great deal if you want to spend some time hiking in the canyon and don't mind driving into town for food and entertainment. If you're arriving in town without a car, a few good budget choices are served by Taos's Chile Line bus, which caters to skiers in the winter, from down on the southern end of town all the way up to the ski valley.

## CENTRAL TAOS
### Under $100

Not a hotel at all, but simply a clutch of well-maintained one- and two-bedroom private casitas, **Taos Lodging** (109 Brooks St., 575/751-1771, www.taoslodging.com, $75 studio) is in a quiet, convenient block about a 10-minute walk north from the plaza. Here, eight cottages, arranged around a central courtyard, have assorted floor plans, but all have porches, full kitchens, and living rooms, as well as access to a shared outdoor hot tub. The smallest, a 350-square-foot studio, sleeps two comfortably; the largest ($130 for two) sleep up to six. Plus, the same group manages two additional properties nearby, for those who want a larger condo.

Of the various motels on the south side, none are very good, but **Sun God Lodge** (919 Paseo del Pueblo Sur, 575/758-3162, www.sungodlodge.com, $69 d) can be fine. Maintenance can be spotty, but rooms are set around a big grassy, tree-shaded courtyard and, in back, a hot tub; there's also a laundry. But note that this can foster a somewhat rowdy atmosphere, especially in ski season or after big summer events.

### $100-150

Walking distance from the plaza, ◖ **El Pueblo Lodge** (412 Paseo del Pueblo Norte, 575/758-8700, www.elpueblolodge.com, $100 s, $120 d) is a budget operation with nice perks such as free laundry. Rooms vary from a snug nook in the oldest adobe section to new, slick motel rooms complete with gas fireplaces. Those in the 1960s motel strip are a good combo of atmosphere and tidiness. The grounds are pleasant, with a heated outdoor pool, a hot tub, and hammocks slung between the big cottonwoods in the summertime.

Unlike Taos Pueblo up the road, this pueblo has electricity and running water.

© ZORA O'NEILL

© ZORA O'NEILL

the front door of the Mabel Dodge Luhan House

In addition to being a tourist attraction, the ◖ **Mabel Dodge Luhan House** (240 Morada Ln., 575/751-9686, www.mabeldodgeluhan. com, $105 d) also functions as a homey bed-and-breakfast. Even the least expensive rooms, in a 1970s outbuilding, feel authentically old and cozy, with wood floors and antique furniture. In the main house, Mabel's original bedroom ($200) is the grandest (you can even sleep in her bed). But for those who don't mind waking at the crack of dawn, the upstairs solarium ($130) is gloriously sunny, with gorgeous views of the mountain. Either way, you'll feel a little like you're bunking in a museum (which means those who want modern amenities like air-conditioning should look elsewhere). Breakfast is a cut above standard B&B fare.

**Inn on the Rio** (910 E. Kit Carson Rd., 575/758-7199, www.innontherio.com, $140 d) might be more accurately called Motel on the Creek. But what a motel: Each of the 12 thick-walled rooms is meticulously decorated with an artistic eye. Rich colors liven up the walls, and vintage Southwestern knickknacks add flair without being kitschy. The vintage wall heaters, still cranking from the old motor-court days, keep the rooms as toasty as a fireplace would. A hot tub between the two wings, plus luxe sheets and locally made bath gels, add unexpected luxury. Pair this with longtime resident owners and a great morning meal, and you have all the benefits of a bed-and-breakfast without the feeling that you have to tiptoe in late at night.

### $150-250

**La Posada de Taos** (309 Juanita Ln., 575/758-8164, www.laposadadetaos.com, $159 d) hits the sweet spot between luxury comforts and casual charm—all the amenities are here, such as wood fireplaces (in five of the six rooms) and whirlpool tubs (in three), but the overall atmosphere is very homey and informal, and the decor is distinctly Taos without being heavy-handed, with sparing country touches. The price is right too, coming in on the lower end compared to other places with the same perks. El Solecito, in the older adobe section with its own back terrace, is particularly nice.

Of the two landmark hotels in town, **Hotel La Fonda de Taos** (108 S. Plaza, 575/758-2211, www.lafondataos.com, $159 d) has a few more modern perks, such as gas fireplaces and mostly reliable Internet. Plus, you can feel quite grand opening your balcony doors over the plaza (though you may also be subjected to predawn street-cleaning noise). Don't miss the small collection of D. H. Lawrence's erotic paintings (10am, noon, 2pm, 4pm, and 6pm; $3 admission). But the **Historic Taos Inn** (125 Paseo del Pueblo Norte, 575/758-2233, www. taosinn.com, $165 s, $185 d), established in 1936 in the former home of the town doctor, has a cozier feeling, even if it is slightly overpriced. Rooms in the main building are more historic feeling and cheaper; in the courtyard section or other outbuildings, you may get a kiva fireplace.

If you like eye candy, you'll love **Casa Gallina** (613 Callejon, 575/758-2306, www. casagallina.net, $185-250 d), a collection of five guest cottages, each decorated with an artist's eye for color and texture to showcase beautiful handicrafts from Taos and around the globe. Kitchens can be stocked with occasional goodies from the garden and eggs from resident hens (they're also pressed into service for the fresh and delicious breakfasts). And it doesn't hurt that the meticulous owner also happens to be a massage therapist.

An experiment in sustainable development, **El Monte Sagrado** (317 Kit Carson Rd., 575/758-3502, www.elmontesagrado.com) is a soothing retreat that's still walking distance from the plaza. If the solar panels and the ingenious water-reuse system weren't pointed out to you, you'd probably never even notice them. Instead, eclectic style draws the eye, especially in the five artist-decorated casitas ($209), which sport odd details like hand-painted trout, or in a lavish global suite ($429) filled with Chinese antiques. The standard Native American suites ($259) and Taos Mountain rooms ($209) are a little less exciting, with their white-linens-and-dark-wood look, but they carry a reasonable price for entry into the swank grounds, which include a lovely spa.

## RANCHOS DE TAOS

At the south edge of Ranchos de Taos, **Adobe & Pines Inn** (4107 Hwy. 68, 575/751-0947, www. adobepines.com) is built around an 1830s hacienda, shaded by old trees and overlooking a lush garden. Of the eight rooms, six are quite large (from $179), with especially lavish

bathrooms. But even the two smallest rooms ($109 and $119) have fireplaces—and everyone gets the exceptionally good breakfasts, with fresh eggs from the on-site chickens.

## ARROYO SECO

The best lodging bargain in the area is **The Abominable Snowmansion** (Hwy. 150 in Arroyo Seco, 575/776-8298, www.abominablesnowmansion.com). Conveniently set midway to the Taos Ski Valley in bustling "downtown" Arroyo Seco, this cheerful place offers bunks in dorm rooms ($25) and private rooms (from $50). In the summer, you can also camp (from $20) or sleep in a tepee ($55), and nosh on veggies from the hostel garden. But as the name suggests, winter sports fanatics are the main clientele, and if you don't want to be woken by skiers racing for the Chile Line bus outside, opt for an individual cabin with shared bath ($45).

## RIO GRANDE GORGE

For an only-in-Taos experience, stay the night in an **Earthship** (U.S. 64, 575/751-0462, www.earthship.com, $130 d). Four of the curvy, off-the-grid homes are available, with room for up to six people in the largest one. Not only does an Earthship feel like a Hobbit house with banana trees (in the south-facing greenhouse areas), but you're out in the larger, all-Earthship subdivision, with great views of the mountain. And yes, there's running water, refrigerators, and all the other comforts.

# Food

For a town of its size, Taos has a very broad selection of restaurants. If you're in town during a holiday or the peak ski season, you might want to make reservations, but otherwise they're not necessary, and the whole Taos dining scene is casual, with waiters often inquiring about your day skiing along with your preference for red or white wine. At one of the New Mexican places, be sure to try some *posole*—it's more

common here than in Albuquerque or Santa Fe, often substituted for rice as a side dish alongside pinto beans. Also, the breakfast burrito—a combo of scrambled eggs, green chile, hash browns, and bacon or sausage in a flour tortilla—is commonly wrapped up in foil and served to go, perfect if you want an early start hiking or skiing. Taos runs a cash economy—many smaller places don't take plastic.

# CENTRAL TAOS
## Café

The location of **World Cup** (102-A Paseo del Pueblo Norte, 575/737-5299, 7am-7pm daily, $3) on the corner of the plaza makes it a popular pit stop for both tourists and locals—the latter typically of the drumming, dreadlocked variety, lounging on the stoop.

## Breakfast and Lunch

**Michael's Kitchen** (304-C Paseo del Pueblo Norte, 575/758-4178, 7am-2:30pm Mon.-Thurs., 7am-8pm Fri.-Sun., $8) is famous for New Mexican breakfast items like huevos rancheros and blue-corn pancakes with pine nuts, served all day, but everyone will find something they like on the extensive menu at this downhome, wood-paneled family restaurant filled with chatter and the clatter of dishes. "Health Food," for instance, is a double order of chile cheese fries. The front room is devoted to gooey doughnuts, cinnamon rolls, and pie.

**Taos Diner** (908 Paseo del Pueblo Norte, 575/758-2374, 7:30am-2:30pm daily, $9) is as straight-ahead as its name. The pleasant surprise: Much of the enchiladas, egg plates, pancakes, and other typical diner fare is prepared with organic ingredients. Plus, the largely local scene provides good background theater to your meal—the servers seem to know everyone. There's a second outpost, **Taos Diner II** (216-B Paseo del Pueblo Sur, 575/751-1989, 5pm-10pm Thurs.-Sun.), just south of the plaza, that's also open for dinner.

Euro-Latino might be the best catch-all term for the menu at **◖ Gutiz** (812-B Paseo del Pueblo Norte, 575/758-1226, 8am-3pm Tues.-Sun., $10), which borrows from France and Spain and adds a dash of green chile. Start your day with a chocolate croissant or an impressive tower of scrambled eggs and spinach. Lunch sees traditional *croques monsieurs* or cumin-spiced chicken sandwiches.

At the homey **Dragonfly Café** (402 Paseo del Pueblo Norte, 575/737-5859, 11am-9pm Mon.-Sat., 9am-3pm Sun., $17), you can choose your table according to which novelty set of salt and pepper shakers you prefer. The menu is eclectic and hearty (a tender lamb kebab, for instance, or an elaborate kale salad); Sunday brunch features delicious baked goods and house-smoked trout. Early mornings (9am-11am), the front counter is open just for coffee and pastries.

Just west of the plaza, **El Gamal** (112 Doña Luz St., 575/613-0311, 9am-5pm Mon.-Wed., 9am-9pm Thurs.-Sun., 11am-3pm Sun., $7) brings the best of Israeli street snacks to Taos, with *shakshuka* (spicy scrambled eggs) and bagels for breakfast and falafel and *sabich* (eggplant and egg) sandwiches at lunch, washed down with a fizzy yogurt soda. There's also more standard hippie fare on the menu: homemade granola and the like.

In the Taos Inn, elegant **Doc Martin's** (125 Paseo del Pueblo Norte, 575/758-1977, 11am-10pm Mon.-Fri., 7:30am-2:30pm and 4pm-10pm Sat.-Sun., $10) is fine at dinner, but weekend brunch is when the kitchen really shines—especially on dishes like the Kit Carson (poached eggs on yam biscuits topped with red chile) or blue-corn pancakes with blueberries. The lunch menu is also tasty and doesn't reach the stratospheric prices of dinner.

## American

**5 Star Burgers** (1032 Paseo del Pueblo Sur, 575/758-8484, 11am-9pm Sun.-Thurs., 11am-10pm Fri.-Sat., $9) may occupy an old fast-food building, but that's where the resemblance to McD's ends. The place has been repainted with rich yellows and purples, and the menu boasts of hormone-free beef and local produce. The burgers are succulent, whether standard beef or Maryland crab, and vegetarians can choose from two excellent options. The final classy touch: wine and beer to wash it all down.

## Fresh and Local

**Graham's Grille** (106 Paseo del Pueblo Norte, 575/751-1350, 11am-9pm Mon.-Thurs., 10am-9pm Fri.-Sun., $18) is always busy because its menu satisfies simple cravings—for mac-and-cheese with green chile, say—in a hearty yet fresh way. There's a good selection of vegan and gluten-free dishes too. Spacious and airy, with lots of blond wood, the space is restful.

TAOS

Close to the entrance to Taos Pueblo, Tiwa Kitchen serves native foods.

There are two entrances and two separate dining rooms, as well as a patio near the back entrance (in the alley off the plaza).

**❰ The Love Apple** (803 Paseo del Pueblo Norte, 575/751-0050, 5pm-9pm Tues.-Sun., $20) wears its local, organic credentials on its sleeve, and the food delivers in simple but powerful flavor combinations, such as a quesadilla made sweet with apple and squash, and *posole* enriched with local lamb and caramelized onions. The atmosphere is like early-days Chez Panisse filtered through a northern New Mexican lens: a thick-walled adobe chapel, with candles glimmering against wine bottles along the walls. In summer, the restaurant is open seven nights a week, but it can get hot inside, so go early to snag a patio table.

## Italian

**Taos Pizza Out Back** (712 Paseo del Pueblo Norte, 575/758-3112, 11am-10pm daily, $8) serves up the best pie in town, using mostly local and organic ingredients. A glance at the menu—with items like green chile and black beans, and the popular portobello-gorgonzola combo—often makes first-timers blanch, but after a bite or two they're converts, like everyone else in town. Soups and a good Greek salad are also available, if you want to round out your meal.

## Mexican

*New* Mexican items may be on the menu at **❰ Antonio's** (122 Doña Luz St., 575/751-4800, 11am-9pm Mon.-Sat., $15), but the real good stuff here is from south of the border: rich *rellenos en nogada* (stuffed poblano peppers in walnut sauce), *carnitas* (crispy pork) with a tangy green salsa, and succulent *barbacoa de borrego* (pit-roasted lamb). Summer in the courtyard patio is lovely, with seats upstairs and down, and the interior is cozy in the winter.

For a more casual bite, hit tiny **❰ La Cueva** (135 Paseo del Pueblo Sur, 575/758-7001, 10am-9pm daily, $8), with its fantastically fresh and homemade-tasting dishes like chicken mole enchiladas, as well as exceptionally savory beans. No alcohol, though.

## New Mexican

A small, festively painted place on the north side of town, the family-run **Orlando's** (1114 Don Juan Valdez Ln., 575/751-1450, 10:30am-3pm and 5pm-9pm daily, $10) is invariably the first restaurant named by anyone, local or visitor, when the question of best chile comes up. That said, there are occasional whisperings about inconsistency (heresy!). But Orlando's still generally serves very satisfying, freshly made New Mexican standards, such as green-chile chicken enchiladas. The *posole* is quite good too—perfectly firm, earthy, and flecked with oregano. It's always busy, but a fire pit outdoors makes the wait more pleasant on cold nights.

On the road to Taos Pueblo, **Tiwa Kitchen** (575/751-1020, 7am-3pm Wed.-Mon., $13) is a friendly place serving all the usual chile-laced goods, plus nice hyper-local touches like fry bread with chokecherry syrup, or stuffed with buffalo meat. I've heard reports of inconsistency here, but it's well worth a stop.

## Fine Dining

◖ **El Meze** (1017 Paseo del Pueblo Norte, 575/751-3337, 5:30pm-9:30pm Mon.-Sat., $23) just might be Taos's best restaurant, thanks to both its exceptional food and tiny touches such as complimentary mineral water and plush blankets for cool evenings outside. Chef Frederick Muller shows the link between New Mexico, Spain, North Africa, and the Middle East, in dishes that are both brainy and deep-down satisfying: Delectable mountain trout is seasoned with Spanish paprika and served with a lavish herb salad, while fried green olives stuffed with blue cheese are the bar snack to beat in all of New Mexico. The setting is cozy in winter, inside a thick-walled hacienda, and expansive in summer, with a large patio with a view of Taos Mountain.

Open since 1988 but relatively new to this cozy adobe-house space, **Lambert's** (123 Bent St., 575/758-1009, 11:30am-2:30pm and 5:30pm-9pm daily, $32) is a Taos favorite, where everyone goes for prom, anniversaries, and other landmark events. Its New American menu is a bit staid, but everything is executed perfectly.

Get one of the game-meat specials if you can; otherwise, the signature pepper-crusted lamb is fantastic. A full liquor license means good classic cocktails, which you can also enjoy upstairs at the **Treehouse Lounge** (5pm-close).

## RANCHOS DE TAOS

Just off the plaza near the church, **Ranchos Plaza Grill** (6 St. Francis Plaza, 575/758-5788, 11am-3pm and 5pm-8:30pm Tues.-Sat., 11am-3pm Sun., $11) is a casual spot, known for its red *chile caribe,* made from crushed, rather than ground, chiles, for a really rustic effect.

Across the road, the chile at **Old Martina's Hall** (4140 Hwy. 68, 575/758-3003, 7am-9:30pm Wed.-Mon., $20) may be dialed down for out-of-state palates, but the place has other redeeming qualities. The once-derelict adobe theater with a soaring ceiling has been lovingly redone, and now hosts special events, and serves the likes of goat-cheese salads, farro risotto, and truffle fries. It's more casual for breakfast and lunch ($10 for sandwiches), and the light is lovely. Snoop around to see all the rooms and levels. The building is in Ranchos de Taos, across the road from the turn to the church.

## ARROYO SECO

◖ **Abe's Cantina y Cocina** (489 Hwy. 150, 575/776-8643, 7am-5:30pm Mon.-Fri., 7am-1:30pm Sat., $4), a creaky old all-purpose general store/diner/saloon, has earned fans all over for its satisfying and cheap breakfast burritos. There's a full menu of tacos and green-chile cheeseburgers, if you care to eat in, and a nice back patio. And don't miss the sweet, flaky empanadas next to the cash register in the store.

For coffee, though, you'll want to go next door to **Taos Cow** (485 Hwy. 150, 575/776-5640, 7am-6pm daily), a chilled-out coffee bar par excellence, with writers scribbling in one corner and flute players jamming in another. But it's the ice cream that has made the Taos Cow name (you'll see it distributed all around town, and elsewhere in New Mexico and Colorado). The most popular flavors are tailored to local tastes: Café Olé contains cinnamon and Mexican chocolate chunks, while

Cherry Ristra is vanilla with piñon nuts, dark chocolate, and cherries. Sandwiches ($9) are an option too, if you want real sustenance.

## TAOS SKI VALLEY

For nourishment by the ski area, fortify yourself with a green-chile cheeseburger or bowl of smoky-hot green-chile stew at the **Stray Dog Cantina** (105 Sutton Pl., Taos Ski Valley, 575/776-2894, 8am-9pm daily, $12), which gets busy after 3pm, when tired skiers come down from a day on the slopes. In the summer, it doesn't open till 11am on weekdays, but it's a nice destination for a drive, as you can sit on the deck and listen to the river flow by.

More adventurous drivers can head for **Bavarian Lodge** (100 Kachina Rd., 575/776-8020, 11:30am-9pm daily in ski season, Thurs.-Sun. only in summer, $15), way up Twining Road near the southeast edge of the ski area and Kachina Lift 4. You'll need four-wheel drive in winter; in summer, the huge front deck is a lovely place to have a beer (served by actual German speakers) in the pines. The menu is typical Wiener schnitzel and spaetzle.

"downtown" Arroyo Seco

Bavarian Lodge's deck is a fine spot for a beer.

# West on U.S. 64

Coming through the mountains on U.S. 64 gives you a dramatic descent into the Chama Valley, where U.S. 84 is one of the more spectacular drives in northern New Mexico. (It starts getting good down south in Abiquiu.)

## TRES PIEDRAS

This settlement about 30 miles west of Taos is only a handful of houses scattered around the crossroads of U.S. 64 and U.S. 285, but the **Chili Line Depot Café** (38429 U.S. 285, 575/758-1701, 8am-8pm daily, $7), just north of the intersection, is a bright spot for food in the wilderness, with friendly staff and hearty burritos. Call ahead to check hours.

## TIERRA AMARILLA AND LOS OJOS

U.S. 64 climbs up and over the Brazos Mountains, the view from the pass taking in the sheer limestone of 3,000-foot-high cliffs to the north. Descending into the golden valley along the Rio Chama, you soon reach the junction with U.S. 84 and the village of Tierra Amarilla, off the east side of the highway. Next door to the courthouse is the cool little **Three Ravens Coffeehouse** (15 Hwy. 531, 575/588-9086, 7am-4pm Mon.-Fri.), a labor of love and active community center; ask the owner about how he renovated the ancient adobe building.

Just a few miles north of Tierra Amarilla and west of the highway, Los Ojos is a two-block-long main street of adobe and Victorian wood-frame buildings, most connected in some way with **Ganados del Valle,** a cooperative established in 1983 to preserve the economy in the region, which for hundreds of years had been based on raising sheep and selling their products. But young people could no longer earn a living from this, and many of the most traditional weaving and spinning techniques had

already been lost. The cooperative was gradually able to provide employment for dozens of artists, administrators, and sheepherders, and in 1990, one of its founders, Maria Varela, who got her start as a Chicana activist in the Student Nonviolent Coordinating Committee in the 1960s, earned a MacArthur "genius grant" for her efforts.

One Ganados project, **Tierra Wools** (91 Main St., 575/588-7231, www.handweavers. com, 9am-6pm Mon.-Sat., 11am-4pm Sun. Apr.-Nov., 10am-4pm Mon.-Sat. Nov.-May), has become a pilgrimage site for anyone engaged in fiber arts. The shop showcases the work of village women—rugs, pillows, ruanas—as well as brilliantly dyed skeins of hand-woven wool yarn from the hardy, four-horned Churro sheep, a breed that the conquistadors introduced to New Mexico. If you're interested in the process, ask to see the dye vats out back. The last weekend in April, the **Spring Harvest Festival** involves demonstrations of sheep-shearing, hand-spinning, and more, along with music and other entertainment. The shop also offers two lodgings in a sweet rental **casita** (from $75), for those who'd like a taste of village life.

## EL VADO LAKE AND HERON LAKE STATE PARKS

These two reservoirs west of Tierra Amarilla are nearly linked. Of the two, **El Vado Lake State Park** (575/588-7247, www.nmparks. com, $5/car) is smaller but busier, as motorboats are permitted here, and it's a popular recreation spot, with large **campgrounds** at its south end (accessible via Hwy. 112, 17 miles southwest of Tierra Amarilla).

A 5.5-mile hiking trail leads from Shale Point, north of all of the campgrounds, up along the Rio Chama, across a bridge, up past Heron Dam, and into the south end of **Heron Lake State Park** (575/588-7470), which is also

© ZORA O'NEILL

**dramatic weather outside Tierra Amarilla**

TAOS

accessible via U.S. 64/84 and Highway 95. This lake is much quieter, as boat traffic is more restricted. It's a favored spot for wintering bald eagles and hawks, and several pairs of rare and enormous ospreys (raptors with wingspans of nearly five feet) settle here as well. During the week, free ranger-led hikes are available on request—ideally, call ahead to the park office to let the staff know you're coming. There are scores of attractive campsites all along the banks here.

Both lakes offer excellent fishing, though you'll need to arrange for a boat at **Stone House Lodge** (Hwy. 95, 575/588-7274, www.stonehouselodge.com, from $55/4 hours), as there are no rentals at the lake itself. The stretch of the Chama River from El Vado Dam to Abiquiu Lake is a very good rafting run, one of the best places in the state for a multiday trip. **Kokopelli Rafting Adventures** (505/983-3734, www.kokopelliraft.com) in Santa Fe and **Los Rios River Runners** (575/776-8854, www.losriosriverrunners.com) in Taos both run

trips through these remote canyons; expect to pay about $350 for a two-day outing.

## CHAMA

A tiny high-mountain town, Chama is a perfect getaway for people who find Durango or Silverton, Colorado, too crowded. With just 1,200 residents, the place was and still is focused on the railroad that begins here and threads its way between the mountains to Antonito, just over the state line. Even if the train isn't your thing, you can drive north on Highway 17 for the views.

And Chama can't grow much more, as it's hemmed in on both sides by land belonging to the Jicarilla Apache. The tribe operates an elite hunting ranch, The Lodge at Chama, that's a favorite politico getaway. But the natural attractions here are accessible to all—with the Rio Chama running right through town, you could theoretically walk out the front door of your (very affordable) rental cabin, snag a trout, and cook it up for dinner. On a day visit, the star of

## King Tiger and the *Mercedes*

The pastoral village of **Tierra Amarilla** gives little indication that it was once a battleground in the Chicano rights movement and the local Hispano fight for land-grant restitution. The Tierra Amarilla *merced* (land grant) was established in the 19th century, and when Nuevo México became a U.S. territory in 1848, the Treaty of Guadalupe Hidalgo specified it would be preserved. But cattle ranchers and the national forest system gradually appropriated it, so that, by the 1960s, many families in largely Hispano Rio Arriba County found themselves landless and subsisting on less than $1,500 per year.

Around this time, Reies López Tijerina, a charismatic activist in the growing Chicano movement, took up the land-grant cause. In 1967, he and more than 150 local men stormed the Tierra Amarilla courthouse, calling themselves the Political Confederation of Free City States and bearing a banner proclaiming "Give Us Our Land Back." Their plan was to make a citizen's arrest of the district attorney. But the DA was nowhere around, the activists wound up taking everyone in the courthouse hostage, and 300 National Guard troops were called in. The incident made headlines across the country, and Tijerina was an overnight legend. The press dubbed him King Tiger, and he was praised in the ballad "El Corrido de Rio Arriba," penned within weeks by the band Los Reyes de Albuquerque.

Trials the next year were equally gripping: Tijerina wept on the witness stand, a lawman present at the raid turned up murdered, and even New Mexico's governor gave heartfelt testimony. Tijerina came away with a minimal sentence for second-degree kidnapping. He went on to lead the Chicano faction as part of Martin Luther King Jr.'s Poor People's Campaign.

In Tierra Amarilla, meanwhile, the battle lines became hopelessly tangled. With seed money from a generous donor, the Sierra Club announced in 1970 that it would donate a new "land grant" to the area, but it failed to materialize—perhaps because environmentalists soon were battling the local sheepherders over the effects of grazing. In 1995, a local shepherd successfully sued Sierra Club for the never-applied donation, and the economic situation in the valley has somewhat improved. But many people must lease land on which to graze their sheep, resentments run deep, and the heroism of King Tiger is still recalled with feeling.

the show is the great steam train and its depot. If you stay a little longer, you'll have a chance to appreciate the remarkable vistas—particularly in the fall, when the mountains are blanketed with a thick patchwork of color.

### ◖ Cumbres & Toltec Scenic Railroad

The biggest attraction in Chama is the historic steam-driven **Cumbres & Toltec Scenic Railroad** (575/756-2151, www.cumbrestoltec. com), which has been running 64 miles from Chama up to Antonito, Colorado, since 1880. It is now jointly owned by the two neighboring states and maintained as a sort of museum.

You can travel the route in several ways, depending on how much of a train ride you want. The shortest ride is the four-hour Sunday Express, running only that day in summer. The year-round standard outing is from Chama to the midpoint, the ghost town of Osier, just over the state border—you hop off there, have lunch, stroll around, and get back on the train for the ride back down the pass ($79 adults, $39 kids). The whole trip takes a little more than six hours. Hardcore rail fans can go the whole way to Antonito—stopping in Osier for lunch—and return to Chama by bus, which takes eight hours ($95 adults, $49 kids); this way, you'll get to see the dramatic Toltec Gorge, just north of Osier.

Trains run most frequently in June, July, and early August, then again from late September

© ZORA O'NEILL

The Cumbres & Toltec steam train descends to Chama.

TAOS

to mid-October, for the autumn leaf season. Reservations are advised, and you can choose from three classes of service (windows open in tourist class, which is fun, but soot from the steam engine can make things a little gritty). The hot lunch included in the ticket price is pretty generous, with turkey and all the standard vegetables, plus buttermilk pie to finish.

You can also prowl around the depot and rail yards. Pick up a flyer at the station that identifies all the structures, as well as distinguishes between drop-bottom gondolas, flangers, and other specialized train cars.

## Recreation

Elk are prevalent throughout the mountains around Chama, and in the fall, the elk's distinctive mating call, or bugle, can be heard. Just off the north edge of town, the **Sargent Wildlife Management Area** has a viewing spot just inside the borders of the reserve, overlooking a big basin where the animals often graze. You can also hike into the center of the 20,000

acres, along the Rio Chama (for excellent fishing)—ask at the Chama visitors center for more information, and other area hiking spots.

## Accommodations

Chama has a reasonable selection of places to stay. The south side of town is largely devoted to rustic riverside cottage operations. **Chama River Bend** (2625 Hwy. 64, 575/756-2264, www.chamariverbendlodge.com) is probably the best maintained, with rooms in a motel-like strip (from $79), as well as cabins closer to the water (from $109), joined by an immaculate lawn.

Up near the depot, the lodging is a bit less rustic. The pretty ☾ **Chama Station Inn** (423 Terrace Ave., 575/756-2315, www.chamastationinn.com, $85 d) is just across from the train. Most of the nine rooms have wood floors, and all are decorated sparingly with country touches; the extra $10 for a deluxe room is well worth it, as it gets you a fireplace, a graceful high ceiling, and a little more space.

One of the least expensive beds can be found at **The Hotel** (501 S. Terrace Ave., 575/756-2416, www.thehotel.org, $64 d), a 1930s building with small, low-ceiling rooms that are nonetheless very clean, and a pleasant throwback—they match the train, in a way. At press time the business was for sale—check that a change in owners hasn't changed quality.

Campers will do well at the **Rio Chama RV Park** (U.S. 64, 575/756-2303, May-mid-Oct.), on the north edge of town, where tent sites ($14) are nestled amid tall trees and the river flows right by.

## Food

For an honest steak and potato, plus not-so-carnivorous items like grilled trout and cold beer, head to the **High Country Restaurant & Saloon** (2299 S. Hwy. 17, 575/756-2384, 11am-10pm daily, $10-20), a big wood-paneled operation that's popular with through-bikers as well as locals. It serves a massive breakfast buffet on Sunday 8am-noon.

**Sonny's Café** (2000 Hwy. 17, 575/756-1064, 7am-10pm daily, $12) serves "Spanish" (a.k.a. New Mexican) food, as well as tourist-friendly stuff like chicken-fried steak and burgers. Don't be put off by the industrial exterior; inside has a cabin vibe. Sometimes the food is a bit greasy, but given the shortage of dining options, it can be fine.

## Information and Services

Chama's **visitors center** (575/756-2235, 8am-6pm daily) is located at the junction of U.S. 64/84 and Highway 17, on the southern edge of town. In addition to maps and other info (for the whole state), it also provides free Internet access, coffee, and even apples from the tree outside, if you're there in the fall. In the winter, the office closes one hour earlier.

## JICARILLA APACHE NATION

The village of **Dulce** is the main town of the 750,000-acre **Jicarilla Apache Nation** (575/759-3242, www.jicarillaonline.com), which stretches north to the state line and south almost to the town of Cuba. The area is not the ancestral homeland of this band of Apache—originally, they had lived around the Platte and Arkansas Rivers in what is now central Colorado. But they were pushed south by white settlers in the 19th century, eventually scattering to live with other tribes as far south and east as Tucumcari. The current reservation wasn't designated until 1887, when the band's numbers had dwindled to just 330 and the group had split into two factions. Although the land was hard-won, it proved very fortunate when oil and gas were discovered on it in the 1930s. Profit from these resources, as well as a casino in Dulce and the luxurious Lodge at Chama, has made this a relatively prosperous reservation.

The tribe now numbers about 3,500 members, with 2,500 or so based in Dulce. The village is set in a high, grassy valley that feels hidden away from the rest of the world, with bison, cattle, and sheep grazing beneath the snowcapped Rockies.

## Festivals and Events

On the third week in July, the **Little Beaver Roundup** is a well-attended powwow and rodeo in Dulce that's open to visitors, and photography is permitted. Similar events, plus traditional footraces, mark **Go-Jii-Ya**, the tribe's feast day on September 15; it takes place at Stone Lake.

## Recreation

Most visitors come here to hunt mule deer and elk on the reservation lands, or to fish in one of the many lakes; contact **Jicarilla Game and Fish** (575/759-3255, www.jicarillahunt.com) for hunting and fishing rules and permits. **Stone Lake** ($5, or free with fishing and hunting licenses), 18 miles south of Dulce, has pretty campsites around its three miles of shoreline.

## Getting There

Dulce is 25 miles west of Chama on U.S. 64, about 30 minutes away.

TAOS

# The Enchanted Circle

The loop formed by U.S. 64, Highway 38, and Highway 522 is named for its breathtaking views of the Sangre de Cristo Mountains, including Wheeler Peak. The area is a cultural shift from Taos, much of it settled by Anglo ranchers and prospectors in the late 1800s and currently populated by transplanted flatlander Texans enamored of the massive peaks. The main towns on the route—Angel Fire and Red River—are just ski resorts. As the scenery is really the thing, you can drive the 84-mile route in a short day, with time out for a short hike around Red River or a detour along the Wild Rivers scenic byway.

If you head counterclockwise around the loop, you can take in the dramatic scene at the end of the drive, descending into the Taos Valley from Questa. But if you want to stop for

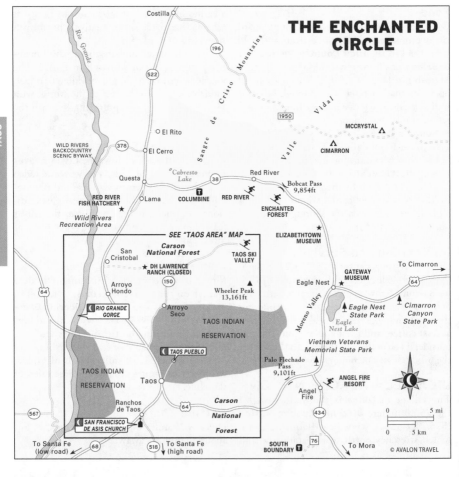

© AVALON TRAVEL

a meal, you should probably do it in Angel Fire, where the best eating options currently are.

To start, head east on Kit Carson Road, which turns into U.S. 64, winding along next to the Taos River and past numerous campgrounds and hiking trails. At Palo Flechado Pass, the road descends into the high Moreno Valley, a gorgeous expanse of green in early spring, and a vast tundra in the winter.

## ANGEL FIRE

A right turn up Highway 434 leads to this tiny ski village, a cluster of timber condos at the base of a 10,600-foot mountain. **Angel Fire Resort** (800/633-7463, www.angelfireresort. com, $66 full-day lift ticket) looks like a molehill in comparison with Taos Ski Valley, with a vertical drop of 2,077 feet. But it does have the asset of being far friendlier to snowboarders, and it has two freestyle terrain parks. For those with no snow skills at all, the three-lane, 1,000-foot-long tubing hill provides an easy adrenaline rush.

In summer, the resort transforms itself with activities like fishing at **Monte Verde Lake** ($25/person) and an elaborate zipline course ($105), the only one in New Mexico. Off the slopes, **Roadrunner Tours** (Hwy. 434 in town, 575/377-6416, www.rtours.com) does trail rides into the high mountains.

But the main warm-weather diversion is mountain biking, on the mountain itself, and on the storied **South Boundary Trail** (no. 164), which runs from a trailhead off Forest Road 76 south of Angel Fire. The route to Taos is about 5 vertical-seeming miles up and over the pass, then another 22 or so back to El Nogal trailhead on U.S. 64, a couple of miles east of Taos. **Gearing Up** (129 Paseo del Pueblo Sur, 575/751-0365) offers shuttle service, so you can bike one-way.

### Food

For lunch, **Hail's Holy Smoked BBQ** (3400 Hwy. 434, 575/377-9938, 11am-7pm Tues.-Thurs., 11am-8pm Fri.-Sat., $9) represents Texan cuisine, with smoked brisket, as well as *posole*, meatloaf, and homemade desserts.

**Hatcha's Grill** (3469 Hwy. 434, 575/377-7011, 10am-8pm Mon.-Tues. and Thurs.-Sat., 10am-7pm Sun., $9) represents good home-style New Mexican. If you happen to be around for dinner, check **The Pub 'n Grub** (52 N. Angel Fire Rd., 575/615-5446, 3pm-8pm daily in winter, 5pm-9pm daily in summer) for fresh, hearty bar food like buffalo burgers; it's closed October and November.

### Information

The Angel Fire CVB maintains a **visitors center** (3365 Hwy. 434, 575/377-6555, www. angelfirefun.com, 8am-5pm Mon.-Sat., 9am-3pm Sun.) just south of the T intersection with Angel Fire Road. The **Angel Fire Chamber of Commerce** (3407 Hwy. 434, 575/377-6353, www.angelfirechamber.org, 9am-5pm Mon.-Fri.) has its own office where the lobby is open 24 hours, so you can pick up brochures and maps anytime.

## VIETNAM VETERANS MEMORIAL STATE PARK

Back on U.S. 64, a few miles past the turn for Angel Fire, a swooping white structure rises on the hill to your left. This is the **Vietnam Veterans Memorial State Park** (575/377-2293, www.nmparks.com, 9am-5pm daily, chapel open 24 hours), built by Victor Westphall as a remembrance for his son David, who died in the war. When Westphall commissioned Santa Fe architect Ted Luna to design the graceful white chapel in 1968, it was the first such memorial for the casualties of Vietnam; an adjacent visitors center was built later and has expanded over the years. The complex is a site of pilgrimage for many, and the front grounds and bulletin boards testify to veterans' and families' devotion, as they are covered with additional informal monuments and messages.

## EAGLE NEST

At the junction of U.S. 64 and Highway 38, **Eagle Nest** is just a small strip of wooden buildings, all that's left of what was a jumping gambling town in the 1920s and 1930s, when bars hosted roulette and blackjack, and

© ZORA O'NEILL

Vietnam Veterans Memorial State Park

enterprising businessmen would roll slot machines out on the boardwalks to entice travelers en route to Raton and the train. The small lake here is the main focus of fun, but there's also good hiking just east in Cimarron Canyon State Park.

### Eagle Nest Lake State Park

East of U.S. 64, south of town, **Eagle Nest Lake** was created in 1918 with the construction of a privately financed dam on the Cimarron River. In addition to agricultural and mining uses, the lake supplied an ice-block industry in the winter. Today it's a state park, stocked with trout, and a popular summertime recreation spot (the Fourth of July fireworks display is legendary). For the marina and **visitors center** (575/377-1594, 8am-4:30pm daily, $5/car day use), look for the turn off U.S. 64 marked by a large RV park sign. Stop here for an exhibit on the dam, as well as camping ($10).

### Gateway Museum

The community **Gateway Museum** (U.S. 64, 575/377-5978, www.gatewaymuseum.org, 9:30am-4pm Mon.-Sat., 11am-4pm Sun., donation), at the east edge of town, gives a basic overview of the good old days and often hosts events, such as a mountain-man rendezvous.

### Accommodations and Food

**Laguna Vista Lodge** (575/377-6522, www.lagunavistalodge.com, $85-125 d) has standard motel rooms connected by a screened porch, as well as cabins and apartments with a view of the lake.

Retro **Kaw-Lija's** (Therma Dr., 575/377-3424, 11am-3pm Wed., 11am-8pm Fri.-Tues., $6) is the most reliable place to eat here, with burgers and the like. Opening hours can be erratic, and it closes in the winter. In the town's oldest hotel, built out of old railroad ties, **Calamity Jane's** (51 Therma Dr., 575/377-9530, 11am-9pm daily, $10) is the town's main restaurant and bar hangout, though the steakhouse food is inconsistent.

© ZORA O'NEILL

Eagle Nest Lake State Park

## Information

The **Eagle Nest Chamber of Commerce** (51 Therma Dr., 575/377-2420, www.eaglenest-chamber.org, 10am-4pm Mon.-Sat.) has an enthusiastic staff.

## ELIZABETHTOWN

Blink and you'll miss it: A small sign on the right side of the road 4.8 miles past Eagle Nest points to a left turn to the former gold-rush site of Elizabethtown, the first incorporated village in New Mexico. When gold was discovered in 1866, it grew to more than 7,000 people, then faded to nothing after a dredge-mining project failed in 1903. It's now a ghost town overshadowed by the stone ruins of the Mutz Hotel, the former center of social activity. The only signs of life are, ironically, in the **cemetery,** which is still used by residents of Colfax County and contains graves dating as far back as 1880. The quirky **Elizabethtown Museum** (575/377-3420, 10am-5pm daily June-Aug., $2 donation) details Elizabethtown's brief but lively history with items collected from local families'

troves, from the gold-rush years and much later (vintage pinball machines!).

## RED RIVER

As you descend into the valley, a somewhat bizarre apparition awaits: tidy rows of wooden buildings, all done up in Old West facades, complete with boardwalks and swinging saloon doors. No, it's not Elizabethtown of yore, it's the ski village of Red River. **Red River Ski & Snowboard Area** (575/754-2223, www.redriverskiarea.com, $66 full-day lift ticket) may be a baby hill compared with Taos, but it's nothing if not convenient: The trails run right into town, so it's walking distance from anywhere to the chairlift.

Like Elizabethtown, Red River was once a community of wild prospectors, carving copper, silver, and gold out of the hillsides. When that industry went bust, the town salvaged itself by renting out abandoned houses to vacationers escaping the summer heat at lower elevations. Just when air-conditioning started to become widespread in the 1950s,

a mountain-man rendezvous at the Gateway Museum in Eagle Nest

TAOS

the ski area opened, saving the town from a major slump. Red River still thrives, with a year-round population of only about 450. The town hosts a rowdy Memorial Day Motorcycle Rally, as well as a large Fourth of July parade and a Mardi Gras street party; contact the **Red River Chamber of Commerce** (575/754-2366, www.redrivernewmex.com) for more details.

### Cross-Country Skiing

On Highway 38 east of town, midway through Bobcat Pass, the **Enchanted Forest** cross-country ski area (575/754-6112, www.enchanted-forestxc.com, 9am-4:30pm, $16 full-day pass) has more than 20 miles of groomed trails through the trees and up the mountainside. Nonskiers can rent snowshoes. And, for a special overnight experience, you can trek in to a **yurt** ($50-85, depending on season), nicely appointed with a wood stove. It's available year-round, and snowmobile delivery of your gear is an option in winter.

### Hiking

This is the back side of Wheeler Peak, so the ascents are much more gradual, while still yielding dramatic views. Stop in at the **visitors center** (100 E. Main St., 575/754-3030, www.redriver.org, 8am-5pm daily), in the town hall, for area maps and trail guides. The least strenuous hiking option is the **Red River Nature Trail,** which starts in town at Brandenburg Park and runs two miles one-way, with signs identifying plants and geological formations.

### Food

Red River has the largest selection of lunch options on the Enchanted Circle, but none of them are particularly remarkable. Business turnover can be high here, but at least **Texas Reds** (400 E. Main St., 575/754-2922, 4:30pm-9pm Mon.-Thurs., 11:30am-3pm and 4:30pm-9pm Fri.-Sun., $17) is consistent; it has relocated twice and still packs 'em in for big steaks in a wood-paneled Western-look room, the floors scattered with peanut shells. For something lighter, **Dairy Bar** (417 E. Main St., 575/754-2479, 11am-4pm daily, $5) does burgers, chile, quesadillas, and of course soft-serve ice cream.

### Information

The chamber of commerce staffs a **visitors center** (100 E. Main St., 575/754-3030, 8am-5pm daily) inside the town hall, off the north side of the main drag.

## QUESTA

Arriving in Questa, at the junction of Highway 38 and Highway 522, you're back in Spanish New Mexico. The town, which now has a population of about 1,700, was established in 1842 and is still primarily a Hispano farming village, though a few Anglo newcomers have set up art galleries here. The heart of town is the 1841 **San Antonio Church,** which has been undergoing a multiyear restoration. When one wall first collapsed in 2008, the community split over whether to save the adobe structure or raze it; finally, a new priest managed to unify a volunteer crew, which has

the liveliest spot in the old mining camp of Elizabethtown

been at work gradually rebuilding on nights and weekends.

The few eating options here can't be recommended, though a new restaurant, **Los Amigos** (2422 Hwy. 522, 575/586-2165, 9am-7pm Mon.-Sat., 9am-5pm Sun., $7), at the main intersection, had just opened at press time.

## Wild Rivers Recreation Area

The **Wild Rivers Recreation Area** is a portion of Carson National Forest, accessible via a road north of Questa. It encompasses the confluence of the Rio Grande and Red River, where the two flows have forged dramatic canyons. Steep trails lead down into the gorge and along the river, so you can make a full loop, and white-water rafting is very popular here in the Class III rapids of the Red River Confluence run. Five developed **campgrounds** (but no RV hookups; $7/car) on the rim can be reached by car, or you can hike in to campsites by the river ($5).

The area feels very remote and wild, especially once you get down one of the trails—you will probably see red-tailed hawks circling over the gnarled, centuries-old piñon and juniper trees, and perhaps even river otters, reintroduced into the Rio Grande here in 2008. The easiest way to explore is along the 1.7-mile **Pescado Trail,** south along the Red River rim and down to the Red River Fish Hatchery, past Questa.

The access road to the recreation area is three miles north on Highway 522 from the main Questa intersection, then west on Highway 378, which leads through the town of El Cerro and to the area's **visitors center** (575/586-1150, 9am-6pm daily June-Aug., $3/car day use).

## D. H. Lawrence Ranch

After Questa, the view opens up as you descend into the valley, with mesas stretching far to the west. Five miles east on a rutted road is the 160-acre **Kiowa Ranch,** where English writer and provocateur D. H. Lawrence lived in 1924 and 1925 with his wife, Frieda, and the painter Dorothy Brett. Unfortunately, the University of New Mexico, which manages the ranch, has closed the site to regular visitors. To be honest, though, there wasn't a lot to see: two tiny cabins (one where painter Dorothy Brett lived), a gnarled pine that inspired Georgia O'Keeffe's painting *The Lawrence Tree,* and "that outhouse of a shrine," as Mabel Dodge Luhan referred to the building where the writer's ashes are mixed into a concrete slab.

# Information and Services

## TOURIST INFORMATION

The **Taos Visitors Center** (1139 Paseo del Pueblo Sur, 575/758-3873, www.taos.org, 9am-5pm daily) is an expansive and helpful place a few miles south of the plaza. Stop here for flyers and maps galore, free coffee, and the very thorough weekly news and events bulletin (also posted online), which includes gallery listings, music, and more.

### Books and Maps

**Moby Dickens** (124-A Bent St., No. 6 Dunn House, 575/758-3050, 10am-6pm daily) is Taos's best bookstore, well informed on local history and culture and stocking plenty of maps, as well as rare books, a good CD collection, and assorted gifts.

### Local Media

The *Taos News* comes out every Thursday, and it contains the *Tempo* entertainment section, with music, theater, and film listings. Many hotels offer free copies of *Tempo* to their guests. The *Albuquerque Journal* publishes a special northern edition daily, focused on local issues.

### Radio

While you're in town, don't miss tuning in to **KTAO** (101.9 FM), a local radio station that's all solar-powered. The musical programming is broad, and you're sure to learn interesting tidbits about the community as well.

## SERVICES
### Banks

**US Bank** (120 W. Plaza, 575/737-3540, 9am-5pm Mon.-Fri.), just off the southwest corner of the plaza, is the most convenient bank and ATM while on foot. The drive-through service at **Centinel Bank of Taos** (512 Paseo del Pueblo Sur, 575/758-6700, 9am-5pm Mon.-Fri.) is easily accessible from the main drag.

### Post Offices

The Taos **post office** (710 Paseo del Pueblo Sur, 575/751-1801, 9am-1pm and 2pm-4:30pm Mon.-Sat.) is on the south side; there's another on the north side (318 Paseo del Pueblo Norte, 575/758-2081, 8:30am-5pm Mon.-Fri.), next to the Dragonfly Café.

### Internet

**Wired?** (705 Felicidad Ln., 575/751-9473, www.wiredcoffeeshop.com, 8am-5pm daily), behind Albertson's off La Posta Road, is a laid-back Internet café and business center with a big garden, good veggie and raw-food meals, and free wireless access for laptops; computer use is $2 for 15 minutes.

# Getting There and Around

## BY CAR

From Santa Fe, the drive to Taos takes about 1.5 hours (70 miles) along the most direct route, which is the "low road" through the river valley (via Española, U.S. 84/285 to Hwy. 68). If taking the high road (via Chimayó and Truchas, mostly on Hwy. 76), plan on at least 2 hours for the 80-mile drive.

From Albuquerque, add at least an hour's travel time for the 60-mile drive up I-25 (the most direct route).

Once in Taos, you will need a car to get to outlying sights, but will also have to bear the daily traffic jam on Paseo del Pueblo. There are paid parking lots close to the plaza, and a free one down Kit Carson Road less than a quarter mile. For rental cars, **Enterprise** (1350 Paseo del Pueblo Sur, 575/758-5333, www.enterprise.com, 8am-5pm Mon.-Fri., 9am-noon Sat.) has a convenient office.

## BY BUS AND SHUTTLE

For pickup at the Albuquerque airport, **Twin Hearts Express** (575/751-1201, $50 one-way) runs a shuttle four times a day (11:30am, 1:30pm, 3:30pm, and 5:30pm), with drop-offs at most hotels. Allow at least 2.5 hours for travel time.

From Santa Fe, there's great weekend service from city-sponsored **Taos Express** (575/751-4459, www.taosexpress.com, $10 round-trip), which runs from Taos and back once on Friday afternoon, and again on Saturday and Sunday, completing a loop in the morning and another in the afternoon. The one-way trip takes 1 hour and 40 minutes.

In Santa Fe, the bus picks up passengers near the Rail Runner main depot (Montezuma at Guadalupe) and at the South Capitol station. In Taos, it drops off at the Loretto parking lot, one block west of the plaza; going back south, it also picks up passengers at the Sagebrush Inn (1508 Paseo del Pueblo Sur). The schedule follows the Rail Runner's arrival in Santa Fe (and it can carry bicycles), making it a potentially seamless three-hour trip all the way from Albuquerque. It can also stop at the Santa Fe airport. Reservations are required.

Within Taos, the **Chile Line bus** runs north-south from the Ranchos de Taos post office to the Taos Pueblo, approximately every 40 minutes 7:30am-5pm Monday-Friday. The fare (exact change only) is $0.50. Mid-December-April, a **ski shuttle** ($1) runs to Taos Ski Valley, with five buses daily making stops at key motels en route to the mountain; not all buses stop at all hotels. Contact the city (575/751-4459, www.taosgov.com) for maps and schedules.

TAOS

# LAS VEGAS AND THE NORTHEAST

Historically and geographically, the northeast section of the state bridges central New Mexico and the great American plains. The alpine Pecos Wilderness forms a natural barrier east of Santa Fe, then the land levels out into a rolling, grassy vista stretching to the horizon. This was the northern border for the Spanish, and only after Mexico gained its independence

© ZORA O'NEILL

# HIGHLIGHTS

LOOK FOR ◖ TO FIND RECOMMENDED SIGHTS, ACTIVITIES, DINING, AND LODGING.

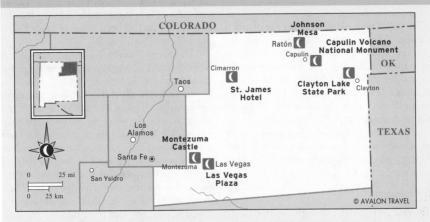

© AVALON TRAVEL

◖ **Las Vegas Plaza:** The heart of "Meadow City" is this grassy spread surrounded by grand territorial and old adobe buildings. It's so well preserved, it has been used frequently as a movie set—but it's blessedly free of souvenir shops (page 174).

◖ **Montezuma Castle:** The glamour of the early railroad era is captured in this Queen Anne-style confection built as a resort hotel, now used as a college student center. Schedule a tour of the interior if possible, and don't miss the nearby hot springs (page 175).

◖ **Clayton Lake State Park:** Stop by this oasis in the prairie to stand in—or at least near—the footsteps of giants. Dinosaurs left their immense tracks in the prehistoric mud here 100

million years ago (page 184).

◖ **Capulin Volcano National Monument:** To get a great view across the plains, wind your way along the unnervingly narrow road that spirals up this perfectly round peak. You can also hike down into the crater (page 187).

◖ **Johnson Mesa:** Outside of Taos, this is probably the most striking scenery in northern New Mexico—the Rockies rise up to the north, and the plains slip away far below the edge of this empty pastoral expanse (page 189).

◖ **St. James Hotel:** The history of Cimarron, and its present social life, is intrinsically caught up with this old inn, the state's best 19th-century hotel (page 194).

NORTHEAST

in 1821 were traders' wagon trains welcome to enter the area from Kansas. For the three decades when the Santa Fe Trail was at its peak of activity, then the subsequent prosperity brought in by the railroad, northeastern New Mexico was a lively place.

Now, though, especially since the Dust Bowl ate away at the eastern edge, it's a relatively silent swath of territory, traversed only by cattle

and motorists. The latter usually stick to the interstate that runs north to Colorado. A few people stop to visit the town of Raton, at the base of a precipitous pass over the Rockies, or Cimarron, deeper in the mountains and that much more untouched by time. Just off I-25 in the lowlands, Las Vegas is the region's biggest center of activity. No bright lights and high rolling here: This Vegas is a college town with a population of about 14,000, a sedate place extending from a tree-shaded plaza edged with colonial and Victorian buildings that manage to be well preserved without feeling like a theme park. This can be refreshing after Santa Fe's enforced historicism.

The other major landmark on the plains is Capulin Volcano, which was active 60,000 years ago. Its cinder cone rises a thousand feet above the surrounding land, and from its rim you can see the earth fall away to the edge of the Sangre de Cristo Mountains. This area may not exude the barren drama of New Mexico's western desert or the thrill of the rugged mountains, but these placid flatlands, interrupted by only a few roads and small towns, offer a sense of space and tranquility unmatched elsewhere in the state.

## HISTORY

Dinosaurs traipsed through in the Early Cretaceous (most notably leaving footprints north of Clayton), and Comanche and other Plains Indians crisscrossed the area for hundreds of years before the Spanish arrived. But northeast New Mexico is even more indelibly marked by the Santa Fe Trail. The trade route proved to be the thin end of the wedge that opened up the West to American domination. First came goods from Missouri to the hungry market in Santa Fe (previously restricted to trading only with Spain), then came military supplies during the Mexican-American War, followed by homesteaders, prospectors, and entrepreneurs.

It was these prospectors who caused substantial trouble in the Rocky Mountains when, in 1866, gold was discovered not far from the northern branch of the Santa Fe Trail. Scores of hopeful miners flooded in—never mind the strike was on the Maxwell Land Grant, 1.7 million acres of private property. By the 1870s, a battle was brewing between the land-grant owners and the squatting miners. The resulting Colfax County War involved assassinations, lynchings, and Republican conspiracies in Santa Fe. Finally, an 1887 Supreme Court ruling gave squatters the boot, along with Spanish

families who had been settled for generations. But by then, the railroad was bringing surer money than gold anyway—as well as another point of conflict. Anglo businessmen piled off the train in Raton and East Las Vegas, buying up land and earning the wrath of the Hispano shepherds who had been living in a much simpler economy for centuries.

Meanwhile, homesteaders on the plains northeast of Las Vegas had set the stage for another drama. Beginning in 1862, when the Homestead Act doled out 160-acre parcels to any family with enough nerve to take them, the would-be farmers struggled to work the thin topsoil that lay over limestone bedrock. They were able to displace the native Plains Indian tribes in many areas, but they had no defense against the drought that struck in the 1920s. Soon, this was the western edge of the Dust Bowl, where the sky turned black for days at a time and children died from inhaling the grit. It was an unrivaled economic and environmental disaster that emptied the region of all but the ranchers who had initially settled the area for the United States.

After many decades, the northern plains' fortunes finally turned again, with the discovery of carbon-dioxide fields and the expansion of cattle ranching. But the area remains sparsely populated, just as much of the former Maxwell Land Grant is still relative wilderness.

## PLANNING YOUR TIME

On the surface, Clayton, Las Vegas, Raton, and Cimarron are all one-night towns, as there are few formal sights and little to do in the evenings. But you could easily settle down somewhere for a few days (Cimarron or Las Vegas are the strongest candidates) while you investigate the spaces in between, hiking, fishing, or just driving the pretty back roads. The drive to Las Vegas on I-25 is a fairly dull one just for a day trip from Santa Fe, but the town is a great diversion if you're staying a while or heading farther into the plains. Few tourists make it all the way to Clayton, in the farthest corner. But if you think of it as a point of contrast with central, mountainous New Mexico,

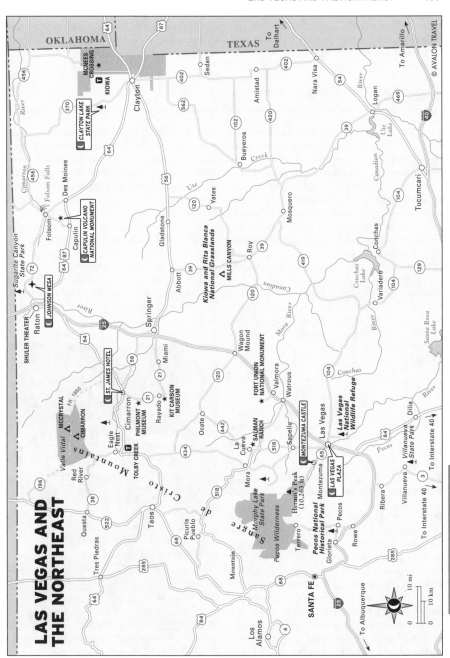

# LAS VEGAS AND THE NORTHEAST

NORTHEAST

it can be a worthwhile journey. Winter can be harsh here: Tourist services in Raton and Cimarron are severely curtailed beginning in September and lasting through the end of April, and a cold snap in early fall is not uncommon.

# Pecos and Villanueva

Santa Fe backs up against the 223,000 acres of the Pecos Wilderness, the second-largest nature reserve in New Mexico (after the Gila, in the southwest). The mountain streams seethe with trout, and elk ramble through emerald-green meadows. In the 2011 Pacheco Fire, a chunk in the center of the forest burned, but the wilderness is still fine in many accessible spots. Villanueva, a small village near a gem of a state park, is a short drive southeast.

On the drive out on I-25, near exit 295, you pass the site of the westernmost Civil War battle in the United States. The Battle of Glorieta Pass raged March 26-28, 1862, part of a Confederate plan to invade the West with a force of Texans—a plan that was foiled in this decisive rout. The fight is reenacted here annually.

## PECOS

The gateway to the wilderness area is the former logging town of Pecos, where mountain men rub shoulders with alternative healers and monks. To reach the village, head east along I-25 to Glorieta (exit 299) and Highway 50; or take the alternate route via Highway 63 (exit 307), which passes the ruins of Pecos Pueblo, the regional power before the Spanish arrived.

### Pecos National Historical Park

When the Spanish made first contact with local people in 1540, Pecos was the largest pueblo in the region, population 2,000, in four- and five-story stone buildings sealed with mud. In **Pecos National Historical Park** (Hwy. 63, 505/757-7200, www.nps.gov/peco, 8am-6pm daily June-Aug., 8am-5pm Sept.-May, $3), the ruins of this complex community are accessible to visitors via a 1.5-mile paved interpretive trail that winds through the remnants of the Pecos

Pueblo walls, a couple of restored kivas, and, most striking, the shell of a Franciscan mission. Free **guided tours** around various parts of the site run daily at 10am and at 2pm during the summer and Friday-Sunday at 1:30pm in winter. In winter, the visitors center closes at 4:30pm.

On a ridge looking out on the plains to the northeast and the mountains behind, the park provides a beautiful view today; around 1100, when the area was being settled with the first villages, it also provided a livelihood. The ridge was part of a natural trade path between the Rio Grande farmers and the buffalo hunters of the Great Plains. Both groups met in Pecos,

ruins of a Franciscan mission inside Pecos National Historical Park

itself an agricultural community, to barter. What began as a series of small villages consolidated in the 14th century into a city, with a layout so orderly it appears to have been centrally planned, and by 1450, the fortress of Pecos was the major economic power in the area.

Perhaps it was the city's trading culture and relative worldliness that made the Pecos Indians welcome Francisco Vásquez de Coronado and his men in 1540 with music and dancing rather than bows and arrows. Nearly 60 years later, Don Juan de Oñate visited the area and ordered a mission church built—a giant structure with six bell towers and buttresses 22 feet thick in some spots. The building was destroyed during the Pueblo Revolt, however, and the Pecos people dug a kiva smack in the middle of the ruined convent area—symbolic architecture, to say the least.

But the Spanish came back, and they were even welcomed and aided at Pecos. When they built a new church in the early 1700s, it was noticeably smaller, maybe as a form of compromise. But even as a hybrid Pueblo-Spanish culture developed, the Indian population was falling victim to disease and drought. When the Santa Fe Trail opened up in 1821, Pecos was all but empty, and in 1838, the last city dwellers marched to live with fellow Towa speakers at Jemez Pueblo, 80 miles west; their descendants still live there today.

## Pecos Wilderness

Stop in at the **Pecos Wilderness ranger station** (Hwy. 63, 505/757-6121, 8am-4:30pm Mon.-Fri.) on the south end of Pecos town to get maps and information on trail conditions, as well as the eight developed campgrounds. Fires and floods in 2013 had caused serious damage to some of the main trails accessible via Highway 63.

At this high elevation, summer temperatures are rarely above 75°F and can dip below freezing at night, so pack accordingly. Budget cuts mean many outhouses and trash bins are locked; be prepared to dig holes as necessary, and pack out your trash.

Highway 63 runs north out of town,

following the Pecos River past several fishing access points. In the tiny settlement of Terrero is a **general store** (1911 Hwy. 63, 505/757-6193, 8am-6pm daily in summer). The road then narrows and rises to reach the onetime mining camp of Cowles—now just a wide spot in the road. Immediately north, Forest Road 223 leads 4.5 miles to Iron Gate Campground and **Hamilton Mesa Trail** (no. 249), a fairly level 3.8-mile hike to a wide-open meadow—look for strawberries among the wildflowers.

At the end of Highway 63 (bear right where the dirt road forks), **Cave Creek Trail** (no. 288) runs out of Panchuela Campground. It's an easy 3.6-mile out-and-back that follows a small waterway up to some caves that have been carved out of the white limestone by the stream's flow. If you go past the caves, up a steep hillside, you reach an area burned in the 2013 Jaroso Fire; this is not recommended, due to the danger of falling trees. Another short out-and-back is **Jack's Creek Trail** (no. 257), out of the campground of the same name. Turn back at the junction with Dockweiler Trail (no. 259), about four miles in, to avoid the burned area. All trails in this area require a $2 trailhead parking fee; additional fees apply for camping or picnicking, depending on the spot.

## Accommodations and Food

For staying the night, the **Benedictine Monastery** (Hwy. 63, 505/757-6600, www.pecosmonastery.org, $75 s) maintains simple rooms with beautiful views; the rate is a suggested donation and includes meals. Several mountain lodges, such as **Los Pinos Ranch** (505/757-6213, www.lospinosranch.com, $145 pp), offer multiday packages with all meals and a variety of outdoor activities.

At the main crossroads in Pecos, where Highway 50 meets Highway 63, **Frankie's at the Casanova** (Hwy. 63, 505/757-3322, 8am-2pm daily, 5:30pm-8:30pm Fri.-Sat., $9) is the town social center, serving massive breakfasts, lunches, and dinners, which range from plain old enchiladas to pasta Alfredo with shrimp. During summer, dinner is served on a few weeknights as well.

## SOUTH TO VILLANUEVA

From exit 323 off I-25, 14 miles past Pecos, Highway 3 is a beautiful drive south. The two-lane road runs through a narrow valley with rich red earth cut into small farm plots. Villages such as Ribera and El Pueblo were founded in the late 18th century, after the establishment of the San Miguel del Vado Land Grant in this valley. Named for a ford *(vado)* on the Pecos River, this area later became the official customs point for caravans entering Mexican territory via the Santa Fe Trail.

You'll also pass 【 **La Risa Café** (Hwy. 3, 575/421-3883, 11am-8pm Thurs.-Sat., 8am-6pm Sun., $9), where the shady screened patio is a popular stop for locals and day-trippers to enjoy spicy New Mexican food and astounding slices of pie. Farther along is the tiny, family-run **Madison Winery** (Hwy. 3, 575/421-8028, 10am-5pm Sat., noon-5pm Sun. in summer, other times by appointment), between El Pueblo and Sena.

**Villanueva,** centered on its own historic church, is the largest settlement along the road; it has a small general store, handy if you're staying at the nearby campground.

### Villanueva State Park

The small but beautiful **Villanueva State Park** (575/421-2957, www.nmparks.com, $5/car) occupies a bend in the Pecos River against 400-foot-tall sandstone cliffs. Because the parkland is small, it doesn't draw big crowds—even in the summer, it's busy only on the weekends. Otherwise, you'll probably have the 2.5-mile Canyon Trail to yourself and the choice of **camping** ($8) on the cottonwood-shaded river bottom (near flush toilets and shower), or up on the canyon rim amid juniper and piñon. The river is stocked with trout and can be deep enough for canoeing. Spring comes early, filling trails with wildflowers by late April; fall is a burst of red scrub oak and yellow cottonwood leaves, in sharp contrast to the evergreens.

# Las Vegas

The city in New Mexico that suffers most from misplaced expectations, Las Vegas is a quiet community about 50 miles northeast of Santa Fe. Its centerpiece is a tree-shaded plaza, and nearly a thousand registered historic buildings stand in the surrounding blocks.

Set near Starvation Peak—a landmark butte on the Santa Fe Trail—the city was a Spanish settlement well before it was a stop on the trade route. In the middle of town, the Gallinas River still marks the historic division between the 1835 settlement of Nuestra Señora de los Dolores de las Vegas (Our Lady of Sorrows of the Meadows) and the railroad boom town of East Las Vegas, begun in 1879. The old Hispano plaza-centered town and the new, largely Anglo community didn't merge until 1970—probably because for decades, East Las Vegas was huge, anarchic, and populated with cattle rustlers, scam artists, and outlaws like Doc Holliday, who owned a saloon here for

a year. Poor relations between the two towns were exacerbated by fights over land use. A band of Hispano vigilantes called the Gorras Blancas (White Caps) went around snipping through Anglo fencing in the night, so that their sheep could continue to graze.

But the changes wrought by the railroad were irrevocable, and along with Anglo economic supremacy came telephones, an electric streetcar, an opera house, and other trappings of modern life. For a period in the late 19th century, "Meadow City" was the biggest metropolis between Missouri and San Francisco, with an opera theater and a huge Harvey House hotel, the Castañeda. Times have changed (that hotel is now derelict), but the New Mexico Normal School, established during this early boom period to train teachers, is now Highlands University, and philanthropist Armand Hammer established a branch of the United World College system outside of town

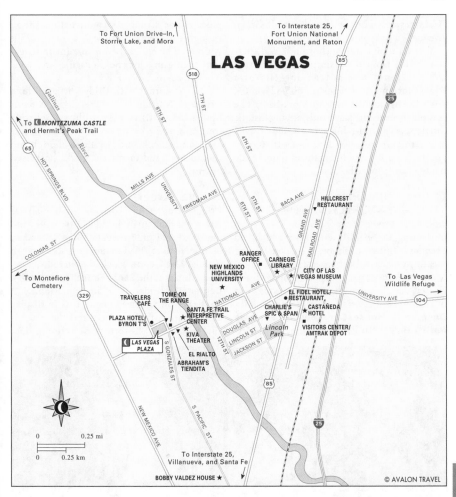

To Fort Union Drive-In,
Storrie Lake, and Mora

To Interstate 25,
Fort Union National
Monument, and Raton

**LAS VEGAS**

518

85

25

8TH ST

7TH ST

Gallinas River

To **C** *MONTEZUMA CASTLE*
and Hermit's Peak Trail

65

HOT SPRINGS BLVD

4TH ST

MILLS AVE

UNIVERSITY

FRIEDMAN AVE

5TH ST

6TH ST

BACA AVE

GRAND AVE

RAILROAD AVE

HILLCREST
RESTAURANT

COLONIAS ST

To Montefiore
Cemetery

329

RANGER
OFFICE

NEW MEXICO
HIGHLANDS
UNIVERSITY

CARNEGIE
LIBRARY

CITY OF LAS
VEGAS MUSEUM

AVE

NATIONAL

To Las Vegas
Wildlife Refuge

UNIVERSITY AVE

104

TRAVELERS
CAFE

TOME ON
THE RANGE

SANTA FE TRAIL
INTERPRETIVE
CENTER

PLAZA HOTEL/
BYRON T'S

**C** LAS VEGAS
PLAZA

KIVA
THEATER

S GONZALES ST

DOUGLAS AVE

LINCOLN ST

12TH ST

JACKSON ST

CHARLIE'S
SPIC & SPAN

Lincoln
Park

EL FIDEL HOTEL/
RESTAURANT

CASTAÑEDA
HOTEL

VISITORS CENTER/
AMTRAK DEPOT

EL RIALTO

ABRAHAM'S
TIENDITA

85

NEW MEXICO AVE

S PACIFIC ST

25

0        0.25 mi

0        0.25 km

To Interstate 25,
Villanueva, and Santa Fe

BOBBY VALDEZ HOUSE ★

© AVALON TRAVEL

in the 1980s. Together, the two institutions cater to several thousand students, who give the town a lot of its life.

## SIGHTS

The best way to explore Las Vegas and appreciate its historic architecture is on foot. Start on the old plaza and notice how the building styles and the street layouts change as you head east across Bridge Street, which leads toward the New Mexico Highlands University campus. Douglas Avenue, two blocks south, is the main shopping district on the east side; still farther east are the rail yards, now relatively derelict but at one time the liveliest part of town.

If Las Vegas looks vaguely familiar, maybe it's because you watched the Cold War scare flick *Red Dawn* too many times, or you're a fan of Tom Mix Westerns such as *The Tenderfoot's Triumph*. The city was the setting for scores of silent films shot in the early 20th century, as well as later productions such as *Easy Rider, All the Pretty Horses,* and *No Country for Old Men. Red Dawn* used the area most thoroughly; the

"Calumet Says Howdy" mural just off Grand Avenue is a relic of the shoot.

You can pick up a thorough walking-tour guide from the visitors center or from the **Citizens' Committee for Historic Preservation** (116 Bridge St., 505/425-8803, www.lvcchp.org, 10am-3pm Mon.-Sat.). The pamphlet covers the plaza and outlying historic districts, each with a distinctive building style; some structures date back as far as 1846. The group also occasionally organizes tours inside many of the private homes.

### Las Vegas Plaza

The large, tree-edged **Las Vegas Plaza** on the west side of town shows only a few remnants of the original Spanish settlement, which had been built entirely of adobe, in a defensive ring meant to be sealed off against Apache raids. Many buildings later got spruced up with territorial details when the railroad brought in bricks, tin cornices, and other modern details. **Desmarais House/Our Lady of Sorrows Parish Hall** (1810 E. Plaza) is one of the few older adobe structures (built before 1883), though the curvy roofline is a bit of 1930s whimsy. The old *acequia madre* (main irrigation ditch) runs along South Pacific Street, one block south of the plaza.

On the corner with Bridge Street, **Plaza Drugs** (178 Bridge St., 505/425-5221, 8am-6pm Mon.-Sat.) is a great old-school soda fountain and pharmacy. Sip a cherry-lime soda and check out the Lego model and the house-brand medicinal herbs, harvested nearby.

### Bridge Street

**Bridge Street,** which leads toward the Gallinas River, was built up in the mid-19th century and now mixes old and new: A tattoo parlor and an herb store have filled in empty spaces next to Popular Dry Goods, which deals in rodeo wear. The exhibits at the **Santa Fe Trail Interpretive Center** (116 Bridge St., 10am-3pm Mon.-Sat.) are heavy on yellowed documents in display cases. But entrance is free, and the place is run by the local historic preservation group,

relaxing on Las Vegas Plaza

© ZORA O'NEILL

NORTHEAST

members of which are happy to answer questions of all kinds.

## East Las Vegas

New Mexico Highlands University occupies either side of the street once you cross the river. Up the hill and past the campus, you enter some of the finer residential districts, with many examples of beaux arts and Queen Anne architecture—the best is around **Carnegie Park** (4th St. and National Ave.). The park's green lawn surrounds the elegant domed **Carnegie Library** (500 National Ave., 505/426-3304, 8am-5pm Mon.-Fri., 8am-noon Sat.), a mini-Monticello. Of the more than 2,500 libraries around the world funded by steel magnate and philanthropist Andrew Carnegie, it's one of the few that still houses the public library, and only one of three in the state to have survived.

About five blocks south is Douglas Avenue, where the commercial buildings range from sleek 1940s storefronts to the enormous Romanesque **Masonic Temple** (514 Douglas Ave.) of 1895. Farther south still, **Lincoln Park** (Lincoln and 7th Sts.), is another square surrounded by gracious large homes.

## City of Las Vegas Museum and Rough Riders Memorial Collection

It takes almost more time to say the name of the **City of Las Vegas Museum and Rough Riders Memorial Collection** (727 Grand Ave., 505/426-3205, www.lasvegasmuseum.org, 10am-4pm Tues.-Sat., $2 donation) than it does to tour it, but the exhibits are informative and based on well-chosen artifacts. It starts with a glass case of pots and baskets from the pre-Columbian era, but quickly gets to Vegas's glam years in the late 19th century, when the town supported two opera houses and had all the trappings of high society and general civilization, including the first telephone line in the state, installed in 1879.

One room is dedicated to souvenirs from Teddy Roosevelt's Rough Riders, the spirited regiment he led in the Spanish-American War of 1898. The soldiers, chosen for their skills with horses and guns, were volunteers from all over the West, with the majority from New Mexico; they chose Las Vegas as the site of their first reunion and continued to gather over the years, until the last soldier died in 1975.

## Montefiore Cemetery

On the west edge of town at the end of Colonias Street (you'll probably want to drive), the rambling **Montefiore Cemetery** is an interesting place to visit, especially the back corner, dedicated to the sizeable Jewish population that settled here in the mid-1800s and set up stores and other trade operations. After walking around downtown, you'll recognize many of the names: Charles Ilfeld, for instance, and Samuel Nahm of the Stern & Nahm building on Bridge Street. Although this community established the first synagogue in the state, Congregation Montefiore, in 1881, only about 40 Jews are left in Las Vegas today.

## Bobby Valdez House

Connoisseurs of visionary oddness should stop by the **Bobby Valdez House** (521 S. Pacific St.) where the resident artist keeps his yard neat and tidy, to show off the weird, painted cement figures he's been sculpting since he retired from the military, about 20 years ago. If he's out and about, he'll introduce you to his creations.

## ◖ Montezuma Castle

About six miles north of town (head north off the plaza on Hot Springs Blvd.), **Montezuma Castle** is a 10,000-square-foot architectural confection perched on the mountainside. The turreted Queen Anne-style building stands as a reminder of more glamorous travel days, when the Atchison, Topeka & Santa Fe Railroad envisioned an elite resort here, connected to the main line with a spur track. The firm of Burnham & Root (one of whose principals went on to make his name with the Chicago World's Fair complex of 1893) created the spectacular building, which opened to guests in 1885. But despite the patronage of Billy the Kid as well as American presidents, the place closed after less than 20 years. It later became

Montezuma Castle, now home to the United World College of the American West

© ZORA O'NEILL

the Montezuma Baptist College, then a Jesuit seminary for Mexican priests until 1972.

It was nearly in ruins when the **Armand Hammer United World College of the American West** (505/454-4221, www.uwc-usa.org) acquired it in 1981 and invested more than $10 million in its restoration. Historically accurate, but with modern touches such as vivid Dale Chihuly chandeliers, the interior is as lavish as the exterior—it's well worth seeing if your schedule allows. It is open to visitors only during free twice-monthly tours, on Saturday afternoons—call or check the website for the schedule.

Also on the college grounds is **Dwan Light Sanctuary** (505/454-4200), which *is* open to the public between 6am and 10pm. The serene meditation space is at its most remarkable during daylight, when it dazzles with prism installations by Charles Ross, an artist who is building an earthwork sculpture nearby called *Star Axis* (www.staraxis.org). Register first at the visitors booth.

What makes the drive up more worthwhile are the **Montezuma Hot Springs** (5am-midnight, free), the waters that first inspired the construction of the castle resort. They're alongside Highway 65—just drive half a mile past the main school entrance and look for signs and breaks in the guardrail on the right side of the road. Those farthest along are the most appealing, a series of round concrete pools, screened from the road with a basic fence.

In the winter, Montezuma Pond, just west of the campus, may be frozen solid enough for **ice skating** (call 505/454-4200 for info). The pond was originally built by the hotel for ice harvesting.

## ENTERTAINMENT AND EVENTS

Even though it's a college town, Las Vegas isn't particularly rambunctious, and it rolls up its sidewalks entirely on Sunday.

### Nightlife

In the summer, the plaza hosts live music on Friday afternoons (4pm-6pm), after which you could check out the **Fort Union Drive-In** (3300 7th St., 505/425-9934, Fri.-Sun. May-Sept.), a great little relic of cinematic history, and a bargain at $7 per carload. The year-round movie option is the **Kiva Theater** (109 Bridge St., 505/425-5482, www.kivatheater.com), which has °been open since 1912, making it the second-oldest cinema in the state, after the Fountain Theater in Mesilla.

After the nightly movie, you could head to **Byron T's** (230 N. Plaza, noon-midnight daily), the bar at the Plaza Hotel, which has dark wood paneling, big show windows overlooking the square, and a great mix of local drinkers. **El Rialto** restaurant (141 Bridge St., 505/454-0037) has a more modern-feeling bar.

### Festivals and Events

On the second Saturday evening of each month, Bridge Street gets lively with the town **Artwalk,** when galleries and shops are open late.

If you're in town over Fourth of July weekend, you'll see the **Fiestas de las Vegas,** when

NORTHEAST

vendors of traditional foods (as well as fair staples like caramel apples) set up all around the plaza and down Bridge Street, and bands perform in the gazebo. Festivities last five days, beginning with Mass at Our Lady of Sorrows Church, one block west of the plaza, and ending with the crowning of the Reina de las Fiestas.

## SPORTS AND RECREATION

For maps and current conditions in the mountains, visit the **Pecos/Las Vegas Ranger District office** (1926 N. 7th St., 505/425-3534, 8am-5pm Mon.-Fri.).

### Santa Fe National Forest

North of town, Highway 65 winds up an ever-narrowing valley to the borders of Santa Fe National Forest and **El Porvenir Campground,** in a pretty patch of pine forest, with campsites ($8) near a stream shaded by ponderosas. **Hermit's Peak Trail** (no. 223) leads 9.5 miles to the 10,263-foot summit. The peak's name refers to wandering mendicant Giovanni Maria Agostini, who was born in Italy and traveled all over the Americas on foot. He walked from Kansas City to Las Vegas with a wagon train in the 1860s; he eventually wound up in the Organ Mountains near Las Cruces, where he was mysteriously killed.

### Storrie Lake State Park

Just a few miles north of town, **Storrie Lake State Park** (Hwy. 518, 505/425-7278, www.nmparks.com, $5/car) is heavily used for waterskiing and windsurfing. But as a place to camp, you can do much better, as it's rather barren, and campsites are so close to the highway that you hear the rush of traffic. As long as you're not hauling an RV, head instead to **Morphy Lake State Park** (575/387-2328, www.nmparks.com, $5/car), which is much quieter.

### Las Vegas National Wildlife Refuge

Southeast of town via Highway 104, the remarkably lush **Las Vegas National Wildlife Refuge** is part of a chain of wetlands cultivated to accommodate migratory birds. A number of bald eagles winter here, and Swainson's hawks and more than 10 other species of raptors pass through every fall. A rectangular driving route cuts through the 8,672-acre area, passing **McAllister Lake,** where you can also camp. The second half of the circuit is unpaved and can get quite muddy.

Stop in first at the **visitors center** (Hwy. 281, 505/425-3581, 8am-2pm Mon.-Fri.) to get an idea what birds are visiting; ask, too, if the secondary driving route is open, as it occasionally is in the late fall. To stretch your legs, take the short **Prairie Trail,** which begins next to the gate at the center's driveway, or the half-mile **Gallinas Canyon Trail,** in the southwest corner of the refuge. The latter hike descends into a small canyon, where you can usually spot prairie falcons and swallows; register first (weekdays only) at the visitors center.

## ACCOMMODATIONS

Just about all of Las Vegas's hotels and motels are on North Grand Avenue. The newest chain operations are on the far end, at exit 347.

Las Vegas has two historic hotels. **El Fidel Hotel** (500 Douglas Ave., 505/425-6761, $45 s, $63 d) gets less press than its rival on the plaza, but you can't beat the price. Rooms are pretty basic, and some windows don't open, but the vast tile-floor lobby is relaxing. (You can get Wi-Fi, but not in the rooms.) You're also right next to an excellent restaurant, and there's pretty much always a vacancy. And did I mention the low, low rates?

But if budget allows, the ◖ **Plaza Hotel** (230 N. Plaza, 505/425-3591, www.plazahotel-nm.com) is beautiful, the first building on the main square to get a solid rehab in the 1960s, and still the grandest. The standard rooms (officially $149, lower if you book online) are perfectly nice, but the deluxe rooms and suites ($174 and $199), in the original building, have the most atmosphere, with towering ceilings, velvet drapes, and stately antiques. Rates include a basic hot breakfast in the hotel's sunny dining room.

# FOOD

Aside from the chains on Grand Avenue, dining choices are limited in Las Vegas, but there are a couple of gems.

## Cafés

**Charlie's Spic & Span Bakery and Café** (715 Douglas Ave., 505/426-1921, 6am-6pm Mon.-Sat., 7am-3pm Sun., $8) is a roomy restaurant where the glass cases burst with monster-size éclairs, jelly doughnuts, and cinnamon buns. But the real specialty is the flour tortilla—be sure to get one with whatever you order, whether it's chile-smothered eggs (breakfast is served all day) or spicy green-chile stew, or just a green-chile cheeseburger. After tasting the delectably fluffy things, you'll be ruined for the supermarket variety, so pick up a to-go bag at the door.

On the plaza, the all-purpose **Travelers Café** (1814 S. Plaza, 505/426-8638, 7:30am-4:30pm Mon.-Sat., $5) is the place for a coffee, Wi-Fi, and veggie-sandwich fix.

Up on the north side, not far from the freeway, the family-run diner **Hillcrest Restaurant** (1106 N. Grand Ave., 505/425-7211, 6am-8:30pm daily, $9) is a wonderful time capsule, and its food will satisfy anyone, as it smoothly switches between Americana (hot turkey sandwiches) and great New Mexican classics—the same way all the local customers chat in Spanish and English. It's open a bit later in the summer.

## New Mexican

Get goodies to eat in the park from **Abraham's Tiendita** (151 Bridge St., 505/425-0930, 8am-4pm Mon.-Fri., $5), a tiny storefront that doles out empanadas, tamales, and other handheld treats. Its ATM burrito packs a punch.

## Fine Dining

For dinner, the Plaza Hotel's **Landmark Grill** (230 N. Plaza, 505/425-3591, 5pm-9pm daily $14) is popular with local politicians and the like for its steaks, pork chops, and chiles rellenos, served up in a wood-trimmed dining room off the hotel's lobby. The restaurant also

Charlie's Spic & Span, at the sign of the giant cream puff

© ZORA O'NEILL

NORTHEAST

does breakfast (7am-11am daily), lunch (11am-2pm), and Saturday and Sunday brunch (11am-2pm), all quite good—a fine option if you're not staying at the hotel but want to enjoy its atmosphere.

A welcome addition to the generally down-home dining scene, **⬛ El Fidel Restaurant** (510 Douglas Ave., 505/425-6659, 11am-2pm and 5pm-10pm Mon.-Fri., 5pm-10pm Sat., 9am-2pm and 5pm-10pm Sun., $14-24) feels like it was beamed in from a much bigger city, with a crisp black-and-white interior and jazz playing softly. This could seem pretentious, but the semiorganic menu is both creative and satisfying, with great flavor combos such as lamb meatballs with walnut-mint pesto. If you're coming from Santa Fe, you might not be stunned, but if you're coming in from the country, it's like an oasis of urbanity.

## INFORMATION

The Las Vegas **visitors center** (1224 Railroad Ave., 505/425-8631, www.lasvegasnewmexico.com, 9am-6pm Mon.-Fri., 11am-7pm Sat.,

noon-6pm Sun.), run by the chamber of commerce, occupies a tiny office in the former rail depot where Lincoln Avenue dead-ends at the tracks.

**Tome on the Range** (158 Bridge St., 505/454-9944, 10am-5:30pm Mon.-Fri., 10am-5pm Sat., noon-4pm Sun.) is an excellent bookstore, with a fine selection of local history and other Western lore, along with all the best sellers.

## GETTING THERE

By car, Las Vegas is 65 miles (about 1 hour) northeast of Santa Fe on I-25, and 107 miles (1.5 hours) south of Raton. From Taos over the pass through Mora is 75 miles (nearly 2 hours).

**Amtrak** (800/872-7245, www.amtrak.com) stops at the nicely remodeled old train depot, with service once daily each way from Chicago and Los Angeles. As a weekend trip, you could take the train up from Albuquerque—it takes about three hours and costs $27. There is no Greyhound service.

# Mora Valley

Highway 518 heads north from Las Vegas, along the Sangre de Cristo foothills. It eventually turns west to begin the ascent over the mountains—here you'll find the communities of La Cueva and Mora, which are culturally and historically linked with the Hispano towns on the other side of the range, such as Peñasco. A drive through here will take only a few hours (or the better part of a day, if you come during raspberry season), but several mountain retreats might entice you to stay a while.

## MORPHY LAKE STATE PARK

Gem-like **Morphy Lake State Park** (575/387-2328, www.nmparks.com, $5/car) used to be one of the most difficult-to-reach parks in New Mexico. The narrow road up to the lake, off Highway 94 (turn in Sapello), has finally been paved, but it's still not navigable by RVs.

Once you get there, the lake is open only to rowboats or craft with electric engines, so the quiet isn't disturbed. The deep-blue water is stocked with trout and ringed with tall ponderosa pines, which provide shade for the primitive **campsites** ($8).

## LA CUEVA

At the junction of Highways 518 and 442, **La Cueva** is no longer a town, but a national historic site. It was settled as part of the Mora Land Grant in the early 19th century, and the old mill, built in the 1870s, still creaks and clanks as the acequia streams over the waterwheel, which generated electricity for nearby homes until 1949. To the northeast, the small adobe **San Rafael Mission Church** displays the French Gothic windows in vogue in 1862, when it was built. **Salman Ranch**

NORTHEAST

© ZORA O'NEILL

The water wheel at La Cueva Mill has been running since the 1870s.

(575/387-2900, www.salmanraspberryranch. com) occupies some of the La Cueva outbuildings, and it has built beautiful rambling gardens inside the mill complex's old adobe walls. These are a wonderful place to stretch or enjoy a picnic in the summertime. The **you-pick raspberry farm** is open from early August to mid-October, depending on the weather, as is a basic café to feed hungry pickers. Year-round, the **farm store** (9am-5pm daily July-Dec., 9am-4pm Thurs.-Mon. Jan.-June) sells raspberry jam and vinegar, fresh berries (in season), and other local foodstuffs.

## MORA AND CLEVELAND

The center of the 1835 land grant and of the lush valley, the town of Mora is also the county seat—though it's no bustling metropolis. Visitors often come for **Tapetes de Lana**

(Main St., 575/387-2247, www.moravalleyspinningmill.com, 7:30am-4pm Mon.-Sat., 10am-2pm Sun.), at the main intersection in Mora. Inside, locally spun yarn, from the nearby mill, and handwoven rugs are for sale. The group works with Churro sheep and locally raised alpaca wool.

Some of this wool comes from **Victory Ranch** (Hwy. 434, 575/387-2254, www.victoryranch.com, 10am-4pm daily mid-Mar.-Dec., $3), up the road about a mile from the highway junction. With feedings of the fuzzy little camelids at 11am, 1pm, and 3pm, it's a great place to take the kids.

About a mile down the road in the neighboring village, the **Cleveland Roller Mill Museum** (Hwy. 518, 575/387-2645, www.clevelandrollermillmuseum.com, 10am-3pm Sat.-Sun. June-Aug., free) is a two-story adobe structure built around 1900 and kept in use until the mid-1950s. It doesn't look too impressive from the outside, but the building houses a complex system of heavy-duty machinery, from the massive steel rollers that crushed the wheat to the "sock dusters" that absorbed the potentially explosive flour dust. Everything's intact and put into use every Labor Day for the annual Millfest, when there's also live music and arts and crafts booths.

### Accommodations and Food

At the south end of Mora, **Hatcha's Café** (Hwy. 518 at Hwy. 434, 575/387-9299, 10am-7pm Mon.-Fri., 8am-2pm Sun., $8) does a mean green-chile stew. Across from the Cleveland Roller Mill Museum, **Mora Inn & RV Park** (Hwy. 518, 575/387-5230, www.morainn.com) is a quiet spot to bunk for the night, with motel rooms ($65 d) as well as campsites for RVs ($20) and tents ($10). It also has a good café, **Krystal's Korner Kafe** (7am-6:30pm Mon.-Fri., 7:30am-6:30pm Sat., 7:30am-3pm Sun., $7), where the pinto beans are especially good.

# The Northern Plains

New Mexico's plains are a subtly shifting blanket of gold, brown, or green, depending on the season. This requires a certain mind-set to appreciate. The trick is to stop craving switchbacks, vertigo-inducing views, and all the other adrenaline-fueled drama of the mountains. Then you'll find this area incredibly relaxing, as the low-hanging, puffy clouds scud out to the horizon. After a bit of driving, you'll begin to discern the smallest changes: a shimmer of silver where a certain grass flourishes, or the brief contrast afforded by a dark rock outcropping.

Granted, there's very little to do. The major public lands, the Kiowa and Rita Blanca National Grasslands, are virtually indistinguishable from the surrounding private ranches and offer little in the way of recreation. The whole area is home to herds of pronghorn, some elk, and thousands and thousands of cows, the lifeblood of the economy. It's modern cowboy country, but it's also scarred by the traumatic Dust Bowl years, when dirt lay in drifts up to the fence posts. Some of the older locals still recall those hard times. In the unreconstructed small towns, there are few galleries or other signs of modern gentrification. If you're interested in prehistoric goings-on, though, the place is fascinating. Dinosaurs roamed through the mud, and then so-called Folsom Man hunted bison during the last ice age; you can see the lingering evidence in several places.

## FORT UNION NATIONAL MONUMENT

On a barren plain 80 miles from Santa Fe, **Fort Union National Monument** (Hwy. 161, 505/425-8025, www.nps.gov/foun, 8am-5pm daily June-Aug., 8am-4pm daily Sept.-May, $3) was the largest military depot in the Southwest, located strategically where the two branches of the Santa Fe Trail joined. Built largely of adobe, the fort has melted away, leaving not much more than the outlines of the buildings;

however, you can still get an idea just how vast the complex was, and the experience is heightened by audio clips that play in front of buildings like the jail and the latrine.

It took three tries to build the fort. The first, made of logs, was built in 1851 as a base for campaigns against Apache raiders, but it soon rotted away. A second was a star-shaped earthen fortification built in a hurry to defend against a rumored Confederate attack in 1861; fortunately, the Union triumphed in the Battle of Glorieta Pass, just a year later, and the troops could abandon the muddy hovel.

The third structure, the stone and adobe outlines of which are preserved today, had relatively luxurious officers' quarters and plenty of room for both a military post and a very busy supply depot for items on the trade route. But like so many settlements in New Mexico, Fort

© ZORA O'NEILL

NORTHEAST

old adobe walls at Fort Union National Monument

## Along the Santa Fe Trail

Whether Bing Crosby is crooning about it, Ronald Reagan riding along it, or a modern traveler retracing it, the Santa Fe Trail has earned a certain golden glow in American popular culture. The route, which cut across the frontier from Missouri to the middle of New Mexico, was used for less than 60 years, but it has become one of the great symbols of American westward expansion, all bundled up with the era when the cowboy and his horse were the masters of the new land.

The trail holds up well under the pressure of symbolism, especially when you consider the effort it took to traverse its 900 miles. A certain entrepreneur named William Becknell is credited with making the first trading trip, in 1821, without even knowing yet that the Mexican government, newly independent from Spain, had opened the borders of Nuevo México to outsiders. When Becknell was welcomed in Santa Fe, rather than imprisoned, and made a profit of 2,000 percent on his first load of calico cloth, it wasn't long before wagons loaded with more than three tons of goods were groaning across the plains.

Not that it was easy money. On this highway, wagons took close to three months to make the trip. At the far edge of Kansas, traders had to make a choice: the slow-going Mountain Route through frigid Colorado and the brutal Raton Pass, or the level and easy Cimarron Cut-off, where wagon trains faced scarce water and attacks by Comanche and Apache raiders. The biggest wagon trains, bursting with everything from basic cotton cloth to fripperies like parasols and playing cards, had no choice but to take the latter. Despite the dangers, the traders forged on, driven by dreams of profit. In the process, they also carried the dreams of the expansionist United States—an abstract concept until the U.S. Army used the Santa Fe Trail for supply caravans when it went to war with Mexico in 1846.

So many tons of trade goods and, later, settlers to the new American territory were hauled along the plains that in places, the earth is still scored by wagon ruts. But even such an influential, profitable trail was not a permanent one. First the trail shortened as America's frontier border moved west; then the railroad displaced it entirely. But perhaps the very fact that the Santa Fe Trail was outmoded so quickly by more modern technology is what has fixed it so well in the American imagination.

Union became obsolete when the railroad was laid through the state, and by 1891, after less than three decades of use, the massive installation was decommissioned.

Walk out northeast from the ruins to see the ghostly imprints of wagon ruts from the Santa Fe Trail—they're most visible early or late in the day.

## EAST FROM WAGON MOUND

Named for a rock outcropping that faintly resembles a Conestoga wagon, the small town at exit 387 is the turning point for Roy—a pretty route to Clayton, preferable to U.S. 56 from Springer. There's not much here but a couple of gas stations, though on Labor Day weekend,

Wagon Mound hosts **Bean Day** (www.wagonmoundnm.com), a harvest celebration more than a century old, with rodeos, a free barbecue, and a big parade—bigger than the tiny downtown can hold, so it runs through twice.

## Highway 120 to Roy

You're really getting off here for Highway 120, which heads east across flatlands that are often surprisingly green. Another surprise: the dip down into Canadian River Canyon, striated with red and white. The road then heads to **Roy**—home to not quite 500 people, giving it the dubious title of the largest town in Harding County. Its last claim to fame was that Western-swing bandleader

Bob Wills penned "San Antonio Rose" here in 1927, as he worked as a barber by day. At the time, Roy was a shipping point for coal to Tucumcari and a major dry-ice manufacturing site, thanks to its location on top of the Bravo Dome carbon-dioxide field.

## La Frontera del Llano Scenic Byway

Although the drive from Wagon Mound is arguably more awe-inspiring, Highway 39, which runs north and south from Roy, is an *official* scenic route, a section of La Frontera del Llano Scenic Byway. To the south and east, the "Edge of the Plains" route goes to the cattle-ranching centers of **Mosquero** and **Bueyeros,** passing pink-striped buttes, a string of beautiful old churches, and dilapidated little bars. At Bueyeros, you can turn south to follow the byway to its end at Logan (near Ute Lake State Park and I-40), or head north to make a roundabout route up to Clayton.

Back at Roy, the byway follows the northern stretch of Highway 39 through the **Kiowa and Rita Blanca National Grasslands.** The 230,000 acres of short-grass prairie are federally managed to maintain the natural flora, so as to avoid a repeat of the 1930s devastation. The land is home to quail, bobcats, and lots of pronghorn, but don't expect pristine wilderness—cattle are still allowed to graze here. You can camp at **Mills Canyon,** 10 miles north of Roy on Highway 39, then about 10 miles west, where a narrow, rocky road leads 800 feet down into the canyon. A former commercial farm, the sheltered river bottom still harbors a few fruit trees, as well as wildlife such as mule deer and Barbary sheep, introduced in 1950. During dry summers, the campground can be closed due to fire danger—call the grasslands headquarters in Clayton (575/374-9652) to check the status before heading out.

Highway 39, and the scenic byway, ends at the town of Abbott, at the junction with U.S. 56—from here, it's virtually a straight shot east to Clayton.

## SPRINGER

At the I-25 exit for U.S. 56, which runs directly to Clayton, the tiny town of Springer was formerly named Maxwell, for Lucien B. Maxwell, whose land grant covered all of Colfax County. It was also the county seat between 1882 and 1898 (Raton now holds the title). When political power moved away, so did most of the action. Now there's not much here except a handful of antiques stores, the largest and most obsessively organized of which is **Jespersen's Cache** (403 Maxwell Ave., 575/483-2349).

There is also allegedly a Santa Fe Trail museum, north on the main drag, but it is never open….

## CLAYTON

Only 12 miles from Texas, Clayton is a place where most of the 2,900 people in town spend their days on horseback or otherwise engaged in the large cattle operations on the surrounding ranches and feedlots. (If the wind blows the wrong way, the smell is hard to ignore, though on a crisp autumn evening, there's a positive spin: You definitely get a sense of place.) By night, attention focuses on the gem of a vintage movie theater or the high school football stadium. The big annual event is the rodeo on Fourth of July weekend, and there are easily more churches than restaurants in town. In short, you're a long way from Santa Fe.

Clayton was established relatively late by New Mexican standards—in 1888, well after the railroad cut through. But it soon rocketed to notoriety as the place where outlaw Thomas "Black Jack" Ketchum met his end, two years after he was picked up for attempting to rob a train near Folsom.

### Sights

Bone up on local history at the interesting **Herzstein Memorial Museum** (S. 2nd St. at Walnut St., 575/374-2977, 10am-5pm Tues.-Sun., free), a collection of local ephemera bequeathed to the town by a prominent shopkeeper. Spread over two floors of a stately 1919 Methodist church, the displays are kept sparkling

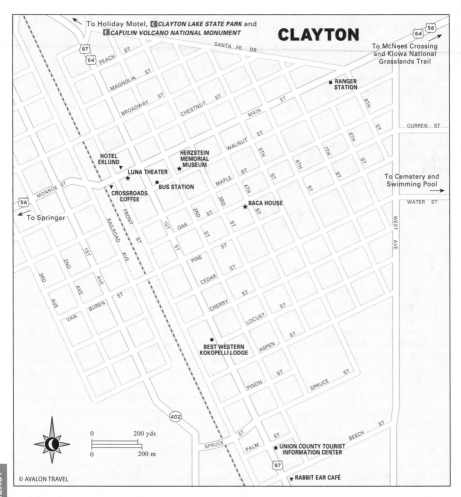

To Holiday Motel, **CLAYTON LAKE STATE PARK** and
**CAPULIN VOLCANO NATIONAL MONUMENT**

# CLAYTON

To McNees Crossing
and Kiowa National
Grasslands Trail

SANTA FE DR

PEACH ST
MAGNOLIA ST
BROADWAY ST
CHESTNUT ST
MAIN ST
WALNUT ST
MAPLE ST
OAK ST
PINE ST
CEDAR ST
CHERRY ST
LOCUST ST
ASPEN ST
PINON ST
SPRUCE ST
PALM ST
BEECH ST

RANGER STATION

CURREN ST

To Cemetery and
Swimming Pool

WATER ST

To Springer

HOTEL EKLUND
HERZSTEIN MEMORIAL MUSEUM
LUNA THEATER
BUS STATION
CROSSROADS COFFEE
BACA HOUSE

BEST WESTERN KOKOPELLI LODGE

UNION COUNTY TOURIST INFORMATION CENTER

RABBIT EAR CAFÉ

0   200 yds
0   200 m

© AVALON TRAVEL

and dust-free, with period furniture, clothing, and medical equipment alongside vitrines dedicated to local luminaries such as Cowgirl Hall of Famer and single mom Bernice McLaughlin. There's also a small but fascinating display on the Dust Bowl. Tucked away in a small hall are photographs of Black Jack Ketchum being hanged on the courthouse square in 1901, a grisly event that ended in his accidental beheading. Ketchum (both parts) is buried in the **cemetery** (Princeton Ave.), in the southeast corner of town.

The thorough sightseer can also cruise the **Baca House** (320 Oak St.), where the fence and gate are the work of Dionicio Rodríguez, a folk artist known for his elaborate faux-bois cement creations, particularly in Brackenridge Park in San Antonio, Texas, as well as in Little Rock and Memphis. The Oak Street work dates from the early 1940s, commissioned by a well-traveled land speculator who'd seen Rodríguez's work in Texas.

## Clayton Lake State Park

Fifteen miles north of Clayton, sunk down

the quirky trim of the Baca House

Dinosaur tracks dot Clayton Lake State Park.

just below the level of the surrounding plain, **Clayton Lake State Park** (Hwy. 370, 575/374-8808, www.nmparks.com, $5/car, $8 camping) is a lovely haven for day use or camping. But the real attraction is the **dinosaur footprints** in the sandstone at the east end of the lake. Made some 100 million years ago in what was then mud, they are part of a long series of tracks from Mosquero Creek in Harding County up to Fort Collins, Colorado, a route that ran along the edge of an ancient sea. They're accessible via a quarter-mile-long paved trail—look for signs to the right as you enter the park. Try to go early in the morning or in late afternoon, when the longer shadows make the prints stand out more clearly. The visitors center at the park also has a small display about dinosaur life in this area.

## Sports and Recreation

**McNees Crossing** gets frequent mention in tourist literature, but even true Santa Fe Trail enthusiasts will find the trail ford a bit underwhelming; look for the marker on Highway 406, east and north of Clayton. Better to head for the **Kiowa National Grasslands Hiking Trail,** which leads to some better-preserved wagon ruts, as well as a ruined homestead. Getting there requires zigzagging along dirt ranch-access roads. Head east on U.S. 64/56, then 13 miles north on Highway 406; turn left (west) on Campbell Road and go 3 miles, then north 1 mile to a small pullout for parking. On your way out of Clayton, you might want to stop at the grasslands' **ranger station** (714 Main St., 575/374-9652) for a map.

Should you need to cool off, the **municipal swimming pool** (Water St., 12:30pm-5:30pm Tues.-Fri., noon-6pm Sat., 1pm-6pm Sun.) is a good-sized outdoor facility with a kiddie slide. It's on the east side of town—go through the gate to the armory and the airport.

## Entertainment

If you're a vintage cinema buff, don't miss the **Luna Theater** (4 Main St., 575/374-2712), under the neon winking moon. Built in 1916, it was redone in 1935, complete with a ballroom

NORTHEAST

in the basement. Pay the $7 admission regardless of what's showing, just to see the glowing interior, set with art deco sconces and the beautiful original embroidered velvet curtain. You can also try knocking during the day—if someone's there, they'll show you around. Shows are Friday-Sunday only.

## Accommodations

Clayton has a remarkable number of fine places to sleep. Locally owned independent **Holiday Motel** (U.S. 87, 575/374-2558, $45 s, $69 d) is a gem, well kept up and scrupulously clean. The owners are so enthusiastic, they fold the towels into elephants. It's on the northwest edge of town, about a quarter mile out from the big bridge.

Downtown at the main crossroads, **Hotel Eklund** (15 Main St., 575/446-1939, www.hoteleklund.com, $90 d) is a three-story trove of history, with a cool saloon. Rooms are spare, with metal bedsteads, lace curtains, and nice new bathrooms that only look old, with their honeycomb tiles and pedestal sinks. Rooms on the front or east side are preferable to those on the west, to dampen freight-train noise. Rates include a basic chain-motel-style breakfast.

If you want a pool, head to **Best Western Kokopelli Lodge** (702 S. 1st St., 575/374-2589, www.bestwestern.com, $125 d). It's a million times nicer than it has to be, considering the feeble competition from the other chain hotels: big outdoor swimming area, wireless Internet, a free hot breakfast buffet, and plush, spacious rooms.

## Food

The **Hotel Eklund** (15 Main St., 575/446-1939, 10:30am-2pm and 4pm-9pm Mon.-Fri., 10:30am-9pm Sat.-Sun., $10) is a major hub for lunch and dinner, and a great excuse to sit in the front saloon (though, sadly, the 1850s wood bar can only serve beer and wine now). The menu has the usual mix of steaks ($15-18), New Mexican standards, and burgers, but a lot is made from scratch, including dangerously sweet desserts.

The other popular spot, open for breakfast too, is the **Rabbit Ear Café** (1201 S. 1st St., 575/374-3277, 7am-8pm Tues.-Sat., 10:30am-2pm Sun., $10)—which doesn't mean it's great. It's inconsistent, but when it's good, the chile is hot and the burritos are stuffed. Either way, it's a good slice of life in Clayton.

The other option is **Crossroads Coffee** (2 S. Front St., 575/374-5282, 6:30am-3pm Mon.-Fri., 8am-11am Sat., $7), a funky wood-paneled place in the old feed store that also happens to be an unlikely outpost of espresso with house-roasted beans. It serves a different sandwich, soup, and salad every day; breakfast burritos and biscuits and gravy are on offer in the morning.

## Information

The **Clayton-Union County Tourist Information Center** (1103 S. 1st St., 575/374-9253, www.claytonnewmexico.net, 8am-5pm Mon.-Fri.) has a few brochures, plus souvenir Dust Bowl postcards and free wireless Internet.

## Getting There

By car, Clayton is 84 miles (1.5 hours) east along U.S. 56/412 from Springer at I-25, and about the same distance from Raton via U.S. 64/87. From Santa Fe, it's about 220 miles (3.5 hours).

**Greyhound** (800/231-2222, www.greyhound.com) runs through once a day, but only via Amarillo, Texas, dropping you off at the station (113 E. Walnut St., 575/374-6207, 8am-5pm Mon.-Fri.).

## WEST TO RATON

U.S. 64/87 heads roughly northwest out of Clayton, another hypnotizing drive through golden prairie. The terrain changes a bit halfway along, as defunct volcanoes punctuate the horizon. The most distinctive is the perfectly conical peak of Capulin; a drive up to the top (an adventure in itself) gives you a break from all the flatness, as well as a stunning view.

From Capulin, you can detour north to the ghost town of Folsom, a starting point for two smaller, more scenic roads. Backtrack east along a rough byway through the washes and ridges

© ZORA O'NEILL

The cone of Capulin Volcano is visible for miles around.

strung along the border with Colorado, or keep heading west on Highway 72, which takes you across a dramatic high mesa, the perfect way to meet the mountains at Raton.

### ◖ Capulin Volcano
### National Monument

Unmissable on the skyline, the soft dome of **Capulin Volcano National Monument** (575/278-2201, www.nps.gov/cavo, 8am-5pm daily June-Aug., 8am-4:30pm daily Sept.-May, $5/car) reaches 8,182 feet above sea level and stands approximately as tall as the Empire State Building. About 60,000 years ago, Capulin spewed hot ash and rock into the air, which settled into an almost perfect cone—its top edge looks like a carefully opened soft-boiled egg. At the summit, you can walk a short trail down into the crater, where steam vents are noticeable in the winter, as the surrounding patches are covered with greenery. Or hike up around the rim: From this vantage point you can see more clearly how this whole region was shaped by volcanic activity, from the lava-topped mesas

to the hulking Sierra Grande. The latter formation is another dormant volcano, about a million years old, that's also the largest lone mountain in the United States, covering 50 square miles and rising 2,200 feet above the surrounding plain. Guided tours of the crater in summer at 11am and 1pm can point out more details.

But to reach the top of Capulin, you have to negotiate a two-mile road that spirals up the side of the volcano. It's narrow and doesn't have as many guardrails as you might expect; put your steeliest driver in charge, and take it slow. It's much easier coming down, as you're on the inside lane. Also watch out for mule deer in the road around the base. The area at the top has limited parking, so if you're visiting in the busy months of July and August, go very early or late in the day, or you'll have to wait to drive up.

### Folsom

Hard by the railroad tracks, late-19th-century Folsom drew cattle-traders and outlaws—most notably "Black Jack" Ketchum, whose gang held up trains three times here. In 1908, a flood demolished a good part of the town, and even claimed the life of the village telephone operator, who stayed at her post to warn residents of danger. Around the same time, floods also uncovered a collection of bison skeletons embedded with spear points in a wash west of town. When the site was excavated in 1927, the spear points were determined to be at least 10,000 years old—a shock to archaeologists, who'd previously thought American Indians had arrived on the continent only around 2000 BC.

In an old general store at the intersection of Highways 325 and 456, **Folsom Museum** (575/278-2122, www.folsomvillage.com, 10am-5pm daily June-Oct., 10am-5pm Sat.-Sun. May and Oct., $1.50) tells these stories in more detail, if not always in the most illuminating way. Some collections (carefully labeled river rocks) are surreal and cryptic; others, such as the one on slave-turned-cowboy-and-accidental-archaeologist George McJunkin, are genuinely illuminating. Perhaps the best item is the odd diorama of the Ketchum hanging.

## Dry Cimarron Scenic Byway

A network of rural highways stretching into Colorado and Oklahoma, this route roughly follows the path of the Dry Cimarron River, with Highway 456 as the backbone; it eventually winds up back in Clayton.

About 3.5 miles northeast of Folsom on Highway 456, on the right (southeast) side of the road, look for a pullout and a sign warning against swimming. A small trail leads a short way to **Folsom Falls,** where water pours directly out of the rock face. It's visible from the edge of the shallow canyon, but you'll need to clamber down the rocks to get to the water's edge.

From here, Highway 456 zigzags across the river bottom as it heads east. At the junction with Highway 370, you can drive south to Clayton Lake State Park, but if you continue east, you'll pass towering buttes dubbed Battleship and Wedding Cake. You then loop back to Clayton via Highway 406.

"busy" downtown Folsom

a lone church atop Johnson Mesa

## ◖ Johnson Mesa

If time (and weather) permits, don't skip the drive along Highway 72 out of Folsom, one of the most beautiful in New Mexico. The narrow paved byway dips and rises, roller-coaster-like, as it gradually climbs the foothills, and then you're deposited on the top of **Johnson Mesa,** a bucolic expanse of grazing land studded with smaller hills, including the perfectly round Red Mountain. At one point, the road passes close to the mesa edge, and you can see the land plunge away. About the only evidence of human habitation up here is a small stone church, **St. John's Methodist,** built in 1897. No one lives on the mesa regularly now, though a few hardy souls come up for the summer along with the livestock. If you drive this way at dusk, watch out for deer on the road, even on the outskirts of Raton.

# The Rockies

Where the laden caravans of traders struggled through Raton Pass on the Santa Fe Trail's mountain route, drivers now zip up with ease. Raton is still a watering hole, but it sates visitors with fast-food restaurants and travel centers; go beyond the off-ramp economy to see the town's century-old core, laid out along the railroad depot. South and west of Raton, smaller Cimarron was another stopping point on the mountain route, and one that wears its history well.

## RATON

The glowing red RATON sign on the hilltop on the northwest side of town suggests a bit more glitz than this mountain burg currently has. But traces of past glamour remain in the sturdy downtown, in the art deco fire station

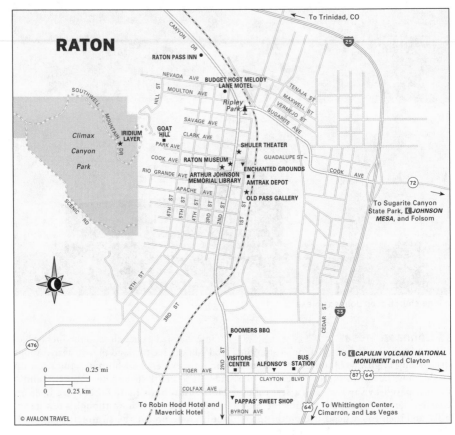

on North 2nd Street, for instance, the quirky castle facade of the El Raton Theatre, and the elegant Colfax County Building on North 3rd Street.

Raton is defined entirely by the mountain behind it. In 1866, an entrepreneur by the name of Richens Wootton took it upon himself to blast out a proper road through the mountains over Raton Pass, wide enough to accommodate wagon trains—then he set up a toll gate and charged Santa Fe Trail traders to come through. "Uncle Dick," as he was known, sold his road to AT&SF Railroad for $1 and a lifetime grocery stipend. The railroad helped keep the town of Raton in money too, and some wealth came from coal mining in the surrounding mountains, though nothing like the giddy get-rich-quick silver and gold mines in the south. All of this was enough to bring big theaters and the first public school in the state—though, like everywhere in the late-19th-century West, it had its fair share of lynchings, mob violence, and more.

Now it's more peaceful, overlooking the plains to the east, but with its heart in the Rockies. If you are just passing through, note that nearly everything shuts on Sundays—you'll be hard-pressed to find somewhere to eat outside of the usual chains.

## Sights

The gem of 2nd Street is the rococo **Shuler**

Raton's stately Shuler Theater

of local life are nicely presented, along with vintage dolls, works by Taos painters and some good *santero* carvings in the front upstairs area.

Pick up a walking-tour brochure here to guide you along 1st Street, Raton's **historic downtown** where the handsome old storefronts are trimmed in cast-iron garlands, graceful figureheads, and jutting cornices. Business isn't exactly booming, but there are a few antiques shops and the **Old Pass Gallery** (145 S. 1st St., 575/445-2052, www.ratonarts.org, 10am-4:30pm Tues.-Sat.), run by the local arts council. It occupies a renovated Wells Fargo office, and next door is the train depot, the only surviving building of a huge complex that used to manage the comings and goings of more than 60 trains a day.

You could also seek out the **Arthur Johnson Memorial Library** (244 Cook Ave., 575/445-9711, 1pm-6pm Mon., 10am-6pm Tues.-Wed. and Fri.-Sat., 10am-9pm Thurs.), between 2nd and 3rd Streets, a neoclassical structure built as a post office in 1917, then converted to a library under the Carnegie program. It houses a good collection of Southwest-themed art, including some of the early Taos artists.

By car, you can head up **Goat Hill,** where the RATON sign is perched; take Moulton Avenue west to Hill Street. This hill is geologically famous, as it has a visible stripe of iridium running through it—the stripe of detritus that marks the meteorite crash that ended the dinosaurs. Just before the top of the hill, bear right rather than left at the fork—this dirt road will carry you around the ridgeline a few miles to a marked spot and a scenic overlook.

**Theater** auditorium (131 N. 2nd St., 575/445-4746, www.shulertheater.com), beautifully restored by the town and used for live performances. Visitors can tour the theater weekdays 9am-5pm—definitely worth a stop to see the 1930s lobby murals and the beautiful cloud-studded "sky" above the proscenium. Three of the original drop curtains survive as well—they're painted with scenes depicting a Roman villa, the palisade cliffs near Cimarron, and Raton's Ripley Park. Building the theater was a bit of a battle, as the city council used money that had been earmarked for a new city hall. Later, the municipal auditorium was named in honor of the mayor who'd perpetrated the boondoggle, in a council resolution that was worded to effectively tell Raton residents, "See, we told you you'd love it."

The main thoroughfare for cars is 2nd Street, where the **Raton Museum** (108 S. 2nd St., 575/445-8979, 10am-4pm Tues.-Sat. in summer, 10am-4pm Wed.-Sat. in winter, free), occupies two large tin-ceiling shop fronts. Displays about the coal camps and other facets

## Entertainment

A quirky castle facade marks **El Raton Theatre** (115 N. 2nd St., 575/445-7008, www.elraton-theatre.com), a movie palace built in 1929, now souped up with a digital projector for first-run films. If you want a peek inside during the day, just knock—if someone's free, they're happy to let you in and show you around.

## Sports and Recreation

An eight-mile drive from Raton, **Sugarite**

Canyon State Park (211 Hwy. 526, 575/445-5607, www.nmparks.com, $5/car) encompasses 3,600 acres along either side of Chicorica Creek and Lake Maloya, for trout fishing and casual boating. The area is also beautiful in spring, when the mountain slopes are dotted with wildflowers. From behind the visitors center, two miles up Highway 526, the **Coal Camp Trail** runs through the ruins of a mining settlement and up to two old mine shafts; a few longer trails lead up to the bluffs that line the road—ask at the visitors center for maps.

Hunting is a very big deal in the high mountains around Raton. **Whittington Center** (Hwy. 64, 575/445-3615, www.nrawc.org), a 52-square-mile complex established in 1973 by the National Rifle Association, is a starting point for many hunters. It's the largest gun club in the United States, offering classes for beginners and experts, target and skeet shooting (from $20/day), plus real-life hunting for deer, antelope, and even mountain lions. There's also space to camp (from $12) or simple cabins (from $14/person).

## Accommodations

Most chain motels are on Clayton Boulevard, which runs from exit 451 off I-25—but some of the old-time independent options here, at the north and south ends of town, will restore your faith in American roadside hospitality. On the north side, **( Raton Pass Inn** (308 Canyon Dr., 575/445-3641, www.ratonpassinn.com, $60 d) is an excellent choice, though it's open only mid-April through mid-October. The owner is obsessively clean, and she has spruced up the 1950s exterior with jazzy green-and-salmon paint; inside, the 14 large rooms are decorated with a special touch and include Wi-Fi, mini fridges, and microwaves. Reservations, even if only on the same day, are absolutely required—a phone call is the best way to arrange.

Just to the south, the **Budget Host Melody Lane Motel** (136 Canyon Dr., 575/445-3655, www.budgethost.com, $55 d) is remarkable for its groovy slant-ceiling rooms, eight of which have a vintage steam sauna built into the tub, a real treat after a long drive. The motel changed

hands in 2013, though, and it was yet to be seen whether the new owners would keep the place up to the same standards; check current reviews online.

On the south side of town, **Robin Hood Motel** (1354 S. 2nd St., 575/445-5577, www.robinhoodmotelusa.com, $68 d) is yet another fine old-style inn, though a touch more up-to-date than others. Behind butter-yellow doors are fairly standard modern motel trappings, though the groovy original orange linoleum shows in some bathrooms. There's also a small outdoor pool (summers only).

Finally, at the southernmost edge, just by the I-25 on-ramp, the **( Maverick Motel** (1510 S. 2nd St., 575/445-3792, $44 s, $64 d) is the greatest throwback of all, a block of 10 snug rooms straight from the 1940s, maintained by a man who seems stuck in that decade himself. Pale-blue chenille bedspreads, screen doors, and even an old soda machine will make you feel like you're sleeping in a museum, in the best way. This place trumps even the motels in Tucumcari for retro charm; go before the owner decides to retire.

the well-tended Robin Hood Motel

© ZORA O'NEILL

Boomers has good barbecue and creative architecture.

## Food

Raton's restaurants have limited opening hours, and if you don't plan well, you'll be relegated to the fast-food joints on Clayton Boulevard. For morning coffee, **Enchanted Grounds Espresso Bar** (111 Park Ave., 575/445-2129, 7am-2pm Mon., 7am-4:30pm Tues.-Fri., 7:30am-4:30pm Sat.) is the place to go; it also serves French toast, egg sandwiches, and light lunches.

The architecture may be a mash-up of a horse trailer and a gas station, but the food at ◖ **Boomers BBQ** (1117 S. 2nd St., 575/445-2881, 11am-8pm Mon.-Sat., $9) is pure, unadulterated Texan meat love. Order from the window in the trailer, and then take your foam container of brisket, pork, chicken, or sausage (plus sides!) to eat outside, or in the onetime gas station office. The brisket is succulent, the sauce is light and tangy, and the price is right.

**Pappas' Sweet Shop** (1201 S. 2nd St., 575/445-9811, 11:30am-2pm and 5pm-8pm Mon.-Fri., 5pm-7:30pm Sat., $10) bears mention just because it has been around so long. In fact, the atmosphere can be a bit geriatric, but

fair enough, since it's been going since 1923. It has a (freshly revived) vintage soda fountain, and classics like chicken salad on the menu.

**Alfonso's** (412 Clayton Rd., 575/445-8022, 7am-9pm Mon.-Sat., 8am-8pm Sun., $8) is open a little bit later than other places—though you'll be dining in one end of a Conoco gas station. The setup is fast-food-y, but the food is good, authentic Mexican.

## Information

The **New Mexico visitor information center** (100 Clayton Blvd., 575/445-2761, www.raton.info, 8am-5pm daily) is maintained by both the Raton chamber of commerce and the state tourism board.

## Getting There

By car, Raton is 83 miles (1.5 hours) from Clayton (about 20 minutes longer if you go via Johnson Mesa). From Santa Fe, it's 175 miles (2.5 hours) via I-25, and 220 miles (3.25 hours) from Denver. Cimarron is 40 miles (45 minutes) away, and Taos is 95 miles (2 hours).

NORTHEAST

**Amtrak** (800/872-7245, www.amtrak.com) trains pull in to the historic depot on 1st Street once each day on the eastbound and westbound routes. The trip from Albuquerque takes about 4.5 hours and costs $44. The only direct **Greyhound** (800/231-2222, www.greyhound.com) buses come in from Denver and Amarillo, Texas, and drop you off at the station (542 Clayton Blvd., 575/445-9071, 8am-9am and 11am-1pm daily).

## VALLE VIDAL

South of Raton, U.S. 64 bears west, away from I-25 and deeper into the mountains. About 35 miles along (5 miles east of Cimarron) is the turn for Forest Road 1950. This dirt road is the only access route (and a circuitous one) to Valle Vidal, a 102,000-acre chunk of the Carson National Forest that straddles some of the highest peaks in the Sangre de Cristo range. For anyone seeking pristine wilderness, Valle Vidal is perhaps the last, best place to get a sense of what New Mexico was like before mining and ranching took off in the 19th century. The area is home to the state's largest elk herd, and its watershed is essential for the now-rare Rio Grande cutthroat trout.

Though little visited, it is probably one of the best-known public lands in New Mexico, as the area was the topic of strenuous debate from 1982, when Pennzoil traded the land to the National Forest Service in exchange for tax breaks, until 2006, when a long grassroots campaign finally got a law passed to prohibit mining and drilling for natural gas.

There are no services in the wilderness, very few trails, and only two formal camping areas with no services but toilets. Coming from U.S. 64, the first one you reach is **McCrystal Campground** ($8), set on a flat plain, with a few ponderosas providing shade; this is where people exploring on horseback often camp. If you want more privacy, head eight more miles to the 35 sites at the higher-elevation **Cimarron Campground** ($10), which are tucked amid trees; many trout-fishing creeks are right nearby. For current conditions and advisories (parts of the valley are closed seasonally to protect the elk), contact the **Questa Ranger District office** (575/586-0520), on the west side, which manages the whole area.

## CIMARRON

This community of less than a thousand people still feels like a 19th-century mountain town. A few times a year, the streets are filled with horses being driven to various pastures on the vast Philmont ranch that adjoins the community, and the assorted rivalries of the Colfax County War are spoken of as though they happened yesterday—perhaps because so much of the town's social life takes place at the old St. James Hotel, where the ceiling is pocked with bullet holes.

But more than this violent history, the wilderness is what defines Cimarron. Established in 1861 by Lucien Maxwell, the town was the most substantial settlement on the giant land grant that Maxwell would later own outright. The surrounding mountains (and all the wildlife they harbor) still press in close; when the sun starts to set and the stars glimmer overhead, you're reminded just how small the town is. Amid so much empty land, you have to wonder what all the fighting was about...and was that a bear rustling in the trees?

By day, you can visit a handful of galleries on 9th Street, one block north of U.S. 64 and the old acequia, or watch the fish jump in the Cimarron River. You can hike between granite cliffs or tour the mansion of the oilman who ran Philmont ranch and dedicated it to the Boy Scouts of America. But at the end of the day, you'll likely be back at the St. James, drinking a beer and talking about the past.

### ◖ St. James Hotel

The center of Cimarron's social life, past and present, is the **St. James Hotel** (Hwy. 21, 575/376-2664), a beautifully maintained building that's as packed with legends, lore, and (perhaps) ghosts as it is with beautiful antiques and stuffed buffalo heads. Opened first as a saloon by a French chef named Henri Lambert

the Old Mill Museum in Cimarron

It was, and it only got more so, as some 200 people were killed trying to settle the debate over who got to live on the Maxwell Land Grant.

All that history still feels very present in the chandelier-lit hallways lined with peeling wallpaper. Visitors are welcome to poke around on the ground floor, where some of the guest-room doors are left open. You can also pick up a **walking-tour guide** to other, far less preserved monuments in the "old town" part of Cimarron.

### Old Mill Museum

Round out the local history with a visit to the **Old Mill Museum** (Hwy. 21, 575/376-2913, 10am-5pm Mon.-Wed. and Fri.-Sat., 1pm-5pm Sun. June-Aug., weekends only May and Sept., $3), four floors of fun just across the street from the hotel. Built by Lucien Maxwell in 1864, the structure now houses Boy Scouts memorabilia, relics of the Colfax County War, and a two-headed calf.

You can also visit the **cemetery,** a short walk south on Highway 21, where the grave of settler-rights supporter Reverend Franklin Tolby sits alongside more recent (and longer-lived) Cimarron residents.

### Sports and Recreation

West of town about 12 miles, straddling U.S. 64 and stretching nearly to Eagle Nest, **Cimarron Canyon State Park** (575/377-6271, www.nmparks.com, $5/car) is known for its excellent trout fishing in the Cimarron River and its tributaries, as well as the dramatic granite palisades that form the canyon walls. Backcountry camping is not permitted, and the only established campgrounds are several spots fairly close to the road.

Hiking, however, is excellent, especially on **Clear Creek Trail,** a 7-mile out-and-back you can do in about three hours. The route runs along a creek and passes several small waterfalls while gaining about a thousand feet; it's particularly nice in the fall, when the aspens turn yellow. Look for a signed pullout on the

(former employer: Abraham Lincoln) in 1872, the St. James became a Wild West playground bar none, with just about every famed outlaw passing through its swinging doors. Buffalo Bill Cody met Annie Oakley in the saloon, Jesse James always requested the same room, and Billy the Kid, "Black Jack" Ketchum, and Wyatt Earp all signed the guest register. Cimarron was considered calm and quiet when three days passed without the sound of gunfire in the St. James; bullets are still embedded in walls and ceilings, particularly in the main dining room.

Specifically, one act of the **Colfax County War** played out here, when in 1875 the ranch hand and freelance gunman Clay Allison killed Francisco Griego in alleged self-defense, as Griego was seeking vengeance for the murder of his nephew, the constable Cruz Vega, whom Allison had lynched, in retaliation for his alleged participation in the murder of Franklin Tolby, a young minister who supported the rights of the local settlers. Sound complicated?

© ZORA O'NEILL

NORTHEAST

© ZORA O'NEILL

a beacon in the wilderness: Colfax Tavern

south side of the road, around mile marker 292. Running about 6 miles one-way, **Tolby Creek Trail** makes a longer outing, but most of the trek is pleasantly shaded and damp, ending in beautiful high meadows. This trail is not so clearly marked—you should double-check the route at the **park office,** across the highway from the trailhead at the western park boundary, just before you reach the town of Eagle Nest.

## Accommodations

The **St. James Hotel** (Hwy. 21, 575/376-2664, www.exstjames.com) is the obvious pick here, even if the 12 rooms in the main building have been very gently remodeled in recent years, so in most cases the floors still creak atmospherically, but the bathrooms, with small tubs, are new and shiny. Most have private baths ($120-155), and a few share a more deluxe facility in the hall ($85-100). If you can't live without a TV, phone, and a/c, opt for one of the 10 modern rooms in the annex ($95-105). Room rates include a breakfast buffet with good biscuits and gravy.

Just up the road, the excellent-value **Cimarron Inn & RV Park** (U.S. 64, 575/376-2268, www.cimarroninn.com) offers a different taste of history: Its main building is a converted old motel with snug, thick-walled rooms, each one in a different Western theme. Four small rooms ($49) are a steal for solo travelers or couples, while the eight larger rooms ($69 d) are divvied up like tiny apartments, so there's a wall separating beds. Families or groups might like the Cowboy Cabin ($135), which sleeps up to six people, or the Casita ($240), with room for a dozen.

## Food

Cimarron has few dining options. As usual, the main action, especially at night, when it's the only game in town, is at the **St. James Hotel** (Hwy. 21, 575/376-2664, 7am-10:30am and 11am-9pm daily, $8-20). Unfortunately the food—burgers, steaks, burritos, pizza—is pretty uninspired. The bar here is the only one in town; it's open from 11am till midnight, or "whenever the bartender gets tired of looking at people."

The only other dinner option, and even then it's an early one, is eight miles up the road toward Raton, at the **Colfax Tavern** (32230 U.S. 64, 575/376-2229, 11am-"when we feel like it" Wed.-Sat., noon-evening Sun., $9), better known as Cold Beer, due to these very words painted in extremely large letters on the front of the building. Monday is spaghetti night, its pizza gets praise, and bands play on weekends.

For breakfast or lunch, **( The Porch** (636 E. 9th St., 575/376-2228, 7:30am-2pm Mon.-Fri., 10am-2pm Sat., 10am-1pm Sun. June-Aug., 10am-2pm Mon.-Fri. Sept.-May, $6) sets you up right with strong coffee, pastries, and great chicken salad, and a small market sells local produce. The porch in question faces U.S. 64, but the entrance is on the street one block north.

## Information
Cimarron's **visitors center** (575/376-2417, www.cimarronnm.com, 10am-5pm Mon.-Sat., 1pm-5pm Sun. May-Aug., 10am-4pm Tues.-Sat. Sept.-Apr.) occupies a small house just off U.S. 64 at Lincoln Avenue. You can pick up a walking-tour brochure here, along with other background info. To really get into the history of the place, you could take the **Legends by Lantern Light** tour (575/445-8373, www.legendsbylantern.com, 7:30pm Sat. in summer, $8) to hear the tales of local outlaws.

## Getting There
From Raton, Cimarron is 40 miles southwest, about a 45-minute drive on U.S. 64. Taos is 55 miles away to the west, also on U.S. 64; the drive takes about 1.5 hours.

## PHILMONT SCOUT RANCH
South out of Cimarron, Highway 21 takes the roundabout way back to Springer at

I-25. The first leg roughly follows the old Santa Fe Trail route, passing the headquarters of **Philmont Scout Ranch** (575/376-2281, www.philmontscoutranch.org), the 127,000-acre spread that's now the property of Boy Scouts of America. More than 21,000 scouts come for backpacking trips every year. Practically an independent village, the place has its own post office, fire brigade, and hospital.

Visitors are welcome at **Philmont Museum & Seton Memorial Library** (575/376-1136, 8am-5:30pm daily June-Aug., 8am-5pm Mon.-Fri. Sept.-May, free), which displays a history of the ranch, photos of the Santa Fe Trail, and the art collection of Ernest Thompson Seton, a cofounder of the Boy Scouts. Fans of lavish manors will want to make reservations with the Philmont Museum to see **Villa Philmonte** (call for tour schedule, free), the vacation home of Oklahoma oilman Waite Phillips, the Boy Scouts' benefactor. His Spanish

the Kit Carson Museum in Rayado

© ZORA O'NEILL

Mediterranean manse was built in 1926, and it's still chockablock with European antiques, as well as Waite's collection of Western paraphernalia.

Philmont Scout Ranch also manages the **Kit Carson Museum** (Hwy. 21, 9am-5pm Thurs.-Mon. June-Aug., free), about seven miles farther down Highway 21. The adobe building is near where Lucien Maxwell and his friend Kit Carson set up a camp in the late 1840s, to deal with Santa Fe Trail traders (ruts are still visible where the trail crosses the Rayado River), and the museum re-creates life in that period, with costumed "mountain men" demonstrating how to fire a black-powder rifle, forge a horseshoe, and cook up a meal on a campfire.

# NAVAJO NATION AND THE NORTHWEST

American Indian culture is often relegated to museums, its crafts and relics preserved behind glass or mounted on walls. But in northwestern New Mexico, native traditions are lived every day. The Navajo Nation, the largest reservation in the United States, occupies much of this region and stretches across 27,000 square miles into Arizona and Utah, while the

# HIGHLIGHTS

LOOK FOR ◖ TO FIND RECOMMENDED SIGHTS, ACTIVITIES, DINING, AND LODGING.

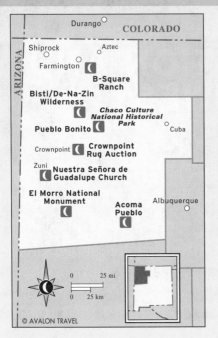

beautiful piece of handmade craftsmanship, and a good story while you're at it. This monthly auction in a Navajo village is a shopping event like no other (page 207).

◖ **El Morro National Monument:** *"Pasó por aquí,"* Don Juan de Oñate scratched in stone in 1605. He was just one of the many famous travelers who left their mark on this cliff face, making it New Mexico's de facto guestbook over the centuries (page 209).

◖ **Nuestra Señora de Guadalupe Church:** Stunning murals decorate the whitewashed walls of Zuni Pueblo's oldest adobe church. Colorful and intricately detailed, the kachinas look vividly real (page 211).

◖ **B-Square Ranch:** Tom Bolack's mind-bogglingly huge collection of taxidermy and his son's museum of electrical relics make for one of the oddest, and most passionate, roadside attractions in the state (page 225).

◖ **Bisti/De-Na-Zin Wilderness:** Hiking this windswept landscape of dusty gray, red, and black stones is like taking a trip to another planet. There are no marked trails, but the weird mushroom-shaped rocks make good landmarks (page 228).

◖ **Acoma Pueblo:** This windswept village on a mesa west of Albuquerque is one of the oldest communities in the United States. Visit for the views as well as for the delicate black-on-white pottery made only here (page 203).

◖ **Crownpoint Rug Auction:** Pick up a

◖ **Pueblo Bonito:** The largest set of ruins at **Chaco Culture National Historical Park,** this 12th-century complex was also the largest building in North America in pre-Columbian times, marking the center of a vast, complex network of trade and culture (page 238).

Acoma, Laguna, and Zuni reservations are three outlying Puebloan communities. Visitors can appreciate a remarkable continuity of culture, from ancient ruins to contemporary powwows. The backdrop is slablike mesas, jagged canyons, spired red-rock buttes—the sort of classic Southwestern scenery that has photographers, mountain bikers, and hikers all reaching for their gear.

The most common route around the area begins on I-40 west out of Albuquerque, toward Acoma Pueblo. A thousand-year-old settlement atop a natural fortress of stone, "Sky City" is one of the most striking spots in New Mexico, rivaling Taos for the title of oldest inhabited town in the United States. Farther on, Gallup is the self-proclaimed Indian capital of the world, a major business hub for more than

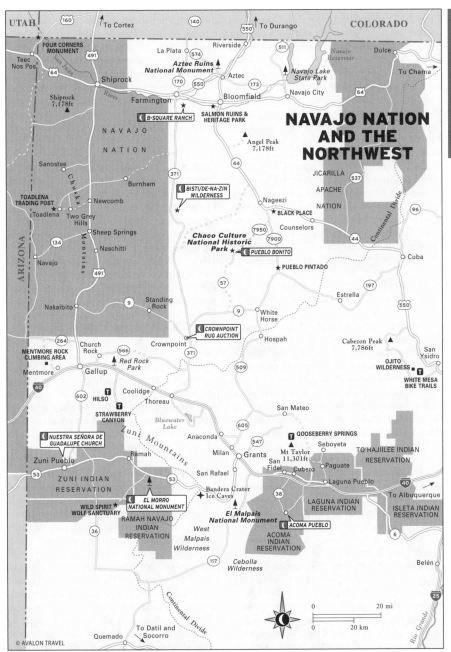

a hundred years. Along with its old-fashioned trading posts, it's emerging as a great outdoor destination, thanks to some excellent trails and rock-climbing sites nearby.

Heading north along a dead-straight and nearly empty highway brings you into the heart of Diné Bikéyah (Navajo land) and past Shiprock, a great plume of volcanic stone sticking straight out of the plain that, like so many natural features in this area, is the subject of scores of legends and tales.

Just beyond the eastern border of the reservation, Farmington is a small town with an outdoorsy bent. It makes a good base for exploring the last big site on the circuit: Chaco Canyon, where between AD 850 and 1250, the ancestral Puebloans (Anasazi) built a nine-mile-long city, a metropolis that served as the ceremonial and religious capital for this influential culture.

## HISTORY

Northwestern New Mexico shows evidence of human occupation as early as 8000 BC, but it was not until the middle of the 9th century AD that people really began to flourish here: AD 850 marks the approximate point when the residents of Chaco Canyon moved from their sunken pit houses into larger, above-ground complexes that grew into multistory blocks. These made up a network of communities as far north as Mesa Verde and as far south as Zuni, all displaying a similar architectural style and connected by skillfully engineered roads. For unknown reasons, though, they eventually left these towns behind and dispersed, some toward the Rio Grande, some to Zuni, and some onto the Hopi lands in what is now Arizona.

Meanwhile, bands of Navajo had migrated from northern climes into the desert a bit west of Chaco. No one has been able to pinpoint the date of their arrival here; the tribe's oral tradition says that Chaco was still inhabited, but archaeological evidence suggests the Navajo were not in their current territory until after Chaco was empty, around 1300, and perhaps not even until shortly before the Spanish made their first *entrada,* in 1540. In any case, the Navajo settled in quickly, and when the Spanish brought

livestock, they added sheepherding—as well as raiding on horseback—to their already highly developed agricultural lifestyle.

Simply because the region was farther away from Santa Fe and the trade routes along the Rio Grande, it avoided some of the worst suffering brought by Spanish rule. The real trouble began when the United States took control of the New Mexico territory in 1846, and optimistic homesteaders began flooding into the lands occupied by often hostile Navajo, Apache, and others. It didn't help that the American expansionists had already discovered rich mineral deposits in the Navajo homeland. The worst confrontations came in the 1860s, the era when federal Indian agent Kit Carson embarked on a scorched-earth campaign, burning crops, slaughtering sheep, and chopping down orchards. On the brink of starvation, the Navajo began to surrender in 1863, and Carson promptly marched them all, in the dead of winter, 400 miles southeast to Fort Sumner. Thousands died during "the Long Walk" and in the following years of captivity. They finally returned to a federally granted reservation in 1868.

Much of modern Navajo history takes place in Arizona, where wrangling with the federal government, private energy interests, and the neighboring Hopi people over the use of coal deposits has been going on for more than a century—but these same factors (minus the Hopi) are constantly at play in New Mexico as well.

## PLANNING YOUR TIME

The driving distances are not so great here, so you could cover this territory in as little as three days, staying one night in Zuni or Gallup and the next in Farmington. But this would leave you time to see only, say, Acoma Pueblo the first day, a long scenic drive including Four Corners the next, and the ruins at Chaco Canyon on the third. If you really want to appreciate how this part of New Mexico is culturally different from the rest of the state, four days will give you a little more time to stop and catch your breath, and maybe take a hike or two. A full week would of course be giving the place its proper due. For anyone with more than a passing interest in ancient archaeological sites, Chaco can take a whole day, or even three. Mountain bikers and hikers could concentrate on the trails around Gallup—a great mix of mountains and rugged rock, and a couple of good places to hang out in town at night.

As there are few mountain ranges, a lot of the terrain in this region is devoid of shade. If you're planning any outdoor activities, try to avoid passing through at the peak of summer. The lower elevations relative to the rest of the state mean that most of this area does not get heavy snow in the winter, but the road to Chaco will be more difficult.

# West to Gallup

I-40 climbs the West Mesa out of Albuquerque and heads straight across a plateau lined with flat mesas—archetypal Southwest scenery. Although it's somewhat dull freeway driving, the destination of ancient Acoma Pueblo is well worth it. Built on top of one of these mesas, it's an amazing place to visit and meet the people whose ancestors have lived here for nearly a thousand years. At the small town of Grants, you can turn south from the highway to enter the volcanic badlands of El Malpais; nearby is El Morro National Monument, a natural pool amid cliffs adorned with centuries-old graffiti. If you're on this loop on Highway 53, you'll next reach Zuni Pueblo, and Gallup (and I-40) is straight north from there.

## LAGUNA PUEBLO

About 18 miles west of Albuquerque, I-40 crosses the border onto the 45 square miles of **Laguna Pueblo** (505/552-6654, www.lagunapueblo.org), on which 7,000 Keresan-speaking Ka-waikah (Lake People) live in six villages. From the highway, the only impression you get of Laguna is its Dancing Eagle Casino, but if you have time, get off at exit 114 to visit the **San José Mission Church.** Established in 1699 when the Laguna people requested a priest (unlike any other pueblo), it stands out for its stark white stucco coating, but this is a relatively recent addition, following a 19th-century renovation. It was mudded and whitewashed every year until the 1950s, when the boom in uranium mining in the area left

no time for this maintenance; it's now sealed with stucco.

Inside, between a packed-earth floor and a finely wrought wood ceiling, the late-18th-century altar screen commands the room. It's the work of the so-called Laguna Santero, an unidentified painter who made the innovation of placing icons inside a crowded field of decorative borders and carved and painted columns, creating a work of explosively colorful folk art that was copied elsewhere in the region in subsequent decades.

If you're lucky, **Alfred Pino,** a local artist and informal guide, will be hanging around the church and offer you a personal tour and explanation of the symbols on the altar and the painted elk hides on the walls, in exchange for a tip and donation to the church. The church is officially open 8am to 4:30pm weekdays (after a 7am morning Mass), but it can be open later and on weekends if Alfred's around.

Each of the six villages of Laguna celebrates its own feast day, and then the whole pueblo turns out at the church September 17-19 for the Feast of San José, one of the bigger pueblo events in the Albuquerque area.

## ◖ ACOMA PUEBLO

At exit 102 off I-40, visitors to Acoma turn south. The road crosses up and over a ridge, and you may feel as though you've crossed through a pass into a Southwestern Shangri-la, for none of this great basin is visible from the highway. Down in the valley, the route runs

## Ceremonial Dances

This is only an approximate schedule for ceremonial dances—dates can vary from year to year. Annual feast days typically involve carnivals and markets in addition to dances. Confirm details and start times—usually afternoon, but sometimes following an evening or midnight Mass—with the **Indian Pueblo Cultural Center** (505/843-7270, www.indianpueblo.org) before setting out. For the Navajo dances in Shiprock, check with the organizers of the **Northern Navajo Nation** Fair (505/368-3727, www.northernnavajonationfair.org).

- **January 6** - Laguna (Old Laguna): Feast of Los Tres Reyes
- **March 19** - Laguna (Old Laguna): Feast of San José
- **Easter** - Most pueblos: various dances
- **July 26** - Laguna (Seama): Feast of Saint Anne
- **August 1** - Acoma (Acomita): Feast of San Lorenzo
- **August 15** - Laguna (Mesita): Feast of the Assumption

- **September 2** - Acoma (Sky City): Feast of San Esteban
- **September 8** - San Ildefonso: corn dances; Laguna (Encinal): Feast of the Nativity of the Blessed Virgin Mary
- **September 19** - Laguna (Old Laguna): Feast of San José
- **September 25** - Laguna (Paguate): Feast of Saint Elizabeth
- **Early October** - Shiprock: Yei Bichei dances
- **October 17** - Laguna (Paraje): Feast of Saint Margaret Mary
- **October 24-27** - Laguna (Old Laguna): harvest dance
- **Late November/early December** - Zuni: Shalako
- **December 24** - Acoma (Sky City): luminaria display; Laguna: dances after evening Mass
- **December 25-28** - Acoma (Sky City): Christmas dances; Laguna: Christmas dances, all villages

directly toward a flat-topped rock that juts up like a tooth.

Atop the rock is the original **Acoma Pueblo,** the village known as **Sky City.** The community covers about 70 acres and is built entirely of pale, sun-bleached adobe, as it has been since at least 1100. Only 50 or so people live on the mesa top year-round, given the hardships of no running water or electricity, but many families maintain homes here, and the place is thronged on September 2, when the pueblo members gather for the **Feast of San Esteban.** The rest of the 2,800 Acoma (People of the White Rock, in their native Keresan) live on the valley floor, which is used primarily as ranchland.

### Visiting Sky City

The fragile nature of the windswept village accounts in part for the particularly stringent tourism policies. All visitors must stop at the **Sky City Cultural Center and Haak'u Museum** (Indian Rte. 23, 800/747-0181, www.acomaskycity.org, 9am-5pm daily Mar.-mid-Nov., 9am-5pm Fri.-Sun. mid-Nov.-Feb.) on the main road, which houses a café and shop stocked with local crafts, along with beautiful rotating exhibits on Acoma art and tradition. From here, you must join a guided tour ($23), which transports groups by bus to the village. The road to the top is the one concession to modernity; previously, all goods had to be hauled up the near-vertical cliff faces. The tour lasts about an hour and a half, after which visitors may return by bus or hike down one of the old trails, using hand- and footholds dug into the rock centuries ago. In summer, tours start at 9:30am and depart every 45 minutes or so, with the last one going at 3:30pm. In the winter, the first tour begins at 10:15am, and they go about hourly until 3pm. Definitely call ahead to check that the tours are running and verify times, as the pueblo closes to visitors periodically.

The centerpiece of the village is the **Church of San Esteban del Rey,** one of the most iconic of the Spanish missions in New Mexico. Built between 1629 and 1640, the graceful, simple structure has been inspiring New Mexican architects ever since. (Visitors are not allowed inside, however, nor into the adjoining cemetery.) As much as it represents the pinnacle of Hispano-Indian architecture in the 17th century, it's also a symbol of the brutality of Spanish colonialism, as it rose in the typical way: forced labor. The men of Acoma felled and carried the tree trunks for the ceiling beams from the forest on Mount Taylor, more than 25 miles across the valley, and up the cliff face to the village.

Acoma is well known for its pottery, easily distinguished by the fine black lines that sweep around the curves of the creamy-white vessel. On the best works, the lines are so fine and densely painted, they shimmer almost like a moiré. The clay particular to this area can be worked extremely thin to create a pot that will hum or ring when you tap it. Throughout the village, you have opportunities to buy pieces. Given the constraints of the tour, this can feel slightly pressured, but in many cases, you have the privilege of buying work directly from the artisan who created it.

### Accommodations and Food

The cultural center contains the **Y'aak'a Café** (9am-4pm daily Mar.-mid-Nov., Fri.-Sun. only mid-Nov.-Feb.), which serves earthy local dishes like lamb stew, tamales, and corn roasted in a traditional *horno* oven—as well as Starbucks coffee. Acoma Pueblo operates the small-scale **Sky City Casino & Hotel** (888/759-2489, www.skycity.com, $99 d), also at exit 102. Its rooms are perfectly clean and functional, and there's a little pool.

## Acoma vs. Oñate: Grudge Match

The early history of the conquistadors with Acoma was one of brutal back-and-forth attacks, each purportedly as revenge for an earlier one. The prime Spanish actor was Don Juan de Oñate, the first governor of Spain's newest province. In a 1599 attack, after many previous skirmishes, his men killed hundreds of Acoma, more than decimating the hilltop village.

But Oñate was not content. After the battle, he brought his enemies into a makeshift court and tried them for murder. The sentence for the inevitable guilty verdict was that every male in Acoma over the age of 25 would have one foot cut off; everyone between the ages of 12 and 25 was pressed into slavery; and the children were sent to convents in Mexico.

Oñate was eventually recalled from his post and chastised for his actions. But in 1640, as if to add insult to injury, the Spanish friars presented the Church of San Esteban del Rey—built by Acoma slaves, over more than a decade—to the maimed pueblo population as "restitution" for Oñate's cruelties. As a further gift of salvation, the friars publicly purged and hanged the village's spiritual leaders in the churchyard.

Variations on this treatment happened up and down the Rio Grande, eventually inspiring the Pueblo Revolt of 1680. But Oñate's particular brand of viciousness is probably the most remembered. Shortly after a monument to the conquistador was erected north of Española in 1998, the right foot of the bronze statue turned up missing—someone had snuck in at night and sawed it clean off. An anonymous letter to newspapers stated that the act was "on behalf of our brothers and sisters at Acoma Pueblo." Rumor adds that the prankster vandals also left behind at the statue two miniature feet made of clay, attached to a shield inscribed with the words "The Agony of Defeat."

# GRANTS

This town of 8,000 has gone through several career changes since its start in the 1880s. It began as a railroad camp, but it soon grew into a lumber town, based on the rich forests of the Zuni Mountains to the south. In the 1940s, logging restrictions kicked in, and locals turned to farming, mustering the questionable boast of "carrot capital of the world."

But just a decade later, Grants reinvented itself as the much more *au courant* "uranium capital of the world," after a local sheepherder happened across some of that valuable ore just outside of town. It turned out to be one of the largest uranium fields in the world. With the best ore depleted in the 1980s and the last mine closed in 1999, Grants is now retired, so to speak. (But recent interest in alternatives to fossil fuel might bring it back for one last job.) Meanwhile, Grants welcomes guests for a meal and a story or two about its past before they carry on to Gallup or Albuquerque. Mount Taylor just to the north is also a destination for hikers.

## New Mexico Mining Museum

If you're just driving through town, try to make time for the surprisingly good **New Mexico Mining Museum** (100 N. Iron Ave., 505/287-4802, 9am-4pm Mon.-Sat., $3), where you descend below the earth into a mock mine shaft. The narration from former miners gets pretty technical, but the narrow tunnels and clanking machinery give you a very real appreciation for the physical labor and risk involved in mining. The museum is on the west side of town, at the corner of Santa Fe Avenue, the main east-west drag.

## Mount Taylor

Heading north out of town, 1st Street (Hwy. 547) turns into Roosevelt Avenue then Lobo Canyon Road, headed toward **Mount Taylor**, a.k.a. Tsoodzil (Turquoise Bead) to the Navajo, who count it as one of their nation's four sacred mountains (although it is not technically on the reservation). Just past mile marker 10

on Highway 547, **Coal Mine Campground** (505/287-8833, May-Sept.) is thick with pines and has some nice shady sites, with a stream running nearby.

Just as the pavement on Highway 547 ends, a right turn onto gravel Forest Road 193 takes you five miles to the head of **Gooseberry Springs Trail** (no. 77). From here, you can hike 3.5 miles to the mountain's summit, at 11,301 feet. Although the elevation gain is 2,400 feet, it's not a very strenuous climb, and it delivers an incredibly rewarding view—on a clear day, you can see as far as the Arizona border. Allow about three hours for the round-trip.

## Food

**Badlands Burgers & Tortas** (519 W. Santa Fe Ave., 505/287-5557, 10am-8pm Mon.-Sat., $7), near the center of town, does a mean green-chile cheeseburger—it won a 2009 championship at the state fair, thanks to its double patties, bacon, and guacamole, along with the green stuff. Its Mexican-style tortas are good too, and not quite as overwhelming.

For coffee, **Coco Bean Café** (333 Nimitz Dr., 505/285-4143, 7am-7pm Mon.-Fri., 8am-4pm Sat., 9am-2pm Sun., $4) is a good excuse to get off the main road through town. Look for Nimitz on the east side of town; turn north and follow the road as it curves and crosses a small bridge.

Farther along, at exit 79 (really Milan, just west of Grants), **Wow Diner** (1300 Motel Dr., 505/287-3801, 6am-midnight Tues.-Sun., $8) is a true old-style diner, its stainless steel gleaming in the sun. The menu has something for everyone, from pork *carnitas* to spinach salad to old-fashioned ice cream shakes.

## Information

Definitely stop in at the helpful and attractive **Northwest New Mexico Visitor Center** (1900 E. Santa Fe Ave., 505/876-2783, 9am-6pm daily in summer, 8am-5pm daily in winter), just south of I-40 at exit 85. Pick up maps, brochures, and suggested driving routes and hiking tours in this corner of the state.

## CROWNPOINT RUG AUCTION

The curiously named town of **Thoreau** (pronounced thu-ROO) at exit 53 inspires no Walden-style reveries, but it is the turnoff for one of the best shopping experiences in northwestern New Mexico. Twenty-five miles north is a small Navajo community, home of the **Crownpoint Rug Auction** (505/786-7386, www.crownpointrugauction.com), which has been connecting buyers and sellers from all around the region since 1968. Even if you have no interest in buying, it's a great cultural experience, and an opportunity to see some beautiful work up close.

The sales, in the school gym on the second Friday of the month (usually; check the website), draws casual shoppers as well as big gallery owners from Santa Fe. Jewelers and potters set up tables in the hall, and vendors sell food in the parking lot, giving the event a bit of a fair feel. It's easy to find the school in the tiny town—turn left from Highway 371 and look for lots of parked cars. Rugs are on view from 4pm to 6:30pm; bidding starts at 7pm and usually lasts till around 10pm. Often with more rugs on offer than customers, there's a good chance you'll find something you like for a reasonable price—a good 4-foot-by-6-foot rug can go for $300 or so, and small sampler rugs can go for $30. Cash is the only payment accepted; there's an ATM in the gas station across from the school, but don't rely on it for any big purchase.

There's nowhere to stay in Crownpoint; Grants and Gallup (preferable for lodging options) are both about an hour's drive, and Farmington is due north on Highway 371, about an hour and a half away.

## EL MALPAIS NATIONAL MONUMENT

The product of three volcanic events, the lava-strewn landscape of the **El Malpais National Monument** (505/783-4774, www.nps.gov/elma, free) is not exactly the barren terrain *el malpaís* (el-mal-pie-EES, literally, the badlands) suggests. A surprising amount of greenery has

© ZORA O'NEILL

taking offers at the Crownpoint Rug Auction

NORTHWEST

© ZORA O'NEILL

the natural arch at El Malpais National Monument

taken root in the millennia since the last eruption, between 2,000 and 3,000 years ago, and in the spring, wildflowers stand out against the jagged black rock. The lava fields are riven with deep, cave-like tubes that formed as the hot rock cooled. Some of the most scenic areas are along the monument's eastern border, where the lava meets red sandstone cliffs, as well as New Mexico's largest natural arch.

For those who just want a quick look, the easiest access point is **Sandstone Bluffs Overlook,** where, on a short walk along the edge of the eastern cliffs, you can admire the lava fields, and see north to Mount Taylor. It's about 11 miles south from I-40 on Highway 117. Drive another 7 miles to reach **La Ventana Arch,** a great sandstone arc; a short trail leads to a scenic viewing spot.

If you'd like a longer hike or drive into the park, stop first at the **Northwest New Mexico Visitors Center** (1900 E. Santa Fe Ave., 505/876-2783, 9am-6pm daily in summer, 8am-5pm daily in winter), near I-40 at exit 85, midway between the two highways

that access different parts of the badlands. National Park Service employees can give you detailed maps and current conditions, and from there you can decide whether to take Highway 53 or Highway 117 south into the monument area. The monument **information center** (505/783-4774, 8am-4:30pm daily) is less conveniently located on Highway 53, 23 miles south of I-40.

In addition to the hikes detailed below, there are more demanding but worthwhile places to explore outside the borders of the national park, in the BLM land designated **Cebolla Wilderness** (off the southeast border of the park) and **West Malpais Wilderness** (to the south and west)—ask at the visitors center for details on these areas as well.

### Zuni-Acoma Trail

By far the most strenuous hike, the shadeless 7.5-mile **Zuni-Acoma Trail** cuts across the lava beds roughly along the path used for centuries by the Puebloans in this region. It's rough going because the ground is so uneven, but if you're interested in the plants and animals that thrive in El Malpais, this can be a rewarding trek. The eastern trailhead is on Highway 117, before you reach La Ventana Arch; the western one is on Highway 53.

## Lava Falls Area

For the best up-close look at the lava, head farther south on Highway 117 to the **Lava Falls Area.** Here you can still make out the swirls and eddies of the molten stuff as if it had cooled yesterday; the variety of shapes and textures is fascinating, as are the odd pockets of stunted trees that manage to flourish here. The three-mile route (a mile-long loop with a one-mile spur) is marked only by rock cairns, so bring a compass, as it's easy to get disoriented.

## El Calderon Area

At the **El Calderon Area** on Highway 53, a three-mile loop trail heads to **El Calderon Cinder Cone,** the area around the lava vent, and then back to the parking lot via a dirt road. Calderon Crater, the oldest of the three lava flows that make up the area, dates back some 115,000 years—as a result, the rock is more weathered, and not the stark black found around younger McCartys Crater. This is also the area where lava tubes are closest to the road—a short walk from the car reveals the entrance to **Junction Cave,** a tube that partially collapsed—you see a sliver of daylight on the other end. The famous **Bat Cave,** less than a mile from the parking area, still has a circling cloud of the nocturnal critters at sunset, though not as many as in the past.

## Big Tubes Area

The **Big Tubes Area,** a network of 17 miles of lava caves on the west side of the monument, has by far the weirdest terrain, but it was closed at the time of research, again due to the bat fungus. Even if it does reopen, you'll need a high-clearance truck to get here, as well as headlamps (with extra batteries), sturdy boots, and heavy work gloves to protect your hands from the jagged rocks.

## Bandera Crater Ice Caves

A family-run tourist attraction that was grand-fathered in when El Malpais was made a national monument, the **Bandera Crater Ice Caves** (Hwy. 53, 888/ICE-CAVE, www.ice-caves.com, 9am-5pm daily Mar.-Oct., 9am-4pm daily Nov.-Feb., $11) are an impressive natural sight, especially during the heat of summer, when you can descend from 90°F outside to 31°F underground, the chill emanating from a permanent layer of greenish ice at least 20 feet thick. Although the same phenomenon is visible elsewhere in El Malpais (for much less money), this is the most accessible spot, and generally more impressive. The other half of the attraction, Bandera Crater, 750 feet deep, is actually not much to look at—literally, just a big hole in the ground.

## ◖ EL MORRO NATIONAL MONUMENT

This area may seem like relative wilderness today, but in fact, it has always been a fairly well-traveled route. The proof is at the **El Morro National Monument** (Hwy. 53, 505/783-4226, www.nps.gov/elmo, 9am-5pm daily, free), where Don Juan de Oñate carved his name in the bluff *(morro)* and darkened the inscription with lamp soot, as a way of passing the time while his men rested and horses drank at the natural pool formed by snowmelt. It's also a vivid image of the early Spanish power in the Southwest—Oñate made his mark in 1605, seven years after his first official colonizing mission, and two years before the English even set foot in the New World. In the centuries since, seemingly every celebrity of the American West, major and minor, has left a graffiti autograph: Don Diego de Vargas was here in 1692, early in his campaign to reclaim Nuevo México following the Pueblo Revolt of 1680. P. Gilmer Breckenridge, who led an experimental caravan of 25 camels from Texas to California, visited in 1857, and his compatriot, E. Pen Long, left a curlicue signature that gets the prize for best penmanship.

The half-mile **Inscription Loop Trail** is paved and leads first to the year-round pool

NORTHWEST

© ZORA O'NEILL

**historic American graffiti at El Morro National Monument**

at the base of the rocks, then along the cliff face. The longer you stare at the rocks, the more names—as well as figures, carved by the Zuni centuries earlier—pop out. The natural ground level has sunk over the centuries too, so the graffiti crawls up the cliffs well above your head. For a view, continue on up to the top of the bluffs on the **Headland Trail.** The loop, which takes another hour, passes Atsinna, the ruins of a small pueblo occupied by the Zuni in the 13th and 14th centuries.

## Accommodations and Food

With just nine primitive sites, El Morro public **campground** (free) is usually very quiet—though it can be difficult to get a spot in the summer, when it's first-come, first-served. The water is shut off after the first freeze, usually in October.

If the public campground is full, or you just want a little more comfort, **El Morro RV Park & Cabins** (Hwy. 53, 505/783-4612, www.el-morro-nm.com), immediately east of the national monument, is a great place to stay in the

wilderness. Tent campsites are $15 per night, while tidy little cabins with queen and double beds start at $79; RV sites are $25. The on-site **Ancient Way Café** (9am-5pm Sun.-Tues. and Thurs., 9am-8pm Fri.-Sat., $8) has tasty brisket and beans, and good veggie options; weekend dinners are one set entrée (jerk chicken, for instance), and you should call to reserve.

Just east on the highway a few miles is the excellent ☾ **La Tinaja Navajo Café** (Hwy. 53, 505/783-4349, 11am-9pm Tues.-Fri., 9am-9pm Sat.-Sun., $10), which uses locally raised beef and other goodies for everything from "Navajo fajitas" to German sausage specials to home-baked zucchini bread. Look for the big barn on the south side of the road.

## RAMAH

Twelve miles west of El Morro, Ramah (pronounced RAY-muh) was originally settled by Mormons, though now part of the Navajo reservation. The local Ramah Navajo Weavers Association, like the collective in Tierra Amarilla in northern New Mexico, has helped revive an economy based on sheep, particularly the old Churro breed. The settlement's history is told in the tiny **Ramah Museum** (505/783-4215, 1pm-4pm Fri.); at the curve in town, turn north.

## Wild Spirit Wolf Sanctuary

Just before you reach Ramah, you pass the turn for the **Wild Spirit Wolf Sanctuary** (505/775-3304, www.wildspiritwolfsanctuary.org, 10am-5pm Tues.-Sun., $7), where you can hang out with some 50 captive-bred wolves and wolf-dogs that would otherwise go homeless. **Guided tours** (required) run at 11am and 12:30pm, 2pm, and 3:30pm. You can also **camp** here ($15 for tents or RVs)—then you're here in the morning to help feed the animals (reserve ahead; $25 pp). Signs off Highway 53 point to Mountainview and Pine Hill; it's another 12 miles on Indian Route 125 and 120.

# Zuni Pueblo

Covering more than 600 square miles and with a population of more than 10,000, Zuni is the largest of the pueblos. For centuries, the Zuni people were spread over a wide area in several settlements. The pueblo Halona:wa (Anthill), around which the modern town of Zuni is based, was established long ago, but did not become the center of population until 1692, after the people made a peace agreement with Don Juan de Oñate and gathered here. With plenty of new, cinder-block construction, the town doesn't look immediately appealing, but if you stay overnight (it's the only pueblo where you can do so), you'll have a better appreciation for the community. If you can't spend the night, certainly take the tour of the small historic core of the village—otherwise Zuni's appeal may be lost in the dust.

Isolation from the Rio Grande-area pueblos has helped keep Zuni culture more distinct—its *"olla* maidens," for instance, perform a traditional dance with pots balanced on their heads. Zuni is also famous for its delicate inlay jewelry, called "needlepoint," in which the tiniest bits of turquoise, coral, and other stones are set in intricate patterns on a silver field; the texture almost resembles beadwork. Collectors also hold Zuni kachinas (figurines of spirit beings) and fetishes (tiny carved animals) in high esteem. If you're coming here to shop, though, avoid late June and late December, when a period of fasting called Deshkwi bans buying or selling.

## SIGHTS

Register first at the **visitors center** (Hwy. 53, 505/782-7238, www.zunitourism.com, 8:30am-5:30pm Mon.-Fri., 10am-4pm Sat., noon-4pm Sun.), midway through town on the north side of the road. Here you can get information on artists' studios as well as arrange a number of tours, including the highly recommended **walking tour** around Old Zuni (Middle Village).

All tours require advance notice, but if you have a particular interest, they are a wonderful way of seeing a different side of Zuni. The visitors center can arrange a 2.5-hour **artist workshop tour** ($75 for up to four people), based on your preferred medium (silver, stone, etc.), as well as a **traditional meal** ($12 pp) featuring local tamales, bread, and more. The former requires three days' notice; the latter, seven. Archaeological site visits are also possible, to **Hawikku,** where ancestral Zuni lived and where Coronado thought one of the "Cities of Gold" might be; and to the **Village of the Great Kivas,** inhabited in the 11th century. Both are $75 for up to four people and require a week's notice.

### ◖ Nuestra Señora de Guadalupe Church

The core of the historic area called the Middle Village is the **Nuestra Señora de Guadalupe Church,** where the walls, first erected in 1629 and rebuilt in 1692, are painted with larger-than-life Shalako figures and other elements of the Zuni tradition as they function in the four seasons. The brilliantly colored murals, created over more than 20 years beginning in 1970, are the work of one esteemed pueblo artist, Alex Seowtewa, and his sons. Together with the blankets and buffalo heads, this is one of the most syncretic churches in the state— a beautiful, fervent expression of faith over millennia.

The church is accessible only by **guided tour** (10am, 1pm, and 3pm Mon.-Sat., 1pm and 3pm Sun.), which departs from the Zuni visitors center. Theoretically, two separate tours are offered: one around the old town and one to the church, each for $10. But in practice, all visitors are usually lumped into a single tour of everything for $15. The whole combined tour takes a little over an hour.

### A:shíwi A:wan Museum and Heritage Center

Zuni's small **A:shíwi A:wan Museum and Heritage Center** (2 E. Ojo Caliente Rd., 505/782-4403, www.ashiwi-museum.org, 9am-6pm Mon.-Fri., free) is fascinating. It tells the story of the Zuni people, from creation myths through more contemporary issues with archaeologists and other researchers, such as Frank Cushing, who brought the pueblo to broader attention in the 19th century and became a local hero for a time. Cushing's endeavors are portrayed in a few hilarious cartoons by a Zuni artist. Also on display are artifacts from the ancestral settlement of Hawikku, excavated in 1916. They had been whisked away to a basement in a branch of the Smithsonian; Zuni leaders negotiated for this selection to be returned, leaving the remainder to be better preserved at the Smithsonian.

The museum is just south of Highway 53: Turn at the major stop sign on the west end of town; the museum is at the next big intersection, on the northwest corner, across from Halona Plaza.

## FESTIVALS AND EVENTS

The largest event of the year, the ritual of **Shalako** (also spelled Sha'la'ko) marks the end of the agricultural season and the beginning of winter in late November or early December. Although many of the prayers and dances take place in areas closed to visitors, it is still a remarkable time to visit the pueblo.

The Shalako, part of the extensive pantheon of kachinas, act as messengers between man and gods; when they depart the village, they are bearing the Zuni prayer for rain in the spring. For this ceremony, they are men who are elected each year to impersonate these godlike forces, and they spend the entire year preparing. The 24-hour ritual begins around noon, but the real excitement comes at dusk, when the men descend from the sacred mesa south of town. With giant eagle-feather masks with goggle eyes and wooden beaks, they are transformed into frightening, noisy, 10-foot-tall creatures; they are an awesome sight as they swoop through the crowds and the bonfires, their beaks clacking and the drums pounding behind them. As they proceed around the village, lit only by bonfires, the effect is transporting.

Shortly after Shalako, the whole community gathers for the **Give-Away,** to thank the clans involved in the ritual—preparation is a massive expense. People bring specific gifts as well as all manner of unused items, from deer meat to refrigerators, which are redistributed according to need. Again, it's a ceremony that outsiders may not entirely get, but it's a festive time to be in town.

Other secular events throughout the year include the **Zuni Cultural Arts Expo,** in late July or early August; the **McKinley County Fair,** also in August; the **Ancient Way Fall Festival,** an arts and harvest festival all along Highway 53 in early October; and the **Holiday Arts Market,** in early December. The visitors center can confirm dates.

## ACCOMMODATIONS AND FOOD

Unlike most pueblos, where visitors are welcome for the day or as casino customers, Zuni offers a unique opportunity to stay overnight and just soak up the atmosphere of the place: wood smoke, red dirt, and sparkling stars. The supremely comfortable 🌙 **Inn at Halona** (23-B Pia Mesa Rd., 505/782-4418, www.halona. com, $79) is run by a French native whose late wife had century-old roots on the reservation. The older main house has five rooms (no. 4 upstairs is beautifully sunny, while the basement no. 5 is big yet cozy-feeling), but you might prefer the side house if you prefer to sleep late, because the scene in the main house's breakfast room can get pretty animated. Guests dig in to what seems like an endless array of breads, eggs,

meats, and the signature blue-corn pancakes. Book well ahead if you plan to be in town during any special events.

The main place to eat is the adjacent general store, **Halona Plaza**, where the deli counter serves up excellent fried chicken ($6) with smoky-hot red-chile sauce on the side—New Mexican fusion at its finest. There's a bit more of a social scene at night down at **Chu-Chu's** (1344 Hwy. 53, 505/782-2100, 11am-10pm, Mon.-Sat., $8), on the east end of the town, where there's pizza, subs, and a nice little patio.

The seriously food-curious should also stop in to **Paywa's Bakery** (noon-5pm Wed.-Fri.), down a dirt road opposite Chu-Chu's. The operation bakes sourdough and sweet pies in a giant adobe *horno*.

# Gallup

Initially just a wide spot along the railroad, Gallup took its name from the man who doled out cash in exchange for the coal that companies hauled in from the surrounding mines in the 1880s. By the 1920s, Gallup was known for its exceptionally pure coal, which meant higher wages for workers, who flooded in from Britain, China, Italy, Greece, and scores of other places, making the town a polyglot community from early on. The mining business has slowed, but at least a hundred trains still rumble through every day—it's a near-constant background noise, and as the freight loads cruise right through the center of town, you often have the disconcerting sensation of looking down a street and seeing the background in motion.

Gallup's other disconcerting effect is the sense you've stepped onto a movie set. The place was a popular Hollywood location from the 1930s on through the Route 66 heyday, and it's not hard to see why, what with the glowing neon, the red sandstone cliffs, and the jagged Hogback Mountains, which inspire visions of Wild West adventure. Less glamorously, in

the 1970s and 1980s, Gallup struggled with high unemployment, and astronomical rates of drunk driving and alcoholism. But one get-tough mayor started a turnaround, and now downtown is clean and lively, and the civic pride is palpable.

## SIGHTS

The railway and I-40 divide Gallup in two, but most of what visitors want is on the south side: The historic downtown area is on Highway 66 and Coal Avenue, lined with the most notable buildings and shops. The far east and west ends of town cater to through travelers on the interstate, with all the chain hotels and restaurants.

You can cover most of Gallup's attractions on foot after parking downtown. Some of the best art is outdoors, in the many murals around town, some painted by the WPA in the 1930s and others put up in the 21st century. There's one dedicated to the Navajo code talkers on South 2nd Street just south of Highway 66, as well as a great modern one on the side of the city hall (Aztec Avenue at South 2nd Street)

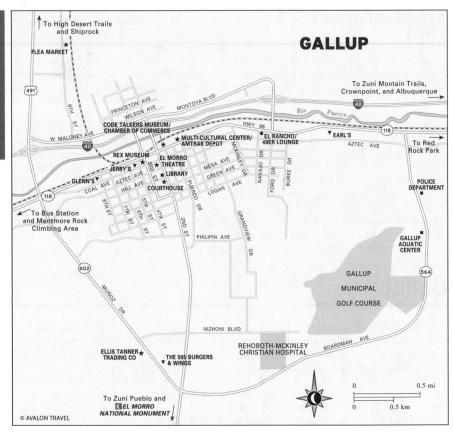

that evokes modern life in Gallup: kids in pickup trucks, road construction, and rodeo events.

## McKinley County Courthouse

Downtown is anchored by the Pueblo Revival **McKinley County Courthouse** (207 W. Hill St.), one block south of Coal Avenue. If you ask nicely and it's a slow day, you can walk around inside the courthouse and admire the tile work, the punched-tin light fixtures, and the 2,000-square-foot WPA mural in the main courtroom. Painted by Lloyd Moylan, it's the largest surviving work from that period in the state.

## WWII Navajo Code Talkers Museum

Adjoining the chamber of commerce, the **WWII Navajo Code Talkers Museum** (103 W. Hwy. 66, 505/722-2228, 8am-5pm Mon.-Fri., free) is a large collection of memorabilia arranged in fluorescent-lit glass cases—ask the chamber employees to turn the lights on. No frills here: The room is mostly used for business meetings, but the collected papers, photographs, and clippings trace the use of the Navajo language as code through the fight. Given the importance of the code to the success of the U.S. campaign, it's a little depressing to realize this is one of the largest permanent exhibits on the

the Pueblo Revival McKinley County Courthouse in Gallup

© ZORA O'NEILL

subject (there's another inside the Burger King in Kayenta, Arizona).

## Multi-Cultural Center

The old Santa Fe Rail station has been converted into a well-used community arts center. Visitors will enjoy the **Storyteller Museum** (201 E. Hwy. 66, 505/863-4131, 10am-4pm Tues.-Sat., free) upstairs. The nifty collection of dioramas—scenes involving model trains, a replica trading post—are accompanied by headphones to listen to a local's explanation of the scene. You'll also find a café, a visitors info desk, a music shop, and the **Ceremonial Gallery,** which exhibits local student art.

Between Memorial Day and Labor Day, free guided **walking tours** of downtown depart from here, usually at 10am daily.

## Rex Museum

Like many small-town collections, the **Rex Museum** (300 W. Hwy. 66, 505/863-1363, 9am-6pm Mon.-Fri., $2 donation) is a hodgepodge, from roller skates to programs from the Inter-Tribal Ceremonial. But perhaps it's most interesting to see the traces of the various immigrant groups that have settled in Gallup, from Chinese to Greeks.

## Red Rock Park

East of town about six miles, **Red Rock Park** is Gallup's public party spot, with rodeo grounds and an outdoor amphitheater. It also has the surprisingly large **Red Rock Museum** (505/722-3839, 8am-noon and 1pm-5pm Mon.-Fri., $2 donation), which feels as though it was set up in the 1970s, then left to its own devices. The display cases, filled with information on the Zuni, Hopi, and Navajo, are a little dusty; you'll probably have to turn the lights on yourself. It houses one of the most elaborate displays of Zuni kachinas anywhere—all the figurines labeled, and their roles explained. There's also a model hogan (the traditional Navajo home) and a selection of local jewelry styles. Access the park via the frontage road (E. Hwy. 66), from exit 33 or exit 26 off I-40, then turn north on Highway 566.

## The Navajo Code Talkers

© ZORA O'NEILL

**the memorial to the Navajo Code Talkers and victims of the Bataan Death March, in downtown Gallup**

The ingenuity and heroism of the Navajo code talkers of World War II has only come to full light in recent decades. As a result, this team of more than 300 men (and one Anglo fighter fluent in Navajo) have become a novel footnote in the history of the war, rather than a crucial element in the U.S. military's victory. In fact, the never-broken code, based on Navajo vocabulary, was an essential part of the Battle of Iwo Jima, and the code talkers were involved in every Marine battle in the Pacific.

Twenty-nine recruits formed the first team of code talkers, who also developed the code. At its core, the system used Navajo words to represent letters of the alphabet—these could be used to spell, or combined to form larger words and concepts. For instance, *w* was represented by the Navajo word for weasel, *gloe-ih*.

To say "when," the code talker said "weasel" and "hen": *gloe-ih-na-ah-wo-hai;* "will" was *gloe-ih-dot-sahi,* or "sick weasel." Military terms required more creativity: a *bish-lo,* or "iron fish," was a submarine.

The advantage of Navajo was that it was a highly complex yet completely oral language, with only a handful of nonnative speakers. Moreover, it was extremely fast to transmit, because unlike previous systems, it didn't require a machine at either end. The code talkers have long been a point of pride for the Navajo, especially as symbols of the power of speaking the ancestral language. A **mural** by Be Sargent on South 2nd Street in Gallup depicts the code in visual form, showing the original 29 code talkers along with the various animals and objects used as keys in the code.

# ENTERTAINMENT AND EVENTS

On an average day, the streets of Gallup are not exactly hopping. You will notice a significant rush on weekends, though, as people from surrounding communities come into town to do business. And expect crowds during the two big annual events, a powwow and a balloon rally. The landmark **El Morro Theatre** (110 W. Aztec Ave., 505/726-0050, www.elmorrotheatre.com) is downtown, built in 1926 in the Spanish colonial revival style. It's a venue for films as well as local theater and music.

## Nightlife

Gallup's past alcohol problems mean liquor laws are strict, and few places stay open very late. Even **Coal Street Pub** (303 W. Coal Ave., 505/722-0117, 11am-10pm Sun.-Wed., 11am-11pm Thurs.-Sat.), the main bar downtown, serves only beer and wine. It's a convivial place in the evening, often with some kind of live music on the weekends.

The **49er Lounge** (1000 E. Hwy. 66, 5pm-1am daily) in the El Rancho Hotel does serve booze, but you might not need it because the setting is dizzying enough—like the rest of the hotel, this place exudes an almost overwhelming aura of decaying Western glamour. Go early, as it tends to close before the posted time if business is slow.

On weekends, you might also find mellow live music at **Angela's Café** (201 E. Hwy. 66, 505/722-7526, 9am-5pm Mon.-Thurs., 9am-9pm Fri., 11am-5pm Sat., $7).

## Festivals and Events

Every night at 7pm between Memorial Day and Labor Day, Navajo, Hopi, and other dance and music groups perform in the plaza in front of the courthouse, for free.

For four days in late July or early August, Gallup hosts the **Inter-Tribal Indian Ceremonial** (www.theceremonial.com), which draws more than 20,000 participants from various tribes in Canada and Mexico, as well as all over the United States. Also on the schedule

are a beauty pageant, a fashion show, and lots of music.

The other big annual event is the **Red Rock Balloon Rally** (www.redrockballoonrally.com), on the first weekend in December. With about 200 participating hot air balloons, it has been going strong since 1981, probably because the setting, against the vibrant sandstone at Red Rock Park, is unbeatable. The balloonists often need extra volunteers, so it's a good chance to get a free ride or join a chase crew—show up early and ask around.

# SHOPPING

With a historic trading post or overstocked pawnshop seemingly every 10 feet, Gallup can be an exciting or overwhelming place to shop, depending on your point of view. But even if you don't feel up to sifting through treasure troves of Navajo turquoise, the **trading posts,** some in business for the better part of a century and still doing business primarily with the local Indian population, are worth a visit simply as another town attraction. They're stocked with everything from hand-spun skeins of wool to crisp new blue jeans, and of course, heaps and heaps of jewelry.

One of the oldest, most respected trading posts downtown is **Richardson's Trading Co. & Cash Pawn** (222 W. Hwy. 66, 505/722-4762, 9am-6pm Mon.-Sat.), where the warren of storefronts is permeated with the smell of old leather.

Another shopping hotspot is **City Electric Shoe Shop** (230 W. Coal Ave., 505/863-5252, 10am-6pm Mon.-Sat.), where you can pick up a pair of street-ready moccasins in butter-soft suede or an embossed leather belt—both are made in a workshop in the basement.

On the south side, **Ellis Tanner Trading Co.** (1980 Hwy. 602, 505/863-4434, 8am-7pm Mon.-Sat.) has deep roots in Gallup; check inside for a huge mural by local artist Chester Kahn, honoring locals who have been good role models. You can pick up roasted piñon nuts, Diné-English children's books, vintage dance regalia, and more.

But perhaps the best shopping experience

© ZORA O'NEILL

grilled lamb sandwich and corn stew at the
Gallup flea market

in Gallup is at the 9th Street **flea market**
(505/722-7328) every Saturday on the north
side of town. It's a great swap meet where you
can pick up anything from a beaded necklace to
a wolf-mix puppy to a bale of hay—not to mention all kinds of traditional foods. Vendors get
rolling around 10am, and wind up in the mid-
afternoon. To get there, head north on U.S.
491, then cut east to North 9th Street on West
Jefferson Avenue.

## SPORTS AND RECREATION

The city of Gallup has developed great trails
on the nearby sandstone bluffs and in the pon-
derosa-covered Zuni Mountains. There's a lot
to do in a relatively small area, and it's all still
crowd-free. For additional details to what follows, see the **Adventure Gallup website** (www.
adventuregallup.org), or pick up a comprehensive map from the chamber of commerce.

### Biking

The main mountain biking network is the

**High Desert Trail System.** The three inter-
connecting loops, each rated for a different
skill level, run along the mesas northwest of
town. In addition to great views over cliff
edges and some tricky constructed switchbacks, the trails are marked by occasional
public art—so just when you think the weird
rock formations are sculpture enough, you
might look up to see a black steel bobcat peer-
ing down at you. The main trailhead, called
Gamerco, is two miles north on U.S. 491, then
left on Chino Loop; the gravel parking lot is
on the left side of the road.

For shady forest biking, head to the **Zuni
Mountain Trail System,** a patch of national
forest southeast of Gallup. From exit 33 on
I-40, Highway 400 runs south about six
miles to Hilso Trailhead, the beginning of
several climbs up through ponderosa forests and aspens; nearly all intersect up on
the ridgeline, so you can come back a different way.

In town, **Brickyard Park** (700 E. Aztec Ave.)
is a mountain-bike terrain park in Gallup's old
clay quarry. Come here to practice your skills
on dirt tracks and jumps.

### Hiking

Hikers are also welcome on the High Desert
and Zuni Mountain trails, though two-wheelers have the right-of-way. In the latter area,
**Strawberry Canyon Trail** is a shady, easy 1.5-
mile hike up to a lookout tower, and it runs
along a rough forest road, so there's room for
both bikers and hikers. Follow Highway 400
past Hilso Trailhead, up to mile marker 0; just
past the entrance to McGaffey Campground is
a parking area on the right.

At two accessible trails close to town, you get
the whole place to yourself. They both start in
Red Rock Park: **Pyramid Rock Trail** is a 1.7-
mile hike up to 7,487 feet, atop an aptly named
butte. **Church Rock Trail** is 2.2 miles round-
trip (a stem with a loop at the end)—it's less of
a climb, working around the base of some dramatic rocks. An optional connector trail (1.3
miles) links the two routes, making a full hike
of three to four hours.

East of town, Pyramid Rock Trail leads up Gallup's sandstone rocks.

### Rock Climbing
A well-maintained public park east of town, **Mentmore Rock Climbing Area** is frequented by only a handful of local regulars. With 31 sport routes and 50 bolted top-rope climbs spread over six different walls, along with quite a few bouldering options, there's more than enough fun to go around. At least some of the rocks get sun all the time, so it's climbable in the winter, but check the weather before heading out. The sandstone is fragile when wet, so local policy is to stay off the rocks for a couple of days after heavy rain. To get there, take exit 16 from I-40 and head west on Highway 66 for half a mile; turn north on County Road 1, then bear west as it turns into Mentmore Road, leading directly to the parking area.

### Swimming
**Gallup Aquatic Center** (620 S. Boardman Ave., 505/726-5460, $4) is a kid's dream, with curvy slides galore, cactus-shaped sprinklers, and even a "lazy river" setup; adults get a separate competition-size pool for laps. It's all indoors, but still a lot of fun.

## ACCOMMODATIONS
Even if you don't plan to spend the night, do stop in at **El Rancho Hotel** (1000 E. Hwy. 66, 505/863-9311, www.elranchohotel.com, $92 s, $102 d). The lobby alone is a Western fantasia of rustic wood paneling, furniture made of bull horns, a giant stone fireplace, and glossy photos of all the Hollywood actors who passed through the doors back in Gallup's heyday as a movie backdrop. (It helped that the man who built the place in 1937 was D. W. Griffith's brother.) Rooms named after Kirk Douglas, Ronald Reagan, and others are kitted out with wagon-wheel headboards and vintage bathroom tile; some even have back porches.

A separate motel wing has significantly less character but perfectly clean and functional rooms—rates here start at $60. Guests at both have access to a decent swimming pool, and there's (sometimes spotty) wireless Internet access in the lobby. Practically speaking, rooms in the main hotel seem faintly overpriced. But for sheer atmosphere, this is one of the best places in the state to get a taste of what tourism must've been like back when New Mexico really was the wild frontier. Ignore the unreliable online booking engine (which doesn't show the motel rooms)—just call to reserve.

## FOOD
As with the hotels, all the chain places (and a couple of vintage diners) are near the freeway exits. You definitely get more local flavor, in every sense, if you venture into the center of town.

### Cafés
The whitewashed **Coffee House** (203 W. Coal Ave., 505/726-0291, 7am-8:30pm Mon.-Sat., $6) has an old tin ceiling, contemporary photography on the walls, and a mellow atmosphere where Navajo artists and fleece-clad mountain bikers mingle. Evenings often see some local singer-songwriter. The menu ranges

© ZORA O'NEILL

The El Rancho Hotel is a marvel of yesterday.

from fresh salads and big sandwiches to a full breakfast.

With a nice small-town diner vibe, **Angela's Café** (201 E. Hwy. 66, 505/722-7526, 9am-5pm Mon.-Thurs., 9am-9pm Fri., 11am-5pm Sat., $7), in the cultural center in the former train station, serves burgers and a good selection of craft beers to locals. Despite its opening hours, it doesn't really do breakfast—just an egg sandwich for waiting train passengers. In the evenings, there's occasionally acoustic music.

◖ **Glenn's Bakery** (900 W. Hwy. 66, 505/722-4104, 6am-9pm Mon.-Sat., $3-10) is impressive first for its dazzling doughnut case, which includes wonderfully flaky cinnamon rolls. If you need more than a sugar fix, settle in alongside locals reading the morning papers for breakfast burritos, pizza, or one of the daily specials, such as lamb stew.

Aside from the fact that all burgers are served well-done, **The 505 Burgers & Wings** (1981 Hwy. 602, 505/722-9311, 11am-7pm Mon.-Fri., 11am-3pm Sat., $9) is pretty good, with

hand-cut fries, pretzel-bread buns, and nice fresh sides. And, with an almost entirely local clientele, it's a good glimpse of regular life in Gallup. Look for it in a small strip mall on the south side of town.

### New Mexican

Family-owned, with a battered neon sign, ◖ **Jerry's Café** (406 W. Coal Ave., 505/722-6775, 8am-9pm Mon.-Sat., $8) has a crowd of dedicated followers (read: addicts) who drive miles for the stuffed sopaipilla, drenched in superhot red-chile sauce. The place is tiny and often packed with courthouse employees during lunchtime, so go late or early.

It may not have the absolute best food in town, but **Earl's** (1400 E. Hwy. 66, 505/863-4201, 6am-8:30pm Mon.-Sat., 7:30am-6:30pm Sun., $8) has a timeless atmosphere that can't be beat. Since 1947, it has been serving biscuits and gravy, Navajo tacos, and enchiladas. It's conveniently close to the east-side freeway exit, and gets packed after the Saturday flea market. You'll either love or hate the fact that local artisans go table to table selling their wares.

If you're not staying at El Rancho, you could pop in for a perfectly good meal at the **El Rancho Restaurant** (1000 E. Hwy. 66, 505/863-9311, 6:30am-10pm daily, $11), where all the dishes are named after Hollywood stars. New Mexican food is your best bet, including *atole* (cornmeal mush) for breakfast; the margaritas ($7 for "top shelf" with fresh lime juice) are dangerously strong.

## INFORMATION

Conveniently located right downtown, the staff at the **chamber of commerce** (106 W. Hwy. 66, 505/722-2228, www.thegallupchamber. com, 8:30am-5pm Mon.-Fri.) can answer just about any question. From Memorial Day to Labor Day, it's also open Saturdays, from 8:30am to 5pm.

## GETTING THERE

By car, Gallup is two hours (140 miles) west of Albuquerque on I-40, and nearly three hours (187 miles) east of Flagstaff, Arizona. From Farmington, it's a two-hour drive south (120 miles).

Trains stop at Gallup's station on Highway 66 once a day, eastbound and westbound. From Albuquerque, the trip takes about 2.5 hours and costs $24, making it a pleasant option for a car-free outing. The station, which is used as the Multi-Cultural Center, is not staffed; you'll have to contact **Amtrak** (800/872-7245, www.amtrak.com) for tickets and train status.

**Greyhound** (800/231-2222, www.greyhound.com) serves Gallup from Albuquerque, with departures from a mini-mart on the west side (3060 W. Hwy. 66, 505/863-9078) three times daily.

# Navajo Nation

Covering some 27,000 square miles in New Mexico, Arizona, and Utah, the Navajo Nation is the largest reservation in the United States, and with nearly 300,000 people claiming Navajo ancestry (about 175,000 of whom live on the reservation), the Navajo are the largest tribe in the country. They call themselves Diné (The People); the term Navajo came from Tewa via the Spanish, translating as "cultivated field," for which these settled people were already well known when the conquistadors met them.

Although the reservation was granted in 1868, the Navajo Nation didn't take on its current shape until decades later, when the eastern border was expanded through a series of complex land swaps with the U.S. government—the ruins at Chaco Canyon, for instance, are on federal land but surrounded by Navajo territory. This fringy edge is often referred to as the Checkerboard. Some portions of the reservation, such as Ramah, near Zuni, are completely separate from the rest of the "Big Rez."

The main route through New Mexico's Navajo land is U.S. 491 north from Gallup. Until 2003, the highway was known as U.S. 666, but the Department of Transportation reportedly got sick of the chronic sign theft and changed the number. It still hasn't completely shaken its nickname, the Devil's Highway, due to regular car crashes and tales of people being attacked by "skinwalkers" (Navajo shape-shifters) along its most remote stretches.

The drive north to Shiprock is beautiful but solitary, passing only a few chapter houses (reservation administrative centers), and the occasional hogan, the traditional Navajo ceremonial building. With their straight, faceted sides, hogans resemble the cliffs that often tower above them, and their doors always face the sunrise.

The terrain shifts to a sandy pink as you head north, punctuated by the Chuska Mountains, to the west on the border with Arizona, then the occasional mesa. Finally, there is Shiprock, a dramatic spike that does look like a prow gliding through the sandy sea—or, as the Navajo see it, a "rock with wings" (Tse' Bit'a'i).

## TOADLENA TRADING POST

The community of Two Grey Hills is widely considered to be the source of some of the finest rugs in the Navajo tradition—delicately shaded neutral tones, often undyed wool carefully selected for its natural color, then woven into intricate geometric patterns rich with symbolic meaning. Some can be so thin and tightly woven, they resemble paper. The creaky old **Toadlena Trading Post** (505/789-3267, 9am-6pm Mon.-Sat.) near Newcomb is one of the main places where Two Grey Hills rugs are sold, and in addition to exquisite work for sale, it has a museum dedicated to skilled artisans of New Mexico. The exhibit changes every two years—a show about Spanish and Mexican textiles, including work by Navajo weavers taken as slaves by the Spanish, is up till mid-2015. It's a nice excuse to drive off the highway and into the foothills of the Chuskas.

On U.S. 491, look for the Shell station around mile marker 60; head west on the paved road, about 10 miles, and follow it as it turns south through the village of Toadlena.

The trading post is on a small hill, a few curves after the road turns to dirt. From there, rather than completely backtracking, you can continue on the dirt road as it heads back southeast, passing through Two Grey Hills proper, where its own **trading post** (505/789-3270, 8am-6pm Mon.-Sat.) is less artfully arranged but also holds some treasures. Look for it just past the intersection with a paved road leading north. This northbound road drops you back on the paved Toadlena road, to connect back to U.S. 491.

## SHIPROCK

Not to be confused with Window Rock (the Navajo Nation capital in Arizona), the town of Shiprock is the largest community in the Navajo Nation, home to 8,300 people, Diné College, a regional hospital, and a major Bureau of Indian Affairs office. Visitors won't find a lot going on, though, unless they're in town for the **flea market,** in the parking lot at the intersection of U.S. 491 and U.S. 64—it's appealing not just for the random assortment

Toadlena Trading Post sits in the foothills of the Chuska Mountains.

© ZORA O'NEILL

of merchandise (CDs from Navajo rock bands, as well as crafts and jewelry) but also for the seriously traditional Navajo food, such as blue-corn mush and stewed sumac. If you're staying in Farmington, the flea market is definitely worth the short drive over. It allegedly runs daily (8am to 5pm), but it's still biggest and most interesting on Saturdays.

The big annual event is **Northern Navajo Nation Fair** (505/368-4301, www.northern-navajonationfair.org), celebrated for more than a century. It happens the first weekend in October, when there's a major powwow, the Miss Northern Navajo pageant, a free barbecue, and a fry bread cook-off, as well as the nine-day Ye'iibichei dance ritual.

The rest of the time, Shiprock is as good a place as any to fill up on gas and admire the view across the San Juan River and desert plateau. In the strip mall at the intersection with U.S. 64, look for **Navajo Fine Jewelry and Collectibles** (9am-8pm Mon.-Sat., noon-6pm Sun.). It may not have the charm of an old trading post, but as a project of the Navajo Nation government, it's very well priced and shows some excellent work. Look for rugs patterned with tall, skinny Yei deities—they're a specialty of the Shiprock region.

### Food

If you miss the flea market, you can get mutton stew and fry bread tacos at **Mannings Thatsaburger** (U.S. 491, 505/368-4019, 10am-8pm daily, $7) and at **KFC** (U.S. 491, 505/368-4805, 10am-9pm Sun.-Wed., 10am-10pm Thurs.-Sat., $4). Honestly, the stuff is better at Mannings, but there's still novelty value in subverting the fast-food establishment by marching up to the plastic KFC counter and ordering the local goods.

In the summer, keep an eye out for roadside vendors of fresh produce and "kneel down bread," fresh corn pudding steamed in corn husks.

## FOUR CORNERS MONUMENT

In 2009, the **Four Corners Monument** (U.S. 160, 928/871-6647, 8am-7pm daily May-Sept., 8am-5pm daily Oct.-April, $3) where the state boundaries of New Mexico, Arizona, Utah, and Colorado all meet came under scrutiny, as analysis of old surveying techniques suggested that the point might be a good 2.5 miles off. But rebuttal from the National Geodetic Survey settled the matter, and the monument rests easy again. It's not much to see, though: Even after a renovation, it's recommended only for aficionados of roadside Americana, fans of Twister, and land surveyors.

It does at least provide an excuse to tour around the barren, butte-spiked lands up here, and you'll be wanting to get out and stretch your legs just about the time you pass by the entrance on U.S. 160. And what a stretch you'll get, as you put one limb in each state and pose for your travel companion's camera. There's also a gift shop and some fry bread vendors (but no public water source).

Nearby, farther north on U.S. 160, just past the San Juan River, be sure to stop at the scenic overlook for an awesome view across the flatlands to Shiprock (occasionally marred by smog from the power plant).

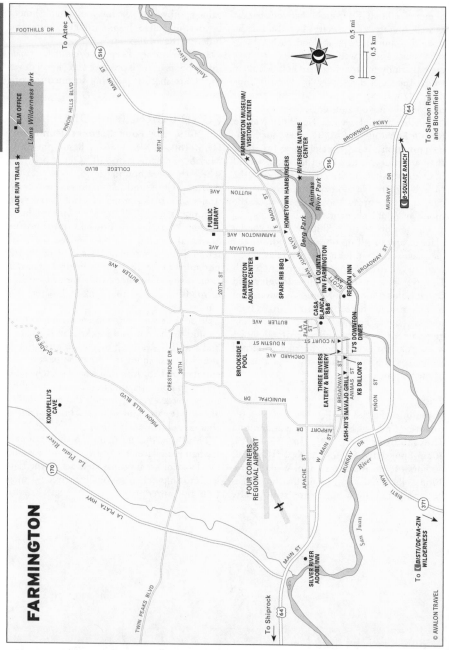

# FARMINGTON

To Aztec

FOOTHILLS DR

To Shiprock

To Salmon Ruins
and Bloomfield

To BISTI/DE-NA-ZIN
WILDERNESS

© AVALON TRAVEL

0          0.5 mi
0          0.5 km

BLM OFFICE
GLADE RUN TRAILS
Lions Wilderness Park
KOKOPELLI'S CAVE
PUBLIC LIBRARY
FARMINGTON AQUATIC CENTER
SPARE RIB BBQ
CASA BLANCA B&B
FARMINGTON MUSEUM/ VISITORS CENTER
RIVERSIDE NATURE CENTER
HOMETOWN HAMBURGERS
LA QUINTA INN FARMINGTON
REGION INN
TJ'S DOWNTOWN DINER
THREE RIVERS EATERY & BREWERY
ASH-KII'S NAVAJO GRILL
KB DILLON'S
BROOKSIDE POOL
FOUR CORNERS REGIONAL AIRPORT
SILVER RIVER ADOBE INN
B-SQUARE RANCH

Animas River
La Plata River
San Juan River
Berg Park
Animas River Park

PINON HILLS BLVD
E MAIN ST
516
COLLEGE BLVD
30TH ST
BUTLER AVE
20TH ST
HUTTON AVE
FARMINGTON AVE
SULLIVAN AVE
SAN JUAN BLVD
E MAIN ST
SCOTT AVE
E BROADWAY ST
BUTLER AVE
LA PLATA ST
N DUSTIN ST
N COURT ST
ORCHARD AVE
W BROADWAY ST
ANIMAS ST
PINON ST
MURRAY DR
CRESTRIDGE DR
30TH ST
GLADE RD
MUNICIPAL DR
APACHE ST
W MAIN ST
AIRPORT DR
MAIN ST
TWIN PEAKS BLVD
LA PLATA HWY
170
BROWNING PKWY
MURRAY DR
BISTI HWY
371
64
516
64

# Farmington

Even though (or perhaps in part because) it's set right against the border of the Navajo Nation, Farmington has an entirely different feel from Shiprock. The largely Anglo population of 45,000 prospers from coal, oil, and natural-gas deposits, and the nearby Four Corners Power Plant is a major employer. It's the most common base for visiting the ruins at Chaco Canyon to the south, and a pleasant enough city in its own right, tidy and filled with parks.

Farmington's first settlers, from England, were attracted by the fertile land around the confluence of the San Juan, La Plata, and Animas Rivers (the Navajo name for the area is Tótah for "the place where the waters meet"). The first well was drilled in the 1890s—but the investor was dismayed to hit gas rather than the water he'd been looking for. The Farmington Oil & Gas Co. was established in 1906, but it wasn't until 1922 that the industry really got any attention, with a wildcat well in Hogback producing crude so pure that cars could run on the stuff, no refining necessary. In the meantime, though, Farmington's growth was based on the prosperous farms and orchards in the surrounding river valley. The 1950s marked the first real oil boom, when many of the orchards were plowed under to make room for new houses; another came in the 1970s, thanks to the limited supply from overseas. And with current tensions in the world oil market, it's doing quite well once again.

## SIGHTS

The town proper has only a handful of typical attractions; pick up the *Footloose in Farmington* brochure for a walking tour of some of the nicer historic buildings downtown. The town of Aztec and the ruins there are just 30 minutes by car, so it's easy to hit the highlights in one day.

### Farmington Museum

In the same building as the convention and visitors bureau, the **Farmington Museum** (3041 E. Main St., 505/599-1174, www.farmingtonmuseum.org, 8am-5pm Mon.-Sat., free) has some pretty slick exhibits. The centerpiece is *From Dinosaurs to Drill Bits*, a rather loud and overtly gee-whiz display, complete with video holograms, about the oil and gas industry—underwritten by major corporations, naturally. Once you get away from the hissing steam and chattering touch-screen games, you'll find a tasteful display on Farmington's general history, as well as an interesting replica trading post and information on just how the posts' complex, usually cashless economies functioned.

### ◖ B-Square Ranch

A 12,000-acre spread, **B-Square Ranch** (3901 Bloomfield Hwy./U.S. 64, www.bolackmuseums.com, 505/325-4275, tours by appointment only, 9am-3pm Mon.-Sat., free) is home to two of the weirdest museums in New Mexico. It's not exactly the contents of the museums (hunting trophies and electrical gizmos) that are

downtown Farmington

odd—it's the glimpse you get into the obsessive minds of the men behind them.

At the main ranch house, the **Bolack Museum of Fish & Wildlife** is the work of Tom Bolack, oilman and erstwhile lieutenant governor of New Mexico, who until his death was an outspoken environmentalist—and a passionate hunter. One-hour tours begin with Bolack's "big five" hunting trophies from Africa and carries on through a veritable menagerie of taxidermy, with thousands of specimens from all over the globe, as well as tiger-skin rugs, elephant-foot spittoons, and specimen trays of Indonesian flying lizards. And then there's the whole display of marine life, including a shark.

On the other side of the property, Tom Bolack's son, Tommy, is steadily adding to the **Bolack Electromechanical Museum,** a jumbled but awesome array of obsolete or near-obsolete technology: electric meters, radio antennae, TV cameras, a vintage DC-3, and one of Elvis's Cadillacs. The walk through the collection takes two hours and is peppered with odd information about the family and Tommy's interests, which include country music and pyrotechnics (he sets off a massive display every Fourth of July).

The Bolack Electromechanical Museum walks a fine line between hoarding and collecting.

The ranch driveway is immediately west of Browning Parkway, running south, marked by a small sign. Make reservations for tours at least a day ahead, and at least four days ahead for a Saturday tour.

## Salmon Ruins & Heritage Park

Ten miles east of Farmington, the **Salmon Ruins & Heritage Park** (6131 U.S. 64, 505/632-2013, www.salmonruins.com, 8am-5pm Mon.-Fri., 9am-5pm Sat.-Sun., $3) is not exactly the best place to contemplate the mysteries of the ancients, what with the traffic drone from the highway and the dilapidated mobile homes that clutter the view behind the 11th-century semicircular complex.

But the site is intriguing for this very reason: Here, the layers of accumulated culture include the present day, as well as homesteaders' cabins and a gnarled apple orchard planted in the 19th century. And even though the area feels crowded now, you can see why the spot, next to the San Juan River and towering cottonwoods, must have appealed to each wave of settlers. The buildings from the earliest period, between 1088 and 1263 (when the place was abandoned following a major fire), were probably built by colonists from Chaco, as they use the same masonry style and a similar layout. There are more than 300 rooms in a single large block.

The "heritage park" includes the rough timber home of George Salmon, whose family helped preserve the ruins, as well as facsimile hogans, tepees, and other examples of local architecture over the millennia. The small **museum** here is also quite good, with its emphasis on tools and daily life. In the winter (Nov.-April), the ruins don't open till noon on Sunday.

The **San Juan County Archaeological Research Center and Library,** based at Salmon Ruins, runs small-group tours around Chaco Canyon as well as some of the more obscure sites on Navajo land. Rates for an eight-hour outing, including a sandwich lunch, are typically $295 for one or two people.

© ZORA O'NEILL

Salmon Ruins & Heritage Park

## ENTERTAINMENT AND EVENTS

Farmington turns in early—if you can't find fun at the places mentioned here, there's always the mall and multiplex cinema on East Main Street, on the north side of town.

### Nightlife

Your best bet for a relaxed bar scene is **Three Rivers Brewery & Tap Room** (101 E. Main St., 505/324-2187, noon-midnight daily), where most people play pool while savoring pints of the house-made Chaco Nut Brown Ale and other brews. Also downtown, **K. B. Dillon's** (101 W. Broadway, 505/325-0222, 11am-9pm Mon.-Sat.) is a bit rowdier; there's a steakhouse attached, if you need something to soak up the beer. On summer weekends, the locals (and bored long-stay oilmen) head to the track at **Sunray Park & Casino** (39 Rd. 5568, 505/566-1200, www.sunraygaming.com) for the horse races. And every Friday and Saturday afternoon in the summer, there's **live music** on the small square

at the corner of Main Street and Orchard Avenue.

### Festivals and Events

Farmington's main get-together is the **Totah Festival** (totahfestival.farmingtonnm.org), a Navajo art market on Labor Day weekend. The city also hosts the **Connie Mack World Series** (www.cmws.org), in August, the final contest of the youth baseball teams that aren't in the Little League.

## SPORTS AND RECREATION

With three rivers and dramatic sandstone formations nearby, as well as a few in-town parks, the Farmington area is good for getting out and about. For maps, permits, fishing licenses, and more information on these and other activities, stop in at the **BLM Farmington field office** (6251 College Blvd., 505/564-7600, 8am-5pm Mon.-Fri.).

### Hiking

The relatively wild-feeling **Animas River Park**

runs along the riverbank on the east side of town, with trails winding through the trees. It's a pretty place for a morning run or a sunset stroll, and the paved waterside path, dotted with picnic tables, runs a full five miles. The easiest access to this walk is at **Berg Park,** on the west bank of the river, off Scott Avenue; on the east bank, the **Riverside Nature Center** (505/599-1422, 10am-6pm Tues.-Sat., free) has more trails, as well as a village of fat prairie dogs. It's also open Sundays, 1pm-5pm, in summer.

## Mountain Biking

Local mountain bikers developed the BLM-managed Glade Run Trail System through the sandstone cliffs north of the city. It's the site of the venerable **Road Apple Rally** (505/599-1140, www.roadapplerally.com), which has run every October since 1981 (back then, competitors rode single-speed, fat-tire cruisers). You can do the rally route on your own, or one of several other loops through the foothills.

It's easy to get lost in the network of singletrack and dirt roads—download a map from www.4corners.info. An expert at **Cottonwood Cycles** (4370 E. Main St., 505/326-0429, 10am-6pm Mon.-Fri., 10am-5pm Sat.) should be able to get you oriented better. The Glade Run trails are also open to hikers, though bicyclists get the right-of-way.

## ◖ Bisti/De-Na-Zin Wilderness

Some 45,000 acres of barren shale hills and weird rock formations, this wilderness area is about 30 miles south of Farmington, most directly accessible by Highway 371. You have to be self-sufficient to enjoy this place—there are no marked trails, no bicycles or groups of more than eight people allowed, and no services, water, or information at the access points. But if you can commit a few hours to a hike (or better, camp on a moonlit night), you will find it one of the more fascinating terrains in the state. It's also relatively easy to navigate, as the ravines and washes form natural paths, and the larger formations and hills are good landmarks (though definitely bring a compass).

The BLM-managed patch of land has two access points. The **Bisti** side (36.5 miles south on Hwy. 371, then 2 miles east on gravel Road 7297) is less than stunning when you get out of your car—you probably passed more intriguing hoodoos (wind-eroded pillars of sandstone) on the drive down. The land in front of the small parking area looks like eroded pavement, and the low hills resemble mud-caked elephants. Farther off, deep red hills are a by-product of intensely hot coal fires millions of years ago.

Walk roughly southeast about 30 minutes (two miles), and you're surrounded by precarious-looking towers of rock and undulating walls of ravines; another 1.5 hours due east from here, and you pass all of the best formations. Keep an eye out for fossils in the rocks and chunks of petrified wood on the ground.

The other access point, the **De-Na-Zin** side, is on County Road 7500, 14 miles east from Highway 371, and 10.9 miles west of U.S. 550. The pull-off on the north side of the dirt road is marked only by a small sign that's easy to miss. Here, you must hike across about half a mile of low scrub before you turn down into the washes.

## ACCOMMODATIONS

Many of Farmington's visitors are here for work, which creates a market for decent hotels in all price brackets—though none are particularly cheap. All the chain hotels are represented, on the east and north fringes of town.

## Under $100

In the budget category, independent ◖ **Region Inn** (601 E. Broadway, 505/325-1191, www.theregioninn.com, $92 d) matches all the chain hotels in amenities but charges a bit less; there's free wireless Internet, and even an outdoor pool. Not far from downtown and the river walk along the Animas, the location is very convenient, and the on-site Mexican restaurant, **Tequila's,** is not bad. If it's full, your next best option is **La Quinta Inn Farmington** (675 Scott Ave., 505/327-4706, www.lq.com, $75 d), which is in very good shape. It's on the north side, behind the mall.

## $100-150

If you can find it, down a precipitous little gravel road just off U.S. 64 on the west side of town, **Silver River Adobe Inn** (3151 W. Main St., 505/325-8219, www.silveradobe.com, $115 d) makes a wonderful, natural oasis. The breakfast room, packed floor to ceiling with plants, overlooks the river, and the whole place has a pleasant, hand-built-in-the-1970s feel, complete with solar panels, as well as exposed adobe-brick walls in the two rooms and one suite.

In a quiet residential neighborhood, ◖**Casa Blanca Inn** (505 E. La Plata St., 505/327-6503, www.4cornersbandb.com, $149 d) encompasses three separate properties—humdrum split-level ranch homes on the outside, but completely transporting inside, with a tasteful and un-cluttered mix of hand-carved furniture, brick and wood floors, and decorative treasures like Guatemalan bedspreads, Indian headboards, and Chinese vases. The main "hacienda" has two separate garden areas and includes the Vista Grande suite, with a wraparound sun porch. Across the street are two smaller properties, with two rooms each. Main Street is easy walking distance down the hill.

## Over $150

For sheer novelty value, you can't beat **Kokopelli's Cave** (3204 Crestridge Dr., 505/326-2461, www.bbonline.com/nm/koko-pelli, $260 d), a "luxury cave dwelling" in the cliffs on the north side of town. To get to your fully appointed, 1,650-square-foot home, you have to edge along a sandstone path down the side of a cliff face—so once you're in, you'll probably stay in for a night or two. But with a full kitchen, a barbecue grill, a hot tub, and a deck with a great view, you're pretty well set.

## FOOD

Meals in Farmington are rarely anything to write home about, but there are a few reliable options among the scores of fast-food outlets.

## Breakfast

Satisfying breakfasts can be had at **TJ's Downtown Diner** (119 E. Main St., 505/327-5027, 5:30am-2:30pm Mon.-Fri., 6am-12:30pm Sat., $8), a sunny spot on a corner on the edge of downtown.

## American

For a tasty sandwich and hand-cut fries, the tiny white building that is **Hometown Hamburgers** (2133 E. Main St., 505/326-5580, 10am-10pm Mon.-Sat., 11am-6pm Sun., $4) is the place to go. It beats McDonald's in quality *and* quantity: Really hearty eaters can order a one-pound patty.

It's a little disorienting to walk into **Spare Rib BBQ** (1700 E. Main St., 505/325-4800, 10am-8pm Tues.-Sat., $8), which looks exactly like a roadside joint somewhere in the South—except the picnic tables are indoors, on carpeting. Hush puppies, sweet tea, and collard greens are all on the menu next to succulent pulled pork.

## New Mexican

A rare opportunity to eat Navajo food, made by and for Navajo, the very popular **Ash-Kii's Navajo Grill** (123 W. Broadway, 505/326-3804, 11am-5pm Mon.-Fri., $7) is a cheerful diner run by a family that used to sell food at flea markets—all the favorites are here, with squash stew, Navajo tacos, and mutton sandwiches. But there are a few novelties too, like the Ace pizza, topped with bits of lamb. Wash it down with Navajo tea (an herb called *cota*).

## Three Rivers Brewery

In a stately old downtown block that once housed a drugstore and the daily *Times-Hustler,* the sprawling ◖ **Three Rivers Brewery** (E. Main St.) takes up the better part of a block, with a bar, brewery, sit-down restaurant, and pizzeria—all with separate menus and entrances along Main Street. The main **restaurant** (101 E. Main St., 505/324-2187, 11am-9pm Mon.-Sat., noon-9pm Sun., $20), on the corner with North Orchard Street, is a lovely old tin-ceiling room, with an original soda fountain, serving house-made root beer for kids, and real beer for grownups. The menu shows a love of drink with items like the super-marinated Drunken

Steak. Sandwiches are fresh-tasting items like herbed chicken salad.

Next door is the bargain **pizzeria** (107 E. Main St., 505/325-0308, 11am-10pm Sun.-Thurs., 11am-11pm Fri.-Sat., $7), where you can build your own pie with a stupendous array of toppings, from garlic-pistachio cream to homemade meatballs. From a brick oven, they're nice and crispy, and very reasonably priced. And if *that* doesn't satisfy, it also has a whole menu of New Mexican items, plus pinball and old arcade games to distract the kids.

Finally, you can toddle down to the **tap room** (113 E. Main St., 505/325-6605) for a game of pool, or just a beer in the backyard.

## INFORMATION
The **Gateway Park Visitors Center** (3041 E. Main St., 505/326-7602, www.farmingtonnm.org, 8am-5pm Mon.-Sat.), in the same building as the Farmington Museum, is the place to pick up flyers and maps, including a very detailed one published by the chamber of commerce.

## GETTING THERE AND AROUND
By car, Farmington is three hours (180 miles) northwest from Albuquerque on U.S. 550 and two hours (120 miles) east from Gallup on I-40. It's only about one hour (50 miles) south from Durango, Colorado, on U.S. 550, and a little more than 30 minutes east to Shiprock on Highway 64/489.

Thanks to the oil and gas industry, **Four Corners Airport** (FMN), on the west side of town, receives flights from Denver on Great Lakes Airlines (800/554-5111, www.flygreatlakes.com). National car rental chains have branches at the airport.

# Aztec

A half-hour drive northeast from Farmington, Aztec nearly counts as a suburb. But with its pretty restored main street lined with brick-front shops, including a giant historical museum, this town of 7,000 has its own character. Like Farmington, a lot of the economy is based on the gas industry. In 1921, Aztec became the first town in the state to use natural gas to heat homes.

## SIGHTS
The scenery around here is a study in dusty tones, with white and beige rocks studded only with sagebrush and the occasional piñon tree—a stark backdrop for the Ancestral Puebloan ruins on the north side of town that are worth the visit for the great kiva alone.

### Aztec Ruins National Monument
The "place by flowing waters" was misnamed Aztec by American settlers in the 19th century, who assumed people from central Mexico had established this place. **Aztec**

downtown Aztec

© ZORA O'NEILL

© ZORA O'NEILL

a kiva at Aztec Ruins National Monument

**Ruins National Monument** (84 County Rd. 2900, 505/334-6174, www.nps.gov/azru, 8am-6pm daily in summer, 8am-5pm daily in winter, $5) doesn't have the dramatic setting of Chaco Canyon or Mesa Verde, but it's the best place to see Anasazi (Ancestral Puebloan) architecture if you can't make it to those more remote spots.

The main excavated area is only a portion of a larger city. When you're up on a high point looking over the surrounding ground, you'll see that the other "hills" are really unexcavated rubble. The cleaned-up **West Ruin** contains some 400 rooms, as well as a few nice details that show off the Ancestral Puebloans' knack for building. As you walk out of the visitors center and along the side wall of the great house, for instance, notice the band of green stone embedded in the wall, apparently an intentional bit of decoration. This is also a rather neat place to explore because you can go inside many of the rooms, some of which have their original ceilings: 800-year-old timber, insulated with mud-daubed twigs. The interior

walls would have been plastered; some were painted as well.

But the really fascinating detail here is the fully reconstructed **great kiva,** a submerged room 40 feet across, the roof of which originally weighed 95 tons. Descending the stairs into the gloom, stepping onto the packed earth of the floor, you can easily imagine the whole community (or at least the men) gathered together for meetings and ceremonies.

Culturally, Aztec appears to have been first affiliated with Chaco Canyon; later, its construction style imitated that used at Mesa Verde in Colorado. It was occupied only for about two centuries and abandoned before 1300.

A number of burials found in the lower rooms led archaeologists to reexamine the long-held assumption that these buildings—and similar complexes at other Ancestral Puebloan sites—functioned like apartment blocks. According to that theory, lower rooms were most often used for storage. But here at Aztec, the ritually prepared bodies suggest that the rooms had a more specialized use, and that perhaps these stone buildings were dedicated to ceremonies and city administration, while people lived in outlying structures made of perishable materials that haven't stood the test of time.

The small **museum** addresses this issue, just one in the ever-changing field of archaeology, with a small item in one corner noting that the exhibits have yet to be updated to reflect the new ideas about the use of great houses. No matter, as the items on display are particularly interesting regardless of what theory they prop up. There's a shred of a woven reed mat, a portion of a blanket made of turkey feathers and rabbit fur, and an original ladder (rare, because they were so heavily used and usually left out in the elements), among other small comforts of life eight centuries ago.

### Aztec Museum & Pioneer Village

The ultimate in small-town historical collections, the **Aztec Museum & Pioneer Village** (125 N. Main Ave., 505/334-9829, www.aztecmuseum.org, 10am-4pm Tues.-Sat. June-Sept., 10am-4pm Thurs.-Sat. Oct.-May, $3) has the usual array of old telephone switchboards, vintage eyeglasses, and farming implements—but it has an enormous number of them, all obsessively laid out in what seems like an endless series of rooms.

And just when you thought you were done browsing through the complete interior of an old barbershop and the large gun room, you go outside to find...an entire town. Set in orderly rows, all the usual Old West establishments are there, built at a slightly smaller scale: the sheriff's office, the one-room schoolhouse, the general store, the village doctor, even the church, which in this case was a real building from a nearby community that was moved here and scaled down to fit with the others. And of course, each building is kitted out with period-specific knickknacks.

## SPORTS AND RECREATION

The mountain biking and hiking trail called **Alien Run** traces a route up Hart Canyon, past the site of an alleged UFO crash. It's a scenic bit of single-track, with a few patches of slick sandstone. It's a nine-mile loop, and about four miles in, a plaque marks the site where in 1948 the remnants of a 100-foot-wide disc were spotted, along with dead creatures resembling small humans; according to locals, the crash was swiftly followed by heavy-breathing military reps who whisked all the evidence away—though apparently the site does register a slightly abnormal amount of radiation. To reach the trailhead, take U.S. 550 north four miles, then turn right on County Road 2770. Follow this three miles to a left turn, then it's half a mile up a hill and another half mile right along the fence to a gate and parking lot. There's an annual **bike race** (www.alienrun.com) on the trail in early May, and **Cottonwood Cycles** (200 South Main Ave., 505/334-2703, 10am-6pm Mon.-Fri., noon-5pm Sat.) can provide advice and gear.

## ACCOMMODATIONS AND FOOD

At the **Step Back Inn** (103 W. Aztec Blvd., 505/334-1200, www.stepbackinn.com, $98 d), the rooms nod to the past with Victorian-style armoires and reproduction wallpaper; you get homemade cinnamon rolls at breakfast. For those on a budget, the motel-style **Enchantment Inn** (1800 W. Aztec Blvd., 505/334-6143, $58 s, $65 d) looks a little barebones outside, but the rooms are modern and clean.

**Atomic Espresso & Bistro** (122 N. Main Ave., 505/334-0109, 7am-2:30pm Mon.-Fri., 8am-noon Sat., $8), also known as the Main Street Bistro, is across the street from the Aztec Museum. It offers good strong coffee, homemade pastries, and quiche. For New Mexican, head to **Rubio's** (116 S. Main Ave., 505/334-0599, 11am-9pm. Mon., 7am-9pm Tues.-Thurs., 7am-10pm Fri.-Sat., $11), which takes up the better part of a block and has a lovely patio.

## INFORMATION

The **Aztec Welcome Center** (110 N. Ash St., www.aztecchamber.com, 505/334-9551, 8am-5pm Mon.-Fri.), run by the chamber of commerce, can answer all pressing questions.

## GETTING THERE

Aztec is 16 miles (30 minutes) northeast of Farmington via Highway 516, and 9 miles (15 minutes) north of Bloomfield on U.S. 550.

# Bloomfield

The town of Bloomfield (www.bloomfieldnm.com), at the intersection of U.S. 64 and U.S. 550, is about the same size as Aztec but doesn't really present any strong reason for visitors to stop. It's the gateway to the best state park in the region, though.

## ANGEL PEAK SCENIC AREA

Think of **Angel Peak Scenic Area** (free) as the cheater's version of Bisti/De-Na-Zin—a great place to take in northwestern New Mexico's unique geology, from the comfort of your car. The area gives you the big picture, down into a dramatic expanse of striated sandstone, rather than the ground-level view you get at Bisti. The landscape of peaks and pinnacles, carved by ancient rivers and millennia of wind, is a short drive south of Bloomfield, accessible by a road winding along the canyon edge for about six miles. Each turn yields new photo-worthy vistas; you'll also find several sets of picnic shelters. At the end of the road is a tidy primitive **campground** (no water), with nine sites. From U.S. 550, 15 miles south of Bloomfield, turn east on County Road 5175.

© ZORA O'NEILL

the view into the canyon at Angel Peak Scenic Area

## NAVAJO LAKE STATE PARK

Approaching **Navajo Lake State Park** (1448 Hwy. 511, 505/632-2278, www.nmparks.com, $5/car), Highway 539 crosses the dam itself in an unnerving, guardrail-free swoop. The lake is the second largest in the state (after Elephant Butte), its 15,500 acres of water stretching like fingers up into Colorado. The glassy surface reflects the sky and year-round snow on the Rocky Mountains to the north. The main access point (of three) is **Pine Site,** just across the dam on Highway 511, with a visitors center and a large developed **campground** ($10, $14 with electric) that has great views over the lake, although it's somewhat removed from the water's edge. This entrance also leads to the main **marina,** offering houseboat rentals and a snack bar. This area can get pretty packed in the summertime, but the shoulder seasons can be beautifully empty. The alternate access to the lake is at **Sims Mesa Site,** on the east side via Highway 527, which has a significantly smaller camping area and can be a little quieter in high season.

houseboats on Navajo Lake

© ZORA O'NEILL

### Fishing

The park encompasses a portion of the San Juan River that's renowned for its fishing: rainbow, cutthroat, and brown trout, as well as kokanee salmon and largemouth bass. The San Juan's "quality waters," as they're called, have special regulations: The first quarter mile after the dam is catch-and-release only, and in the next 3.5 miles, you may use only flies with a single barbless hook, and keep only one fish of 20 inches or more. There are pull-offs for riverbank access all along Highway 511. On the opposite bank (reached via Road 4280 off Highway 173) is pretty, tree-shaded **Cottonwood Campground,** with nearly 50 sites. You can pick up a fishing license at any of the lodges and guide shops in the community of Navajo Dam, at the junction of Highways 173 and 511.

### SIMON CANYON

Technically not part of the state park but accessible by the same road as Cottonwood Campground, **Simon Canyon** is BLM land that has been labeled an "area of critical environmental concern," due to the presence of golden eagles, prairie falcons, and other treasured species. Use is restricted to hikers and anglers, and the trails are not frequently used. The main route, up through the canyon that runs due north where Road 4280 dead-ends, also passes a Navajo defensive fort, built in the 18th century on a pillar of rock.

### ACCOMMODATIONS AND FOOD

**Best Western Territorial Inn & Suites** (415 S. Bloomfield Blvd., Bloomfield, 505/632-9100, www.bestwestern.com, $105 d) is the closest you can stay to Chaco Canyon without camping.

Just east of the last turn to Navajo Lake from U.S. 64, **The Monastery of Our Lady of the Desert** (10258 U.S. 64, 505/419-2938, www. ourladyofthedesert.org, $40 pp) has four spare, newly built retreat rooms. Guests are also given meals. The price is a suggested donation, and guests are encouraged to do some light chores.

# Chaco Culture National Historical Park

State politicians make periodic threats to pave the two rutted access roads to **Chaco Culture National Historical Park** (505/786-7014, www.nps.gov/chcu, 7am-sunset, $8/car, good for seven days), but fortunately this has not yet come to pass. Much of the appeal of Chaco is its location in a valley that has remained relatively untouched since the Ancestral Puebloans (Anasazi) departed sometime in the 13th century. The long, bumpy ride to this hidden valley gives you time to get into the right frame of mind—you're turning back the calendar 800 years as you drive.

Arriving via the northern route, Chaco finally appears through a small pass in the reddish rocks, with the striking Fajada Butte directly in front of you. The long valley, bordered with sheer cliff faces, was once home to more than 6,000 people, and now just you and

the other visitors who made the drive are there to appreciate the ruins.

## HISTORY

The first people to settle in Chaco Canyon arrived sometime between 5,000 and 10,000 years ago, but a distinctive Chacoan culture (also called Anasazi and Ancestral Puebloan) only developed around AD 850. In an arid valley with a harsh climate and very little water, the people of Chaco worked extremely hard to build a society that supported thousands of residents and spread its influence all over the region.

Aerial surveys done in the 1980s revealed a network of roads connecting the settlements here with some 150 outlying communities, farms, and forests where timber was gathered. The roads were perfectly straight (even going up and over cliffs and mesas, rather than

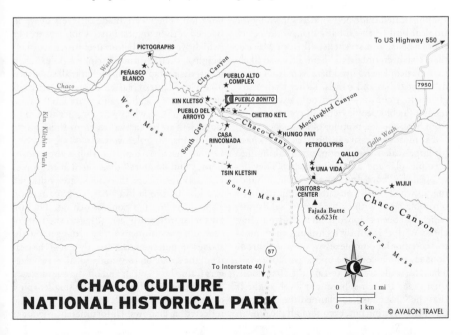

**CHACO CULTURE NATIONAL HISTORICAL PARK**

## The Anasazi and the Cannibalism Debate

The popular conception of the Ancestral Puebloans (previously known as the Anasazi) has been of a peaceful, egalitarian society based on agriculture. But a theory advanced by physical anthropologist Christy Turner suggests the Pueblo Indians might be better off disavowing their ancestors. In his 1999 book *Man Corn: Cannibalism and Violence in the Prehistoric American Southwest,* Turner proposed that the Anasazi culture was a violent one obsessed with ritual consumption of human flesh. Granted, the cannibalism could have been introduced by a Mexican culture, perhaps the Toltecs, and used against the Anasazi as a means of terrorizing them. In any case, his theory proposed an answer to a nagging question: What about all those piles of mangled human bones and fire-blackened skulls found at Chaco Canyon, Mesa Verde, and other Anasazi sites?

Many of Turner's colleagues were skeptical, if not downright shocked, and Pueblo Indians were, and still are, outraged at the accusations about their people. Turner and other archaeologists were banned from excavations in Mesa Verde. In the years since Turner published *Man Corn,* however, evidence to support his theory seems to have grown. For instance, other researchers found coprolites (preserved human feces) that tested positive for human proteins. Whether or not cannibalism was a regular part of Anasazi life, the evidence Turner uncovered does create a bleak and violent picture of life in what today appear to be peaceful valleys and canyons.

around) and up to 30 feet wide—a great deal of effort for a culture that did not have wheels or beasts of burden. Chaco was at the center of a sophisticated trade network, as shown by the tropical bird feathers, baby macaw skeletons, copper bells, and seashells, all from Mexico, that have been uncovered here. It is also likely that the people who lived here were from many different tribes and bands, rather than a single distinct culture—this would explain how today's Pueblo people, who all claim ancestry from here, speak a number of languages.

Far more impressive is the Chacoans' knack for large-scale construction, often taking into account solar and lunar alignments. They developed the **"core and veneer"** style of building, in which walls consisted of an inner mass of rubble faced with thin panels of sandstone, which had been chipped from the surrounding cliffs. With this sturdy technique, they raised the ceremonial complexes we now call **great houses,** which could be up to five stories tall. That the walls were thickest on the first floors, then taper at each subsequent level, suggests that the Chacoans had planned the construction before setting out, even though the growth

of the largest great houses, such as Pueblo Bonito, took place over a couple of centuries.

Chacoan ceilings were another durable innovation. They were made of layers of wood stacked at right angles: First, whole tree trunks (which were dried before use, to reduce their weight), then thinner, stripped poles, then twigs, then scraps of juniper bark, all smoothed over with a layer of plaster. Many of these roofs survive, nearly a thousand years later—even more impressive when you consider that most wood had to be carried in from the Chuska Mountains, 50 miles west.

The Chacoans' sophistication is also evident in the **"sun daggers"** discovered at the top of Fajada Butte. There, three rocks are positioned to allow light to fall in a particular pattern on a spiral drawn on a boulder behind. The sun falls on it differently according to the time of year. On the summer solstice, a dagger of light shone through the rocks directly across the center of the spiral; on the winter solstice, two daggers framed the spiral; and on the equinoxes, a smaller dagger of light marked a smaller spiral off to one side. The cycles of the moon are also reflected in shadows. Unfortunately, the rocks shifted in recent years, in part due to visitors wearing away the dirt at their base, and the daggers are no longer aligned; the butte is now closed off.

The pace of construction slowed in the 12th century, and by 1300 or so, the canyon seems to have been empty, and the Chacoans dispersed, some to what is now Hopi territory in Arizona, some south to Zuni, others to the Rio Grande pueblos. No one has determined for certain whether the migration was due to environmental degradation, attacks from outside, or some other factor, and every new archaeological discovery seems to open up more possibilities, rather than confirm any one theory.

## VISITING THE PARK

This is one of New Mexico's greatest treasures, and even if you're not a big fan of ruins, the remote setting makes the place well worth the drive for an afternoon visit. If you're intrigued by ancient culture or wildlife, then you may want to allot several days, pitching a tent at the campground near the entrance to the valley.

Chaco Culture National Historical Park

And regardless of how long you stay, don't get too caught up in following trail guides or hitting all the spots on a map. Unless you're a specialist, you won't discern much difference in the various settlements in the valley, so don't burn yourself out trying to see every one. Better to spend time in one quiet spot, listening to the rush of ravens' wings, the whisper of the breeze, and the other subtle sounds of this now-empty place.

### Visitors Center

Stop first at the **visitors center** (8am-5pm daily) to pay the $8 entrance fee, pick up a map, find out what birds and animals have been spotted recently, and get a free backcountry permit if you think you'll be hiking. You can also join a ranger-led tour of Pueblo Bonito (free). If your schedule allows, time your visit with a **Chaco Night Sky Program,** a periodic event that takes advantage of Chaco's location, more than 75 miles from any population center. Visitors can peer through a number of high-powered telescopes, and the sky positively glitters at night.

### Una Vida

The small **Una Vida** ruins, accessible via a 1.6-mile trail behind the visitors center, represent the earlier phase of great-house building in Chaco, begun around 850. They're worth a quick look, if only to see how an unexcavated (yet well-preserved) site differs from one where all the debris has been cleared. Blowing sand has gradually accumulated, just as the walls have slowly crumbled. You can see evidence of later occupation, probably by shepherds in the 19th century—the slabs of stone have been freshly piled up, in a different style from the original building. If you follow the trail behind the ruins, you'll see a few petroglyphs chiseled into the rock.

### Accommodations and Camping

Before you reach the visitors center, **Gallo Campground** offers 49 sites ($10), water, restrooms, and a dump station for RVs.

Outside the park on the south side (on Hwy.

9), **Chaco Outlier** (505/655-3246, www.chaco-outlier.com) has pretty campsites ($20) as well as a few cabins ($40). The closest hotels, all about a two-hour drive, are in Bloomfield and Farmington north on U.S. 550; Cuba, south on U.S. 550; and in Grants on I-40 to the south.

## CANYON LOOP DRIVE

A nine-mile one-way loop runs up to the northwest end of the canyon and back, with parking areas near each great house.

### Hungo Pavi

Like Una Vida, **Hungo Pavi** is one of the earlier complexes in the valley, built between 940 and 1040; also like the other ruins, it's largely unexcavated. If you're short on time, you can easily skip this, though the gentle curve of the back wall and the numerous tiny windows in it are rather striking.

### Chetro Ketl

The defining element of **Chetro Ketl**, built over a century beginning around 1010, is its huge raised plaza. The elevated platform, some 12 feet high, required tons of packed earth and stone in its construction. With more than 500 rooms, it's the second largest great house in Chaco. It also displays a long colonnaded wall—a very rare style in this region, and perhaps an idea borrowed from Paquimé, in northern Mexico, a city with which the Chacoans are known to have traded. You can also walk from Chetro Ketl to Pueblo Bonito (the next stop on the ruins road), along a flat, quarter-mile trail that passes clusters of petroglyphs on the canyon wall.

### ◖ Pueblo Bonito

The largest complex in the canyon and the pinnacle of Chacoan engineering, **Pueblo Bonito** is thought to be the ceremonial heart of the ancient community. It began in the mid-800s as a sliver of an arc, a few rooms deep, and by the 12th century grew into a compound with more than 600 rooms, at least 30 kivas, and walls up to five stories tall in some sections. Roads lead straight to it from every smaller settlement in the area. The various masonry styles used in construction make it clear where the various phases begin and end, and where, for instance, an old wall and a new one converge to enlarge the arc. In some sections, the masonry is as regular as brick; in others, you can see where worn stone has been reused.

The 0.6-mile trail leads first through an alarming array of sandstone boulders that seem to have just yesterday tumbled down from the cliff above. (In fact, they fell in 1941, crushing part of the compound.) The route then continues through the Pueblo Bonito complex, including some of the enclosed rooms, but it is hard to get a true sense of the scale of the place from the ground. If you have time and energy, hike to the mesa top via the Pueblo Alto trail.

### Wetherill Cemetery

One of the few relics in this valley from a more recent era, the tiny **Wetherill Cemetery** near the end of the ruins road is easily overlooked. It is the final resting place of Richard Wetherill, a Colorado rancher turned profiteering archaeologist. He was the first to bring Cliff Palace at Mesa Verde to national attention, and in 1896, the American Museum of Natural History hired him to dig up relics at Chaco Canyon. Wetherill is also credited with being the first to apply the name Anasazi to the people who inhabited the Four Corners area between the 9th and 12th centuries.

At that time, archaeology was only just developing as a science, and many academics in the field saw Wetherill—who worked on his own, removing pots and other valuable items as he pleased—as a threat to the accurate study of these ancient places. It was irrelevant that Wetherill was often far more knowledgeable about the area and the culture than they were. Wetherill was disparaged as a "pot-hunter," and the Antiquities Act of 1906 was devised to designate national monuments and keep people like him out—Wetherill had actually staked a homestead claim on the land around Pueblo Bonito. He was operating a trading post there when he was shot and killed by a Navajo man in 1910. His wife, Marietta, is also buried here, along with several unnamed Navajo.

## Pueblo del Arroyo

This is a beautiful spot in spring or summer during the rains, when the tall cottonwoods are thick from the water in the wash that gives **Pueblo del Arroyo** its name. The large, rounded stones used in many of the rooms indicate a slightly later construction than Pueblo Bonito and Chetro Ketl, which are built of the thin, regular, sharp-edged slabs that was easily collected from the mesa top. This stone was eventually used up, forcing a switch to the rounder, more irregular stone found here. For the most part erected in the early 12th century, the complex also displays some of the "tri-wall" construction that is more common in Mesa Verde.

## Kin Kletso

If you've been noting the different styles of masonry throughout the various great houses, then you should also stop at **Kin Kletso**, at the far north end of the road, and a short walk from the parking lot. It displays the clearest example of what's dubbed the McElmo style of masonry (after the McElmo Valley in Colorado), associated with Mesa Verde. Its presence in Chaco Canyon is taken as an indication that the two communities were in regular contact (although now archaeologists debate who influenced whom). Whereas the best Chacoan stone walls incorporate thick rubble cores and exceptionally regular facing stones, McElmo masonry is characterized by a relatively thin rubble core and the use of large, rounded pieces of sandstone on the surface, chinked with tiny, irregular bits of rock. It was first used at Chaco in the early 1100s.

## Casa Rinconada

Relatively isolated from the other great houses, **Casa Rinconada** is an enormous great kiva, meant to hold hundreds of people. Unlike other kivas, it stands alone, rather than as part of a larger complex, and it is aligned on a north-south axis with the great house of New Alto,

on the opposite mesa top. It displays all the signature elements, from the wall niches to the two raised floor vaults, which may have been topped with wood to create large drums.

To visit just the kiva, bear right at the fork in the trail shortly after it begins. The trail then loops south, past a number of small villages, similar to the great houses, but on a much more limited scale. The oral histories of the contemporary Pueblo people—Zuni, Acoma, Hopi, etc.—all refer to Chaco Canyon as their ancestors' home; however, the Puebloans represent such a variety of languages and traditions that Chaco must have been home to a mix of peoples even then. Some archaeologists have proposed that these distinct villages near Casa Rinconada were inhabited by one of the different peoples.

## HIKING

For all the longer hikes, you must have a permit, available from the visitors center, or, if you're indecisive, at the trailhead. There's no fee, and no limit on numbers—this is just a way for rangers to keep track of who's out in the wilderness.

## Pueblo Alto

This 5.1-mile loop hike, which runs off the north end of the valley from behind Kin Kletso (park at Pueblo del Arroyo), is definitely the most worthwhile of the day hikes, as long as you can handle the first clamber up the cliff face to the canyon rim. From here, it's a level walk back along the mesa top to a point where you can peer down on Pueblo Bonito—the geometry of the buildings and the successive layers of development all pop into focus from this perspective. You can backtrack from the Pueblo Bonito overlook, which makes for a 3.2-mile hike, or carry on to the **Pueblo Alto Complex site.** The trail then passes by stairs and ramps the Anasazi carved in the cliffs, through a slot canyon, and back up to the mesa edge for a view over Chetro Ketl. You finish by climbing back down the same route to Kin Kletso. Allow between three and four hours for the full hike.

## Peñasco Blanco

From the Pueblo de Arroyo parking lot at the north end of the ruins road, this longer out-and-back leads to seldom-visited Chacoan and Navajo petroglyphs (rock carvings) and pictographs (paintings on the rock), and the unexcavated ruins of **Peñasco Blanco**, the third-largest great house in the canyon, with a unique oval layout. It's a bit of a drab hike just for this, but mostly level. The first batch of pictographs is two miles in. The whole hike, 7.2 miles round-trip, will take between four and six hours; it can be especially tiring due to the sandy ground along most of the route.

## South Mesa

This 3.6-mile loop in parts follows some old Chacoan roads, from near Casa Rinconada on the west side of the canyon to the unexcavated great house **Tsin Kletsin**, which appears to have been used as a lookout and signal post, as the view from its main kiva has sightlines to six other great houses. The trail first rises to the mesa top, about 450 feet, then descends through South Gap via one of the ancient roads. The full trip can take up to four hours, or you can just hike up to Tsin Kletsin and back in about two.

## Wijiji

A perfectly flat hike (also accessible to bicyclists), this trail leads 1.5 miles through a natural wash to a **great house** from AD 1100. It's a piece of wholly planned architecture, apparently built in a single phase, unlike the other great houses in the area. Though relatively small, it is exceptional for its symmetry. Allow between two and three hours.

## PUEBLO PINTADO

A separate, unexcavated great house about 20 miles southeast of Chaco and technically part of the same park, **Pueblo Pintado** is recommended for completists only. If you come here after an extensive visit to Chaco, you will almost certainly wonder why you made the drive; however, if you happen to be going to nearby Crownpoint for the rug auction, then you might want to stop in.

## GETTING THERE

The only way to reach Chaco is by car and you should allow ample time for the drive—at least two hours from Farmington, Cuba, or Grants. There are two approaches: the better-used northern route from U.S. 550 and the often bumpier southern route, up from I-40. Some maps and GPS devices suggest that Highway 57 provides access to Chaco Canyon on the north side. It does not.

The **northern** route is from U.S. 550 near Nageezi, onto County Road 7900, which is paved. After eight miles you turn onto the smaller County Road 7950 (well signed), and the paving gives out. The full drive is 21 miles and takes no more than 45 minutes when conditions are good.

From the **south,** the approach is via paved Highway 371 from Thoreau and Highway 9, then 20 miles on dirt Highway 57. But you'll want a high-clearance vehicle, and patience—the top practical speed on this bumpy road is 35 miles per hour at best. Call ahead (505/786-7014) to check conditions before taking this route.

# U.S. 550 South to Bernalillo

The drive back south to the Albuquerque area is a scenic one, with a couple of possible stops in some lesser-visited wilderness areas.

## THE BLACK PLACE

Fans of Georgia O'Keeffe may recognize the **gray-black hills** hills along U.S. 550, about two miles south of the junction with County Road 7900 (the turn to Chaco). Off either side of the road around mile marker 111 are shadowy arroyos, hollowed-out cliffs, and silvery buttes, just ripe for abstract painting.

## CUBA

Forty-eight miles south of the turn to Chaco Canyon (County Road 7900), Cuba is an old Hispano town, founded in the late 18th century. You can get a good meal here, and a good deal on a bed—handy before or after a Chaco visit.

## Accommodations

Cuba is a handy place to sleep before or after visiting Chaco Canyon. On the north side of town, the **Frontier Motel** (U.S. 550, 575/289-3474, $60 s, $70 d) is a bargain, and most of its 33 rooms (in two complexes, across the road from each other) had been renovated as of late 2013, with new carpet, firm beds, and flat-screen TVs. Families will like the two-bedroom suite with a kitchen. If the Frontier is full, the next best option is **Cuban Lodge** (6332 U.S. 550, 575/289-3269, $66 d), on the south edge of town. It shows its age, but it is clean and has very nice management.

If you don't mind a bit more winding driving, then the B&B **Sueños Encantados** (off County Rd. 11, 575/289-3327, www.suenos-encantados.com, $80 d) makes a lovely rural retreat, out on an old adobe homestead about 6.5 miles off of U.S. 550, just south of Cuba. To-go lunches are an option, nice if you're headed to Chaco.

## Food

The Hispano roots have yielded the exemplary ☾ **El Bruno's** (6449 Main St., 575/289-9429, 11am-10pm daily, $12), where every fall a team of women hand-preps all the green chile the restaurant will use for the rest of the year. In this season, you can order a bowl of "Hazel's green chile," which is really just a bowl of the stuff, barely seasoned with pork and tomato. The rest of the year, the chile works its way into stuffed sopaipillas, tamales, and a Cubita sandwich (a play on the classic ham-and-Swiss cheese *cubano*). There are occasional reports of bad meals, but when it's good, it's great—and you can't really argue, as it's one of the few restaurants for miles around.

## CABEZON PEAK

West of U.S. 550, this 2,000-foot-tall "big head" butte is popular for **rock climbing,** or you can **hike** up to the peak for a view as far as Mount Taylor. According to Navajo legend, Mount Taylor represents a slaughtered giant whose head rolled to form Cabezon, while his blood settled into El Malpais. To reach the trailhead, turn west off U.S. 550 at County Road 279, about 20 miles north of San Ysidro. Then go 12 miles southwest to BLM Road 1114, which leads to the parking area in 3 miles.

## OJITO WILDERNESS

These badlands were designated the **Ojito Wilderness** in late 2005, so they are still relatively unmarked by trails. The terrain is mostly stark, striped red hills, scored by rivulets of glittering white gypsum—not quite as dramatic as Bisti/De-Na-Zin, but also not as remote. The partial skeleton of the herbivore *Seismosaurus* was discovered here in 1979, and you may spot fossils in the canyon walls.

From U.S. 550, turn onto Cabezon Road (County Road 26), south of San Ysidro, then bear left at the fork—the parking area for the wilderness is about 10 miles in, on the left. On the way (about 4 miles in), you reach the parking area and trailhead for **White Mesa Bike Trails,** an eerie range of gray gypsum hills traced by 15 miles of single- and double-track. The system runs in two concentric loops. About a third of it, the "Dragon's Back"

section, is exceptionally challenging, while the rest is fairly accessible to all riders. Although the trails were laid out for two-wheelers (and a stretch for horses), they're also open to hikers.

Both Ojito and Cabezon are managed by the **BLM Rio Puerco field office** in Albuquerque (435 Montaño Blvd. NE, 505/761-8700).

# LAS CRUCES AND THE SOUTHWEST

Driving south from Albuquerque along I-25, your perception of New Mexico may shift dramatically: Here in the river basin, the land is green and lush. All the way to the city of Las Cruces, where New Mexico State University is known for its agriculture program, the Rio Grande nurtures alfalfa fields and pecan and pistachio orchards, as well as acres and acres of green chile.

© ZORA O'NEILL

# HIGHLIGHTS

LOOK FOR ◖ TO FIND RECOMMENDED SIGHTS, ACTIVITIES, DINING, AND LODGING.

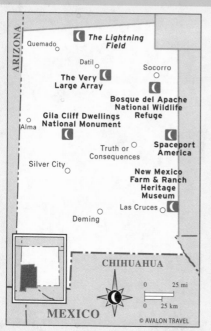

for free at the operation's visitors center (page 251).

◖ **The Lightning Field:** An equally innovative, yet completely different, use of these central plains, Walter de Maria's mesmerizing sculpture requires a long drive and a 24-hour time commitment (page 253).

◖ **Bosque del Apache National Wildlife Refuge:** Some of the best bird-watching in the state happens on these wetlands near the Rio Grande. Time your visit with the arrival of the sandhill cranes in October (page 254).

◖ **Spaceport America:** Technically, flights are set to depart only to low-Earth orbit for now, but still, the desert near Truth of Consequences is the future of space travel (page 257).

◖ **New Mexico Farm & Ranch Heritage Museum:** Ancient tractors, actual livestock, and crafts demonstrations are among the attractions at this vast museum that tells the history of New Mexico in a practical yet fascinating way (page 269).

◖ **Gila Cliff Dwellings National Monument:** The cliffside ruins are not too striking, but they're a good starting destination within the immense Gila Wilderness, the state's largest (page 292).

◖ **The Very Large Array:** Studding the plains west of Socorro, 27 giant radio telescopes look into deep space. You can see them up close

Turning out tons of the stuff every year, the town of Hatch is a pilgrimage site for the chile-addicted. To the north, the Bosque del Apache is a vast river-fed bird sanctuary that attracts sandhill cranes and other migratory birds.

But beyond the reach of irrigation is the Chihuahuan Desert, the largest in North America, which begins around Socorro and stretches south all the way to Zacatecas in Mexico. From a car window, the view can be monotonous and dreary—no wonder Spaniards along the Camino Real trade route called this waterless stretch the Jornada del Muerto (Dead

Man's Trail). Up close, though, the terrain is studded with a surprising variety of yucca and cactus, as well as roadrunners, jackrabbits, and coyotes. And when the scenery does shift, as in the Florida Mountains near Deming or at the strange outcroppings called the City of Rocks, it is all the more striking in this barren expanse.

Farther west rise the mountain ranges of the Continental Divide, where the ancient Mogollon people made their home—you can see their old living spaces at the Gila Cliff Dwellings. Elsewhere in the Gila Wilderness, the largest reserve in the state, are remnants of

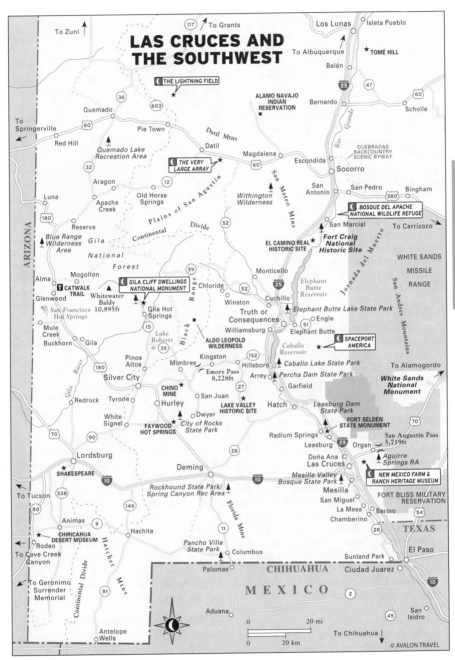

# LAS CRUCES AND THE SOUTHWEST

To Zuni

117 To Grants

Los Lunas    Isleta Pueblo

To Albuquerque    ★ TOMÉ HILL

Belén

☾ THE LIGHTNING FIELD

25    47

36    603    ALAMO NAVAJO INDIAN RESERVATION    Bernardo    Scholle    60

Quemado

Pie Town    Datil Mtns

To Springerville    60    Red Hill    Datil    Magdalena    Escondida    QUEBRADAS BACKCOUNTRY SCENIC BYWAY

Quemado Lake Recreation Area    ☾ THE VERY LARGE ARRAY    60    Socorro

32    Aragon    12    Old Horse Springs    San Mateo Mtns    San Antonio    San Pedro    Bingham

Luna    Withington Wilderness    San Marcial    380    ☾ BOSQUE DEL APACHE NATIONAL WILDLIFE REFUGE

Apache Creek    Plains of San Agustin    52    To Carrizozo

180    Reserve    Continental    Divide    EL CAMINO REAL HISTORIC SITE    Fort Craig National Historic Site

☀ Blue Range Wilderness Area    Gila    WHITE SANDS MISSILE RANGE

National    Forest    Monticello    25    Elephant Butte Reservoir    Jornada del Muerto    San Andres Mountains

Alma    Mogollon    59    ☾ GILA CLIFF DWELLINGS NATIONAL MONUMENT    Chloride    52

ⓣ CATWALK TRAIL    Whitewater Baldy 10,895ft    Winston    ★ Elephant Butte Lake State Park

Glenwood    Gila Hot Springs    Truth or Consequences    Engle

San Francisco Hot Springs    15    Lake Roberts    Williamsburg    51    Elephant Butte    ☾ SPACEPORT AMERICA

Mule Creek    Gila    Buckhorn    ALDO LEOPOLD WILDERNESS    Caballo Reservoir

Pinos Altos    Kingston    152    ★ Caballo Lake State Park    To Alamogordo

Gila River    35    Mimbres    Emory Pass 8,228ft    Hillsboro    ☀ Percha Dam State Park    White Sands National Monument

Silver City    27    Arrey    Garfield

Redrock    Tyrone    CHINO MINE    San Juan    LAKE VALLEY HISTORIC SITE    Hatch    Leasburg Dam State Park

Hurley    Dwyer    70

White Signal    FAYWOOD HOT SPRINGS    City of Rocks State Park    FORT SELDEN STATE MONUMENT

90    26    Radium Springs    San Augustín Pass 5,719ft

Lordsburg    Deming    Leasburg    25    Organ    Aguirre Springs RA

★ SHAKESPEARE    10    Doña Ana    Las Cruces    ☀ NEW MEXICO FARM & RANCH HERITAGE MUSEUM

To Tucson    338    Rockhound State Park/ Spring Canyon Rec Area    10    Mesilla Valley Bosque State Park    FORT BLISS MILITARY RESERVATION

80    146    Mesilla    San Miguel    54

Animas    9    La Mesa    Berino

CHIRICAHUA DESERT MUSEUM    Hachita    11    Chamberino    28    TEXAS

To Rodeo    Cave Creek Canyon    Pancho Villa State Park    Columbus    Sunland Park    El Paso

To Geronimo Surrender Memorial    81    Palomas    CHIHUAHUA    Ciudad Juarez    10

Antelope Wells    MEXICO    2

Aduana    0      20 mi    45    San Isidro

0      20 km    To Chihuahua

© AVALON TRAVEL

ARIZONA

Florida Mtns    Hatchet Mtns    Continental Divide

the phenomenal, if short-lived, mining boom of the late 19th century. Silver City, on the southern edge of the Gila, has held up quite well and now harbors a laid-back creative community that holds "Carpe mañana" as its unofficial motto.

Along the north side of the Gila Wilderness, the mountains level onto the Plains of San Agustín, a great empty bowl dotted with herds of pronghorn—as well as the giant white radio telescopes that make up the Very Large Array, a major space research center. This is ranch land, with an independent ethos held over from the rough-and-tumble mining days and range wars. Landowners in Catron County are required by law to carry a gun, and it's not uncommon to see folks swaggering around with full hip holsters. But even the most weatherbeaten Westerner will sweeten up in Pie Town, where, just as you'd hope, you can get a fresh slice of America's favorite dessert.

## HISTORY

This corner of New Mexico saw the first extensive human habitation in the American Southwest, with the Mogollon (moh-gui-YONE) and Mimbres cultures (named for the places in which relics of their culture were first discovered) settling here around AD 700. With the exception of the late-era Gila Cliff Dwellings and the remnants of a few pit houses, however, these ancient people left few traces. Around 1300, about the same time that the ancestral Puebloans (Anasazi) left Chaco and Bandelier, the Mogollon abandoned their territory, for reasons that are still not clear. Presumably they moved east to the Rio Grande to meld with and expand the Pueblo culture that had just started there.

They were replaced (or perhaps edged out) by the Apache, a nomadic people spread across what's now Arizona, New Mexico, and northern Mexico. The Chiricahua and the Mimbres bands ranged over what's now the Gila Wilderness, and Geronimo, the best-known Apache, said he was born on or near the Gila River in 1829. Their raiding culture put them at odds with the Mexican government, then the American one, which was keen to protect the gold miners who'd arrived in the new territory in the 1850s.

The U.S. Army was soon engaged in a small-scale war with the most tenacious Apache leaders, such as Cochise, Victorio, the woman fighter Lozen, and Mangas Coloradas (Red Sleeves). Instrumental in the fight was the African American cavalry, better known as the Buffalo Soldiers; they also helped build many of the forts in southern New Mexico. In the meantime, Apache women and children were being forced on to trains and resettled as far away as Florida and Alabama; the Chiricahua were the only American Indians who were not granted a reservation.

Geronimo finally surrendered in 1886, but violence continued. The mining boomtowns (now focused on silver) that sprang up were brutal, lawless places. Then the towns faded rapidly when silver currency was replaced with the gold standard in 1893. Meanwhile, south of the mountains, the growing cattle-ranching industry had its own share of vicious infighting, which consumed big businessmen, mercenary cattle rustlers, hit men, and every politician in the southern flatlands; assassinations were not uncommon. And the small town of Columbus, on the border with Mexico, was all but demolished by Pancho Villa in a 1916 raid.

These early battles have moved to the courtroom, where preservationists face off against cattle ranchers. As the long-term damage of overgrazing has become more obvious, environmentalists have been able to successfully sue to take more wilderness acreage out of ranchers' control. Longstanding debates—over reintroduction of the Mexican gray wolf, for instance—have yet to be resolved, making the contrast all the more stark between deep-rooted families who've lived on and worked the land for generations and transplants who've moved here for the natural beauty.

## PLANNING YOUR TIME

Given the driving distances, it's difficult to visit New Mexico's southwest if you're also interested in Santa Fe or other northern destinations. You're better off focusing on this area exclusively, perhaps even flying in to El Paso and working your way north, rather than driving down from Albuquerque. You can lounge around Truth or Consequences for a couple of days, and Las Cruces and Silver City both merit a long weekend, though you could get the spirit of each place in a day. What will interest most visitors is the Gila Wilderness, where hiking and relaxing in hot springs can occupy a day or a whole week.

Relatively speaking, the plains west of Socorro hold less appeal, but it's nice to at least cruise through this ranching area if you can (and it does complete a logical driving loop), as it's a sharp contrast to the hippie-holdover outlook in Silver City. Likewise, Deming and points west could be left off an arts- or hiking-focused itinerary. As pure empty desert, the bootheel south and west of Lordsburg appeals largely to naturalists.

Even if you're not planning to hike, at least make time to drive Highway 152 to Silver City, or, for hardier drivers, the Bursum Road to Mogollon and beyond. The I-25 frontage road south of Truth or Consequences gives you a closer look at the chile heartland.

# South from Albuquerque

The desert terrain beyond Albuquerque on I-25 doesn't look immediately promising, and there's no escaping to a more scenic frontage road in this stretch. Los Lunas and Belén have their own heritage, in farming and railroads, but in recent years they have become bedroom communities for Albuquerque. By exit 152, though, you can strike out into truly remote New Mexico along the Quebradas Scenic Backcountry.

## ISLETA PUEBLO

The southernmost of the pueblos, Tiwa-speaking **Isleta Pueblo** (505/869-3111, www.isletapueblo.com) had a good deal of interaction with the first Spanish settlers and was the only community that didn't participate in the Pueblo Revolt of 1680, during which many of its people fled to Hopi lands and intermarried. Notably, Isleta was home to civil rights hero Miguel Trujillo, who in 1948 successfully sued the New Mexico government for American Indians' right to vote, ending 24 years of the state's disregard for federal law.

Visitors can see the whitewashed **St. Augustine Church,** a beautiful example of early mission architecture. Established in 1612, it was rebuilt in 1716, and it now glows with whitewashed walls and a sky-blue back wall.

Take exit 215, heading south on Highway 47, then west on Highway 147 to the village. The pueblo celebrates the **Feast of St. Augustine** (Aug. 28-Sept. 4), with the biggest dances on the first and last days.

## LOS LUNAS AND BELÉN

The Rail Runner train has made these towns an easy outing from Albuquerque. Of the two, Belén is the more interesting destination, and more accessible by train (as the Los Lunas Rail Runner station is in a residential neighborhood). In Belén, the **Harvey House Museum** (104 N. 1st St., 505/861-0581, 12:30pm-3:30pm Tues.-Sat., 1pm-3pm Sun., donation) is across Reinken Avenue (walk over the bridge) and just south of the depot. It tells the story of the town's past as a major rail hub. Just across the street, **Pete's Café** (105 N. 1st St., 505/864-4811, 11am-8pm Mon.-Thurs., 11am-8:30pm Fri.-Sat., $9) has been open since 1949. Chile con queso—a melty, Velveeta-heavy mess—starts every meal, and everything else is similarly basic and popular, up to the homemade pies for dessert.

Walk south one block to reach Becker Avenue, Belén's historic main drag. Not much is hopping here, though feminist artist Judy Chicago lives in the old Belen Hotel

THE SOUTHWEST

building and runs the nonprofit arts organization **Through the Flower** (107 Becker Ave., 505/864-4080) across the street; its archive is open by appointment. A few more blocks east is the **Art League Gallery** (509 Becker Ave., 505/861-0217), and one block north is **Buckland Pharmacy** (600 Dalies Ave., 505/864-7434, 8:30am-6:30pm Mon.-Fri., 8:30am-3pm Sat.), which runs a nice old-fashioned soda fountain.

## Tomé Hill

Midway between Los Lunas and Belén, east of I-25 and the Rio Grande, **Tomé Hill** is an important pilgrimage site, especially on Good Friday; it is topped with three 16-foot-high crosses. A natural lookout point, the hill was a landmark on the Camino Real, and that history is commemorated with a sculpture at the base of the trail. A 20-minute climb gives a good view down the Rio Grande; keep an eye out for petroglyphs on the rocks near the top. Take exit 203 from I-25, head east, then south about three miles on Highway 47 and turn east. Tomé's old town church is across Highway 47 to the west.

## QUEBRADAS BACKCOUNTRY BYWAY

This 24-mile dirt road, which runs in a jagged arc down to U.S. 380, just south of Socorro, more than makes up for the previous miles of dreary highway driving. The rounded hills here are striped with rainbow hues, and the scrub desert teems with hawks, mule deer, and foxes. Requiring two to three hours, the route makes a good slow way to the Bosque del Apache if you're planning late-afternoon bird-watching (or you could come back up this way after a morning tour). Don't attempt the drive if it has rained recently—the route is named for the deep "breaks," or drainage channels it crosses, and the mud in the bottoms can be impossible to pass. Look out for sandy patches at all times, as well as the occasional hardy mountain biker.

Leave I-25 at Escondida (exit 152), then go north for 1.3 miles on the east-side frontage road; turn east at Escondida Lake and continue for 0.8 mile, crossing the river, to Pueblito, where you turn right at a T intersection. After about a mile, you see a sign for the byway beginning on your left (west); the road ends on U.S. 380 about 10 miles east of San Antonio and the road to the *bosque*. Coming north, the start is easier to find: From the intersection of the *bosque* road (Highway 1) in San Antonio, in front of the Owl Café, head east on U.S. 380 for just over 10 miles; then turn north on County Road A-129, the beginning of the byway.

# Socorro and the Plains of San Agustín

The small town of Socorro is the gateway to the Plains of San Agustín, a prehistoric lake bed that's now a vast bowl of grazing land. U.S. 60 used to be a well-used cross-country route. Now this part of the state is seldom visited and holds few of the typical charms for visitors (and even fewer services)—but it is beautiful, especially after a wet winter or a good summer rainy season, when the plains turn into lush fields of wildflowers. The tiny ranching communities that mark the west edge of the plains—Datil, Pie Town, and Quemado—are, not coincidentally, a day's horseback ride apart.

## SOCORRO

Once a pueblo that offered food to conquistador Don Juan de Oñate, Socorro (Succor, or Relief) now shelters people en route to the Bosque del Apache (about 20 miles south), as well as the students of the **New Mexico Institute of Mining & Technology** (a.k.a. New Mexico Tech, 575/835-5011, www.nmt.edu), which has been training engineers since 1889.

© ZORA O'NEILL

Socorro's Capitol Bar, a quality saloon

The town has a small time-warp historic plaza, but the mission-style campus is scenic as well. To reach it, turn west from the main north-south route, California Street, onto Bullock Street and follow it toward the hills.

## Entertainment

Wet your whistle at the **Capitol Bar** (575/835-1193, noon-2am Mon.-Sat., noon-midnight Sun.) on the plaza, which doesn't seem to have changed much in its century of doing business—this is one of those dim, creaky-wood-floor saloons that you thought existed only on movie sets.

Socorro also has a revamped old movie theater, the **Loma Cinema** (107 Manzanares St., 575/835-0965, $5), which looks vintage on the outside, but inside has stadium seating and usually has two or three movies on the schedule per day.

## Accommodations

Socorro has one B&B, with only two rooms: **Socorro Old Town B&B** (114 Baca St.,

575/838-2619, www.socorrobandb.qwestoffice.net, $125 d), in a renovated bungalow with a nice back patio. If it's full, chain motels are the only real options. As for the numerous motels, **San Miguel Inn** (916 N. California St., 575/835-0211, $35 d) is a fairly decent independent one, and **America's Best Value Inn** (1009 N. California St., 575/835-0276, $51 d) has a few chips in its furniture but is otherwise well kept up, and especially nice for the price.

## Food

For your caffeine fix, **⟨ Mountain Coffeehouse** (110 Manzanares St., 575/838-0809, 7am-8pm daily), just off the plaza, has the necessary espresso, as well as house-made gelato, sandwiches, full breakfasts, and occasional Indian dinner specials. The vibe is distinctly nerdy-intellectual.

For a full meal, try **Socorro Springs** (1012 N. California St., 575/838-0650, 11am-10pm daily, $12), a brewpub on the north end of the main drag through town with a diverse menu, from morning coffee and omelets through

THE SOUTHWEST

El Camino restaurant is open 24 hours.

late-night flame-grilled burgers and creative pizzas. Just down the road, **Bodega Burger** (606 N. California St., 575/838-2087, 11am-9pm Mon.-Sat., 10am-8pm Sun., $11) is not quite as good on the food front, but it does have a full bar, so you can get a good margarita ($9) here.

Vintage Americana fans—or anyone hungry after 9pm or 10pm—should head for **El Camino** (707 N. California St., 575/835-1180, 24 hours, $6), an all-night diner that's plucked straight from the early-faux-wood-paneling era. And finally, **Sofia's Kitchen** (105 Bullock St., 575/835-0022, 6am-9pm Mon.-Fri., 7am-9pm Sat.-Sun., $7) does especially good New Mexican. Bands play Friday, Saturday, and Sunday on a small stage in the corner, in what's otherwise a pretty generic-looking diner.

### Getting There
Socorro is 80 miles south of Albuquerque on I-25, a bit more than an hour's drive. If you're heading west from here on U.S. 60, through Magdalena and on to the Very Large Array, be sure to fill up your gas tank, as there's only one station farther west, in Datil, and it's very expensive.

## MAGDALENA
An escape for those who find Socorro too bustling, Magdalena sits on the edge of the plains, a small clutch of houses under a great sky. Established in 1884, the town was a commercial hub: Ranchers drove cattle here, and miners shipped ore, to be loaded on a rail spur from the main line at Socorro. But the last cattle drive happened in 1970, and the rails were torn out in 1981. More recently, Magdalena came to symbolize the current drought hanging over the West, as its well literally ran dry in the summer of 2013. After the summer rains started, the aquifer was mildly replenished, but the town was still on severe water watch at the time of research, as the thousand or so people here are learning to live with less.

For orientation: U.S. 60 becomes 1st Street in town; Main Street runs north-south in the center.

### Sights
Follow signs south from U.S. 60 to the **Box Car Museum** (Main St., 575/854-2261, 10am-6pm Tues. and Thurs.-Fri., 10am-8pm Wed., 10am-4pm Sat., donation), a small collection of historical artifacts, including some items from the remote Alamo Navajo reservation (29 miles north), set next to the former train depot.

### Sports and Recreation
The little-visited mountains south of town provide a great chance to hike or mountain bike in solitude. The main trail access point is **Water Canyon Campground,** reached via Forest Road 235, which runs south from U.S. 60 11 miles east of Magdalena. Southwest of Magdalena in the San Mateo Mountains, the remote **Withington Wilderness** is almost always devoid of people. For info on trails here and closer to town, visit the **Magdalena Ranger District office** (575/854-2281, 8am-4:30pm Mon.-Fri.), on the east side.

© ZORA O'NEILL

Vestiges of Magdalena's boom years as a cattle station remain.

## Accommodations

Of the two motels in Magdalena, the **Western Motel & RV Park** (404 1st St., 575/854-2417, www.thewesternmotel.com, $42 s, $52 d) is preferable, with flower boxes and lace curtains in the windows, though the all-over pine paneling may be a bit overwhelming for some (there's one adobe room, the former maternity hospital).

Three miles west of town, **Rancho Magdalena** (U.S. 60, 575/854-3091, www. ranchomagdalena.com, $115 d) is a B&B with three cozy rooms with corner fireplaces, all in a recently built house set on a small rise, overlooking rolling ranchland. The same owners also offer a rental house in Magdalena proper ($175), and two other cabins ($175) farther out. For the B&B, turn south near mile marker 109.

## Food

For coffee, lunch, and general tourist information, stop in at **Bear Mountain Coffee House** (902 W. 1st St., 575/854-3310, 9am-3:30pm

Wed.-Sun., $7), on the west end of town. It's a redone saloon, made cozy with a reading nook and outgoing women who run an information center and art gallery.

Dinner can be had a couple of nights a week at the **Magdalena Café and Steakhouse** (109 S. Main St., 575/854-2696, 7am-1:30pm Mon.-Wed., 7am-1:30pm and 5pm-7pm Thurs.-Fri., 7am-12:30pm Sat., $9), set in a pretty old building with shiny wood floors and cozy booths. At press time, local dinner favorite M&M Grill was in the process of moving; if it reopens, you'll find rustic burgers, fruit smoothies, and tortilla soup.

## ◖ THE VERY LARGE ARRAY

A little more than 20 miles west of Magdalena, strange structures jut out of the plains. These are the 27 radio telescopes—which look like enormous satellite dishes—that compose The Very Large Array, a research center devoted to the study of deep space. Reach the **visitors center** (575/835-7243, www.vla.nrao.edu, 8:30am-sunset daily) by turning south onto Highway 52 and following signs to the VLA access road. The center explains, first of all, just what radio astronomy is, as well as how the telescopes are focused to see deep into the Milky Way and show images as precise as shading on Mercury's poles that may be ice. Then you can walk up close to one of the telescopes, as large as a baseball diamond and weighing 230 tons; with any luck, the array will be refocusing, and you'll get to see the massive structure slowly, grindingly turn, eerily in synch with all the others stretching up to 20 miles away. The first Saturday of the month, there are free guided tours at 11am, 1pm, and 3pm.

For a long back-road drive, continue south on Highway 52, passing through a 600-acre private elk reserve and the ghost towns of Winston and Chloride, to eventually connect with I-25 just north of Truth or Consequences.

## DATIL

For visitors and Datil's 50 or so locals, life centers on the **Eagle Guest Ranch** (U.S. 60,

THE SOUTHWEST

© ZORA O'NEILL

**Radio telescopes on the Plains of San Agustín**

575/772-5612, 7am-9pm Mon.-Sat.), an all-purpose motel, gas station, saloon, diner, and taxidermy shop. Radio techies from the VLA rub shoulders with hunting parties, and the motel rooms ($48 s, $55 d) will do in a pinch. It's a chummy, frontier-feeling place, but most people blow right through on their way to....

## PIE TOWN

Aside from Truth or Consequences, no other town name in New Mexico looks as intriguing on a map as Pie Town. In fact, "town" is overstating it, as it has a population of about 45, a single working pay phone, and two cafés. The second weekend in September is the annual **Pie Festival.**

The place got its name in the 1920s, when an entrepreneur began dishing out a sweet pick-me-up to famished homesteaders and, later, intrepid cross-country motorists. But after the federal interstate diverted traffic, the pie market dried up, and the place went pie-less for decades. In 1994, a disappointed

visitor to Pie Town took matters into her own hands and opened the ( **Pie-O-Neer Café** (U.S. 60, 575/772-2711, 11am-4pm Thurs.-Sun.). The daily roster of pies is dazzling—apple-cranberry, double cherry, pecan-oat, to name just a few—and each one is encased in perfectly flaky crust. So you might want a slice to eat in, and another to go. Also on the menu, in case you don't want to head straight to dessert: green-chile stew, and a vegetarian quiche. Call ahead, though—the hours can be erratic.

It doesn't have the cute backstory, but **Good Pie Café** (U.S. 60, 575/772-2700, 10am-5pm Mon.-Thurs., 3pm-8pm Fri.) is the town's more steady operation, with a selection of New Mexican and diner standards along with the sweets; consult the "pie chart" to see what varieties are available that day. This is also the hangout for some of Catron County's crustiest ranchers; keep your cool when folks swagger in with guns strapped to their hips. Friday dinner requires a reservation.

© ZORA O'NEILL

Who wouldn't stop in Pie Town?

## QUEMADO

Quemado is little more than a wide spot along the highway, but it does provide some basic services for travelers. The **Largo Motel** (U.S. 60, 575/773-4686, $65 d), on the west edge of town, has very comfortable beds. Its **café** (6am-9pm Mon.-Wed., 6am-11pm Thurs.-Sat., 7am-9pm Sun.) is quite good—its "Mexican cheeseburger" is the stuff of legend, a patty wrapped in a flour tortilla and smothered in green chile and cheese.

You can also camp at **Quemado Lake Recreation Area,** about 20 miles south of U.S. 60 on Highway 32; the 131-acre lake is stocked with trout, and camping facilities range from RV hookups to pleasantly shady spots for tents. A hiking trail heads to a lookout tower in the ponderosa forest above. Bears can be a problem here during dry summers, and the camping facilities may be closed; check with the **Quemado Ranger District office** (575/773-4678, 8am-4:30pm Mon.-Fri.), just off U.S. 60 at the intersection with Highway 36.

### ◖ *The Lightning Field*

Quemado is also the unlikely starting point for a visit to an elaborate work of land art called *The Lightning Field* (505/898-3335, www.lightningfield.org, May-Oct.). Sculptor Walter de Maria laid out the work in 1977, setting 400 stainless-steel poles in a grid measuring one mile by one kilometer. The light glints off the poles, and summer storms create a field of crackling, brilliant electricity across their pointed tips. De Maria envisioned an immersive experience, in which the viewer, in pure isolation, watches the light shift over the course of the day. To this end, casual visitors are not allowed, and the road to the site is unmarked; you must make reservations for an overnight stay and leave your car in Quemado. At $150 per person ($250 during the prime storm months of July and August), the basic accommodations may seem a bit steep, but this ranks as one of the state's most remarkable places to spend the night, not to mention one of the great places to meditate on New Mexico's phenomenal landscape.

## SAN ANTONIO

As I-25 continues south from Socorro, the highway passes alongside Bosque del Apache, one of the largest nature reserves in the United States. Access is via Highway 1, south from U.S. 380, where the small town of San Antonio, just a blip on the map, provides a couple of lunch spots for hungry birders.

### ◖ Bosque del Apache National Wildlife Refuge

Occupying more than 57,000 acres on either side of the Rio Grande, the **Bosque del Apache National Wildlife Refuge** is in a sense a manufactured habitat: Controlled flooding creates the marshes that draw the birds, which find food on farm plots dedicated to tasty grains. But this is really restoring a process that happened naturally before the Rio Grande was dammed. The birds certainly have no objection. Arctic geese, sandhill cranes, bald eagles, and a whole variety of ducks happily settle in for the winter. In the spring, migratory warblers and pelicans stop off on their way back to points north, while great blue herons make their spring nests here. Summer is relatively quiet, as only the year-round species remain: hummingbirds, swallows, flycatchers, and the like.

Five miles inside the north border of the reserve, you pass the **visitors center** (575/835-1828, www.friendsofthebosque.org, 7:30am-4pm daily), where you can pick up maps and find out which birds have been spotted that day. A bit farther south on Highway 1, a 12-mile paved car loop passes through all the marshlands and the grain fields; at certain points along the drive, you can get out and hike set trails, such as a quarter-mile boardwalk across a lagoon or a trail to the river. Some areas are open to mountain bikers. The **loop drive** ($5/car) opens when birdlife is at its best, one hour before sunrise; cars need to be out by an hour after dark. With all its marshland, the *bosque* could just as well be called a mosquito sanctuary—slather on plenty of repellent before you start your drive.

The biggest event of the year is the arrival of the sandhill cranes—they were the inspiration for the refuge, as their population had dwindled to fewer than 20 in 1941. But now more than 15,000 of these graceful birds with six-foot wingspans winter over in the *bosque.* They're celebrated annually at the five-day **Festival of the Cranes** (www.festivalofthecranes.com) in November, when birders gather to witness the mass morning liftoffs and evening fly-ins.

### Accommodations

If you want to wake up and get straight to the birds, **Casa Blanca B&B** (13 Montoya St., 575/835-3027, www.casablancabedandbreakfast.com, $80 d) can put you up for the night in one of three cozy rooms in an 1880 Victorian farmhouse. It's closed May-September, but rambling, Western bonanza **Fite Ranch** (Fite Ranch Rd., 575/838-0958, www.fiteranchbedandbreakfast.com, $110 d), about seven miles east of San Antonio, is open year-round. It has a two-night minimum.

For camping, **Bosque Birdwatchers RV Park** (575/835-1366, $15) is bare bones (no showers), but just 100 yards north of the reserve border on Highway 1.

### Food

San Antonio manages to support two legendary green-chile cheeseburger joints: the **Owl Bar & Café** (U.S. 380, 575/835-9946, 8am-9pm Mon.-Sat., $6), which has always gotten all the press, and relative upstart but now genuine rival **Buckhorn Burgers** (U.S. 380, 575/835-4423, 11am-7:50pm Mon.-Fri., 11am-3:30pm Sat., $6), just across the street. Both serve beer and burgers, both have chummy local staff and plenty of lore—so how to choose? Go to the Owl if you like your burgers thin, to Buckhorn if you like them a little fatter. Actually, the Owl gets an extra point for historic detail: The bar here is from the world's first Hilton hotel—not part of Conrad Hilton's international chain, but the one opened by his father when he moved here in the 1880s; Conrad was born shortly thereafter, grew up to be his father's business partner, and went on to develop hotel properties around the world. The Owl's owners salvaged the bar after the structure surrounding it burned.

If, for some reason, you're not in the mood for a burger, follow the signs for **San Antonio Crane** (17 Pino St., 575/835-2208, 10am-4pm Tues.-Sat., noon-3pm Sun., $8), one block south off U.S. 380, for homemade New Mexican food (including especially good tamales) served in a tiny dining room.

## EL CAMINO REAL

South of the Bosque, the Chihuahuan Desert scenery takes over, with dusty grasses occasionally punctuated by yucca trees. Highway 1, the interstate frontage road now designated **El Camino Real National Scenic Byway,** grants a quieter perspective and leads directly to the two major sights in this area: the remains of a Civil War-era fort and a monument to El Camino Real de Tierra Adentro (the Royal Road of the Interior) forged between central Mexico and Santa Fe during the Spanish colonial period. Just one of a network of trade routes through Spanish territory in the Americas, this north-south trail brought fur and silver into the heart of Mexico, from where it was shipped out to

© ZORA O'NEILL

El Camino Real Historic Site

seaports. I-25 parallels the old route, which was so heavily traveled that wagon ruts are still visible. Unfortunately the casual tourist won't see them, as most of these hallowed spots fall within the bounds of Armendaris Ranch and Ladder Ranch, both owned by Ted Turner, who promotes bison grazing and management of endangered wildlife on his million-plus acres.

## Fort Craig National Historic Site

One of the largest forts in the Southwest and the staging point for the crucial Battle of Valverde during the Civil War, **Fort Craig National Historic Site** (dawn-dusk daily, free) is a long way to drive for precious little to see. Only true military buffs will have the imagination to bring the few building outlines and crumbling earthworks to life. As a place to stretch your legs, though, you could do worse: The site is near the Rio Grande (a bit of a walk over level ground), in view of Black Mesa to the north. In the days of the Camino Real, this striking landmass came to be known as the Mesa del Contadero, as its position next to the river formed a natural chute for counting livestock herds. In February 1862, the north side of the mesa saw the Battle of Valverde, in which the fort's forces managed to damage a Confederate supply train, setting the stage for a more decisive Union victory in the Battle of Glorieta about a month later.

## El Camino Real Historic Site

Hidden from view about 2.5 miles east of I-25 (exit 115), the **El Camino Real Historic Site** (575/854-3600, www.caminorealheritage.org, 8:30am-5pm Wed.-Sun., $5) is well worth a detour. The stark modern museum stands on a windswept bluff with no sign of human population in sight—a fitting locale for this tribute to the often-difficult Spanish trade route that for centuries linked Zacatecas, Mexico, with the frontier town of Santa Fe. Inside the heritage center, the information-packed exhibits describe the major points along the royal road; outside are traditional gardens, a dramatic vista on the Chihuahuan Desert, and a six-mile trail north to Fort Craig.

# Truth or Consequences

For decades, the town of Hot Springs was just a dot on the map 150 miles south of Albuquerque. Its bathhouses had once been packed with health-seekers enjoying the underground reservoir of mineral-rich water, but by the mid-20th century, the place had slumped into obscurity. Around this time, the popular radio show *Truth or Consequences* was offering national publicity to any town willing to change its name to match the show's, and the Hot Springs council took the bait. The stunt was completed in the spring of 1950, with host Ralph Edwards and a convoy of press and celebrities on hand. National notoriety faded, but T or C (as it's commonly known) has managed to hang on, acting as a diversion from the interstate for through travelers and a bargain retirement spot for people fleeing frigid Minnesota and Dakota winters.

In the 21st century, the town has gotten a bit of a boost, from two sides. One is from the younger artists who have relocated here from the coasts, helping revive the small downtown area with galleries and hot-springs operations. The other is from Richard Branson, whose Virgin Galactic is the anchor tenant at the Spaceport America east of town; the growing industry has brought fresh interest in the town. While space tourists line up for the eventual first launch (perhaps in 2014), T or C is a pleasant, if a bit ramshackle, place to spend a night or two.

## Orientation

Drivers will enter T or C either at its farthest north end (exit 79), where Highway 181 turns into the long commercial strip known as North Date Street, or on the south side (exit 76), where Highway 187 runs through an adjunct town called Williamsburg, then turns into Broadway in T or C. Both routes lead downtown, bounded by Main Street and Broadway, where the galleries are located (note that many

are closed at least Monday and Tuesday). Most of the commercial bathhouses and hotels with springs are on or south of Main Street.

## SIGHTS

T or C's must-see sight is **Geronimo Springs Museum** (211 Main St., 575/894-6600, 9am-5pm Mon.-Sat., noon-4pm Sun., $6). A fantastic small-town collection, it documents both the monumental and the mundane in T or C since its founding. Seven rooms display everything from mammoth skulls to portraits of local bankers to an authentic log cabin. Local rebel Geronimo gets a lot of attention, as does town-maker and radio and TV host Ralph Edwards.

In the semicircle bordered by Main Street and Broadway, a good portion of the Depression-era storefronts have been revived with galleries and quirky shops. Of the more than 15 galleries, **RioBravoFineArt** (110 N. Broadway) is the oldest, representing, among others, the town's best-known painter, Delmas Howe, who made his name with lush murals and homoerotic cowboy portraits.

For even older artwork, peek in the always-open **post office** (300 Main St.) for a somewhat eerie 1938 mural of an American Indian dance, by Lithuanian immigrant Boris Deutsch.

The town's **Civic Center** (W. 4th Ave. between Grape St. and N. Foch St.) is covered in Delmas Howe's signature flower blooms. On the south side, the **Exotic Cactus Ranch** (1600 S. Broadway, 575/894-0790, 9am-3pm Thurs.-Sun. in summer, call for winter hours) is a small but well-stocked nursery, as much as a museum of obscure flora as a beloved resource for local gardeners. Also in this area is **Veterans Memorial Park** (996 S. Broadway, 575/894-7640, www.torcveteransmemorial.com), which contains a half-scale replica of the Vietnam Memorial in Washington DC, as well

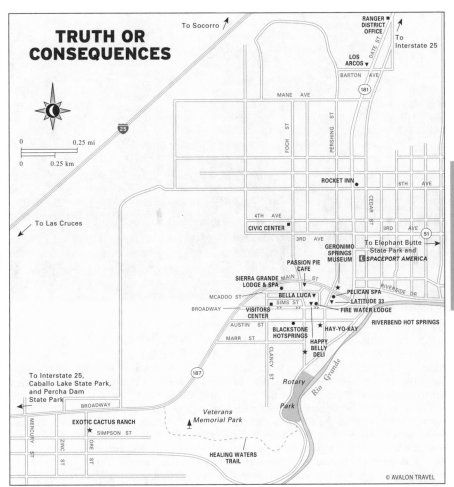

# TRUTH OR CONSEQUENCES

To Socorro

To Interstate 25

RANGER DISTRICT OFFICE

LOS ARCOS

BARTON AVE

181

MANE AVE

FOCH ST

PERSHING ST

DATE ST

0    0.25 mi

0    0.25 km

25

ROCKET INN

6TH AVE

CEDAR ST

4TH AVE

CIVIC CENTER

3RD AVE

To Las Cruces

3RD AVE

51

GERONIMO SPRINGS MUSEUM

To Elephant Butte State Park and
**(** SPACEPORT AMERICA

PASSION PIE CAFE

SIERRA GRANDE LODGE & SPA

MAIN ST

RIVERSIDE DR

BELLA LUCA

PELICAN SPA

MCADOO ST

SIMS ST

LATITUDE 33

BROADWAY

VISITORS CENTER

FIRE WATER LODGE

AUSTIN ST

BLACKSTONE HOTSPRINGS

HAY-YO-KAY

RIVERBEND HOT SPRINGS

MARR ST

HAPPY BELLY DELI

To Interstate 25,
Caballo Lake State Park,
and Percha Dam
State Park

187

CLANCY ST

Rotary

Rio Grande

BROADWAY

Park

MERCURY ST

ZINC ST

ORE ST

EXOTIC CACTUS RANCH

SIMPSON ST

Veterans
Memorial Park

HEALING WATERS TRAIL

© AVALON TRAVEL

as a **museum of military history** (10am-4pm Tues.-Sat., noon-4pm Sun., free).

## **(** Spaceport America

Practically speaking, you may not be able to visit this supposedly must-see sight—or you may find the tour price too high. But it is nonetheless marvelous to contemplate **Spaceport America** (www.spaceportamerica. com), the first commercial space-flight hub in the world. Could there be a more fitting setting than southern New Mexico, with all its empty space and its history of rocket research and alleged alien spacecraft activity? Tucked into the desert about 30 miles southeast of Truth or Consequences, the facility was still waiting for passengers as this book was going to press, and it was accessible by guided bus tour, only driving around the perimeter. If you're reading this after mid-2014, space flights may have gotten off the ground, and presumably, tours can also visit the

© ZORA O'NEILL

Spaceport America keeps a low profile.

building itself. **Space Place** (www.spacepla-cenm.com, $59) is in charge of the bus tours, currently scheduled for twice a day Friday and Saturday, and once on Sunday; this may of course change as the spaceport opens.

The project has been in the works for almost 20 years, though the current structure is the more recent work of British architect Norman Foster, known for his swooping curves and use of organic materials—this explains, perhaps, why the structure looks like a giant horseshoe crab, half-buried in the sand.

The spaceport is most closely associated with another, far more famous Brit, Richard Branson. His Virgin Galactic company will launch civilians—who have paid upwards of $200,000 and undergone a week of training— into low-Earth orbit for only a few minutes, just high and long enough to see the curve of the blue-green Earth against the black void of space.

## ENTERTAINMENT AND EVENTS

T or C's version of nightlife is the outdoor group pool at **Riverbend Hot Springs** (100 Austin St., 575/894-SOAK, www.nm-hotsprings.com, 8am-10pm daily). The most festive night out is the downtown **Second Saturday Art Hop** (Main St. and Broadway, 6pm-9pm), every month, year-round. Doors stay open late, and residents toddle from spot to spot, sharing gossip and free refreshments.

The biggest annual event is the **Ralph Edwards Fiesta** (575/740-7542, www.torcfiesta.com), celebrated with style on the first weekend in May every year since 1950. Edwards himself attended until 1999, often with assorted TV and movie personalities in tow. Even without him (he died in 2005), the festivities are pretty grand for such a small town, pulling together what feels like all of T or C's disparate population of 8,000, with the Old Time Fiddlers Association marching alongside youngsters dressed as aliens. Expect lots of goofy floats, art cars, Spam-craft contests, and more.

## SPORTS AND RECREATION

Truth or Consequences caters largely to the layabout, what with all the warm baths. Sports aficionados have in the past enjoyed the artificial lakes just minutes from town—but low water levels due to droughts have curtailed some of the fishing and boating.

If you'll be heading west into the Gila National Forest from here, stop by the **Black Range Ranger District office** (1804 N. Date St., 575/894-6677, 8am-4:30pm Mon.-Fri.), in the Lakeway Shopping Center, to pick up maps and other info.

### Hot Springs

Of the dozen or so spots to take the waters, **Riverbend** (100 Austin St., 575/894-SOAK, www.nmhotsprings.com, 8am-10pm daily) is the best if you prefer the open air. Perched at the water's edge, the cascading communal pools ($10/hour) offer a range of water temperatures. If you're feeling less social, opt for one of three private tubs, similarly open-air and facing the river ($15/hour).

**Sierra Grande Lodge & Spa** (501 McAdoo St., 575/894-6976, www.sierragrandelodge. com, $25/hour) is pricey, but its pools—indoors and out—are especially nice. You must make reservations ahead of time, as the pools are drained and filled fresh for every visitor.

For cheap and historic, head for **Hay-Yo-Kay** (300 Austin St., 575/894-2228, www.hay-yo-kay.com, 8am-noon and 4pm-8pm Wed.-Fri., 10am-8pm Sat.-Sun.), a restored bathhouse from the 1920s—the indoor pools for one or two people are cramped but clean; rates start at $6 for half an hour. Out back, the "longhouse" is one very large tub in a semi-open shelter, shielded from the weather.

### Healing Waters Trail

This three-mile walking route around and a bit out of town is half history, half nature. Downtown, the route passes many of the iconic hot springs and historic buildings, with markers at crucial points. Across the river, southeast of downtown, a dirt trail winds through wetlands and into the scrub-covered hills, giving a good view over the old part of town. Signs along the way tell the story of how the favorite Apache bathing spot became the town of Hot Springs. Pick up a map at the museum or the visitors center on Broadway.

### Elephant Butte Lake State Park

Named for a distinctive rock formation in the center of the water, 40-mile-long Elephant Butte Lake is the largest body of water in New Mexico—in a good year, anyway. Recent droughts have left it dramatically reduced and curtailed the usual fishing and boating. One bonus of low water: Sandy beaches appear. If/when the weather turns, the lake will return to its usual summertime buzz, with the party spilling over to the small town of Elephant Butte, immediately north of Truth or Consequences on Highway 181.

**Elephant Butte Lake State Park** (575/744-5923, www.nmparks.com, $5/car) contains a huge number of **campsites** ($10-14), though of course in the current state, they're all quite far from the water. Follow the frontage road along the west edge of the lake to quieter campsites such as North and South Monticello Point.

Campers and day-trippers alike should stop first at the **visitors center** (575/744-5421, 7:30am-4:30pm daily) near the south end, to pay fees and check on current conditions. Major services are here too, at the marinas or in town. **Marina del Sur** (101 S. Hwy. 195, 575/744-5567, www.marinadelsur.info) rents pontoons, houseboats, and kayaks.

### Caballo Lake State Park

This **smaller lake** (Hwy. 187, 575/743-3942, www.nmparks.com, $5/car) 16 miles south of Truth or Consequences is quieter than Elephant Butte, frequented mainly by anglers out for white bass and walleye. The Lakeside Recreation Area has boat access and a few easy hiking trails. The developed sites at **Stallion Campground** ($8 for tents, $14 for RVs), overlooking the lake, are preferable to those at

Appaloosa, and the primitive camping area is fairly private; you can also park your car about a mile north of the park entrance and hike in to camp at **Eagle Point.**

South of Caballo Dam, the **Riverside Recreation Area** has fairly attractive developed camping spots right on the water, though the spaces are not particularly private-feeling. The best ones are at the far south end of the recreation area.

### Percha Dam State Park

Five miles south of Caballo Lake, this small recreational area is a **birding** hot spot for vermilion flycatchers, among other rare migratory birds. Otherwise, the area is not particularly lush and can feel a little dusty despite the big old cottonwood trees that line the river.

## ACCOMMODATIONS

Places with in-room hot springs are all downtown, cheaper options are on North Date Street, and a few chain hotels are very close to the interstate.

### Under $100

A renovated old motor court, **❰ Blackstone Hotsprings** (410 Austin St., 575/894-0894, www.blackstonehotsprings.com) has seven rooms decorated (tastefully) in retro-TV themes, from the black-and-white Twilight Zone ($75) to the 1950s space-age Jetsons ($135). Some setups have patios and/or kitchenettes, and private hot springs fill every room's large soaking tub.

In a similar motor-court setting, **Fire Water Lodge** (311 Broadway, 575/740-0315, www.firewaterlodge.com) doesn't look like much from the outside, but its rooms are some of the most attractive and well-priced in town—the walls are painted in glowing colors, and the hand-carved furniture fits perfectly in each space. All have hot spring-fed tubs built in (from $90); two are outdoors. Some have kitchens too, though breakfast at the bagel place next door is included.

**Riverbend Hot Springs** (100 Austin St., 575/894-7625, $70 d) has rooms for rent too,

for more efficient commuting to its nice outdoor soaking facilities. The "artist rooms" are their cheapest option, built in mobile homes but with all new furnishings; casitas and suites (from $105) with kitchenettes are also available.

Just out of the downtown loop, the **❰ Rocket Inn** (605 N. Date St., 575/894-2964, $49 s, $51 d) is a very well-tended old motor court from 1948, with all-new insides. Sparkling bathrooms, ceiling fans, and fantastic beds are all a steal at this price—and the owners are efficient and friendly. You can walk to hot springs downtown (guests get a discount at Riverbend).

If these places are full, try the **Pelican Spa** (306 S. Pershing St., 575/894-0055, www.pelican-spa.com, $55 s, $95 d), which has 31 rooms and apartments in several properties around downtown. This might be spread too thin—we received a complaint of (ironically) a lack of hot water, as well as shabby furniture. Note that unlike other downtown hotels, only one has an in-room soaking tub; all other guests share a large separate spa area at the South Pershing address.

The Rocket Inn is pretty down to earth.

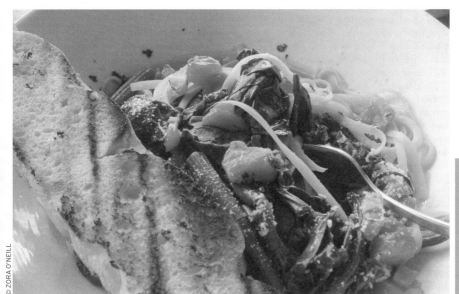

© ZORA O'NEILL

THE SOUTHWEST

pasta at BellaLuca

## $100-150

By far the ritziest choice in T or C, **Sierra Grande Lodge & Spa** (501 McAdoo St., 575/894-6976, www.sierragrandelodge.com, $129 d, $279 suite) occupies a historic hotel building, with 16 wood-floor rooms decorated in a spare Southwest style, plus a separate casita. Rooms on the front upstairs have balconies with a view of the mountains. Hotel rates include a one-hour soak in the spa, which has indoor and outdoor baths. Room rates drop slightly during the week.

## FOOD

Start your day right with an "Elvis waffle" (banana slices and peanut butter sauce), or perhaps even more brilliantly, a waffle with bacon in the batter, and real maple syrup on the side. **Passion Pie Café** (406 Main St., 575/894-0008, 7am-3pm daily, $6) is where this magic happens, plus plenty more (Greek salads, cupcakes, etc.), all fresh and homemade.

For a hearty lunch, head to **Happy Belly Deli** (313 Broadway, 575/894-3354, 7am-3pm Mon.-Sat., $6), where the New Yorker proprietors pride themselves on quality bagels, meaty sandwiches, and other standards. Friday and Saturday nights (5pm-9pm), they also serve pizza.

Vegetarians should look for **White Coyote Café** (113 Main St., 575/575-3004, 8am-2pm Fri.-Mon.), which keeps somewhat erratic opening hours and months (sometimes it closes for the whole summer). But when it's open, it's fresh and creative.

**BellaLuca** (303 Jones St., 575/894-9866, 11am-9pm Mon. and Wed.-Thurs., 11am-10pm Fri.-Sat., 11am-8pm Sun., $14) serves crispy-crust pizzas, inventive pastas and more, in a very sleek setting with floor-to-ceiling windows and art on the walls. Not everything hits the mark, but the food is always fresh (organic eggs and more) and appealing.

To call **Latitude 33** (304 S. Pershing St., 575/740-7804, 11am-2pm Mon.-Thurs., 11am-2pm and 5pm-9pm Fri.-Sat., $11) an "Asian fusion" restaurant conjures up something too grand—this is creative, home-style food that happens to have ingredients like coconut milk and ginger. The cabbage salad is packed with flavor, as is the Thai-style iced tea. Note: no booze at research time; beer and wine may come.

In the mood for a hefty dry-aged steak, shrimp cocktail, and deep-fried zucchini strips? Seek out the time-warp steakhouse **Los Arcos** (1400 N. Date St., 575/894-6200, 5pm-9:30pm Sun.-Thurs., 5pm-10:30pm Fri.-Sat., $12), where the calendar seems never to have changed from opening day in 1970. Nonetheless, the food is fresh and satisfying.

## INFORMATION AND SERVICES

Stop in at the helpful **visitors center** (529 Broadway, 575/894-1968, www.sierracountynewmexico.info, 9am-4:30pm Mon.-Sat., noon-4pm Sun.) for a map of the town and scads of brochures to surrounding attractions, including the Geronimo Trail.

For local reads and more, **Black Cat Books and Coffee** (128 Broadway, 575/894-7070, 8am-5pm Fri.-Mon.) stocks new and used titles.

# Geronimo Trail

Named for the fearsome leader who held out against the Southern Apache Agency until 1886, longer than any other American Indian fighter, this **scenic route** (www.geronimotrail.com) winds through the former territory of his tribe, including the Black Range, the longest

© ZORA O'NEILL

the northern branch of the Geronimo Trail

and most rugged stretch of mountains in the state, where many of the battles between U.S. troops and the Apaches were waged. But you'll see little evidence of that period, except in place names such as Massacre Canyon. More prevalent are the relics of the short-lived silver boom of the late 19th century. Some of the saloons, general stores, and banks from that era still stand, empty and listing dangerously or propped up and turned into museums.

The route is technically a loop, but the west side of the circuit (Forest Road 150) is 46 miles of rudimentary dirt that can't be recommended for standard cars. Most people will drive the northern section to Chloride, Winston, and Monticello, or traverse just the southern section, through Hillsboro and Kingston, and winding over the pass to Silver City. Many of the more interesting sights are short side trips off the main trail. Before you head out, fill your tank—there are no gas stations on the route west of T or C.

## THE NORTHERN ROUTE

Head north out of T or C along the I-25 frontage road, then turn west into the Cuchillo Mountains on Highway 52.

### Winston and Chloride

After passing through **Cuchillo,** founded in the

1850s, the road winds up and over the mountains to Winston. A picturesque array of wood buildings set on a wide plain, Winston got its name from a generous shop-owner who gave credit to residents suffering through the crash of 1893, when silver was devalued and prospectors lost everything. Now it's a relatively lively community—at least compared with neighboring Chloride, a few miles up the road. Established in 1879, Chloride went bust less than 20 years later. The "hanging tree" still stands in the middle of Wall Street, and the **Pioneer Store Museum** (575/743-2736, 10am-4pm daily, donation) is stocked as it would have been in the 19th century. The museum owners can advise on nearby trails up to abandoned mines.

The bank building is now the excellent **Chloride Bank Café** (575/743-0414, 11am-7pm Wed.-Sat., 11am-5pm Sun., $7), with fresh, homemade, and creative food—including new pies and cakes every day.

## Monticello

Backtrack on Highway 52 about halfway, then cut east on dirt Tortilla Flats Road to Las Placitas and, farther northwest on Highway 142, Monticello. This is a pretty farming community that was an early Spanish settlement. Ringed with lavender plots and grape arbors, it is still centered on the traditional plaza established in the 1850s. One farm, **The Darland Company** (www.organicbalsamic.com), specializes in balsamic vinegar, and also has a few rental casitas (from $110) that are lovely escapes, though best for very independent travelers—you must bring all food and anything else you might need.

You can then return to T or C via Highway 142.

## THE SOUTHERN ROUTE

Twelve miles south of Truth or Consequences, Highway 152 heads west into the Black Range, passing a couple of old mining towns. The mountain scenery is striking, though west of Kingston, the area was hard hit by a forest fire in 2013, so hiking is limited.

The road is serpentine and best driven in the daytime.

## Hillsboro

Seventeen miles along the road, Hillsboro has an Old West feel. It became the seat of Sierra County in 1884, then managed to weather the silver devaluation and a bitter murder trial in 1899, as cattlemen's feuds and other range rivalries split the whole region. But in the early 20th century, it suffered floods and the flu epidemic, and after a long legal struggle, lost its county-seat status to Hot Springs (later T or C) in 1936, along with most of its remaining population. Just to be certain there was no going back, the courthouse was dismantled; you can still see its ruins along the "high road" through town.

On the east edge of town, the exceedingly dusty **Black Range Museum** (Hwy. 152, 575/895-5233, 11am-4pm Thurs.-Sat., 1pm-5pm Sun., $2 donation) merits a poke around if you happen to arrive during its open hours. The haphazard collection includes fittings from "The Chinaman's Café" that occupied this building after legendary madam-made-good Sadie Orchard sold the property to Tom Ying. The **Hillsboro General Store Café** (10697 Hwy. 152, 575/895-5306, 8am-3pm Fri.-Wed., $7) is good for a snack, a homey place in an 1879 building (that still works as a store as well). Road-food standards like burritos and grilled cheese with green chile are on the menu.

## Lake Valley Historic Site

From the main junction in Hillsboro, Highway 27 detours south, out of the mountains and into the rolling hills around **Lake Valley Historic Site** (Thurs.-Mon.), an especially well-kept relic. The slumping buildings with rusted tin roofs are all the evidence that remains of the richest single silver mine ever discovered, in 1881: a glittering cavern lined with solid ore that prospectors dubbed The Bridal Chamber. The find was marred by typical tragedy for that period, as George Daly, the man who'd led the exploration, was killed by Apaches the same day the trove was unearthed.

the Hillsboro General Store Café

© ZORA O'NEILL

The strike prompted all the usual expansion, with saloons, stagecoach and railroad service, and plenty of gunfights. Although the silver crash and a catastrophic fire in 1895 ruined this town, Lake Valley was inhabited by a few hardy old-timers until as recently as 1994. As a result, some of the buildings are in recognizable shape, and the schoolhouse is still used for special events. Stewards should be on-site to give you a walking-tour map and answer questions; if not, you can usually find copies of the map at the entrance to the site.

Highway 27 ends at the intersection with Highway 26, and the alleged town of Nutt—all that's there is the aptly named **Middle of Nowhere Bar** (19160 Hatch Hwy., 575/267-4567, 10am-9pm Wed.-Sat., noon-9pm Sun.). Head east to Hatch (18 miles) or southwest to Deming (28 miles).

## Kingston

Back in Hillsboro, continue nine miles west on Highway 152 to where a Dead End sign points to Kingston. A population of more than 7,000

made this the largest town in New Mexico in 1890, when the surrounding mountains were being stripped of their silver in mines called Ready Pay and Opportunity. Butch Cassidy, Mark Twain, and Billy the Kid all passed through, and Lillian Russell performed in the opera house, but the market panic in 1893 inspired a mass exodus. All that's left now is a community even smaller than Hillsboro, a clutch of buildings along a narrow road. The only one that looks just as it did during the boom years is the faithfully restored 1884 **Percha Bank** (575/895-5652, 11am-3pm Fri.-Sun. June-Aug., free), complete with all the woodwork and fittings, as well as an enormous working vault. A gallery space exhibits local art.

The **Black Range Lodge** (119 Main St., 575/895-5652, www.blackrangelodge.com, $95 s, $105 d) is an atmospheric mountain outpost where you'll get a real sense of the outdoors. The main building, with its heavy stone walls and wood ceiling beams, may inspire memories of summer camp. The bedrooms upstairs are far better than bunks, however, with sensible, not-too-frilly antiques, old quilts, and cozy radiant heat in the floors. A separate building showcases the owners' expertise in straw-bale construction; the upstairs guesthouse has a full kitchen and a deck, while the downstairs studio has a kitchenette. A larger property across the street can sleep up to 14. Kids will appreciate the foosball in the game room. Full breakfast (with eggs from the resident chickens) is provided; for dinner, you're welcome to cook your own food in the kitchen.

## West to Silver City

After Kingston, Highway 152 snakes up to Emory Pass (elev. 8,228 feet), which was hardest hit by the 2013 Silver Fire. The route can be tedious and tiring in even the best of weather. If you anticipate heavy rain, better to take the southern route to Silver City; snow often closes the pass entirely.

Continuing to Silver City through the Mimbres Valley, you will pass Chino Mine.

# Mesilla Valley

Heading due south from T or C on I-25 (or, more scenically, on Highway 187 and Highway 185), you return to the fertile river valley and the heartland of New Mexico's distinctive cuisine. This is chile country, where the bulk of the state's crop is grown and processed. In the summer, the fields are hot and still and solidly green. By the fall harvest, the air is almost noticeably spicy (those with allergies, beware!).

## HATCH

This community has earned a much bigger name than its population of 2,000 would suggest. Every Labor Day weekend, the **Hatch Chile Festival** celebrates the town's most famous crop. As you'd imagine, food vendors are plentiful, but you can also shop for chile-themed crafts and wave to the Chile Festival Queen. The tiny **Hatch Museum** (149 W. Hall St., 575/267-3638, 9am-3pm Mon.-Fri., donation) should document this a bit more, but instead features locally made doilies, and a whole wall full of rocks and minerals.

If your visit doesn't coincide with the fiesta, head to **Valley Café** (335 W. Hall St., 575/267-4798, 8am-3pm Mon.-Fri., 7:30am-3pm Sat., $6), which serves chiles rellenos and other green-chile standards hot and fast. It has only five tables, though, so if it's full, or you want takeout anyway, opt for **B&E Burritos** (303 N. Franklin St., 575/267-5191, 7am-4:30pm Mon.-Fri., 7am-3pm Sat., $6),

another one of the more esteemed places to eat the hot stuff in Hatch. Its rellenos are dangerously greasy, but the chile-meat burrito is good, and if you like the salsa, you can buy whole jars of it. It's on the right when coming in from I-25, set back a bit at the corner of West Hill Street.

You can buy chile all year round in Hatch,

the year's green-chile crop in Hatch

## Utopia on the Rio Grande

Even before the Hog Farm and other communes were established in the 1960s, New Mexico was a destination for visionaries. In 1882, a New York City dentist named John Newbrough claimed angels had channeled his hands to type almost a thousand pages of revelation in a manuscript he called *Oahspe*. The text lays out an elaborate cosmology in which, among other things, the earth moves along with the sun through different regions of space, each having a spiritual effect on the human race. It also details a plan for dealing with the world's orphans, through the building of a model village called the Shalam Colony that would be dedicated to children's education.

*Oahspe*'s text inspired followers, who called themselves Faithists, and with 20 of these people Newbrough set about realizing Shalam Colony on the banks of the Rio Grande, about a mile from the village of Doña Ana, north of Las Cruces. A wealthy Bostonian put up the money for 1,500 acres of rich farmland, and the Faithists built some 35 buildings, plus innovations such as heated chicken pens, and a grand residence for the children. But farming proved difficult for the inexperienced colonists, and they were able to relocate only about 50 orphans. When Newbrough died of the flu in 1891, Shalam was already suffering. His wife and the Boston investor (who married in 1893) struggled to keep the place afloat, but the group dispersed in 1901, and the few remaining children were shipped to orphanages in Texas and Colorado.

A few Faithists carried on and settled in other parts of the West, but the only remnant of the Shalam Colony's social experiment is a historic marker on Highway 185.

whether freshly roasted in late August and early September, or frozen or dried and ground. One well-stocked shop is **Hatch Chile Sales** (265 W. Hall St.), which also sells pint jars of great homemade salsa.

## FORT SELDEN STATE MONUMENT

Established in 1865, **Fort Selden State Monument** (1280 Ft. Selden Rd., 575/526-8911, 8:30am-5pm Wed.-Sun., $3), 22 miles south of Hatch and 16 miles north of Las Cruces, was never the site of a dramatic battle—but that doesn't mean a visit here is dull. On the contrary, because the small museum isn't bogged down in troop maneuvers, it has space to dedicate to the humdrum details of life on the 19th-century frontier. Here you learn, for instance, that women often accompanied their husbands to forts, and that a soldier's diet consisted of not much more than flour, bacon grease, and the occasional apple. Recipes, building fixtures, and remnants of letters flesh out the portrait of the soldiers stationed here to escort trading caravans. The adobe fort itself has melted to the outlines of a few walls surrounding a central parade ground; a monument to the Buffalo Soldiers, many of whom were stationed here, sits adjacent.

# Las Cruces

Built along the Rio Grande, with mountains jutting up to the east, Las Cruces resembles a miniature Albuquerque in its geography. But this city of 97,000 is distinct in several respects. As the home of New Mexico State University, which has a dedicated Chile Pepper Institute, this is a farm town and proud of it. And while Las Cruces may not literally abut Mexico (El Paso, Texas, 42 miles south, gets in the way), the neighboring country's influence is strongly felt here, in a cross-border culture that's distinct from the Hispano communities in the northern part of the state.

## SIGHTS

Although Las Cruces was founded in 1849, few relics remain. The most notable landmarks are its mural-adorned water towers—you'll see a few coming in from the north on I-25. The historic area is the adobe enclave of Mesilla on the city's east side, technically a separate town, though functionally just a particularly scenic neighborhood.

### Mesilla

For the most scenic approach, drive to Mesilla via University Avenue in the south. Fields line the road, and you'll feel as if you have indeed arrived in a different town when you turn north on Calle de El Paso. The historic village, which has largely preserved its original adobe architecture, centers on a trim plaza that's more sedate than Albuquerque's or Santa Fe's, but also less plagued with tourist tackiness. The twin-spired **Basilica of San Albino** (575/526-9349, 1pm-3pm Mon.-Sat.), which dates from 1906, stands on the north side of the plaza. It replaced an earlier adobe built in the mid-19th century, when the settlement of Mesilla had finally attained, after seven years, some security from Apache raids, as well as legal surety when the Gadsden Purchase settled the dispute over the land on which Mesilla sat.

For more on Mesilla's historic buildings, stop in at the **visitors center** (2231 Avenida de Mesilla, 575/524-3262 ext. 117, www.vivamesilla.org, 9:30am-4:30pm Mon.-Thurs., 10am-2pm Fri.-Sat.), inside the town hall, for an annotated map. It will point out such venerable spots as the Fountain Theatre, off the southeast corner of the plaza. It was established by Albert Jennings Fountain, the powerful political leader who lived in Mesilla with his Mexican wife; his family performed melodramas on its stage. Fountain later disappeared, along with his young son, a victim of the range wars; his presumed murder prompted a contentious 1899 trial of cattleman Oliver Lee in the town of Hillsboro.

After you've toured around the plaza, walk west, to the residential section, where you'll get an idea what the all-adobe village looked like 150 years back. (Be respectful when taking photos, though.)

### Downtown Museums

The heart of old Las Cruces doesn't look like much, but it has been through a lot. It once looked just like Mesilla, all old adobes and "modern" mercantiles. But a 1960s urban renewal scheme razed all that and installed a covered pedestrian mall that made the whole area dark and hard to reach. Starting in 2005, this was gradually reversed, and Main Street is finally emerging into a slightly livelier place, with a few anchor theaters and a farmers market on Saturday mornings.

The city runs three adjacent museums downtown—none exactly thrilling, but a good excuse to visit the area. The **Branigan Cultural Center** (501 N. Main St., 575/541-2154, 9am-4:30pm Tues.-Sat.) hosts special events and houses a concise history of the city. Next door to the south, the **Las Cruces Museum of Art** (491 N. Main St., 575/541-2137, 9am-4:30pm Tues.-Sat., free) shows off local talent, and next door to that (doors on both Main Street and Water, in the back) is the **Las Cruces Museum**

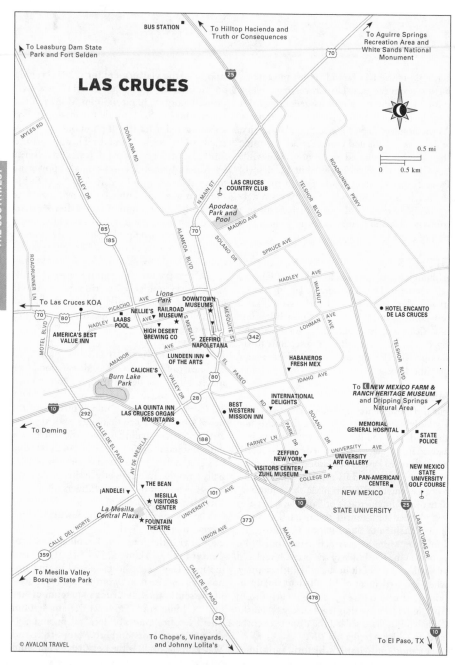

# LAS CRUCES

BUS STATION ■

To Hilltop Hacienda and
Truth or Consequences

To Aguirre Springs
Recreation Area and
White Sands National
Monument

To Leasburg Dam State
Park and Fort Selden

MYLES RD

DONA ANA RD

VALLEY DR

ROADRUNNER PKWY

70

25

85

185

ROADRUNNER LN

MOTEL BLVD

To Las Cruces KOA

70

80

AMERICA'S BEST
VALUE INN

PICACHO    AVE

HADLEY

Lions
Park

NELLIE'S
LAABS
POOL

RAILROAD
MUSEUM

DOWNTOWN
MUSEUMS ★

HIGH DESERT
BREWING CO

ZEFFIRO
NAPOLETANA

N. MAIN ST

ALAMEDA   BLVD

SOLANO DR

LAS CRUCES
COUNTRY CLUB

Apodaca
Park and
Pool

MADRID AVE

MADRID AVE

SPRUCE AVE

HADLEY    AVE

WALNUT

MESQUITE ST

S. MESILLA

342

HOTEL ENCANTO
DE LAS CRUCES

TELSHOR BLVD

LOHMAN    AVE

AMADOR

CALICHE'S

Burn Lake
Park

LUNDEEN INN
OF THE ARTS

VALLEY DR

EL PASO

28

80

HABANEROS
FRESH MEX

IDAHO   AVE

To ◖ NEW MEXICO FARM &
RANCH HERITAGE MUSEUM
and Dripping Springs
Natural Area

TELSHOR BLVD

10

292

CALLE DE EL PASO

AV DE MESILLA

To Deming

LA QUINTA INN
LAS CRUCES ORGAN
MOUNTAINS

188

BEST
WESTERN
MISSION INN

INTERNATIONAL
DELIGHTS

FARNEY   LN

PARK    RD

SOLANO   DR

UNIVERSITY    AVE

MEMORIAL
GENERAL HOSPITAL ■

STATE
POLICE

ZEFFIRO
NEW YORK

ZEFFIRO
NEW YORK

VISITORS CENTER/
ZUHL MUSEUM

UNIVERSITY
ART GALLERY

COLLEGE DR

PAN-AMERICAN
CENTER ■

NEW MEXICO
STATE
UNIVERSITY
GOLF COURSE

THE BEAN

¡ANDELE! ▾

MESILLA
VISITORS
CENTER

La Mesilla
Central Plaza ★ FOUNTAIN
THEATRE

CALLE DEL NORTE

359

To Mesilla Valley
Bosque State Park

101    AVE

UNIVERSITY

373

10

MAIN ST

UNION AVE

NEW MEXICO

STATE UNIVERSITY

25

LAS ALTURAS DR

CALLE DE EL PASO

28

To Chope's, Vineyards,
and Johnny Lolita's

478

10

To El Paso, TX

0         0.5 mi

0        0.5 km

© AVALON TRAVEL

THE SOUTHWEST

© ZORA O'NEILL

a renovated theater in Las Cruces' downtown strip

**of Nature and Science** (450 N. Water St., 575/522-3120, 9am-4:30pm Tues.-Sat., free), which gives a good overview of the ecosystems in this part of New Mexico, illustrated with terrariums showcasing native reptiles.

The old Santa Fe depot houses the **Las Cruces Railroad Museum** (351 N. Mesilla St., 575/647-4480, 9am-4:30pm Thurs.-Sat., free), with some nice period details in the furniture. But of course the real fun is in the model-train room, which re-creates the AT&SF line around Las Cruces.

### New Mexico State University

Founded in 1888, **New Mexico State University** (NMSU), home of the Aggies, is on the south side of town in the triangle formed by the intersection of I-10 and I-25, on a modern campus with a few Spanish and Southwestern touches. On the northwest corner, next to the visitors center (where it's easiest to park), look in at the **Zuhl Museum** (775 College Dr., 575/646-3616, www.nmsu.edu/zuhl, 8am-5pm Mon.-Fri., free), a collection of

geological items; particularly beautiful are the slabs of petrified wood. In Williams Hall, on University Avenue just east of Solano Drive, the **University Art Gallery** (575/646-2545, www.nmsu.edu/artgal, noon-4pm Tues. and Thurs.-Sat., noon-4pm and 6pm-8pm Wed., free) has a beautiful collection of painted wood *retablos* (saint portraits) from the 19th century. Just opposite to the west, in Kent Hall, the **University Museum** (575/646-3739, noon-4pm Tues.-Sat., free) displays recent archaeological finds.

### New Mexico Farm & Ranch Heritage Museum

Even avowed city slickers will find something intriguing at the **New Mexico Farm & Ranch Heritage Museum** (4100 Dripping Springs Rd., 575/522-4100, www.frhm.org, 9am-5pm Mon.-Sat., noon-5pm Sun., $5), on the east edge of town near the Organ Mountain foothills. Indoors, trace the history of agriculture in New Mexico by peeking inside a traditional Mogollon pit house, then hearing the personal histories of homesteaders who replaced

© ZORA O'NEILL

THE SOUTHWEST

Get rural at the New Mexico Farm & Ranch Heritage Museum.

the Spanish in the 1860s. Space is given to Blackdom, the African American farmers' settlement begun in the Pecos Valley and relocated to Las Cruces in 1921, as well as the travails of other immigrant groups. Ag geeks can admire giant cotton pickers and learn more about the Spanish acequia system of irrigation. Outside, the museum sprawls for acres, encompassing a dairy barn and goats and longhorn cattle. Look out for demonstrations of sheep shearing, blacksmithing, home canning, and the like. Throughout, the volunteer docents have the zeal of missionaries—you too may have a real appreciation for vintage tractors by the time you leave.

## ENTERTAINMENT AND EVENTS

With a student body of more than 16,000, NMSU is a strong influence on local nightlife, so casual bars with free-flowing beer are the norm. Special events highlight the city's ties to Mexican culture.

### Nightlife

"None of our beers suck," boasts **High Desert Brewing Co.** (1201 W. Hadley Ave., 575/525-6752, 11am-midnight Mon.-Sat., noon-10pm Sun.), but they needn't set standards so low. This brewpub's products are all quite savory, and they wash down good basic bar grub. There's live music Tuesday, Thursday, and Saturday, though you'd never guess it from the outside of the place, which looks like an office.

On the plaza in Mesilla, **El Patio Cantina** (2171 Calle de Parian, 575/526-9943, 5pm-11pm Mon., 4pm-11pm Tues., 2pm-2am Wed.-Sat., noon-midnight Sun.) is a good old-fashioned bar. Wednesday night is jazz night, and weekends are usually booked with classic-rock cover bands that get a cross-section of Las Cruces.

### Performing Arts

Downtown on Main Street is a fine movie palace of yore, the Italianate **Rio Grande Theatre** (213 N. Main St., 575/523-6403, www.riograndetheatre.com). It now hosts live performances. Nearby too is the old **State Theater,** home to the long-running Las Cruces Community Theatre (313 N. Main St., 575/523-1200, www.lcctnm.org).

### Cinema

In Mesilla, the **Fountain Theatre** (2469 Calle de Guadalupe, 575/524-8287, www.mesillavalleyfilm.org, $7) has been open since 1870 and operating as a cinema since 1905. It's a tiny, anonymous adobe building, the anti-movie palace, but a cool place to see a film, as you settle in between walls painted with murals of the Rio Grande. The place is entirely run by volunteers, with all kinds of interesting international films shown nightly at 7:30pm.

### Festivals and Events

The premier annual event in Las Cruces is the **Whole Enchilada Fiesta** (575/526-1938, www.enchiladafiesta.com), over three days in late September. The festival of *lucha libre* (Mexican wrestling), motorcycle shows, and food vendors takes place in the city recreation area east of downtown and culminates in the construction of the world's largest enchilada, using 750 pounds of cornmeal, 175 pounds of grated cheese, and 75 gallons of red-chile sauce.

Other city parties have a more traditional south-of-the-border flavor. Mesilla's plaza celebrates Mexico's victory in the 1862 Battle of Puebla on **Cinco de Mayo,** with fireworks, music, piñatas, and folk-dancing performances on the weekend closest to May 5. Likewise, the **Diez y Seis de Septiembre Fiesta** commemorates Mexico's independence movement with all the usual fun on the weekend nearest September 16. At the end of October, the colorful fun of **Dia de los Muertos,** the Day of the Dead, gives kids a chance to see a different sort of Halloween.

NMSU's Pan-American Center fills with the blare of trumpets for four days in November, for the **Las Cruces International Mariachi Conference & Festival** (www.lascrucesmariachi.org), which draws a long roster of musicians from northern Mexico, California, and across the Southwest. The daytime shows in Young Park are convivial.

## SPORTS AND RECREATION

The mountains' proximity makes Las Cruces a very outdoorsy town. The **Southwest Environmental Center** (275 N. Main St., 575/522-5552, www.wildmesquite.org, 9am-6pm Mon.-Fri.) is a great resource for anyone interested in the wild areas around the city—ask here for trail recommendations, and learn what the latest efforts to protect the desert have yielded.

### Biking

Las Cruces is flat and relatively slow-paced, making it very easy to get around on two wheels; empty roads and rugged trails nearby cater to any recreational style. **Ride On Sports** (525 S. Telshor Blvd., 575/521-1686, www.rideonsports.com, 10am-8pm Mon.-Fri., 9am-8pm Sat., 11am-6pm Sun.) is the best local shop, offering all kinds of gear and plenty of tips on where to ride.

One of the best-loved mountain biking trails

is north of the city, just off Highway 185 in the Robledo Mountains on the west side of the Rio Grande. **Robledo Trail** (also known as SST Trail) is 6.5 miles of single-track (13 miles round-trip) with lots of technical challenges—definitely for experienced riders. Ask Ride On Sports for precise directions to the trailhead. A more accessible circuit, **"A" Mountain Trail** (also signed as Tortugas Mountain Trails) starts just 10 minutes east of the NMSU campus and loops around a cone-shaped hill bedecked with a big red capital "A." The counterclockwise route around the low peak is the easier option, though beginning riders might still have to walk in a couple of spots.

### Bird-Watching

Encompassing three miles of wetlands on the west side of the Rio Grande, **Mesilla Valley Bosque State Park** (5000 Calle del Norte, 575/523-4398, 7am-4pm Wed.-Sun., $5/car) was known as one of the best birding spots in southern New Mexico well before it was established as a state park in 2007. Entrance is via the visitors center on the northern side, where **guided hikes** go out at 2:30pm on weekends, and birding tours run at 7:30am on Saturday; take Calle del Norte (Hwy. 359) west from central Mesilla, then drive south 1.2 miles within the park.

### Hiking

The most accessible day hikes are in the foothills of the Organs, directly east of Las Cruces. **Dripping Springs Natural Area** (575/522-1219, 8am-7pm Apr.-Sept., 8am-5pm Oct.-Mar., $5/car) is 10 miles east of the city, at the end of Dripping Springs Road. The visitors center is also the head of the 1.5-mile Dripping Springs Trail, which winds through the ruined buildings of the 19th-century resort that gives the area its name. Just before you reach the visitors center, **La Cueva Picnic Area** is high enough that it affords a fine view across the basin. A trail from here leads past a cave that was the home of an Italian hermit for a few years in the 1860s, until he was found dead with a knife in his back; his murder was never solved.

© ZORA O'NEILL

the Organ Mountains, east of Las Cruces

Running six miles up and over the mountains to the east side, **Baylor Pass Trail** is a bit more challenging. It begins in the foothills east of Baylor Canyon Road—look for the turn 1.9 miles south of U.S. 70. After ascending about 1,600 feet to the pass, you have a view of both the Mesilla Valley to the west and White Sands to the east, then the trail descends over two miles to end in **Aguirre Springs Recreation Area** (575/525-4300, $5/car), a campground on the east side of the mountains. It takes about four hours to traverse; alternatively, you could make a shorter—but steeper—hike by starting on the east end and going only up to the pass and back, about 2.5 hours. From the same campground, you have access to **Pine Tree Trail**, a 4.5-mile loop that's a little shadier, without much altitude gain—it takes only about three hours to do the circuit.

### Rock Climbing

With the near-vertical Organ Mountains always in view, it's no wonder Las Cruces has a strong climbing scene—in fact, when considered with Hueco Tanks closer to El Paso, it's one of the best areas for bouldering and climbing in the United States. The options are too many to detail here, so your best bet is to contact **Outdoor Adventures** (1424 Missouri Ave., 575/521-1922, www.outdooradventures-lc.com, 10am-6pm Mon.-Fri., 10am-5pm Sat.) for guidance and maps.

### Swimming

Las Cruces has several public pools. **Laabs** (701 W. Picacho Ave., 575/524-3168) is a modern outdoor pool with slides, open only during the summer. Admission is $4 for adults, $2 for children.

## ACCOMMODATIONS

Las Cruces is short on distinctive lodging. Of the chain operations, the most conveniently located ones are on Avenida de Mesilla, before you reach Mesilla proper.

### Under $100

Campers can set up at the **Las Cruces KOA**

(814 Weinrich Rd., 575/526-6555, www.las-crucescampgrounds.com), west of the city just south of U.S. 70, with fantastic views of the mountains, a heated swimming pool, and wireless Internet. Cabins ($58) and tent sites (from $29) are available. You can also camp at **Leasburg Dam State Park** (Hwy. 157, 575/524-4068, www.nmparks.com), 15 miles north of town adjacent to Fort Selden. The park runs along a series of irrigation canals and is favored by kayakers and bird-watchers; it has 31 developed campsites ($8 for tents, $14 for RVs).

Of the many chain hotels in town, the cheapest that can be recommended—in the otherwise dubious stretch of Picacho Avenue—is **America's Best Value Inn** (2160 W. Picacho Ave., 575/524-8627, www.abvi.com, $60 s, $70 d), fairly recently renovated and sporting a swimming pool—plus a giant red chile sculpture out front.

Near Mesilla, **La Quinta Inn & Suites Las Cruces Organ Mountains** (1500 Hickory Dr., 575/523-0100, www.lq.com, $69 d) is in excellent shape and has a small pool. The **Best Western Mission Inn** (1765 S. Main St., 575/524-8591, www.bwmissioninn.com, $85 d) is older but well kept, and its large rooms have nice little Southwestern details like tile mirror frames. Rates include a full breakfast, and you can often get very good online discounts.

## $100-150

Walking distance from downtown, the rambling, Spanish-style **Lundeen Inn of the Arts** (618 S. Alameda St., 575/526-3326, $89 s, $125 d) has been open for decades, and the walls crowded with paintings reflect that age. The place feels a bit dim and dusty, but the owner, an architect, is interesting, and the history is also palpable. Some rooms have fireplaces.

The road to **Hilltop Hacienda** (2600 Westmoreland Ave., 575/382-3556, $125 d), on the northeast fringe of the city, cuts through barren desert. But the B&B itself is set amid beautifully tended gardens full of honeysuckle, wildflowers, and pomegranate and cypress trees. Watch the sunset from one of several quiet patios or the hot tub, perched on the hillside. The three guest rooms share a private kitchen, and guests also have access to private trails around the hacienda's 17 acres.

The city's plushest hotel, **Hotel Encanto de Las Cruces** (705 S. Telshor Blvd., 575/522-4300, www.hotelencanto.com, $129 d) perches on a hill, affording great views across the valley. Inside, the decor is a rich palette of tan and wine, with a hint of Spanish colonial style, and the beds are particularly comfortable. Request either a west-facing top-floor room for a great sunset view or something on the pool level, where patios open onto the swimming area. The only drawback is that its location on the east side is a bit isolated, and the only place in walking distance is the Mesilla Valley Mall.

## FOOD

As with sightseeing, eating is a little livelier in Mesilla, with a couple of landmark spots clustered around the plaza. But central Las Cruces has a few hot (as in spicy-hot) spots as well. Also consider **Chope's** (Hwy. 28, 575/233-3420, 11:30am-1:30pm and 5:30pm-8:30pm Tues.-Fri., 5:30pm-8pm Sat., $8), in the village of La Mesa, only about 20 minutes' drive south of Mesilla.

### Mesilla

First, two recommendations for the food: **Emilia's on the Plaza** (2290 Calle de Parian, 575/652-3007, 11am-8pm Mon.-Sat., $10) is a homey little place with a nice patio. The menu has chiles rellenos and other New Mexican goodies, as well as lighter things like BLTs and Cuban sandwiches. A few blocks north of the plaza, **iAndele!** (1950 Calle del Norte, 575/526-9631, 8am-2:30pm Mon., 8am-9pm Tues.-Sun., $10) specializes in delicious *tacos al carbon* (with meat fresh off the grill) and rich, red-chile-flecked *posole*. The main restaurant is a room-upon-room, ever-expanding place, and just south, across Calle del Norte, is the smaller **iAndele!'s Dog House** (1983 Calle del Norte, 575/526-1271, 11am-9pm daily, $10), which has the same menu, plus Mexican-style hot

© ZORA O'NEILL

THE SOUTHWEST

¡Andele!'s Dog House serves spicy Mexican hot dogs.

dogs (wrapped in bacon and doused in jalapeños and other goodies). And, true to its name, it's canine-friendly and has a nice patio where pooches are welcome.

All that said, the plaza in Mesilla is also home to two landmark restaurants, the sort of places where Las Cruceños have gone for special-occasion meals for decades. While the food can only be recommended with reservations, they both have stellar ambience. At **Double Eagle** (2355 Calle de Guadalupe, 575/523-6700, 11am-10pm Mon.-Sat., noon-9pm Sun., $24) it's all chandeliers and fogged mirrors. Though its fancy-steakhouse menu is expensive and only mediocre, it's worth stopping in at least for a drink or an appetizer, to soak up the grand atmosphere and poke through all the ghostly rooms. During the day, the more budget-friendly option is the casual New Mexican café **Peppers** (575/523-4999, $12), which occupies two smaller front rooms of the Double Eagle, as well as its central courtyard with a fountain; it's a bit uneven, though.

**La Posta** (2410 Calle de San Albino, 575/524-3524, 11am-9pm Sun.-Thurs., 11am-9:30pm Fri.-Sat., $11), just across the plaza, dishes up New Mexican standards in an old adobe that was a stop on the Butterfield Overland Mail & Stage route. The rambling compound (unspool a string to find your way back from the bathroom) is decked out with parrots and knickknacks, the mariachi music is nonstop, and the margarita menu is two-pages long. You could do worse.

Finally, for coffee and community, **The Bean** (2011 Avenida de Mesilla, 575/523-5155, 7am-3pm daily, $3) is the most popular place to chill out with a cup of joe. Set in an old gas station, the coffeehouse hosts an array of quirky regulars, while serving up pastries, omelets, and grilled sandwiches.

### Las Cruces

As pizza purists demand, it's all about the crust at ◖ **Zeffiro Pizzeria Napoletana** (136 N. Water St., 575/525-6757, 11am-2pm and 5pm-8pm Mon.-Thurs., 11am-2pm and 5pm-9pm Fri.-Sat., $9). Pies come out of the wood oven with almost comically blistered and bubbling edges. Toppings run from typical pepperoni to lemon slices and asparagus; there's pasta too. The place gets busy early, especially if there's a concert at the nearby Rio Grande Theatre. The same team runs the student-friendly **Zeffiro New York Pizzeria** (901 University Ave., 575/525-6770, 11am-9pm Mon.-Sat., noon-7pm), where you can get a somewhat greasier pizza by the slice.

The **farmers market** on Main Street usually has a number of good snack vendors—tamales and more. It sets up Wednesday and Saturday (8am-noon), with more activity on the latter day.

Chef Alfredo does just about everything at ◖ **Habaneros Fresh Mex** (1275 S. Solano Dr., 575/524-1829, 8am-9pm Mon.-Sat., 10am-4pm Sun., $6), a converted drive-up place that now dishes out gorditas, house-made mole, carne asada fries, and more. It's all hot and fresh, and a fantastic bargain—you even get free "welcome soup."

**Nellie's** (1226 W. Hadley Ave., 575/524-9982, 8am-2pm, Tues.-Sat., $7) promises "chile with an attitude," though the service is perfectly pleasant; equal parts meat and green fire, it's the chunky "four-alarm chile" that really gets in your face. Huevos rancheros are a slightly mellower way to start your day.

Las Cruces is short on global cuisine, but **International Delights** (1245 El Paseo Rd., 575/647-5956, 8am-11pm daily, $8) satisfies a lot of cravings. The menu includes Middle Eastern standards like falafel along with familiar deli combos and a good selection of coffee, tea, and pastries, including baklava with local flair: date pecan, vanilla piñon, and more. Look for it in the back corner of a strip mall next to Albertson's supermarket.

On a hot summer night, there's no better place to be than **Caliche's** (590 S. Valley Dr., 575/647-5066, 11am-10pm daily, $4), which serves frozen custard under pink and blue neon. A caliche (Spanish for hard clay) is the local equivalent of a St. Louis-style concrete, a shake so thick you have to eat with a spoon. Of course there are New Mexican mix-ins such as pine nuts and red chile.

## INFORMATION AND SERVICES

**Las Cruces Convention & Visitors Bureau** (211 N. Water St., 575/541-2444, www.lascrucescvb.org, 8am-5pm Mon.-Fri.) has free high-speed Internet service, along with a helpful staff and piles of brochures.

On the old plaza, the excellent **Mesilla Book Center** (2360 Calle Principal, 575/526-6220, 11am-5:30pm Tues.-Sat., 1pm-5pm Sun.) has perhaps every book you'd ever want to read about the American West and the Mexican border, plus current and classic fiction, guides to horse care and bike repair, and plenty more. Downtown, **COAS: My Bookstore** (317 N. Main St., 575/524-8471, 9am-6pm Mon.-Sat., 11am-5pm Sun.) is crammed with secondhand titles of every kind.

## GETTING THERE AND AROUND

By car, Las Cruces is 225 miles (3 hours) south of Albuquerque on I-25 and U.S. 85, and 45 miles (about 45 minutes) north of El Paso, Texas. From Alamogordo, it's 68 miles (1 hour) west on Highway 70; from Deming, it's 60 miles (1 hour) east on I-10; and from Truth or Consequences, 75 miles (1.25 hours) south on I-25.

Rather than making the drive from the Albuquerque airport, many visitors to Las Cruces fly into El Paso (ELP). **Las Cruces Shuttle** (575/525-1784, www.lascrucesshuttle.com) runs an airport transport service 10 times daily. Rates are $45 one-way, or $70 round-trip. Despite its optimistic name, Las Cruces International Airport (LRU) receives only private planes.

The **Greyhound bus** (800/231-2222, www.greyhound.com) stops at the Chucky's convenience store (800 E. Thorpe Rd., 575/524-8518, 7am-11pm daily). Two buses run daily from Albuquerque; six run from El Paso.

**RoadRunner Transit** (575/541-2500) is the city bus system, though buses run infrequently, and only until 7pm Monday through Friday, till 6pm on Saturday, and not at all on Sunday. Fare is $1 (exact change, bills accepted), and buses are equipped with front bike racks. Route no. 40 runs to Mesilla from downtown; visit www.las-cruces.org for a full schedule and map.

THE SOUTHWEST

## South of Las Cruces

© ZORA O'NEILL

**Get your espresso fix in the fields south of Las Cruces.**

Drive south out of Mesilla on Calle de El Paso (Highway 28), and you're almost immediately in lush agricultural land: Pecan orchards, vineyards, and cotton fields sprawl almost all the way to the Texas border. The two-lane road winds by you-pick farms, corn mazes, and other seasonal entertainment. Year-round, you can break up the drive with stops at wineries, such as **Rio Grande Vineyards** (5321 Hwy. 28, 575/524-3985, noon-5:30pm Fri.-Sun.), closest to Mesilla, or **La Viña** (4201 Hwy. 28, 575/882-7632, noon-5pm Thurs.-Tues.), the oldest vineyard in New Mexico, in La Union. Both stock other local products, such as honey and chiles, in addition to wine.

Just south of La Viña, red-painted **Johnny Lolita's** (3200 S. Hwy. 28, 915/929-4008, 7:30am-3pm Tues.-Sun., $3) pops out in the middle of the fields. This coffeehouse roasts its own beans, and it makes a good turnaround point for the drive. The place hosts a farmers market most Sunday mornings in season, and a "thieves market" of local crafts and vintage goods on the first Saturday and Sunday of each month.

Wind up with a meal at **Chope's** (Hwy. 28, 575/233-3420, 11:30am-1:30pm and 5:30pm-8:30pm Tues.-Fri., till 8pm Sat., $8), back close to Las Cruces, in the village of La Mesa. It's a down-at-the-heels roadhouse and restaurant, famous for its heavily egg-battered chiles rellenos, red chile beans, and rural New Mexican ambience. The restaurant is in the house to your left; you can also eat in the bar, and even if you don't, you should have a beer there just to people-watch.

# West to the Bootheel

Heading west from Las Cruces, I-10 runs through the flatlands up to the Chiricahua Mountains on the Arizona border. Most of the area is unrelenting desert punctuated by spikes of mountains, such as the Floridas rising 2,800 feet above the surrounding plain. The area is known for dust storms and shimmering heat, but in the southwestern corner of the state, a little stub of virtually untouched wilderness juts farther south. Jaguars have been spotted here on very rare occasions, and critters like coatimundi, tarantulas, rattlesnakes, and particularly enormous locusts thrive. By late August, when the summer rains are strong enough, the desert turns a lush green; avoid May and June, however, before the rains have started, as this is the hottest, driest period.

## DEMING

"Pure water and fast ducks" boast billboards advertising Deming's charms, and surely no other town in the United States can make such a claim to fame. The water comes from a large aquifer under the city of 15,000; as for the speedy birds, they're part of the Great American Duck Race, the city's biggest annual event. The business leaders who came up with the scheme in 1980 (to rival Ruidoso's horse-racing industry) admit the initial brainstorming session did involve liquor.

Deming is popular with retirees from the upper Midwest, and its greater cityscape is one of RV and trailer parks, as well as truck stops. But its old downtown, south of the intersection of Pine and Gold, shows a surprising elegance, and it's a great place to pull off the highway for

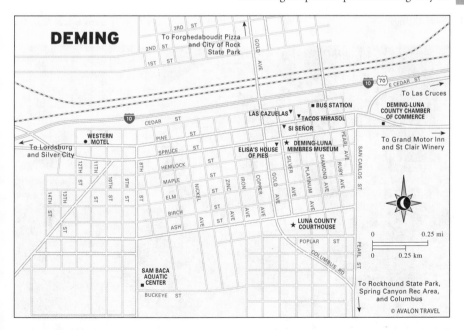

© AVALON TRAVEL

THE SOUTHWEST

authentic Mexican food. Street addresses with directionals (SW, NE, etc.) are outside of town, not in central Deming.

## Sights

Most visitors start with the **Deming-Luna Mimbres Museum** (301 S. Silver Ave., 575/546-2382, 9am-4pm Mon.-Sat., 1:30pm-4pm Sun., closed Sun. July-Aug., donation), one block south of Pine Street. Set in a 1917 armory, the museum is the county's vast repository of historic flotsam, lovingly curated and carefully arranged. Novelty whiskey bottles, nutcrackers, geodes, beautiful Mimbres pottery—it's all here, in incredible detail and profusion.

At the end of South Silver Street, the red-brick **Luna County Courthouse,** restored in 2006, looks like it would be more at home in Iowa. It was built in 1910, then in 1916 saw the trial of many of Pancho Villa's alleged accomplices in the rebel leader's raid on Columbus, New Mexico; four of the "Villistas" were subsequently hanged on the green lawn in front of the building.

The **St. Clair Winery** (1325 De Baca Rd. SE, 575/546-2408, 9am-6pm Mon.-Sat., noon-6pm Sun.), established by a French family in 1984, occupies 15 acres a few miles outside of town (head east on Pine Street) and is an easy hop off the interstate. This is just part of some 120 acres the group owns, to produce most of the grapes for winemakers all over the state (shh, it's a bit of a dirty secret!). You can taste a wide range of wines; the better ones are under the D. H. Lescombes label—especially the syrah, which does well in the sun here.

## Entertainment and Events

Deming's annual hoedown is the last weekend in August, when the **Great American Duck Race** (www.demingduckrace.com) takes over. In addition to the headline duck sprint, festivities include a cash-prize tortilla toss, outhouse races, a parade with more fake foam beaks than you can count, and a balloon rally.

## Sports and Recreation

Beat the summer heat at **Sam Baca Aquatic**

St. Clair Winery is a short detour off the highway near Deming.

© ZORA O'NEILL

**Center** (815 W. Buckeye St., 575/546-7958, $2), which has three big outdoor pools and a water slide, with frolicking kids segregated from the lap-swimmers. It's open summers from mid-May through the end of September; call for hours.

For a more outdoorsy experience, head southeast to the Florida (Flowering) Mountains, so named for the colorful wildflowers that blanket their steep slopes in springtime. In summer, though, they can feel a bit barren and hot, and nowhere more so than at **Rockhound State Park** (9880 Stirrup Rd. SE, 575/546-6182, www.nmparks.com, $5/car). Its setting in the foothills is picturesque, especially around sunset, but a day poking around with a pickax (you're allowed to carry out 15 pounds of finds) is rewarding only for the truly geologically minded. Everyone else will probably be satisfied with the exhibits of geodes and other mineral miracles in the visitors center.

For more scenic hiking and good bird-watching, head to **Spring Canyon Recreational Area** (8am-4pm Wed.-Sun.), immediately adjacent to Rockhound. While you're out, you have a slim chance of spotting an ibex, a variety of goat with large curving horns. The Department of Game and Fish imported them from Iran and released them here in 1970, as part of a now-discontinued program to create an exotic game-hunting industry; about 400 of the animals live in the mountains now.

## Accommodations

Travelers seldom plan to spend the night in Deming, but if you're deciding between here and Lordsburg for the night, Deming is the better bet, with a larger selection both at the lower end and in more upmarket chain options. Ordinarily, you should have no trouble rolling into town without a reservation, but book ahead when the duck races are on at the end of August.

Of the independent hotels, **Western Motel** (1207 W. Pine St., 575/544-8811, $45 d) is older but quite clean, and kept with more care than most motels in this category. Rooms have a microwave, coffee maker, and fridge. The place is brightened up with flowers planted outside the rooms. On the east side of town, **Grand Motor Inn** (1721 E. Pine St., 575/546-2632, www.grandmotorinndeming.com, $52 d) delivers excellent value for money—though, oddly, it charges $1 for toiletries. You get a nice big room, with a mini-fridge, and even a swimming pool.

## Food

Deming doesn't look like a promising gourmet stop, but it is a good place to sample some Mexican (as opposed to *New* Mexican) food. **Tacos Mirasol** (309 E. Pine St., 575/544-0646, 9am-9pm daily, $5) is a tiny but sparkling-clean roadside hut that does tacos, of course, but also Mexican-style sandwiches *(tortas)*, which consist of a choice of meat on a soft fluffy roll, usually slathered with avocado, mayonnaise, and a thin layer of refried beans. Both come with a tangy-hot tomatillo salsa; cut the heat with a banana milkshake or fresh limeade.

For a heartier meal, head for ◖ **Las Cazuelas** (108 N. Platinum St., 575/544-8432, 11am-7pm Tues.-Sat., 7am-4pm Sun., $8), a cheery Mexican restaurant hidden in the back of a meat market. Of course you can get a big *churrasco* platter of grilled meats, but you can go smaller, with a burger or a spicy soup, as well as burritos and other goodies. Everything's fresh and homemade-tasting.

For New Mexican, the time-warp **Si Señor** (200 E. Pine St., 575/546-3938, 9:30am-8pm Mon.-Sat., 10am-3pm Sun., $7) shouldn't be discounted for its walls tiled like a 1970s bathroom. On the plus side: low prices, huge portions, and an ingenious platter of chicken-fried steak slathered with green chile and cheese (the "milanesa"). Regulars also recommend the carne adovada-stuffed sopaipilla.

In a side alley by the Wells Fargo parking lot, cozy **Elisa's House of Pies & Restaurant** (208 S. Silver Ave., 575/494-4639, 10am-6pm Mon.-Fri., 10:30am-7pm Sat., 11am-4pm Sun., $7) is not kidding about the pies: pecan, lemon meringue, millionaire (cream pie with pecans and pineapple), and more. Elisa and her husband also dish out a full soul-food menu that includes barbecue ribs, collard greens, and red

© ZORA O'NEILL

City of Rocks State Park

beans and rice. The sides are good for vegetarians—a nice break from cheese enchiladas. In summer, the place is open until 7pm Monday through Friday (Sunday hours are the same).

Finally, if you've got a car full of kids (and/or you just can't face another enchilada), **Forghedaboudit Pizza** (2020 Hwy. 26, 919/780-1334, 11:30am-9pm Mon.-Thurs., 11:30am-10pm Fri.-Sat., $10) is worth a detour. Solo diners can ask for a 12-inch pizza (not on the menu), and the homemade meatballs and tomato sauce are good. There are also hot sandwiches and salads.

### Information

Make your first stop in town the **Deming-Luna County Chamber of Commerce** (800 E. Pine St., 575/546-2674, www.demingchamber.com, 9am-5pm Mon.-Fri., 9am-11am Sat.), where you'll find a chatty staff, free coffee and Wi-Fi, and answers to all your area questions.

### Getting There

By car, Deming is 60 miles (one hour) west of Las Cruces via I-10; it's another 60 miles west to Lordsburg. Silver City is 53 miles (one hour) north via U.S. 180. The **Greyhound bus** (800/231-2222, www.greyhound.com) comes in twice a day from Las Cruces and drops you at the Shell station (420 E. Cedar St., 7am-10pm daily).

## CITY OF ROCKS STATE PARK

Bristling out of the flat basin north of Deming, **City of Rocks State Park** (327 Hwy. 61, 575/536-2800, www.nmparks.com, $5/car) does indeed resemble a metropolis. Hardened lava, eroded over 35 million years, forms towering pinnacles and bulbous growths, creating a skyline straight out of Dr. Seuss. With expansive views across the flatlands and all sorts of birds and other wildlife to check out up close, City of Rocks makes a great spot for a picnic and short hike, or an overnight in one of the 52 campsites (10 have water and electrical hookups). The visitors center is well equipped, with showers for overnighters. The park is 24 miles from Deming

© ZORA O'NEILL

Faywood Hot Springs

(28 miles from Silver City) on U.S. 180, then 4 miles northeast on Highway 61.

### Faywood Hot Springs

On the road to City of Rocks is **Faywood Hot Springs** (Hwy. 61, 575/536-9663, www.faywood.com); the springs are a bit less wild-feeling than those in the Gila, but they are also much easier to reach, as the route here from surrounding towns is a straight highway. Long ago, the springs were harnessed for a posh resort, but that building was razed—now the pools are perched around a small rise, shaded with small trees. Public pools (10am-10pm daily, $12.50/day) are split between clothing-optional and swimsuits-required; private pools ($25/hour) are also available. There are very nice **campsites** ($18.75 pp) and **cabins** ($99) with access to the pools included. Bring your own water, snacks, and towels; a visitors center was under construction at research time, but progress looked slow.

## COLUMBUS

Devastated in a raid by Pancho Villa in 1916, the border town of Columbus is still not exactly jumping. It's centered on a park and a WPA-built town hall, with most of its commerce and community linked with Mexico in some way. As you drive south from Deming on Highway 11, the terrain grows sandier, more dotted with cactus and yucca, and generally more like what people imagine Mexico to look like. You may see a giant white blimp in the sky—it's an aerostat, a balloon-borne radar system used by the U.S. Border Patrol.

### Pancho Villa State Park

The southeast corner of the main crossroads (Highways 9 and 11) in Columbus, formerly a U.S. Army encampment, has been transformed into small **Pancho Villa State Park** (Hwy. 9, 575/531-2711, www.nmparks.com, $5/car). It includes an excellent **museum** (8am-5pm daily) dedicated to Villa's 1916 attack, in which 90 of Columbus's 400 residents were killed. The subsequent manhunt for the Mexican rebel leader, led by General John J. Pershing, involved some 2,000 troops traveling by car and airplane—the first mechanized military campaign in history. The museum does a great job of portraying both the personal tragedy felt in Columbus and the impressive scale of Pershing's military operation, which was a crucial training ground for World War I. South of the museum and a large cactus garden are 79 **campsites** ($8 car, $14 RV) with good facilities but in somewhat spartan surroundings.

## Columbus Historical Society Museum

Round out your cultural experience with a quick visit to the **Columbus Historical Society Museum** (575/531-2620, 10am-4pm daily Sept.-Apr., 10am-1pm daily May-Aug., donation), across the intersection from the state park. Housed in the old train depot, it has nifty train paraphernalia, as well as some morbidly interesting items, such as a replica death mask of Pancho Villa and a diorama showing the wreckage of the town in 1916.

## PALOMAS

The town of Palomas, Mexico, is not particularly remarkable, but it's somewhat illuminating to see just how different it is from its sister American town. Immediately past the customs gates and the dead-straight border fence is a five-block strip of dentist offices, pharmacies, fruit-pop vendors, and taco shops. One mega-mart, the impossible-to-miss **Pink Store** (575/531-7243, 9am-6pm daily), sells crafts from all over Mexico, plus the obligatory margaritas at the in-house restaurant. Crossing the border is usually as easy as being waved through; coming back to American soil, however, you'll need to show your passport, and your car may be subject to X-ray. It's a lot easier to walk over (technically, you need a passport, but no one checks pedestrians). Free parking is available just before the border, and the Pink Store can arrange a golf-cart escort if you buy too much to carry yourself.

## Accommodations and Food

In this relative middle of nowhere, there are two good places to sleep. Homey **Martha's Place** (204 Lima Rd., 575/531-2467, www.marthasplacebedandbreakfastcolumbusnewmexico.com, $60 d) is a great surprise—in fact, you might want to make the detour from Deming if you prefer B&Bs. Each of the five sunny rooms has a balcony. Across Highway 11, another Martha runs **Hacienda de Villa** (220 S. Hwy. 11, 575/531-1000, $55 d), a nicely kept, if somewhat standard, little motel that's a real bargain. The main building used to house the town's museum.

For meals, you can eat breakfast at **Martha's Place** ($9, or $4.50 for all-you-can-eat pancakes), or at the **Patio Café** (211 Broadway, 575/531-2495, 9pm-3pm Mon.-Sat., $7). The namesake outdoor area is shady and filled with flowers, a respite from the desert outside. Half-pound burgers are the centerpiece of the menu, but green-chile stew and any breakfast dish are generally winners as well.

For dinner, it's practical—and preferable—

Hacienda de Villa

© ZORA O'NEILL

just to walk to Mexico, and have great *barbacoa* and more at the various street carts and restaurants.

## LORDSBURG

Aesthetically, Lordsburg is lacking—a quick cruise around town suggests this is where the chain-link-fence salesman made his first million. It's also a bit tragic economically, as the freight train industry that drove the place has all but died, leaving a desolate strip of 1st Street (now Motel Drive) running parallel to the tracks. Why stop? Well....

### Sights

The **Lordsburg-Hidalgo County Museum** (710 E. 2nd St., 575/542-9086, 1pm-5pm Mon.-Fri., free) has a fascinating exhibit on the history of POW camps in New Mexico during World War II. One was located near Lordsburg, and German and Italian prisoners were put to work farming. The rest of the museum is a bit of a jumble, though there are some relics from local mines (another defunct Lordsburg industry).

Two and a half miles south of Lordsburg on Highway 494, the ghost town of **Shakespeare** (575/542-9034, www.shakespeareghosttown. com, $4) is in perhaps the ideal state of repair—just enough to spark the imagination, but not so polished as to seem museum-like. What's even more interesting is how the typical Old West buildings such as the saloon, the assay office, and the blacksmith's shop are overlaid with the history of the family that has owned and maintained the place since 1935. There's also a dance studio, where a generation of Lordsburg girls took classes, and a shack that the family matriarch squatted in to protest the expansion of I-10. The result is a more poignant monument to the fading American West than you find in most ghost towns. The place is open only one or two weekends a month—check the schedule online. If you go on a reenactment day ($5, four weekends a year), you'll also get to see shootouts and maybe a mock hanging.

### Accommodations and Food

Thanks to the U.S. Border Patrol setting up

Special tours at the ghost town of Shakespeare end with shootouts.

headquarters here, Lordsburg's accommodation options are better than they were five years ago. **Best Western Western Skies Inn** (1303 S. Main St., 575/542-8807, www.bestwestern.com, $70 d) and **Comfort Inn & Suites** (400 Wabash St., 575/542-3355, www.comfortinnlordsburg.com, $90 d) are both in good shape; both have pools.

For New Mexican food, head into town to ( **Ramona's** (904 E. Motel Dr., 575/542-3030, 8am-8pm Tues.-Fri., 8am-2pm Sun., $7), a tiny café with pretty curtains in the windows. On Sundays, they serve a fantastic menudo. Another great option is **Triple J Café** (228 E. Motel Dr., 575/542-3073, 11am-9pm daily), where you can watch the trains rumble right through downtown while you eat. Peppery green-chile stew is a treat, and à la carte burritos are a good choice for lighter eaters.

## RODEO

The gateway town, such as it is, to New Mexico's "bootheel" is a string of barely a dozen buildings along Highway 80, fronting now-vanished railroad tracks and the Arizona state line. Rodeo sits in a dramatic bowl between small but spiking mountain ranges; coming over the small pass into the valley affords one of the more awe-inspiring views in southern New Mexico, especially in late afternoon when the sun glints off the crags. This flat terrain, which develops temporary shallow lakes (called playas) in the wet season, is hospitable to a huge range of birds. Nine miles away is Portal, Arizona, world-famous as a birding destination.

### Sights

Two miles north of Rodeo proper, the **Chiricahua Desert Museum** (4 Rattlesnake Canyon Rd., 575/557-5757, 9am-5pm daily, $5) is a herper's dream—dedicated to all things reptilian. The entry fee allows access to two rooms full of live, rare rattlesnakes and lizards, as well as a profusion of herpetology tchotchkes—from Steve Irwin memorabilia to vintage snake-bite kits. Also on display are beautifully detailed paintings and prints of snakes by noted wildlife illustrator Tell Hicks.

© ZORA O'NEILL

You can't miss the Chiricahua Desert Museum, home to the world's largest rattlesnake (tail).

For those who get nervous just reading about snakes, there's a large gift shop to browse (plenty of local guides and more) and a garden with rare cacti (free).

Ten miles over the border in Arizona, alongside Highway 80, the **Geronimo Surrender Memorial** is the final chapter to the Apache leader's story, lived so vividly around New Mexico. For nearly 30 years, Geronimo fought against the incursions into Apache lands after Mexicans killed his family; he finally submitted to American terms in 1886, effectively ending the Indian Wars. After his surrender, he was taken prisoner and toured as an exotic attraction, including at the 1904 World's Fair in St. Louis. Just as Geronimo's birth monument is not at the "headwaters of the Gila," but in an accessible parking lot, the stone memorial pillar is placed for convenience by the highway. The actual surrender site is in **Skeleton Canyon,** in the Peloncillo Mountains, accessible by dirt road and a short hike. Look for

Skeleton Canyon Road, a mile south of the memorial.

## Sports and Recreation

The wilderness areas around here are almost completely devoid of trails; if you fancy adventure (and carrying plenty of water), the **Big Hatchet** and **Animas** ranges to the south await.

If you prefer a bit more structure, make the short drive past Portal and on to **Cave Creek Canyon** in the Coronado National Forest, strikingly lush, teeming with birds, and lined on either side with sheer cliffs pocked with caves. To get there, take Highway 533 (Portal Rd.) west from Highway 80, directly across from the Chiricahua Desert Museum.

Stop first at the **visitor information center** (Forest Rd. 42, 8am-4pm Fri.-Sun.) for maps and a bird checklist. (Note that Arizona does not observe daylight saving time; in summer, the closing time is really 5pm New Mexico time.)

Up the road a couple of miles is the turn for **South Fork Trail** (no. 243), a birding pilgrimage site because the rare elegant trogon is often in residence along the creek here. Even if you're not interested in our feathered friends, it's hard not to love the elegant trogon, which lives up to its name with its scarlet breast with a long chestnut-brown tail. The area is also lovely in the fall, when the maple leaves turn. The full trail length is nearly seven miles, with an elevation gain of 2,500 feet, but the first mile or so is level.

For more local information and books, stop off at the **Southwestern Research Station,** an ecologists' camp maintained by the American Museum of Natural History. Its **Chiricahua Nature Shop** (520/558-2396, 8:30-noon and 1pm-4:30pm Wed.-Sat.) is a good place to find out what interesting critters have been spotted here. Farther up the road from here is another good walk, **Herb Martyr Trail** (no. 247); at 2.8 miles it's much shorter than the South Fork route, but more strenuous.

## Accommodations and Food

Reason alone to drive all this way, the lovely **Casa Adobe** (Hwy. 80, 575/557-7777, www.casaadobe.net, $150 d) fulfills every get-away-from-it-all fantasy. Rodeo has no cell phone coverage, and there's no Internet in this beautiful casita, leaving you free to sit and admire the dramatic mountains on either side. The whole house is yours, impeccably decorated with rustic furniture and stocked with goodies like eggs from the hosts' chickens. Similar digs on better-trod paths in the state would cost at least twice as much. The rate is for two nights minimum.

For meals and a bit of social contact, head to the **Rodeo Grocery & Café** (Hwy. 80, 575/557-2295, 7:30am-5pm Mon.-Sat., $7), which posts its food specials for the month—school-cafeteria-style, but so much tastier. For dinner, the **Rodeo Tavern** (Hwy. 80, 575/557-2229, 4pm-10pm Wed.-Sat., $12) makes excellent fried chicken, and also has a pool table and a varied crew of regulars.

With 24 hours' notice, you can also eat at the cafeteria at the **Southwestern Research Station.**

# Silver City

Called just "Silver" by the locals, this casual mountain burg ranks high on quality-of-life lists. It has lured a portion of its 11,000 population from out of state with a near-utopian combination of outdoor activities, an educated populace (Western New Mexico University is here), and beautiful housing stock that dates from the city's boom in the late 19th and early 20th centuries. Unlike more slapdash towns, Silver was built to last, and its stone and cast-iron structures have helped the town maintain its grandeur. Over the decades, it has been home to Billy the Kid, who came here in 1873 at about age 13 and got into trouble from the

THE SOUTHWEST

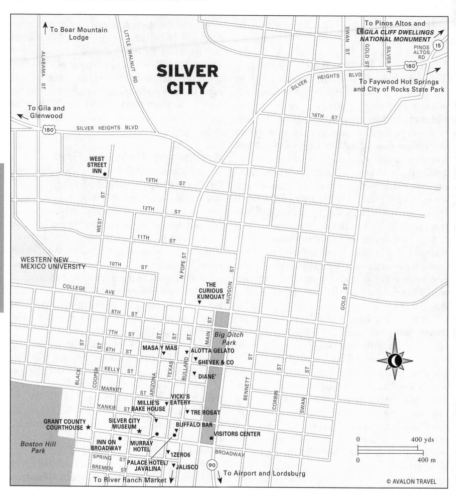

start, then many wealthy tuberculosis patients in the 1890s.

Contemporary hippies have set the mellow pace downtown and drive the local food co-op and other local institutions, while rat-race dropouts, young artists, and a small gay and lesbian community have bought up the territorial-style bungalows and downtown storefronts, repainted them in candy colors, and created a distinctive, unpretentious cultural scene. It also happens to encourage culinary creativity as well—there are more exceptional restaurants here than you'd expect in a town this size.

Navigating Silver is not immediately intuitive because the main downtown drag is Bullard Street, though Hudson Street, a couple of blocks east, is larger and runs directly south from U.S. 180. The original Main Street, which ran parallel to and between Bullard and Hudson, was washed away in a series of floods between 1895 and 1903, leaving what's evocatively called the Big Ditch. A greenery-filled chasm some 50 feet below the street level, it's

creatively painted shopfronts in Silver City

an unorthodox park for an unorthodox populace. Most of the rest of Silver's attractions are on the west side of it.

## SIGHTS

The first stop in learning about the town, the **Silver City Museum** (312 W. Broadway, 575/538-5921, 9am-4:30pm Tues.-Fri., 10am-4pm Sat.-Sun., $3 donation) is an intriguing, polished collection in an old Victorian home. You'll see photos of Main Street before and after it became the Big Ditch, a fascinating exhibit on the culture and economy of tuberculosis treatment in New Mexico, and more than you thought you wanted to know about mining history and science. Be sure to climb up to the cupola to take in the view of the whole town.

Just up the hill at the end of Broadway, the **Grant County Courthouse** is a small but elegant building. The highlight is 1934 murals depicting the local ranching and mining industries.

Farther afield, the **WNMU Museum** (1000 W. College Ave., 575/538-6386, 9am-4:30pm Mon.-Fri., 10am-4pm Sat.-Sun., free) has an excellent collection of Mimbres pottery, on which critters like coatis, turkeys, and pronghorns dance. Not to mention a grand antique urinal in the basement men's room. The museum is in Fleming Hall. Head west on 10th Street; on campus, look for the building near the top of the hill on the right.

## ENTERTAINMENT AND EVENTS

Although it's a college town, Silver City isn't too rowdy at night. A few bars strung out along Bullard give a good mix of evening options within a few blocks. And many people make the drive to Pinos Altos for music at the saloon there.

For a late-night drink, the bare-bones **Buffalo Bar** (211 N. Bullard St., 575/538-3201, 10am-2am Mon.-Sat., 10am-midnight Sun.), better known as "The Buff," has pool tables and a long bar propped up by regulars.

As for events, Silver is internationally known for the **Tour de Gila** (www.tourofthegila.

com), a race that, thanks to its winding routes through the surrounding mountains, is known as a warm-up for the Tour de France. If you're a cycling fan, this is a great time to see teams sweat up close. Plan well ahead around this time: All hotels are packed for the event, and surrounding highways are restricted on certain days.

Later in May, Silver's biggest cultural event is the **Silver City Blues Festival** (www.mimbres-arts.org), over Memorial Day weekend. Since 1995, it has gained a strong reputation, and the likes of Odetta and the Holmes Brothers have graced the stage at Gough Park, the Buffalo Bar, and the Buckhorn Saloon in Pinos Altos.

In mid-September, the **Gila River Festival** (575/538-8078, www.gilaconservation.org) rallies an excellent roster of musicians and artists for an environment-friendly party in mid-September. While the center of the action is Silver City, activities such as guided hikes, bird-watching, and archaeological tours take place in the forest to the north. It's a great opportunity to explore less-visited spots in the company of experts.

## SPORTS AND RECREATION

Surrounded on almost every side by the Gila National Forest, Silver is an outdoorsy town. The **Silver City Ranger District office** (3005 Camino del Bosque, 575/388-8201, 8am-4:30pm Mon.-Fri.) is just north of U.S. 180 off the 32nd Street Bypass on the east side of town.

### Biking

The staff at **Gila Hike & Bike** (103 E. College Ave., 575/388-3222, 9am-5:30pm Mon.-Fri., 9am-5pm Sat., 10am-4pm Sun.) are veterans, with lots of tips on where to ride in the area. Ambitious road cyclists can trace some of the routes of the Tour de Gila, while mountain bikers can head to **Little Walnut Picnic Area,** north of town via Little Walnut Road from near the intersection of U.S. 180 and Highway 90. This is the starting point for a couple of short, relatively easy outings, as well as one seven-mile loop that's more challenging. You can get detailed trail guides from Gila Hike &

Bike or at www.silvercity.org (select Activities, then Cycling).

### Hiking and Horseback Riding

In town, you can stroll up **Boston Hill,** a network of trails around the abandoned mines that started Silver. The view from the top of the hill is fine. The trailhead nearest to downtown is at the end of Spring Street, just off Cooper Street.

For more in-depth or complex excursions, Chiricahua Apache guide Joe Saenz runs **Wolf Horse Outfitters** (Arenas Valley Rd., 575/534-1379, www.wolfhorseoutfitters.com) specializing in low-impact, educational trips into the wilderness. His excellent services range from a half-day hike ($95) to custom pack-horse adventures (from $210/day).

## ACCOMMODATIONS

Downtown Silver has a couple of excellent lodging options. Most chain hotels and motels are on U.S. 180 on the east side of town (also called Silver Heights Boulevard), which is not walkable to downtown.

### Under $100

The **Palace Hotel** (106 W. Broadway, 575/388-1811, www.silvercitypalacehotel.com, $51 s, $68 d) embodies the phrase "faded charm," but it is moderately priced and full of historic ambience—even if the beds can be a bit saggy. Noise from Bullard Street and Broadway can be a problem; the quietest of the 22 rooms are no. 61 ($51), a cozy hideaway with one double bed in the back of the building, and no. 59 ($82), a two-room suite. A basic continental breakfast is included in the rate.

### $100-150

Silver's "newer" historic hotel is the ◖**Murray Hotel** (200 W. Broadway, 575/956-9400, www.murray-hotel.com, $109 s, $149 d), a glamorous slab of a building erected in the late 1930s. It reopened in 2012, after major renovation, and its rooms are both comfortable and fabulously located. Room 426 has beautiful glass bricks in the bathroom.

As for B&Bs, the 1883 **Inn on Broadway**

(411 W. Broadway, 575/388-5485, www.innonbroadwayweb.com) is in a fine location, across from the Silver City Museum. Three sunny rooms upstairs ($120-150) are spacious, with especially nice bathrooms (although some might find the old-fashioned hand shower in the Hummingbird Room a bit of a nuisance). The cozier downstairs room ($130) has a marble fireplace. Decorating styles range from subdued Victorian to subdued Western.

If you'll be in town for a few nights, or just want the full comforts of home, consider **West Street Inn** (1303 West St., 575/534-2302, www.weststreetinn-nm.com), which contains three well-kept apartments with full kitchens. Casa Bonita ($125) is good for groups or families, with two bedrooms and a yard; the other two apartments ($105) are one-bedrooms with king beds.

## Over $150

Set on 178 acres up against the national forest, **Bear Mountain Lodge** (60 Bear Mountain Ranch Rd., 575/538-2538, www.bearmountainlodge.com, $160 d) is a homey retreat where you can get a taste of the Gila in comfort—trails crisscross the land, or you can just enjoy the room from your balcony. The beautiful adobe main building was built in the mid-1920s. The creative, unpretentious café here is open to non-guests with prior reservations.

## FOOD

Silver has a large number of amazing places to eat, all in the downtown area—so many, it's hard to designate just one as a top pick. Note that most restaurants close early, and some of the best are open only a few days a week.

### Cafés

Get your java at **Javalina** (201 N. Bullard St., 575/388-1350, 6am-6pm Sun.-Thurs. 6am-9pm Fri.-Sat., $3), a rambling, old-style coffeehouse with wood floors, lots of couches, and people sitting for hours over a game of chess or the daily paper. In the evenings, you might catch a bluegrass group or other performer here.

Set in the former Elks Lodge, **Vicki's Eatery** (315 N. Texas St., 575/388-5430, 7am-3pm Mon.-Sat., 8am-2pm Sun., $9) is a prime spot for lunch, with big sandwiches that range from familiar and hearty (green-chile turkey melt) to the more exotic (chutney and turkey). It's also one of the few places open for breakfast on Sunday.

Head a bit off the main drag for the icebox pie of your dreams: **Millie's Bake House** (215 W. Yankie St., 575/597-2253, 10am-5pm Tues.-Sat., $4) is a fantastically home-style operation, with nice sandwiches and salads to balance out the myriad sugar-fix options.

At the south end of Bullard, **River Ranch Market** (300 S. Bullard St., 575/597-6328, 10am-6pm Wed.-Sat., $12) is more of a store for locally produced meat and nuts, but it shows off its grass-fed beef in a hearty, spicy bowl of chili, and a few other treats. Take food to go, or eat in the little back garden.

### Fresh and Local

Silver residents love long-established **Ⅽ Diane's** (510 N. Bullard St., 575/538-8722, 11am-2pm and 5:30pm-9pm Tues.-Sat., 11am-4pm and 5:30pm-9pm Sun., $17). It's the go-to spot for familiar flavors like meatloaf and lasagna, in a pleasant atmosphere. The adjacent "parlor" hosts live music some evenings.

Newer to the scene but nearly as popular, **Tre Rosat** (304 N. Bullard St., 575/654-4919, 11am-9pm Mon.-Fri., 9am-9pm Sat., $10) serves upscale bar food, such a green-chile poppers, big burgers, and a "bulgogi hoagie"; gluten-free bread is an option.

### International

These three restaurants are Silver's most eclectic, and are worth planning a trip around. Decked out with Bollywood art and Mexican crafts, **Ⅽ 1zero6** (106 N. Texas St., 575/313-4418, www.1zero6.com, 5pm-8:30pm Fri.-Sun., $17) is small and thoroughly personal. Each night's menu has just a few options, but they could be anything from tortellini Bolognese to Indonesian chicken in a banana leaf, all cooked from scratch, and with such a reverence for flavor you'd think there's a grandmother in the kitchen. Check the menu on the website on Wednesday, and call to put dibs on the dishes you want.

Equally globe-trotting, ◖ **The Curious Kumquat** (111 E. College Ave., 575/534-0337, 11am-4:30pm and 5:30pm-8:30pm Tues.-Sat., $17) is the domain of Chef Rob Connoley, who forages locally and buys meat from the 4-H. But dishes may have Indian, Filipino, or Korean flavors. Once a month, he pulls out the stops for a ten-course hypermodern menu. Lunch is more familiar (green-chile corn chowder), but just as delicious. And no matter what, get some sweet treat—this is the chef's not-so-secret passion.

Long-established ◖ **Shevek & Co.** (602 N. Bullard St., 575/534-9168, 5pm-8:30pm Sun.-Tues., 5pm-9pm Fri.-Sat., $18) has a refined, personal menu that goes all around the Mediterranean for inspiration, mixing in lots of saffron and garlic. Soups are especially good. Vegetarians will find plenty to like, and every dish can be had in a range of sizes (three "tapa" portions make a good meal). The wine list is carefully selected to match the food. The elegance of the food isn't always matched by the decor, which can run to standard plastic furniture on the back patio. But don't be deterred—Shevek knows his stuff.

### New Mexican and Mexican

**Masa y Mas** (601 N. Bullard St., 575/538-5555, 8am-5pm Mon.-Sat., 8am-1:30pm Sun., $8) cranks out fresh tortillas daily, and it serves Mexican (not *New* Mexican) plates, such as barbacoa tacos, at a few plastic-covered tables. It's super casual, but packed with flavor.

Occupying a string of old storefronts on the south end of downtown, ◖ **Jalisco Café** (103 S. Bullard St., 575/388-2060, 11am-8:30pm, $12) is the most popular New Mexican joint in town. Along with a small selection of seafood dishes, you'll get all the green- and red-chile-smothered classics, though they're not nearly

as hot as the menu warns, and the green chile is typical of southern New Mexico, all mellow and creamy—a relief for some diners, a travesty for others. Everyone can agree on the sopaipillas, which are huge and perfectly pillowy.

### Dessert

No meal is complete without a scoop or two from **Alotta Gelato** (619 N. Bullard St., 575/534-4995, noon-9pm Sun.-Thurs., noon-10pm Fri.-Sat., $3), where the devoted owners craft the richest flavors possible and preside over a sugar-buzzed clientele of addicted locals. The pistachio comes with an elaborate warning—you may never have tasted something so intensely nutty. Thoughtfully, there's a perfectly reasonable child-size scoop for those who may have previously gorged themselves at Silver's other excellent dining options.

## INFORMATION

The **Silver City Visitors Center** (201 N. Hudson St., 575/538-5555, www.silvercitytourism.org, 9am-5pm Mon.-Fri., 10am-4pm Sat.-Sun.) is just east of Big Ditch Park at Broadway. It's open on weekends only if there's a special event on, but there's info available out front all the time, and its website is very thorough.

## GETTING THERE

By car, Silver City is closest to Deming, about 60 miles (1 hour) south via U.S. 180. From Truth or Consequences, the closest town on I-25, it's 88 miles west, but the drive takes more than 2 hours on the winding road over Emory Pass; count on 4.5 hours from Albuquerque via I-25. Tucson, Arizona, is 200 miles (3 hours) west, and El Paso is 2.5 hours east.

**Grant County Airport** (SVC), about 10 miles southeast of Silver City, receives flights once or twice daily from Phoenix on Great Lakes Airlines (800/554-5111, www.greatlakesav.com).

# Trail of the Mountain Spirits

A romantic name for the usual driving circuit out of Silver City, the **Trail of the Mountain Spirits** (www.tmsbyway.com) runs north on Highway 15 through the little town of Pinos Altos, then up to Gila Cliff Dwellings National Monument and many hiking trails into the wilderness. After backtracking from the cliff dwellings, the route continues through the pine forest east on Highway 35, past Lake Roberts, over the Continental Divide to Bear Canyon Lake, and through the village of Mimbres. Highway 152 then leads back west to Silver City via the region's modern mining center around Bayard.

## PINOS ALTOS

About seven miles north on Highway 15, a sign points to the optimistically named Pinos Altos Business Loop. In fact, this tiny community offers just a couple of commercial attractions, and

Hearst Church in Pinos Altos

© ZORA O'NEILL

that's the way folks like it. "P.A.," as the town is known, is the retreat for those who think Silver is too big and busy.

In terms of sights, you can stop in at the obligatory **Pinos Altos Museum & Curio Shop** (33 Main St., 575/388-1882, 11am-5pm daily, $2), an 1860s log cabin packed with cast-iron gewgaws; it sets the tone for the rest of the buildings in the area, which are functional if not always accurate replicas of what used to stand here in the 19th century.

Across the street, the **Buckhorn Saloon** (32 Main St., 575/538-9911, www.buckhornsaloonandoperahouse.com, 5pm-10pm Mon.-Sat.) serves burgers ($11) and steaks ($28) in a wood-paneled, Wild West setting; it's open for drinks starting at 3pm and continuing past the dinner hour, with very well attended live music starting around 7pm in the adjacent **Pinos Altos Opera House.**

Also look for **Hearst Church** (Golden Ave., 10am-5pm Fri.-Sun. May-Oct.), an odd pitched-roof adobe structure built in 1898 by William Randolph Hearst's mother, Phoebe, who had gained her family fortune from a gold mine in the area. It's now home to the **Grant County Art Guild** (575/538-8216, www.gcag.org). It's west of the main street—follow Historic Route signs as you come into town.

## GILA HOT SPRINGS

A small collection of services for wilderness visitors, the village of Gila Hot Springs is the last chance to stock up before heading farther north. **Doc Campbell's Post** (575/536-9551, 10am-4pm daily) sells basic provisions, books, fishing and hunting licenses, and homemade ice cream.

Just south of here are two semi-developed hot springs—but they flooded in 2013, so check on their status before making a special trip. Just south of mile marker 39, look for a turn labeled "Access Road" and signs to **Gila Hot Springs Campground** (575/536-9551, www.

THE SOUTHWEST

inside the Gila Cliff Dwellings

gilahotspringsranch.com). The three riverside pools ($4 pp), kept at different temperatures, are barely developed—so didn't lose much in the floods. There are a few tent campsites here ($5 pp), which should be reserved ahead; the same owners run Doc Campbell's Post, and an RV campground and rental apartments there, away from the river, as well as a horseback-riding operation ($40/half day). The tranquility of the springs can sometimes be disrupted by groups of riders setting off from here.

An earlier right turn, at the four-way intersection down the hill from Highway 15, leads to **Wildwood Retreat & Hot Springs** (575/536-3600, www.wildwoodhotspringsretreat.com), which was more developed and so will need a bit more refurbishing post-flood. The springs are channeled into paved pools ($7/day). You can camp here ($12 pp), or rent a rustic cabin (from $40 s) or a more developed hogan or house (from $60). There's also a nice shared kitchen area. But note that the whole place is closed during the winter months.

One safety note: The hot springs water harbors a rather nasty amoeba that can cause a fatal brain infection—but don't panic! The amoeba can only enter your system through your nose—so as long as you keep your head above water, you'll be fine.

## GILA CLIFF DWELLINGS NATIONAL MONUMENT

The big destination on the byway is the **Gila Cliff Dwellings National Monument** (8:30am-5pm daily June-Aug., 9am-4pm daily Sept.-May, $3), just past Gila Hot Springs and 44 miles north of Silver City. Compared with the ruins at Bandelier National Monument or Chaco Canyon, these are relatively small and in a less spectacular setting, but if these are the only cliff settlements you'll be near on your trip, don't miss them. The drive up from Silver, along a narrow road often with no center stripe, takes up to three hours.

Stop in first at the **visitors center** (575/536-9461, www.nps.gov/gicl, 8am-4:30pm daily), which gives a basic overview of the environment as well as the Mogollon culture that inhabited the cliff dwellings for only a generation near the end of the 13th century, through excavated relics of daily life such as reed mats and mosaic work. The rock cairn in the parking lot is a discreet monument to the Apache chief Geronimo, born far up the canyon ("at the headwaters of the Gila," as he said) in 1829.

A two-mile drive gets you to the pay station ($3 pp or $10/family) at the **trailhead** and a basic nature center, where enthusiastic rangers will let you know what kind of animals are out and about. You reach the **caves** via a mile-long loop trail that takes about an hour to walk. The route is level for the first half, then increasingly steep as it winds up and through the dwellings. The trail passes three of the five caves, which once housed up to 60 people in about 40 rooms; the central one is a large, bilevel arrangement that included the central ceremonial chambers. Much of the wood you see in the rooms is original, preserved perfectly in the dry air; the Mogollon, who did not have steel, shaped it by burning it and hacking it with stone tools.

## Recreation

This is the most easily accessible part of the Gila Wilderness, with some very scenic hiking along canyon bottoms. Check the status of trails and hot springs at the visitors center—as of fall 2013, fire and flooding had done yet-to-be-determined damage to some routes.

### HIKING

The three forks of the Gila River converge near the cliff dwellings, and the canyons formed by the water are usually a nice place to walk, though there was massive flooding in 2013, which may have shifted routes and changed scenery. In any case, be prepared for wet and muddy stream crossings and in summer, plan to hike in the morning, so you're not caught in canyons during afternoon rainstorms.

At 34 miles, the **West Fork Trail** (no. 151) is the longest in the Gila wilderness. The first three miles provide a pleasantly varied, fairly easy day hike. The trail begins at Scorpion Campground, across from the Gila Cliff Dwellings. Just off the trail to the south after the first river crossing, a small ruined cabin sits next to the grave of one William Grudging, murdered in 1893—eerie evidence of the violent past of this otherwise peaceful setting. Further traces of past inhabitants can be seen at a small cliff dwelling on the west side, which marks the turnaround point for most day hikers. Others do the full length as a multiday backpacking trek.

Given the complex network of trails in this area, it's easy to make a number of loop hikes through varied terrain. Ask for suggestions in the visitors center, where you can also pick up a topographical map and check which areas might still show flood damage.

### HOT SPRINGS

A refreshing warm bath in the great outdoors is a fine motivator for a hike, and there are several natural springs in the vicinity of the cliff dwellings' visitors center—although they too were washed out in the 2013 floods, and may or may not be accessible. The closest ones to the visitors center are **Lightfeather Hot Spring,**

just half a mile up the Middle Fork Trail; however, the water here is scalding hot, and you may have to reroute the river water to dilute it to a usable temperature. The deep pools of **Jordan Hot Springs** are worth the longer hike (about eight miles) up the same trail; you can shorten the trip by starting at the trail behind TJ Corral, farther up the road to the cliff dwellings, but get precise directions from the visitors center.

## LAKE ROBERTS

Heading east from the intersection with Highway 35, you reach **Lake Roberts**, a pristine 69 acres stocked with trout. Shaded heavily by tall pine trees, it's a popular getaway during the summer months; you can **camp** at the lake, in developed sites ($7) or undeveloped ones (free), which have no water. There are also several lodges in the area. The first you reach, at the intersection with Highway 15, is ⓒ**Little Toad Creek Inn & Tavern** (1122 Hwy. 35, 575/536-9649, www.littletoadcreek.com). The restaurant here is a great place to stop for a meal on weekends, when breakfast has items like house-smoked salmon; downstairs, the tavern (noon-8pm Wed.-Mon.) serves its house-distilled vodka and rum. Hours scale back in fall and spring—call ahead. The inn's rooms ($50 d) are as nice as can be, considering most are in mobile homes; the more solid-feeling ones ($80 d) are attached to the lodge. All are functional, clean, and well priced. Plus, there's no better place to wake up if you love birds, as the main lodge building is surrounded by feeders and draws just about every species in the Gila to the floor-to-ceiling windows. During the **Hummingbird Festival** in mid-July, the lodge is packed; call for exact dates and be sure to book ahead.

## MIMBRES VALLEY

The wide, green valley surrounding the village of Mimbres is the epicenter of the ancient culture of the same name, best known for its elegant black-on-white pottery designs, done about a thousand years ago. One of the sites where these were unearthed is the **Mimbres**

© ZORA O'NEILL

Chino Mine, east of Silver City, is one of the world's largest open-pit mines.

**Valley Cultural Site** (14 Sage Dr., 11am-3pm daily, free). The earth has been so churned over by excavations, it takes a trained eye to see the outlines of any ancient settlement, but you can also see two more recent (19th-century) homesteads. Look for the turn off the north side of the road. Now, though, you're most likely to think of it as a place to fill up your tank at one of the gas stations here. The **Gila Wilderness Ranger District office** (Hwy. 35, 575/536-2250, 8am-4:30pm Mon.-Fri.) is here.

Just after the turnoff to the old Spanish settlement of **San Lorenzo,** Highway 35 dead-ends at Highway 152, which runs west to Silver City.

## CHINO MINE

Off the east side of Highway 152, you can't help but notice the monumentally altered landscape around the **Chino Mine,** the pit of which measures more than a mile across. The oldest continuously mined claim in the United States,

it was first known by Apaches, who took copper from the area. In 1799, the Spanish, with the help of convict labor, began extracting copper and sending it to Mexico. Production was so great that the majority of the early 19th-century copper coins from Mexico and Spain can be traced back to Santa Rita del Cobre, as the mine was known then. Open-pit mining began in 1910, eventually swallowing up the town of Santa Rita that had grown adjacent to the mine.

The hole now reaches 1,600 feet into the ground, dwarfing the trucks and shovels that toil on its terraces, and the majority of Grant County's population is employed here in some capacity. You can't miss Chino from the road, but if you want an up-close look, stop at the observation point maintained by Phelps Dodge, just south of mile marker 6. If you're able to ignore the obvious environmental ravages, you could call it an impressive piece of land art.

# Gila National Forest

From Silver City, U.S. 180 runs north about 45 miles to the junction with Highway 12 and the town of Reserve. For much of the drive, the road is surrounded by the **Gila National Forest**, the larger region surrounding the more tightly controlled Gila Wilderness. Its 2.7 million acres stretch west to Arizona and north as far as Quemado. Passing through rolling grassy plains and between mountain peaks, this is a beautiful—and often empty—drive.

## GILA

Not to be confused with Gila Hot Springs, the village of Gila is often a jumping-off point for trips into the wilderness area or down the Gila River to the southwest; it's also close enough to Silver City that it counts as a sort of suburb.

Set on 90 acres with a stream running through, ( **Casitas de Gila** (50 Casita Flats, 575/535-4455, www.casitasdegila.com) is a great way to enjoy the area in comfort. Nightly rates go down the longer you stay—and once you get a glimpse of the night sky from the hot tub, you'll probably want to settle in. The apartments, furnished with custom Mexican woodwork, have kiva fireplaces, kitchens stocked with breakfast food, and private patios. Foldout couches in the living rooms make the standard casitas ($160) family-friendly, while a larger two-bedroom option ($225) can sleep six.

## SAN FRANCISCO HOT SPRINGS

The **San Francisco Hot Springs** are some of the most beautiful in the area, a large warm pool tucked in a canyon about 1.5 miles from the trailhead. The hot water bubbles out of

THE SOUTHWEST

## Exploring the Gila Wilderness

Covering 558,000 acres, the Gila Wilderness is the largest such protected area in any state but Alaska, and it's also the first. With the adjacent 200,000 acres of the Aldo Leopold Wilderness, plus the Gila National Forest to the south and north, it's an almost overwhelming place to explore. The terrain ranges from piñon forests dotted with spring wildflowers to the flat beds of the three forks of the Gila River. Fires and massive flooding in 2013 burned trails and changed watercourses—so any exploration should start with a check with the visitors center at the Gila Cliff Dwellings, or one of the national forest district offices.

The most common access point to the wilderness is on the south side, via Highway 15 north of Silver City. This serpentine road makes its way up through pine trees to the Gila Cliff Dwellings National Monument and several well-used trailheads.

While you're driving or hiking around, keep your eyes open for the area's rich wildlife. At lower elevations, javelinas (small wild pigs) are plentiful, as are packs of coatimundis. Nimble, raccoon-like animals with long snouts, coatis usually live in more tropical climates; southern New Mexico is the only area they're found in the United States. You might see one scampering across the road, or napping in a tree. Less exotic, skunks are plentiful (four different species, in fact), and you'll surely encounter at least the traces of one at some point on your trip. In the higher mountains, you may see herds of mule deer and elk. The eponymous Gila monster, a venomous lizard that can grow up to two feet in length, makes its home here, as do lots of rattlesnakes. Be alert in the springtime, when the snakes have just come out of hibernation and are on the prowl for mates. Wear boots that come above your ankles, and don't place your feet between rocks or in crevices when hiking.

the river plain, and the specific pool locations may change from year to year, but the general spot is easy to reach. Look for the turn west off U.S. 180, about five miles south of Glenwood, around mile marker 58. A dirt road leads to a well-marked trail. Avoid the area during summer rainstorms—not only is there a risk of flash flooding, but the trail is heavy clay that's a slog when wet. If you happen to miss the turn, you can always stop in the Glenwood ranger office and ask directions—and check the status.

## GLENWOOD

The road north from Gila skirts the mountains and races through grasslands, reaching the small town of Glenwood after about 30 miles. It's got the basics: gas station, café, and a few motels.

Based just north of Glenwood, Leah Jones of **Gila Wilderness Ventures** (575/539-2800, www.gilawildernessventures.com) runs day horse rides as well as multiday pack trips in the Gila. For info on local trails, stop in at or call the **Glenwood Ranger District office** (575/539-2481, 8am-4:30pm Mon.-Fri.).

### Catwalk Trail

Ordinarily, this place is a must-see, but due to fires deeper in the wilderness in 2012, then flooding in 2013, the trail was closed at research time; call the Glenwood rangers for news. A Civilian Conservation Corps project in the 1930s, the **Catwalk Trail** is a hanging walkway over a stream for the first half of its 1.1 miles, sometimes suspended more than 20 feet above the water and pink canyon walls pressing in close on either side. The catwalk follows the route of a water pipeline built in the 1890s as part of a mining operation. The first, easiest part is also wheelchair-accessible. Normally, the entrance fee is $3 per car, and the turnoff for the trail is in the middle of Glenwood, well marked as Highway 174 (Catwalk Road).

### Accommodations and Food

For an overnight stay, the **Whitewater Motel** (U.S. 180, 575/539-2581, www.whitewatermotel.com), next to the post office near the south

entrance to the town, is a simple place where the owners clearly care about details. Beds are a bit springy, but the 10 rooms are tidy, comfortable, and trimmed with lace curtains, with back porches overlooking a shady garden and stream. Configurations range from one double bed ($52) to three twin beds and a double ($69), great for families or groups. You can also camp in the area at **Bighorn Campground,** adjacent to the Catwalk trailhead; however, it has just five tent spots (and no room for RVs), and no water.

The only real dining option in town is **Golden Girls Café** (U.S. 180, 575/539-2561, 7am-11am Sun.-Wed., 7am-11am and 4pm-8pm Thurs.-Sat., $5), which is cozy and very, very inexpensive. Homemade jelly is a highlight, and coffee is $1, like it ought to be—but you pay extra for milk. The menu is limited; if you're headed north, you may want to press on to Alma Grill.

## MOGOLLON

Unlike many old mining towns, Mogollon bursts with color and cheer—at least on weekends between May and October, when the businesses up here are open. Its old buildings, including the **Silver Creek Inn** (www.silver-creekinn.com, $110 d), the **Purple Onion Café** (575/539-2710, 9am-5pm Fri.-Sun.), and the village archives, are painted in vibrant shades. It's a great place to get away for a night or two, as it feels quite cut off from the world.

In fact it *is* quite cut off from the world, nine miles up Highway 159, which locals call the **Bursum Road.** The road washed out due to floods in 2013, and it is very often closed with snow in the winter. From a turn east about three miles north of Glenwood, it starts off easily enough, crossing rolling scrub, but then it ascends steeply into the mountains. About halfway into the climb, the road reduces to a harrowing single lane with steep switchbacks and no guardrails.

But the view across the rolling grasslands below is stunning. Hardier drivers can carry on past Mogollon, where the road grows increasingly rough and enters aspen glades that glow

© ZORA O'NEILL

the view from the Bursum Road to Mogollon

for miner James Cooney and a few of his men, who were killed here by Apaches in 1880.

On the east side of the road, **Alma Grill** (U.S. 180, 575/539-2233, 6am-3pm Fri.-Wed., $6) serves all the necessary food for a good road trip: enchiladas, biscuits, and more.

## RESERVE

Hunting is big business in the Catron County seat, with expeditions leaving from here and plenty of taxidermy shops in town. **Reserve**, first settled by Mexican homesteaders in the early 1800s, is notorious for an 1884 shootout between 80-odd Texan cowboys and the local deputy sheriff, Elfego Baca, who held off the gang for 36 hours, until they ran out of ammunition. In what many saw as a blatantly racist move, Baca was later brought to trial for murdering one of the cowboys; he was finally acquitted when he displayed the bullet-riddled door he'd hidden behind. Look for a memorial to Baca at the main crossroads.

The **Reserve Ranger District office** (575/523-6232, 8am-4:30pm Mon.-Fri.), on Highway 12 just west of town, has information on the Gila National Forest, as well as the wilderness area.

For food, ◖ **Adobe Café and Bakery** (U.S. 180., 575/533-6146, 7am-8pm Sun.-Mon., 7am-3pm Thurs.-Fri., $8), just south of Reserve, on U.S. 180 about a quarter-mile from the junction with Highway 12, is a real treat, with a fresh, varied menu of breakfast goodies, salads, and creative sandwiches. Service can be a bit slow, though. It usually closes February through mid-April. The same owners run the adjacent **Hidden Springs Inn** (www.thehiddenspringsinn.com, $69 d), a very good deal, and nicely kept.

For dinner, **Ella's** (96 Main St., 575/533-6111, 7am-8pm Tues.-Sat., 7am-2pm Sun.-Mon., $8), in Reserve proper, will do just fine—locals in Carhartts and hats dig in to chicken-fried steak and enchiladas.

gold in the fall—but forest fires have stripped the trees and increased the risk of falling logs. Give the area a few years to clear up, and wind your way very, very carefully back down the way you came in. Avoid doing this at sundown, however, as the glare just adds to the risk.

## ALMA

Once a hideout for Butch Cassidy, this wide spot in the road is the turnoff for a good hiking trail into the Gila, the **Mineral Creek Trail.** The first 1.5 miles are an easy family hike and the scenery beyond gets even better, but its course may have changed due to flooding—check with the rangers in Glenwood. To reach the trail (no. 201), turn east in Alma onto Mineral Creek Road, a dirt track; this turns into Forest Road 701 and dead-ends at the trailhead after 5.5 miles. Just before mile 5, look for "Cooney's tomb," a giant boulder made into the gravesite

# CARLSBAD CAVERNS AND THE SOUTHEAST

Barren land stretches between the few major tourist sights in southeastern New Mexico. But those sights are often far from typical: the vast, bat-filled spaces of Carlsbad Caverns National Park, the ghostly gypsum dunes at White Sands National Monument, a museum dedicated to UFOs and an even better one dedicated to contemporary art, both in Roswell. In short, you'll

© ZORA O'NEILL

# HIGHLIGHTS

LOOK FOR ◖ TO FIND RECOMMENDED SIGHTS, ACTIVITIES, DINING, AND LODGING.

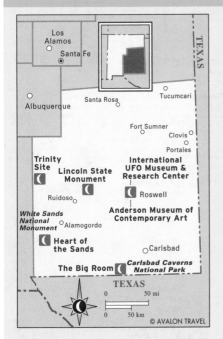

◖ **International UFO Museum & Research Center:** Mysteries of deep space revealed! Government conspiracies uncovered! Plush alien dolls for sale! Roswell's most popular museum may seem campy, but it takes its mission very seriously (page 316).

◖ **Anderson Museum of Contemporary Art:** Roswell is also home to this excellent collection of artwork in every media, which rivals the galleries in Santa Fe in quality and wins for sheer gutsy enthusiasm (page 317).

◖ **The Big Room:** Some 600,000 visitors a year tour the main cave at **Carlsbad Caverns National Park**—for good reason. It's amazing in both its vast scale and its smallest details, such as clusters of tiny stalactites as delicate as lace. Silence is requested on the tour—not hard, as you'll be too awed to speak (page 326).

◖ **Heart of the Sands:** Visiting the eerie landscape at the center of **White Sands National Monument** is like going to the beach and the North Pole both at once. It's certainly unlike any place you've ever seen (page 336).

◖ **Lincoln State Monument:** The late 19th century's "most dangerous town in America" is now a quiet place, half of its main-street buildings preserved as museums that conjure life in Billy the Kid's era, without all the usual Wild West kitsch (page 343).

◖ **Trinity Site:** You can visit the site of the first atomic bomb blast (fittingly set in a stretch of the stark Jornada del Muerto desert) only two days a year, but it's an essential stop if your schedule allows (page 346).

THE SOUTHEAST

find surprising things here if you make the drive.

And what a long drive it is. The blank expanse the Spanish dubbed the Llano Estacado starts in Fort Sumner (where sharpshooter Billy the Kid finally met his end in 1881) and stretches east and south into Texas. The roads are straight, the horizon unbroken, and soon you can't tell if you've been driving for 20 minutes or two hours. The occasional oil derrick, wind turbine, or herd of cattle breaks up the monotony, and tiny towns loom up suddenly and disappear in the rear-view mirror just as fast. Portales, center of the "peanut basin of the Southwest," is a rare green spot, thanks to a deep aquifer. Roswell is the area's largest settlement, and perhaps its strangest, as many people are still obsessed with an alleged crash-landing of an alien spacecraft here in 1947.

Southwest of Roswell, the Sacramento Mountains spike along the edge of the plains. Here, the resort towns of Cloudcroft

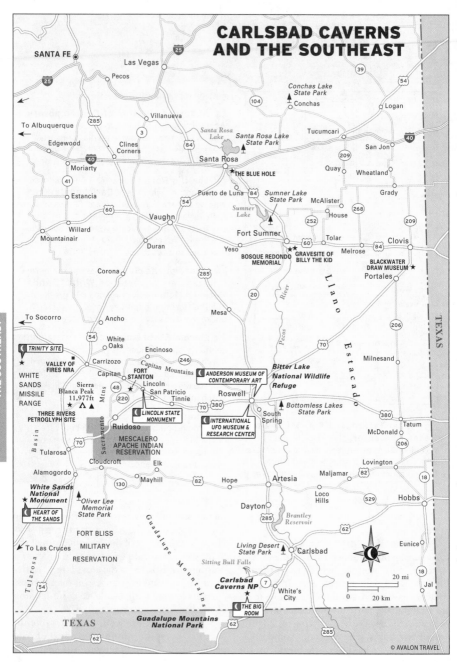

# CARLSBAD CAVERNS AND THE SOUTHEAST

THE SOUTHEAST

SANTA FE
Las Vegas
Pecos
To Albuquerque
Edgewood
Clines Corners
Moriarty
Estancia
Willard
Mountainair
Duran
Corona

Villanueva
Santa Rosa Lake
Santa Rosa Lake State Park
Santa Rosa
★THE BLUE HOLE
Puerto de Luna
Vaughn
Yeso

Conchas Lake State Park
Conchas
Logan
Tucumcari
San Jon
Quay
Wheatland
Grady
Sumner Lake State Park
McAlister
House
Sumner Lake
Fort Sumner
Tolar
Melrose
Clovis
BOSQUE REDONDO MEMORIAL
GRAVESITE OF BILLY THE KID
BLACKWATER DRAW MUSEUM ★
Portales

To Socorro
Ancho
Mesa
TRINITY SITE
VALLEY OF FIRES NRA
White Oaks
Encinoso
Carrizozo
Capitan
FORT STANTON
Lincoln
San Patricio
Tinnie
ANDERSON MUSEUM OF CONTEMPORARY ART
Bitter Lake National Wildlife Refuge
Roswell
LINCOLN STATE MONUMENT
Ruidoso
MESCALERO APACHE INDIAN RESERVATION
INTERNATIONAL UFO MUSEUM & RESEARCH CENTER
South Spring
Bottomless Lakes State Park
McDonald
Tatum

WHITE SANDS MISSILE RANGE
Sierra Blanca Peak 11,977ft
THREE RIVERS PETROGLYPH SITE
Tularosa
Cloudcroft
Elk
Mayhill
Hope
Artesia
Maljamar
Lovington
Hobbs

Alamogordo
White Sands National Monument
HEART OF THE SANDS
Oliver Lee Memorial State Park
Dayton
Loco Hills
Brantley Reservoir

To Las Cruces
FORT BLISS MILITARY RESERVATION
Living Desert State Park
Carlsbad
Eunice

Sitting Bull Falls
Carlsbad Caverns NP
White's City
Jal

THE BIG ROOM
Guadalupe Mountains National Park

TEXAS

Llano Estacado

Milnesand

Pecos River

0    20 mi
0    20 km

© AVALON TRAVEL

and Ruidoso cater to Texans who've fled the maddening flatlands. The steep trails at Ski Apache, with a base elevation of 9,600 feet, provide winter entertainment. At the base of the mountains, orderly Alamogordo is home to the International Space Hall of Fame and the closest town to White Sands, a 275-square-mile landscape that's fascinating as a natural attraction, but also inextricably linked with the world's first atomic bomb test, which took place in this desert in 1945.

Carlsbad Caverns, another natural wonder, fortunately has no such legacy. Getting there requires the longest drive of all, nearly to the Texas border in the south. But when you see the so-called Big Room, the vast main cave that drips with stalactites and takes more than an hour to explore, you'll know there's nothing else like it in New Mexico, nor in the whole country.

## HISTORY

Hundreds of millions of years ago, southeastern New Mexico's modern history was already set in stone: The dinosaurs that roamed the swampy banks of the sea were eventually transformed into the fossil fuel that many a contemporary Lovingtonian or Artesian makes a living extracting today.

In between, New Mexico's southern plains and mountain ranges saw much the same patterns as the rest of the state. The U.S. Army set upon the resident Indian tribes, and General James Carleton ordered Kit Carson, "All Indian men of that [Mescalero] tribe are to be killed whenever and wherever you can find them." Billy the Kid got up to no good and eventually died here, at the age of 21. And railroad lines and highways (especially the legendary Route 66) brought modern thrills to previously untouched patches of plain.

But a single cataclysmic event really marked the area. Just before sunrise one summer morning in 1945, White Sands was lit brighter than high noon by a towering mushroom cloud—the successful test of the first atomic bomb, which was then deployed over Japan to win World War II. During the Cold War, White Sands was the proving ground for some essential technology in the space race. In this respect, the region is an odd juxtaposition of humankind's most current obsessions against timeless landscape.

## PLANNING YOUR TIME

If you're focusing on Carlsbad, White Sands, and even Cloudcroft or Ruidoso, it can make sense to fly in to El Paso (ELP), then stay in Las Cruces (one hour's drive) your first night; the town of Carlsbad also receives commuter flights from Albuquerque.

Driving from Albuquerque, you could take the leisurely route via the Salinas Pueblo missions and Carrizozo, reaching Ruidoso or Alamogordo by dinnertime, then carrying on to White Sands the next day—or you could cruise down the interstate and get straight to White Sands by the afternoon. In any case, allow about three hours for a basic visit to the park, or more if you plan to do any hiking or photography. Carlsbad Caverns calls for the better part of a day to see just the basics, though the more adventurous small-group tours are well worth allotting a second day. Both these places get busy in the summer, and the caverns can feel crowded; the sands absorb crowds better. At any rate, if you can push your visit till mid-August, you may miss some crowds (as kids head back to school), and also see the landscape a bit greened by summer rains.

# East on the Interstate

After crossing the pass between the Sandia and Manzano Mountains east of Albuquerque, I-40 heads into the high plains. Get used to the scenery, because it won't change until well into Texas. The wind blows constantly across gold tufts of grass, and the barbed-wire fences are clotted with tumbleweeds. The most excitement along this stretch is counting down the billboards to truck stops like the Flyin' C, where you can stock up on everything from moccasins to fireworks. It's not quite the glamour of Route 66 of old, but the combination of tacky signage, big sky, and a whole lot of nothing says "American road trip" like nothing else.

## EDGEWOOD

Off exit 187 in Edgewood, **Wildlife West Nature Park** (505/281-7655, www.wildlifewest.org, 10am-6pm daily mid-Mar.-Oct., noon-4pm daily Nov.-mid-Mar., $7) is a better-than-average roadside attraction. This "enhanced zoo" is a 122-acre wildlife sanctuary for wolves, cougars, elk, and other native animals.

For solid road food at the same exit, **Katrinah's East Mountain Grill** (150 Hwy. 344, 505/281-9111, 7am-8pm Tues.-Sat., 8am-2pm Sun., $8) has a menu of standard diner goodies, from enchiladas to veggie wraps, all made from fresh ingredients. Look for it three miles north of I-40, just past Walmart.

## SANTA ROSA

This town of 2,500 is easy to cruise past on I-40. But for a refreshing swim, take time out for the "City of Natural Lakes," where cool springs well up alongside the Pecos River. From 1901, Santa Rosa was a stop on the Chicago, Rock Island & Pacific freight line, and in the 1930s, the place began to grow as Route 66 travelers passed through. John Steinbeck set a scene of *The Grapes of Wrath* here, which was then re-created for film in the town in 1940. Its stretch of the historic highway, which runs parallel to I-40 to the south, is lined with stately old warehouses and lurid neon.

### The Blue Hole

Most people come to Santa Rosa for an unexpected natural attraction: **The Blue Hole** (dawn-dusk daily), an 81-foot-deep pool of water that's a constant 64°F year-round. Only about 80 feet across, it doesn't look like much from the surface, but it's more impressive when you consider that water is gushing from the spring at the bottom at 3,000 gallons per minute (check the overflow channel on the south side to get an idea just what that number means). The steady temperature and perfect clarity of the water makes it a popular place for scuba divers—who create an incongruous image with the tumbleweeds blowing by in the background. And the place is popular with local kids, who can spend a whole summer day doing cannonballs off the high rocks on one side. (There are less adventurous ways of getting into the water, including cement stairs.)

Admission is free, but to dive you'll need a **permit** ($8), available from the visitors center or the dive shop, both adjacent to the Blue Hole. To reach the area, get off at exit 278 or 275 and follow signs to Blue Hole Road (also a section of Historic Route 66).

If you want more room to play, backtrack on Blue Hole Road to **Park Lake,** an adjacent natural spring that's the town's biggest recreation spot. Zip down the free waterslide, rent a pedal boat, or just jump into the cool, clear water. (Compared with these natural springs, **Santa Rosa Lake State Park,** the product of a dam on the Pecos River north of town, is quite dull.)

### Route 66 Auto Museum

For car buffs, the **Route 66 Auto Museum** (2866 Historic Rte. 66, 575/472-1966, www.route66automuseum.com, 7:30am-6pm Mon.-Sat., 10am-5pm Sun. Apr.-Oct., 8am-5pm Mon.-Sat., 10am-5pm Sun. Nov.-Mar., $5), on the east side of town, is a showroom of a couple dozen curvaceous machines from the heyday of American road-tripping; some are for sale.

## Accommodations

Santa Rosa has the normal chain places, with a couple, such as **Comfort Inn** (2524 Historic Rte. 66, 575/472-5412, www.comfortinn.com, $69 d), in better condition than their counterparts in Tucumcari. If you want a vintage Route 66 motel, **La Loma Inn** (1709 Historic Rte. 66, 575/472-4379, $43 s, $50 d) and all-nonsmoking **La Mesa Inn** (2415 Historic Rte. 66, 575/472-3021, $38 s, $42 d) are both decent options, well tended by longtime local owners. Still, if your taste runs to vintage, there are better places in Tucumcari.

## Food

Santa Rosa boasts of its PDL chile, a special strain grown just to the south in the village of Puerto de Luna; it's usually eaten in its green form. Unfortunately, there's nowhere reliable to eat it. **Comet II** (217 Historic Rte. 66,

575/472-3663, 11am-9pm Tues.-Sun., $8), bathed in neon, has potential for simple, diner-style New Mexican, but doesn't always deliver, and the landmark **Joseph's Bar & Grill** (865 Historic Rte. 66, 575/472-3361, 7am-10pm daily, $7), is better for its kitschy decor (including its "Fat Man" logo, salvaged from a Depression-era restaurant) than its food. Still, if you're headed east on I-40, this is about your last chance for chile before blander Texan-style fare takes over.

## Information

Next to the Blue Hole, the **Santa Rosa Visitors Center** (1085 Blue Hole Rd., 575/472-3763, www.santarosanm.org, 8am-5pm Mon.-Fri., 8am-noon Sat.) sells dive permits, in addition to stocking all the usual brochures.

## PUERTO DE LUNA

Santa Rosa's historic roots are in this tidy collection of tin-roofed adobe buildings in a protected valley 10 miles south of I-40 on Highway 91. There's nothing precisely to see here, but,

THE SOUTHEAST

© ZORA O'NEILL

Puerto de Luna

as part of the larger **Mesalands Scenic Byway**, which zigzags across I-40 between Santa Rosa and Tucumcari, it's a pretty way to head south to Fort Sumner, through red-striped rocky hills and chile fields. (The next legs of the byway are U.S. 84 back north to I-40, then Highway 156 from Santa Rosa and Highway 209 north to Tucumcari.)

Founded in 1842, Puerto de Luna was the county seat in the 1880s and later the childhood home of writer Rudolfo Anaya, who described the place in detail in his seminal novel *Bless Me, Ultima*. It's also alleged to be the place Billy the Kid enjoyed his last Christmas dinner, while Pat Garrett was taking him to jail in Lincoln.

## SUMNER LAKE STATE PARK

A welcome bit of lushness amid the dry grasses, **Sumner Lake State Park** (Hwy. 203, 575/355-2541, www.nmparks.com, $5/car) is an excellent birding spot, as it's on a major migration route (check the canyon below the dam in summer). The **camping** spots ($8-18), spread out in four areas amid cottonwoods and junipers, are very pretty. The state park is midway between Santa Rosa and Fort Sumner, six miles west of U.S. 84 via Highway 203.

## FORT SUMNER

A small town bedecked in Old West-style detailing, **Fort Sumner** is 42 miles south of I-40 and Santa Rosa via U.S. 84. It's best known as the final resting place of Henry McCarty, a.k.a. Henry Antrim, a.k.a. William H. Bonney, a.k.a. Billy the Kid. It was here in 1881 that Lincoln County Sheriff Pat Garrett finally tracked down the gunfighter and shot him (in ambush, in the dark, the Kid's fans will point out), to mete out justice for the 21 men Billy had allegedly killed in his short life—he was only 21, in fact, when he died in a farmhouse kitchen.

For more than a century, this legend of a Wild West antihero had all but obliterated the memory of what Fort Sumner had first been: a failed reservation-turned-concentration-camp for about 9,000 Navajo and 500 Mescalero

Apache for five years during the Civil War. In 2005, a state monument finally gave more public recognition to this tragic period in the settling of the American West.

### Sights

In town proper, seek out the **WPA murals** in the De Baca County Courthouse (514 Ave. C, 575/355-2601, 8am-4:30pm Mon.-Fri.), just northeast of the main intersection in town. Inside the redbrick building, head upstairs to see vivid images of the taming of the Western frontier. On the main street is the **Billy the Kid Museum** (1435 E. Sumner Ave., 575/355-2380, www.billythekidmuseumfortsumner.com, 8:30am-5pm daily mid-May-Sept., 8:30am-5pm Mon.-Sat. Oct.-mid-May, $4), a tourist outpost of the highest order: room upon room of antique gewgaws, a gift shop, and a replica of Billy the Kid's grave.

The real deal is down the road: Head 3 miles east of town on U.S. 84, then 3.5 miles south on Billy the Kid Road, and you reach the *real* **gravesite of Billy the Kid** (free), in a desolate little cemetery behind the so-so **Old Fort Sumner Museum** (575/355-2942, 9am-5pm daily, $3.50). Perhaps due to his repeated jailbreaks in life, William Bonney is now penned in by a wrought-iron fence as well as cemented over, along with a couple of his "pals." Also buried nearby: Lucien B. Maxwell, owner of the enormous Maxwell Land Grant in northern New Mexico, as well as this property, after the fort was decommissioned. It was in Maxwell's son's home, less than a mile toward the river, that Billy the Kid was fatally shot. The museum offers yet another collection of Old West relics and plenty more detail about the young star of the Lincoln County War.

### Bosque Redondo Memorial

Immediately south on the road from here, the **Bosque Redondo Memorial** (3647 Billy the Kid Rd., 575/355-2573, www.nmmonuments.org, 8:30am-4:30pm Wed.-Mon., $3) is a long-overdue museum and monument to the exceptional misery endured by most of the Navajo and a handful of Mescalero Apache, beginning

Bosque Redondo Memorial

in 1863. Force-marched in to this reservation from the northern corners of the state, the people endured what the Navajo came to call the Long Walk, a midwinter trek of hundreds of miles, during which the weakest were shot for holding up the group and many women and children were sold into slavery.

The two bands, which had little in common culturally and shared only a history of raiding each other, were penned in here and told to make a life together. But the allotted stretch of river basin was not enough land to support so many, so crops failed and disease tore through the overcrowded communities. The Mescalero Apache defied the U.S. military and left as a group two years into the terrible experiment. Nearly 3,000 Navajo—almost a third of the tribe—died in what they named H'weeldi (Place of Suffering) before they were allowed to return to their homelands.

The museum is a conceptual modern building—Navajo hogan meets Apache tepee—with a detailed exhibit on the camp, plus extra room for rotating displays on other low points

in human rights history. Out back, a path leads past the site where the Navajo leaders finally signed the treaty that released them (and established the Navajo Nation) in 1868, and into the greenery alongside the river, where the fort itself used to stand. It's a deceptively pretty setting.

## Food

**Rodeo Grill** (451 W. Sumner Ave., 575/355-8000, 7:30am-3pm Mon.-Fri., $9), a few blocks east of the main intersection, serves burgers and hand-cut fries, as well as nice breakfast burritos, heated till the tortilla gets crispy on the grill, in a casual room hung with lariats and saddles. But if you're visiting on a weekend, your best bet is **Fred's** (1408 Sumner Ave., 575/355-7500, 11am-8pm Tues.-Sat., $7), a big cinderblock building on the east side that, despite its unwelcoming facade, draws raves for its chile, guacamole, and chicken-fried steak; check out the neat old wood bar in the back. On Sunday, you're left with **Sadie's** (257 Sumner Ave., 575/355-1461, 11am-2pm and 5pm-7pm Mon. and Thurs.-Fri., 9am-2pm and 5pm-9pm Sat.-Sun., $7), on the west end of town, but that's not a bad deal at all—it's good for New Mexican food. But note that awkward closure between lunch and dinner—in short, if you're hungry in Fort Sumner on a Sunday afternoon, you're out of luck.

## Information

Visit the **De Baca Chamber of Commerce** (707 N. 4th St., 575/355-7705, www.fortsumner-chamber.com, 9am-4pm Mon.-Fri.) for all the basic tourist details.

## TUCUMCARI

For the California-bound on Route 66, Tucumcari was the first real stop on New Mexico's stretch of the Mother Road. "Tucumcari Tonite!" urged the billboards leading up to the town's neon-lined strip—and they still do today. The neon glow is not quite what it once was, but Americana buffs should definitely get off the highway here, to see the Tepee Curios shop and other architectural oddities,

© ZORA O'NEILL

**vintage Route 66 architecture in Tucumcari**

THE SOUTHEAST

and bunk down in one of the well-preserved old motor courts. Dinosaur freaks will find a great museum.

Tucumcari's existence predates Route 66: Main Street is oriented with the old railroad depot, north of the highway. When the tracks were being laid, this spot on the plains was dubbed Six-Shooter Siding, but the gunplay quieted down a little once regular trade got going, and the place took the name of nearby Tucumcari Mountain. The railroad provided steady employment until it closed operations here in 1999. But the residents of the sturdy, low bungalows that line the wide side streets have kept the town from being blown away in the wind—they are stubborn and dedicated to keeping the place alive.

### Sights
After you've cruised the neon signs on Historic Route 66 (a.k.a. Tucumcari Boulevard), check out the *other* main drag: Turn north on 1st Street and drive about eight blocks up to **Main Street** and the train depot; along the way,

elaborate photo-realistic **murals,** most by a husband-and-wife team, adorn many buildings.

The surprisingly spiffy **Mesalands Dinosaur Museum** (222 E. Laughlin St., 575/461-3466, www.mesalands.edu, 10am-6pm Tues.-Sat. Mar.-Aug., noon-5pm Tues.-Sat. Sept.-Feb., $6.50) is in this area too, just east of 1st Street and two blocks north of Tucumcari Boulevard. The exhibit hall contains a huge number of beautiful bronze casts of dinosaur skeletons (neat, because you're allowed to touch them), as well as some dinosaur eggs and lots of other fossils. It also owns a rare, nearly complete 30-foot-long skeleton of the giant carnivore *Torvosaurus.*

Two blocks farther north (look for the windmill), the **Tucumcari Historical Museum** (416 S. Adams St., 575/461-4201, 9am-3pm Tues.-Sat., $5) takes up an entire two-story redbrick house with old saddles, slot machines, and Indian relics, then spills over into a yard full of vintage boxcars, Route 66 paraphernalia, and more.

### Entertainment
Built in 1936, the elegant deco-style **Odeon Theater** (123 S. 2nd St., 575/461-0100, $5.50) is a small-town treasure, with a modest but cool pink neon sign, offset with yellow zia symbols. Shows are every night but Monday at 7pm, and also at 4pm on weekends. The concession stand includes hot dogs, in case you want to make dinner of it (only the Pow Wow is open after the movie lets out).

### Sports and Recreation
In the summer, locals decamp to one of New Mexico's bigger reservoirs, **Conchas Lake State Park** (575/868-2270, www.nmparks. com, $5/car), northwest of town 34 miles on Highway 104. It stretches for about 25 miles, its coastline weaving along many inlets, sandy beaches, and canyons. The setting is rather austere, however, and there's very little shade—it's nicer to visit in the cooler spring or fall, when crowds are lighter as well.

In town, the **public pool** (415 W. Hines St., 575/461-4582) is open summers only, and closes as soon as school is in session, by the third week in August.

## Accommodations

Tucumcari has a handful of excellent-value retro motels—worth a stop just to enjoy a taste of the past. A relic of the Route 66 days, the pink-and-turquoise ( **Blue Swallow Motel** (815 E. Route 66 Blvd., 575/461-9849, www. blueswallowmotel.com, $50 s, $65 d), on the east side of town, dates from 1939, making it perhaps the oldest standing motel on Route 66. The 14 rooms are cozy, with thick plaster walls, tiled showers, and chenille bedspreads; vintage issues of *The Saturday Evening Post* and old phones heavy enough to be weapons round out the historic feel. Guests are often Americana buffs from around the globe. The place closes for about six weeks in January and February.

If you prefer your retro style in the form of midcentury groovy, head to the jaunty cinderblock court of the ( **Motel Safari** (722 E. Route 66 Blvd., 575/461-1048, www.

one of several excellent old motels on the Mother Road

themotelsafari.com, $65 d), with firm beds and flat-panel TVs, plus mod, spindly legged furniture that conjures 1959. One suite nods to Wanda Jackson, the queen of rockabilly.

Just a tiny bit later in the timeline of motel architecture, the **Historic Route 66 Motel** (1620 E. Route 66 Blvd., 575/461-1212, www.rte66motel.com, $42 d) conjures Palm Springs in Tucumcari, and its owners have maintained the minimalist style. It might not have a fabulous neon sign, but rooms have floor-to-ceiling windows and very cool turquoise vinyl chairs that may be from the original 1967 design.

## Food

Look for the big fiberglass steer above the sign at **Del's** (1202 E. Route 66 Blvd., 575/461-1740, 11am-9pm Mon.-Sat., $10), where you'll find a mighty fine chicken-fried steak (lovely crunchy batter; rich mashed potatoes on the side) as well as a nicely appointed soup-and-salad bar. It's been serving locals since 1956, and feels like a chummy living room because of it.

Because it's open late and has a full bar, **Pow Wow Restaurant & Lizard Lounge** (801 W. Route 66 Blvd., 575/461-2587, 6am-10pm Sun.-Thurs., 6am-midnight Fri.-Sat., $8) is a major town hangout. The restaurant serves sandwiches and New Mexican dishes in a pastel Southwest-style dining room. It's a perfectly serviceable place to have lunch or dinner.

For lunch, **Cornerstone Deli** (711 E. Route 66 Blvd., 575/461-3326, 11am-8pm Mon.-Sat., $6) serves sandwiches with ingredients from the local small-scale **Tucumcari Mountain Cheese Factory** (foodies, check it out at 823 E. Main St.), as well as homemade potato chips and super-creamy frozen custard.

For breakfast, it's hard to beat **Kix on 66** (1102 E. Route 66 Blvd., 575/461-1966, 6am-2pm daily, $6), where you can smell the bacon from the parking lot. The old-style diner slings hash browns, biscuits, and other morning standards to regulars in teal vinyl booths or at the long Formica counter. It has the same owners as Del's—you'll recognize the white gravy.

THE SOUTHEAST

If your love of the past doesn't stretch to good old-fashioned American coffee, head to **Circa Espresso** (1620 E. Route 66 Blvd., 575/461-6099, 6:30am-11am daily, $3), at the Historic Route 66 Motel, for your morning blast of steam-powered caffeine. It serves no real food, though.

## Information

The **Tucumcari-Quay County Chamber of Commerce** (404 W. Route 66 Blvd., 575/461-1694, 9am-5pm Mon.-Fri.) has the usual assortment of information.

## Getting There

By car, Tucumcari is 59 miles (less than one hour) east along I-40 from Santa Rosa, 176 miles (three hours) east from Albuquerque, and 113 miles (two hours) west from Amarillo, Texas. By bus, **Greyhound** (800/231-2222, www.greyhound.com) stops in Tucumcari three times a day, at the McDonald's (2608 S. 1st St., 575/461-1350, 5am-midnight daily).

# The Llano

Texans refer to these barren plains as the Llano, and much of this area could be mistaken for the neighboring state, from the fields of cattle (for both beef and dairy) to the oil derricks that dot the horizon. "West West Texas" rarely sees tourists, but some of this land is exceptionally pretty: South on Highway 209 from Tucumcari, for instance, takes you closer to the mesas and leaves the visual clutter of billboards and semitrucks behind. Scored by deep channels, the red earth is studded with cholla cactus and a delicate-looking variety of yucca, as well as black, brushy mesquite. The occasional farmhouse—often built only feet away from a ruined homestead from 50 years ago—shows the optimism required to live in this windy, harshly beautiful landscape. (If you jog west toward Fort Sumner, you'll see the state actually profiting from the rough climate here, through a field of wind turbines that feed into the electricity grid.)

## CLOVIS

Like many other chronically windy spots on the plains, Clovis has a problem keeping its signboards straight, so WELCOMET OCLOVIS will have to do. Busy as it is with rail freight, cattle auctions, and training at the adjacent Cannon Air Force Base, Clovis doesn't really court tourists anyway. It had its big moment in the national spotlight in 1957, when Buddy Holly recorded "That'll Be the Day" in a music studio here. And even though its population is 38,000 and growing, it feels like a fairly small town, especially along its wide, brick-paved Main Street, which dead-ends at the rail yard. The downtown area sports some stylish art deco buildings, including the glamorous Hotel Clovis, once the tallest building between Dallas and Albuquerque, recently converted to lofts, but now overshadowed by grain silos.

## Sights

No one talks about it much today, but in the late 1950s, "the Clovis Sound" was an unmistakable, and deeply influential, musical phenomenon. It was the product of a single recording studio here on the edge of the Texas plains, and it's commemorated in the small but thorough **Norman & Vi Petty Rock & Roll Museum** (105 E. Grand Ave., 575/763-3435, 8am-noon and 1pm-5pm Mon.-Fri., $5). The displays of ephemera tell the story of how local boy Norm Petty and his wife, Vi, scored a hit with their smooth version of "Mood Indigo," then returned here to build a recording studio. Norm was an acoustic obsessive, and his attention to detail came through when he helped an aspiring country star named Buddy Holly, from Lubbock, revamp his tunes into pop hits. After Holly shot to stardom, other hopeful artists beat a path to Clovis to work with the Pettys.

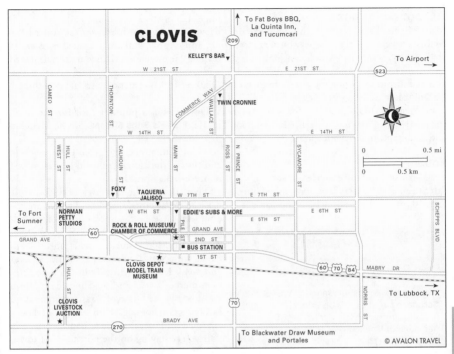

**CLOVIS**

To Fat Boys BBQ,
La Quinta Inn,
and Tucumcari

209

KELLEY'S BAR

To Airport

W 21ST ST     E 21ST ST     523

COMMERCE WAY     TWIN CRONNIE

WALLACE ST

THORNTON ST

W 14TH ST     E 14TH ST

CAMEO ST

0     0.5 mi
0     0.5 km

WEST ST
HULL ST
CALHOUN ST
MAIN ST
ROSS ST
N PRINCE ST
SYCAMORE ST

FOXY
TAQUERIA JALISCO
W 7TH ST     E 7TH ST

NORMAN PETTY STUDIOS
To Fort Sumner

W 6TH ST     EDDIE'S SUBS & MORE     E 6TH ST
E 5TH ST

SCHEPPS BLVD

60
ROCK & ROLL MUSEUM/CHAMBER OF COMMERCE
GRAND AVE

PILE ST

GRAND AVE     2ND ST
BUS STATION
1ST ST

CLOVIS DEPOT MODEL TRAIN MUSEUM
60  70  84     MABRY   DR

HULL ST

NORRIS ST

To Lubbock, TX

CLOVIS LIVESTOCK AUCTION
70

270     BRADY     AVE

To Blackwater Draw Museum
and Portales

© AVALON TRAVEL

THE SOUTHEAST

The Beatles, who saw Holly in concert in 1958, were indelibly marked by the big, clean Clovis Sound, and the young Rolling Stones covered "Rave On." Norman Petty helped launched the careers of Roy Orbison and Waylon Jennings, and kept producing through the 1960s (as rockabilly bands morphed into psychedelia) and the 1970s, and died in 1984.

The museum also contains a re-creation of **Norman Petty Studios** (open only by special request), still standing at 1313 West 7th Street, in what was Petty's father's service station. The museum space is in the basement of the chamber of commerce, which closes for lunch—but if you arrive just before noon, you're welcome to stay in the museum and let yourself out.

Otherwise, Clovis's attractions are just the regular business activities: You can watch the action every Wednesday morning at **Clovis Livestock Auction** (504 S. Hull St., 575/762-4422), south of the tracks at the corner of Brady. Or follow the freight trains' comings and goings from the bridge over Hull Street or at the **Clovis Depot Model Train Museum** (221 W. 1st St., 575/762-0066, www.clovisdepot.com, noon-5pm Wed.-Sun., call for hours in Feb. and Sept., $5 per person or $15 per family). The restored 1950s depot contains a number of operating scale models, and rail fans can listen in to the real-time communications in the yard, as they're piped in over speakers in the depot.

## Entertainment and Events

Local country acts play at **Kelley's Bar** (2208 N. Prince St., 575/762-0044), which also happens to be the only real bar in town. The annual Petty-inspired jam, the **Clovis Music Festival** (575/763-3435, www.clovismusicfestival.net), happens every September and draws a roster of throwback rockabilly and roots acts. The Norman Petty studio is also open during that weekend.

## Accommodations

Most of the cheaper motels in Clovis are on Mabry Drive, parallel to the very busy railroad tracks through town—which can make for a bad night's sleep if you're sensitive to noise. If you can afford it, go for the town's branch of **La Quinta** (4521 N. Prince St., 575/763-8777, www.lq.com, $109 d), one of a few options on the north side of town, with a nice indoor pool and well-kept, suite-layout rooms.

## Food

For Mexican, head to **Taqueria Jalisco** (217 W. 7th St., 575/763-1865, 7am-9pm Sun.-Thurs., 7am-10pm Fri.-Sat., $8), where you can get a

### The *Llano Estacado*

The early explorers on Francisco Vásquez de Coronado's first excursion through the West, in 1541, referred to the stretch east from the Sacramento Mountains as the *llano estacado*, describing the place as an endless sea of green, with grass as high as their horses' bellies. It's an evocative image, but it doesn't explain exactly what the conquistadors may have meant by the word *estacado*.

The common translation is "stockaded" or "staked" plains, which hardly clarifies the issue. Some academics have reasoned that the great green expanse was as disorienting as being at sea, so the Spanish horsemen pounded stakes in the ground to mark their way. Meanwhile, those in the "stockaded" camp reason that the Spanish thought the mesas that punctuated the flatlands—particularly the 300-foot-high Caprock Escarpment near Tucumcari—stood up, straight-walled, like defensive stockades. A third, far less common interpretation proposes that in 16th-century Spanish, *estacado* also had the meaning of "covered in spikes." That is, these were the "stickered plains," due to the spiny yucca plants and thorn-covered mesquite bushes that flourish here. Whatever the case, although the "sea of green" that Coronado traversed is not so green today, the mesas remain as stark and straight.

huge slab of steak and homemade flour tortillas, as well as deep-fried *gorditas*, stuffed *tortas*, and creamy, cinnamon-spiked *horchata* to drink—far more food than you can eat, served with style (the trompe l'oeil mural takes you right to Mexico's Pacific coast), at astonishingly low prices.

Downtown, a popular spot for the noon meal is **Eddie's Subs & More** (517 N. Main St., 575/762-6911, 10:30am-4pm Mon.-Fri., $7), good for hamburgers and green-chile stew—in addition to the aforementioned heroes, served on fresh-baked bread.

Then there's the category of 1950s-style drive-in restaurants, the likes of which are seldom seen these days—especially not of this caliber. **Foxy** (720 W. 7th St., 575/763-7995, 7am-10pm Mon.-Thurs., 7am-11pm Fri.-Sat., 8am-10pm Sun., $5) excels at crispy taquitos and steak fingers, while **Twin Cronnie** (709 Commerce Way, 575/763-5463, 8am-10pm daily, $5) is the home of a tasty combination involving two hot dogs, chili, and a round bun, among a million other menu items.

If you're staying on the north side of town, **Fat Boys BBQ** (901 E. Llano Estacado Blvd., 575/763-9543, 11am-8pm Mon., 11am-9pm Tues.-Sat., 11am-3pm Sun., $12) is a handy dinner spot, with a broader menu than just smoked meat (you can even get a salad!). But it's not quite so stupendous that it's worth a drive north for its own sake.

## Information

The Clovis **chamber of commerce** (105 E. Grand Ave., 575/763-3435, www.clovisnm.org, 8am-5pm Mon.-Fri.) has its offices downtown, in the same building as the Petty Museum.

## Getting There

By car, Clovis is 85 miles (1.5 hours) south from Tucumcari zigzagging on Highway 209; 110 miles (2 hours) northeast from Roswell on U.S. 70, 3.5 hours from Albuquerque, and 2 hours from Lubbock, Texas. Fort Sumner is 60 miles (1 hour) west on U.S. 84.

**Clovis Municipal Airport** (CVN), six miles east of town, receives two flights a day from

the Clovis skyline

Santa Fe on Great Lakes Airlines (800/554-5111, www.greatlakesav.com). **Greyhound** (800/231-2222, www.greyhound.com) stops at Cortez Gas (2207 S. Prince St., 575/762-4584, 9am-5pm Mon.-Sat.); buses come from Las Cruces once a day.

## BLACKWATER DRAW MUSEUM

Midway between Clovis and Portales, the **Blackwater Draw Museum** (42987 U.S. 70, 575/562-2202, 10am-5pm Mon.-Sat., noon-5pm Sun. June-Aug., closed Mon. Sept.-May, $3) shows relics from the "type site" for the ancient culture dubbed Clovis Man, the oldest known culture in the New World—or at least the oldest one that researchers can agree on. Excavations in the late 1940s and early 1950s revealed distinctive fluted spearheads embedded in a mammoth carcass, effectively proving the existence of humans in North America at the end of the last ice age, in roughly 11,300 BC. The site, nearby on Highway 467, is also important because it shows so many layers of occupation: Remnants of the later Folsom Man culture are stacked atop the Clovis points, and early agricultural efforts on top of that. (Your museum admission also gives you access to the site—ask for directions.)

This is all well illustrated in the museum, which explains the logic of archaeology in addition to the ancient history itself. You'll find a reproduction mammoth head—to give an idea of the scale those early hunters were up against—as well as a number of other glass cases illustrating the development of hunting technology in the region. Although the museum is officially shut on Mondays in winter, you may find the door open and the staff inside, tending to their own work but still ready to chat about the exhibits.

## PORTALES

Anchored by Eastern New Mexico University, Portales is also home to some prairie chickens and a whole lot of peanut farmers. The farmland surrounding Portales may produce a mere 30 million pounds of legumes a year—only 1 percent of the nation's peanut crop—but that accounts for 90 percent of the exceptionally tasty red-skinned Valencia variety. Its downtown, fanning out from a deco-goes-West courthouse (look for the cowboy friezes above the windows), is slowly being revitalized, and the most attractive area of town is the campus of dark brick buildings and green lawns in the southwest corner of town. On the 21-mile drive down from Clovis, you might see the biggest tumbleweeds of your trip—just slow down and let 'em roll on by.

### Sights

On the ENMU campus, the **Roosevelt County Museum** (575/562-2592, 8am-noon and 1pm-5pm Mon.-Fri., 10am-4pm Sat., 1pm-4pm Sun., free) is a very manageable size, with some great paintings (see the cowboy's ode to the mountain lion in the main hall) and cool dioramas, along with items from Japan and Peru, donated by well-traveled locals. The museum is at West 2nd Street and University Place. Weekend hours in summer may vary—call ahead. Also

on the campus, upstairs at Golden Library, is the voluminous **Jack Williamson Science Fiction Collection** (8am-5pm Mon.-Fri.), more than a dozen long shelves of sci-fi and fantasy work collected by Williamson, both a fan and author (his lifetime achievement Nebula Award is on display) who happened to live in Portales. Fittingly, the library's style is a bit midcentury space-age—it's a nice place to settle into a low-slung lounge chair and flip through a 1963 Science Fiction back issue.

Equally obscure and similarly impressive, the **Dalley Windmill Collection** (Lime St. at U.S. 70) is the largest private collection in the country, with about 85 of the essential ranch-land machines. At research time, they were in the process of being moved from the Dalleys' front yard (out on East 18th Street, about a mile out of town) to the fairgrounds, on the north edge of town, west of U.S. 70 and the railroad tracks—look for them just past a gas station and Stripes convenience store. And while you're there, you can buy fresh Valencia peanuts at **Borden's** (620 E. Lime St., 575/356-6691,

9am-4:30pm Mon.-Fri.), which has a lot of other locally made snacks as well.

For more of a peanut fix, head two miles northeast of town to **Sunland Peanuts** (42593 U.S. 70, 575/356-6638, 8am-5pm Mon.-Fri.), the area's biggest processing plant. It makes peanut butter and other treats, all available in the gift shop. Visitors are welcome for free tours of the plant (samples included) on Mondays, Wednesdays, and Fridays at 2pm; call ahead to let them know you're interested.

### Festivals and Events

Near the end of October, ENMU and the chamber of commerce sponsor the annual **Peanut Valley Festival** (575/562-2242). It's not *completely* peanut-obsessed, what with distractions like a big craft fair, funnel-cake booths, and the like, but it is a lively time to be in town. In April, birders descend for the **High Plains Lesser Prairie Chicken Festival** (575/762-6997), a get-together of grouse fans to marvel at the birds' mating rituals—it all takes place in nearby Milnesand, which claims to be the Lesser Prairie Chicken Capital of New Mexico.

### Accommodations

Along with a couple of chain hotels, there's **Casa del Sol** (1401 W. 17th St., 575/356-5966, www.casadelsolportales.com, $75 d), an attractive cottonwood-shaded adobe built in the 1940s by architect John Gaw Meem—a lovely outpost of Pueblo Revival style. It has two rooms, one in the main house and another in a more private outbuilding.

### Food

Sample Portales's produce in a deliciously creamy peanut-butter shake at **Pat's Twin Cronnie** (100 N. Chicago Ave., 575/356-5841, 11am-9pm Sun.-Thurs., 11am-10pm Fri.-Sat., $5), where you can also fill up on taquitos, burgers, and chili dogs.

On the plaza, the **Do Drop Inn** (123 S. Main St., 575/226-5282, 7am-7pm Mon.-Thurs., 7am-8pm Fri., 7am-6pm Sat., $6) is a chummy little café that serves supremely gooey

© ZORA O'NEILL

fine specimens from the Dalley Windmill Collection

homemade baked goods and assorted sandwiches. Just across the street, **Roosevelt Brewing Co.** (201 S. Main Ave., 575/226-2739, 11am-9pm Tues.-Thurs. and Sun., 11am-10pm Fri.-Sat., $10) serves a more substantial meal, using local farm products in the timeless combo of wood-oven pizza, house-brewed beer, and killer cupcakes. At research time, the place had been open less than a year, and it still needed to work out some service kinks.

### Information
The **Roosevelt County Chamber of Commerce** (100 S. Ave. A, 575/356-8541, www.portales.com, 8am-5pm Mon.-Fri.) can help you out with maps and brochures.

### Getting There
By car, Portales is 21 miles (20 minutes) southwest of Clovis on U.S. 70; it's about 90 miles (1.5 hours) northeast of Roswell, and 228 miles (3.5 hours) southeast from Albuquerque. **Greyhound** (800/231-2222, www.greyhound.com) drops passengers at

McDonald's (120 W. 1st St.); buses come from Las Cruces once a day.

## TATUM
When you're driving through Tatum, keep an eye on the street signs—the cut-metal silhouettes are the work of **Westcraft Metal Art** (504 W. Broadway, 575/398-5295), which specializes in this decoration that's essential to any well-turned-out ranch gate. You can visit the operation a few blocks west of the main intersection, where the company also sells smaller gift items.

## LOVINGTON
The seat of Lea County, Lovington has a handsome art deco courthouse and tidy streets. The town-operated **Lea County Museum** (103 S. Love St., 575/396-4805, www.leacountymuseum.org, 9am-5pm Tues.-Sat., free), across from the courthouse, contains all the usual pioneer-era items. In addition, one room is dedicated to Western writer Max Evans, who lived until the age of 12 in nearby Humble City, now

© ZORA O'NEILL

**Metal art adorns the streets of Tatum.**

all but vanished (Evans rechristened the place Starvation, Texas, in one of his novels).

If you're hungry in Lovington, hit the **Lazy 6** (102 S. 1st St., 575/396-5066, 10am-2pm Mon.-Fri., $6), where the knickknack-to-customer ratio is 10 to 1, even when the place is packed for lunch. Don't let it distract you from the good home cooking, though. It's one block west of Main Street.

## HOBBS

Yet another oil town with the smell of, shall we say, "money" in the air, Hobbs is just five miles from the Texas border and the largest settlement in Lea County, with more than 40,000 residents. It's a destination only for people working in the industry, students at New Mexico Preparatory College and the College of the Southwest, and fans of gliding—the flat land and empty skies are ideal for delicate sailplanes.

Wild West fanatics will want to pay their respects at the **Western Heritage Museum and Lea County Cowboy Hall of Fame** (5317 Lovington Hwy., 575/392-6730, www.museumshobbsnm.org, 10am-5pm Tues.-Sat., 1pm-5pm Sun., $3), a sleek bit of architecture that renders an oil derrick in green glass. The complex on the north edge of town honors rodeo champions (of which Lea County has a disproportionately high number) and all-around good local citizens. It also gives an interesting overview of the region's history, from dinosaur stomping ground to homesteaded territory to modern source of black gold, first tapped in 1927.

## ARTESIA

To quote the travel cliché, Artesia is a town of contrasts. One of the most discordant views of New Mexico can be had at the junction of U.S. 285 and U.S. 82 in Artesia. Look west and you'll see an attractive, modernized Main Street that boasts an old movie palace, lots of shops, and sturdy old buildings. Look east and you see the state's largest oil refinery, all concrete towers, blinking lights, and plumes of steam and smoke. More practically, Artesia is less than an hour's drive from Carlsbad, and it has two decent hotels—so you could conceivably sleep here, for slightly better value, before or after visiting the caverns. But don't stay here if you're up to no good—Artesia is all about law-abiding behavior, thanks to the presence of a federal law-enforcement training center.

## Sights

If you keep your back to the refinery, you can spend a pleasant hour or two (or more, if you go to a movie), checking out the **Artesia Historical Museum & Art Center** (505 W. Richardson Ave., 575/748-2390, www.artesia-museum.com, 9am-noon and 1pm-5pm Tues.-Fri., 1pm-5pm Sat., free), in a pretty area two blocks south of Main Street.

Larger-than-life bronze statues dot the main drag, including a very cool series of life-size figures in the midst of a cattle-rustling operation, arranged across three intersections.

## Accommodations

**Heritage Inn** (209 W. Main St., 575/748-2552, www.artesiaheritageinn.com, $119 d) is a historic hotel that has been smartly renovated on the points that matter: modern bathrooms and comfy beds. The glitzier **Hotel Artesia** (203 N. 2nd St., 888/746-2066, www.hotelartesia.com, $123 d) looks like it has been beamed in from Miami. The 52 spacious rooms are done in a somewhat generic sleek modern style, with every convenience for business travelers. The lobby lounge is popular after work.

## Food

For caffeine, a slab of German chocolate cake, or a hearty sandwich, head to **The Jahva House** (105 N. 5th St., 575/746-9494, 7am-8pm Mon.-Thurs., 7am-9pm Fri., 10am-4pm Sun., $8), where it's hard to say what is worshiped more: espresso drinks or Jesus. There's a Bible open on the counter, but also an impressively detailed menu of Italian terminology. The groovy marbleized pink sinks in the bathrooms (labeled ADAM and EVE) are so yummy-looking, you'll want an ice-cream sundae as well.

For dinner, pickings are slim. **Piccolino** (201 N. 1st St., 575/748-1100, 10:30am-9pm Mon.-Sat., $11) does passable red-sauce Italian (stick to the pastas), though service can be glacial. Or head to **The Wellhead** brewpub (332 W. Main St., 575/746-0640, 11am-9pm Mon.-Sat., $11) for livelier atmosphere; the menu is pretty standard bar food, though.

## Information

Stop in at the **Artesia Chamber of Commerce** (107 N. 1st St., 575/746-2744, www.artesia-chamber.com, 9am-5pm Mon.-Fri.), in the old train depot for additional info.

# Roswell

Launched into national notoriety in 1947 by an alleged UFO crash (and subsequent government cover-up) on a ranch northwest of town, Roswell has been marked indelibly by the odd events. Popular fascination was renewed with "truth-seeking" exposés in the 1980s, and the town has become a sort of pilgrimage site for true believers and kitsch seekers alike. The city seal sports an alien, the green streetlamps have eyes, and the McDonald's resembles a spaceship about to lift off.

But there's a lot more to this city of 48,000,

the largest metro area in this region. Founded in 1870, it has its roots in ranching, then agriculture, after an artesian well was discovered in 1890; Chaves County is the largest dairy producer in the state. The 1910 courthouse has a tall, green-tiled dome, built by Isaac Hamilton Rapp, who was also instrumental in designing Santa Fe's zoning codes to create a homogenous downtown.

Over the longer term, Roswell has probably been more influenced by the New Mexico Military Institute, established 1891. There's

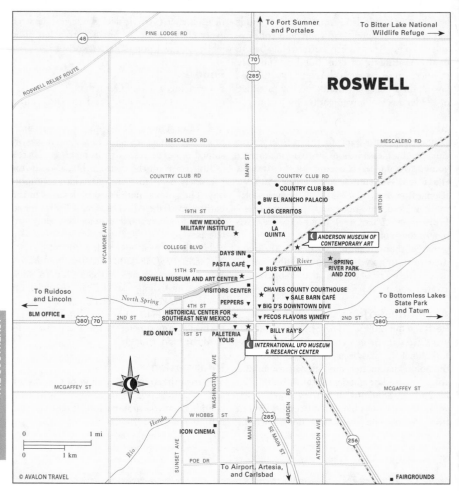

a conservative streak, to the point it's hard to find a bar at night. As if to balance the scales, Roswell has hosted a small clan of contemporary artists every year since the mid-1960s, which has fostered a strong appreciation for the arts and two excellent museums. These disparate elements can keep a visitor entertained for a day or two.

## SIGHTS

The central intersection is at North Main Street (U.S. 285) and West 2nd Street (U.S. 70/380), also the location of the UFO museum. Like debris around a crash site, space-themed gift shops and other attractions dot the surrounding blocks.

### International UFO Museum & Research Center

Most visitors to Roswell make a beeline to the **International UFO Museum & Research Center** (114 N. Main St., 800/822-3545, www. roswellufomuseum.com, 9am-5pm daily, $5), a converted movie theater where the events of

© ZORA O'NEILL

Evidence of alien landings is everywhere in Roswell.

July 1947 are dissected with obsessive care. The museum was founded by two men who were peripherally involved in the incident, and they're occasionally at the front desk, ready to talk shop with anyone who asks. The dense mass of data—newspaper clippings, affidavits, faded photos—is a little overwhelming and presented with a minimum of gloss; an audio tour only heaps on more detail. Related issues such as ancient alien cults, Area 51, abductions, and crop circles get the same thorough documentary treatment.

The mood lightens a bit with a section about Roswell in the movies, and a photo studio where you can have your picture taken being "beamed up." And be sure to press the button for special effects on the central installation of two gawky aliens below a silver disc.

### Roswell Museum and Art Center

The wide-ranging **Roswell Museum and Art Center** (100 W. 11th St., 575/624-6744, www. roswellmuseum.org, 9am-5pm Mon.-Sat., 1pm-5pm Sun., free) is a real treasure. The original gallery space, built in 1937 as a WPA project, is an attraction in itself, with high viga ceilings and tin chandeliers; it contains work by local luminaries like Peter Hurd and Henriette Wyeth, as well as a beautiful collection of Western paraphernalia, such as finely wrought spurs and elaborate beaded deerskin tunics.

The place celebrates science too, with an exhibit on space-flight visionary Robert Goddard, who moved from Massachusetts to Roswell in the 1930s to continue his work on liquid-fueled rockets—his workshop has been re-created, piece by piece, in one room. Adjacent to the main museum, the **Robert H. Goddard Planetarium** (912 N. Main St.), the second-largest in the state, has several public shows a month; call the museum for the schedule.

### ◖ Anderson Museum of Contemporary Art

As good as the Roswell Museum is, it's no match for the 17,000-square-foot **Anderson Museum of Contemporary Art** (409 E. College Blvd., 575/623-5600, www.roswellamoca.org,

## New Mexico's Alien Obsession

In 1947, strange objects were spotted in American skies. First an incident was reported in Washington State, then another in Idaho. When the next one happened, less than a month later, in Roswell, it was all over the press, with stories of a "flying disc," complete with alien crew, crashing on a ranch outside of town. No sooner did journalists descend than stories were revised, the military got involved, and a haze of confusion swirled up around the event.

The military's denial of the event did not squash the story, and soon enough, the United States seemed to be in the grip of a UFO frenzy, as scores of sightings were reported. A 1950 book titled *Behind the Flying Saucers*, by a reporter for *Variety*, Frank Scully, described yet another strange encounter in New Mexico: In March 1948, just nine months after the Roswell incident, the residents of Aztec, near Farmington, apparently had a similar occurrence in their own backyard—although no one actually saw the disc in the sky or at the crash site, as all but a scrap had been whisked away by the military. In fact, Scully was the first to investigate the crash, when he was in the area looking into the "Farmington Armada" spotted earlier in the year.

Two years later, it came out that the spaceship wreckage Scully had seen was actually the work of Silas Newton and Leo Gebauer, who had been seeking investors in their device for finding oil. The crash had been their backstory for the alien technology that allegedly drove their gadget, and they hoped to secure investors in their scheme. The two con men were convicted of fraud in 1953.

That didn't stop UFO enthusiasts from reviving the Aztec story in the 1980s, along with the Roswell incident, which became the subject of fresh fascination. Now both towns have a respectable alien-inspired tourism industry. The general perception in New Mexico toward these and other events (such as the creepy cattle mutilations in the 1970s, and not-uncommon tales of alien abductions) is not one of feverish conviction, nor of outright dismissal. It's more an attitude of resigned acceptance—as if the UFOs are just one more weird happening in a very weird state.

9am-4pm Mon.-Fri., 1pm-5pm Sat.-Sun., free), an invigorating collection from the past four decades, in media ranging from oil paintings to wood inlay. The works on view are representative samples from an artist-in-residence program established in 1967 by oilman Donald Anderson. Since then it has hosted luminaries like abstract expressionist Milton Resnick and sculptor Luís Jiménez (best known for his *Blue Mustang* outside the Denver airport), along with scores of others still working and developing their reputations.

In the museum, many of the products of the "gift of time" (as the foundation calls the residency) are set alongside photos of the artists, posing as a group or relaxing with their families in the compound they're granted on the fringes of town—a sort of yearbook photo, which also pegs the art to a certain period. It's an unorthodox approach (as is the way pieces are hung, packed in close and covering nearly every surface), and it lends an exuberance to the place that's hard to resist, even if you're not generally a fan of contemporary artwork.

### General Douglas L. McBride Military Museum

A visit to this array of military paraphernalia, the **General Douglas L. McBride Military Museum** (800/421-5376, www.nmmi.edu/museum, 8am-4pm Mon.-Fri., free) is more an excuse to get inside the giant fortress that is the New Mexico Military Institute, on North Main Street at College Boulevard. The main building and master plan was designed by I. H. and W. M. Rapp, who also did the courthouse. The institution has about 1,000 high school students from all over the country, and alumni include newscaster Sam Donaldson, hotelier Conrad Hilton, historian Paul Horgan, painter Peter Hurd, actor Owen Wilson, and even Miss New Mexico 2001. The entrance to the museum is in the back of the main building; head west on College, then turn right on Kentucky, then through the gates at Duty Street.

## Historical Center for Southeast New Mexico
The trials of pioneer living are detailed at the **Historical Center for Southeast New Mexico** (200 N. Lea Ave., 575/622-8333, www.hssnm. net, 1pm-4pm daily, free), a 1910 Prairie-style brick bungalow filled with period furniture and mannequins. You can pick up a brochure for a walking tour around Roswell's other historic houses, in a variety of styles.

## ENTERTAINMENT AND EVENTS
You're lucky to find even a restaurant open past 8pm in Roswell, much less a bar. The city lets loose for a couple of annual parties, though. **Icon Cinema** (900 W. Hobbs St., 575/208-2810, www.iconcinemas.com) is a four-screen theater on the south side of town. Given the limited nightlife in Roswell, it's usually pretty packed.

### Nightlife
**Billy Ray's** (118 E. 3rd St., 575/627-0997, 11am-midnight Tues.-Sat.) has a decent scene, with popular karaoke, and live music on the weekends.

You can sample wine from many of the state's best producers at **Pecos Flavors Winery** (305 N. Main St., 575/627-6265, 10am-7pm Mon.-Thurs., 10am-8pm Sat.-Sun.), though the tasting bar shuts at 5pm. Thanks to a handsome antique wood bar and a convivial atmosphere, this feels more like a town hangout than a formal tasting room, and it's a nice place to put your feet up after walking around downtown. It also stocks other local bounty, such as salsas and pistachios, and occasionally hosts live music in the evenings.

## Festivals and Events
The town dedicates Fourth of July weekend to visitors from space, as well as around the world, for the **Roswell UFO Festival** (www.ufofestivalroswell.com), which melds serious science with all the geekiness of a *Star Trek* convention. More than 50,000 space fans gather for an alien costume contest, screenings of vintage sci-fi films, a nighttime disc-golf tourney, and lectures by scientists and assorted actors. By contrast, the **Eastern New Mexico State Fair & Parade** (575/623-9411, www.enmsf.com), at the fairgrounds on the southeast side of town in early October, seems pretty mundane.

## SPORTS AND RECREATION
A big park in town caters to kids, while a state park to the east offers a few opportunities for swimming and mountain biking. Overall, though, the flat terrain around Roswell doesn't lend itself to exciting outdoors activities. The **BLM Roswell field office** (2909 W. 2nd St., 575/627-0272, 8am-4:30pm Mon.-Fri.), on the far west edge of town, is the contact point for questions about nearby public lands.

### Spring River Park and Zoo
Like many small-town zoos, the animal component of **Spring River Park and Zoo** (1306 E. College Blvd., 575/624-6760, 10am-8pm daily in summer, 10am-5:30pm daily in winter, free) might be a little distressing—although the massive prairie dog village (allegedly the largest in the state) is always a crowd-pleaser, and there's a fishing hole just for kids. And the 1926 carousel costs just a quarter, as does the miniature train that loops around the grounds. The park is the head of the **Spring River Trail,** a five-mile paved route to the town golf course.

### Bottomless Lakes State Park
The pools at **Bottomless Lakes State Park** (575/624-6058, www.nmparks.com, $5/car) just east of Roswell are a rare phenomenon in New Mexico. Like the Blue Hole in Santa Rosa, they began as water-filled caverns, then the ceilings collapsed. Lea Lake, the deepest and largest of the pools here, plunges 90 feet. It's

also the only lake open for swimming and diving, but it's a pretty small patch of water for the crowds that descend on it in the summertime.

There's tent **camping** at Cottonwood Lake, adjacent to the park office. (If you're interested in archaeology, ask here for directions to **Garnsey Arroyo,** a barely excavated bison "kill site" from about 500 years ago.) You'll find RV camping farther down the access road at Lea Lake.

**Skidmarks Trail,** good for biking or hiking, runs for a little more than three miles over some of the limestone bluffs on the north edge of the park area. Wildflowers bloom here in the spring, and you'll see lots of water birds. Look for the trailhead just as you turn onto the loop road around the park (if you get to Lazy Lagoon, you've gone too far).

To reach the park, head east of Roswell 12 miles on U.S. 380, then turn south on Bottomless Lakes Road, which loops around the lakes after about 3 miles.

### Bitter Lake National Wildlife Refuge

Established in 1937, the **Bitter Lake National Wildlife Refuge** (4067 Bitter Lakes Rd., 575/622-6755) encompasses nearly 25,000 acres of grasslands, dunes, and wetlands around the Pecos River. As at Bottomless Lakes, there are a number of freshwater sinkholes. The area is great for birding, as well as for spotting more than 90 species of colorful dragonflies and damselflies, best viewed in late summer. There's even a **Dragonfly Festival** in early September. To reach the refuge headquarters, from North Main Street (U.S. 70/285), turn onto East Pine Lodge Road east and follow it until it turns into Bitter Lakes Road and runs into the park. The visitors center is open weekdays only.

## ACCOMMODATIONS

Most of the motels are along the northern section of Main Street (U.S. 70/285); unfortunately, aside from one B&B, the only respectable options are national chains, all typically priced at $100 and up.

### Under $100

Of the chains, the **Best Western El Rancho Palacio** (2205 N. Main St., 575/622-2721, www.bestwestern.com, $76 d) almost always can be booked for under $100. "Palace" may be stretching it, but the rooms, which open onto exterior hallways, are in good shape and fairly modern feeling; those upstairs have nice higher ceilings. Breakfast is included, and there's an outdoor pool.

For about the same price, the **Days Inn** (1310 N. Main St., 575/623-4021, www.daysinn.com, $76 d) is admittedly not quite as sturdy-feeling; walls and ceilings are a bit thin, breakfast is skimpier, and the pool is smaller. But it is well kept, and it's located a bit closer to the center of town, so a good option if you prefer to walk around, rather than drive.

### $100-150

The one B&B in town, **Country Club Bed & Breakfast** (400 E. Country Club Rd., 575/624-1794, www.countryclubbnb.com) occupies a beautiful Victorian house on the far north side of town. There are just two rooms, one with a full bed ($85) and the other with a queen ($102), but they're furnished nicely, without too much lace; bathrooms are on the small side, though.

## FOOD
### American

The one tragedy of ⬛ **Big D's Downtown Dive** (505 N. Main St., 575/627-0776, 11am-9pm Mon.-Fri., $7) is that it's only open on weekdays. Don't be fooled by the name, the casual order-at-the-counter setup, and the walls covered with New Mexico license plates. This is no dive at all, but a gourmet operation in fast-food disguise. "Bergs" (burgers) have toppings like sautéed mushrooms and sherry mayonnaise, salads burst with goodies like toasted pine nuts, the waffle fries are sprinkled with garlic, and even the water is laced with cucumber and lime.

### Italian

As one of the few places serving on a Sunday

night, **Pasta Café** (1208 N. Main St., 575/624-1111, 11am-9:30pm Sun.-Thurs., 11am-10:30pm Fri.-Sat., $13) does solid Italian. Despite the name, the place is a bit more formal than a café, and the menu's not just pasta—it also has well-executed favorites like a delectably light eggplant Parmesan.

## Mexican

A nice dose of Mexico can be had at the **Red Onion** (1400 W. 2nd St., 575/622-3232, 7am-8pm Tues.-Sat., 7am-3pm Sun.-Mon., $7) transports you to Mexico for breakfast or lunch, with big platters of *migas* (scrambled eggs with tortilla bits mixed in) and other standards, with Jarritos sodas to wash it down. It also has a surprisingly appetizing lunch buffet 11am-2pm. Look for it in a half-empty strip mall a bit out of the center on the west side.

**Los Cerritos** (2103 N. Main St., 575/622-4919, 7am-9pm Mon.-Sat., 7am-5pm Sun., $9) is more mainstream mash-up Mexican. The place has all the interior charm of a Denny's, but it does great fresh tableside guacamole and giant refreshing *micheladas* (beer, spicy tomato juice, and lime). On Tuesday evenings, crispy tacos are only $0.50 each.

## New Mexican

Both a meal and a sightseeing opportunity, the **Sale Barn Café** (900 N. Garden St., 575/622-1279, 7am-2pm Mon.-Thurs., 9am-2pm Fri., $7) sits alongside the Roswell Livestock Auction. If you go on a Monday morning, you can watch cattle get sold off, which will either improve or kill your appetite, depending on your outlook. The menu is straight-up diner-style New Mexican, plus a tasty pecan crumble, and an excellent cross-section of characters. On Mondays, closing time is really whenever the auctions end.

**Peppers** (500 N. Main St., 575/623-1700, 11am-10pm Mon.-Sat., $10) is one of the most popular restaurants in town. It feels a bit like a family-owned Chili's, with an all-over-the-place menu. It's strongest on meat, from fajitas

to baby-back ribs, but there's also a good vegetarian burrito and some other solid New Mexican dishes. Wash it all down with a microbrew and get a seat on the patio if you can.

## Dessert

For afternoon refreshment, head to **◖Paleteria Yolis** (510 W. 2nd St., 11am-9pm daily, $2) for a fresh-fruit ice pop or other cold treat. The place feels straight out of Mexico in the best possible way, from the sparkling pink-and-white decor to the case full of flavors like tamarind and *fresas con crema* (strawberries and cream). For a taste sensation, go for a *mango-neada*, mango sorbet doused in sweet-tart-hot sauce and chile. Everything's made fresh (and translated into English).

## INFORMATION AND SERVICES

The **Roswell Convention & Visitors Bureau** (912 N. Main St., 575/624-7704, www.seeroswell.com, 8:30am-5pm Mon.-Fri., 8:30am-4pm Sat., 8:30am-3pm Sun.) has info on all parts of the state and free wireless Internet access.

## GETTING THERE AND AROUND

By car, Roswell is 40 miles (40 minutes) north of Artesia on Highway 285, 185 miles (3.25 hours) northeast of Las Cruces via Highways 54 and 70, and 200 miles (3 hours) southeast of Albuquerque. **American Airlines** (800/443-7300, www.aa.com) operates two flights daily, sometimes more, from Dallas to Roswell (ROW). The airport is five miles south of town. **Greyhound** (800/231-2222, www.greyhound.com) runs one bus a day from Las Cruces to the station (1100 N. Virginia Ave., 575/622-2510, 8am-4pm Mon.-Fri., 11:30am-3:30pm Sat.).

In town, Roswell has a surprisingly good bus system, **Pecos Trails Transit** (575/624-6766, www.roswell-nm.gov). The most useful bus for visitors is no. 1, which runs up and down Main Street roughly every half hour; the no. 2 bus runs west along 2nd Street. Fare is $0.75.

# Carlsbad

Tourists rarely hear the word Carlsbad without "caverns" tacked on the end, which means that few people come to see the town itself (the national park is 30 miles farther south on U.S. 62/180). But the place is pleasant, thanks to an orderly plan laid out in 1888 and the Pecos River rolling through in a broad ribbon.

Shaded with old trees, the river makes a great place to swim in the summer. You'll be excused if you make a beeline for the caves, though.

## SIGHTS

Canal Street is the big north-south route now, but the historic main drag was Canyon Street,

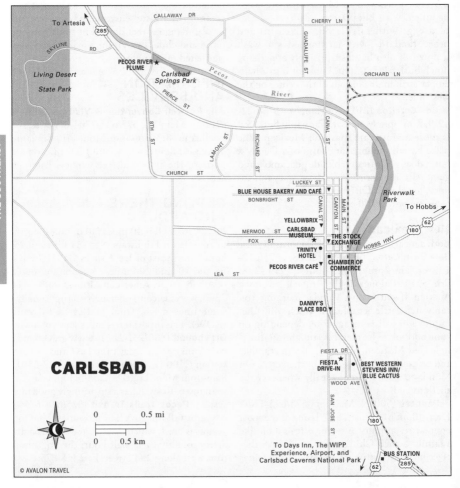

which still has a few cute shops, galleries, and antiques stores, as well as a Pueblo Revival-style courthouse, its front door bordered with cattle brands. The Pecos River glides along the east side. On the north edge of town, the **Pecos River Flume** brings irrigation water to farm plots, erected in wood in 1890 then rebuilt more permanently in 1903; it was the largest concrete structure in the world at the time.

## Carlsbad Museum & Art Center

The town's **Carlsbad Museum & Art Center** (418 W. Fox St., 575/887-0276, 10am-5pm Mon.-Sat., free) holds a small trove of excellent Southwestern art, including some beautiful pieces by Ernest Blumenschein and other early Taos painters. There are also a few early photographs of the caverns, a real stagecoach, and lots of pottery.

## Living Desert State Park

Immediately north of Carlsbad, off U.S. 285, the zoo and gardens at **Living Desert State Park** (1504 Miehls Dr. N., 575/887-5516, www.nmparks.com, 8am-5pm daily June-Aug., 9am-5pm daily Sept.-May, $5) is a great place to familiarize yourself with the area habitat. Planted with endemic cactus, grasses, and yucca, the place also keeps a few rescued native animals in cages, so you can get an up-close look at elk, peccary, and even bobcats and a black bear with a penchant for painting. Last entrance is 3:30pm.

## ENTERTAINMENT AND EVENTS

In the summer, hit the drive-in; in the winter, cruise the Pecos.

### Nightlife

The three-screen **Fiesta Drive-In** (401 W. Fiesta Dr., 575/885-4126, www.fiestadrivein.com) still draws crowds to first-run movies year-round. Fully renovated in 2004, it's high-tech for an outdoor cinema, and the concessions stand includes burgers and fries, in addition to the usual popcorn and candy.

As for bars, **Trinity Hotel** (201 S. Canal St.,

575/234-9891, 5pm-10pm Mon.-Sat.) is a popular gathering place, with a long wood bar in a high-ceiling room. Only beer, wine (most from around New Mexico), and faux cocktails are served, but there's a good selection of snacks to go alongside. For a rowdier night out, the **Blue Cactus Lounge** (1829 S. Canal St., 575/887-2851), in the Best Western Stevens Inn, is the place to go for occasional live music, and an illuminating cross-section of Carlsbadians.

### Festivals and Events

If you're in Carlsbad in the winter, don't miss **Christmas on the Pecos** (575/887-6516, www.christmasonthepecos.com, $12.50 Sun.-Thurs., $17.50 Fri.-Sat.), an extravaganza of twinkling lights, leaping reindeer, and even glowing margarita glasses all strung across more than a hundred homes on either side of the river. You view the spectacle from a pontoon boat gliding along the water; the whole ride takes about an hour. The city has obligingly extended the "Christmas" season from Thanksgiving to New Year's Eve, and you should book tickets in advance, especially on weekends.

## SPORTS AND RECREATION

Essential when the temperature climbs above 90°F in the summer, Carlsbad offers a number of ways to cool off.

### Pecos River

The great **Beach Recreation Area,** at the end of Church Street, is essentially the city's public pool, with protected swimming areas, a little island for diving, and even a few palm trees and seagulls (migrants from the Gulf of Mexico), which lend a beachfront feel. With **Carlsbad Cruise Lines** (800/976-3021, www.carlsbadcruises.com), you can rent pedal boats ($10/30 minutes) and kayaks ($12/hour) or take an hour-long cruise on a pontoon boat ($6). A **river walk** runs 4.5 miles along the water on both banks.

### Sitting Bull Falls

West of town, the 130-foot cascade of **Sitting Bull Falls** (noon-6pm Fri.-Mon., Apr.-Sept.,

© ZORA O'NEILL

the Pecos River in Carlsbad

THE SOUTHEAST

noon-5pm Fri.-Mon. Oct.-Mar., $5/car) is a nice spot for an easy hike on a paved path, a picnic, and a dip in the small, icy pool. Sixteen miles of dirt trails also wind through the area. Look for the turn 12 miles north of town, onto Highway 137. The drive takes about 45 minutes.

## ACCOMMODATIONS

The lodging situation in Carlsbad is dispiriting. Hotels have a captive clientele in the half-million visitors to the caverns every year, and prices reflect that—there is no decent room here under $100, and many hideous rooms go for $150 or so. Moreover, with one exception, none of the independents can be recommended. Just about all hotels are on the southern end of Canal Street and its continuation, National Parks Highway (U.S. 62/180), for an easy start on the drive to the caverns. You might consider staying up the highway in Artesia—although you'll have to allot an extra hour's driving time.

The **Best Western Stevens Inn Carlsbad** (1829 S. Canal St., 575/887-2851, www.

bestwestern.com, $137 d) is a warren of 220 rooms, and maintenance isn't airtight, but overall it's reliable. There's a small pool on the premises.

**Days Inn** (3910 National Parks Hwy., 575/887-7800, $148 d) has everything you need, including cushy beds and an indoor pool. Bathrooms are small but clean, and everything's very well kept up. Rates include a basic continental breakfast.

A bright spot in Carlsbad's dreary hotel scene, **❰ Trinity Hotel & Suites** (201 S. Canal St., 575/234-9891, www.thetrinityhotel.com, $169 s) occupies a stately old bank building downtown. It is the most expensive place in town, but not by much, and it's vastly nicer than anywhere else. Within the historic setting, rooms are thoroughly modern, with sleek black furniture and all the tech trimmings, set under stately high ceilings and other grand old details. Upstairs rooms are preferable; the first-floor ones have large windows facing the street, so you need to keep the drapes shut for privacy. Also, the place is really designed for couples: Only two of the nine rooms have more than one bed.

## FOOD

As with hotels, Carlsbad isn't bursting with choice, and the best options are open only for lunch. Most places are on or very near Canal Street.

### Breakfast and Lunch

Good for a quick coffee and morning pastry, or for a more leisurely meal in the yard, the **❰ Blue House Bakery & Café** (609 N. Canyon St., 575/628-0555, 6am-noon Mon.-Sat., $7) is relaxing and comfortable, tucked away in a residential area. The menu ranges from home-made granola to daily soups and sandwiches.

**Pecos River Café** (409 S. Canal St., 575/887-8882, 6:30am-2pm Mon.-Fri., $8) is better than its architecture (a former Pizza Hut) might suggest. Thanks to its spicy green-chile enchiladas and other New Mexican platters, and its killer cinnamon rolls, it gets packed; try to avoid the noon lunch rush.

## Hot Rocks in Carlsbad

When many New Mexicans think of Carlsbad, they think of an entirely different sort of cave from the ones preserved in the national park here. More than 2,000 feet below ground is a vast, deep salt bed into which 15 miles of storage halls have been carved. This is the Waste Isolation Pilot Plant, a nuclear waste dump just east of town, south of the highway to Hobbs.

Bitterly fought from the day it was proposed in 1979 until after it opened in 1999, the site became a symbol of a sort of New Mexican fatalism. Judging from decades of prior oafishness, corner-cutting, and corruption, most people believed New Mexican leaders were just too incompetent to pull off such a tricky, potentially dangerous operation.

Fortunately, over more than a decade in operation, WIPP hasn't seen any major glitches. It helps that the salt caves are meant to contain low-level waste, such as contaminated lab suits and rubber gloves from Los Alamos National Labs. But because the site has been deemed a success, Governor Martinez has called for testing whether the site can also hold higher level, "hot" material—in part to compensate for the closure of the Yucca Mountain site in Nevada. The idea has geologists and state residents worried that this could cause leaks in the facility—but many local residents support an expansion of WIPP, for the jobs it will offer.

While this debate rages, the Department of Energy office hosts a chipper little exhibit about the current operation, **The WIPP Experience** (4021 National Parks Hwy., 800/336-9477, 8am-4:30pm daily, free), which involves a video and (yippee) free salt samples.

## Barbecue

The eponymous owner of ( **Danny's Place BBQ** (902 S. Canal St., 575/885-8739, 11am-9pm Wed.-Mon., $10) is obsessive, in a good way. He earned a reputation for quality 'cue while operating a pit off the side of the Dairy Queen he managed. Now on his own, he keeps not much more on the menu than smoked meat in a sweet-hot sauce (though the meat's so succulent, it's fine plain). There are the usual sides, including some great bacon-y pinto beans.

## Fine Dining

For a slightly dressed-up dinner scene, the **Trinity Hotel Restaurant** (201 S. Canal St., 575/234-9891, 7am-1:45pm and 5pm-9pm Mon.-Sat., $16) has a familiar menu of pastas and steaks at dinner, and a mix of sandwiches for lunch. It doesn't break any new ground, but it's better than a chain restaurant, and the split-level, wood-floor dining room is elegant and buzzing with conversation. Breakfast is also good, with fresh pastries and sun shining in through the big front windows. There's a free New Mexico wine tasting daily (3pm-7pm).

**The Stock Exchange** (220 W. Fox St., 575/725-5444, 5pm-9pm Tues.-Sat., $18) is a family-friendly steak house that treads a nice line between fancy (dark tablecloths and wood; less-than-standard sides such as sweet potato fries or salted watermelon) and totally laid-back (doughnuts for dessert!). And despite the goofy name, the "Healthy Woman" steak, in a reasonable six-ounce serving, is a welcome option. The price is nice too.

Set in a butter-yellow craftsman bungalow, **Yellowbrix** (201 N. Canal St., 575/941-2749, 11am-2:30pm and 5pm-9pm Sun.-Thurs., 5pm-10pm Fri.-Sat., $9) is Carlsbad's toniest lunch spot, with dishes like French onion soup and poached-pear salad. At night, it aspires to fine dining, which isn't particularly inspired or worth the money ($23 or so for mains)—but there's a good $13 green-chile cheeseburger on the menu, which is a fine excuse to sit out on the front patio.

THE SOUTHEAST

## INFORMATION AND SERVICES

Stop in at the **Carlsbad Chamber of Commerce** (302 S. Canal St., 575/887-6516, www.carlsbadchamber.com, 9am-5pm Mon., 8am-5pm Tues.-Fri.) for a visitors guide and a detailed map.

## GETTING THERE

By car, Carlsbad is 37 miles (40 minutes) south of Artesia on Highway 285, and 207 miles (3.5 hours) east of Las Cruces by the fastest route, I-10 south to Highways 180/62 east via El Paso, Texas (165 miles; 3 hours). From Albuquerque, it's 275 miles (4.25 hours). **Greyhound** (800/231-2222, www.greyhound.com) buses come through from El Paso, Texas, once a day, stopping at Food Jet (3102 National Parks Hwy., 575/628-0768, 5am-midnight daily).

**New Mexico Airlines** (888/564-6119, www.flynma.com) flies in to Carlsbad airport (CNM) from Albuquerque, on two flights daily. The airport is south of town on U.S. 62/180.

# Carlsbad Caverns National Park

One of the country's most awesome natural wonders, Carlsbad Caverns is mesmerizing, even in a two-hour stroll around the biggest cavern. But you could easily spend days here (your entrance ticket is good for three days) visiting ever more obscure underground worlds. The desert scenery around the caverns was severely damaged in a wildfire in 2011, and is still recovering—scenic drives through the area can't really be recommended.

## VISTING THE PARK

The park is 23 miles south of the town of Carlsbad and seven miles in on a winding access road. In prime conditions, it takes about 45 minutes to get to the **visitors center** (727 Carlsbad Caverns Hwy., 575/785-3137, www.nps.gov/cave, 8am-7pm daily June-Aug., 8am-5pm daily Sept.-May, $6). In the peak summer months, allow an extra hour's waiting time at the visitors center. Probably the best time to go is in December, before the holidays, or in January and February, because you'll have the whole place to yourself, in near ghostly silence. One summer treat: Hundreds of thousands of bats fly out every evening, and the 56°F temperature underground is a treat.

Always pack a sweater, no matter how hot it is outside, and wear sturdy shoes, even if you're only going on the main self-guided tours. You might want to pack a lunch too, as the cafeteria at the caverns is pretty institutional. Fill your gas tank in Carlsbad, as once you head south you're at the mercy of one pricey station in White's City.

## The Big Room

The basic entrance ticket gives you access to two major parts of the cave: the **Natural Entrance Trail** (last entrance 3:30pm daily June-Aug., 2pm daily Sept.-May), which descends about 800 feet in the course of a mile, on a paved trail dense with switchbacks, and **The Big Room** (last entrance 5pm daily June-Aug., 3:30pm daily Sept.-May), the largest cave in the Carlsbad complex. If you don't want to hike down, an elevator will whisk you 754 feet down to the cavern floor. Instead of floors, the display panel shows 50-foot increments. The 1.5-hour walk down is preferable if you have time, as it gives you a better sense of what it must have been like for cowboy Jim White to first explore this place in the early 20th century. It also gives an idea of the scale you'll be dealing with once you get underground—at one point, you have to hike for about 30 minutes around Iceberg Rock, a 200,000-ton boulder.

The Big Room is lit in tasteful white lights and glows like a natural cathedral: The ceiling soars up into the dark, and the space is 1.25 miles long. If you think of caves as claustrophobia-inducing, this one will change your mind.

## Guided Tours in Carlsbad Caverns

| TOUR | Cost | Duration | Length | Age Limit | Schedule |
|------|------|----------|--------|-----------|----------|
| King's Palace | $8 | 1.5 hours | 1 mile | 4 and up | 10am and 1pm daily |
| Left Hand Tunnel | $7 | 2 hours | 0.5 mile | 6 and up | 9am daily |
| Lower Cave | $20 | 3 hours | 1 mile, plus 60-ft descent on rope ladders | 12 and up | 1pm Mon.-Fri. |
| Slaughter Canyon Cave | $15 | 5.5 hours, including driving time | 1.75 miles, including steep 0.5-mile hike to entrance | 8 and up | Summer: 8:30am Fri.-Sun.; Winter: 8:30am Sat.-Sun. |
| Hall of the White Giant | $20 | 4 hours | 1 mile, very strenuous | 12 and up | 1pm Sat. |
| Spider Cave | $20 | 4 hours | 1 mile, very strenuous | 12 and up | 1pm Sun. |

(But it's not all natural—there's still a snack bar down on the cave floor, as well as restrooms, discreetly hidden behind rock formations.)

Scientists theorize that The Big Room—and many of the other caverns in this network—began to form more than 20 million years ago, as the petroleum deposits under the Guadalupe Mountains reacted with groundwater to create sulfuric acid, which ate through the stone to form vast hollow spots under the ground. These spaces started to fill with stalagmites and stalactites about 500,000 years ago, and now the intricate formations—still growing in some spots—range from hulking towers that ripple like clay to delicate needles that look more like icicles than stone.

For both routes, you can rent an **audio tour** for $5—it includes some interesting information, but don't get too caught up in listening to every entry. It's just as rewarding to let your imagination roam.

### Ranger-Led Tours

These small-group side tours are an alternative to the crowds in the Big Room. You get a little more quiet and, of course, see a lot more of the caverns. Try to decide on tours before you arrive and make reservations (877/444-6777, www.recreation.gov). Note that if you'd like to see more once you're down in the Big Room, you have to come back up to the surface to buy the extra ticket.

The easiest addition to your itinerary, **King's Palace** is the deepest part of the caves open to the public. Limited to 75 participants, the tour passes giant formations as well as tiny details such as a bat's skeleton grown into a stalagmite. Best of all, it includes a few minutes with the lights turned off, when you get to stand in the cool, smothering black. Unlike all the other ranger-led tours, the trail is paved and not particularly steep except at the entrance.

**Left Hand Tunnel** is best for a sheer sense of discovery. On the trek, limited to 15 people, you carry just a flickering lantern through fantastic rock formations—made all the more bizarre as they loom up out of the darkness. **Lower Cave** requires a bit more exertion, starting with a clamber down 50 feet of rope and narrow ladders. The formations here include

© PETERM / 123RF.COM

Carlsbad Caverns National Park

toothpick-like stalactites and the perfectly round and white formations called "cave pearls."

**Slaughter Canyon Cave** is the only spot not accessible through the visitors center. Instead, you have to drive five miles south of White's City, then turn west onto a well-signed county road; there's also a steep hike to the entrance. Once in the cave, though, the walk isn't too difficult and it goes past formations like the glittering, crystal-covered column dubbed the Christmas Tree.

Finally, for people who aren't afraid of tight spaces, **Hall of the White Giant** and **Spider Cave** are strenuous but rewarding trips. Each one takes about four hours, and you have to bring batteries and gloves (the rangers provide headlamps and helmets). Expect to wiggle through some very narrow tunnels and get muddy in the process.

### Special Events

From late May through mid-October, hundreds of thousands of bats rush out from the depths of the caverns and into the bug-filled twilight. Half an hour before sunset at an amphitheater at the top of the Natural Entrance Trail, rangers give a short talk about the bats (ask at the visitors center or call 575/785-3012 for times). When the **Bat Flight** begins, you hear the soft flapping of their wings and feel the rush of air as they pass overhead. If you're an early riser, you can also come at dawn (well before the visitors center is open) to see the bats return.

Most are of the Brazilian free-tail variety, which migrate to Mexico in the winter. Another group of larger cave *Myotis* live in the Lake of the Clouds, the deepest point in the cave system; they too come out every night, and if you're at the underground cafeteria near closing time, you might feel them whir through. Whether you're underground or at the amphitheater, keep your camera stowed—the flash and auto-focus devices disorient the animals.

Throughout the summer, the park also hosts monthly **Star Party** (www.nps.gov/cave) events, with rangers on hand with telescopes.

## WHITE'S CITY

This so-called town at the junction of U.S. 62/180 and Highway 7 is an unreconstructed tourist trap—there's a bad restaurant, two hopelessly dumpy hotels, a wildly overpriced gas station, and a junk-filled gift shop. Blindfold your kids as you drive past the giant waterslide (for hotel guests only), or you'll never hear the end of it. The **Greyhound** bus can be prevailed upon to pull up here, though it's not a regularly scheduled stop.

## GUADALUPE MOUNTAINS NATIONAL PARK

Adjacent to the caverns land and just over the border in Texas, **Guadalupe Mountains National Park** (915/828-3251, www.nps.gov/gumo, $5) is mentioned here because it's where people usually camp ($8) when visiting Carlsbad Caverns. The largest area, with both tent and RV sites (but no hookups), is **Pine Springs Campground,** near the visitors center, about 35 miles south of White's City on U.S. 62/180.

You can also hike the exceptionally scenic **McKittrick Canyon,** where a 6.8-mile out-and-back trail leads through a narrow limestone canyon thick with deciduous trees—truly stunning in late October, when the leaves turn, though often crowded. The park also encompasses **Salt Basin Dunes,** a glittering landscape similar to White Sands National Monument, but more isolated.

# Cloudcroft

The closest mountains to the Texas flatlands, the Sacramentos have drawn vacationers with a drawl since 1899, when a local railroad man built a resort at Cloudcroft, now accessible by U.S. 82 due west of Artesia. The village is still barely more than a cluster of rustic cabins and a few gift shops—but the view, looking down as far as White Sands, is majestic, especially when the clouds are gathering below you. The view straight up is great too—hence the location of a major solar observatory nearby.

## SIGHTS

The main street in town is Burro Avenue, just north of U.S. 82—here's where you'll find a row of Old West-style false-front buildings along a wooden boardwalk.

### Sacramento Mountains Historical Museum

Across the street from the chamber of commerce, the local **Sacramento Mountains Historical Museum** (U.S. 82, 575/682-2932, www.cloudcroftmuseum.com, 10am-4pm Mon.-Tues. and Fri.-Sat., 1pm-4pm Sun. in

© ZORA O'NEILL

Burro Avenue, Cloudcroft's Old West-style main street

summer, 10am-4pm Fri.-Sat., 1pm-4pm Sun. in winter, $5) is the usual assortment of memorabilia from the past, plus a "pioneer village" made up of several old log cabins, furnished with antique tools and furniture.

## Sunspot

Sixteen miles south of Cloudcroft on Highway 6563 (named for the wavelength of the orange-red light we associate with images of the sun; most people call it Sunspot Highway), **Sunspot National Solar Observatory** and privately owned Apache Point Observatory take advantage of the high altitude and clear skies to spy on deep space. The Sunspot **visitors center** (575/434-7190, 9am-5pm daily Mar.-Jan.) explains how the telescopes work, but ideally, join the guided tour on Saturdays and Sundays in summer, at 2pm.

Even if you're not interested in the science side, the highway is a pretty drive, with dramatic vistas down to White Sands, and you'll pass **Karr Canyon,** another nice place for a picnic. Look for signs en route labeled with the names of planets—they're placed along the road according to their relative distance to one another, at a scale of 1:250 million.

## SPORTS AND RECREATION

Cloudcroft has a lot to do year-round. As long as you're adjusted to the altitude, the hiking trails are not too strenuous. Check current conditions with the **Sacramento Ranger District office** (4 Lost Lodge Rd., 575/682-2551, 8am-4:30pm Mon.-Fri., plus 9am-2:30pm Sat. in summer), one mile up Highway 130 toward the Sunspot Highway.

### Hiking

The old railroad that used to zigzag up the mountain is gone, but the rail bed makes for excellent hiking on the well-maintained 11-mile **Cloud-Climbing Rail Trail.** The **Mexican Canyon Loop** is probably the best introduction—it's just 2.5 miles and leads to the picturesque (and vertigo-inducing) Mexican Canyon Trestle, built in 1899. The trail

starts on the west edge of town, off the south side of the road, by a replica of the original train depot. For a map on the rest of the rails-to-trails network, stop in at the chamber of commerce.

Another popular route is **Osha Trail** (no. 10), maintained by the National Forest Service. It runs three miles through relatively level, shaded forest that's especially pretty when the leaves change in the fall. The trailhead is on the opposite side of the road from the Mexican Canyon trestle.

### Mountain Biking

The 28-mile **Rim Trail** is legendary for its amazing views as it winds along the spine of the mountains, roughly parallel to Sunspot Highway (Hwy. 6563). It climbs about a thousand feet over the course of the whole ride, though it has some zippy downhill sections, as well as some jarring rocky terrain. Only the first 13 or so miles are official Forest Service trail (no. 105), but it runs all the way to Sunspot, then down to Forest Road 90 to the southeast. You can cut in at the observatory and take the paved road back downhill. The trailhead is just off Highway 6563—look for parking on the right side almost immediately after you make the turn from Highway 130.

A handful of other loop trails start in town and nearby. Stop in at the chamber of commerce or the exceptionally helpful **High Altitude Outfitters** (310 Burro Ave., 575/682-1229, 10am-5:30pm Mon.-Thurs., 10am-6pm Fri.-Sat.), a shop that also organizes a race every April, for maps and other guidance.

### Winter Sports

Two miles east of town on U.S. 82, **Ski Cloudcroft** (575/682-2333, www.skicloudcroft.net, $35 full-day lift ticket), has modest ski runs as well as a tubing area. There's more reliable fun in town, at **Cloudcroft Ice Rink** (575/682-4585, 3pm-9pm Fri., 10am-6pm Sat.-Mon.) at the west end of Zenith Park, and tubing all over the hills. Many of the town's rail trails are good for **cross-country skiing.**

## ACCOMMODATIONS

The main type of accommodation in town is the guest cabin. Location isn't too essential, considering how small the town is.

### Under $100

Halfway down the mountain on the way to Tularosa, the excellent **◖Cloudcroft Mountain Park Hostel** (1049 U.S. 82, 575/682-0555, www.cloudcrofthostel.com) has three rooms with eight bunks each ($17 pp), as well as two basic private rooms ($30) and one big family room ($50), all with access to shared baths and a big common area and kitchen. Everything's clean and colorfully painted, with a casual but orderly atmosphere.

**Summit Inn** (Chipmunk Ave. at Curlew Pl., 575/682-2814, www.summitinn-nm.com, $55 s, $72 d) has clean and tidy, if dated, rooms, with tiny kitchenettes, vintage TVs, and showers (no tubs). Don't bother with the cabins, though—they're relatively expensive and short on charm.

At the east end of town, **Spruce Cabins** (100 Lynx Ave., 575/682-2381, www.sprucecabins.com, $75 d) are pleasant enough standalone apartments with a faintly rustic feel. The wood paneling has a certain 1970s mobile home vibe, but that's offset by attractive quilts on the beds and cozy wood-burning fireplaces.

Smack in the center of town, **◖Cloudcroft Hotel** (306 Burro Ave., 575/682-3414, www.cloudcrofthotel.com, $89 s, $114 d) is affordable and very well kept. Each of the eight rooms is carefully decorated and fastidiously clean; all have claw-foot tubs and lots of pine paneling. There are a couple of odd rooms that don't have windows to the outside—potentially dreary, but a bargain and a bit quieter than those on the front of the building (though room no. 1, for $139, with access to the front balcony, is a gem). The hotel also runs four cabins (from $160), across the road, kept to the same high standards.

**Burro Street Boardinghouse** (608 Burro Ave., 575/682-3601, $89) has just three rooms, but each one is very nicely done, with choice antiques and details like vanity sinks. The building is a big, airy pine-paneled A-frame, and the owner is an old Cloudcroft hand.

### $100-150

At the top of the hill—and the price range—**The Lodge** (601 Corona Pl., 800/395-6343, www.thelodgeresort.com, $145 d) is a fairly well-restored relic from the early railroad era. The current structure, with its vaguely Tyrolean look, was built in 1911 by the Alamogordo & Sacramento Railway. With lots of chintz, brocade, and dark wood, the style may be historically accurate, but some of the 58 rooms can feel cramped, especially the standard queens. Rooms in the Retreat wing (from $265) are newer construction and have fireplaces and whirlpool tubs. Down the hill, the Pavilion is the oldest section, a large wood cabin with a wraparound porch—the rooms here are a bit more rustic, and rates (from $135) include breakfast at Rebecca's, the resort's main restaurant.

## FOOD

Cloudcroft's unofficial social center, the **Western Bar & Café** (304 Burro Ave., 575/682-9910, 6am-9pm daily, $7) satisfies just about every social need, whether you want a breakfast omelet, a cold beer, or a crazy night of karaoke (the bar is open till 11pm during the week and 1am on Friday and Saturday). The vibe is friendly and the crowd is eclectic.

For a somewhat healthier meal, seek out **◖ Cloud Café** (505 Burro Ave., 575/682-5843, 10am-4pm Mon.-Sat., noon-4pm Sun., $8), which is actually off Burro Avenue, down a side alley. Pies with proper butter crust are a big draw, or, if you want savory, go for the chicken pastry pie, a sort of rustic tart. Crepes are also an option, as well as hot sandwiches and fresh salads. It's also blessedly free of mountain-lodge kitsch.

Up the hill at The Lodge, **Rebecca's** (575/682-2566, 7am-10:30am, 11:30am-2:30pm, and 5:30pm-9pm Mon.-Sat., 7am-2pm Sun.) has historic ambience, though the prices for only average sandwiches and steaks are high ($12 at lunch, $24 and up at dinner). But it's a good spot for a drink and a snack.

## INFORMATION

Cloudcroft's **chamber of commerce** (U.S. 82, 866/874-4447, www.cloudcroft.net, 10am-5pm Mon.-Sat.) occupies a tiny cabin on the east side of town and has just about any info on the town you could need.

## GETTING THERE

Cloudcroft is 20 miles (30 minutes) by car from Alamogordo via U.S. 82 east and 90 miles (1.5 hours) west from Artesia.

# Alamogordo

For most visitors, Alamogordo functions as the gateway to the stunning White Sands National Monument, the largest field of pure gypsum in the world. It also has a couple of interesting sights of its own. Founded in 1899 as a railroad stop, the town has been shaped more by the early space industry and Holloman Air Force Base, which also trains German pilots. It fits between the railroad tracks and the foothills of the Sacramento Mountains, with some 41,000 residents in a low-rise sprawl—though it feels much smaller.

## SIGHTS

Navigating Alamogordo is straightforward: Almost everything is located on or very near White Sands Boulevard (U.S. 54/70), which runs roughly north-south through town. On New York Avenue, one block east, is Alamogordo's historic downtown, along a couple of blocks south of 10th Street. The space museum is far up in the foothills, but it's visible from a long way off.

### New Mexico Museum of Space History

The state-run **New Mexico Museum of Space History** (Hwy. 2001, 575/437-2840, www.nmspacemuseum.org, 9am-5pm daily, $6) began in 1976 as a hall of fame for astronauts, including the first chimpanzee in space, who's buried here. Then it expanded into this comprehensive look at space exploration—which in many ways got its start in rocket tests in the Tularosa Basin below. Working your way down through four floors, you pass assorted relics from the space race, a chunk of moon rock, and more. But perhaps the most interesting items are those that hint at what everyday life in zero gravity is like, such as the space station interior model and a space-flight hygiene kit. It's a surprisingly un-high-tech museum. The cobbled-together rockets and patched-up spacesuits serve as a reminder just how mechanical and hardware-driven space exploration has been—not a sleek, digital process at all.

The current state of space exploration looks a little slicker: The bottom floor of the museum is devoted to the X Prize, which encourages commercial space flights, and a hangar outside contains a model of the first winner: glossy, bulbous SpaceShipOne, covered in corporate-sponsor logos. Next to it, a 1940s accelerator for testing G-forces looks brutally primitive.

### Toy Train Depot

You can't miss Alamogordo's nifty miniature train: It runs straight through town, parallel to White Sands Boulevard. The northern endpoint is the **Toy Train Depot** (1991 N. White Sands Blvd., 575/437-2855, www.toytraindepot.homestead.com, noon-4:30pm Wed.-Sun., $6), the model-train collection of a retired rocket scientist. One of the layouts shows the old route up to Cloudcroft. But the real fun is outside on the larger-scale tracks, where two trains run down to Alameda Park and back, and a smaller-gauge one runs loops around the yard. Kids might get to drive it themselves, if they're well behaved.

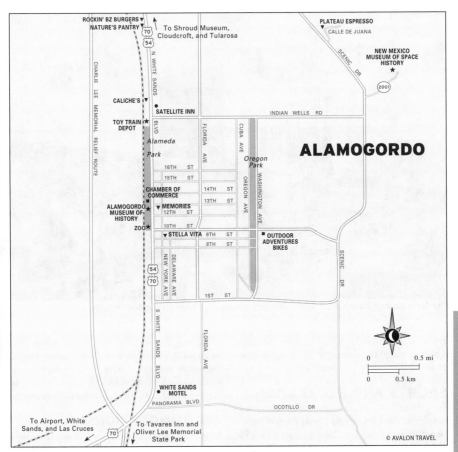

## Alamogordo Museum of History

In the usual assortment of pioneer gear and old furniture is the **Alamogordo Museum of History** (1301 N. White Sands Blvd., 575/434-4438, www.alamogordohistory.com, 10am-4pm Mon.-Fri., 10am-3pm Sat., 1pm-3pm Sun., free); the highlight of the collection is an American flag with 47 stars. There's also some information about Trinity Site, as well as the older Hispano community of La Luz, just north of Alamogordo.

## Alameda Park and Zoo

**Alameda Park and Zoo** (1321 N. White Sands Blvd., 575/439-4290, 9am-5pm daily, $2.50) is the oldest in the Southwest. It has about 90 species on view, including some frisky otters and even some kangaroos, which don't look too out of place in this desert. There's also a nice shaded picnic area inside. The entrance is on 10th Street just west of White Sands Boulevard.

## Shroud Exhibit and Museum

Tucked inside the White Sands Mall is Alamogordo's most surprising attraction, the **Shroud Exhibit and Museum** (3199 N. White Sands Blvd., 575/415-5206, 1pm-6pm Tues.-Fri., 2pm-4pm Sun., free) devoted to a photo-replica of the Shroud of Turin, the work of a

The New Mexico Museum of Space History showcases space-race technology.

group of researchers, based in New Mexico, who examined the shroud in 1978 using state-of-the-art imagining technology.

## SPORTS AND RECREATION

For general info on trails and other recreation, stop in at the **Lincoln National Forest** supervisor's office (3463 Las Palomas Rd., 575/434-7200, 7:30am-4:30pm Mon.-Fri.) or **Outdoor Adventures Bikes & Sports** (1516 10th St., 575/434-1920, 10am-6pm Mon.-Fri., 10am-5pm Sat.), where you can also rent gear.

### Hiking

The one big rec area nearby is **Oliver Lee Memorial State Park** (409 Dog Canyon Rd., 575/437-8284, www.nmparks.com, $5/car), 12 miles south of Alamogordo. The 5.5-mile **Dog Canyon Recreational Trail** begins at the visitors center and leads through a surprisingly lush canyon where you'll see everything from moss to orchids growing, if you look closely. It then heads up to a ridge with great views of the desert basin—a strenuous climb, with an elevation gain of 3,100 feet. Many hikers just go about 2.5 miles in to a stone cowboy cabin, then turn around. There are also more than 40 developed **campsites** ($8-14)—the closest camping to White Sands National Monument.

## ACCOMMODATIONS

A rare case in which an eye-catching neon sign actually points to quality lodging, **❰ White Sands Motel** (1101 S. White Sands Blvd., 575/437-2922, www.whitesandsmotel.biz, $50 s, $60 d) is a tidy little shell of an old motel court, nicely updated inside. The rooms are snug, but they're kept clean, and many are well back from the main road, for slightly less traffic noise. Rooms all have mini-fridges, microwaves, and wireless Internet.

On the south edge of town, **Tavares Inn** (153 San Pedro Dr., 575/437-8779, www.tavaresinn.com, $105 d) puts the "breakfast" back in bed-and-breakfast, with a massive morning spread. The three rooms are in a rambling white ranch house, with an indoor pool and horses and more out back.

Kid-size trains are the draw at the Toy Train Depot.

## FOOD

It's slim pickings for distinctive dining in Alamogordo—and no surprise most people wind up eating at the chain restaurants on White Sands Boulevard. For a pick-me-up after the Space Museum, **Plateau Espresso** (2724 N. Scenic Dr., 575/434-4466, 6am-9pm daily) will do the trick, while providing awesome views over the city from its patio.

Diners with text anxiety might not like the ordering system at **Rockin' BZ Burgers** (3005 N. White Sands Blvd., 575/434-2375, 11am-8pm, $7), which involves filling out a form to select burger toppings and sides. If in doubt, go for the signature Champ burger, which has made an excellent showing in the state fair green-chile cheeseburger cook-off in recent years; it adds grilled onions to the mix. Another nice touch: buttered buns.

For a healthy lunch, the deli counter at the back of **Nature's Pantry** (2909 N. White Sands Blvd., 575/437-3037, 11am-3pm Mon.-Sat., $7) makes vegetarian-friendly wraps and sprout-stuffed sandwiches, which you can wash down with a shot of wheatgrass juice or a smoothie—a great antidote to standard road food.

**Caliche's** (2251 N. White Sands Blvd., 575/439-1000, 11am-10pm daily, $4) is an outpost of the frozen-custard specialist in Las Cruces. It's no balanced meal, but given the options in Alamogordo, you're excused if you have a thick shake for dinner.

All matte gray and faux stone, **Stella Vita** (902 New York Ave., 575/434-4444, 11am-2pm Mon.-Wed., 11am-2pm and 5pm-9pm Thurs.-Fri., 5pm-9pm Sat., $10) is by far the most stylish place in Alamogordo. The menu is slightly fancy Americana. At lunch, the menu is heavy on salads. At dinner (three nights a week), you can get steaks and pork chops (about $25 per entrée). Service is very attentive.

Set in a homey bungalow, **Memories** (1223 New York Ave., 575/437-0077, 11am-9pm Mon.-Sat., $12) is a bit of a time-warp restaurant, with a menu of baked-potato soup and prime rib, and, at lunch, hot turkey sandwiches.

It requires a 20-minute drive to the south edge of Tularosa, but for its *carne adovada* ribs alone, **Casa de Sueños** (35 St. Francis Dr., 575/585-3494, 11am-8pm Mon.-Thurs., 11am-8:30pm Fri.-Sat., 10:30am-8pm Sun., $12) is worth the trek. This fusion of traditional New Mexican chile with barbecue savor is just one of several tasty (and very meaty) dishes on the menu. You can also get the usual enchiladas and rellenos, as well as burritos to go. The ambience is warmly lit, with a pretty patio out back.

## INFORMATION

The **Alamogordo Chamber of Commerce** (1301 N. White Sands Blvd., 575/437-6120, www.alamogordo.com, 8am-5pm Mon.-Fri.) dispenses a very detailed free map.

## GETTING THERE AND AROUND

By car, Alamogordo is 68 miles (1.25 hours) east from Las Cruces via U.S. 70, and 215 miles (3.25 hours) via I-25 from Albuquerque.

THE SOUTHEAST

© ZORA O'NEILL

Cloudcroft is about 20 miles (30 minutes) due east up the mountains, and Ruidoso is 50 miles (1 hour) northeast. **Greyhound** (800/231-2222, www.greyhound.com) connects Alamogordo to Las Cruces once a day, stopping at the station (3500 N. White Sands Blvd., 575/437-3050, 7am-11am and 4pm-8pm Mon.-Fri., 7am-9am and 5pm-8pm Sat.-Sun.).

# White Sands National Monument

White Sands, 275 square miles of blinding, shimmery gypsum, is a surreal and magnificent place. At every turn, you have to remind yourself what you're really looking at. In the summer, temperatures exceed 100°F, but the sand looks like no desert you've ever seen. On a cool winter day, especially after rainwater has pooled along the road, your brain can't stop thinking snow and ice. For the best photography, as well as a break from the heat, you'll probably want to visit either early or late in the day—but there is also something appropriately overwhelming about this featureless landscape at high noon.

Although the barren dunes at the core of the park are the most popular image of the place, there's a surprising amount of life here, from tiny kangaroo mice to the beleaguered tufts of skunkbush sumac that are the last holdouts as the sand shifts around them. A number of nature trails lead off the eight-mile-long Dunes Drive, and if you have time, you should definitely join one of the ranger-led walks—usually near sunset.

## VISITORS CENTER

Stop in at the pleasantly old-fashioned **visitors center** (575/479-6124, www.nps.gov/whsa, 8am-7pm daily mid-Apr.-Aug., 9am-6pm Mar.-mid-Apr. and Sept.-Oct., 9am-5pm Nov.-Feb., $3) at the main gate to check the schedule of ranger tours and maybe pick up a plastic sled from the gift shop, for sliding down the dunes. Among the ranger outings is a car trip to **Lake Lucero** ($3, reserve ahead), the crystal-filled lake bed that's the source of the sands, as well as the occasional full-moon **bicycle tour** ($5). If you plan to do any backcountry hiking, you'll need to get a permit at the center ($3)—there's only one designated hike-in camping

area, about a mile from the road, so check for a vacancy.

## DUNES DRIVE

Open 7am to sunset, the road leads from the shaggy, brush-covered hills at the edge of the white desert into the pure dunes at the center. In between is the transition area, where hills are being carved away by wind, and yuccas teeter on lone sand pedestals. As long as you park in one of the designated pullouts, you're welcome to walk wherever you like, but make careful note of landmarks; even in the areas with lots of vegetation, it's easy to wind up walking in circles.

The first stop on the drive, **Playa Trail** runs 500 yards along the border where the gypsum meets the regular desert terrain, ending up at a playa, the term for a depression that forms a temporary lake after rainfall. These playas are all over White Sands, as well as in the desert areas of the rest of New Mexico. Of all the trails, this may be the least remarkable—skip it if you're not planning to spend all day here.

The one-mile-long **Dune Life Nature Trail** does a quick loop up to the top of a dune and past the most typical types of vegetation. At least stop to pick up one of the trail guides, which can help you identify animal tracks. The **Interdune Boardwalk** is another quick trail—a very easy way to check out some of the more common plants, without trudging through sand.

## ◖ HEART OF THE SANDS

This is the main destination inside the park. You can set up camp in one of the mod metal picnic shelters (which include grills), then go out to clamber, slip, and slide down the pristine white hills. (There are also restrooms out here, but no water.) From the end of the parking area, the **Alkali Flat Trail** is a 4.6-mile loop into the most austere part of the dunes. This can be extremely disorienting—heed the stern warnings to turn back if you can't see the orange trail markers, which periodically get covered with sand. Allow about three hours for the whole hike, and be sure to register at the trailhead before you proceed.

# Ruidoso

North of Alamogordo and east on U.S. 70, Ruidoso (Noisy) is named for the audible stream that flows through a canyon in the center. Like Cloudcroft, it's a patch of Texas in the high mountains—but it's quite a bit bigger and, at least in spots, substantially more upscale. It's very much a resort town, dedicated to golf (at five courses in the immediate area), horse racing, and skiing on southern New Mexico's highest mountain. Don't go for culture, but for cool air and a cabin in the woods. And brace yourself for cutesy kitsch—the number of tree-trunk bear sculptures is higher per capita than anywhere else in the state.

On the drive up on U.S. 70, you pass through the Mescalero Apache reservation, established in 1883 on some 463,000 acres. The tribe (which got its name from the Spanish, who remarked on its ritual use of peyote, or mescal) operates the ski area as well as a resort and casino about 20 minutes' drive south of town.

## SIGHTS

Ruidoso's main drags are Sudderth Drive (east-west) and Mechem Drive, running north from the west end of Sudderth, to form a big L. The town is divided into districts by the

THE SOUTHEAST

© ZORA O'NEILL

Ruidoso is the unofficial state capital of tree-trunk art.

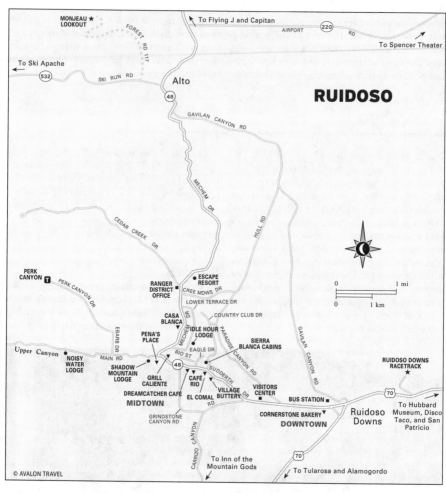

To Flying J and Capitan
To Spencer Theater
AIRPORT (220) RD
MONJEAU ★
LOOKOUT
FOREST RD 117
To Ski Apache
(532)
SKI RUN RD
Alto
(48)
**RUIDOSO**
GAVILAN CANYON RD
MECHEM DR
CEDAR CREEK DR
HULL RD
PERK CANYON ⊤
PERK CANYON DR
● ESCAPE RESORT
RANGER DISTRICT OFFICE
CREE MDWS DR
LOWER TERRACE DR
COUNTRY CLUB DR
CASA BLANCA ▼
IDLE HOUR LODGE
MECHEM DR
PARADISE CANYON RD
SIERRA BLANCA CABINS
GAVILAN CANYON RD
PENA'S PLACE
EBARD DR
Upper Canyon
● NOISY WATER LODGE
MAIN RD
EAGLE DR
RIO ST
(48)
SUDDERTH DR
RUIDOSO DOWNS RACETRACK ★
SHADOW MOUNTAIN LODGE
GRILL CALIENTE
CAFE RIO
VILLAGE BUTTERY ▼
VISITORS CENTER
(70)
DREAMCATCHER CAFÉ
**MIDTOWN**
EL COMAL RD
BUS STATION ■
To Hubbard Museum, Disco Taco, and San Patricio
GRINDSTONE CANYON RD
CARRIZO CANYON
CORNERSTONE BAKERY ▼
**DOWNTOWN**
Ruidoso Downs
To Inn of the Mountain Gods
(70)
To Tularosa and Alamogordo
© AVALON TRAVEL

0                    1 mi
0              1 km

major intersections. Uptown is lower Mechem and the west end of Sudderth (higher address numbers); Midtown, the densest business area, refers to the stretch of Sudderth from up near Mechem to Carrizo Canyon Road. Finally, Downtown is the east end of Sudderth (the lowest street numbers), and "the Y" is the junction of Sudderth and U.S. 70, where most of the chain businesses are. Farther east along U.S. 70, Ruidoso Downs is technically a separate town, but there is no physical gap between it and its neighbor.

## Hubbard Museum of the American West

The small **Hubbard Museum of the American West** (26301 U.S. 70 W, 575/378-4142, www.hubbardmuseum.org, 10am-4:30pm daily, $6), the only real "sight" in Ruidoso, is the collection of a local woman who loved all things equine, and had good taste in Native American crafts. Her assortment of horse-drawn carriages, from a sulky to a chuckwagon to a hearse, fills the downstairs, but don't miss the back hall, with some especially beautiful kachinas. Upstairs is space for temporary, Western-themed exhibitions.

## ENTERTAINMENT

Midtown is the place to be at night, but the track is where the action is on weekend afternoons. In Alto, **Flying J Ranch** (575/336-4330, www.flyingjranch.com, June-Aug.) is unapologetically cheesy, but it may be just the thing if you have kids to delight. Expect pony rides, staged gunfights, and gold panning, followed by a whole lotta grub and a wholesome, Opry-style stage show. The price is actually relatively old-timey, too: $27 for adults, $15 for kids.

### Nightlife

For margaritas, **Casa Blanca** (501 Mechem Dr., 575/257-2495, 11am-9pm daily) is the top spot, enhanced by a great patio surrounded by tall pines. After the first round of drinks and dinner, action usually moves to the two dueling megabars in Midtown: **The Quarters** (2535 Sudderth Dr., 575/257-9535) and **Win, Place and Show** (2516 Sudderth Dr., 575/257-9982), which play both kinds of music (that'd be country *and* western) to inspire some speedy two-stepping around the dance floors. The Quarters also has pool tables.

### Spencer Theater for the Performing Arts

Just up the road from Ruidoso in the satellite community of Alto, the **Spencer Theater for the Performing Arts** (108 Spencer Rd., 575/336-4800, www.spencertheater.com) seats 514, and hosts touring musical productions as well as local performers. The building alone, a white wedge jutting from the plain, is an attraction; the architect is New Mexican Antoine Predock. The interior features a number of Dale Chihuly glass sculptures. Free tours run on Tuesdays and Thursdays at 10am (call to reserve).

## SPORTS AND RECREATION

For details on national forest areas, contact the **Smokey Bear Ranger District office** (901 Mechem Dr., 575/257-4095, 7:30am-4:30pm Mon.-Fri.). Birders should keep an eye out for hummingbirds, which summer here in great numbers.

Sure, there are *real* golf courses in the area, but **Funtrackers** (101 Carrizo Canyon Rd., 575/257-3275, 10am-9pm daily in summer, Sat.-Sun. in winter) has 18 miniature holes, as well as go-carts, an arcade, a human-scale maze, and more. Even Ruidoso's **public swimming pool** (515 Sudderth Dr., 575/257-2795, noon-4:45pm, $3) is pretty fun, with a giant loop-de-loop slide; but it closes when the school year starts, in mid-August.

### Hiking and Biking

Intense wildfires in 2012 closed off much of the forest around Ruidoso, so recreation is limited while the area recovers. In town, **Two Rivers Park,** right behind the **visitors center** (720 Sudderth Dr.), is a little walking trail along the river all the way into Upper Canyon, sometimes so far below the main road level that you forget you're in the middle of town.

Handy **Perk Canyon Trail** begins basically in people's backyards and runs about three miles up to some open meadows. To get to the trailhead, follow Main Road to Ebarb Drive (next to Story Book Cabins); turn right, go about 0.3 mile to Perk Canyon Road, and turn left. The paved road dead-ends at the trail.

### Horse Racing

Memorial Day through Labor Day, **Ruidoso Downs** (26225 U.S. 70, 575/378-4431, www.ruidownsracing.com) hosts races Thursday-Sunday, starting at 1pm. There are a few thoroughbred meets, but historically Ruidoso has been a quarter-horse track. The All-American Futurity, which draws nearly 20,000 people to town over Labor Day weekend, has been dubbed the world's richest quarter-horse race, thanks to its purse of more than $1 million—not bad money for 21 seconds of running. (As in any futurity, owners start the gambling early—they buy into the race as soon as a horse is born, with incremental payments over the next two years.)

THE SOUTHEAST

© ZORA O'NEILL

Quarter horses put Ruidoso on the map.

## Winter Sports

Head 18 miles north to **Ski Apache** (575/464-3600, www.skiapache.com, $51 full-day lift ticket), which can get more than 15 feet of snow a year. Of the 55 trails, 45 percent are advanced, with a vertical drop of 1,900 feet across the mountain. Snowboarders have the run of the trails, as well as the Boneyard, a special park with all kinds of rails and jumps. Don't go driving up here just on a lark, though—Ski Run Road is dangerously narrow, so uphill traffic is banned 3pm-6pm during ski season.

## ACCOMMODATIONS

The signature lodging of Ruidoso is the cozy wood cabin, with kitchen and fireplace, and most of these are in what's called Upper Canyon, on Main Road, which follows the river up a narrowing route. If country-cute is not to your taste, you might prefer the guesthouses at the Hurd La Rinconada Gallery in San Patricio, 20 miles east of town. The majority of the chain hotels are at the east end of town, around the Y, but it's hard to find anything decent for less than $100.

### Under $100

The cheapest lodging in Ruidoso is of course camping. Head five miles up Ski Run Road to **Oak Grove** ($6), with 24 sites, including a few walk-in spots that are wonderfully secluded under oak trees; you'll have to bring your own water.

### $100-150

Set on the river in the Midtown area, **Sierra Blanca Cabins** (215 Country Club Rd., 575/257-2103, www.ruidoso.net/sbcabins, $119 d) are nicely outfitted one- and two-bedroom cabins that have lovely views, and a prime location not too far from Sudderth. The cabins were overhauled by new owners in 2013, with brand-new beds and other fresh details.

A key feature of **Idle Hour Lodge** (112 Lower Terrace Dr., 575/808-8484, www.idlehourlodge.com, $129 d) is its location, tucked away from the main roads yet still easy walking distance to a grocery store and restaurants in Uptown. The 14 cabins come in one- and two-bedroom configurations, in typical Ruidoso style, with wood paneling, quilts on the beds, and little porches out front.

Of the cabins in Upper Canyon, **Shadow Mountain Lodge** (107 Main Rd., 575/257-4886, www.smlruidoso.com, $125-145) is conveniently located at the near end, so you can easily walk into town, if you're so inclined. You have a choice of rooms in the central lodge or in standalone cabins. All are geared to couples, with king beds in the pine-paneled lodge and queens in the cabins, which are more modern but still rustic enough. There are fireplaces and kitchenettes in all the rooms.

### $150-250

There's only one true alternative to mountain-cabin style in town: **Escape Resort** (1016 Mechem Dr., 575/258-1234, www.theescaperesort.com, $229 d), a cluster of five minimalist Southwest-style casitas. Each one is enormous,

Sierra Blanca Cabins are typical of Ruidoso's riverside lodging.

with a full living room, a small kitchen, and a patio, in addition to a lavish bedroom (or two) and bath with separate tub and steam shower. Yes, it's definitely Ruidoso's upper end—but a bargain compared with what you'd pay for such digs in Santa Fe.

The other alternative is **Inn of the Mountain Gods** (287 Carrizo Canyon Rd., 800/545-9011, www.innofthemountaingods.com, $189 d), run by the Mescalero Apache. On paper, it's a lovely place, overlooking a small lake south of town, but maintenance has gone off, and the rooms no longer seem like such a bargain. We include it here as a minor warning—and in case it makes a comeback, as it has done in the past. (The resort's casino and theater are still quite popular entertainment spots.)

## FOOD

Ruidoso's best dining is at the casual end. Many places cater to blander Texan palates— you'll see green chile on the menu, but it's the mildest possible form.

## Cafés

Hidden away at the small traffic circle where Sudderth Drive turns into Main Road, tiny **Peña's Place** (2963 Sudderth Dr., 575/257-4135, 7:30am-2pm Thurs.-Sun., $8) is a homey operation, a labor of love where the owner has made the wood-slab tables himself. Like everywhere in Ruidoso, the chile on the huevos rancheros packs exactly zero punch, but it's balanced out by stupendously good blueberry-pecan whole-wheat pancakes. The eggs benedict (weekends only) are also solid. There are only 24 seats inside, and a dozen more on the front deck, so go early or be prepared to wait.

**Cornerstone Bakery & Café** (359 Sudderth Dr., 575/257-1842, 7am-3pm daily, $8) helps you start the day right—with French toast, for instance, a BEST sandwich (bacon, eggs, spinach, and tomatoes), or a supersticky sweet roll. This is many residents' and regular visitors' morning favorite, so the atmosphere is chummy, and you see a good slice of the town.

Good thing **Village Buttery** (2107 Sudderth Dr., 575/257-9251, 10:30am-2:30pm Mon.-Sat., $8) doesn't open too early, or you might be tempted to start your day with pie. For lunch, you can get hearty soups, quiches, and sandwiches with a Texan twist (pimento cheese, say) before you embark on a tour of the pie case. Despite the café's name, the crusts aren't bursting with butter—pies with crumb crusts are preferable.

The best place in town to get a fresh salad and an interesting sandwich, **Dreamcatcher Café** (2629 Sudderth Dr., 575/802-2222, 11am-9pm Thurs.-Sat., 11am-dusk Sun., $8) does a solid gyro, and its salads are topped with all kinds of goodies.

## Italian

For pizza, head to super casual **Café Rio** (2547 Sudderth Dr., 575/257-7746, 11:30am-8pm daily, $8), which earns the local vote for best pie. All the usual toppings are on offer, along with rarer treats like artichoke hearts and capers, and the rest of the menu reflects the owners' quirky outlook, with items like shrimp jambalaya and Portuguese kale soup. You can wash it all down with a big milkshake—it does not serve beer. It often closes Wednesdays in spring and fall. Cash only.

## Mexican

Just east around the bend from the Hubbard Museum, the low-atmosphere, high-flavor **Disco Taco** (26341 U.S. 70, 575/378-4224, 10am-8:45pm Thurs.-Tues., $5-8) is named not for its soundtrack of choice, but for the meat it cooks on a round griddle (a *disco*). You can get meaty tacos, hangover-curing menudo, and other reasonably authentic *norteño*-style food, as well as assorted egg dishes.

For enchiladas and tamales in a more convenient location, **El Comal** (2117 Sudderth Dr., 575/258-1397, 11am-7pm Mon. and Wed.-Sat., 11am-3pm Sun., $9) is known for its tamales and its *enmoladas,* tortillas doused in rich mole sauce. Look for it in the Gazebo shopping center, and enjoy a seat on the back porch.

For a slightly lighter, fancier take on Mexican food, visit **Grill Caliente** (2800 Sudderth Dr., 575/630-0224, 11am-2:30pm and 5pm-9pm.)

Tues.-Sun., $14) for dishes like stuffed poblano peppers and mushroom tacos. Like much food in Ruidoso, it can veer toward bland, but at least it's veggie-friendly and has nice outdoor seating (much preferable to inside, where the light is harsh).

## INFORMATION

The Ruidoso chamber of commerce operates a very cheery **visitors center** (720 Sudderth Dr., 575/257-7395, www.ruidosonow.com), positively bursting with information and helpful staff. The lobby section is even open 24 hours.

## GETTING THERE

By car, Ruidoso is 74 miles (1.25 hours) east from Roswell on U.S. 70, 170 miles (3 hours) from Albuquerque via I-25 south and east on U.S. 380, and 115 miles (2 hours) from Las Cruces via U.S. 70 east. **Greyhound** (800/231-2222, www.greyhound.com) stops at the station (138 Service Rd., 575/257-2660, 9am-5pm Mon.-Fri., 9am-noon Sat.) once a day from Las Cruces.

# Billy the Kid Trail

This scenic driving route forms a triangle with Ruidoso, Tinnie, and Capitan at the points. The loop is an easy day's drive, meandering through orchards, horse farms, and deep forest. If you're feeling thorough, you can stop first at the **Billy the Kid Interpretive Center** (U.S. 70, 575/378-5318, 10am-5pm Thurs.-Tues.) in Ruidoso Downs, next to the Hubbard Museum.

## SAN PATRICIO

This bucolic village in a valley 20 miles east of Ruidoso glows with the sort of light painters praise—no surprise, then, that it was the home of artists Peter Hurd and Henriette Wyeth, daughter of N. C. Wyeth. One of their children owns the family ranch and operates ◖ **Hurd La Rinconada Gallery** (100 Rinconada Ln.,

800/658-6912, www.wyethartists.com), which displays the family's work. It also rents some beautiful guest homes, scattered over the Wyeth land. These are an excellent alternative to staying in Ruidoso—the smallest ones ($140) cost little more than you'd pay at the high end in town, and they're much larger and more attractive overall, furnished with original art and antiques.

## HONDO

The **Hondo Iris Farm** (575/635-4062, 8am-5pm Tues.-Sat., 10am-4pm Sun.) is a lovely garden oasis, dedicated in part to growing iris bulbs (they're best in late spring). But just as important is the owner's gallery of dramatic handmade jewelry, all of pewter. It's a pretty place to shop and enjoy the greenery.

# TINNIE

Just east of the junction of U.S. 70 and U.S. 380, Tinnie is a dot on the map with one attraction. Folks from Ruidoso drive up here for a fancy night out or big brunch at **Tinnie Silver Dollar** (575/653-4425, 10am-9pm Mon.-Wed., 10am-10pm Thurs.-Sat., 10am-3pm Sun., $28), the old town general store that was restored and expanded into a restaurant in the 1950s, with German stained glass and a gorgeous hardwood bar from Chicago. During the day, you can stop in at the deli and have a sandwich on the wraparound porch.

# ◖ LINCOLN STATE MONUMENT

More of an open-air museum than a town, **Lincoln State Monument** is an artfully preserved Old West village where many of the buildings on the main street have been turned into public monuments. A stroll up and down the road is a rare chance to meditate on history without the distraction of souvenir vendors.

During the Lincoln County War (1878-1881), when the area was wracked by retaliatory killings triggered by a struggle to control the town dry-goods business, the national press dubbed this "the most dangerous town in America." The local feud also put Billy the Kid, who'd been causing low-grade trouble around New Mexico, in the spotlight. He burnished his outlaw reputation when he took sides with the upstart Tunstall faction and the band of "Regulators" who later sought vengeance for Tunstall's murder. Near the end of the war, Billy made a daring escape from the town jail, killing two guards in the process.

## Anderson-Freeman Visitors Center & Museum

You can learn all about the Kid's exploits—as well as the Mexican families who first settled the town in 1846, and the Buffalo Soldiers who bunked at nearby Fort Sumner—at the **Anderson-Freeman Visitors Center & Museum** (U.S. 380, 8:30am-4:30pm daily, $5). Then tour the other buildings in town, which have been filled with period furnishings

and a few smaller historical displays. (A couple of them are open only April-October.) The Tunstall Store—which started the whole fracas—is kitted out with 19th-century stock, and you can see the holes in the courthouse wall where Billy the Kid fired bullets as he made his getaway.

## Accommodations and Food

"No guests gunned down in over 100 years," boasts the **Wortley Hotel** (U.S. 380, 575/653-4300, www.wortleyhotel.com, $95 d), which was formerly owned by Sheriff Pat Garrett. The historic building is smack in the middle of town, so after visiting the museums, you can toddle over here and settle into a rocking chair on the porch, and feel like you're part of the exhibit. The seven whitewashed rooms, all with corner fireplaces, are simply furnished with appropriate antiques. The **restaurant** (8am-3pm Wed.-Sun.) serves a great breakfast (included in the room rate) and lunch. The other option is the **Ellis Store** (U.S. 380, 800/653-6460, www.ellisstore.com), an atmospheric tumble-down stone complex at the east edge of town, where you can stay in the main house with private baths ($99-109) or share a bathroom for less in the rambling mill house ($89).

The beautiful **Dolan House** (U.S. 380, 575/653-4670, 9am-3:30pm Fri.-Tues., $9), a restored adobe in the center of the village, also serves a good breakfast and lunch. If you do stay overnight in Lincoln, note that only the Ellis Store serves dinner for guests; otherwise you're on your own.

# FORT STANTON

A well-signed detour off U.S. 380, **Fort Stanton** is one of the largest historic military outposts in the West. Its buildings were made of stone, rather than adobe, so the complex looks remarkably intact, and the tree-shaded grounds are pleasant for a picnic. A small but interesting **museum** (10am-4pm Thurs.-Mon., free) details the fort's myriad uses, from staging ground for the Indian Wars to a tent hospital for tuberculosis patients to internment camp for hundreds of German sailors in World War

Spend a night at the museum in Lincoln's Wortley Hotel.

II (alas, the swimming pool these industrious men built is in ruins). It stops short of more recent uses—as a women's prison and drug-rehab center—before it was made a state monument in 2007.

Past the fort is a wilderness reserve most remarkable for being set over the third-largest cave system in the state (experienced cavers must get a permit from the BLM field office in Roswell). More accessibly, the area is cut through with numerous horse and hiking trails—you can pick up a map at the fort museum.

## CAPITAN

Capitan is all about Smokey Bear, the tiny cub discovered clinging to a tree after a fire raged across 17,000 acres in the Capitan Mountains in 1950. Badly burned, the cub was nursed back to health, dubbed "Smokey," and eventually shipped off to the National Zoo in Washington, D.C., where a generation of school kids got to visit the living symbol of fire prevention. (The image of Smokey Bear was

invented in 1944—but the campaign didn't catch on until the real, adorable bear took over the mantle.) Smokey died in 1976, but, like Elvis, his spirit lives on, especially here in Capitan, where he's buried, and where nearly every business name is some ursine pun. The place really goes crazy for **Smokey Bear Days,** on the first weekend in May.

The state forestry office operates **Smokey Bear Historical Park** (118 W. Smokey Bear Blvd., 575/354-2748, www.smokeybearpark. com, 9am-5pm daily, $2). It's a bit dry, in a 1970s-education way, though kids will probably be impressed by the displays of forest-fighting gear, and adults might be interested to see how the fire-prevention ads have changed over the years. There's also a short walking trail to Smokey's grave.

### Food

A lovely surprise in this tiny town, **Renee's Real Food** (435 Smokey Bear Blvd., 575/973-0351, 8am-3pm Wed.-Sat., 10am-2pm Sun., $7) is just that—an eclectic, unpretentious menu cooked from scratch. Depending on the chef's whim, you may encounter shrimp po'boys, meatball sandwiches, and, at weekend brunch, crème brûlée French toast. One

constant is handmade bagels, hot and fresh at opening time. At research time, it had only been open a few months; call to check hours, as they may have changed or expanded.

# Northern Tularosa Basin

Both U.S. 70 and U.S. 380 descend to meet U.S. 54, which runs north through a broad, dry valley between the Sacramento and San Andres Mountains. Much of it is part of the White Sands Missile Range, which does industrial and military testing.

## THREE RIVERS PETROGLYPH SITE

Five miles off U.S. 54, in an unremarkable stretch between Tularosa and Carrizozo, the BLM-managed **Three Rivers Petroglyph Site** (8am-7pm daily Apr.-Oct., 8am-5pm Nov.-Mar., $5/car) is easy enough to drive right past. A trail leads up to a series of low

hills, marked by volcanic rock that appears to cover the ridgeline like scabs. Look carefully, and you'll soon see why these 50 acres are now protected: The dark rocks are scored with thousands of intricate designs—lizards, mountain goats, snakes, checkerboards, spirals. Because it's so far from any modern settlement, the area has barely been marred by more recent carving (as the West Mesa in Albuquerque has). Archaeologists estimate that the inscriptions here date from between 900 and 1400, when the Mogollon people had a settlement nearby (a separate short trail leads to its remnants), and the farther

petroglyph at Three Rivers

off the trail you go, the more pure carvings you'll see.

Farther down County Road B-30 about eight miles, just at the base of massive Sierra Blanca, **Three Rivers Campground** ($7) is a very pretty place with 14 tent or RV sites, a creek running nearby, and trails up into the hills. Unlike campgrounds at higher elevations, this one is open year-round, and it's rarely crowded.

## CARRIZOZO

The seat of Lincoln County, Carrizozo was a booming railroad town until the early 1950s, but now is perhaps most notable for the dispenser of the best ice cream sodas in the state: **Roy's Gift Gallery** (1200 Ave. E, 575/648-2921, 10am-12:30pm and 2:30pm-6pm Mon.-Fri., 12:30pm-5:30pm Sat.). The eponymous Roy, a charming Carrizozo native who has been at his craft since 1978, works at an old marble counter, with fountain fixtures from the 1930s. Once the town drugstore, the 1909 building is still outfitted with all its original display cabinets.

If you haven't given yourself a stomachache, you could also cruise the handful of galleries and shops on 12th Street (just north across the main road from Roy's), all painted in party colors, or stop in at the **Carrizozo Heritage Museum** (103 12th St., 575/648-1105, 10am-3pm Wed.-Sun. Mar.-Nov.), which has a small collection devoted to local history, some model trains, and a very large collection of barbed wire.

At the corner of Central Avenue and Airport Road, one block south of the intersection of U.S. 54 and U.S. 380, the **chamber of commerce** (575/648-2732, www.carrizozochamber.org, 10am-2pm Thurs.-Sat.) has its office in a vintage caboose. If it's not open, you can grab brochures from the display outside—one is a very detailed walking/driving tour of all the old buildings in town.

## VALLEY OF FIRES NATIONAL RECREATION AREA

Four miles west of Carrizozo on U.S. 380, the little-visited **Valley of Fires National Recreation Area** (575/648-2241, $3 pp or $5/car) are far smaller than El Malpais National Monument, west of Albuquerque. But they're much more striking because they're the product of an explosion just 1,500 years ago: The rocks are shinier, craggier, and often a very dramatic black, unlike the duller, almost purple hue of older volcanic stone. Up close, you'll be surprised at how much scrubby greenery has managed to grow up around the flow—a short **nature trail** leads around part of the site.

The **campground** ($7-18) has 19 sites, most with electricity hookups, as well as showers and restrooms. The tent sites are in a very nice secluded gully.

## TRINITY SITE

This portion of **White Sands Missile Range,** where the first atomic bomb was detonated on July 16, 1945, is open to the public only on the first Saturday in April and October, 8am-2pm. If this happens to coincide with your schedule, do try to go. At first, it doesn't seem like there's much to see beyond the ranch house where the bomb was assembled and the small depression left in the sand by the explosion, but then small details, such as shards of the green glassy substance created on the desert floor by the heat of the bomb, pop out the more you look around. Perhaps the most disturbing thing about the place is just how normal it looks.

Access is via the Stallion Gate to the missile range, off U.S. 380, at a turn south 53 miles west of Carrizozo or 12 miles east of San Antonio. Contact the missile range **public affairs office** (575/678-1134, www.wsmr.army.mil) to confirm dates and directions. A car convoy makes the 72-mile drive from Alamogordo, starting in the Tularosa High School parking lot; contact the **chamber of commerce** (575/437-6120) for details.

## WHITE OAKS

It's worth the nine-mile detour to White Oaks for a lesson in impermanence: Unbelievably, this used to be the second-largest city in New Mexico, after Las Vegas, and now it's a rough settlement of a couple dozen hardy creative types. Its social heart is the **No Scum Allowed Saloon** (575/648-5583, 11am-8pm Wed.-Thurs., noon-late Fri.-Sat., noon-8pm Sun.), cheerier than its name suggests and also well worth the drive—you might stumble on amazing fiddle playing or a biker bash.

The bar is open year-round, but the rest of this former mining settlement is near-silent in the off-season. At the end of April, it opens up with its annual **artist studio tour** (www.whiteoaksnewmexico.com). The most intriguing buildings—such as spooky, fenced-off Hoyle's Castle to the south, and the equally looming Gumm House, on a hill on the north side—are closed to visitors, but the brick school-house and a little miner's home both contain small museums that are open weekends in the summer. On Fridays in

New Mexico's friendliest bar

summer, the **White Oaks Rascal Fair** is a farmers market and sometime swap meet.

Look for the turn for White Oaks off U.S. 54 three miles north of Carrizozo; head east on Highway 349.

THE SOUTHEAST

# BACKGROUND

## The Land

Sharp peaks, deep gorges, harsh desert, sweeping plains—everything about New Mexico's landscape is dramatic. The light glints off surfaces at surprising angles, and the scenery can change at any bend in the road. The altitude ranges from around 2,800 feet down by the Texas border to more than 13,000 at Wheeler Peak north of Taos, but the average is about 5,700 feet, more than a mile high. So even if the scenery doesn't make you gasp for breath, the thin air might.

### GEOGRAPHY AND GEOLOGY

Much of New Mexico's landscape is the product of volcanic activity, beginning hundreds of millions of years back and ceasing (at least for now) only about 1,500 years ago. The main mountain ranges, which form part of the **Continental Divide**, are relatively young, pushed up in the Eocene era between 55 million and 34 million years ago, when shock waves from the collision of the North American plate and the Farallon plate caused the continent to heave. Just a few million years later, the **Rio Grande Rift**—one of the biggest rift valleys in the world—formed, as eras' and eras' worth of accumulated rock was pulled apart by shifting faults, leaving the perfect path for the river when it began to flow

© ZORA O'NEILL

about 3 million years ago. The water carved deep canyons, such as the 800-foot-deep Rio Grande Gorge west of Taos, that are perfect slices of geologic time, layers of limestone, sandstone, clay, and lava neatly stacked up. Just 1.2 million years back, a volcano's violent eruption and subsequent collapse created the huge **Valles Caldera,** and even as recently as AD 500, molten lava hardened into black badlands in the Tularosa Basin.

Beneath all this is evidence of a more stable time. For some four billion years, the land was completely underwater, then spent hundreds of millions of years supporting prehistoric sea life—hence the marine fossils found at the top of the Sandia Mountains, 10,000 feet above the current sea level. Dinosaurs, too, flourished for a time. One of the first, the nimble meat-eater *Coelophysis,* lived during the Triassic period around Abiquiu, and

heftier herbivores left their tracks all along the northeast part of the state.

## CLIMATE

More than simple latitude, the relative altitude determines the climate in New Mexico, where river-bottom central Albuquerque can be crisp and cloudless while Sandia Peak, 20 miles away and almost 5,000 feet up, is caught in a blinding snowstorm. (Yes, it snows plenty in New Mexico.) Nowhere, though, is it a particularly gentle climate—expect sudden changes in weather and temperature extremes.

At all but the very lowest elevations, winter is cold—days usually between 40°F and 55°F—but rarely cloudy, with a few snowstorms that never add up to as much moisture as people hope. Come spring, which starts in late April or May, the number of wildflowers that dot the hills is a direct reflection of the previous winter's precipitation. Little rain falls in May and June, typically the hottest and windiest months of the year, with temperatures climbing into the 90s—though it can still drop 40 degrees at night.

By early July, the so-called monsoon season brings heavy, refreshing downpours and thunderstorms every afternoon for a couple of months. It's remarkable—if a bit dismaying—to see how quickly all the water vanishes after each torrential rain. If you're out hiking in this season, steer clear of narrow canyons and arroyos during and after rains, as they can fill with powerful, deadly flash floods in a matter of minutes. September, October, and November are again dry, with the temperature dipping lower each month.

The higher the elevation, the later the spring: At 8,500 feet, snow could still be on the ground in May. Summer nights are rarely warm, and winter chill sets in sooner too, with fresh snow often falling in late October or November, although it takes well into December for a good base layer to build up at the ski areas.

Kasha-Ketuwe Tent Rocks National Monument

© ZORA O'NEILL

© ZORA O'NEILL

"No water" has been a steady complaint during New Mexico's multiyear drought.

## ENVIRONMENTAL ISSUES

The state's unforgiving climate and geography have been a perpetual challenge for human inhabitants. For thousands of years, New Mexicans have faced a water shortage. In prehistoric times, farming in the river valley was relatively easy, if subject to flooding. But at higher elevations, mountain streams had to be channeled into irrigation ditches. This system was perfected by Spanish settlers, who called their ditches acequias, a word they'd learned from the Arabs *(al-saqiya)*, who used the system to cultivate the Iberian Peninsula.

Today, as an ever-growing population demands more amenities, traditional ways of managing water have given way to more complex legal wranglings and outright hostility ("No chingen con nuestra agua"—don't f—k with our water—reads a license plate on some farmers' trucks in northern New Mexico). Some 49 billion gallons are pumped out of the middle Rio Grande aquifer every year, and only a portion of that is replenished through mountain runoff. Albuquerque

## Leave No Trace

So as not to upset the rather precarious environmental balance in much of New Mexico, you should internalize the ethic of "leave no trace"–even if you're just out for a short stroll. Let the phrase first guide your trip in the planning stages, when you equip yourself with good maps and GPS tools or a compass, to avoid relying on rock cairns or blazes. Backpackers should repackage food and other items to minimize the waste to pack out. And everyone should try to keep group size under six people; pets should not go in wild areas.

On the trail, resist the urge to cut across switchbacks or slog through the center of the trail, even if it has been widened by others trying to avoid mud. Be quiet, to avoid disturbing wildlife and other hikers. Leave what you find, whether plants, rocks, or potsherds.

Camp only where others have, in durable areas, at least 200 feet from water sources; dig cat holes 200 feet away, too. Pack out your toilet paper and other personal waste, and scatter dishwater and toothpaste. Safeguard food in "bear bags" hung at least 15 feet off the ground. Campfires are typically banned in New Mexico–please honor this policy, and keep a close eye on camp stoves. Pack out all cigarette butts.

Day hikers should also maintain a strict policy regarding litter. Tossing an orange peel, apple core, or other biodegradable item along the trail may not cause an environmental disaster, but it reminds other hikers that humans have been there and intrudes on the natural solitude of New Mexico's wilderness.

started using filtered river water in late 2008. "Smart growth" gets lip service in city council meetings, although construction continues apace on Albuquerque's arid West Mesa. Neo-homesteaders are installing cisterns to catch rain, as well as systems to reuse gray water, but these features are still far from standard.

Years of relative drought have made tinder-boxes of the forests. Within a few weeks in the summer of 2011, several wildfires swept across large swaths of forest. The Las Conchas Fire, near Los Alamos, burned more than 150,000 acres, the largest incident in New Mexico history by far. And it happened on the same terrain that had burned just over a decade before.

Visitors to New Mexico can help by following local environmental policies—complying with campfire bans in the wilderness, for instance, and keeping showers short. Golfers may want to consider curtailing their play here. New courses are springing up in every new casino resort and high-end residential development, despite the fact that they're intense draws on the water table.

# Flora and Fauna

Just as humans have managed to eke a life out of New Mexico, so have plants and animals—and a rather large variety of them. The state supports the fourth most diverse array of wildlife in the country.

## FLORA

Although much of the plant growth in New Mexico is nominally evergreen, the landscape skews toward brown, until you get up into the wetter alpine elevations.

### Vegetation Zones

Below 4,500 feet, New Mexico's **Lower Sonoran** zone, in the river valleys in the southern part of the state, is dotted with cactus, yucca, and scrubby creosote bushes. The **Upper Sonoran** zone, covering the areas between 4,500 and 7,000 feet, is the largest vegetation zone in the state and includes the high plains in the northeast and most of Albuquerque and Santa Fe, where the Sandia and Sangre de Cristo foothills are covered with juniper and piñon trees. The **Transition** zone, from 7,000 feet to 8,500 feet, sees a few more stately trees, such as ponderosa pine, and the state's more colorful wildflowers: orange Indian paintbrush, bright red penstemon, purple lupine. Above 8,500 feet, the **Mixed Conifer** zone harbors that sort of tree, along with clusters of aspens. The **Subalpine** zone, starting at 9,500 feet, is home to Engelmann spruce and bristlecone pine, while 11,500 feet marks the tree line in most places and the beginning of the **Alpine** zone, where almost no greenery survives. At 11,973 feet, the top of Sierra Blanca, near Ruidoso, is the southernmost example of this zone in the United States.

### Trees and Grasses

Trees are the clearest marker of elevation. In low areas—such as the Chihuahuan Desert outside of Las Cruces—you'll see almost no trees, only assorted cacti, such as the common **cane cholla;** the spiky **yucca** plant, which produces towering stalks of blooms in May; and the humble **tumbleweed.** Along the Rio Grande and the Pecos River, thirsty **cottonwoods** provide dense shade; the biggest trees, with their gnarled, branching trunks, are centuries old. In spring, their cotton fills the air—hell for the allergic, but source of a distinctive spicy fragrance—and in fall, their leaves turn pure yellow. Willow and olive are also common.

In the foothills, **piñon** (also spelled "pin-yon"), the official state tree, is everywhere, a slow-growing, drought-resistant scrub evolved to endure the New Mexican climate. When burned, its wood produces the scent of a New Mexico winter night, and its cones yield tasty nuts. Alongside piñon is **shaggy-bark juniper,**

© ZORA O'NEILL

prickly pear cactus fruit

identifiable by its loose strips of bark, sprays of soft needles, and branches that look twisted by the wind. In season, it's studded with purple-gray berries—another treat for foraging humans and animals alike. At ground level in the foothills, also look for clumps of sagebrush and bear grass, which blooms in huge, creamy tufts at the ends of stalks up to six feet tall.

Up in the mountains, the trees are a bit taller—here you'll find the towering **ponderosa** pine, tall trees with thick, almost crusty chunks of reddish-black bark; the crevices smell distinctly of vanilla. At slightly higher elevations, dense stands of **aspens** provide a rare spot of fall color in the evergreen forests. The combination of their golden leaves and white bark creates a particularly magical glow, especially in the mountains near Santa Fe. The highest mountain areas are home to a number of dense-needled hardy pines, such as blue-green **Engelmann spruce, corkbark fir, bristlecone pines,** and **subalpine fir,** with its sleek, rounded pinecones. Hike your way up to stands of these, which are tall but with

sparse branches, and you'll know you're close to the peak.

## FAUNA

As with plants, what you see depends on whether you're down in the desert or up on the mountain slopes. And you'll have to look carefully, because a lot of the animals that have survived here this long are the sort that have blended in with their surroundings—which means there are a lot of brown critters.

### Mammals

In the open, low-elevation areas on city fringes (and sometimes in the occasional vacant urban lot), look for **prairie dogs,** which live in huge underground warrens. When you're camping, the first creatures you'll meet are **squirrels** and **chipmunks**—at higher elevations, look out for Abert's squirrel, with its tufted ears and extra-fluffy tail. Long-haunched, clever, and highly adaptable, **coyotes** roam the lower elevations and are not shy about nosing around backyards; they make a barking yelp at night.

a cinnamon-colored black bear roaming through a New Mexico forest

On the plains, you may see **pronghorns** (often called antelope, though they are not related to Old World antelope) springing through the grasses, while hefty **mule deer** flourish in mountain forests, such as the Pecos Wilderness. Herds of even larger **elk** live in the high valleys; Rocky Mountain elk are common, thanks to an aggressive reintroduction effort in the early 20th century to make up for overhunting. A group of the largest variety, Roosevelt elk, whose fanlike antlers are the stuff of dreams for trophy hunters, roams in Valles Caldera. **Bighorn sheep** live in the mountains around Taos and in the Gila Wilderness.

**Black bears** crash around the forests, though their name is misleading—at any given time, they can be brown, cinnamon-red, or even nearly blond. Smokey Bear, the mascot of the National Forest Service, was from New Mexico, a cub rescued from a forest fire in Capitan. Drought has on many occasions driven the omnivorous beasts into suburban trash cans to forage, with tragic results for both people and the animals. If you're camping, take thorough measures to keep your food away from your camp and out of reach of animals.

And then there's the elusive **jackalope,** a jackrabbit hare sporting elaborate antlers. Alas, it seems now to appear only on postcards, although you may occasionally see a taxidermied head in a curio shop.

## Birds

New Mexico's state bird is the **roadrunner,** which can grow up to two feet long, nests in the ground, feeds on insects and even rattlesnakes, and has feet specially adapted to racing on the sands of the lower desert elevations in which it lives. Blue-and-black **Steller's jays** and raucous all-blue **piñon jays** are common in the foothills and farther up in the mountains, where you can also see **bluebirds, black-masked mountain chickadees,** and **Clark's nutcrackers,** which hoard great stashes of piñon nuts for winter. Also look around for **woodpeckers,** including the three-toed variety, which lives at higher elevations. On the highest peaks are **white-tailed ptarmigans,** which blend in with their snowy environment. But you can't miss the yellow-and-red **Western tanager,** a vivid shot of tropical delight in the Transition zone forests.

In late summer, keep an eye out for tiny, red-throated **Rufous hummingbirds** on their way to Mexico for the winter, along with hundreds of other birds that use the center of the state as a migratory corridor. The Sandia Mountains and the Las Vegas National Wildlife Refuge, among other spots, are on the flight path for **red-tailed hawks, eagles,** and other raptors, especially numerous in the springtime.

With more than 450 species spotted in New Mexico, this list is only scraping the surface. If you're a dedicated birder, first contact the **Randall Davey Audubon Center** (505/983-4609, nm.audubon.org) in Santa Fe, which leads bird walks, or the **Rio Grande Nature Center** in Albuquerque. **Bosque del Apache National Wildlife Refuge,** south of Albuquerque, is a must in the winter when thousands of **sandhill cranes**—and even the

occasional rare **whooping crane**—rest in the wetlands. Jim West of **WingsWest Birding** (800/583-6928, www.wingswestnm.com) is a reputable guide who has been leading groups around New Mexico since 1996.

## Fish

**Trout** is the major endemic fish, found in the cold waters of the Rio Grande as well as the San Juan, Chama, and Pecos Rivers. The cutthroat is particularly beloved in New Mexico—the only variety of trout originally found on the eastern side of the Continental Divide, whereas the more aggressive rainbow and brown trout are interlopers. The Rio Grande cutthroat, the official state fish, is now quite uncommon. Another local fish in jeopardy is the **Rio Grande silvery minnow,** listed as endangered since 1994. The last of the Rio Grande's five native fish, it's in such a dire state that biologists scoop them out of the water individually during bad dry spells and take them to the Albuquerque aquarium for safekeeping.

## Reptiles

One can't step foot in the desert without thinking of **rattlesnakes,** and New Mexico has plenty of them, usually hidden away under rocks and brush, but very occasionally sunning themselves in full view. The predominant species in the Rio Grande Valley, the **Western diamondback,** can grow to be seven feet long. Although its venom is relatively weak, it has an impressive striking distance of almost three feet. Around Taos and Santa Fe, the main species is the **prairie rattlesnake,** which is only four feet long at most, and the threatened **New Mexico ridgenose** is only about two feet long.

More benign cold-blooded critters include **lizards,** such as the **short-horned lizard** (a.k.a. horny toad), a miniature dinosaur, in effect, about as big as your palm. Look for it in the desert and the scrubby foothills.

## Insects and Arachnids

Because it's so dry, New Mexico isn't teeming with bugs. The ones that are there, however, can be off-putting, particularly if you chance

© ZORA O'NEILL

Reptiles like this lizard thrive in the southern desert.

upon the springtime **tarantula migration,** usually in May. It's not a true seasonal relocation, just the time when males come out of their dens to prowl for mates. The fist-size spiders move hundreds at a time, and occasionally back roads are closed to let them pass. If you'll be camping in the desert in the spring, ask the ranger's office about the status. Though they're big and hairy, they're not poisonous.

**Scorpions,** though, can be somewhat toxic, if very rarely deadly. In the southern desert areas, the most common variety is the bark scorpion, which nestles in rock crevices and woodpiles and can find its way into your shoes or the bottom of your sleeping bag. Its sting can cause anything from severe pain to difficulty breathing and should be treated with antivenin as soon as possible. Hard-shelled, segmented **desert centipedes** are another local creepy-crawly; they're often out at night and can grow up to nine inches long.

# History

The historical and cultural continuity in New Mexico is remarkable. The state has been transformed from ice-age hunting ground to home of the atom bomb, but many people claim roots that stretch back hundreds, even thousands, of years.

## ANCIENT AND ARCHAIC CIVILIZATION

New Mexico was one of the first places to harbor humans after the end of the last **ice age.** Archaeological findings indicate that some 12,000 years ago, people were hunting mastodons and other big game across the state. Mammoth bones, arrowheads, and the remains of campfires have been found in the Sandia Mountains east of Albuquerque; Folsom, in northeastern New Mexico; and Clovis, in the south. Sometime between 8000 and 5000 BC, these bands of hunters formed a small temporary settlement just north of Albuquerque, but it was not enough to stave off the decline of that ancient culture, as climatic shifts caused the big game to die off. Nomadic hunter-gatherers, seeking out smaller animals as well as seeds and nuts, did better in the new land, and by 1000 BC, they had established communities built around clusters of pit houses—sunken, log-covered rooms dug into the earth.

Along with this new form of shelter came an equally important advance in food: Mexican people gave corn kernels (maize) and lessons in agriculture to their neighbors, the **Mogollon,** who occupied southern New Mexico and Arizona. By AD 400, the Mogollon had begun growing squash and beans as well and had established concentrated communities all around the southern Rio Grande basin. This culture, dubbed the Basketmakers by archaeologists, also developed its own pottery, another skill learned from the indigenous people of Mexico. So when the Mogollon made contact with the Ancestral Puebloans (also known as the Anasazi) in the northern part of the state, they had plenty to share.

## THE PUEBLOS FORM

The year 700 marks the beginning of the **Pueblo I** phase, when disparate groups began to form larger communities in the upland areas on either side of the northern Rio Grande. Pit houses were still in use, but aboveground buildings of clay and sticks were erected alongside them. Increasingly, the pit houses were sacred spaces, chambers in which religious ceremonies were carried out; these are now known as kivas and are still an integral part of pueblo life.

The **Pueblo II** era begins in 850 and is distinguished by the rise of Pueblo Bonito in Chaco Canyon, northwest of Santa Fe, into a full-scale city and perhaps capital of a small state. It was home to an estimated 1,500 people ruled by a religious elite. But Chaco abruptly began to crumble around 1150, perhaps due to drought, famine, or warfare. This shift marked the **Pueblo III** period, when the people who were to become today's Puebloans began building their easily defended cliff dwellings—most famously in the Four Corners area, at Mesa Verde, but also farther south, on the Pajarito Plateau in what's now Bandelier National Monument, and in Puyé, on Santa Clara Pueblo land. A drought at the end of the 13th century cleared out the Four Corners at the start of the **Pueblo IV** era, provoking the population to consolidate along the Rio Grande in clusters of sometimes more than a thousand interconnected rooms. These communities dotted the riverbank, drawing their sustenance both from the river water and from the mountains behind them.

## THE SPANISH ARRIVE

These settlements were what the Spanish explorer **Francisco Vásquez de Coronado** and his crew saw when they first ventured into the area in 1540. Their Spanish word for the villages, *pueblos,* stuck and is still the name for

© ZORA O'NEILL

**Don Juan de Oñate was one of the early Spanish governors.**

both the places and the people who live in them. Coronado wasn't impressed, however, because the pueblos were made out of mud, not gold as he had been hoping. So after two years and a couple of skirmishes with the natives, the team turned around and headed back to Mexico City.

It took another 50 years for the Spanish to muster more interest in the area. This time, in 1598, Don Juan de Oñate led a small group of Spanish families to settle on the banks of the Rio Grande, at a place they called San Gabriel, near Ohkay Owingeh (which they called San Juan Pueblo). About a decade later, the settlers moved away from their American Indian neighbors, to the new village of Santa Fe. The territory's third governor, Don Pedro de Peralta, made it the official capital of the territory of Nuevo México, which in those days stretched far into what is now Colorado and Arizona.

This time the colonists, mostly farmers, were motivated not so much by hopes of striking it rich but simply of making a living. Moreover, they were inspired by Catholic zeal, and Franciscan missionaries accompanied them to promote the faith among the Puebloans. It was partly these missionaries and their ruthless oppression of the native religion that drove the Indians to organize the **Pueblo Revolt** of 1680. The Franciscans' "conversion" strategy involved public executions of the pueblos' medicine men, among other violent assaults on local traditions. But the Spanish colonists were no help either. In their desperation to squeeze wealth out of the hard land, they exploited the only resource they had, the slave labor of the Indians, who were either conscripts or stolen from their families. (The Indians did their share of poaching from Spanish families too, creating a violent sort of cultural exchange program.)

The leader of the Pueblo Revolt was a man named Popé (also spelled Po'pay), from San Juan Pueblo. Using Taos Pueblo as his base, he traveled to the other communities, secretly meeting with leaders to plan a united insurrection. Historians theorize he may have used Spanish to communicate with other Puebloans who did not speak his native Tewa, and he distributed among the conspirators lengths of knotted rope with which to count down the days to the insurrection. Although the Spanish captured a few of the rope-bearing messengers (Isleta Pueblo may never have gotten the message, which could explain its being the only pueblo not to participate), they could not avert the bloodshed. The Puebloan warriors killed families and missionaries, burned crops, and toppled churches. Santa Fe was besieged, and its population of more than 1,000 finally evacuated in a pitiful retreat.

The Spanish stayed away for 12 years, but finally a new governor, Diego de Vargas, took it upon himself to reclaim the land the Spanish had settled. He managed to talk many pueblos into peaceful surrender, meeting resistance only in Taos and Santa Fe, where a two-day fight was required to oust the Indians from the Palace of the Governors. The Spanish strategy in the post-revolt era was softer, with more compromise between the Franciscans and their intended flock, and a fair amount of cultural and economic exchange. The threat of raiding Comanche, Apache, and Navajo also forced both sides to cooperate. Banding together for defense, they were finally able to drive the Comanche away, culminating in a 1778 battle with Chief Cuerno Verde (Green Horn). The decisive victory is celebrated in the ritual dance called Los Comanches, still performed in small villages by Hispanos and Puebloans alike.

The other bonding force was trade. The Spanish maintained the **Camino Real de Tierra Adentro** (Royal Road of the Interior), which linked Santa Fe with central Mexico—the route follows roughly the line carved by I-25 today. Caravans came through only every year or two, but the profit from furs, pottery, textiles, and other local goods was enough to keep both cultures afloat, if utterly dependent on the Spanish government.

## MEXICAN INDEPENDENCE AND THE FIRST ANGLOS

Spain carefully guarded all of its trade routes in the New World, even in a relatively unprofitable territory like Nuevo México. The only outside trade permitted was through the Comancheros, a ragtag band who traded with Comanche and other Plains Indians, working well into what would later be Oklahoma and even up to North Dakota. The Spanish governor encouraged them because their tight relationship with the Comanche helped protect New Mexico and Texas against intruders.

Interlopers were not welcome. Only a few enterprising fur trappers, lone mountain men in search of beaver pelts, slipped in. Spy-explorer **Zebulon Pike** and his crew were captured (perhaps intentionally, so Pike could get more inside information) and detained in Santa Fe for a spell in 1807. But in 1821, Mexico declared independence from Spain, liberating the territory of Nuevo México along with it. One of the first acts of the new government was to open the borders to trade. Initially just a trickle of curious traders came down the rough track from St. Louis, but soon a flood of commerce flowed along the increasingly rutted and broad **Santa Fe Trail,** making the territory's capital city a meeting place between Mexicans and Americans swapping furs, gold, cloth, and more.

## THE MEXICAN-AMERICAN WAR AND AFTER

Pike's expedition, conducted just as Lewis and Clark returned from their march across the Louisiana Purchase, not only gave the U.S. government new information on the locations of Spanish forts, it also helped fuel the country's expansionist fervor. By the 1840s, **"manifest destiny"** was the phrase on every American's lips, and the government was eyeing the Southwest. It annexed Texas in 1845, but New Mexico, with its small population and meager resources, didn't figure heavily in the short-lived war that followed. The Mexican governor surrendered peacefully to General Stephen Kearny when he arrived in Santa Fe in 1846. In Taos, the transition was not accepted so readily, as Hispano business leaders and Taos Pueblo Indians instigated a brief but violent uprising, in which the first American governor, Charles Bent, was beheaded.

During the **Civil War,** New Mexico was in the way of a Texan Confederate strategy to secure the Southwest, but the rebels were thwarted in 1862 at the Battle of Glorieta Pass. The territory stayed in the hands of the Union until the end of the war. At any rate, people were more concerned with the local, increasingly brutal skirmishes with the Apache and the Navajo, in which the U.S. Army tried to subdue the tribes and protect the homesteaders and profitable gold, silver, and coal mining claims that were being developed. This latter industry indirectly bred further violence in the 1870s in the form of the Lincoln County War and the Colfax County War, two extended brawls in which some of the era's most notorious outlaws were involved.

Even more significant to New Mexico's development was the arrival of the **railroad** in 1880, as it was laid through Raton Pass, near Santa Fe, and close to Albuquerque. Virtually overnight, strange goods and even stranger people came pouring into one of the more remote frontier outposts of the United States. Anglo influence was suddenly everywhere, in the form of new architecture (red brick was an Eastern affectation) and new business. Albuquerque, almost directly on the new railway tracks, boomed, while Santa Fe's fortunes slumped and Taos all but withered away, having peaked back in the late days of the Camino Real.

But while wheeler-dealers were setting up shop in central New Mexico, some more intrepid souls were poking around in the less-connected areas farther north. These tourists were artists who valued New Mexico not for its commercial potential but for its dramatic landscapes and exotic populace who seemed untouched by American ways. From the early 20th century on, Santa Fe and Taos were cultivated as art colonies, a function they still fulfill today.

## FROM STATEHOOD TO WORLD WAR II

Based on its burgeoning economy, New Mexico became the 47th state in the union in 1912, effectively marking the end of the frontier period,

The Castañeda Hotel in Las Vegas is a relic of New Mexico's early railroad history.

ⒸZORA O'NEILL

a phase of violence, uncertainty, and isolation that lasted about 300 years, longer here than anywhere else in the United States. In addition to the painters and writers flocking to the new state, another group of migrants arrived: tuberculosis patients. Soon the state was known as a health retreat, and countless people did stints in its dry air to treat their ailing lungs.

One of these patients was J. Robert Oppenheimer, whose mild case of TB got him packed off to a camp near Pecos for a year after high school. He loved northern New Mexico and got to know some of its more hidden pockets. So when the U.S. Army asked him if he had an idea where it should establish a secret base for the **Manhattan Project,** he knew just the place: a little camp high on a plateau above Santa Fe, named Los Alamos. This was the birthplace of the atomic bomb, a weird, close-knit community of the country's greatest scientific minds (and biggest egos), working in utter secrecy. Only after the bomb was tested at White Sands and Fat Man and Little Boy were dropped over Japan was the mysterious camp's mission revealed.

## CONTEMPORARY HISTORY

With the invention of the A-bomb, New Mexico was ushered into the modern era. This wasn't just because it produced world-changing technology, but also because the high-paying jobs at Los Alamos and Kirtland Air Force Base in Albuquerque helped pull some of the population out of subsistence farming and into a life that involved cars and electricity. But even so, the character of the state remained conservative and closed, so when the 1960s rolled around and New Mexico's empty space looked like the promised land to hippies, the culture clash was fierce. Staunch Catholic farmers took potshots at their naked, hallucinogen-ingesting neighbors who fantasized about getting back to the land but had no clue how to do it. After a decade or so, though, only the hardiest of the commune-dwellers were left, and they'd mellowed a bit, while the locals had come to appreciate at least their enthusiasm. Even if the communes didn't last, hippie culture has proven remarkably persistent—even today, distinctly straight Hispanos can be heard saying things like, "I was tripping out on that band, man," and the state still welcomes Rainbow Gatherings, would-be Buddhists, and alternative healers.

The end of the 20th century saw unprecedented growth in New Mexico's bigger cities. As usual, Albuquerque got the practical-minded development, such as the Intel plant and the services headquarters for Gap Inc., while Santa Fe was almost felled by its own artsiness, turned inside-out during a few frenzied years when movie stars and other moneyed types bought up prime real estate. In just a matter of months in the early 1990s, rents went up tenfold and houses started selling for more than $1 million. Santa Fe has yet to work out the imbalance between its creative forces, which did save the city from utter decline, and economic ones, though it implemented a living-wage law in 2009.

Meanwhile, Taos and Las Cruces have grown slowly but steadily, as have the pueblos, thanks to the legalization of gambling on their lands, but all of these communities still have an air of old New Mexico, where the frontier flavor and solitude can still be felt.

# Government and Economy

New Mexico doesn't look so good on paper, what with high statistics for corruption, nepotism, and poverty. But these issues have also inspired a good deal of activist sentiment, and politics are lively as the economy has begun to slip out of some of its old restrictive patterns.

## GOVERNMENT

New Mexico's political scene is as diverse as its population, a fractious mix of Democrats, Republicans, Greens, Libertarians, anarchists, independents, and irredeemable cranks. The presidential contests of 2000 and 2004 were too close to call, requiring recounts to determine the winners by a hair (Gore in 2000, Bush in 2004). In 2008, the election went squarely to Obama, after he rallied Hispanics with the slogan "Obamanos!" Then-governor Bill Richardson was tapped as a potential cabinet member, but then withdrew after insinuations of corruption. He stepped aside in 2010 for Republican Susana Martinez, New Mexico's first woman governor. (The election would've been historic either way: Her opponent was also a woman.) Reacting to post-crash economic woes, Martinez rapidly swung policies to the right, undoing some of her predecessor's environmental efforts in the name of boosting business. That swing continued in the 2012 presidential election, as counties skewed extremely red or blue; former governor and Libertarian Gary Johnson took 3.5 percent of the vote, his highest stake in the nation.

New Mexico is notable for its high Hispanic representation in every level of government, including the state legislature, which is 44 percent Hispanic. This nearly matches the state Hispanic population of about 45 percent, and it has helped keep the immigration debate at a polite pitch—unlike in neighboring Arizona, where the Hispanic population is 30 percent, but only 16 percent in the legislature.

On a local level, corruption charges and entrenched cronyism are still rampant—or at least perceived as such. When any scandal breaks (nepotistic assignment of highway repair contracts, for instance, or politicians repeatedly arrested for DUIs, and then cleared), pundits can't help but comment that the old Spanish *patrón* system, in which small-town bosses dole out benefits to their loyal supporters, seems to still be at work. "New Mexico is a third-world country" is another common quip.

The system is muddled by the American Indian reservations, each of which acts as a sovereign nation, with its own laws, tax regulations, police forces, and government. Indians vote in U.S. and state elections, but in the pueblos, most domestic issues are decided by a tribal governor, a war chief, and a few other officials elected by a consensus of men in the kiva. The Navajo Nation, perhaps due to the fact that it has more than 250,000 people to manage, as well as a substantial cache of natural resources, does practice direct democracy. In its system, the reservation, which reaches into Arizona and Utah, is divided into "chapters," and their representatives, voted on by men and women alike in a popular election, participate in the Navajo Council, which convenes in the capital at Window Rock, Arizona. Since a reform in 1991, the Navajo system has had three branches, like the American one. In 2006, Lynda Lovejoy was the first woman to run for nation president; she made a strong showing against incumbent Joe Shirley. In 2010, she lost by a small margin to former vice president Ben Shelly.

## ECONOMY

New Mexico has always lagged at the bottom of the country's economic ratings: In 2010, 19 percent of the population was living below the poverty level, compared with the national average of 14.3 percent. It's also near the bottom in the number of high school and college graduates per capita. Statistics in the pueblos and reservations are even grimmer, with up to 50 percent unemployment in some areas—though this is changing due to casino-fueled development. The Navajo Nation has extensive landholdings, but due to an infrastructure that's more 19th than 21st century, no businesses are interested in investing here. The same could in fact be said for many of the rural sections of the state, on Indian land or no.

The 2008 recession hit the state hard, but its overall unemployment rate has been lower than the national average, in part because Albuquerque continues to be a **manufacturing** center for computer chips, mattresses, specialty running shoes, and more. And the city where Microsoft was founded (then Bill Gates and Paul Allen moved back to Seattle to be close to their families) does foster **technology** development, as a range of tech specialists cater to Sandia National Labs. **Aerospace** manufacturing parks are growing outside Albuquerque and Las Cruces. At press time, private space flights were on the brink of departure from Spaceport America near Truth or Consequences.

Significant profits from coal, copper, oil, and natural-gas extraction keep the economy afloat. That's the big money, but the **agricultural** sector, from dairy cows in the south to apple orchards along the Rio Grande to beef jerky from the numerous cattle ranches, contributes a decent amount to the pot. And Santa Fe's **arts** sector shouldn't be overlooked—galleries post sales of $200 million every year, though they're criticized for sending much of that money right back to artists who live and work out of state. Governor Richardson actively courted the **film industry,** nicknamed "Tamalewood," with tax rebates. This led to a boom in movies shot against the dramatic backdrops of the state, and the development of Albuquerque Studios, one of the largest production facilities in the country. Governor Martinez curtailed the rebate program, however, and the industry has shrunk again.

Even if the economic situation isn't ideal, it's nothing New Mexicans aren't used to—low income has been the norm for so long that a large segment of the population is, if not content with, at least adapted to eking out a living from very little (the median family income is only around $44,600, compared with the U.S. median of $52,700). In this respect, the state hasn't lost its frontier spirit at all.

# People and Culture

New Mexico's 1.8 million people have typically been described as a tricultural mix of Indians, Spanish, and whites. That self-image has begun to expand as residents have delved deeper into history and seen that the story involves a few more threads.

## DEMOGRAPHY

The typical labels of Indian, Spanish, and Anglo are used uniquely in New Mexico. First, **Indian:** This is still commonly used, as "Native American" never fully caught on. You'll see "American Indian" in formal situations, but even the "American" part is a bit laughable, considering "America" wasn't so named until Christopher Columbus made his voyage west. "Indian" refers to a number of different peoples who do not share a common culture or language: Navajo on the west side of the state, Jicarilla and Mescalero Apache, and the Puebloans of the Rio Grande and west as far as Acoma and Zuni. (The latter term, "Pueblo," is another problematic one, as it refers not to a particular tribe, but to a larger group of people who speak four distinct languages but are banded together by a common way of living.) With about 10 percent of the population claiming American Indian ancestry (nearly 10 times the national average), traditions are still strong. Though of course they've changed, as neon-dyed feathers trim kids' ceremonial headdresses, and wealth from casinos funds new housing projects.

**Spanish** really means that: the people,

The "tricultural" image of New Mexico is changing, as historians show contributions of other groups over time.

primarily in northern New Mexico, whose ancestors were pure-blood Spaniards, rather than the mestizos of Mexico. For many families, it's a point of pride similar to that of *Mayflower* descendants. Over the years, particularly during the 20th century, a steady influx of Mexican immigrants blurred racial distinctions a bit, but it also reinforced the use of Spanish as a daily language and inspired pride in the culture's music and other folkways. In some circles, the word **Hispano** is used to label New Mexico's distinct culture with centuries-old Iberian roots, which includes the **Basques,** who came here both during the conquest (Don Juan de Oñate, the first Spanish governor, was Basque) and in the early 20th century as sheepherders. The recent discovery of families of **crypto-Jews** (Spanish Jews who nominally converted to Catholicism but fled here to avoid the Inquisition) has added another fascinating layer to the Spanish story, along with the knowledge that many of the first Spanish explorers likely had Arab blood as well.

**Anglo** is the most imprecise term of all, as it can mean anyone who's not Spanish or Indian. Originally used to talk about the white traders who came to hunt and sell furs and trade on the Santa Fe Trail, it still refers to people who can't trace their roots back to the conquistadors or farther. If you're a Vietnamese immigrant in Albuquerque, you could be Anglo. If you're a Tibetan refugee in Santa Fe, you could be Anglo. And even if you're an African-American farmer who settled here after the Civil War, people will at least joke that you're Anglo. (As of 2011, about 40.2 percent of the population was non-Hispanic white; Asians were only 1.6 percent, and African Americans made up 2.5 percent.) But all Anglo culture is shot through with Spanish and Indian influence, whether among the organic garlic farmers from California who rely on their acequias for water or the New Age seekers who do sweatlodge rituals.

Even with a liberal application of "Anglo," the tricultural arrangement is limiting, as it

© ZORA O'NEILL

doesn't assign a place to contemporary immigrants from Mexico and other Latin American countries, and their numbers are growing steadily. It also doesn't acknowledge the strong Mexican-American **Chicano** culture that's shared across the Southwest, from Los Angeles through Texas. The U.S. census form lumps both newer arrivals and old Spanish under "Hispanic"—a category (distinct from race) that made up 46.7 percent of the population in 2011.

## RELIGION

Four hundred years after the arrival of the Franciscan missionaries, New Mexico is still a heavily **Catholic** state—even KFC offers a Friday-night fish fry during Lent. But the relative isolation of the territory produced some variances that have disturbed the Vatican. In both Indian and Spanish churches, the pageantry of medieval Christianity is preserved. Las Posadas, the reenactment of Mary and Joseph's search for lodging in Bethlehem, is a festive torch-lit tradition every December, and during the annual Holy Week pilgrimage to Chimayó, devoted groups stage the stations of the cross, complete with 100-pound wood beams and lots of fake blood.

The Pueblo Indians play on church-as-theater too: During Christmas Eve Mass, for instance, the service may come to an abrupt end as the priest is hustled off the pulpit by face-painted clowns making way for the parade of ceremonial dancers down the aisle. In both cultures, the Mexican Virgin of Guadalupe is highly revered, and a number of saints are honored as intercessors for all manner of dilemmas, from failing crops to false imprisonment.

Eastern religions have a noticeable presence in New Mexico as well, and even a bit of political clout. A community of primarily American-born converts to **Sikhism** in Española, for example, is a major donor to both parties. Santa Fe is home to a substantial number of **Buddhists,** both American converts and native Tibetan refugees who have relocated to this different mountainous land. Stupas can be found up and down the Rio Grande.

© ZORA O'NEILL

mementos at the top of the Catholic pilgrimage site of Tomé Hill

## The Secret Brotherhood: New Mexico's Penitentes

Most Hispano villages in northern New Mexico have a modest one-story building called a *morada*—the meeting place of Los Hermanos Penitentes (The Penitent Brothers), a lay Catholic fraternity with deep roots in medieval Spain and a history that has often put it at odds with the church.

The Penitentes developed in New Mexico in the early colonial era and were at the height of their influence during the so-called Secular Period (1790-1850), when the Franciscans had been pushed out by church leaders in Mexico but no new priests were sent to the territory. Members of the brotherhood cared for the ill, conducted funerals, and settled petty disputes and even elections. They maintained the spiritual and political welfare of their villages when there were no priests or central government to do so.

What the Penitentes are best known for is their intense religious ritual, which includes self-flagellation, bloodletting, and mock crucifixion—activities that took place in public processions for centuries but were driven underground in the late 19th century following official church condemnation. The secrecy, along with sensational journalism by visitors from the East Coast, fueled gruesome rumors. For their crucifixion reenactments, it was said Penitentes used real nails, and the man drawn by lot to be the *Cristo* had a good chance of dying—though no eyewitness ever recorded the practice on paper. One well-documented ritual involves pulling *la carretera del muerte*, an oxcart filled with rocks and a wooden figure of Doña Sebastiana, the Angel of Death. Morbid imagery bred morbid curiosity: Photos in a *Harper's* magazine story from the early 20th century show Anglos looking on agog as Penitentes clad in white pants and black hoods whip themselves.

In 1947, after years of concerted lobbying (but not an official renunciation of its rituals), the Penitentes were again accepted into the fold of the Catholic Church. The *hermanos mayores* (head brothers) from all of the *moradas* convene annually in Santa Fe, and the group, which has an estimated 3,000 members, functions as a political and public-service club.

The rituals do continue, most visibly during Holy Week, when the group's devotion to the physical suffering of the human Jesus is at its keenest. The Penitentes reenact the stations of the cross and the crucifixion, and although ketchup is more prevalent than real blood and statues often stand in for the major players, the scenes are solemn and affectingly tragic. On some days during Holy Week, the *morada* is open to non-Penitentes—a rare chance for outsiders to see the meeting place of this secretive group.

## LANGUAGE

**English** is the predominant language, especially off the beaten track, **Spanish** is commonly used—about 30 percent of the population speaks it regularly. Spanish-speakers in northern New Mexico were for centuries only the old Hispano families, communicating in a variant of Castilian with a distinct vocabulary that developed in isolation. This "Quixotic" dialect changed little until the 20th century, when immigrants arrived from Mexico and elsewhere in Latin America. For much of the 20th century, English was the only permissible classroom language, although many school districts required Spanish as a foreign language. Since the 1990s, education policy has shifted to include bilingual classrooms.

Additionally, you'll occasionally hear Indians speaking their respective languages. Of the four main Pueblo tongues, **Tewa, Tiwa,** and **Towa** are part of the Tanoan family of languages (Kiowa, spoken by Plains Indians, is the fourth member). They are related but mutually unintelligible, roughly equivalent to, say, French, Spanish, and Italian. Tewa is the most widely spoken, used in all of the pueblos just north of Santa Fe: Ohkay Owingeh, San Ildefonso, Santa Clara, Pojoaque, Tesuque, and Nambé. Four pueblos speak Tiwa—Taos and Picurís share one dialect, while Isleta and Sandia, in an odd pocket near Albuquerque, speak a different dialect. Towa is now spoken only at Jemez Pueblo. Part of the greater Athabaskan family, the **Navajo** and **Apache** languages are related to each but distinct from one another.

**Keresan** (spoken in Laguna, Acoma, Cochiti, Kewa, San Felipe, Santa Ana, and Zia) and **Zuni** (spoken only at that pueblo) are what linguists call "isolates." Like Basque, they are not connected to neighboring languages, nor to any other language. Additionally, each Keresan-speaking pueblo has developed its own dialect, so immediately adjacent communities can understand each other, but those farthest apart cannot.

One interesting characteristic of the Pueblo languages is that they have remained relatively pure. Tewa vocabulary, for instance, is still less than 5 percent loan words, despite centuries of Spanish and English influence. This is probably due to the way speakers have long been forced to compartmentalize, using Tewa for conversation at home and switching to English or Spanish for business and trade. For centuries, the Franciscan priests, then the U.S. government, attempted to stamp out Native American languages. Following the Civil War, Puebloan children were moved forcibly to boarding schools, where they were given Anglo names and permitted to speak only English, a policy that continued for decades.

Only in 1990, with the passage of the **Native American Languages Act,** were American Indian languages officially permitted in government-funded schools—indeed, they are now recognized as a unique element of this country's culture and encouraged. In Taos, where the Tiwa language is a ritual secret that outsiders are not permitted to learn, one public school has Tiwa classes for younger students, open only to tribe members and taught by approved teachers; as an added measure against the language being recorded, the classroom has no chalkboard. Less-formal instruction within the pueblos as well as on the Navajo Nation has also helped the Indian languages enjoy a renaissance.

# The Arts

New Mexico is a hotbed of creativity, from Santa Fe's edgy contemporary art scene to traditional Spanish folk artists working in remote villages, using the same tools their great-grandfathers did, to whole American Indian villages, such as Zuni, devoted to the production of fine silverwork. Here's what to look out for in the more traditional arenas of pottery, weaving, jewelry, and wood carving.

## POTTERY

New Mexico's pottery tradition thrives, drawing on millennia of craftsmanship. About 2,000 years ago, the **Mogollon** people in the southern part of the state began making simple pots of brown coiled clay. A thousand years later, the craft had developed into the beautiful black-on-white symmetry of the **Mimbres** people. Later, each of the pueblos developed its own style.

By the 20th century, some traditions had died out, but almost all felt some kind of renaissance following the work of San Ildefonso potter **María Martinez** in the first half of the 20th century. Along with her husband, Julian, Martinez revived a long-lost style of lustrous black pottery with subtle matte decoration. The elegant pieces, which looked at once innovative and traditional, inspired Anglo collectors (who saw the couple's work at the 1934 Chicago World's Fair, among other places) as well as local potters. Today, many artists make their livings working with clay.

The various tribal styles are distinguished by their base clay, the "slip" (the clay-and-water finish), and their shape. Taos and Picurís

## Luminarias or *Farolitos?*

© SUMIKOPHOTO/123RF.COM

**Regional dialect quiz: Name this beloved Southwestern holiday decoration.**

The cultural differences between Santa Fe and Albuquerque don't apply just to the number of art galleries per square block and whether you eat *posole* or rice with your enchiladas. Every Christmas, a debate rears its head: What do you call a paper bag with a bit of sand in the bottom and a votive candle inside? These traditional holiday decorations, which line driveways and flat adobe rooftops in the last weeks of December, are known as luminarias in Albuquerque and most towns to the south, and as *farolitos* in Santa Fe and all the villages to the north.

To complicate matters, another common holiday tradition in Santa Fe and other northern towns is to light small bonfires of piñon logs in front of houses. And Santa Feans call these little stacks of wood...luminarias. *Farolitos*, they

argue, are literally "little lanterns," an accurate description of the glowing paper bags–and under this logic, the use of the term *farolito* has spread a bit in Albuquerque, at least among people who weren't raised saying luminaria from birth.

But Albuquerqueans have Webster's on their side; the dictionary concurs that luminarias are paper-bag lanterns and notes the tradition comes from Mexico, where the bags are often colored and pricked with holes. (Perhaps Albuquerque's relative proximity to the border–and its larger proportion of Mexican immigrants– has shaped the language over the years?) In any case, because this author's loyalties are to Albuquerque, the argument is settled, at least in these pages: Luminaria it is.

pueblos, for instance, are surrounded by beds of micaceous clay, which lends pots a subtle glitter. (It also helps them withstand heat well; they're renowned for cooking beans.) Acoma specializes in intricate black-and-white painted designs. Pottery from Ohkay Owingeh (formerly San Juan) is typically reddish-brown with incised symbols. And Santa Clara developed the "wedding jar," a double-neck design with a handle. Traditional Navajo pottery is distinguished by pitch glaze (a coating of pine resin for a shiny, waterproof finish) and "fire clouds," the grayish smudges left when burning wood has pressed against the clay during firing.

## TEXTILES

After pottery, **weaving** is probably the state's largest craft industry. Historically, Indian and Spanish weaving styles were separate, but they have merged over the centuries to create some patterns and styles unique to the Rio Grande Valley. The first Spanish explorers marveled at the Navajo cotton blankets, woven in whole panels on wide looms; Spaniards had been working with narrow looms and stitching two panels together. Spanish weavers introduced the hardy Churro sheep, with its rough wool that was good for hand-spinning, as well as new dyes, such as indigo (although the blue-tinted rugs are often called **Moki** rugs, using a Navajo word).

In the early 1800s, in an attempt to make a better product for trade, the Spanish government sent Mexican artists north to work with local weavers. Out of this meeting came the distinctive **Saltillo** styles (named for the region the Mexican teachers came from), such as the running-leaf pattern, which Rio Grande weavers alternated with solid-color stripes. In the 1880s, New Mexican artisans first saw quilts from the eastern United States, and they adapted the eight-pointed star to their wool rugs. Another popular motif from the 19th century is a zigzag pattern that resembles lightning.

One item that shows up in antique shops is the **Chimayó blanket,** an invention of the tourist age in the early 20th century, when Anglo traders encouraged local Hispano weavers to make an affordable souvenir to sell to visitors looking for "Indian" blankets. They're handsome, single-width rugs with a strong central motif, perhaps the iconic Southwestern-look rug.

Also look for **colcha** work, a Spanish style in which a loose-weave rug is decorated with wool embroidery. It was revived in the 1930s by Mormons, and you will occasionally see beautiful examples from this period in collectors' shops. Contemporary weaving can draw on any and all of these innovations and is practiced just as often by a young Anglo as a Hispano grandmother. A strong small-batch wool industry in New Mexico helps the scene tremendously—expect to see vivid color-block contemporary pieces alongside the most traditional patterns.

## JEWELRY

Despite a long native tradition, the familiar forms of jewelry seen today date only from the mid-19th century, when the Navajo of western New Mexico pioneered silversmithing (it's thought they learned it during their internment at Fort Sumner) and taught it to the Pueblo Indians. The most iconic piece of Southwestern jewelry, a signature Navajo design, is the turquoise-and-silver **squash-blossom necklace,** a large crescent pendant decorated with flowerlike silver beads. Actually derived from Spanish pomegranate decorations, rather than native plant imagery, it's readily seen in every Southwest jewelry store.

Look also for shell-shaped **concho belts** (also spelled "concha"), silver "shells" linked together or strung on a leather belt, and the San Felipe specialty, **heishi,** tiny disks made of shell and threaded to make a ropelike strand. The Zuni carve small animal **fetishes**—bears, birds, and more—often strung on necklaces with heishi. In addition to turquoise, opals are a popular decorative stone, along with brick-red coral, lapis lazuli, and black jet and marble. Whatever you buy, the gallery or artisan should supply you with a written receipt of its components—which stones, the grade of silver, and so forth.

Raw turquoise and shells for jewelry are on sale at the Gallup flea market.

## Turquoise

Although New Mexico's turquoise is all mined out, the stone is still an essential part of local jewelry-making; most of it is imported from mines in China. It is available in shades from lime-green to pure sky-blue, and much of it has been subjected to various processes to make it more stable and versatile, which affects the price.

Rare gem-grade turquoise is the top of the line—a high-quality, deeply spiderwebbed piece from now-empty mines like Lander or Lone Mountain can cost $350 per carat. "Gem-grade" applies only to **natural stones** (those that have not been chemically treated in any way) and is based on the piece's luster, hardness, and matrix, the term for the web of dark veins running through it, which you should be able to feel in any natural turquoise, regardless of grade. Highest-quality stones from still-functioning mines in China or Tibet will cost significantly less ($10-20 per carat) but will be of the same quality as some premium American stones. Slightly less splendid natural

stones are graded jewelry-quality, high-quality, or investment-quality—but they are not quite hard enough to guarantee they will not change color over decades. They cost $2-5 per carat. For any natural stone, the seller must provide you with a written certificate of its status.

Because good natural turquoise is increasingly difficult to come by and turquoise is such an unreliable stone, various treatments are a common and acceptable way of making a great deal of the stuff usable. **Treated turquoise** refers to any stone that has added resins, waxes, or other foreign elements. A certain proprietary treatment, **enhanced turquoise,** also called "Zachary process turquoise," is usually applied to medium-grade or higher stones.

Turquoise that has been **stabilized,** or submerged in epoxy resin to harden it and deepen the color, makes up the bulk of the market. Because it's less expensive, it allows for a little waste in the carving process, and good-quality stabilized turquoise is often found in expensive jewelry with elaborate inlay. Average-quality stabilized stone, the next grade down, is used by perhaps 70 percent of American Indian artisans—it can stand up to being carved and is very well priced. Though it ranks relatively low in the range of turquoise available, it produces an attractive piece of jewelry—perhaps not with the elaborate spiderwebbing of a rare piece, but with an overall good color and luster.

Below this are low-quality stabilized stones that have been artificially colored (often called "color shot," or, more confusing, "color stabilized"). **"Synthetic"** stones are actually real turquoise—small chunks mixed with a binding powder of ground turquoise or pyrite, then pressed into shapes and cut. The result is surprisingly attractive, with natural spiderwebbing, but it should be clearly labeled as synthetic. And of course there is the turquoise that isn't at all—plastic stuff that can be quite convincing.

Aside from the synthetic stuff, don't worry too much about getting "bad" or "cheap" turquoise—because each stone is different, the more important thing is to find a piece that's attractive to you and is priced to reflect its quality. Just remember that the words "genuine," "authentic," or "pure" have no real meaning. Only "natural" is legally defined and commands a premium, and the phrase "authentic Indian handmade" is legally defined—any variation on this wording (such as "Indian crafted") is likely some kind of ruse. Shopping in New Mexico provides many opportunities to buy direct from the artisan—under the portal at the Palace of the Governors in Santa Fe, for instance. Otherwise, just avoid shopping in too-good-to-be-true stores that are perpetually "going out of business" or "in liquidation."

## WOOD AND TINWORK

When Spanish colonists arrived in New Mexico, they had few resources, little money, and only the most basic tools. A group of settlers would typically include one carpenter, whose skills helped fill everyone's houses with heavy wood **furniture** (still made today). But the carpenter also helped the group to worship—for chief among the wood-carvers was (and is) the *santero* or *santera*, who carves images of saints. These so-called **santos** can be either flat *(retablos)* or three-dimensional *(bultos)* and are typically painted in lively colors, though some outstanding work has been produced in plain, unpainted wood.

Santo styles have shown remarkable continuity over the centuries. The most notable break from tradition was by Patrocinio Barela, whose WPA-sponsored work in the 1930s was almost fluid, utilizing the natural curves and grains of the wood. His sons and grandsons practice the art today. For centuries, the piousness of the *santero* was valued at least as much as his skill in carving, though many contemporary carvers do their work for a large market of avid collectors. One popular figure is San Isidro, patron saint of farmers, from 12th-century Spain.

Look also for **straw marquetry,** another product of hard times in the colonial period, in which tiny fibers of "poor man's gold" replaced precious metals as inlay to make elaborate geometric designs on dark wood. Tinwork is another ubiquitous craft, found in inexpensive votive-candle holders as well as elaborately punched and engraved mirror frames and chandeliers.

# ESSENTIALS

## Getting There

### BY AIR

**Albuquerque International Sunport** (ABQ; 505/244-7700, www.cabq.gov/airport) is the main access point to the region. It's served by all major U.S. air carriers, including Southwest Airlines and JetBlue. Fares fluctuate on the same schedule as the rest of the country, with higher rates in summer and over holidays; in the winter, it's wise to choose a connection through a more temperate hub, such as Dallas (American) or Salt Lake City (Delta).

Small **Santa Fe Municipal Airport** (SAF; 505/955-2900), west of the city, receives direct flights from Dallas and Los Angeles with American Eagle, and from Denver with United and Great Lakes. For visiting the southern half of the state, you might find it easier to fly into **El Paso International Airport** (ELP; 915/780-4749, www.elpasointernationalairport.com), Texas, just an hour's drive from Las Cruces.

### BY TRAIN

**Amtrak** (800/872-7245, www.amtrak.com) runs the Southwest Chief daily between Chicago and Los Angeles, stopping in **Raton, Las Vegas, Lamy** (18 miles from Santa Fe), **Albuquerque,** and **Gallup.**

© ZORA O'NEILL

Albuquerque—so if the train is running behind, you'll be late arriving in Lamy but generally will still get to Albuquerque on schedule.

## BY BUS

**Greyhound** (800/231-2222, www.greyhound. com) connects New Mexico with adjacent states and Mexico. Routes run roughly along I-40 and I-25, with little service to outlying areas. If you're coming from elsewhere in the Southwest, you may want to investigate **El Paso-Los Angeles Limousine Express** (915/532-4061 in El Paso, 626/442-1945 in Los Angeles, 505/247-8036 in Albuquerque, www.eplalimo.com), the biggest operator of bargain bus service for the Mexican immigrant population—its route runs east-west from El Paso to Los Angeles, stopping in Las Cruces and Deming. It also connects Denver and Albuquerque. It's both less expensive and more comfortable than Greyhound.

## BY CAR

Conveniently, New Mexico is crisscrossed by interstates: **I-40** and **I-10** run east-west, and **I-25** cuts roughly down the center, north-south. Denver, Colorado, to Santa Fe is 450 miles, about a 6-hour drive; add another hour to reach Albuquerque. El Paso, Texas, to Albuquerque is 275 miles, about 4 hours. Coming from Flagstaff, Arizona, Albuquerque is 325 miles along I-40, about 4.5 hours; from Amarillo, Texas, it's just slightly less distance in the other direction.

Southwest road-trippers often combine New Mexico with southwestern Colorado, in which case **U.S. 550** makes a good route south from Durango, and **U.S. 84** runs from Pagosa Springs. From Tucson, Arizona, a nice route into New Mexico is to cut north off I-10 at Lordsburg, following Highway 90 to Silver City.

© ZORA O'NEILL

Two interstates cross in Albuquerque.

Amtrak's Sunset Limited train, from Florida to Los Angeles via the southern edge of the state, is significantly less useful—it requires a bus transfer from El Paso to **Las Cruces,** and then makes stops in **Deming** and **Lordsburg.**

Arriving in Albuquerque, you're in the middle of downtown, in a depot shared with Greyhound. There are lockers here (occasionally full), and city bus service and taxis are available just up the block. Lamy (the stop nearest Santa Fe) is no more than a depot—though it is a dramatic and wild-feeling place to get off the train. Amtrak provides an awkwardly timed shuttle service to Santa Fe hotels (passengers arriving on eastbound trains must wait for passengers from the westbound train, an hour later). From Chicago, Amtrak pads its schedule heavily between Lamy and

# Getting Around

Practically speaking, you will need a car. Traveling between towns by bus or train is feasible, but it certainly limits what you can see. Within Albuquerque and Santa Fe, you can often get around by walking, biking, or public transport, but getting to or around anywhere smaller requires your own wheels.

## REGIONAL AIRLINES

To cover the longer distances, flying is a possibility; **New Mexico Airlines** (888/564-6119, www.flynma.com) and **Great Lakes Airlines** (800/554-5111, www.flygreatlakes.com) provide some regional service.

## BY BUS

Between Santa Fe and Taos (and communities around and in between, including the pueblos), the **North Central Regional Transit District** (866/206-0754, www.ncrtd.org) offers commuter bus service. It's not very frequent, but it covers a lot, making it an option for the hardcore car-free traveler.

Another option for the dedicated car-avoider, the **Navajo Transit System** (928/729-4002, www.navajotransit.com) can get you around the northwest and into Arizona—with *a lot* of planning.

**Greyhound** (800/231-2222, www.greyhound.com) connects Albuquerque with Santa Fe and Las Cruces, as well as a few other midsize towns. Anything off the interstate in the southeast will require a transfer in Las Cruces. **El Paso-Los Angeles Limousine Express** (1611 Central Ave. SW, 505/247-8036, www.eplalimo.com) offers good alternative service to Las Cruces.

## BY TRAIN

The **Rail Runner** (866/795-7245, www.nmrailrunner.com) commuter train connects Belén, Albuquerque, and Santa Fe, with convenient downtown stations in both cities, making a car-free visit quite feasible, or even a day trip. The train passes through odd pockets of Albuquerque and stunning, untouched pueblo lands. Tickets are based on a zone system; the 90-minute ride between downtown Albuquerque and Santa Fe costs $8, or $9 for a day pass. Via **Amtrak** (800/872-7245, www.

© VISIONS OF AMERICA LLC/123RF.COM

You never know what you'll see when driving New Mexico's scenic byways.

amtrak.com), Gallup, Raton, and Las Vegas are feasible destinations from Albuquerque.

## BY CAR

Driving New Mexico's scenic byways is definitely one of the pleasures of traveling here. Parking can be somewhat limited in Santa Fe, and you can get around the center of town very easily on foot, so it's best to rent a car only for the days you plan to go out of the city. In Albuquerque, you can live without a car for a few days, but it takes planning and rules out some of the sights. Central Taos is small, but sights are spread out on the fringes, and only the most dedicated can manage without a car. All of the major car-rental chains are at Albuquerque's airport, in a single building; see the respective city chapters for other rental companies and offices.

All but a few roads are passable year-round. You won't need four-wheel drive, but be prepared in winter for ice and snow anywhere other

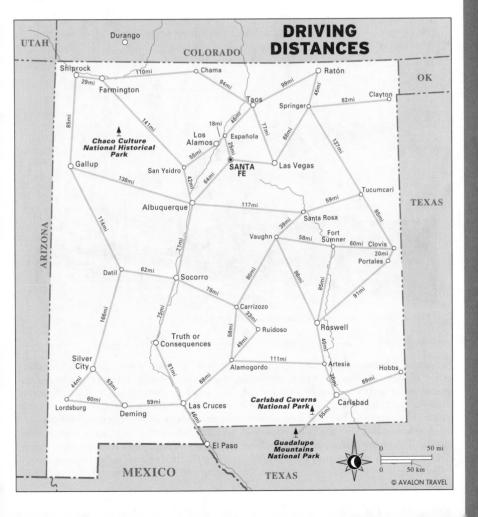

# DRIVING DISTANCES

© AVALON TRAVEL

## Riding the Rails

Traveling by train in New Mexico, if you have the time to do it, is a rewarding experience. You'll get a great sense of the state's emptiness—as well as what a dramatic change the railroad made when it arrived in 1880.

The **Belen Main Street** organization (www.belenmainstreet.org) publishes a map with major sites of train history, along with a suggested seven-day all-train itinerary, visiting Belén, Gallup, Santa Fe, and Las Vegas. It's feasible because the Amtrak departs Albuquerque midday, so you arrive at a reasonable hour.

For the corridor between Santa Fe and Belén, the **Rail Runner** commuter train (www.nmrailrunnervacations.com) offers periodic guided day tours, brochures for self-guided exploration, and package deals on hotels, and other discounts, when you show your ticket.

Going by train does rule out some parts of the state, but it also opens up whole areas you would never see by car. And nothing's more relaxing than watching the scenery roll by. In the words of one Amtrak fan, "It's like having your own chauffeur!"

© ZORA O'NEILL

The Rail Runner connects Albuquerque and Santa Fe.

than central Albuquerque and the southernmost section of the state. Also check your car rental agreement for restrictions on driving on dirt roads—a rare clause in the United States, but occasionally employed by smaller companies. Needless to say, this is a liability, as it's almost impossible to go anywhere interesting in New Mexico without winding up on a dirt road.

Get in the habit of topping off your tank. In the southern half of the state, especially along the Mexican border and anywhere away from I-10 and I-25, there are long stretches of smaller roads without gas stations, and prices can range by as much as $0.40 per gallon between convenient city locations and more remote areas. Contrary to logic, fuel is vastly more expensive in the southeastern side of the state around Hobbs and Artesia, where many oil wells are.

## BY BIKE

With beautiful vistas, often deserted roads, and a strong community of both road cyclists and mountain bikers, New Mexico can be a great place to get around on two wheels, as long as it's not your main form of transport. Whether you'll be riding your own bike or renting one here, always pack a patch kit, and consider installing tire liners. Goathead thorns and broken glass are particular scourges of the highway shoulder.

Central Albuquerque and Santa Fe are both manageable by bicycle, with separate lanes. Las Cruces is moderately accommodating.

# Accommodations and Food

## ACCOMMODATIONS

Whether you want to lay your head in a refurbished Airstream trailer or a cave carved in a cliff face, you can do it in New Mexico. Throughout the book, these distinctive choices (along with many exceptionally comfortable bed-and-breakfasts, lodges, and small hotels) are emphasized over chain options as much as possible. But just because the chains are not listed doesn't mean they're not available—and in many small towns, they're the only option.

The prices listed are the official high-season rack rates—that is, what you'd pay if you just walked in off the street, with no discounts; tax is not included. Most often, the numbers are the least expensive room for one person in one bed (a single, abbreviated *s*) and two people in two beds (a double, abbreviated *d*). **High season** is usually June-August and, in the mountains, the **ski season** is January-March, keeping prices relatively high in Taos and Santa Fe. Expect higher rates in the week following Christmas and during special events, such as Indian Market in Santa Fe, but overall you will probably be able to secure lower rates than those listed simply by looking online or calling the hotel directly.

Note that while many hotels tout their swimming pools, they are often forced to leave them empty due to water restrictions imposed during severe droughts. If you've booked at a hotel specifically for the pool, call to check the status before your trip, so you don't wind up paying a premium for a service you can't use. Santa Fe is the strictest area in the state, and it also limits hotels to changing towels and bed linens only every four days during your visit.

## FOOD

New Mexicans love their food so much, they have been known to enshrine it on lottery tickets, with scratch cards named Chile Cash, Chips and Salsa, and Sopaipilla Dough (promising "lots of honey and plenty of money"). The state cuisine is a distinctive culinary tradition that shouldn't be confused with Tex-Mex, Californian Mex, or south-of-the-border Mexican—even though most locals will say they're going out for "Mexican" when they mean they want a bowl of purely *New* Mexican green-chile stew. (But if you're eating *mole* or *ceviche*, that's "*Mexican* Mexican," and you can get more of it the farther south you drive.) Don't expect bean-and-meat chili, mango-flavored anything, or even all that much guacamole—you can get it, but avocados are expensive here.

### All Chile, All the Time

The cuisine's distinguishing element is the **New Mexico chile pepper**. The best-known variety is the Hatch chile, named for the southern New Mexican town that's the center of the industry. In the north, Chimayó is another big chile-producing town, with its own heirloom strain.

When the chile is picked green, it is roasted and peeled, then used whole to make chiles rellenos (stuffed with cheese and fried in batter) or cut into chunks and cooked in sauces or used as the base of a meaty green-chile stew.

## Red-Chile Sauce

Use only freshly ground New Mexico red chile for this sauce—not the "chile powder" sold in most grocery stores. The sauce will keep in the refrigerator for a month, and you can use it to top eggs or steaks, or devote the whole batch to a tray of enchiladas. (If you're doing the latter, you'll want to keep the sauce relatively runny, so you can easily coat the tortillas with sauce before filling them.) The flavor is best if it is prepared ahead and left to sit overnight.

*Yield: 2 cups*

½ c. New Mexico red chile powder
1 tsp. ground cumin
1 tsp. ground coriander
2 Tbsp. all-purpose flour
2 Tbsp. vegetable oil (or lard)
2 or 3 cloves garlic, crushed or minced
2 c. chicken stock or water
1 tsp. dried oregano (optional)

Measure the chile, cumin, coriander, and flour into a heavy-bottomed saucepan and place over medium-high heat. Stir continuously until the spices are just fragrant and the flour has darkened slightly. Remove the chile-flour mix to a small bowl. Put the oil or lard in the pan, and when it has warmed, add the garlic and stir until fragrant. Then stir the chile-flour mix into the oil-garlic mixture—you will have a very coarse paste. Stirring constantly, slowly add half of the stock or water. The mixture should thicken and become velvety. Add the remaining stock or water and the oregano, mix well, turn heat to low, and let sauce simmer for about 20 minutes, until it is somewhat reduced and thickened to your liking. If the mixture becomes too thick, simply add more water.

In northern New Mexico, that sauce is pure chile, maybe thinned with chicken broth; in the southern part of the state, it's more like a green-chile gravy, often with a base of cream-of-mushroom soup.

The same chiles can be left to ripen, then dried in the sun, where they turn dark red and leathery. The dry red chiles are strung up whole in long chains called *ristras* or ground into powder or for use in sauces or marinades.

While some dishes, such as *carne adovada* (pork shoulder marinated with red chile), are only ever made with one type, most other items—enchiladas, burritos, and eggs (huevos rancheros), to name a few—can be ordered with either variety of chile, so a standard question in restaurants is "Red or green?" You can have both, a style some people have in recent decades taken to calling "Christmas," though old-timers still call it "Mexican flag."

The chile is coupled with the traditional Native American triad of **corn, squash,** and **beans.** The beans are typically brown, meaty pintos, served whole in a stew or mashed up and "refried" (not actually fried twice—the term is a mistranslation of Spanish *refrito,* which means "really fried"). Corn takes the form of tortillas as well as hulled kernels of hominy, called *posole* here and often cooked into a stew with chile, oregano, and meat. Ground corn paste (masa) is whipped with lard (or Crisco, if you're "healthy") and wrapped around a meaty filling, then tied in a corn husk and steamed to make a **tamale.** Squash comes in a common side dish called **calabacitas,** sautéed with onions and a touch of green chile. Spanish settlers brought lamb, which finds its way into tacos and stews.

American Indian cuisine isn't so distinct from what everyone else eats—its one major element is **fry bread,** a round of deep-fried dough served with honey or filled with ground meat, cheese, and lettuce to make an "Indian taco"; a "Navajo taco" often uses shredded lamb or mutton in place of ground beef. Bread baked in a traditional domed adobe *horno* oven is also popular, and the Zuni make a distinctive sourdough this way. On the reservations, you'll see these mud ovens in the yards of even modern houses. Game meat, such as deer, is also a major component of Indian cooking, though you'll rarely see it in restaurants.

Green chile makes its way into standard American fare as well. It's a popular pizza

© ZORA O'NEILL

*Hornos,* or outdoor adobe ovens, are a common sight in New Mexico.

topping (great with pepperoni or ham), and the **green-chile cheeseburger** is a top choice everywhere. Also look out for **breakfast burritos,** big flour tortillas filled with scrambled eggs, hash browns, and some kind of meat—bacon, crumbled sausage, or sometimes Mexican chorizo, a spicy pork sausage. Some places sell them as to-go food, wrapped in foil with green chile added to the mix. At sit-down places, you get the thing smothered in either red or green chile.

**Sopaipillas** are another New Mexican specialty. They're palm-sized pillows of deep-fried dough, used to mop up chile and beans during the main meal, then slathered with honey for dessert. (In a disturbing trend, some restaurants are switching to a honey-flavored corn syrup, because it's cheaper and doesn't crystallize—if you encounter this, complain at top volume.) *Bizcochitos,* little anise-laced cookies, are the state's official sweet treat. Wash it all down with a **margarita,** which purists insist should involve only lime, tequila, and triple sec and be served on the rocks in a salt-rimmed glass. (Restaurants with only a beer-and-wine license

often offer an agave-wine margarita—OK flavor, but pretty weak.)

## How to Take the Heat

When your server plunks down a heavy white ceramic plate covered in chile and melted cheese, the words "this plate is very hot" cover only half of the story. Every year the harvest varies a bit, and the chile can be mild or so spicy as to blister lips and produce a dizzying (and addictive) endorphin rush. Locals look back on particularly incendiary seasons with that mixture of awe, fear, and longing that junkies reserve for their best scores. In general, green chile tends to be hotter than red, but it's best to ask your server what to expect.

You can protect yourself against chile-induced burns by ordering a side of sour cream with your enchiladas or burrito—although be warned that this is seen as a "Texan" affectation and may be derided by your fellow diners. Locals usually just reach for a **sopaipilla,** the starch from which can absorb some of the chile oils. Don't gulp down water, which only spreads the searing oils around your mouth. Beer is a marginal improvement, and margaritas are at least distracting.

### Fine Dining and Wine

While there are plenty of time-warp diners and mom-and-pop hole-in-the-wall joints in New Mexico, dining can also be very sophisticated, keeping pace with the national trend toward local and organic produce. This movement hasn't been such a huge leap here: Many small family farms didn't have to "go organic," because they were never industrialized in the first place. At white-tablecloth places, Southwestern fusion is still common, with chile working its way into foie gras appetizers and even high-concept desserts. The fine dining scene is enhanced by a burgeoning wine industry, initiated by Spanish settlers in the 17th century but enjoying a resurgence since the 1980s. Gruet Winery in Albuquerque is the best-known New Mexico producer, especially for its excellent sparkling wine. This makes for a nice little perk of New Mexico dining: You can get inexpensive bubbly by the glass almost everywhere. The **New Mexico Wine Growers Association** (www.nmwine.com) has information on more wineries, and you can read more about the high-end and organic food scene in *Local Flavor,* a monthly tabloid, and the quarterly *Edible Santa Fe* (www.ediblesantafe.com).

### Vegetarian Food

New Mexican food isn't meat-centric, but vegetarians will have to be vigilant, as many chile dishes are traditionally made with beef or chicken stock as well as lard for flavoring. The closer you get to Texas, the more likely it is that red chile sauce will contain bits of meat. Decades of hippie influence, though, have resulted in many menus stating clearly whether the chile is meatless. Some restaurants have an unreconstructed 1970s worldview, with alfalfa sprouts and squash casseroles galore.

# Conduct and Customs

New Mexico is a part of the United States, but it can sometimes feel quite foreign, particularly in the high mountain Spanish villages and in the Indian pueblos. Regardless, basic courtesy rules, and in smaller communities, modest dress is appreciated, especially at the older Catholic churches.

Some Pueblo Indians, as well as Navajo, find loud voices, direct eye contact, and firm handshakes off-putting and, by the same token, may not express themselves in the forthright way a lot of other Americans are used to. Similarly, a subdued reaction doesn't necessarily mean a lack of enthusiasm.

New Mexico is not a wealthy state, and the gap between rich and poor can be wide. In general, people don't appreciate conspicuous displays of wealth, and it's doubly rude to flash cash, fancy gadgets, and jewelry in tiny villages and pueblos (and public cell-phone use is still considered tacky). Be thoughtful when taking photos, particularly of people's homes—always ask permission, and consider that some of the more "scenic" elements of New Mexico are also the products of poverty, which some people may not be proud to have captured on film.

You can help the local economy by favoring New Mexican-owned businesses, rather than chain operations. Also try to buy directly from artisans wherever possible. In these situations, don't get too bent on bargaining—the item you're buying represents not just raw materials and hours of work, but a person's particular talent, skill, and heritage; insisting on an extra-low price belittles not just the item, but the artisan as well.

## PUEBLO AND RESERVATION ETIQUETTE

Visiting pueblos and reservations calls for particular behavior. Remember that you are not at a tourist attraction—you are walking around someone's neighborhood, so peeking in windows and wandering off the suggested route isn't polite. If you want to take photos, you'll need a camera permit, for an additional fee. Always ask permission before taking photos of people, and ask parents, rather than children, for their consent. Virtually all pueblos ban alcohol.

Some pueblos are more welcoming than others. San Ildefonso, for instance, is open year-round, whereas Jemez is completely closed, except for some feast days. So it's flawed logic to seek out the less-visited places or go in the off times in order to have a less "touristy" experience. In fact, the most rewarding time to visit *is* on a big feast day—you may not be the only tourist there, but you have a better chance of being invited into a local's home.

# Tips for Travelers

## CLASSES AND VOLUNTEERING

From afternoon cooking workshops to intensives on adobe building techniques, the opportunities to learn in northern New Mexico are broad.

### General Education

Look first into the art, music, and outdoors programs at **Ghost Ranch** (877/804-4678, www.ghostranch.org), the beautiful property in Abiquiu. Santa Fe and Albuquerque are both home to renowned alternative healing, herbal medicine, and massage schools, more than can be listed here; visit **Natural Healers** (www.naturalhealers.com) for a list. The El Rito campus of **Northern New Mexico College** (575/581-4115, www.nnmc.edu), north of Abiquiu, runs the **Heritage Retreat Center,** offering Spanish immersion classes and short-term workshops in traditional crafts.

### Cooking

**Santa Fe School of Cooking** (125 N. Guadalupe St., 505/983-4511, www.santafeschoolofcooking.com) offers day classes in contemporary Southwestern cuisine, as well as traditional Native American cooking and New Mexican standards; nice farmers market trips and restaurant walking tours are offered too.

In Dixon, **Comida de Campos** (505/852-0017, www.comidadecampos.com) offers classes on cooking in a traditional outdoor *horno,* and occasionally on clay-pot cooking, all in a beautiful farm setting.

### Permaculture and Alternative Construction

If you're interested in New Mexico's solar architecture movement, you can take a three-day **Earthship Seminar** (575/751-0462, www.earthship.org), a crash course in building the off-the-grid rammed-earth houses that are springing up around Taos. The Earthship Biotecture organization also accepts volunteers.

## FOREIGN TRAVELERS

As for any destination in the United States, check before departure whether you'll need a **visa** to enter; most European nationals do not need one.

New Mexico uses the **United States dollar**, and currency exchange is available at most banks as well as in better hotels, though the rates in the latter case will not be as good. For the best rates and convenience, withdraw cash from your home account through **automatic teller machines** (ATMs); check first, though, what fee your home bank and the ATM's bank will charge you for the transaction, including any fee for a foreign-currency transaction.

**Tipping** is similar to elsewhere in the country: 15 percent to cab drivers, and 15-20 percent on restaurant bills. For larger groups, often restaurants will add 18 percent or so to the bill; this is suggested, and you may refuse it or write in a lower amount if service was poor. Add $1 or so per drink when ordered at the bar; $1 or $2 to staff who handle your luggage in hotels; and $1 or $2 per day to housekeeping in hotels—envelopes are often left in rooms for this purpose, though if you don't see one, don't assume a tip won't be appreciated. **Bargaining** is usually accepted only if you're dealing directly with an artisan, and sometimes not even then—it doesn't hurt to ask, but don't press the issue.

**Electricity** is 120 volts, with a two-prong, flat-head plug, the same as Canada and Mexico.

## ACCESS FOR TRAVELERS WITH DISABILITIES

Wheelchair access can be frustrating in some historic properties and on the narrower sidewalks of Santa Fe and Taos, but in most other respects, travelers with disabilities should find no more problems in New Mexico than elsewhere in the United States. Public buses are wheelchair-accessible, an increasing number of hotels have ADA-compliant rooms, and you can even get out in nature a bit on paved trails such as the Santa Fe Canyon Preserve loop, the Paseo del Bosque in Albuquerque, or part of the Catwalk Trail in Glenwood. If you'll be visiting a lot of wilderness areas, you should get the National Park Service's **Access Pass** (888/467-2757, www.nps.gov), a free lifetime pass that grants admission for the pass-holder and three adults to all national parks, national forests, and the like, as well as discounts on interpretive services, camping fees, fishing licenses, and more. Apply in person at any federally managed park or wilderness area; you must show medical documentation of blindness or permanent disability.

## TRAVELING WITH CHILDREN

Though the specific prices are not listed in this guide, admission prices at major attractions are almost always lower for children than for adults. Hispanic and American Indian cultures are typically very child-friendly, so your little ones will be welcome in most environments, including restaurants and hotels. The only exceptions would be some of the more formal restaurants in Santa Fe and Albuquerque. Kids are sure to be fascinated by ceremonial dances at the pueblos, but be prepared with distractions, because long waits are the norm. Prep children with information about American Indian culture, and brief them on the basic etiquette at dances, which applies to them as well. Kids will also enjoy river rafting (relaxing "floats" along placid sections of the Rio Grande and Rio Chama are good for younger ones). For skiing, Taos Ski Valley has a very strong program of classes for youngsters.

## SENIOR TRAVELERS

Senior discounts are available at most museums and other attractions. If you'll be visiting a number of wilderness areas, look into a **Senior Pass** ($10), a lifetime pass for people 62 and older that grants free admission for the pass-holder and three additional adults to national parks, National Forest Service lands, and many other areas, as well as a 50 percent discount on activities such as camping and boat-launching. The pass can be purchased only in person at any federally managed wilderness area; for more information, contact the **National Parks Service** (888/467-2757, www.nps.gov).

**Road Scholar** (800/454-5768, www.road-scholar.org), formerly known as Elderhostel, runs more than 20 reasonably priced group trips in northern New Mexico, from a five-day general introduction to Santa Fe history to longer tours focusing on the legacy of Georgia O'Keeffe, for instance, or Tony Hillerman's landscape.

## GAY AND LESBIAN TRAVELERS

Santa Fe is one of the major gay capitals in the United States, second only to San Francisco in the per-capita rates of same-sex coupledom, and particularly popular with lesbians. There are no designated "gay-borhoods" (unless you count RainbowVision Santa Fe, a retirement community) or even particular bar scenes—instead, gay men and lesbian women are well integrated throughout town, running businesses and serving on the city council. Two weeks in June are dedicated to Pride on the Plaza, a festive time of gay-pride arts events and parades.

Albuquerque also has a decent gay scene, especially if you want to go clubbing, which is not an option in quieter Santa Fe. As for smaller towns and pueblos, they're still significantly more conservative.

Gay culture in the state isn't all about cute shops and cabarets. One big event is the annual **Zia Regional Rodeo,** sponsored by the **New Mexico Gay Rodeo Association** (505/720-3749, www.nmgra.com). It takes place every June in Albuquerque, with all the standard rodeo events, plus goat dressing and a wild drag race.

In late 2013, after several county clerks performed gay marriages (on the logic that the law didn't explicitly ban it), the New Mexico supreme court ruled that gay marriage was legal statewide.

# Health and Safety

Visitors to New Mexico face several unique health concerns. First and foremost are the environmental hazards of **dehydration, sunburn,** and **altitude sickness.** The desert climate, glaring sun, and thinner atmosphere conspire to fry your skin and drain you of all moisture. (On the plus side, sweat evaporates immediately.) Apply SPF 30 sunscreen daily, even in winter, and try to drink at least a couple of liters of water a day, whether you feel thirsty or not. Remember to ask for water in restaurants—it's usually brought only on demand, to cut down on waste. By the time you start feeling thirsty, you're already seriously dehydrated and at risk of further bad effects: headaches, nausea, and dizziness, all of which can become full-blown, life-threatening **heatstroke** if left untreated. It doesn't even take serious exertion—just lack of water and very hot sun—to develop heatstroke, so if you're feeling at all woozy or cranky (another common symptom), head for shade and sip a cold drink like Gatorade or a similar electrolyte-replacement drink.

Staying hydrated will also help stave off the effects of the high elevation, to which most visitors will not be acclimated. The mildest reaction to being 7,000 feet or more above sea level is lethargy or lightheadedness—you will probably sleep long and soundly on your first night in New Mexico. Some people do have more severe reactions, such as a piercing headache or intense nausea, especially if they engage in strenuous physical activity. Unfortunately, there's no good way to judge how your body will react, so give yourself a few days to adjust, with a light schedule and plenty of time to sleep.

More obscure hazards include **West Nile virus** (wear a DEET-based insect repellent if you're down along the river in the summer); **hantavirus,** an extremely rare pulmonary ailment transmitted by rodents; and the even rarer **bubonic plague** (a.k.a. The Black Death), the very same disease that killed millions of Europeans in the Middle Ages. Luckily, only a case or two of the plague crops up every year, and it's easily treated if diagnosed early. **Lyme disease** is so far nonexistent, as deer ticks do not flourish in the mountains.

If you'll be spending a lot of time hiking or camping, take precautions against **giardiasis** and other waterborne ailments by boiling your water or treating it with iodine or a SteriPen (www.steripen.com), as even the clearest mountain waterways may have been tainted by cows upstream. **Snake bites** are also a small hazard in the wild, so wear boots that cover your ankles, stay on trails, and keep your hands and feet out of odd holes and cracks between rocks. Only the Western diamondback rattlesnake is aggressive when disturbed; other snakes typically will not bite if you simply back away quietly.

General **outdoor safety rules** apply: Don't hike by yourself, always register with the ranger station when heading out overnight, and let friends know where you're going and when you'll be back. Pack a good topographical map and a compass or GPS device; people manage to get lost even when hiking in the foothills, and if you're at all dehydrated or dizzy from the altitude, any disorientation can be magnified to a disastrous degree. Also pack layers of clothing, and be prepared for cold snaps and snow at higher elevations, even in the summer.

## CRIME AND DRUGS

Recreational drug use is not uncommon in New Mexico—generally in a relatively benign form, with marijuana fairly widespread. (Former governor and Republican presidential candidate Gary Johnson, though no longer a user himself, has been a strenuous advocate for its legalization.) But as in much of the rural United States, crystal methamphetamine is an epidemic, and some villages in northern New Mexico have also been devastated by heroin use, with overdose deaths at a rate several hundred times higher than the national average. None of this affects travelers, except that petty theft, especially in isolated areas such as trailheads, can be an issue; always lock your car doors, and secure any valuables in the trunk. Don't leave anything enticing in view.

Drinking and driving is unfortunately still common, especially in rural areas; be particularly alert when driving at night. A distressing number of crosses along the roadside *(descansos)* mark the sites of fatal car accidents, many of which had alcohol involved.

# Information and Services

## MAPS AND TOURIST INFORMATION

For pre-trip inspiration, the New Mexico Tourism Board publishes the monthly **New Mexico** magazine (www.nmmagazine.com), which covers both mainstream attractions and more obscure corners of the state.

If you plan to do a lot of hiking, you can order detailed topographical maps from the **National Forest Service** office in New Mexico (505/842-3292) or from the Bureau of Land Management's **Public Lands Information Center** (www.publiclands.org). Santa Fe's **Travel Bug** (839 Paseo de Peralta, 505/992-0418, 7:30am-5:30pm Mon.-Sat., 11am-4pm Sun.) bookstore also stocks maps. Many smaller towns' chambers of commerce can also be extremely helpful.

Albuquerque, Santa Fe, and Farmington use the area code 505, while most of the rest of the state uses 575.

## TELEPHONE AND INTERNET

Mobile phones on the GSM network (AT&T, T-Mobile) get very poor or no reception in rural areas. The corridor between Albuquerque and Santa Fe is fine, but if you'll be spending a lot of time outside of these two cities, you might consider a CDMA phone (Verizon is best), particularly if you're counting on it for emergencies. Likewise, don't count on data service on your smartphone.

Internet access is widespread, though DSL and other high-speed service is still not necessarily the norm. Many cafés have wireless hot spots, and the city of Albuquerque even maintains a few free ones, but thick adobe walls can be a hindrance to consistent reception.

## TIME ZONE

New Mexico is in the **mountain time** zone, one hour ahead of the West Coast of the United States and two hours behind the East Coast. It's -7 GMT during the winter and -6 GMT in summer, when daylight saving time is followed statewide. Note that neighboring Arizona does not follow daylight saving time, which can lead to confusion around the border.

# RESOURCES

## Glossary

*abierto:* Spanish for "open"

**acequia:** irrigation ditch, specifically one regulated by the traditional Spanish method, maintained by a *mayordomo,* or "ditch boss," who oversees how much water each shareholder receives

**adobe:** building material of sun-dried bricks made of a mix of mud, sand, clay, and straw

**arroyo:** stream or dry gully where mountain runoff occasionally flows

*asado:* stew (usually pork) with red-chile sauce

*atrio:* churchyard between the boundary wall and the church entrance, usually used as a cemetery

*bizcochito:* anise-laced shortbread, traditionally made with lard

**bosque:** Spanish for "forest," specifically the cottonwoods and trees along a river

*bulto:* three-dimensional wood carving, typically of a saint

**caldera:** basin or crater formed by a collapsed volcano

*canal:* water drain from a flat roof; pl. *canales*

**carne adovada:** pork chunks marinated in red chile, then braised; meatier and dryer than *asado*

*cerrado:* Spanish for "closed"

*chicharrón:* fried pork skin, usually with a layer of meat still attached

**chile:** not to be confused with Texas chili, Cincinnati chili, or any other American concoction; refers to the fruit of the chile plant itself, eaten green (picked unripe and then roasted) or red (ripened and dried)

**chimichanga:** deep-fried burrito; allegedly invented in Arizona

*colcha:* style of blanket, in which loom-woven wool is embellished with long strands of wool embroidery

**concho belt:** belt made of stamped, carved silver medallions; also "concha," Spanish for "shell"

*convento:* residential compound adjoining a mission church

**enchilada:** corn tortilla dipped in chile sauce, filled with cheese or meat, and topped with more chile; can be served either rolled or flat (stacked in layers)

*farolito:* in Santa Fe and Taos, a luminaria

*genízaro:* during Spanish colonial times, a detribalized Indian (usually due to having been taken as a slave) who lived with Spaniards and followed Catholic tradition

*gordita:* a variation on the taco, with a thicker tortilla-like shell, sometimes deep-fried; these are a more traditionally Mexican dish (though in that case rarely fried) and are available only in the southern part of the state

*heishi:* fine disk-shaped beads carved from shells

*horno:* traditional dome-shaped adobe oven

*jerga:* Spanish-style wool blanket or rug, loosely woven and barely decorated, meant for daily use

**kachina:** ancestral spirit of the Pueblo people as well as the carved figurine representing the spirit; also spelled "katsina"

**kiva:** sacred ceremonial space in a pueblo, at

least partially underground and entered by a hole in the ceiling

**latillas:** thin saplings cut and laid across vigas to make a solid ceiling

**lowrider:** elaborately painted and customized car with hydraulic lifts

**luminaria:** in Albuquerque, lantern made of a sand-filled paper bag with a votive candle set inside; in Santa Fe and Taos, refers to small bonfires lit during the Christmas season

**menudo:** tripe soup, said to be good for curing a hangover

**morada:** meeting space of the Penitente brotherhood

**nicho:** small niche in an adobe wall, usually meant to hold a santo

**Penitente:** member of a strict Catholic brotherhood

**petroglyph:** rock carving

**pictograph:** painting on a rock surface

**piñon:** any of several fragrant varieties of pine tree that grow in New Mexico

**portal:** the covered sidewalk area in front of a traditional adobe structure; pl. *portales*

**posole:** stew of hulled corn (hominy), pork, and a little chile, either green or red

**pueblo:** Spanish for "village," referring to the various communities of American Indians settled in the Rio Grande Valley; also, capitalized, the people themselves, though they speak several different languages

**rajas:** rough-hewn slats laid over vigas to form a ceiling; also, strips of roasted chile

**ramada:** simple structure built of four sapling posts and topped with additional saplings laid flat to form a shade structure and a place to hang things to dry

**reredos:** altar screen, usually elaborately painted or carved with various portraits of Christ and the saints

**retablo:** flat portrait of a saint, painted or carved in low relief, usually on wood

**ristra:** string of dried red chiles

**santero/santera:** craftsperson who produces santos

**santo:** portrait of a saint, either flat (a *retablo*) or three-dimensional (a *bulto*)

**sipapu:** hole in the floor of a kiva, signifying the passage to the spirit world

**sopaipilla:** square of puffed fried dough, served with the main meal for wiping up sauces and with honey for dessert

**tamale:** corn husk filled with masa (hominy paste) and a dab of meat, vegetables, or cheese, then steamed; usually made in large quantities for holidays

**terrón:** building material of bricks cut out of sod and dried in the sun, similar to adobe, but less common

**Tewa:** language spoken by the majority of Pueblo Indians; others in the Rio Grande Valley speak Tiwa, Towa, and Keresan

**torreón:** round defensive tower built in Spanish colonial times

**vato:** cool Chicano, usually driving a lowrider

**viga:** ceiling beam made of a single tree trunk

**zaguán:** long central hallway

# Suggested Reading

## ART AND CULTURE

Clark, Willard. *Remembering Santa Fe.* Layton, UT: Gibbs Smith, 2004. A small hardback edition of selections from the Boston artist who stopped off in Santa Fe in 1928. He stayed to learn printmaking and produce this series of etchings depicting city life.

Eaton, Robert. *The Lightning Field.* Boulder, CO: Johnson Books, 1995. Eaton served as a forest ranger in Chaco Canyon for five years, so his eye is for the empty and the starkly beautiful destinations around the state, including the art installation of the title (in Quemado, in western New Mexico). His essays, each focusing on a different destination, combine history and strong description. Seek this title out if you want to get well off the usual track.

Gandert, Miguel. *Nuevo México Profundo: Rituals of an Indo-Hispanic Homeland.* Santa Fe: Museum of New Mexico Press, 2000. Like Enrique Lamadrid's work, but with a slightly broader scope. There's an attempt at scholarly analysis in the text, but it's really about the 130 beautiful photographs.

Hammett, Kingsley. *Santa Fe: A Walk Through Time.* Layton, UT: Gibbs Smith, 2004. A light, largely visual tour of the capital's history and rich trove of weird legends, as told through its buildings.

Lamadrid, Enrique. *Hermanitos Comanchitos: Indo-Hispano Rituals of Captivity and Redemption.* Albuquerque: University of New Mexico Press, 2003. Fascinating documentation, in descriptive prose and rich black-and-white photos, of the traditional Spanish dances of northern New Mexico, such as Los Comanches and Los Matachines.

Lummis, Charles F. *A Tramp Across the Continent.* Lincoln: University of Nebraska Press, 1982. In 1884, fledgling journalist Lummis decided to walk from Cincinnati to his new job in Los Angeles; this book chronicles his trip. The sections on New Mexico shine, and Lummis was so entranced that he later moved to the territory. He was the first to write stories about the Penitente brotherhood in the national press.

Myers, Joan. *Pie Town Woman: The Hard Life and Good Times of a New Mexico Homesteader.* Albuquerque: University of New Mexico, 2001. The biography of a woman captured in famous Farm Security Administration photos from 1940, this book also muses on the power of memory and photography.

Padilla, Carmella, and Juan Estevan Arellano. *Low 'n Slow: Lowriding in New Mexico.* Santa Fe: Museum of New Mexico Press, 1999. Lovingly lurid color photographs by Jack Parsons are the centerpiece of this book, which pays tribute to New Mexico's Latino car culture—an art form that has even landed a lowrider from Chimayó in the Smithsonian.

Parhad, Elisa. *New Mexico: A Guide for the Eyes.* Los Angeles: EyeMuse Books, 2009. Informative short essays on the distinctive things you see in New Mexico and then wonder what the backstory is: concho belts, beat-up pickup trucks, blue sky. The richly illustrated book makes good pre-trip reading, or a souvenir when you return.

Price, V. B. *Albuquerque: A City at the End of the World.* Albuquerque: University of New Mexico Press, 2003. Journalist and poet Price writes a travel guide to New Mexico's biggest metropolis but disguises it as a discourse on urban theory, recommending his favorite spots in the context of the city's unique position and growth processes. Black-and-white photographs by Kirk Gittings highlight the stark landscape.

Robinson, Roxana. *Georgia O'Keeffe: A Life.* Lebanon, NH: University Press of New England, 1998. A strong and intimate biography, focusing on the celebrated painter's role as a protofeminist and her difficult relationships.

## FOOD

Feucht, Andrea. *Food Lovers' Guide to Santa Fe, Albuquerque & Taos.* Guilford, CT: Globe Pequot, 2012. A good companion for adventurous eaters, with especially good coverage of Albuquerque's more obscure ethnic restaurants. The author maintains an update website (www.foodloversnm.com).

Frank, Lois Ellen. *Foods of the Southwest Indian Nations.* Berkeley, CA: Ten Speed Press, 2002. Beautiful photographs are a highlight of this thorough documentation of a little-covered cuisine. They help make an ancient culinary tradition accessible and modern without subjecting it to a heavy-handed fusion treatment. For good reason, it earned a James Beard Award.

Kagel, Katharine. *Cooking with Café Pasqual's: Recipes from Santa Fe's Renowned Corner Cafe.* Berkeley, CA: Ten Speed Press, 2006. Re-create your best meals from the legendary restaurant that set the standard for Santa Fe fusion cooking. Chef Kagel is a charming contrarian too, which makes for great reading.

## HISTORY

Childs, Craig. *House of Rain: Tracking a Vanished Civilization Across the American Southwest.* New York: Little, Brown, 2007. The story of the Anasazi (ancestral Puebloans), as told by a curious naturalist, becomes less a solution to an archaeological puzzle than a meditation of why we romanticize "lost" civilizations. His more recent book, *Finders Keepers: A Tale of Archaeological Plunder and Possession* (Little, Brown, 2010), takes the drama to the academy, with tales of scholarly intrigue.

Egan, Timothy. *The Worst Hard Time: The Untold Story of Those Who Survived the Great American Dust Bowl.* New York: Mariner Books, 2006. The town of Clayton features a bit in the pages of this highly readable history that conveys the misery and environmental folly of the period.

Hordes, Stanley. *To the End of the Earth: A History of the Crypto-Jews of New Mexico.* New York: Columbia University Press, 2008. An exhaustive but intriguing account of the Jewish families who fled the Inquisition and lived in the Southwest as Catholic converts. The communities, some still practicing distinctly Jewish rituals, came to light only a few decades ago.

Horgan, Paul. *Great River.* Middletown, CT: Wesleyan University Press, 1991. Two enormous tomes (*Vol. 1: The Indians and Spain* and *Vol. 2: Mexico and the United States*) won the Pulitzer Prize for history. They're packed with drama, on a base of meticulous analysis of primary sources.

Martinez, Esther. *My Life in San Juan Pueblo.* Champaign: University of Illinois Press, 2004. Born in 1912, Martinez has a lot of stories to tell. This free-flowing book incorporates her memories with larger pueblo folklore, and a CD with recordings of some of her stories is included.

Poling-Kempes, Lesley. *Valley of Shining Stone: The Story of Abiquiu.* Tucson: University of Arizona Press, 1997. Georgia O'Keeffe fans will like the personal stories of those in her circle in the 1930s, while historians will appreciate the detailed, linear second half of the book, about the transformation of this remote valley into an artists' haven.

Sides, Hampton. *Blood and Thunder: An Epic of the American West.* New York: Doubleday, 2006. Working from the story of Kit Carson and the campaign against the Navajo, including the Long Walk, Sides tells the gripping story of the entire American West. He's an excellent storyteller, and the 480 pages flow by in a rush of land grabs, battles on horseback, and brutality on all sides.

Simmons, Marc. *New Mexico: An Interpretive History.* Albuquerque: University of New Mexico Press, 1988. The state's historian laureate presents an easy, concise overview of the major historical events. Also look into his more specialized titles, such as *The Last Conquistador: Juan de Oñate and the Settling of the Far Southwest* (Norman: University of Oklahoma Press, 1993).

Usner, Donald J. *Sabino's Map: Life in Chimayó's Old Plaza.* Santa Fe: Museum of New

Mexico Press, 1995. A balanced and gracefully written history of the author's hometown, illustrated with fond photos of all the craggy-faced characters involved. Usner's follow-up, *Benigna's Chimayo: Cuentos from the Old Plaza* (Santa Fe: Museum of New Mexico Press, 2001) relates his grandmother's story of the village and her trove of folktales.

## LITERATURE AND MEMOIR

Anaya, Rudolfo. *Bless Me, Ultima.* New York: Warner, 1994. Anaya's story of a young boy coming of age in New Mexico in the 1940s is beautifully told. The book, first published in 1973, launched Anaya into his role as Chicano literary hero; his later books, such as *Alburquerque* (1992), are not quite so touching, but they have a lot of historical and ethnic detail.

Blume, Judy. *Tiger Eyes.* New York: Delacorte, 2010. A young girl with family troubles relocates to Los Alamos, giving a great teen's-eye-view on the landscape of New Mexico.

Evans, Max. *Hi-Lo to Hollywood: A Max Evans Reader.* Lubbock, TX: Texas Tech University Press, 1998. Prolific Western author Evans coined the term "Hi-Lo Country" for the "high lonesome" eastern plains of New Mexico, and all of his works, whether essay or fiction, somehow reflect the rolling expanse and the particular dilemmas of the modern cowboys who work on them. A ranch kid himself, he has an eye for detail and a direct and affectionate tone; this reader includes many of his own favorite pieces.

Goodman, Tanya Ward. *Leaving Tinkertown.* Albuquerque: University of New Mexico Press, 2013. A poignant memoir of growing up in the wondrous folk-art assemblage outside Albuquerque. The author's father, Ross Ward, died of early-onset Alzheimer's disease, and this book logs that medical tale, unflinchingly, alongside the larger-than-life artist's own story.

Hillerman, Tony. *Skinwalkers.* New York: HarperTorch, 1990. Hillerman's breakout detective novel, set on the Navajo Nation, weaves a fascinating amount of lore into the plot—which comes in handy when Tribal Affairs police Joe Leaphorn and Jim Chee investigate homicides. Hillerman spun Leaphorn and Chee into a successful franchise, and all of the books show the same cultural depth.

Mallery, Barbara Vogt. *Bailing Wire and Gamuza: The True Story of a Family Ranch near Ramah, New Mexico.* Albuquerque: University of New Mexico, 2004. Arranged like a family scrapbook, this memoir recounts the author's homesteading life between 1905 and 1986.

Pillsbury, Dorothy. *Roots in Adobe.* Santa Fe: Lightning Tree Press, 1983. Pillsbury's charming stories capture the strangeness and warmth of Santa Fe culture in the 1940s. The author tells hilarious stories of settling into her little home and the characters she meets.

Silko, Leslie Marmon. *Ceremony.* New York: Penguin, 1988. Silko's classic novel about the impact of the atomic bomb on Native Americans' worldview (and that of all Americans) is brutal, beautiful, and bleak.

## NATURE AND THE ENVIRONMENT

Coltrin, Mike. *Sandia Mountain Hiking Guide.* Albuquerque: University of New Mexico Press, 2005. A print version of Coltrin's meticulously maintained website (www.sandiahiking.com), with thorough trail descriptions, GPS coordinates, and a foldout map of the east and west slopes of the mountain.

Julyan, Robert, and Mary Stuever, eds. *Field Guide to the Sandia Mountains.* Albuquerque: University of New Mexico Press, 2005. A thorough guide illustrated with color photographs, detailing birds, animals, plants, even insects of the Sandias. Most of it applies to the Santa Fe area too.

Kricher, John. *A Field Guide to Rocky Mountain and Southwest Forests.* New York: Houghton Mifflin Harcourt, 2003. A Peterson Field Guide, covering both flora and fauna: trees, birds, mammals, you name it. It's illustrated with both color photos and drawings. It's not encyclopedic, but it's a great basic reference. Peterson guides are also available for narrower categories such as reptiles and amphibians or butterflies.

McFarland, Casey, and S. David Scott. *Bird Feathers: A Guide to North American Species.* Mechanicsburg, PA: Stackpole Books, 2010. While not New Mexico-specific, it is the only guide of its kind, and its authors grew up in the state and know the birdlife well. Great for serious birders and curious hikers, with detailed photographs.

Nichols, John. *On the Mesa.* Layton, Utah: Gibbs Smith, 2005. Best known for his comic novel *The Milagro Beanfield War,* Nichols here writes some visionary nonfiction about traditional life and environment near his home in Taos.

Price, V. B. *The Orphaned Land: New Mexico's Environment Since the Manhattan Project.* Albuquerque: University of New Mexico Press, 2011. Journalist Price examines New Mexico's droughts and other trials—in the same vein as Reisner's *Cadillac Desert.*

Reisner, Marc. *Cadillac Desert: The American West and Its Disappearing Water.* New York: Penguin, 1993. Not specifically about New Mexico, but an excellent analysis of the Southwest's water shortage and how the U.S. government's dam-building projects exacerbated it. Apocalyptic, sarcastic, and totally compelling.

Sibley, David Allen. *The Sibley Field Guide to Birds of Western North America.* New York: Knopf, 2003. The New Mexican birder's book of choice, with 810 species listed, about 4,600 color illustrations, and a handy compact format. Generally beats out Peterson's otherwise respectable series.

Tekiela, Stan. *Birds of New Mexico: Field Guide.* Cambridge, MN: Adventure Publications, 2003. A great book for beginning birders or curious visitors, with 140 of the state's most common species listed, many illustrated with photographs.

# Internet Resources

## TRAVEL INFORMATION

### Albuquerque Convention and Visitors Bureau
**www.itsatrip.org**
The official intro to the city and surrounding areas, with events listings as well as hotel-booking services.

### Four Corners Geotourism
**www.fourcornersgeotourism.com**
A directory of sustainable tourism, sponsored by *National Geographic.*

### Hiking in the Sandia Mountains
**www.sandiahiking.com**
Mike Coltrin hiked every trail in the Sandias over the course of a year, covering about 250 miles. He detailed each hike, complete with GPS references, here.

### Indian Country New Mexico
**www.indiancountrynm.org**
A coalition of tourism groups in northwestern New Mexico maintain this basic overview website.

## New Mexico Board of Tourism
**www.newmexico.org**
The best of the official sites, this one has thorough maps and suggested itineraries.

## Public Lands Information Center
**www.publiclands.org**
Buy USGS, Forest Service, and other topographical maps online from the Bureau of Land Management's well-organized website. Good stock of nature guides and other travel books too.

## Sangres.com
**www.sangres.com**
Scores of articles and travel details about the mountain communities, culture, and history of northern New Mexico, as well as southern Colorado.

## Santa Fe Convention and Visitors Bureau
**www.santafe.org**
Near-exhaustive listings of tourist attractions and services on this slickly produced site.

## Santa Fe Creative
**www.santafecreativetourism.org**
The Santa Fe Arts Commission's listings of arts classes, workshops, and other special events while you're in this creative hub.

## Southern New Mexico Travel & Tourism
**www.southernnewmexico.com**
This site offers heaps of information about even the most obscure towns in the southern half of the state, but many of the articles are quite old, so it's hard to tell whether facts are current.

## Taos Visitors Guide
**www.taos.org**
A thorough directory and events listings, but the visitors center, in Taos itself, is handier.

## Visit Los Alamos
**visit.losalamos.com**
The online version of the chamber of commerce's useful handbook, with business listings and an events calendar.

## Happy Trails!

See New Mexico through a focused lens, with these specialized guides to the state.

- **Birding Trail:** (wildlife.state.nm.us) A map and road signs for feathered friends.
- **Clay Arts Trail:** (www.claytrail.org) Under development at research time, in the southwest corner of the state.
- **Fiber Arts Trails:** (www.nmfiberarts.org) Three routes around this wool-loving state.
- **Green Chile Cheeseburger Trail:** (www.newmexico.org) You'll never go hungry again.
- **Film Trails:** (www.newmexico.org) Six regional routes to movie locations, plus *Breaking Bad*.
- **Space Trail:** (www.nmspacemuseum.org) Wherever a rocket was launched, it's on the map.

## NEWS AND CULTURE

### Albuquerque Journal
**www.abqjournal.com**
The state's largest newspaper is available free online after answering survey questions.

### Alibi
**www.alibi.com**
Albuquerque's oldest free weekly has been cracking wise since 1992, taking a critical look at politics and culture. Its annual "Best of Burque" guide is a good listing of local recommendations.

### Chasing Santa Fe
**www.chasingsantafe.blogspot.com**
The glamorous Santa Fe lifestyle, lovingly documented: local chefs, new shops, and fashion spotting.

### Duke City Fix
**www.dukecityfix.com**
This Albuquerque-centric discussion forum

covers everything from politics to gossip about the restaurant scene.

### Las Cruces Sun-News
**www.lcsun-news.com**
The paper of record in Las Cruces, covering issues all across the southern half of the state, especially border debates.

### New Mexico Politics with Joe Monahan
**www.joemonahan.com**
Analyst Monahan's obsessive, snarky blog charts the circus that is state politics, with plenty examples of why New Mexico still can't shake its "third-world country" rep.

### Roundhouse Roundup
**www.roundhouseroundup.blogspot.com**
A music critic and political reporter for the *Santa Fe New Mexican* relates often funny tales of congressional intrigue.

### Santa Fe New Mexican
**www.santafenewmexican.com**
Santa Fe's main newspaper. The gossip column El Mitote documents celebs in Santa Fe.

### Santa Fe Reporter
**www.sfreporter.com**
Santa Fe's free weekly is politically sharp and often funny. Get opinionated reviews and news analysis here, along with appropriately snarky blogs.

### Smithsonian Folkways
**www.folkways.si.edu**
This enormous online music archive has a number of traditional treasures from the state, including the excellent *Music of New Mexico: Hispanic Traditions* and *New Mexico: Native American Traditions*.

### Steppin' Out
**www.steppinoutnewmexico.com**
Covering all of southern New Mexico, this Socorro-published paper and website has exhaustive cultural listings and arts news.

# Index

# List of Maps

# Acknowledgments

Thanks as always go first to the staff at Avalon, who do such great work with words, graphics, and maps to make the book a great-looking finished project. Thanks to Debbie Reeves, for Portales advice—sorry I had to scoot through town without meeting again. Thanks to John Nichols, for pointing me even farther down the road, to the Geronimo monument and beyond. Thanks to Bob Tollefson, who finally got me to the Hillcrest—next time, hot roast beef. Thanks to Peter Moskos, for enduring. Thanks to the whole state of New Mexico, for always revealing more. And finally, more than anything, thanks to all the readers, for sending feedback. It helps the book immensely, and I'm happy to know it's in good hands.

# MAP SYMBOLS

| | | | | | |
|---|---|---|---|---|---|
| ═══ Expressway | ( Highlight | ✈ Airport | ⚓ Golf Course |
| ─── Primary Road | ○ City/Town | ✈ Airfield | ℙ Parking Area |
| ─── Secondary Road | ◉ State Capital | ▲ Mountain | ▲ Archaeological Site |
| ┄┄┄ Unpaved Road | ⊛ National Capital | ✛ Unique Natural Feature | ⛪ Church |
| ╌╌╌ Trail | ★ Point of Interest | | ⛽ Gas Station |
| ⋯⋯ Ferry | • Accommodation | 🗻 Waterfall | 🐟 Dive Site |
| ═══ Railroad | ▼ Restaurant/Bar | ▲ Park | Mangrove |
| ═══ Pedestrian Walkway | ■ Other Location | ⊓ Trailhead | Reef |
| ⊞⊞⊞ Stairs | Λ Campground | 🗼 Lighthouse | Swamp |

# CONVERSION TABLES

°C = (°F − 32) / 1.8
°F = (°C x 1.8) + 32
1 inch = 2.54 centimeters (cm)
1 foot = 0.304 meters (m)
1 yard = 0.914 meters
1 mile = 1.6093 kilometers (km)
1 km = 0.6214 miles
1 fathom = 1.8288 m
1 chain = 20.1168 m
1 furlong = 201.168 m
1 acre = 0.4047 hectares
1 sq km = 100 hectares
1 sq mile = 2.59 square km
1 ounce = 28.35 grams
1 pound = 0.4536 kilograms
1 short ton = 0.90718 metric ton
1 short ton = 2,000 pounds
1 long ton = 1.016 metric tons
1 long ton = 2,240 pounds
1 metric ton = 1,000 kilograms
1 quart = 0.94635 liters
1 US gallon = 3.7854 liters
1 Imperial gallon = 4.5459 liters
1 nautical mile = 1.852 km

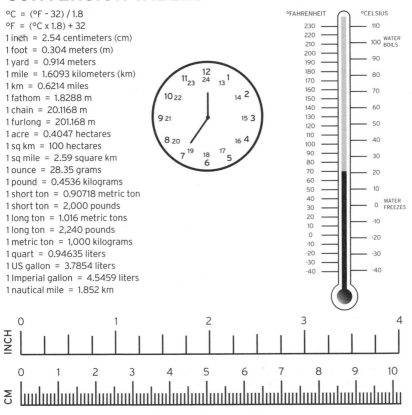

# MOON NEW MEXICO

Avalon Travel
a member of the Perseus Books Group
1700 Fourth Street
Berkeley, CA 94710, USA
www.moon.com

Editor: Sabrina Young
Series Manager: Kathryn Ettinger
Copy Editor: Alissa Cyphers
Graphics Coordinator: Elizabeth Jang
Production Coordinator: Elizabeth Jang
Cover Design: Faceout Studios, Charles Brock
Moon Logo: Tim McGrath
Map Editor: Albert Angulo
Cartographers: Stephanie Poulain, Brian Shotwell
Indexer: Greg Jewett

ISBN-13: 978-1-61238-739-0
ISSN: 1543-6187

Printing History
1st Edition – 1989
9th Edition – July 2014
5 4 3 2 1

## KEEPING CURRENT

If you have a favorite gem you'd like to see included in the next edition, or see anything that needs updating, clarification, or correction, please drop us a line. Send your comments via email to feedback@moon.com, or use the address above.